Solutions Manual (Chapters 1-17)

Accounting
TWENTY-SECOND EDITION

OR

Financial Accounting
TENTH EDITION

Carl S. Warren
University of Georgia, Athens

James M. Reeve
University of Tennessee, Knoxville

Jonathan E. Duchac
Wake Forest University

THOMSON

SOUTH-WESTERN

Australia · Brazil · Canada · Mexico · Singapore · Spain · United Kingdom · United States

THOMSON
™

SOUTH-WESTERN

Solutions Manual Chapters 1-17

to accompany Accounting, 22e or Financial Accounting, 10e

Carl S. Warren, James M. Reeve, Jonathan E. Duchac

VP/Editorial Director:
Jack W. Calhoun

Publisher:
Rob Dewey

Executive Editor:
Sharon Oblinger

Developmental Editor:
Steven E. Joos

Assistant Editor:
Erin Berger

Editorial Assistant:
Kelly Somers

Marketing Manager:
Robin Farrar

Sr. Production Project Manager:
Cliff Kallemeyn

Associate Manager of Technology:
John Barans

Sr. Technology Project Editor:
Sally Neiman

Sr. Technology Project Editor:
Robin Browning

Art Director:
Bethany Casey

Photo Manager:
Tom Hill

Sr. First Print Buyer:
Doug Wilke

Project Manager:
Malvine Litten
LEAP Publishing Services, Inc.

Printer:
West Group
Eagan MN

For permission to use material from this
text or product, submit a request online
at http://www.thomsonrights.com.

For more information about our
products, contact us at:

Thomson Learning Academic Resource
Center

1-800-423-0563

Thomson Higher Education
5191 Natorp Boulevard
Mason, OH 45040
USA

CONTENTS

PREFACE

The Solutions Manual to accompany Warren/Reeve/Duchac's *Financial Accounting, 10th edition* and *Accounting, 22nd edition* contains the solutions or possible solutions for all of the end-of-chapter items from the textbook, including Eye Openers, Practice Exercises, Exercises, Problems, Comprehensive Problems (total of five), and Continuing Problem in Chapters 1 through 4. This Solutions Manual has been verified three times, once by each of the following individuals: James Emig, Villanova University; Ann Martel, Marquette University; and Gary Bower, Community College of Rhode Island. The difficulty, time to completion, and outcomes tagging were provided by Janice Stoudemire, Midlands Technical College.

SOLUTION'S MANUAL FEATURES

As with every edition, the end-of-chapter has been completely revised with all new solutions.

NEW QUESTION INFORMATION GRID!

At the beginning of each chapter there is a Question Information Grid. As with the test bank and the instructor's manual, the solutions manual provides this helpful resource to aid instructors in creating comprehensive, balanced homework assignments and to assess student outcomes.

General Information: As a helpful reference, this grid includes the relationship to the chapter objective as well as a short description of the exercises, problems, and special activities from the textbook.

Difficulty: To aid in the creation of challenging but well-timed homework assignments, the grid also assigns each end-of-chapter item a level of difficulty (Easy, Moderate, Difficult), and an estimated time to completion.

Course Outcomes: In addition to providing a variety of questions related to each chapter objective, this solutions manual also employs a series of tags that can help design effective, balanced homework by the measure of course outcomes. When using the homework functionality of ThomsonNOW, this tagging makes it possible to run reports by outcome that gauge how well students in a particular section, course, or department are doing in relation to these outcomes and competencies. Note that this same series of tags have been used in the test bank, ThomsonNOW quiz questions, and any other gradable asset in ThomsonNOW.

In terms of the tags applied, the end-of-chapter represented in this solutions manual is tagged to outcomes created by three bodies that provide curriculum guidance for accounting courses: The Association to Advance Collegiate Schools of Business (AACSB), The American Institute of Certified Public Accountants (AICPA), and the Institute of Management Accountants (IMA). See also the Accounting Principles Outcomes (APO) chart in the instructor's manual for a third tier of outcomes tagging geared specifically for the accounting principles course.

Note: These tags were developed by the publisher and applied based on the publisher's interpretation of AACSB International accreditation standards and AICPA/IMA content guidelines. The list of tags follows with references to the sources that inspired them with comments about their application.

All end-of-chapter material is tagged to AACSB outcomes, but only financial material is tagged to AICPA core competencies. See the solutions manual volume with the managerial chapters for coverage of the IMA content specification outlines.

AACSB: Derived from the AACSB Web site "The Assurance of Learning Standards. 15. Management of Curricula"

Tags	Skills
AACSB Communication	• Communication abilities.
AACSB Ethics	• Ethical understanding and reasoning abilities.
AACSB Analytic	• Analytic skills.
AACSB Technology	• Use of information technology.
AACSB Diversity	• Multicultural and diversity understanding.
AACSB Reflective Thinking	• Reflective thinking skills.

AICPA: Derived from the AICPA Web site.

Tags	Skills
Functional Competencies	
AICPA FN-Decision Modeling	Individuals preparing to enter the accounting profession must be able to use strategic and critical approaches to decision-making. They must objectively consider issues, identify alternatives, and choose and implement solution approaches in order to deliver services and provide value.
AICPA FN-Leveraging Technology	Technology is pervasive in the accounting profession. Individuals entering the accounting profession must acquire the necessary skills to use technology tools effectively and efficiently. These technology tools can be used both to develop and apply other functional competencies.
AICPA FN-Measurement	Measures used should be both relevant (that is, bear on the decision to be made) and reliable (consistently measure what they purport to measure). Various measurement and disclosure criteria used by accounting professionals—such as GAAP, OCBOA (Other Comprehensive Basis of Accounting), and tax reporting—have been codified to some degree. Other performance measures (such as Economic Value Added) or stated criteria (for example, investment performance) are used for special purposes. Some measurement criteria (such as effectiveness of internal control) are measured qualitatively, rather than quantitatively.
AICPA FN-Reporting	Communicating the scope of work and findings or recommendations is an integral part of a professional service. An accounting professional in public practice might issue an audit or attestation report, recommendations for improved services, or tax or financial planning advice. An accounting professional in business, industry, or government might analyze operations or provide communications to the board of directors. Communicating clearly and objectively the work done and the resulting findings is critical to the value of the professional service. Some forms of communication are governed by professional standards (such as the form and content of the standard auditor's report or the required communications to the audit committees) or law. Others are based on the service applied and the needs of those to whom the accounting professional reports.
AICPA FN-Research	Although accounting professionals need a foundation in standards and other relevant rules, such guidance is constantly evolving. Many accounting profession functions depend on obtaining information from within and outside of an entity. Accordingly, the individual preparing to enter the accounting profession needs to have strong research skills to access relevant guidance or other information, understand it, and apply it.
AICPA FN-Risk Analysis	Risk analysis and control is fundamental to professional service delivery. The identification and management of audit risk (that is, the risk that the auditor will fail to detect a misstatement caused by inadvertent error or fraud that is material to financial statements) is the basis for the conduct of a GAAS audit. The understanding of business risk (that is, the risk that an entity—either a client or the prospective accounting professional's employer—will fail to achieve its objectives) affects how business strategy is created and implemented.

Broad Business Competencies	
AICPA BB-Industry	Individuals entering the accounting profession should be able to identify (through research and analysis) the economics and broad business financial risks and opportunities of the industry and economic sector in which a given organization operates. Identification of these risks and opportunities should include both issues specific to the enterprise, as well as those pervasive throughout the industry/sector.
AICPA BB-Global	Individuals entering the accounting profession should be able to identify and communicate the variety of threats and opportunities of doing business in a borderless world. The accounting professional of the future must provide services to support and facilitate commerce in the global marketplace.
AICPA BB-Legal	Regulatory forces are being shaped by collaboration, migration, and reform as the various stakeholders globalize, share information, and force their particular needs and viewpoints onto political agendas. Individuals preparing to enter the accounting profession need to be capable of describing the legal and regulatory environment and analyzing the impact of changes in relevant requirements, constraints, and competitive practices.
AICPA BB-Leveraging Technology	Technology alters how organizations operate. To provide the greatest value, today's accounting professional must understand and appreciate the effects of technology on the broader business environment.
AICPA-BB-Marketing	Individuals who are marketing- and client-focused are better able to anticipate and meet the changing needs of clients, employers, customers, and markets. This involves both the ability to recognize market needs and the ability to develop new markets.
AICPA BB-Resource Management	The ability to appreciate the importance of all resources is critical for success. Individuals entering the accounting profession should be able to apply management and human resource development theories to human resource issues and organizational problems. Individuals preparing to enter the accounting profession should be able to identify sources of capital and analyze the impact of participation in the global capital markets.
AICPA BB-Critical Thinking	Critical thinking encompasses the ability to link data, knowledge, and insight together from various disciplines to provide information for decision making. Being in tune with the "big picture" perspective is a necessary component for success. Individuals entering the accounting profession should be able to communicate to others the vision, strategy, goals, and culture of organizations.

Note: The AICPA also includes personal competencies not covered in this course.

Software: Though all Practice Exercises, Exercises, and Problems are included in our online homework program, ThomsonNOW, other software is available for selected items. Specifically, Excel (Exl in the grid) templates are available for over 200 exercises and problems, and Klooster & Allen General Ledger software (formerly PASS, KA in the grid) is available for over 100 Exercises and Problems. Note that the printed solutions that have been printed for reference with General Ledger Exercises and Problems are now included as Word files on the Instructor's Web site and Instructor's Resource CD.

Solutions transparencies are also available.

CHAPTER 1
INTRODUCTION TO ACCOUNTING
AND BUSINESS

QUESTION INFORMATION

Number	Objective	Description	Difficulty	Time	AACSB	AICPA	SS	GL
Q1-1	1-1		Easy	5 min	Analytic	BB-Industry		
Q1-2	1-1		Easy	5 min	Analytic	BB-Industry		
Q1-3	1-1		Easy	5 min	Analytic	BB-Industry		
Q1-4	1-1		Easy	5 min	Analytic	BB-Industry		
Q1-5	1-1		Easy	5 min	Analytic	BB-Industry		
Q1-6	1-2		Easy	5 min	Analytic	FN-Measurement		
Q1-7	1-2		Easy	5 min	Analytic	FN-Measurement		
Q1-8	1-2, 1-3		Easy	5 min	Analytic	FN-Measurement		
Q1-9	1-3		Easy	5 min	Analytic	FN-Measurement		
Q1-10	1-5		Easy	5 min	Analytic	FN-Measurement		
Q1-11	1-5		Easy	5 min	Analytic	FN-Measurement		
Q1-12	1-5		Easy	5 min	Analytic	FN-Measurement		
PE1-1A	1-2	Cost concept	Easy	5 min	Analytic	FN-Measurement		
PE1-1B	1-2	Cost concept	Easy	5 min	Analytic	FN-Measurement		
PE1-2A	1-3	Accounting equation	Easy	5 min	Analytic	FN-Measurement		
PE1-2B	1-3	Accounting equation	Easy	5 min	Analytic	FN-Measurement		
PE1-3A	1-4	Transactions	Easy	10 min	Analytic	FN-Measurement		
PE1-3B	1-4	Transactions	Easy	10 min	Analytic	FN-Measurement		
PE1-4A	1-5	Income statement	Easy	10 min	Analytic	FN-Measurement		
PE1-4B	1-5	Income statement	Easy	10 min	Analytic	FN-Measurement		
PE1-5A	1-5	Statement of owner's equity	Easy	5 min	Analytic	FN-Measurement		
PE1-5B	1-5	Statement of owner's equity	Easy	5 min	Analytic	FN-Measurement		
PE1-6A	1-5	Balance sheet	Easy	10 min	Analytic	FN-Measurement		
PE1-6B	1-5	Balance sheet	Easy	10 min	Analytic	FN-Measurement		
PE1-7A	1-5	Statement of cash flows	Easy	10 min	Analytic	FN-Measurement		
PE1-7B	1-5	Statement of cash flows	Easy	10 min	Analytic	FN-Measurement		
Ex1-1	1-1	Types of businesses	Easy	5 min	Analytic	BB-Industry		
Ex1-2	1-1	Professional ethics	Easy	5 min	Ethics	BB-Industry		
Ex1-3	1-2	Business entity concept	Easy	10 min	Analytic	BB-Industry		
Ex1-4	1-3	Accounting equation	Easy	5 min	Analytic	FN-Measurement		
Ex1-5	1-3	Accounting equation	Easy	5 min	Analytic	FN-Measurement		
Ex1-6	1-3	Accounting equation	Easy	5 min	Analytic	FN-Measurement		
Ex1-7	1-3, 1-4	Accounting equation	Moderate	10 min	Analytic	FN-Measurement		
Ex1-8	1-4	Asset, liability, owner's equity items	Easy	5 min	Analytic	FN-Measurement		
Ex1-9	1-4	Effect of transactions on accounting equation	Easy	5 min	Analytic	FN-Measurement		
Ex1-10	1-4	Effect of transactions on accounting equation	Easy	5 min	Analytic	FN-Measurement		

Number	Objective	Description	Difficulty	Time	AACSB	AICPA	SS	GL
Ex1-11	1-4	Effect of transactions on accounting equation	Easy	5 min	Analytic	FN-Measurement		
Ex1-12	1-4	Transactions	Easy	10 min	Analytic	FN-Measurement		
Ex1-13	1-4	Nature of transactions	Moderate	15 min	Analytic	FN-Measurement		
Ex1-14	1-5	Net income and owner's withdrawals	Easy	5 min	Analytic	FN-Measurement		
Ex1-15	1-5	Net income and owner's equity for four businesses	Moderate	10 min	Analytic	FN-Measurement		
Ex1-16	1-5	Balance sheet items	Easy	5 min	Analytic	FN-Measurement		
Ex1-17	1-5	Income statement items	Easy	5 min	Analytic	FN-Measurement		
Ex1-18	1-5	Statement of owner's equity	Easy	5 min	Analytic	FN-Measurement	Exl	
Ex1-19	1-5	Income statement	Easy	5 min	Analytic	FN-Measurement	Exl	
Ex1-20	1-5	Missing amounts from balance sheet and income statement data	Moderate	10 min	Analytic	FN-Measurement		
Ex1-21	1-5	Balance sheet, net income	Moderate	15 min	Analytic	FN-Measurement	Exl	
Ex1-22	1-5	Financial statements	Easy	5 min	Analytic	FN-Measurement		
Ex1-23	1-5	Statement of cash flows	Easy	5 min	Analytic	FN-Measurement		
Ex1-24	1-5	Statement of cash flows	Easy	10 min	Analytic	FN-Measurement		
Ex1-25	1-5	Financial statements	Moderate	10 min	Analytic	FN-Measurement		
Pr1-1A	1-4	Transactions	Easy	30 min	Analytic	FN-Measurement		
Pr1-2A	1-5	Financial statements	Easy	30 min	Analytic	FN-Measurement	Exl	
Pr1-3A	1-5	Financial statements	Moderate	45 min	Analytic	FN-Measurement	Exl	
Pr1-4A	1-4, 1-5	Transactions; financial statements	Moderate	1 hr	Analytic	FN-Measurement	Exl	
Pr1-5A	1-4, 1-5	Transactions; financial statements	Moderate	1 1/2 hr	Analytic	FN-Measurement	Exl	KA
Pr1-6A	1-5	Missing amounts from financial statements	Difficult	1 1/2 hr	Analytic	FN-Measurement	Exl	
Pr1-1B	1-4	Transactions	Easy	30 min	Analytic	FN-Measurement		
Pr1-2B	1-5	Financial statements	Easy	30 min	Analytic	FN-Measurement	Exl	
Pr1-3B	1-5	Financial statements	Moderate	45 min	Analytic	FN-Measurement	Exl	
Pr1-4B	1-4,1-5	Transactions; financial statements	Moderate	1 hr	Analytic	FN-Measurement	Exl	
Pr1-5B	1-4,1-5	Transactions; financial statements	Moderate	1 1/2 hr	Analytic	FN-Measurement	Exl	KA
Pr1-6B	1-5	Missing amounts from financial statements	Difficult	1 1/2 hr	Analytic	FN-Measurement	Exl	
DM-1		Continuing Problem						KA
SA1-1	1-1	Ethics and professional conduct in business	Moderate	30 min	Ethics	BB-Industry		
SA1-2	1-4	Net income	Easy	10 min	Analytic	FN-Measurement		
SA1-3	1-4	Transaction and financial statements	Moderate	1 hr	Analytic	FN-Measurement		
SA1-4	1-1	Certification requirements for accountants	Easy	15 min	Analytic	BB-Industry		
SA1-5	1-5	Cash flows	Easy	5 min	Analytic	FN-Measurement		
SA1-6	1-5	Financial analysis of Enron Corporation	Moderate	30 min	Reflective Thinking	BB-Critical Thinking		

EYE OPENERS

1. The objective of most businesses is to maximize profits. Profit is the difference between the amounts received from customers for goods or services provided and the amounts paid for the inputs used to provide those goods or services.

2. A manufacturing business changes basic inputs into products that are then sold to customers. A service business provides services rather than products to customers. A restaurant such as Applebee's has characteristics of both a manufacturing and a service business in that Applebee's takes raw inputs such as cheese, fish, and beef and processes them into products for consumption by its customers. At the same time, Applebee's provides services of waiting on its customers as they dine.

3. The corporate form allows the company to obtain large amounts of resources by issuing stock. For this reason, most companies that require large investments in property, plant, and equipment are organized as corporations.

4. The stakeholders of a business normally include owners, managers, employees, customers, creditors, and the government.

5. Simply put, the role of accounting is to provide information for managers to use in operating the business. In addition, accounting provides information to other stakeholders to use in assessing the economic performance and condition of the business.

6. No. The business entity concept limits the recording of economic data to transactions directly affecting the activities of the business. The payment of the interest of $1,850 is a personal transaction of Rebecca Olson and should not be recorded by Aquarius Delivery Service.

7. The land should be recorded at its cost of $88,000 to Dependable Repair Service. This is consistent with the cost concept.

8. a. No. The offer of $725,000 and the increase in the assessed value should not be recognized in the accounting records.
   b. Cash would increase by $725,000, land would decrease by $375,000, and owner's equity would increase by $350,000.

9. An account receivable is a claim against a customer for goods or services sold. An account payable is an amount owed to a creditor for goods or services purchased. Therefore, an account receivable in the records of the seller is an account payable in the records of the purchaser.

10. The business incurred a net loss of $145,000 ($565,000 – $420,000).

11. The business realized net income of $180,900 ($919,500 – $738,600).

12. Net income or net loss
    Owner's equity at the end of the period
    Cash at the end of the period

PRACTICE EXERCISES

PE 1–1A

$37,000. Under the cost concept, the land should be recorded at the cost to Johnson Repair Service.

PE 1–1B

$100,000. Under the cost concept, the land should be recorded at the cost to Duck Repair Service.

PE 1–2A

a.
$$A = L + OE$$
$$\$617,000 = \$382,000 + OE$$
$$OE = \$235,000$$

b.
$$A = L + OE$$
$$+\$114,000 = -\$29,000 + OE$$
$$OE = +\$143,000$$
OE on December 31, 2008 =
$$\$378,000 = \$235,000 + \$143,000$$

PE 1–2B

a.
$$A = L + OE$$
$$\$336,000 = \$172,500 + OE$$
$$OE = \$163,500$$

b.
$$A = L + OE$$
$$+\$75,000 = \$15,000 + OE$$
$$OE = +\$60,000$$
OE on December 31, 2008 =
$$\$223,500 = \$163,500 + \$60,000$$

PE 1–3A

(2) Asset (Cash) decreases by $815; Liability (Accounts Payable) decreases by $815.

(3) Asset (Accounts Receivable) increases by $3,250; Revenue (Delivery Service Fees) increases by $3,250.

(4) Asset (Cash) increases by $1,150; Asset (Accounts Receivable) decreases by $1,150.

(5) Asset (Cash) decreases by $500; Drawing (Pamela Kolp, Drawing) increases by $500.

PE 1–3B

(2) Expense (Advertising Expense) increases by $674; Asset (Cash) decreases by $674.

(3) Asset (Supplies) increases by $280; Liability (Accounts Payable) increases by $280.

(4) Asset (Accounts Receivable) increases by $4,800; Revenue (Delivery Service Fees) increases by $4,800.

(5) Asset (Cash) increases by $1,150; Asset (Accounts Receivable) decreases by $1,150.

PE 1–4A

HERAT TRAVEL SERVICE
Income Statement
For the Year Ended June 30, 2008

Fees earned		$378,200
Expenses:		
Wages expense	$181,500	
Office expense	91,350	
Miscellaneous expense	3,150	
Total expenses		276,000
Net income		$102,200

PE 1–4B

LEOTARD TRAVEL SERVICE
Income Statement
For the Year Ended February 28, 2008

Fees earned		$377,000
Expenses:		
Wages expense	$225,000	
Office expense	156,650	
Miscellaneous expense	6,350	
Total expenses		388,000
Net loss		$ 11,000

PE 1–5A

HERAT TRAVEL SERVICE
Statement of Owner's Equity
For the Year Ended June 30, 2008

Lola Stahn, capital, July 1, 2007		$ 75,000
Additional investment by owner during year	$ 20,000	
Net income for the year	102,200	
	$122,200	
Less withdrawals	12,000	
Increase in owner's equity		110,200
Lola Stahn, capital, June 30, 2008		$185,200

PE 1–5B

LEOTARD TRAVEL SERVICE
Statement of Owner's Equity
For the Year Ended February 28, 2008

Harry Thompson, capital, March 1, 2007		$190,000
Additional investment by owner during year	$ 18,000	
Net loss for the year	(11,000)	
Less withdrawals	(10,000)	
Decrease in owner's equity		(3,000)
Harry Thompson, capital, February 28, 2008		$187,000

PE 1–6A

HERAT TRAVEL SERVICE
Balance Sheet
June 30, 2008

Assets		Liabilities	
Cash	$ 70,800	Accounts payable	$ 15,300
Accounts receivable	24,350		
Supplies	5,350	**Owner's Equity**	
Land	100,000	Lola Stahn, capital	185,200
		Total liabilities and	
Total assets	$200,500	owner's equity	$200,500

6

PE 1–6B

LEOTARD TRAVEL SERVICE
Balance Sheet
February 28, 2008

Assets		Liabilities	
Cash	$ 22,700	Accounts payable	$ 21,000
Accounts receivable	37,750		
Supplies	2,550	**Owner's Equity**	
Land	145,000	Harry Thompson, capital	187,000
		Total liabilities and	
Total assets	$208,000	owner's equity	$208,000

PE 1–7A

HERAT TRAVEL SERVICE
Statement of Cash Flows
For the Year Ended June 30, 2008

Cash flows from operating activities:		
Cash received from customers	$ 350,000	
Deduct cash payments for operating expenses	270,000	
Net cash flows from operating activities		$ 80,000
Cash flows from investing activities:		
Cash payments for purchase of land		(60,000)
Cash flows from financing activities:		
Cash received from owner as investment	$ 20,000	
Deduct cash withdrawals by owner	12,000	
Net cash flows from financing activities		8,000
Net increase in cash during year		$ 28,000
Cash as of July 1, 2007		42,800
Cash as of June 30, 2008		$ 70,800

PE 1-7B

LEOTARD TRAVEL SERVICE
Statement of Cash Flows
For the Year Ended February 28, 2008

Cash flows from operating activities:		
Cash received from customers	$350,000	
Deduct cash payments for operating expenses	365,000	
Net cash flows from operating activities.................		$ (15,000)
Cash flows from investing activities:		
Cash payments for purchase of land.......................		(27,000)
Cash flows from financing activities:		
Cash received from owner as investment...............	$ 18,000	
Deduct cash withdrawals by owner..........................	10,000	
Net cash flows from financing activities		8,000
Net decrease in cash during year...............................		$ (34,000)
Cash as of March 1, 2007		56,700
Cash as of February 28, 2008		$ 22,700

EXERCISES

Ex. 1–1

1. service	6. manufacturing	11. merchandise
2. service	7. service	12. service
3. merchandise	8. manufacturing	13. merchandise
4. manufacturing	9. manufacturing	14. manufacturing
5. service	10. service	15. manufacturing

Ex. 1–2

As in many ethics issues, there is no one right answer. A fired researcher at the company reported on this issue in these terms: "The company covered up the first report, and the local newspaper uncovered the company's secret. The company was forced to not locate here (Collier County). It became patently clear that doing the least that is legally allowed is not enough."

Ex. 1–3

1. F	5. F	9. F
2. X	6. B	10. F
3. S	7. X	
4. B	8. S	

Ex. 1–4

Coca-Cola owners' equity: $31,327 – $15,392 = $15,935
PepsiCo owners' equity: $27,987 – $14,415 = $13,572

Ex. 1–5

eBay	$7,991 – $1,263 = $6,728
Google	$3,313 – $384 = $2,929

Ex. 1–6

a. $300,600 ($85,000 + $215,600)
b. $87,350 ($93,500 – $6,150)
c. $31,225 ($42,500 – $11,275)

Ex. 1–7

a. $650,000 ($950,000 – $300,000)
b. $710,000 ($650,000 + $150,000 – $90,000)
c. $548,000 ($650,000 – $75,000 – $27,000)
d. $823,000 ($650,000 + $125,000 + $48,000)
e. Net income: $355,000 ($1,200,000 – $195,000 – $650,000)

Ex. 1–8

a. asset
b. owner's equity
c. liability
d. owner's equity
e. asset
f. asset

Ex. 1–9

a. Increases assets and increases liabilities.
b. Increases assets and decreases assets.
c. Decreases assets and decreases owner's equity.
d. Increases assets and increases owner's equity.
e. Increases assets and increases owner's equity.

Ex. 1–10

    a. (1)   Total assets increased $70,000.

      (2)   No change in liabilities.

      (3)   Owner's equity increased $70,000.

    b. (1)   Total assets decreased $40,000.

      (2)   Total liabilities decreased $40,000.

      (3)   No change in owner's equity.

Ex. 1–11

1. increase
2. decrease
3. increase
4. decrease

Ex. 1–12

1. c
2. c
3. e
4. d
5. c
6. a
7. e
8. a
9. e
10. e

Ex. 1–13

a. (1) Sale of catering services for cash, $45,000.

   (2) Purchase of land for cash, $20,000.

   (3) Payment of expenses, $16,000.

   (4) Purchase of supplies on account, $3,000.

   (5) Withdrawal of cash by owner, $5,000.

   (6) Payment of cash to creditors, $12,000.

   (7) Recognition of cost of supplies used, $2,500.

b. $8,000 ($27,000 – $19,000)

c. $21,500 (–$5,000 + $45,000 – $18,500)

d. $26,500 ($45,000 – $18,500)

e. $21,500 ($26,500 – $5,000)

Ex. 1–14

It would be incorrect to say that the business had incurred a net loss of $32,200. The excess of the withdrawals over the net income for the period is a decrease in the amount of owner's equity in the business.

Ex. 1–15

Alpha

Owner's equity at end of year	
($2,160,000 – $900,000)...	$1,260,000
Owner's equity at beginning of year	
($1,350,000 – $540,000)...	810,000
Net income (increase in owner's equity)	$ 450,000

Bravo

Increase in owner's equity (as determined for Alpha).....	$450,000
Add withdrawals	120,000
Net income...	$570,000

Charlie

Increase in owner's equity (as determined for Alpha).....	$450,000
Deduct additional investment...	270,000
Net income...	$180,000

Delta

Increase in owner's equity (as determined for Alpha).....	$450,000
Deduct additional investment...	270,000
	$180,000
Add withdrawals	120,000
Net income...	$300,000

Ex. 1–16

Balance sheet items: 1, 2, 4, 5, 6, 10

Ex. 1–17

Income statement items: 3, 7, 8, 9

Ex. 1–18

PICKEREL COMPANY
Statement of Owner's Equity
For the Month Ended June 30, 2008

Lynn Jepsen, capital, June 1, 2008		$682,900
Net income for the month	$196,350	
Less withdrawals..	15,000	
Increase in owner's equity.......................................		181,350
Lynn Jepsen, capital, June 30, 2008		$864,250

Ex. 1–19

GIBLET SERVICES
Income Statement
For the Month Ended February 28, 2008

Fees earned...		$479,280
Expenses:		
Wages expense..	$310,600	
Rent expense...	60,000	
Supplies expense..	6,200	
Miscellaneous expense	11,150	
Total expenses		387,950
Net income		$ 91,330

Ex. 1–20

In each case, solve for a single unknown, using the following equation:
Owner's equity (beginning) + Investments – Withdrawals + Revenues – Expenses
= Owner's equity (ending)

Oscar		
Owner's equity at end of year ($670,500 – $292,500).............		$378,000
Owner's equity at beginning of year ($540,000 – $324,000)..		216,000
Increase in owner's equity..		$162,000
Deduct increase due to net income ($177,975 – $97,200)		80,775
		$ 81,225
Add withdrawals		36,000
Additional investment in the business...............................	(a)	$117,225

Papa		
Owner's equity at end of year ($175,000 – $55,000)...............		$120,000
Owner's equity at beginning of year ($125,000 – $65,000)....		60,000
Increase in owner's equity..		$ 60,000
Add withdrawals		8,000
		$ 68,000
Deduct additional investment...		25,000
Increase due to net income...		$ 43,000
Add expenses..		32,000
Revenue	(b)	$ 75,000

Quebec		
Owner's equity at end of year ($180,000 – $160,000).............		$ 20,000
Owner's equity at beginning of year ($200,000 – $152,000)..		48,000
Decrease in owner's equity...		$(28,000)
Deduct decrease due to net loss ($230,000 – $245,000)........		(15,000)
		$(13,000)
Deduct additional investment...		20,000
Withdrawals from the business	(c)	$(33,000)

Romeo		
Owner's equity at end of year ($248,000 – $136,000).............		$112,000
Add decrease due to net loss ($112,000 – $128,000).............		16,000
		$128,000
Add withdrawals		60,000
Owner's equity at beginning of year		$188,000
Deduct additional investment...		40,000
		$148,000
Add liabilities at beginning of year..		120,000
Assets at beginning of year	(d)	$268,000

Ex. 1–21

a.

BURST INTERIORS
Balance Sheet
March 31, 2008

Assets		Liabilities	
Cash................................	$ 72,000	Accounts payable..........	$ 18,480
Accounts receivable.......	40,800		
Supplies...........................	3,600	**Owner's Equity**	
		Gary Deming, capital.....	97,920
		Total liabilities and	
Total assets.....................	$116,400	owner's equity	$116,400

BURST INTERIORS
Balance Sheet
April 30, 2008

Assets		Liabilities	
Cash................................	$122,400	Accounts payable..........	$ 19,920
Accounts receivable.......	46,950		
Supplies...........................	3,000	**Owner's Equity**	
		Gary Deming, capital.....	152,430
		Total liabilities and	
Total assets.....................	$172,350	owner's equity	$172,350

b.	Owner's equity, April 30...	$152,430
	Owner's equity, March 31	97,920
	Net income	$ 54,510

c.	Owner's equity, April 30...	$152,430
	Owner's equity, March 31	97,920
	Increase in owner's equity	$ 54,510
	Add withdrawal	15,000
	Net income	$ 69,510

Ex. 1–22

Balance sheet: a, b, c, d, f, g, h, i, j, k, m
Income statement: e, l, n, o

Ex. 1–23

1. c–financing activity
2. a–operating activity
3. b–investing activity
4. a–operating activity

Ex. 1–24

WEBSTER CONSULTING GROUP
Statement of Cash Flows
For the Year Ended July 31, 2008

Cash flows from operating activities:		
Cash received from customers	$495,000	
Deduct cash payments for operating expenses	371,500	
Net cash flows from operating activities.................		$123,500
Cash flows from investing activities:		
Cash payments for purchase of land.......................		(40,000)
Cash flows from financing activities:		
Cash received from owner as investment...............	$ 20,000	
Deduct cash withdrawals by owner.........................	9,000	
Net cash flows from financing activities		11,000
Net increase in cash during year...................................		$ 94,500
Cash as of August 1, 2007		46,750
Cash as of July 31, 2008		$141,250

Ex. 1–25

1. All financial statements should contain the name of the business in their heading. The statement of owner's equity is incorrectly headed as "Ora Tasker" rather than Galaxy Realty. The heading of the balance sheet needs the name of the business.

2. The income statement and statement of owner's equity cover a period of time and should be labeled "For the Month Ended November 30, 2008."

3. The year in the heading for the statement of owner's equity should be 2008 rather than 2007.

4. The balance sheet should be labeled as of "November 30, 2008," rather than "For the Month Ended November 30, 2008."

5. In the income statement, the miscellaneous expense amount should be listed as the last expense.

6. In the income statement, the total expenses are incorrectly subtracted from the sales commissions, resulting in an incorrect net income amount. The correct net income should be $9,800. This also affects the statement of owner's equity and the amount of Ora Tasker, capital, that appears on the balance sheet.

7. In the statement of owner's equity, the additional investment should be added first to Ora Tasker, capital, as of November 1, 2008. The net income should be presented next, followed by the amount of withdrawals, which is subtracted from the net income to yield a net increase in owner's equity.

8. Accounts payable should be listed as a liability on the balance sheet.

9. Accounts receivable and supplies should be listed as assets on the balance sheet.

10. The balance sheet assets should equal the sum of the liabilities and owner's equity.

Ex. 1–25 Concluded

Corrected financial statements appear as follows:

GALAXY REALTY
Income Statement
For the Month Ended November 30, 2008

Sales commissions		$103,800
Expenses:		
Office salaries expense	$64,800	
Rent expense	22,000	
Automobile expense	5,000	
Supplies expense	600	
Miscellaneous expense	1,600	
Total expenses		94,000
Net income		$ 9,800

GALAXY REALTY
Statement of Owner's Equity
For the Month Ended November 30, 2008

Ora Tasker, capital, November 1, 2008		$20,800
Additional investment during November	$ 5,000	
Net income for November	9,800	
	$14,800	
Less withdrawals during November	4,000	
Increase in owner's equity		10,800
Ora Tasker, capital, November 30, 2008		$31,600

GALAXY REALTY
Balance Sheet
November 30, 2008

Assets		Liabilities	
Cash	$ 6,600	Accounts payable	$ 7,600
Accounts receivable	28,600		
Supplies	4,000	Owner's Equity	
		Ora Tasker, capital	31,600
		Total liabilities and	
Total assets	$39,200	owner's equity	$39,200

Prob. 1–1A

1.

| | Assets | | | = Liabilities + | Owner's Equity | | | | | | | |
	Cash +	Accts. Rec. +	Supplies =	Accts. Payable +	Doni Gilmore, Capital –	Doni Gilmore Drawing +	Fees Earned –	Rent Exp. –	Sal. Exp. –	Supp. Exp. –	Auto Exp. –	Misc. Exp.
a.	+ 25,000				+ 25,000							
b.			+ 1,150	+ 1,150								
Bal.	25,000		1,150	1,150	25,000							
c.	+ 4,500						+ 4,500					
Bal.	29,500		1,150	1,150	25,000		4,500					
d.	– 1,500							– 1,500				
Bal.	28,000		1,150	1,150	25,000		4,500	– 1,500				
e.	– 600			– 600								
Bal.	27,400		1,150	550	25,000		4,500	– 1,500				
f.		+ 2,250					+ 2,250					
Bal.	27,400	2,250	1,150	550	25,000		6,750	– 1,500				
g.	– 580										– 400	– 180
Bal.	26,820	2,250	1,150	550	25,000		6,750	– 1,500			– 400	– 180
h.	– 1,200								– 1,200			
Bal.	25,620	2,250	1,150	550	25,000		6,750	– 1,500	– 1,200		– 400	– 180
i.			– 770							– 770		
Bal.	25,620	2,250	380	550	25,000		6,750	– 1,500	– 1,200	– 770	– 400	– 180
j.	– 1,000					– 1,000						
Bal.	24,620	2,250	380	550	25,000	– 1,000	6,750	– 1,500	– 1,200	– 770	– 400	– 180

2. Owner's equity is the right of owners to the assets of the business. These rights are increased by owner's investments and revenues and decreased by owner's withdrawals and expenses.

Prob. 1–2A

1.

PEDIGREE TRAVEL AGENCY
Income Statement
For the Year Ended December 31, 2008

Fees earned...		$ 250,000
Expenses:		
Wages expense..	$65,000	
Rent expense	25,000	
Utilities expense	18,200	
Supplies expense	2,800	
Miscellaneous expense....................................	1,500	
Total expenses		112,500
Net income		$ 137,500

2.

PEDIGREE TRAVEL AGENCY
Statement of Owner's Equity
For the Year Ended December 31, 2008

Shiann Ott, capital, January 1, 2008................................		$115,000
Net income for the year..	$137,500	
Less withdrawals...	40,000	
Increase in owner's equity..		97,500
Shiann Ott, capital, December 31, 2008		$212,500

3.

PEDIGREE TRAVEL AGENCY
Balance Sheet
December 31, 2008

Assets		Liabilities	
Cash..................................	$180,000	Accounts payable..........	$ 12,500
Accounts receivable	42,300		
Supplies............................	2,700	**Owner's Equity**	
		Shiann Ott, capital.........	212,500
		Total liabilities and	
Total assets......................	$225,000	owner's equity	$225,000

Prob. 1–3A

1.

MARINER FINANCIAL SERVICES
Income Statement
For the Month Ended January 31, 2008

Fees earned..		$52,400
Expenses:		
Salaries expense	$15,000	
Rent expense	7,500	
Auto expense	4,500	
Supplies expense	455	
Miscellaneous expense..	1,280	
Total expenses		28,735
Net income		$23,665

2.

MARINER FINANCIAL SERVICES
Statement of Owner's Equity
For the Month Ended January 31, 2008

Barry Kimm, January 1, 2008..		$ 0
Investment on January 1, 2008..	$25,000	
Net income for January..	23,665	
	$48,665	
Less withdrawals...	9,000	
Increase in owner's equity..		39,665
Barry Kimm, capital, January 31, 2008		$39,665

3.

MARINER FINANCIAL SERVICES
Balance Sheet
January 31, 2008

Assets		Liabilities	
Cash..............................	$29,140	Accounts payable..........	$ 600
Accounts receivable.......	10,400		
Supplies.........................	725	Owner's Equity	
		Barry Kimm, capital.......	39,665
		Total liabilities and	
Total assets....................	$40,265	owner's equity	$40,265

Prob. 1–3A   Concluded

4. (Optional)

MARINER FINANCIAL SERVICES
Statement of Cash Flows
For the Month Ended January 31, 2008

Cash flows from operating activities:		
Cash received from customers	$42,000	
Deduct cash payments for expenses		
and payments to creditors	28,860*	
Net cash flow used for operating activities		$13,140
Cash flows from investing activities................................		0
Cash flows from financing activities:		
Cash received as owner's investment......................	$25,000	
Deduct cash withdrawal by owner............................	9,000	
Net cash flow from financing activities		16,000
Net cash flow and January 31, 2008, cash balance........		$29,140

*$580 + $7,500 + $5,780 + $15,000

Prob. 1–4A

1.

	Assets		=	Liabilities +		Owner's Equity							
	Cash	+ Supplies	=	Accts. Payable	+ Ginny Tyler, Capital	– Ginny Tyler, Drawing	+ Sales Comm.	– Office Sal. Exp.	– Rent Exp.	– Auto Exp.	– Supp. Exp.	– Misc. Exp.
a.	+ 30,000				+30,000							
b.		+ 2,650		+ 2,650								
Bal.	30,000	+ 2,650		2,650	30,000							
c.	– 1,500			– 1,500								
Bal.	28,500	2,650		1,150	30,000							
d.	+ 36,750						+ 36,750					
Bal.	65,250	2,650		1,150	30,000		36,750					
e.	– 5,200								5,200			
Bal.	60,050	2,650		1,150	30,000		36,750		5,200			
f.	– 8,000					8,000						
Bal.	52,050	2,650		1,150	30,000	8,000	36,750		5,200			
g.	– 3,700									2,500		1,200
Bal.	48,350	2,650		1,150	30,000	8,000	36,750		5,200	2,500		1,200
h.	– 9,250							9,250				
Bal.	39,100	2,650		1,150	30,000	8,000	36,750	9,250	5,200	2,500		1,200
i.		– 1,750									1,750	
Bal.	39,100	900		1,150	30,000	8,000	36,750	9,250	5,200	2,500	1,750	1,200

2.

SELTZER REALTY
Income Statement
For the Month Ended March 31, 2008

Sales commissions		$36,750
Expenses:		
Office salaries expense	$9,250	
Rent expense	5,200	
Automobile expense	2,500	
Supplies expense	1,750	
Miscellaneous expense	1,200	
Total expenses		19,900
Net income		$16,850

SELTZER REALTY
Statement of Owner's Equity
For the Month Ended March 31, 2008

Ginny Tyler, capital, March 1, 2008		$ 0
Investment on March 1, 2008	$30,000	
Net income for March	16,850	
	$46,850	
Less withdrawals	8,000	
Increase in owner's equity		38,850
Ginny Tyler, capital, March 31, 2008		$38,850

SELTZER REALTY
Balance Sheet
March 31, 2008

Assets		Liabilities	
Cash	$39,100	Accounts payable	$ 1,150
Supplies	900		
		Owner's Equity	
		Ginny Tyler, capital	38,850
		Total liabilities and	
Total assets	$40,000	owner's equity	$40,000

Prob. 1–5A

1.

Assets				=	Liabilities	+	Owner's Equity
	Accounts				Accounts		
Cash +	Receivable +	Supplies +	Land	=	Payable	+	Kerry Ulman, Capital
8,500 +	15,500 +	1,600 +	18,000	=	5,200	+	Kerry Ulman, Capital
	43,600			=	5,200	+	Kerry Ulman, Capital
	38,400			=			Kerry Ulman, Capital

This page left intentionally blank.

Prob. 1–5A   Continued

2.

			Assets					=	Liabilities	+	Owner's Equity	
	Cash	+	Accounts Receivable	+	Supplies	+	Land	=	Accounts Payable	+	Kerry Ulman, Capital	Kerry Ulman, – Drawing
Bal.	8,500		15,500		1,600		18,000		5,200		38,400	
a.	+ 30,000										+ 30,000	
Bal.	38,500		15,500		1,600		18,000		5,200		68,400	
b.	– 22,000						+ 22,000					
Bal.	16,500		15,500		1,600		40,000		5,200		68,400	
c.	+ 17,900											
Bal.	34,400		15,500		1,600		40,000		5,200		68,400	
d.	– 3,000											
Bal.	31,400		15,500		1,600		40,000		5,200		68,400	
e.					+ 1,550				+ 1,550			
Bal.	31,400		15,500		3,150		40,000		6,750		68,400	
f.	– 4,950								– 4,950			
Bal.	26,450		15,500		3,150		40,000		1,800		68,400	
g.			+ 12,350									
Bal.	26,450		27,850		3,150		40,000		1,800		68,400	
h.									+ 7,880			
Bal.	26,450		27,850		3,150		40,000		9,680		68,400	
i.	– 8,050											
Bal.	18,400		27,850		3,150		40,000		9,680		68,400	
j.	+ 13,200		– 13,200									
Bal.	31,600		14,650		3,150		40,000		9,680		68,400	
k.					– 1,875							
Bal.	31,600		14,650		1,275		40,000		9,680		68,400	
l.	– 5,000											– 5,000
Bal.	26,600		14,650		1,275		40,000		9,680		68,400	– 5,000

Owner's Equity (Continued)

	Dry Cleaning + Sales –	Dry Cleaning Exp. –	Wages Exp. –	Rent Exp. –	Supplies Exp. –	Truck Exp. –	Utilities Exp. –	Misc. Exp.
Bal.								
a.								
Bal.								
b.								
Bal.								
c.	+ 17,900							
Bal.	17,900							
d.				– 3,000				
Bal.	17,900			– 3,000				
e.								
Bal.	17,900			– 3,000				
f.								
Bal.	17,900			– 3,000				
g.	+ 12,350							
Bal.	30,250			– 3,000				
h.		– 7,880						
Bal.	30,250	– 7,880		– 3,000				
i.			– 5,100			– 1,200	– 800	– 950
Bal.	30,250	– 7,880	– 5,100	– 3,000		– 1,200	– 800	– 950
j.								
Bal.	30,250	– 7,880	– 5,100	– 3,000		– 1,200	– 800	– 950
k.					– 1,875			
Bal.	30,250	– 7,880	– 5,100	– 3,000	– 1,875	– 1,200	– 800	– 950
l.								
Bal.	30,250	– 7,880	– 5,100	– 3,000	– 1,875	– 1,200	– 800	– 950

29

Prob. 1–5A   Continued

3. a.

ARGON DRY CLEANERS
Income Statement
For the Month Ended July 31, 2008

Dry cleaning sales		$30,250
Expenses:		
Dry cleaning expense..	$7,880	
Wages expense..	5,100	
Rent expense	3,000	
Supplies expense	1,875	
Truck expense	1,200	
Utilities expense	800	
Miscellaneous expense...	950	
Total expenses		20,805
Net income		$ 9,445

b.

ARGON DRY CLEANERS
Statement of Owner's Equity
For the Month Ended July 31, 2008

Kerry Ulman, capital, July 1, 2008			$38,400
Additional investment by Kerry Ulman	$30,000		
Net income for July...	9,445	$39,445	
Less withdrawals..		5,000	
Increase in owner's equity............................			34,445
Kerry Ulman, capital, July 31, 2008			$72,845

c.

ARGON DRY CLEANERS
Balance Sheet
July 31, 2008

Assets		Liabilities	
Cash.................................	$26,600	Accounts payable..........	$ 9,680
Accounts receivable	14,650		
Supplies...........................	1,275	**Owner's Equity**	
Land	40,000	Kerry Ulman, capital......	72,845
		Total liabilities and	
Total assets....................	$82,525	owner's equity	$82,525

Prob. 1–5A   Concluded

4. (Optional)

ARGON DRY CLEANERS
Statement of Cash Flows
For the Month Ended July 31, 2008

Cash flows from operating activities:		
Cash received from customers	$31,100*	
Deduct cash payments for expenses		
and payments to creditors	16,000**	
Net cash flow from operating activities		$ 15,100
Cash flows from investing activities:		
Purchase of land...		(22,000)
Cash flows from financing activities:		
Cash received as owner's investment......................	$30,000	
Deduct cash withdrawal by owner............................	5,000	
Net cash flow from financing activities		25,000
Increase in cash...		$ 18,100
Cash balance, July 1, 2008		8,500
Cash balance, July 31, 2008		$ 26,600

 *$17,900 + $13,200
**$3,000 + $4,950 + $8,050

Prob. 1–6A

a. Fees earned, $120,000 ($49,600 + $70,400)

b. Supplies expense, $12,000 ($70,400 – $34,000 – $12,800 – $7,200 – $4,400)

c. Andrea Merkel, capital, June 1, 2008, $0

d. Net income for June, $49,600

e. $209,600 ($160,000 + $49,600)

f. Increase in owner's equity, $185,600 ($209,600 – $24,000)

g. Andrea Merkel, capital, June 30, 2008, $185,600

h. Total assets, $192,000 ($17,800 + $14,200 + $160,000)

i. Andrea Merkel, capital, $185,600 ($192,000 – $6,400)

j. Total liabilities and owner's equity, $192,000

k. Cash received from customers, $120,000; this is the same as fees earned (a) since there are no accounts receivable.

l. Net cash flow from operating activities, $41,800 ($120,000 – $78,000)

m. Cash payments for acquisition of land, ($160,000)

n. Cash received as owner's investment, $160,000

o. Cash withdrawal by owner, ($24,000)

p. Net cash flow from financing activities, $136,000 ($160,000 – $24,000)

q. Net cash flow and June 30, 2008, cash balance, $17,800

1.

	Assets			=	Liabilities	+	Owner's Equity								
	Cash +	Accts. Rec. +	Supplies	=	Accts. Payable	+	Ana Urbin, Capital	– Ana Urbin Drawing	+ Fees Earned	– Rent Exp.	– Sal. Exp.	– Supp. Exp.	– Auto Exp.	– Misc. Exp.
a.	+ 40,000						+ 40,000							
b.			+ 1,500		+ 1,500									
Bal.	40,000		1,500		1,500		40,000							
c.	– 800				– 800									
Bal.	39,200		1,500		700		40,000							
d.	+ 7,250								+ 7,250					
Bal.	46,450		1,500		700		40,000		7,250					
e.	– 2,500									– 2,500				
Bal.	43,950		1,500		700		40,000		7,250	– 2,500				
f.	– 1,400												– 1,000	– 400
Bal.	42,550		1,500		700		40,000		7,250	– 2,500			– 1,000	– 400
g.	– 2,000										– 2,000			
Bal.	40,550		1,500		700		40,000		7,250	– 2,500	– 2,000		– 1,000	– 400
h.			– 1,100									– 1,100		
Bal.	40,550		400		700		40,000		7,250	– 2,500	– 2,000	– 1,100	– 1,000	– 400
i.		+ 9,350							+ 9,350					
Bal.	40,550	9,350	400		700		40,000		16,600	– 2,500	– 2,000	– 1,100	– 1,000	– 400
j.	– 3,000							– 3,000						
Bal.	37,550	9,350	400		700		40,000	– 3,000	16,600	– 2,500	– 2,000	– 1,100	– 1,000	– 400

2. Owner's equity is the right of owners to the assets of the business. These rights are increased by owner's investments and revenues and decreased by owner's withdrawals and expenses.

Prob. 1–2B

1.

ABYSS TRAVEL SERVICE
Income Statement
For the Year Ended June 30, 2008

Fees earned..		$375,000
Expenses:		
Wages expense...	$145,400	
Rent expense	50,600	
Utilities expense	31,200	
Supplies expense	8,250	
Taxes expense	6,400	
Miscellaneous expense...............................	3,150	
Total expenses		245,000
Net income		$130,000

2.

ABYSS TRAVEL SERVICE
Statement of Owner's Equity
For the Year Ended June 30, 2008

Megan Koch, capital, July 1, 2007		$ 60,000
Net income for the year..	$130,000	
Less withdrawals..	50,000	
Increase in owner's equity..		80,000
Megan Koch, capital, June 30, 2008..................................		$140,000

3.

ABYSS TRAVEL SERVICE
Balance Sheet
June 30, 2008

Assets		Liabilities	
Cash..................................	$ 99,500	Accounts payable..........	$ 12,500
Accounts receivable.......	48,750		
Supplies...........................	4,250	**Owner's Equity**	
		Megan Koch, capital......	140,000
		Total liabilities and	
Total assets.....................	$152,500	owner's equity	$152,500

Prob. 1–3B

1.

FIREFLY COMPUTER SERVICES
Income Statement
For the Month Ended May 31, 2008

Fees earned...		$41,250
Expenses:		
Salaries expense	$10,000	
Rent expense	9,000	
Auto expense	3,875	
Supplies expense	1,625	
Miscellaneous expense..............................	1,875	
Total expenses		26,375
Net income		$14,875

2.

FIREFLY COMPUTER SERVICES
Statement of Owner's Equity
For the Month Ended May 31, 2008

Kelly Cassidy, capital, May 1, 2008		$ 0
Investment on May 1, 2008................................	$25,000	
Net income for May..	14,875	
	$39,875	
Less withdrawals..	5,000	
Increase in owner's equity.................................		34,875
Kelly Cassidy, capital, May 31, 2008		$34,875

3.

FIREFLY COMPUTER SERVICES
Balance Sheet
May 31, 2008

Assets		Liabilities	
Cash..................................	$16,500	Accounts payable..........	$ 2,350
Accounts receivable	18,750		
Supplies...........................	1,975	**Owner's Equity**	
		Kelly Cassidy, capital....	34,875
		Total liabilities and	
Total assets.....................	$37,225	owner's equity	$37,225

Prob. 1–3B   Concluded

4. (Optional)

FIREFLY COMPUTER SERVICES
Statement of Cash Flows
For the Month Ended May 31, 2008

Cash flows from operating activities:		
Cash received from customers	$22,500	
Deduct cash payments for expenses		
and payments to creditors..	26,000*	
Net cash flow from operating activities		$ (3,500)
Cash flows from investing activities:.............................		0
Cash flows from financing activities:		
Cash received as owner's investment......................	$25,000	
Deduct cash withdrawal by owner	5,000	
Net cash flow from financing activities		20,000
Net cash flow and May 31, 2008, cash balance...............		$16,500

*$9,000 + $1,250 + $5,750 + $10,000

Prob. 1-4B

1.

| | Assets | | = | Liabilities | + | Owner's Equity | | | | | | | |
	Cash +	Supplies	=	Accts. Payable	+	Britt Quinn, Capital	– Britt Quinn, Drawing	+ Sales Comm.	– Office Sal. Exp.	– Rent Exp.	– Auto Exp.	– Supp. Exp.	– Misc. Exp.
a.	+ 30,000					+30,000							
b.	– 2,200									– 2,200			
Bal.	27,800					30,000				– 2,200			
c.	– 1,850										– 1,200		– 650
Bal.	25,950					30,000				– 2,200	– 1,200		– 650
d.		+ 200		+ 200									
Bal.	25,950	200		200		30,000				– 2,200	– 1,200		– 650
e.	+ 20,800							+ 20,800					
Bal.	46,750	200		200		30,000		20,800		– 2,200	– 1,200		– 650
f.	– 150			– 150									
Bal.	46,600	200		50		30,000		20,800		– 2,200	– 1,200		– 650
g.	– 3,600								– 3,600				
Bal.	43,000	200		50		30,000		20,800	– 3,600	– 2,200	– 1,200		– 650
h.	– 1,500						– 1,500						
Bal.	41,500	200		50		30,000	– 1,500	20,800	– 3,600	– 2,200	– 1,200		– 650
i.		– 160										– 160	
Bal.	41,500	40		50		30,000	– 1,500	20,800	– 3,600	– 2,200	– 1,200	– 160	– 650

37

Prob. 1–4B Concluded

2.

UPTOWN REALTY
Income Statement
For the Month Ended April 30, 2008

Sales commissions		$20,800
Expenses:		
Office salaries expense..	$3,600	
Rent expense	2,200	
Automobile expense...	1,200	
Supplies expense	160	
Miscellaneous expense..	650	
Total expenses		7,810
Net income		$12,990

UPTOWN REALTY
Statement of Owner's Equity
For the Month Ended April 30, 2008

Britt Quinn, capital, April 1, 2008......................................		$ 0
Investment on April 1, 2008	$30,000	
Net income for April..	12,990	
	$42,990	
Less withdrawals..	1,500	
Increase in owner's equity...		41,490
Britt Quinn, capital, April 30, 2008...................................		$41,490

UPTOWN REALTY
Balance Sheet
April 30, 2008

Assets		Liabilities		
Cash...............................	$41,500	Accounts payable..........	$	50
Supplies...........................	40			
		Owner's Equity		
		Britt Quinn, capital		41,490
		Total liabilities and		
Total assets	$41,540	owner's equity		$41,540

Prob. 1–5B

1.

				Assets			=	Liabilities	+	Owner's Equity
Cash	+	Accounts Receivable	+	Supplies	+	Land	=	Accounts Payable	+	Jean Potts, Capital
17,200	+	19,000	+	3,750	+	30,000	=	8,200	+	Jean Potts, Capital
			69,950				=	8,200	+	Jean Potts, Capital
			61,750				=			Jean Potts, Capital

Prob. 1–5B Continued

2.

	Assets					=	Liabilities	+	Owner's Equity	
	Cash	+	Accounts Receivable	+	Supplies	+	Land	=	Accounts Payable	+	Jean Potts, Capital	Jean Potts, – Drawing

	Cash	Accounts Receivable	Supplies	Land	Accounts Payable	Jean Potts, Capital	Jean Potts, Drawing
Bal.	17,200	19,000	3,750	30,000	8,200	61,750	
a.	+ 50,000					+ 50,000	
Bal.	67,200	19,000	3,750	30,000	8,200	111,750	
b.	– 45,000			+ 45,000			
Bal.	22,200	19,000	3,750	75,000	8,200	111,750	
c.	– 4,500						
Bal.	17,700	19,000	3,750	75,000	8,200	111,750	
d.		+ 15,250					
Bal.	17,700	34,250	3,750	75,000	8,200	111,750	
e.	– 5,800				– 5,800		
Bal.	11,900	34,250	3,750	75,000	2,400	111,750	
f.			+ 3,200		+ 3,200		
Bal.	11,900	34,250	6,950	75,000	5,600	111,750	
g.	+ 22,900						
Bal.	34,800	34,250	6,950	75,000	5,600	111,750	
h.	+ 17,250	– 17,250					
Bal.	52,050	17,000	6,950	75,000	5,600	111,750	
i.					+ 16,380		
Bal.	52,050	17,000	6,950	75,000	21,980	111,750	
j.	– 10,500						
Bal.	41,550	17,000	6,950	75,000	21,980	111,750	
k.			– 4,450				
Bal.	41,550	17,000	2,500	75,000	21,980	111,750	
l.	– 6,000						– 6,000
Bal.	35,550	17,000	2,500	75,000	21,980	111,750	– 6,000

Owner's Equity (Continued)

	+	Dry Cleaning Sales	–	Dry Cleaning Exp.	–	Wages Exp.	–	Rent Exp.	–	Supplies Exp.	–	Truck Exp.	–	Utilities Exp.	–	Misc. Exp.
Bal.																
a.																
Bal.																
b.																
Bal.																
c.							–	4,500								
Bal.							–	4,500								
d.		+ 15,250														
Bal.		15,250					–	4,500								
e.																
Bal.		15,250					–	4,500								
f.																
Bal.		15,250					–	4,500								
g.		+ 22,900														
Bal.		38,150					–	4,500								
h.																
Bal.		38,150					–	4,500								
i.			–	16,380												
Bal.		38,150	–	16,380			–	4,500								
j.					–	6,200					–	1,875	–	1,575	–	850
Bal.		38,150	–	16,380	–	6,200	–	4,500			–	1,875	–	1,575	–	850
k.									–	4,450						
Bal.		38,150	–	16,380	–	6,200	–	4,500	–	4,450	–	1,875	–	1,575	–	850
l.																
Bal.		38,150	–	16,380	–	6,200	–	4,500	–	4,450	–	1,875	–	1,575	–	850

Prob. 1–5B   Continued

3. a.

SKIVVY DRY CLEANERS
Income Statement
For the Month Ended November 30, 2008

Dry cleaning sales		$38,150
Expenses:		
Dry cleaning expense	$16,380	
Wages expense	6,200	
Rent expense	4,500	
Supplies expense	4,450	
Truck expense	1,875	
Utilities expense	1,575	
Miscellaneous expense	850	
Total expenses		35,830
Net income		$ 2,320

b.

SKIVVY DRY CLEANERS
Statement of Owner's Equity
For the Month Ended November 30, 2008

Jean Potts, capital, November 1, 2008			$ 61,750
Additional investment by Jean Potts	$50,000		
Net income for November	2,320	$52,320	
Less withdrawals		6,000	
Increase in owner's equity			46,320
Jean Potts, capital, November 30, 2008			$108,070

c.

SKIVVY DRY CLEANERS
Balance Sheet
November 30, 2008

Assets		Liabilities	
Cash	$ 35,550	Accounts payable	$ 21,980
Accounts receivable	17,000		
Supplies	2,500	Owner's Equity	
Land	75,000	Jean Potts, capital	108,070
		Total liabilities and	
Total assets	$130,050	owner's equity	$130,050

Prob. 1–5B   Concluded

4. (Optional)

SKIVVY DRY CLEANERS
Statement of Cash Flows
For the Month Ended November 30, 2008

Cash flows from operating activities:		
Cash received from customers	$40,150*	
Deduct cash payments for expenses		
and payments to creditors	20,800**	
Net cash flow from operating activities		$19,350
Cash flows from investing activities:		
Purchase of land		(45,000)
Cash flows from financing activities:		
Cash received as owner's investment	$50,000	
Deduct cash withdrawal by owner	6,000	
Net cash flow from financing activities		44,000
Increase in cash		$18,350
Cash balance, November 1, 2008		17,200
Cash balance, November 30, 2008		$35,550

 *$22,900 + $17,250

**$4,500 + $5,800 + $10,500

Prob. 1–6B

a. Wages expense, $6,450 ($14,340 − $2,880 − $2,400 − $1,620 − $990)

b. Net income, $13,860 ($28,200 − $14,340)

c. Iris Sigrist, capital, April 1, 2008, $0

d. Investment on April 1, 2008, $54,000

e. Net income for April, $13,860

f. $67,860 ($54,000 + $13,860)

g. Withdrawals, $7,200

h. Increase in owner's equity, $60,660 ($67,860 − $7,200)

i. Iris Sigrist, capital, April 30, 2008, $60,660

j. Land, $43,200 ($62,100 − $17,700 − $1,200)

k. Total assets, $62,100

l. Iris Sigrist, capital, $60,660

m. Total liabilities and owner's equity, $62,100 ($1,440 + $60,660)

n. Cash received from customers, $28,200; this is the same as fees earned since there are no accounts receivable.

o. Net cash flow from operating activities, $14,100 ($28,200 − $14,100)

p. Net cash flow from financing activities, $46,800 ($54,000 − $7,200)

q. Net cash flow and April 30, 2008, cash balance, $17,700

This page left intentionally blank.

CONTINUING PROBLEM

1.

			Assets				= Liabilities +			Owner's Equity		
		Cash	+	Accounts Receivable	+	Supplies	=	Accounts Payable	+	Kris Payne, Capital	Kris Payne, − Drawing +	Fees Earned
Apr.	1	10,000								10,000		
	2	+ 2,500										+ 2,500
Bal.		12,500								10,000		2,500
Apr.	2	− 1,000										
Bal.		11,500								10,000		2,500
Apr.	4	+				+ 350		+ 350				
Bal.		11,500				350		350		10,000		2,500
Apr.	6	− 750										
Bal.		10,750				350		350		10,000		2,500
Apr.	8	− 800										
Bal.		9,950				350		350		10,000		2,500
Apr.	12	− 300										
Bal.		9,650				350		350		10,000		2,500
Apr.	13	− 100						− 100				
Bal.		9,550				350		250		10,000		2,500
Apr.	16	+ 350										+ 350
Bal.		9,900				350		250		10,000		2,850
Apr.	22			+ 1,350								+ 1,350
Bal.		9,900		1,350		350		250		10,000		4,200
Apr.	25	+ 500										+ 500
Bal.		10,400		1,350		350		250		10,000		4,700
Apr.	29	− 240										
Bal.		10,160		1,350		350		250		10,000		4,700
Apr.	30	+ 1,000										+ 1,000
Bal.		11,160		1,350		350		250		10,000		5,700
Apr.	30	− 400										
Bal.		10,760		1,350		350		250		10,000		5,700
Apr.	30	− 350										
Bal.		10,410		1,350		350		250		10,000		5,700
Apr.	30					− 180						
Bal.		10,410		1,350		170		250		10,000		5,700
Apr.	30	− 150										
Bal.		10,260		1,350		170		250		10,000		5,700
Apr.	30	− 800										
Bal.		9,460		1,350		170		250		10,000		5,700
Apr.	30	− 300									− 300	
Bal.		9,160		1,350		170		250		10,000	− 300	5,700

	Music Exp. –	Office Rent Exp. –	Equip. Rent Exp. –	Adver- tising Exp. –	Wages Exp. –	Utilities Exp. –	Supplies Exp. –	Misc. Exp.
Apr. 1								
2								
Bal.								
Apr. 2		– 1,000						
Bal.		– 1,000						
Apr. 4								
Bal.		– 1,000						
Apr. 6				– 750				
Bal.		– 1,000		– 750				
Apr. 8			– 800					
Bal.		– 1,000	– 800	– 750				
Apr. 12	– 300							
Bal.	– 300	– 1,000	– 800	– 750				
Apr. 13								
Bal.	– 300	– 1,000	– 800	– 750				
Apr. 16								
Bal.	– 300	– 1,000	– 800	– 750				
Apr. 22								
Bal.	– 300	– 1,000	– 800	– 750				
Apr. 25								
Bal.	– 300	– 1,000	– 800	– 750				
Apr. 29	– 240							
Bal.	– 540	– 1,000	– 800	– 750				
Apr. 30								
Bal.	– 540	– 1,000	– 800	– 750				
Apr. 30					– 400			
Bal.	– 540	– 1,000	– 800	– 750	– 400			
Apr. 30						– 350		
Bal.	– 540	– 1,000	– 800	– 750	– 400	– 350		
Apr. 30							– 180	
Bal.	– 540	– 1,000	– 800	– 750	– 400	– 350	– 180	
Apr. 30								– 150
Bal.	– 540	– 1,000	– 800	– 750	– 400	– 350	– 180	– 150
Apr. 30	– 800							
Bal.	– 1,340	– 1,000	– 800	– 750	– 400	– 350	– 180	– 150
Apr. 30								
Bal.	– 1,340	– 1,000	– 800	– 750	– 400	– 350	– 180	– 150

Continuing Problem   Concluded

2.

DANCIN MUSIC
Income Statement
For the Month Ended April 30, 2008

Fees earned..		$5,700
Expenses:		
Music expense	$ 1,340	
Office rent expense	1,000	
Equipment rent expense...	800	
Advertising expense..	750	
Wages expense..	400	
Utilities expense	350	
Supplies expense	180	
Miscellaneous expense...	150	
Total expenses		4,970
Net income		$ 730

3.

DANCIN MUSIC
Statement of Owner's Equity
For the Month Ended April 30, 2008

Kris Payne, capital, April 1, 2008.......................................		$ 0
Investment on April 1, 2008	$10,000	
Net income for April..	730	
	$10,730	
Less withdrawals...	300	
Increase in owner's equity..		10,430
Kris Payne, capital, April 30, 2008....................................		$10,430

4.

DANCIN MUSIC
Balance Sheet
April 30, 2008

Assets		Liabilities	
Cash................................	$ 9,160	Accounts payable..........	$ 250
Accounts receivable.......	1,350		
Supplies...........................	170	**Owner's Equity**	
		Kris Payne, capital.........	10,430
		Total liabilities and	
Total assets.....................	$10,680	owner's equity	$10,680

SPECIAL ACTIVITIES

SA 1–1

1. Acceptable professional conduct requires that Chester Hunter supply Belgrade National Bank with all the relevant financial statements necessary for the bank to make an informed decision. Therefore, Chester should provide the complete set of financial statements. These can be supplemented with a discussion of the net loss in the past year or other data explaining why granting the loan is a good investment by the bank.

2. a. Owners are generally willing to provide bankers with information about the operating and financial condition of the business, such as the following:

   - Operating Information:
     - description of business operations
     - results of past operations
     - preliminary results of current operations
     - plans for future operations
   - Financial Condition:
     - list of assets and liabilities (balance sheet)
     - estimated current values of assets
     - owner's personal investment in the business
     - owner's commitment to invest additional funds in the business

   Owners are normally reluctant to provide the following types of information to bankers:

   - *Proprietary Operating Information.* Such information, which might hurt the business if it becomes known by competitors, might include special processes used by the business or future plans to expand operations into areas that are not currently served by a competitor.

   - *Personal Financial Information.* Owners may have little choice here because banks often require owners of small businesses to pledge their personal assets as security for a business loan. Personal financial information requested by bankers often includes the owner's net worth, salary, and other income. In addition, bankers usually request information about factors that might affect the personal financial condition of the owner. For example, a pending divorce by the owner might significantly affect the owner's personal wealth.

SA 1–1   Concluded

b. Bankers typically want as much information as possible about the ability of the business and the owner to repay the loan with interest. Examples of such information are described above.

c. Both bankers and business owners share the common interest of the business doing well and being successful. If the business is successful, the bankers will receive their loan payments on time with interest, and the owners will increase their personal wealth.

SA 1–2

The difference in the two bank balances, $90,000 ($140,000 – $50,000), may not be pure profit from an accounting perspective. To determine the accounting profit for the six-month period, the revenues for the period would need to be matched with the related expenses. The revenues minus the expenses would indicate whether the business generated net income (profit) or a net loss for the period. Using only the difference between the two bank account balances ignores such factors as amounts due from customers (receivables), liabilities (accounts payable) that need to be paid for wages or other operating expenses, additional investments that Dr. Dejong may have made in the business during the period, or withdrawals during the period that Dr. Dejong might have taken for personal reasons unrelated to the business.

Some businesses that have few, if any, receivables or payables may use a "cash" basis of accounting. The cash basis of accounting ignores receivables and payables because they are assumed to be insignificant in amount. However, even with the cash basis of accounting, additional investments during the period and any withdrawals during the period have to be considered in determining the net income (profit) or net loss for the period.

SA 1-3

1.

	Assets		= Liabilities +	Owner's Equity						
	Cash +	Supplies =	Accts. Payable +	Kathy Hoss, Capital –	Kathy Hoss, Drawing +	Service Revenue –	Salary Expense –	Rent Expense –	Supplies Expense –	Misc. Expense
a.	+ 1,500			+ 1,500						
b.	– 250	+ 250								
Bal.	1,250	250		1,500						
c.	– 160							– 160		
Bal.	1,090	250		1,500				– 160		
d.	– 140		+ 60					– 200		
Bal.	950	250	60	1,500				– 360		
e.	+ 1,600					+ 1,600				
Bal.	2,550	250	60	1,500		1,600		– 360		
f.	+ 350					+ 350				
Bal.	2,900	250	60	1,500		1,950		– 360		
g.	– 600						– 600			
Bal.	2,300	250	60	1,500		1,950	– 600	– 360		
h.	– 150									– 150
Bal.	2,150	250	60	1,500		1,950	– 600	– 360		– 150
i.	+ 600					+ 600				
Bal.	2,750	250	60	1,500		2,550	– 600	– 360		– 150
j.		– 100							– 100	
Bal.	2,750	150	60	1,500		2,550	– 600	– 360	– 100	– 150
k.	– 500				– 500					
Bal.	2,250	150	60	1,500	– 500	2,550	– 600	– 360	– 100	– 150

2.

ADVANTAGE
Income Statement
For the Month Ended June 30, 2007

Service revenue		$2,550
Expenses:		
Salary expense..	$600	
Rent expense	360	
Supplies expense	100	
Miscellaneous expense...	150	
Total expenses		1,210
Net income		$1,340

3.

ADVANTAGE
Statement of Owner's Equity
For the Month Ended June 30, 2007

Kathy Hoss, capital, June 1, 2007		$ 0
Investment on June 1, 2007	$1,500	
Net income for June	1,340	
	$2,840	
Less withdrawals..	500	
Increase in owner's equity..		2,340
Kathy Hoss, capital, June 30, 2007		$2,340

4.

ADVANTAGE
Balance Sheet
June 30, 2007

Assets		Liabilities	
Cash..................................	$2,250	Accounts payable	$ 60
Supplies............................	150		
		Owner's Equity	
		Kathy Hoss, capital	2,340
		Total liabilities and	
Total assets	$2,400	owner's equity	$2,400

SA 1–3   Concluded

5.   a. Advantage would provide Kathy with $380 more income per month than working as a waitress. This amount is computed as follows:

Net income of Advantage, per month......................................	$1,340
Earnings as waitress, per month:	
30 hours per week × $8 per hour × 4 weeks	960
Difference	$ 380

   b. Other factors that Kathy should consider before discussing a long-term arrangement with the Racquet Club include the following:

   Kathy should consider whether the results of operations for June are indicative of what to expect each month. For example, Kathy should consider whether club members will continue to request lessons or use the ball machine during the winter months when interest in tennis may slacken. Kathy should evaluate whether the additional income of $380 per month from Advantage is worth the risk being taken and the effort being expended.

   Kathy should also consider how much her investment in Advantage could have earned if invested elsewhere. For example, if the initial investment of $1,500 had been deposited in a money market or savings account at 3% interest, it would have earned $3.75 interest in June, or $45 for the year.

   Note to Instructors: Numerous other considerations could be mentioned by students, such as the ability of Kathy to withdraw cash from Advantage for personal use. Unlike a money market account or savings account, some of her investment in Advantage will be in the form of supplies (tennis balls, etc.), which may not be readily convertible to cash. The objective of this case is not to mention all possible considerations, but rather to encourage students to begin thinking about the use of accounting information in making business decisions.

SA 1–4

Note to Instructors: The purpose of this activity is to familiarize students with the certification requirements and their online availability.

SA 1–5

	First Year	Second Year	Third Year
Net cash flows from operating activities	negative	positive	positive
Net cash flows from investing activities	negative	negative	negative
Net cash flows from financing activities	positive	positive	positive

Start-up companies normally experience negative cash flows from operating and investing activities. Also, start-up companies normally have positive cash flows from financing activities—activities from raising capital.

SA 1–6

As can be seen from the balance sheet data in the case, Enron was financed largely by debt as compared to equity. Specifically, Enron's stockholders' equity represented only 17.5% ($11,470 divided by $65,503) of Enron's total assets. The remainder of Enron's total assets, 82.5%, were financed by debt. When a company is financed largely by debt, it is said to be highly leveraged.

In late 2001 and early 2002, allegations arose as to possible misstatements of Enron's financial statements. These allegations revolved around the use of "special purpose entities" (partnerships) and related party transactions. The use of special purpose entities allowed Enron to hide a significant amount of additional debt off its balance sheet. The result was that Enron's total assets were even more financed by debt than the balance sheet indicated.

After the allegations of misstatements became public, Enron's stock rapidly declined and the company filed for bankruptcy. Subsequently, numerous lawsuits were filed against the company and its management. In addition, the Securities and Exchange Commission, the Justice Department, and Congress launched investigations into Enron.

Note to Instructors: The role of the auditors and board of directors of Enron might also be discussed. However, these topics are not covered in Chapter 1 but are covered in later chapters.

CHAPTER 2
ANALYZING TRANSACTIONS

QUESTION INFORMATION

Number	Objective	Description	Difficulty	Time	AACSB	AICPA	SS	GL
Q2-1	2-2		Easy	5 min	Analytic	FN-Measurement		
Q2-2	2-1		Easy	5 min	Analytic	FN-Measurement		
Q2-3	2-1		Easy	5 min	Analytic	FN-Measurement		
Q2-4	2-1		Easy	5 min	Analytic	FN-Measurement		
Q2-5	2-1		Easy	5 min	Analytic	FN-Measurement		
Q2-6	2-2		Easy	5 min	Analytic	FN-Measurement		
Q2-7	2-1		Easy	5 min	Analytic	FN-Measurement		
Q2-8	2-3		Easy	5 min	Analytic	FN-Measurement		
Q2-9	2-3		Easy	5 min	Analytic	FN-Measurement		
Q2-10	2-4		Easy	5 min	Analytic	FN-Measurement		
Q2-11	2-4		Easy	5 min	Analytic	FN-Measurement		
Q2-12	2-4		Easy	5 min	Analytic	FN-Measurement		
Q2-13	2-4		Easy	5 min	Analytic	FN-Measurement		
Q2-14	2-4		Easy	5 min	Analytic	FN-Measurement		
Q2-15	2-1		Easy	5 min	Analytic	FN-Measurement		
PE2-1A	2-1	Journal entry for purchase of office equipment	Easy	5 min	Analytic	FN-Measurement		
PE2-1B	2-1	Journal entry for purchase of office supplies	Easy	5 min	Analytic	FN-Measurement		
PE2-2A	2-1	Journal entry for fees earned on account	Easy	5 min	Analytic	FN-Measurement		
PE2-2B	2-1	Journal entry for cash received for services rendered	Easy	5 min	Analytic	FN-Measurement		
PE2-3A	2-1	Journal entry for owner's withdrawal	Easy	5 min	Analytic	FN-Measurement		
PE2-3B	2-1	Journal entry for owner's withdrawal	Easy	5 min	Analytic	FN-Measurement		
PE2-4A	2-1	Rules of debit and credit and normal balances	Easy	5 min	Analytic	FN-Measurement		
PE2-4B	2-1	Rules of debit and credit and normal balances	Easy	5 min	Analytic	FN-Measurement		
PE2-5A	2-2	Determining cash receipts	Easy	5 min	Analytic	FN-Measurement		
PE2-5B	2-2	Determining supplies expense	Easy	5 min	Analytic	FN-Measurement		
PE2-6A	2-3	Effect of errors on a trial balance	Moderate	10 min	Analytic	FN-Measurement		
PE2-6B	2-3	Effect of errors on a trial balance	Moderate	10 min	Analytic	FN-Measurement		
PE2-7A	2-4	Correction of errors	Easy	5 min	Analytic	FN-Measurement		
PE2-7B	2-4	Correction of errors	Easy	5 min	Analytic	FN-Measurement		
Ex2-1	2-1	Chart of accounts	Easy	5 min	Analytic	FN-Measurement		
Ex2-2	2-1	Chart of accounts	Easy	5 min	Analytic	FN-Measurement		
Ex2-3	2-1	Chart of accounts	Easy	10 min	Analytic	FN-Measurement		
Ex2-4	2-1	Identifying transactions	Easy	10 min	Analytic	FN-Measurement		

Number	Objective	Description	Difficulty	Time	AACSB	AICPA	SS	GL
Ex2-5	2-1, 2-2	Journal entries	Easy	10 min	Analytic	FN-Measurement		
Ex2-6	2-3	Trial balance	Easy	5 min	Analytic	FN-Measurement	Exl	
Ex2-7	2-1	Normal entries for accounts	Easy	5 min	Analytic	FN-Measurement		
Ex2-8	2-1	Normal balances of accounts	Easy	5 min	Analytic	FN-Measurement		
Ex2-9	2-1	Rules of debit and credit	Easy	5 min	Analytic	FN-Measurement		
Ex2-10	2-1	Capital account balance	Easy	5 min	Analytic	FN-Measurement		
Ex2-11	2-1	Cash account balance	Easy	5 min	Analytic	FN-Measurement		
Ex2-12	2-1	Accounts balances	Moderate	10 min	Analytic	FN-Measurement		
Ex2-13	2-1, 2-2	Transactions	Moderate	15 min	Analytic	FN-Measurement		
Ex2-14	2-1, 2-2	Journalizing and posting	Easy	10 min	Analytic	FN-Measurement		
Ex2-15	2-1, 2-2	Transactions and T accounts	Easy	15 min	Analytic	FN-Measurement	Exl	
Ex2-16	2-3	Trial balance	Moderate	10 min	Analytic	FN-Measurement	Exl	
Ex2-17	2-3	Effect of errors on trial balance	Moderate	10 min	Analytic	FN-Measurement		
Ex2-18	2-3	Errors in trial balance	Difficult	15 min	Analytic	FN-Measurement		
Ex2-19	2-3	Effect of errors on trial balance	Moderate	10 min	Analytic	FN-Measurement		
Ex2-20	2-3	Errors in trial balance	Easy	10 min	Analytic	FN-Measurement		
Ex2-21	2-4	Entries to correct errors	Easy	5 min	Analytic	FN-Measurement		
Ex2-22	2-4	Entries to correct errors	Easy	5 min	Analytic	FN-Measurement		
Pr2-1A	2-1, 2-2, 2-3	Entries into T accounts and trial balance	Moderate	1 1/2 hr	Analytic	FN-Measurement		
Pr2-2A	2-1, 2-2, 2-3	Journal entries and trial balance	Moderate	1 1/2 hr	Analytic	FN-Measurement	Exl	KA
Pr2-3A	2-1, 2-2, 2-3	Journal entries and trial balance	Moderate	1 1/2 hr	Analytic	FN-Measurement	Exl	KA
Pr2-4A	2-1, 2-2, 2-3	Journal entries and trial balance	Moderate	2 hr	Analytic	FN-Measurement	Exl	KA
Pr2-5A	2-3, 2-4	Errors in trial balance	Difficult	2 hr	Analytic	FN-Measurement		
Pr2-6A	2-3	Corrected trial balance	Difficult	1 1/2 hr	Analytic	FN-Measurement	Exl	
Pr2-1B	2-1, 2-2, 2-3	Entries into T accounts and trial balance	Moderate	1 1/2 hr	Analytic	FN-Measurement		
Pr2-2B	2-1, 2-2, 2-3	Journal entries and trial balance	Moderate	1 1/2 hr	Analytic	FN-Measurement	Exl	KA
Pr2-3B	2-1, 2-2, 2-3	Journal entries and trial balance	Moderate	1 1/2 hr	Analytic	FN-Measurement	Exl	KA
Pr2-4B	2-1, 2-2, 2-3	Journal entries and trial balance	Moderate	2 hr	Analytic	FN-Measurement	Exl	KA
Pr2-5B	2-3, 2-4	Errors in trial balance	Difficult	2 hr	Analytic	FN-Measurement		
Pr2-6B	2-3	Corrected trial balance	Difficult	1 1/2 hr	Analytic	FN-Measurement	Exl	
DM-2		Continuing Problem						KA
SA2-1	2-3	Ethics and professional conduct in business	Easy	5 min	Ethics	BB-Industry		
SA2-2	2-1	Account for revenue	Easy	5 min	Analytic	FN-Measurement		
SA2-3	2-1	Record transactions	Easy	5 min	Analytic	FN-Measurement		

Number	Objective	Description	Difficulty	Time	AACSB	AICPA	SS	GL
SA2-4	2-1	Debits and credits	Easy	15 min	Analytic	FN-Measurement		
SA2-5	2-1, 2-2	Transactions and income statement	Moderate	1 hr	Analytic	FN-Measurement		
SA2-6	1-1	Opportunities for ac-countants	Easy	15 min	Reflective Thinking	FN-Research		

1. An account is a form designed to record changes in a particular asset, liability, owner's equity, revenue, or expense. A ledger is a group of related accounts.

2. The terms *debit* and *credit* may signify either an increase or decrease, depending upon the nature of the account. For example, debits signify an increase in asset and expense accounts but a decrease in liability, owner's capital, and revenue accounts.

3. Liabilities and owner's equity both have rights or claims to assets as indicated by the accounting equation, Assets = Liabilities + Owner's Equity. Therefore, the same rules of debit and credit apply to both liabilities and owner's equity.

4. a. Decrease in owner's equity
   b. Increase in expense

5. a. Increase in owner's equity
   b. Increase in revenue

6. a. Assuming no errors have occurred, the credit balance in the cash account resulted from drawing checks for $2,500 in excess of the amount of cash on deposit.
   b. The $2,500 credit balance in the cash account as of January 31 is a liability owed to the bank. It is usually referred to as an "overdraft" and should be classified on the balance sheet as a liability.

7. a. The revenue was earned in February.
   b. (1) Debit Accounts Receivable and credit Fees Earned or another appropriately titled revenue account in February.
      (2) Debit Cash and credit Accounts Receivable in March.

8. The trial balance is a proof of the equality of the debits and the credits in the ledger.

9. No. Errors may have been made that had the same erroneous effect on both debits and credits, such as failure to record and/or post a transaction, recording the same transaction more than once, and posting a transaction correctly but to the wrong account.

10. The listing of $21,630 is a transposition; the listing of $15,000 is a slide.

11. a. No. Because the same error occurred on both the debit side and the credit side of the trial balance, the trial balance would not be out of balance.
    b. Yes. The trial balance would not balance. The error would cause the credit total of the trial balance to exceed the debit total by $450.

12. a. The equality of the trial balance would not be affected.
    b. On the income statement, total operating expenses (salary expense) would be overstated by $5,000, and net income would be understated by $5,000. On the statement of owner's equity, the beginning and ending capital would be correct. However, net income and withdrawals would be understated by $5,000. These understatements offset one another, and, thus, ending owner's equity is correct. The balance sheet is not affected by the error.

13. a. The equality of the trial balance would not be affected.
    b. On the income statement, revenues (fees earned) would be overstated by $80,000, and net income would be overstated by $80,000. On the statement of owner's equity, the beginning capital would be correct. However, net income and ending capital would be overstated by $80,000. The balance sheet total assets is correct. However, liabilities (notes payable) is understated by $80,000, and owner's equity is overstated by $80,000. The understatement of liabilities is offset by the overstatement of owner's equity, and, thus, total liabilities and owner's equity is correct.

14. The preferred procedure is to journalize and post a correcting entry debiting Accounts Payable and crediting Cash.

15. a. From the viewpoint of Peachtree Storage, the balance of the checking account represents an asset.
    b. From the viewpoint of Buckhead Savings Bank, the balance of the checking account represents a liability.

PRACTICE EXERCISES

PE 2–1A

Nov. 23	Office Equipment	13,750	
	Cash		5,000
	Accounts Payable		8,750

PE 2–1B

Mar. 13	Office Supplies	6,500	
	Cash		1,300
	Accounts Payable		5,200

PE 2–2A

| Feb. 2 | Accounts Receivable | 6,300 | |
| | Fees Earned | | 6,300 |

PE 2–2B

| Jan. 21 | Cash | 1,250 | |
| | Fees Earned | | 1,250 |

PE 2–3A

| Oct. 31 | Amy Sykes, Drawing | 4,500 | |
| | Cash | | 4,500 |

PE 2–3B

| July 31 | Paul Wright, Drawing | 7,250 | |
| | Cash | | 7,250 |

PE 2–4A

1. Debit and credit entries, Normal credit balance
2. Debit and credit entries, Normal debit balance
3. Debit entries only, Normal debit balance
4. Credit entries only, Normal credit balance
5. Debit and credit entries, Normal credit balance
6. Credit entries only, Normal credit balance

PE 2–4B

1. Debit and credit entries, Normal debit balance
2. Credit entries only, Normal credit balance
3. Debit entries only, Normal debit balance
4. Debit entries only, Normal debit balance
5. Debit and credit entries, Normal credit balance
6. Debit and credit entries, Normal debit balance

PE 2–5A

Using the following T account, solve for the amount of cash receipts (indicated by ? below).

Cash			
Apr. 1 Bal.	18,750	219,140	Cash payments
Cash receipts	?		
Apr. 30 Bal.	22,175		

$22,175 = $18,750 + Cash receipts – $219,140

Cash receipts = $22,175 + $219,140 – $18,750 = $222,565

PE 2–5B

Using the following T account, solve for the amount of supplies expense (indicated by ? below).

Supplies			
Jan. 1 Bal.	1,035	?	Supplies expense
Cash receipts	2,325		
Jan. 31 Bal.	786		

$786 = $1,035 + $2,325 – Supplies expense

Supplies expense = $1,035 + $2,325 – $786 = $2,574

PE 2–6A

a. The totals are equal since both the debit and credit entries were journalized and posted for $486.

b. The totals are unequal. The debit total is higher by $2,260 ($1,130 + $1,130).

c. The totals are unequal. The credit total is higher by $90 ($2,540 – $2,450).

PE 2–6B

a. The totals are unequal. The credit total is higher by $300 ($1,312 – $1,012).

b. The totals are equal since both the debit and credit entries were journalized and posted for $4,500.

c. The totals are unequal. The credit total is higher by $1,278 ($1,420 – $142).

PE 2–7A

a. Accounts Payable 3,125
      Accounts Receivable   3,125

b. Advertising Expense.. 1,500
      Miscellaneous Expense   1,500

      Advertising Expense.. 1,500
         Cash...   1,500

Note: The first entry in (b) reverses the incorrect entry, and the second entry records the correct entry. These two entries could also be combined into one entry as shown below; however, preparing two entries would make it easier for someone to understand later what happened and why the entries were necessary.

     Advertising Expense....................................... 3,000
         Miscellaneous Expense   1,500
         Cash...   1,500

PE 2–7B

a. Supplies 2,690
      Office Equipment...   2,690

      Supplies 2,690
         Accounts Payable...   2,690

Note: The first entry in (a) reverses the incorrect entry, and the second entry records the correct entry. These two entries could also be combined into one entry as shown below; however, preparing two entries would make it easier for someone to understand later what happened and why the entries were necessary.

     Supplies 5,380
         Office Equipment..   2,690
         Accounts Payable..   2,690

b. Cash 3,750
      Accounts Receivable   3,750

EXERCISES

Ex. 2–1

Balance Sheet Accounts	Income Statement Accounts
Assets	**Revenue**
Flight Equipment	Cargo and Mail Revenue
Purchase Deposits	Passenger Revenue
for Flight Equipment*	
Spare Parts and Supplies	**Expenses**
	Aircraft Fuel Expense
Liabilities	Commissions***
Accounts Payable	Landing Fees****
Air Traffic Liability**	
Owner's Equity	
None	

  *Advance payments on aircraft purchases
 **Passenger ticket sales not yet recognized as revenue
 ***Commissions paid to travel agents
****Fees paid to airports for landing rights

Ex. 2–2

Account	Account Number
Accounts Payable	21
Accounts Receivable	12
Angie Stowe, Capital	31
Angie Stowe, Drawing	32
Cash	11
Fees Earned	41
Land	13
Miscellaneous Expense	53
Supplies Expense	52
Wages Expense	51

Ex. 2–3

Balance Sheet Accounts		Income Statement Accounts	
1. Assets		**4. Revenue**	
11	Cash	41	Fees Earned
12	Accounts Receivable		**5. Expenses**
13	Supplies	51	Wages Expense
14	Prepaid Insurance	52	Rent Expense
15	Equipment	53	Supplies Expense
2. Liabilities		59	Miscellaneous Expense
21	Accounts Payable		
22	Unearned Rent		
3. Owner's Equity			
31	Rebecca Wimmer, Capital		
32	Rebecca Wimmer, Drawing		

Note: The order of some of the accounts within the major classifications is somewhat arbitrary, as in accounts 13–14 and accounts 51–53. In a new business, the order of magnitude of balances in such accounts is not determinable in advance. The magnitude may also vary from period to period.

Ex. 2–4

a. and b.

Transaction	Account Debited		Account Credited	
	Type	Effect	Type	Effect
(1)	asset	+	owner's equity	+
(2)	asset	+	asset	−
(3)	asset	+	asset	−
			liability	+
(4)	expense	+	asset	−
(5)	asset	+	revenue	+
(6)	liability	−	asset	−
(7)	asset	+	asset	−
(8)	drawing	+	asset	−
(9)	expense	+	asset	−

Ex. 2–5

			Debit	Credit
(1)	Cash		30,000	
	Tosha Lewis, Capital			30,000
(2)	Supplies		1,800	
	Cash			1,800
(3)	Equipment...		24,000	
	Accounts Payable			15,000
	Cash			9,000
(4)	Operating Expenses.......................................		3,050	
	Cash			3,050
(5)	Accounts Receivable		15,000	
	Service Revenue			15,000
(6)	Accounts Payable...		7,500	
	Cash			7,500
(7)	Cash		10,000	
	Accounts Receivable			10,000
(8)	Tosha Lewis, Drawing		2,500	
	Cash			2,500
(9)	Operating Expenses.......................................		1,050	
	Supplies			1,050

Ex. 2–6

EOS CO.
Unadjusted Trial Balance
March 31, 2008

	Debit Balances	Credit Balances
Cash..	16,150	
Accounts Receivable...	5,000	
Supplies..	750	
Equipment	24,000	
Accounts Payable		7,500
Tosha Lewis, Capital		30,000
Tosha Lewis, Drawing...	2,500	
Service Revenue		15,000
Operating Expenses	4,100	
	52,500	52,500

Ex. 2–7

1. debit and credit (c)
2. debit and credit (c)
3. debit and credit (c)
4. credit only (b)
5. debit only (a)
6. debit only (a)
7. debit only (a)

Ex. 2–8

a. Liability—credit
b. Asset—debit
c. Owner's equity
   (Boyd Magnus, Capital)—credit
d. Owner's equity
   (Boyd Magnus, Drawing)—debit
e. Asset—debit
f. Revenue—credit
g. Asset—debit
h. Expense—debit
i. Asset—debit
j. Expense—debit

Ex. 2–9

a. debit
b. debit
c. credit
d. debit
e. debit
f. credit
g. debit
h. credit
i. credit
j. debit
k. credit
l. credit

Ex. 2–10

a. Debit (negative) balance of $3,700 ($21,800 − $1,500 − $24,000). Such a negative balance means that the liabilities of Sarah's business exceed the assets.

b. Yes. The balance sheet prepared at December 31 will balance, with Sarah Bredy, Capital, being reported in the owner's equity section as a negative $3,700.

Ex. 2–11

a. The increase of $166,870 ($479,250 – $312,380) in the cash account does not indicate earnings of that amount. Earnings will represent the net change in all assets and liabilities from operating transactions.

b. $75,055 ($241,925 – $166,870)

Ex. 2–12

a. $67,700 ($11,150 + $72,300 – $15,750)

b. $117,000 ($115,000 + $27,500 – $25,500)

c. $5,100 ($60,500 – $77,700 + $22,300)

Ex. 2–13

2007

Oct.	1	Rent Expense	2,500	
		Cash		2,500
	3	Advertising Expense	1,100	
		Cash		1,100
	4	Supplies	725	
		Cash		725
	6	Office Equipment	7,500	
		Accounts Payable		7,500
	10	Cash	3,600	
		Accounts Receivable		3,600
	12	Accounts Payable	600	
		Cash		600
	20	Alfonso Finley, Drawing	1,000	
		Cash		1,000
	27	Miscellaneous Expense	500	
		Cash		500
	30	Utilities Expense	195	
		Cash		195
	31	Accounts Receivable	20,150	
		Fees Earned		20,150
	31	Utilities Expense	315	
		Cash		315

67

Ex. 2–14

a.

	JOURNAL			Page 38

Date	Description	Post. Ref.	Debit	Credit
2008				
July 27	Supplies..	15	1,875	
	Accounts Payable............................	21		1,875
	Purchased supplies on account.			

b., c., d.

Supplies 15

Date	Item	Post. Ref.	Dr.	Cr.	Balance Dr.	Cr.
2008						
July 1	Balance...............................	✓	....	....	735	....
27	....	38	1,875	....	2,610	....

Accounts Payable 21

Date	Item	Post. Ref.	Dr.	Cr.	Balance Dr.	Cr.
2008						
July 1	Balance...............................	✓	....	....	....	11,380
27	....	38	....	1,875	....	13,255

Ex. 2–15

a.

(1)	Accounts Receivable	13,750	
	Fees Earned...		13,750
(2)	Supplies	1,325	
	Accounts Payable		1,325
(3)	Cash	8,150	
	Accounts Receivable		8,150
(4)	Accounts Payable...	800	
	Cash		800

b.

Cash					Accounts Payable			
(3)	8,150	(4)	800		(4)	800	(2)	1,325

Supplies				Fees Earned			
(2)	1,325					(1)	13,750

Accounts Receivable			
(1)	13,750	(3)	8,150

Ex. 2–16

MATICE CO.
Unadjusted Trial Balance
July 31, 2008

	Debit Balances	Credit Balances
Cash	52,350	
Accounts Receivable	112,500	
Supplies	6,300	
Prepaid Insurance	9,000	
Land	255,000	
Accounts Payable		56,130
Unearned Rent		27,000
Notes Payable		120,000
Milton Adair, Capital		259,920
Milton Adair, Drawing	60,000	
Fees Earned		930,000
Wages Expense	525,000	
Rent Expense	180,000	
Utilities Expense	124,500	
Supplies Expense	23,700	
Insurance Expense	18,000	
Miscellaneous Expense	26,700	
	1,393,050	1,393,050

Ex. 2–17

Inequality of trial balance totals would be caused by errors described in (b) and (d).

Ex. 2–18

AWESOME CO.
Unadjusted Trial Balance
December 31, 2008

	Debit Balances	Credit Balances
Cash	26,750	
Accounts Receivable	49,200	
Prepaid Insurance	16,000	
Equipment	150,000	
Accounts Payable		22,360
Unearned Rent		8,500
Sean Milner, Capital		164,840
Sean Milner, Drawing	20,000	
Service Revenue		167,500
Wages Expense	84,000	
Advertising Expense	14,400	
Miscellaneous Expense	2,850	
	363,200	363,200

Ex. 2–19

Error	(a) Out of Balance	(b) Difference	(c) Larger Total
1.	yes	$5,125	debit
2.	yes	1,350	credit
3.	yes	1,375	debit
4.	yes	18	credit
5.	no	—	—
6.	yes	180	credit
7.	no	—	—

Ex. 2–20

1. The debit column total is added incorrectly. The sum is $291,750, rather than $458,250.
2. The trial balance should be dated "for the month ending October 31, 2008," not for the month of October.
3. The Accounts Receivable balance should be in the debit column.
4. The Accounts Payable balance should be in the credit column.
5. The Nolan Towns, Drawing, balance should be in the debit column.
6. The Advertising Expense balance should be in the debit column.

A corrected trial balance would be as follows:

HYBRID CO.
Unadjusted Trial Balance
October 31, 2008

	Debit Balances	Credit Balances
Cash	22,500	
Accounts Receivable	49,200	
Prepaid Insurance	10,800	
Equipment	150,000	
Accounts Payable		5,550
Salaries Payable		3,750
Nolan Towns, Capital		129,600
Nolan Towns, Drawing	18,000	
Service Revenue		236,100
Salary Expense	98,430	
Advertising Expense	21,600	
Miscellaneous Expense	4,470	
	375,000	375,000

Ex. 2–21

		Debit	Credit
a.	Joel Goodson, Drawing	20,000	
	Wages Expense		20,000
b.	Prepaid Rent	3,600	
	Cash		3,600

Ex. 2–22

a. Accounts Payable.. 940
       Supplies Expense   940

    Supplies 940
       Cash   940

b. Cash 5,500
       Fees Earned..   2,750
       Accounts Receivable   2,750

PROBLEMS

Prob. 2–1A

1. and 2.

Cash			
(a)	25,000	(b)	2,000
(g)	3,750	(c)	1,500
		(e)	975
		(f)	1,200
		(h)	240
		(i)	2,500
		(j)	450
		(m)	1,500
		(n)	280
Bal.	18,105		

Accounts Receivable			
(l)	3,150		

Supplies			
(e)	975		

Prepaid Insurance			
(f)	1,200		

Automobiles			
(c)	16,500		

Equipment			
(d)	6,500		

Notes Payable			
(j)	450	(c)	15,000
		Bal.	14,550

Accounts Payable			
(i)	2,500	(d)	6,500
		(k)	750
		Bal.	4,750

Hannah Knox, Capital			
		(a)	25,000

Professional Fees			
		(g)	3,750
		(l)	3,150
		Bal.	6,900

Rent Expense			
(b)	2,000		

Salary Expense			
(m)	1,500		

Automobile Expense			
(n)	280		

Blueprint Expense			
(k)	750		

Miscellaneous Expense			
(h)	240		

3.

HANNAH KNOX, ARCHITECT
Unadjusted Trial Balance
July 31, 2008

	Debit Balances	Credit Balances
Cash	18,105	
Accounts Receivable	3,150	
Supplies	975	
Prepaid Insurance	1,200	
Automobiles	16,500	
Equipment	6,500	
Notes Payable		14,550
Accounts Payable		4,750
Hannah Knox, Capital		25,000
Professional Fees		6,900
Rent Expense	2,000	
Salary Expense	1,500	
Automobile Expense	280	
Blueprint Expense	750	
Miscellaneous Expense	240	
	51,200	51,200

Prob. 2–2A

1.

(a)	Cash	15,000	
	Kara Frantz, Capital		15,000
(b)	Rent Expense..	2,500	
	Cash		2,500
(c)	Supplies	850	
	Accounts Payable		850
(d)	Accounts Payable...	400	
	Cash		400
(e)	Cash	15,750	
	Sales Commissions		15,750
(f)	Automobile Expense	2,400	
	Miscellaneous Expense	600	
	Cash		3,000
(g)	Office Salaries Expense..................................	3,250	
	Cash		3,250
(h)	Supplies Expense...	575	
	Supplies		575
(i)	Kara Frantz, Drawing	1,000	
	Cash		1,000

Prob. 2–2A   Continued

2.

Cash			
(a)	15,000	(b)	2,500
(e)	15,750	(d)	400
		(f)	3,000
		(g)	3,250
		(i)	1,000
Bal.	20,600		

Supplies			
(c)	850	(h)	575
Bal.	275		

Accounts Payable			
(d)	400	(c)	850
		Bal.	450

Kara Frantz, Capital			
		(a)	15,000

Kara Frantz, Drawing			
(i)	1,000		

Sales Commissions			
		(e)	15,750

Office Salaries Expense		
(g)	3,250	

Rent Expense		
(b)	2,500	

Automobile Expense		
(f)	2,400	

Supplies Expense		
(h)	575	

Miscellaneous Expense		
(f)	600	

3.

MUDCAT REALTY
Unadjusted Trial Balance
March 31, 2008

	Debit Balances	Credit Balances
Cash	20,600	
Supplies	275	
Accounts Payable		450
Kara Frantz, Capital		15,000
Kara Frantz, Drawing	1,000	
Sales Commissions		15,750
Office Salaries Expense	3,250	
Rent Expense	2,500	
Automobile Expense	2,400	
Supplies Expense	575	
Miscellaneous Expense	600	
	31,200	31,200

Prob. 2–2A   Concluded

4. a. $15,750
    b. $9,325
    c. $6,425

Prob. 2–3A

1.

JOURNAL

Pages 1 and 2

Date		Description	Post. Ref.	Debit	Credit
2008					
June	1	Cash...	11	18,000	
		Brooks Dodd, Capital...........................	31		18,000
	5	Rent Expense...	53	2,150	
		Cash	11		2,150
	6	Equipment..	16	8,500	
		Accounts Payable..............................	22		8,500
	8	Truck..	18	18,000	
		Cash	11		10,000
		Notes Payable.....................................	21		8,000
	10	Supplies...	13	1,200	
		Cash	11		1,200
	12	Cash...	11	10,500	
		Fees Earned..	41		10,500
	15	Prepaid Insurance	14	2,400	
		Cash	11		2,400
	23	Accounts Receivable.............................	12	5,950	
		Fees Earned..	41		5,950
	24	Truck Expense.......................................	55	1,000	
		Accounts Payable..............................	22		1,000
	29	Utilities Expense...................................	54	1,200	
		Cash	11		1,200
	29	Miscellaneous Expense	59	400	
		Cash	11		400
	30	Cash...	11	3,200	
		Accounts Receivable	12		3,200

Prob. 2–3A Continued

JOURNAL
Pages 1 and 2

Date	Description	Post. Ref.	Debit	Credit
2008				
June 30	Wages Expense	51	2,900	
	Cash	11		2,900
30	Accounts Payable..............................	22	2,125	
	Cash	11		2,125
30	Brooks Dodd, Drawing..........................	32	1,750	
	Cash	11		1,750

2.

GENERAL LEDGER

Cash   11

Date	Item	Post. Ref.	Dr.	Cr.	Balance Dr.	Balance Cr.
2008						
June 1	....	1	18,000	....	18,000	....
5	....	1	....	2,150	15,850	....
8	....	1	....	10,000	5,850	....
10	....	1	....	1,200	4,650	....
12	....	1	10,500	....	15,150	....
15	....	1	....	2,400	12,750	....
29	....	2	....	1,200	11,550	....
29	....	2	....	400	11,150	....
30	....	2	3,200	....	14,350	....
30	....	2	....	2,900	11,450	....
30	....	2	....	2,125	9,325	....
30	....	2	....	1,750	7,575	....

Accounts Receivable   12

Date	Item	Post. Ref.	Dr.	Cr.	Balance Dr.	Balance Cr.
2008						
June 23	....	1	5,950	....	5,950	....
30	....	2	....	3,200	2,750	....

Prob. 2–3A   Continued

Supplies   13

Date	Item	Post. Ref.	Dr.	Cr.	Balance Dr.	Balance Cr.
2008						
June 10	....	1	1,200	....	1,200	....

Prepaid Insurance   14

Date	Item	Post. Ref.	Dr.	Cr.	Balance Dr.	Balance Cr.
2008						
June 15	....	1	2,400	....	2,400	....

Equipment   16

Date	Item	Post. Ref.	Dr.	Cr.	Balance Dr.	Balance Cr.
2008						
June 6	....	1	8,500	....	8,500	....

Truck   18

Date	Item	Post. Ref.	Dr.	Cr.	Balance Dr.	Balance Cr.
2008						
June 8	....	1	18,000	....	18,000	....

Notes Payable   21

Date	Item	Post. Ref.	Dr.	Cr.	Balance Dr.	Balance Cr.
2008						
June 8	....	1	....	8,000	....	8,000

Accounts Payable   22

Date	Item	Post. Ref.	Dr.	Cr.	Balance Dr.	Balance Cr.
2008						
June 6	....	1	....	8,500	....	8,500
24	....	1	....	1,000	....	9,500
30	....	2	2,125	....	....	7,375

Brooks Dodd, Capital   31

Date	Item	Post. Ref.	Dr.	Cr.	Balance Dr.	Balance Cr.
2008						
June 1	....	1	....	18,000	....	18,000

Brooks Dodd, Drawing   32

Date	Item	Post. Ref.	Dr.	Cr.	Balance Dr.	Balance Cr.
2008						
June 30	....	2	1,750	....	1,750	....

Prob. 2–3A Continued

Fees Earned   41

Date	Item	Post. Ref.	Dr.	Cr.	Balance Dr.	Balance Cr.
2008						
June 12	....	1	....	10,500	....	10,500
23	....	1	....	5,950	....	16,450

Wages Expense   51

Date	Item	Post. Ref.	Dr.	Cr.	Balance Dr.	Balance Cr.
2008						
June 30	....	2	2,900	....	2,900	....

Rent Expense   53

Date	Item	Post. Ref.	Dr.	Cr.	Balance Dr.	Balance Cr.
2008						
June 5	....	1	2,150	....	2,150	....

Utilities Expense   54

Date	Item	Post. Ref.	Dr.	Cr.	Balance Dr.	Balance Cr.
2008						
June 29	....	2	1,200	....	1,200	....

Truck Expense   55

Date	Item	Post. Ref.	Dr.	Cr.	Balance Dr.	Balance Cr.
2008						
June 24	....	1	1,000	....	1,000	....

Miscellaneous Expense   59

Date	Item	Post. Ref.	Dr.	Cr.	Balance Dr.	Balance Cr.
2008						
June 29	....	2	400	....	400	....

Prob. 2–3A Concluded

3.

COORDINATED DESIGNS
Unadjusted Trial Balance
June 30, 2008

	Debit Balances	Credit Balances
Cash	7,575	
Accounts Receivable	2,750	
Supplies	1,200	
Prepaid Insurance	2,400	
Equipment	8,500	
Truck	18,000	
Notes Payable		8,000
Accounts Payable		7,375
Brooks Dodd, Capital		18,000
Brooks Dodd, Drawing	1,750	
Fees Earned		16,450
Wages Expense	2,900	
Rent Expense	2,150	
Utilities Expense	1,200	
Truck Expense	1,000	
Miscellaneous Expense	400	
	49,825	49,825

Prob. 2–4A

2. and 3.

			JOURNAL		Pages 18 and 19	

Date	Description	Post. Ref.	Debit	Credit
2008				
Nov. 1	Rent Expense.....................................	52	5,000	
	Cash	11		5,000
2	Office Supplies	14	1,750	
	Accounts Payable.........................	21		1,750
5	Prepaid Insurance	13	4,800	
	Cash	11		4,800
10	Cash..	11	52,000	
	Accounts Receivable	12		52,000
15	Land..	16	90,000	
	Cash	11		10,000
	Notes Payable.............................	23		80,000
17	Accounts Payable................................	21	7,750	
	Cash	11		7,750
20	Accounts Payable.............................	21	250	
	Office Supplies	14		250
23	Advertising Expense	53	2,100	
	Cash	11		2,100
27	Cash..	11	700	
	Salary and Commission Expense	51		700
28	Automobile Expense	54	1,500	
	Cash	11		1,500
29	Miscellaneous Expense	59	450	
	Cash	11		450
30	Accounts Receivable...........................	12	48,400	
	Fees Earned.................................	41		48,400
30	Salary and Commission Expense	51	25,000	
	Cash	11		25,000
30	Ashley Carnes, Drawing......................	32	8,000	
	Cash	11		8,000
30	Cash..	11	2,500	
	Unearned Rent.................................	22		2,500

Prob. 2–4A   Continued

1. and 3.

Cash
11

Date	Item	Post. Ref.	Dr.	Cr.	Balance Dr.	Balance Cr.
2008						
Nov. 1	Balance.............................	✓	....	....	26,300	....
1	....	18	....	5,000	21,300	....
5	....	18	....	4,800	16,500	....
10	....	18	52,000	....	68,500	....
15	....	18	....	10,000	58,500	....
17	....	18	....	7,750	50,750	....
23	....	18	....	2,100	48,650	....
27	....	19	700	....	49,350	....
28	....	19	....	1,500	47,850	....
29	....	19	....	450	47,400	....
30	....	19	....	25,000	22,400	....
30	....	19	....	8,000	14,400	....
30	....	19	2,500	....	16,900	....

Accounts Receivable
12

Date	Item	Post. Ref.	Dr.	Cr.	Balance Dr.	Balance Cr.
2008						
Nov. 1	Balance.............................	✓	....	....	67,500	....
10	....	18	....	52,000	15,500	....
30	....	19	48,400	....	63,900	....

Prepaid Insurance
13

Date	Item	Post. Ref.	Dr.	Cr.	Balance Dr.	Balance Cr.
2008						
Nov. 1	Balance.............................	✓	....	....	3,000	....
5	....	18	4,800	....	7,800	....

Office Supplies
14

Date	Item	Post. Ref.	Dr.	Cr.	Balance Dr.	Balance Cr.
2008						
Nov. 1	Balance.............................	✓	....	....	1,800	....
2	....	18	1,750	....	3,550	....
20	....	18	....	250	3,300	....

Land
16

Date	Item	Post. Ref.	Dr.	Cr.	Balance Dr.	Balance Cr.
2008						
Nov. 15	....	18	90,000	....	90,000	....

Prob. 2–4A Continued

Accounts Payable
21

Date	Item	Post. Ref.	Dr.	Cr.	Balance Dr.	Balance Cr.
2008						
Nov. 1	Balance	✓	....	....	....	13,020
2		18	....	1,750	....	14,770
17		18	7,750	....	....	7,020
20		18	250	....	....	6,770

Unearned Rent
22

Date	Item	Post. Ref.	Dr.	Cr.	Balance Dr.	Balance Cr.
2008						
Nov. 30		19	....	2,500	....	2,500

Notes Payable
23

Date	Item	Post. Ref.	Dr.	Cr.	Balance Dr.	Balance Cr.
2008						
Nov. 15		18	....	80,000	....	80,000

Ashley Carnes, Capital
31

Date	Item	Post. Ref.	Dr.	Cr.	Balance Dr.	Balance Cr.
2008						
Nov. 1	Balance	✓	....	....	....	32,980

Ashley Carnes, Drawing
32

Date	Item	Post. Ref.	Dr.	Cr.	Balance Dr.	Balance Cr.
2008						
Nov. 1	Balance	✓	....	....	2,000	....
30		19	8,000	....	10,000	....

Fees Earned
41

Date	Item	Post. Ref.	Dr.	Cr.	Balance Dr.	Balance Cr.
2008						
Nov. 1	Balance	✓	....	....	....	260,000
30		19	....	48,400	....	308,400

Salary and Commission Expense
51

Date	Item	Post. Ref.	Dr.	Cr.	Balance Dr.	Balance Cr.
2008						
Nov. 1	Balance	✓	....	....	148,200	....
27		19	....	700	147,500	....
30		19	25,000	....	172,500	....

Prob. 2–4A   Continued

Rent Expense   52

Date	Item	Post. Ref.	Dr.	Cr.	Balance Dr.	Cr.
2008						
Nov. 1	Balance.............................	✓	....	....	30,000	....
1	....	18	5,000	....	35,000	....

Advertising Expense   53

Date	Item	Post. Ref.	Dr.	Cr.	Balance Dr.	Cr.
2008						
Nov. 1	Balance.............................	✓	....	....	17,800	....
23	....	18	2,100	....	19,900	....

Automobile Expense   54

Date	Item	Post. Ref.	Dr.	Cr.	Balance Dr.	Cr.
2008						
Nov. 1	Balance.............................	✓	....	....	5,500	....
28	....	19	1,500	....	7,000	....

Miscellaneous Expense   59

Date	Item	Post. Ref.	Dr.	Cr.	Balance Dr.	Cr.
2008						
Nov. 1	Balance.............................	✓	....	....	3,900	....
29	....	19	450	....	4,350	....

Prob. 2–4A Concluded

4.

PASSPORT REALTY
Unadjusted Trial Balance
November 30, 2008

	Debit Balances	Credit Balances
Cash	16,900	
Accounts Receivable	63,900	
Prepaid Insurance	7,800	
Office Supplies	3,300	
Land	90,000	
Accounts Payable		6,770
Unearned Rent		2,500
Notes Payable		80,000
Ashley Carnes, Capital		32,980
Ashley Carnes, Drawing	10,000	
Fees Earned		308,400
Salary and Commission Expense	172,500	
Rent Expense	35,000	
Advertising Expense	19,900	
Automobile Expense	7,000	
Miscellaneous Expense	4,350	
	430,650	430,650

Prob. 2–5A

1. Totals of preliminary trial balance:

Debit	$39,224.40
Credit	$38,336.50

2. Difference between preliminary trial balance totals: $887.90

3. Errors in trial balance:

   (a) Supplies debit balance was listed as $979.90 instead of $997.90.

   (b) Notes Payable credit balance of $6,500.00 was listed as debit balance.

   (c) Martin Tresp, Drawing debit balance of $1,350.00 was listed as credit balance.

   (d) Miscellaneous Expense of $283.50 was omitted.

4. Errors in account balances:

   (a) Accounts Payable balance of $1,077.50 was totaled as $1,225.90.

5. Errors in posting:

   (a) Prepaid Insurance entry of July 9 for $144.00 was posted as $1,440.00 (slide).

   (b) Land entry of July 10 for $12,000.00 was posted as $1,200.00 (slide).

   (c) Cash entry of July 25 for $1,681.30 was posted as $1,683.10 (transposition).

   (d) Wages Expense entry of July 31 for $1,390.00 was posted as $1,930.00 (transposition).

6.

July	31	Advertising Expense	53	125.00	
		Cash	11		125.00

7.

MAINSTAY TV REPAIR
Unadjusted Trial Balance
July 31, 20—

	Debit Balances	Credit Balances
Cash	8,791.00	
Supplies	997.90	
Prepaid Insurance	395.50	
Land	26,625.00	
Notes Payable		6,500.00
Accounts Payable		1,077.50
Martin Tresp, Capital		27,760.20
Martin Tresp, Drawing	1,350.00	
Service Revenue		8,000.40
Wages Expense	2,518.60	
Utilities Expense	436.60	
Advertising Expense	400.00	
Rent Expense	1,540.00	
Miscellaneous Expense	283.50	
	43,338.10	43,338.10

Prob. 2–6A

1.

IBERIAN CARPET
Unadjusted Trial Balance
March 31, 2008

	Debit Balances	Credit Balances
Cash..	6,400*	
Accounts Receivable..	13,720	
Supplies...	2,500	
Prepaid Insurance...	1,230	
Equipment..	56,000	
Notes Payable..		33,600
Accounts Payable..		8,800
Jose Mendrano, Capital..		34,900
Jose Mendrano, Drawing......................................	18,000	
Fees Earned...		122,700
Wages Expense..	70,000	
Rent Expense...	16,600	
Advertising Expense..	7,200	
Gas, Electricity, and Water Expense......................	6,900	
Miscellaneous Expense..	1,450	
	200,000	200,000

*$4,300 + $3,000 (a) – $900 (b)

2. No. The trial balance indicates only that the debits and credits are equal. Any errors that have the same effect on debits and credits will not affect the balancing of the trial balance.

Prob. 2–1B

1. and 2.

	Cash		
(a)	22,500	(b)	4,000
(g)	6,500	(c)	2,500
		(d)	1,200
		(f)	1,600
		(h)	1,800
		(i)	300
		(l)	1,500
		(m)	210
		(n)	200
		(o)	250
Bal.	15,440		

	Accounts Receivable	
(k)	3,500	

	Supplies	
(d)	1,200	

	Prepaid Insurance	
(f)	1,600	

	Automobiles	
(b)	15,300	

	Equipment	
(e)	5,200	

	Notes Payable		
(n)	200	(b)	11,300
		Bal.	11,100

	Accounts Payable		
(h)	1,800	(e)	5,200
		(j)	800
		Bal.	4,200

	Lynette Moss, Capital		
		(a)	22,500

	Professional Fees		
		(g)	6,500
		(k)	3,500
		Bal.	10,000

	Rent Expense	
(c)	2,500	

	Salary Expense	
(l)	1,500	

	Blueprint Expense	
(j)	800	

	Automobile Expense	
(o)	250	

	Miscellaneous Expense	
(i)	300	
(m)	210	
Bal.	510	

3.

LYNETTE MOSS, ARCHITECT
Unadjusted Trial Balance
April 30, 2008

	Debit Balances	Credit Balances
Cash	15,440	
Accounts Receivable	3,500	
Supplies	1,200	
Prepaid Insurance	1,600	
Automobiles	15,300	
Equipment	5,200	
Notes Payable		11,100
Accounts Payable		4,200
Lynette Moss, Capital		22,500
Professional Fees		10,000
Rent Expense	2,500	
Salary Expense	1,500	
Blueprint Expense	800	
Automobile Expense	250	
Miscellaneous Expense	510	
	47,800	47,800

Prob. 2–2B

1.

(a)	Cash	18,000	
	Bill Bonds, Capital		18,000
(b)	Supplies	1,000	
	Accounts Payable		1,000
(c)	Cash	14,600	
	Sales Commissions		14,600
(d)	Rent Expense...	3,000	
	Cash		3,000
(e)	Accounts Payable...	600	
	Cash		600
(f)	Bill Bonds, Drawing	1,500	
	Cash		1,500
(g)	Automobile Expense.....................................	2,000	
	Miscellaneous Expense................................	500	
	Cash		2,500
(h)	Office Salaries Expense...............................	2,800	
	Cash		2,800
(i)	Supplies Expense...	725	
	Supplies		725

Prob. 2–2B Continued

2.

Cash					Sales Commissions		
(a)	18,000	(d)	3,000			(c)	14,600
(c)	14,600	(e)	600				
		(f)	1,500		**Rent Expense**		
		(g)	2,500		(d)	3,000	
		(h)	2,800				
Bal.	22,200						

Supplies					Office Salaries Expense	
(b)	1,000	(i)	725		(h)	2,800
Bal.	275					

Accounts Payable					Automobile Expense	
(e)	600	(b)	1,000		(g)	2,000
		Bal.	400			

Bill Bonds, Capital				Supplies Expense	
		(a)	18,000	(i)	725

Bill Bonds, Drawing			Miscellaneous Expense	
(f)	1,500		(g)	500

3.

GENESIS REALTY
Unadjusted Trial Balance
July 31, 2008

	Debit Balances	Credit Balances
Cash	22,200	
Supplies	275	
Accounts Payable		400
Bill Bonds, Capital		18,000
Bill Bonds, Drawing	1,500	
Sales Commissions		14,600
Rent Expense	3,000	
Office Salaries Expense	2,800	
Automobile Expense	2,000	
Supplies Expense	725	
Miscellaneous Expense	500	
	33,000	33,000

4. a. $14,600

    b. $9,025

    c. $5,575

Prob. 2–3B

1.

<table>
<tr><td colspan="5" align="center">JOURNAL</td><td align="right">Pages 1 and 2</td></tr>
<tr><td>Date</td><td align="center">Description</td><td align="center">Post.
Ref.</td><td align="center">Debit</td><td align="center">Credit</td></tr>
<tr><td>2008
Oct. 1</td><td>Cash..</td><td>11</td><td>20,000</td><td></td></tr>
<tr><td></td><td>Kristy Gomez, Capital ....</td><td>31</td><td></td><td>20,000</td></tr>
<tr><td>3</td><td>Rent Expense.......................................</td><td>53</td><td>1,600</td><td></td></tr>
<tr><td></td><td>Cash ....</td><td>11</td><td></td><td>1,600</td></tr>
<tr><td>10</td><td>Truck...</td><td>18</td><td>15,000</td><td></td></tr>
<tr><td></td><td>Cash ....</td><td>11</td><td></td><td>5,000</td></tr>
<tr><td></td><td>Notes Payable.................................</td><td>21</td><td></td><td>10,000</td></tr>
<tr><td>13</td><td>Equipment..</td><td>16</td><td>4,500</td><td></td></tr>
<tr><td></td><td>Accounts Payable............................</td><td>22</td><td></td><td>4,500</td></tr>
<tr><td>14</td><td>Supplies...</td><td>13</td><td>1,100</td><td></td></tr>
<tr><td></td><td>Cash ....</td><td>11</td><td></td><td>1,100</td></tr>
<tr><td>15</td><td>Prepaid Insurance ....</td><td>14</td><td>2,800</td><td></td></tr>
<tr><td></td><td>Cash ....</td><td>11</td><td></td><td>2,800</td></tr>
<tr><td>15</td><td>Cash..</td><td>11</td><td>6,100</td><td></td></tr>
<tr><td></td><td>Fees Earned....................................</td><td>41</td><td></td><td>6,100</td></tr>
<tr><td>21</td><td>Accounts Payable................................</td><td>22</td><td>2,400</td><td></td></tr>
<tr><td></td><td>Cash ....</td><td>11</td><td></td><td>2,400</td></tr>
<tr><td>24</td><td>Accounts Receivable...........................</td><td>12</td><td>8,600</td><td></td></tr>
<tr><td></td><td>Fees Earned....................................</td><td>41</td><td></td><td>8,600</td></tr>
<tr><td>26</td><td>Truck Expense ....</td><td>55</td><td>875</td><td></td></tr>
<tr><td></td><td>Accounts Payable............................</td><td>22</td><td></td><td>875</td></tr>
<tr><td>27</td><td>Utilities Expense..................................</td><td>54</td><td>900</td><td></td></tr>
<tr><td></td><td>Cash ....</td><td>11</td><td></td><td>900</td></tr>
<tr><td>27</td><td>Miscellaneous Expense ....</td><td>59</td><td>315</td><td></td></tr>
<tr><td></td><td>Cash ....</td><td>11</td><td></td><td>315</td></tr>
</table>

Prob. 2–3B Continued

		Post.		
	JOURNAL			Pages 1 and 2
Date	Description	Ref.	Debit	Credit
2008				
Oct. 29	Cash...	11	4,100	
	Accounts Receivable	12		4,100
30	Wages Expense	51	2,500	
	Cash	11		2,500
31	Kristy Gomez, Drawing	32	3,000	
	Cash	11		3,000

2.

Cash   11

		Post.			Balance	
Date	Item	Ref.	Dr.	Cr.	Dr.	Cr.
2008						
Oct. 1	....	1	20,000	....	20,000	....
3	....	1	....	1,600	18,400	....
10	....	1	....	5,000	13,400	....
14	....	1	....	1,100	12,300	....
15	....	1	....	2,800	9,500	....
15	....	1	6,100	....	15,600	....
21	....	2	....	2,400	13,200	....
27	....	2	....	900	12,300	....
27	....	2	....	315	11,985	....
29	....	2	4,100	....	16,085	....
30	....	2	....	2,500	13,585	....
31	....	2	....	3,000	10,585	....

Accounts Receivable   12

2008						
Oct. 24	....	2	8,600	....	8,600	....
29	....	2	....	4,100	4,500	....

Prob. 2–3B   Continued

Supplies 13

Date	Item	Post. Ref.	Dr.	Cr.	Balance Dr.	Cr.
2008						
Oct. 14	....	1	1,100	....	1,100	....

Prepaid Insurance 14

Date	Item	Post. Ref.	Dr.	Cr.	Balance Dr.	Cr.
2008						
Oct. 15	....	1	2,800	....	2,800	....

Equipment 16

Date	Item	Post. Ref.	Dr.	Cr.	Balance Dr.	Cr.
2008						
Oct. 13	....	1	4,500	....	4,500	....

Truck 18

Date	Item	Post. Ref.	Dr.	Cr.	Balance Dr.	Cr.
2008						
Oct. 10	....	1	15,000	....	15,000	....

Notes Payable 21

Date	Item	Post. Ref.	Dr.	Cr.	Balance Dr.	Cr.
2008						
Oct. 10	....	1	....	10,000	....	10,000

Accounts Payable 22

Date	Item	Post. Ref.	Dr.	Cr.	Balance Dr.	Cr.
2008						
Oct. 13	....	1	....	4,500	....	4,500
21	....	2	2,400	....	....	2,100
26	....	2	....	875	....	2,975

Kristy Gomez, Capital 31

Date	Item	Post. Ref.	Dr.	Cr.	Balance Dr.	Cr.
2008						
Oct. 1	....	1	....	20,000	....	20,000

Kristy Gomez, Drawing 32

Date	Item	Post. Ref.	Dr.	Cr.	Balance Dr.	Cr.
2008						
Oct. 31	....	2	3,000	....	3,000	....

Prob. 2–3B Continued

Fees Earned
41

Date	Item	Post. Ref.	Dr.	Cr.	Balance Dr.	Balance Cr.
2008						
Oct. 15	....	1	....	6,100	....	6,100
24	....	2	....	8,600	....	14,700

Wages Expense
51

Date	Item	Post. Ref.	Dr.	Cr.	Balance Dr.	Balance Cr.
2008						
Oct. 30	....	2	2,500	....	2,500	....

Rent Expense
53

Date	Item	Post. Ref.	Dr.	Cr.	Balance Dr.	Balance Cr.
2008						
Oct. 3	....	1	1,600	....	1,600	....

Utilities Expense
54

Date	Item	Post. Ref.	Dr.	Cr.	Balance Dr.	Balance Cr.
2008						
Oct. 27	....	2	900	....	900	....

Truck Expense
55

Date	Item	Post. Ref.	Dr.	Cr.	Balance Dr.	Balance Cr.
2008						
Oct. 26	....	2	875	....	875	....

Miscellaneous Expense
59

Date	Item	Post. Ref.	Dr.	Cr.	Balance Dr.	Balance Cr.
2008						
Oct. 27	....	2	315	....	315	....

Prob. 2–3B   Concluded

3.

ULTIMATE DESIGNS
Unadjusted Trial Balance
October 31, 2008

	Debit Balances	Credit Balances
Cash	10,585	
Accounts Receivable	4,500	
Supplies	1,100	
Prepaid Insurance	2,800	
Equipment	4,500	
Truck	15,000	
Notes Payable		10,000
Accounts Payable		2,975
Kristy Gomez, Capital		20,000
Kristy Gomez, Drawing	3,000	
Fees Earned		14,700
Wages Expense	2,500	
Rent Expense	1,600	
Utilities Expense	900	
Truck Expense	875	
Miscellaneous Expense	315	
	47,675	47,675

Prob. 2–4B

2. and 3.

			JOURNAL		Pages 18 and 19	

Date		Description	Post. Ref.	Debit	Credit
2008					
Aug.	1	Office Supplies	14	1,500	
		Accounts Payable............................	21		1,500
	2	Rent Expense...	52	2,500	
		Cash	11		2,500
	3	Cash..	11	28,720	
		Accounts Receivable	12		28,720
	5	Prepaid Insurance	13	3,600	
		Cash	11		3,600
	9	Accounts Payable..................................	21	250	
		Office Supplies	14		250
	17	Advertising Expense	53	3,450	
		Cash	11		3,450
	23	Accounts Payable..................................	21	2,670	
		Cash	11		2,670
	29	Miscellaneous Expense	59	500	
		Cash	11		500
	30	Automobile Expense	54	1,500	
		Cash	11		1,500
	31	Cash..	11	1,000	
		Salary and Commission Expense	51		1,000
	31	Salary and Commission Expense	51	17,400	
		Cash	11		17,400
	31	Accounts Receivable............................	12	51,900	
		Fees Earned	41		51,900
	31	Land..	16	75,000	
		Cash	11		10,000
		Notes Payable...................................	23		65,000
	31	Jody Craft, Drawing..............................	32	5,000	
		Cash	11		5,000
	31	Cash..	11	2,000	
		Unearned Rent..................................	22		2,000

Prob. 2–4B Continued

1. and 3.

Cash   11

Date	Item	Post. Ref.	Dr.	Cr.	Balance Dr.	Balance Cr.
2008						
Aug. 1	Balance......................................	✓	....	....	21,200	....
2	....	18	....	2,500	18,700	....
3	....	18	28,720	....	47,420	....
5	....	18	....	3,600	43,820	....
17	....	18	....	3,450	40,370	....
23	....	18	....	2,670	37,700	....
29	....	19	....	500	37,200	....
30	....	19	....	1,500	35,700	....
31	....	19	1,000	....	36,700	....
31	....	19	....	17,400	19,300	....
31	....	19	....	10,000	9,300	....
31	....	19	....	5,000	4,300	....
31	....	19	2,000	....	6,300	....

Accounts Receivable   12

Date	Item	Post. Ref.	Dr.	Cr.	Balance Dr.	Balance Cr.
2008						
Aug. 1	Balance......................................	✓	....	....	35,750	....
3	....	18	....	28,720	7,030	....
31	....	19	51,900	....	58,930	....

Prepaid Insurance   13

Date	Item	Post. Ref.	Dr.	Cr.	Balance Dr.	Balance Cr.
2008						
Aug. 1	Balance......................................	✓	....	....	4,500	....
5	....	18	3,600	....	8,100	....

Office Supplies   14

Date	Item	Post. Ref.	Dr.	Cr.	Balance Dr.	Balance Cr.
2008						
Aug. 1	Balance......................................	✓	....	....	1,000	....
1	....	18	1,500	....	2,500	....
9	....	18	....	250	2,250	....

Land   16

Date	Item	Post. Ref.	Dr.	Cr.	Balance Dr.	Balance Cr.
2008						
Aug. 31	....	19	75,000	....	75,000	....

Prob. 2–4B   Continued

Accounts Payable   21

Date		Item	Post. Ref.	Dr.	Cr.	Balance Dr.	Cr.
2008							
Aug.	1	Balance.............................	✓	....	....	....	6,200
	1	....	18	....	1,500	....	7,700
	9	....	18	250	....	....	7,450
	23	....	18	2,670	....	....	4,780

Unearned Rent   22

Date		Item	Post. Ref.	Dr.	Cr.	Balance Dr.	Cr.
2008							
Aug.	31	....	19	....	2,000	....	2,000

Notes Payable   23

Date		Item	Post. Ref.	Dr.	Cr.	Balance Dr.	Cr.
2008							
Aug.	31	....	19	....	65,000	....	65,000

Jody Craft, Capital   31

Date		Item	Post. Ref.	Dr.	Cr.	Balance Dr.	Cr.
2008							
Aug.	1	Balance.............................	✓	....	....	....	31,550

Jody Craft, Drawing   32

Date		Item	Post. Ref.	Dr.	Cr.	Balance Dr.	Cr.
2008							
Aug.	1	Balance.............................	✓	....	....	16,000	....
	31	....	19	5,000	....	21,000	....

Fees Earned   41

Date		Item	Post. Ref.	Dr.	Cr.	Balance Dr.	Cr.
2008							
Aug.	1	Balance.............................	✓	....	....	....	220,000
	31	....	19	....	51,900	....	271,900

Salary and Commission Expense   51

Date		Item	Post. Ref.	Dr.	Cr.	Balance Dr.	Cr.
2008							
Aug.	1	Balance.............................	✓	....	....	140,000	....
	31	....	19	....	1,000	139,000	....
	31	....	19	17,400	....	156,400	....

Prob. 2–4B   Continued

Rent Expense 52

Date		Item	Post. Ref.	Dr.	Cr.	Balance Dr.	Cr.
2008							
Aug.	1	Balance..............................	✓	....	....	17,500	....
	2	....	18	2,500	....	20,000	....

Advertising Expense 53

Date		Item	Post. Ref.	Dr.	Cr.	Balance Dr.	Cr.
2008							
Aug.	1	Balance..............................	✓	....	....	14,300	....
	17	....	18	3,450	....	17,750	....

Automobile Expense 54

Date		Item	Post. Ref.	Dr.	Cr.	Balance Dr.	Cr.
2008							
Aug.	1	Balance..............................	✓	....	....	6,400	....
	30	....	19	1,500	....	7,900	....

Miscellaneous Expense 59

Date		Item	Post. Ref.	Dr.	Cr.	Balance Dr.	Cr.
2008							
Aug.	1	Balance..............................	✓	....	....	1,100	....
	29	....	19	500	....	1,600	....

Prob. 2–4B   Concluded

4.

EQUITY REALTY
Unadjusted Trial Balance
August 31, 2008

	Debit Balances	Credit Balances
Cash	6,300	
Accounts Receivable	58,930	
Prepaid Insurance	8,100	
Office Supplies	2,250	
Land	75,000	
Accounts Payable		4,780
Unearned Rent		2,000
Notes Payable		65,000
Jody Craft, Capital		31,550
Jody Craft, Drawing	21,000	
Fees Earned		271,900
Salary and Commission Expense	156,400	
Rent Expense	20,000	
Advertising Expense	17,750	
Automobile Expense	7,900	
Miscellaneous Expense	1,600	
	375,230	375,230

Prob. 2–5B

1. Totals of preliminary trial balance:

| | Debit | $39,224.40 |
| | Credit | $38,336.50 |

2. Difference between preliminary trial balance totals: $887.90

3. Errors in trial balance:

   (a) Supplies debit balance was listed as $979.90 instead of $997.90.

   (b) Notes Payable credit balance of $6,500.00 was listed as debit balance.

   (c) Martin Tresp, Drawing debit balance of $1,350.00 was listed as credit balance.

   (d) Miscellaneous Expense of $283.50 was omitted.

4. Errors in account balances:

   (a) Accounts Payable balance of $1,077.50 was totaled as $1,225.90.

5. Errors in posting:

   (a) Prepaid Insurance entry of July 9 for $144.00 was posted as $1,440.00 (slide).

   (b) Land entry of July 10 for $12,000.00 was posted as $1,200.00 (slide).

   (c) Cash entry of July 25 for $1,681.30 was posted as $1,683.10 (transposition).

   (d) Wages Expense entry of July 31 for $1,390.00 was posted as $1,930.00 (transposition).

6.

| July | 31 | Utilities Expense | 53 | 110.00 | |
| | | Cash | 11 | | 110.00 |

Prob. 2–5B Concluded

7.

MAINSTAY TV REPAIR
Unadjusted Trial Balance
July 31, 20—

	Debit Balances	Credit Balances
Cash	8,806.00	
Supplies	997.90	
Prepaid Insurance	395.50	
Land	26,625.00	
Notes Payable		6,500.00
Accounts Payable		1,077.50
Martin Tresp, Capital		27,760.20
Martin Tresp, Drawing	1,350.00	
Service Revenue		8,000.40
Wages Expense	2,518.60	
Utilities Expense	546.60	
Advertising Expense	275.00	
Rent Expense	1,540.00	
Miscellaneous Expense	283.50	
	43,338.10	43,338.10

Prob. 2–6B

1.

EPIC VIDEO
Unadjusted Trial Balance
July 31, 2008

	Debit Balances	Credit Balances
Cash	6,750*	
Accounts Receivable	15,300	
Supplies	2,250	
Prepaid Insurance	1,710	
Equipment	54,000	
Notes Payable		18,000
Accounts Payable		5,580
Carlton Dey, Capital		32,400
Carlton Dey, Drawing	13,500	
Fees Earned		178,020
Wages Expense	102,000	
Rent Expense	20,850	
Advertising Expense	9,450	
Gas, Electricity, and Water Expense	5,670	
Miscellaneous Expense	2,520	
	234,000	234,000

*$6,250 – $5,000 (a) + $5,500 (b)

2. No. The trial balance indicates only that the debits and credits are equal. Any errors that have the same effect on debits and credits will not affect the balancing of the trial balance.

CONTINUING PROBLEM

2. and 3.

			JOURNAL			Page 1

Date			Description	Post. Ref.	Debit	Credit
2008						
May	1		Cash..	11	2,500	
			Kris Payne, Capital........................	31		2,500
	1		Office Rent Expense...........................	51	1,600	
			Cash	11		1,600
	1		Prepaid Insurance	15	3,360	
			Cash	11		3,360
	2		Cash..	11	1,350	
			Accounts Receivable	12		1,350
	3		Cash..	11	4,800	
			Unearned Revenue..........................	23		4,800
	3		Accounts Payable..............................	21	250	
			Cash	11		250
	4		Miscellaneous Expense	59	300	
			Cash	11		300
	5		Office Equipment...............................	17	5,000	
			Accounts Payable............................	21		5,000
	8		Advertising Expense	55	180	
			Cash	11		180
	11		Cash..	11	750	
			Fees Earned...................................	41		750
	13		Equipment Rent Expense	52	500	
			Cash	11		500
	14		Wages Expense	50	1,000	
			Cash	11		1,000

Continuing Problem   Continued

2. and 3.

JOURNAL

Date	Description	Post. Ref.	Debit	Credit
2008				
May 16	Cash......................................	11	1,500	
	Fees Earned.....................................	41		1,500
18	Supplies................................	14	750	
	Accounts Payable...........................	21		750
21	Music Expense..................................	54	325	
	Cash	11		325
22	Advertising Expense	55	800	
	Cash	11		800
23	Cash..	11	750	
	Accounts Receivable..........................	12	1,750	
	Fees Earned.....................................	41		2,500
27	Utilities Expense.................................	53	560	
	Cash	11		560
28	Wages Expense	50	1,000	
	Cash	11		1,000
29	Miscellaneous Expense	59	150	
	Cash	11		150
30	Cash..	11	400	
	Accounts Receivable..........................	12	1,100	
	Fees Earned.....................................	41		1,500
31	Cash..	11	2,800	
	Fees Earned.....................................	41		2,800
31	Music Expense..................................	54	900	
	Cash	11		900
31	Kris Payne, Drawing...........................	32	1,000	
	Cash	11		1,000

Continuing Problem   Continued

1. and 3.

Cash   11

Date	Item	Post. Ref.	Dr.	Cr.	Balance Dr.	Balance Cr.
2008						
May 1	Balance..............................	✓	....	....	9,160	....
1	....	1	2,500	....	11,660	....
1	....	1	....	1,600	10,060	....
1	....	1	....	3,360	6,700	....
2	....	1	1,350	....	8,050	....
3	....	1	4,800	....	12,850	....
3	....	1	....	250	12,600	....
4	....	1	....	300	12,300	....
8	....	1	....	180	12,120	....
11	....	1	750	....	12,870	....
13	....	1	....	500	12,370	....
14	....	1	....	1,000	11,370	....
16	....	2	1,500	....	12,870	....
21	....	2	....	325	12,545	....
22	....	2	....	800	11,745	....
23	....	2	750	....	12,495	....
27	....	2	....	560	11,935	....
28	....	2	....	1,000	10,935	....
29	....	2	....	150	10,785	....
30	....	2	400	....	11,185	....
31	....	2	2,800	....	13,985	....
31	....	2	....	900	13,085	....
31	....	2	....	1,000	12,085	....

Accounts Receivable   12

Date	Item	Post. Ref.	Dr.	Cr.	Balance Dr.	Balance Cr.
2008						
May 1	Balance..............................	✓	....	....	1,350	....
2	....	1	....	1,350	—	—
23	....	2	1,750	....	1,750	....
30	....	2	1,100	....	2,850	....

Supplies   14

Date	Item	Post. Ref.	Dr.	Cr.	Balance Dr.	Balance Cr.
2008						
May 1	Balance..............................	✓	....	....	170	....
18	....	2	750	....	920	....

Prepaid Insurance   15

Date	Item	Post. Ref.	Dr.	Cr.	Balance Dr.	Balance Cr.
2008						
May 1	....	1	3,360	....	3,360	....

Continuing Problem   Continued

Office Equipment   17

Date	Item	Post. Ref.	Dr.	Cr.	Balance Dr.	Balance Cr.
2008						
May 5	....	1	5,000	....	5,000	....

Accumulated Depreciation—Office Equipment   18
This account is not used in Chapter 2.

Accounts Payable   21

Date	Item	Post. Ref.	Dr.	Cr.	Balance Dr.	Balance Cr.
2008						
May 1	Balance..............................	✓	....	....	....	250
3	....	1	250	....	—	—
5	....	1	....	5,000	....	5,000
18	....	2	....	750	....	5,750

Wages Payable   22
This account is not used in Chapter 2.

Unearned Revenue   23

Date	Item	Post. Ref.	Dr.	Cr.	Balance Dr.	Balance Cr.
2008						
May 3	....	1	....	4,800	....	4,800

Kris Payne, Capital   31

Date	Item	Post. Ref.	Dr.	Cr.	Balance Dr.	Balance Cr.
2008						
May 1	Balance..............................	✓	....	....	....	10,000
1	....	1	....	2,500	....	12,500

Kris Payne, Drawing   32

Date	Item	Post. Ref.	Dr.	Cr.	Balance Dr.	Balance Cr.
2008						
May 1	Balance..............................	✓	....	....	300	....
31	....	2	1,000	....	1,300	....

Income Summary   33
This account is not used in Chapter 2.

Fees Earned   41

Date	Item	Post. Ref.	Dr.	Cr.	Balance Dr.	Balance Cr.
2008						
May 1	Balance..............................	✓	....	....	....	5,700
11	....	1	....	750	....	6,450
16	....	2	....	1,500	....	7,950
23	....	2	....	2,500	....	10,450
30	....	2	....	1,500	....	11,950
31	....	2	....	2,800	....	14,750

Continuing Problem   Continued

Wages Expense

Date	Item	Post. Ref.	Dr.	Cr.	Balance Dr.	Balance Cr.
2008						
May 1	Balance..............................	✓	....	....	400	....
14	....	1	1,000	....	1,400	....
28	....	2	1,000	....	2,400	....

Office Rent Expense

51

Date	Item	Post. Ref.	Dr.	Cr.	Balance Dr.	Balance Cr.
2008						
May 1	Balance..............................	✓	....	....	1,000	....
1	....	1	1,600	....	2,600	....

Equipment Rent Expense

52

Date	Item	Post. Ref.	Dr.	Cr.	Balance Dr.	Balance Cr.
2008						
May 1	Balance..............................	✓	....	....	800	....
13	....	1	500	....	1,300	....

Utilities Expense

53

Date	Item	Post. Ref.	Dr.	Cr.	Balance Dr.	Balance Cr.
2008						
May 1	Balance..............................	✓	....	....	350	....
27	....	2	560	....	910	....

Music Expense

54

Date	Item	Post. Ref.	Dr.	Cr.	Balance Dr.	Balance Cr.
2008						
May 1	Balance..............................	✓	....	....	1,340	....
21	....	2	325	....	1,665	....
31	....	2	900	....	2,565	....

Advertising Expense

55

Date	Item	Post. Ref.	Dr.	Cr.	Balance Dr.	Balance Cr.
2008						
May 1	Balance..............................	✓	....	....	750	....
8	....	1	180	....	930	....
22	....	2	800	....	1,730	....

Supplies Expense

56

Date	Item	Post. Ref.	Dr.	Cr.	Balance Dr.	Balance Cr.
2008						
May 1	Balance..............................	✓	....	....	180	....

Insurance Expense

57

This account is not used in Chapter 2.

Continuing Problem   Concluded

Depreciation Expense   58

Date	Item	Post. Ref.	Dr.	Cr.	Balance Dr.	Balance Cr.

This account is not used in Chapter 2.

Miscellaneous Expense   59

Date	Item	Post. Ref.	Dr.	Cr.	Balance Dr.	Balance Cr.
2008						
May 1	Balance	✓	....	....	150	....
4	....	1	300	....	450	....
29	....	2	150	....	600	....

4.

DANCIN MUSIC
Unadjusted Trial Balance
May 31, 2008

	Debit Balances	Credit Balances
Cash	12,085	
Accounts Receivable	2,850	
Supplies	920	
Prepaid Insurance	3,360	
Office Equipment	5,000	
Accounts Payable		5,750
Unearned Revenue		4,800
Kris Payne, Capital		12,500
Kris Payne, Drawing	1,300	
Fees Earned		14,750
Wages Expense	2,400	
Office Rent Expense	2,600	
Equipment Rent Expense	1,300	
Utilities Expense	910	
Music Expense	2,565	
Advertising Expense	1,730	
Supplies Expense	180	
Miscellaneous Expense	600	
	37,800	37,800

SPECIAL ACTIVITIES

SA 2–1

Acceptable ethical conduct requires that Tomas look for the difference. If Tomas cannot find the difference within a reasonable amount of time, he should confer with his supervisor as to what action should be taken so that the financial statements can be prepared by the 5 o'clock deadline. Tomas's responsibility to his employer is to act with integrity, objectivity, and due care, so that users of the financial statements will not be misled.

SA 2–2

The following general journal entry should be used to record the receipt of tuition payments received in advance of classes:

Cash	XXXX	
Unearned Tuition Deposits		XXXX

Cash is an asset account, and Unearned Tuition Deposits is a liability account. As the classes are taught throughout the term, the unearned tuition deposits become earned revenue.

SA 2–3

The journal is called the book of original entry. It provides a time-ordered history of the transactions that have occurred for the firm. This time-ordered history is very important because it allows one to trace ledger account balances back to the original transactions that created those balances. This is called an "audit trail." If the firm recorded transactions by posting ledgers directly, it would be nearly impossible to reconstruct actual transactions. The debits and credits would all be separated and accumulated into the ledger balances. Once the transactions become part of the ledger balances, the original transactions would be lost. That is, there would be no audit trail, and any errors that might occur in recording transactions would be almost impossible to trace. Thus, firms first record transaction debits and credits in a journal. These transactions are then posted to the ledger to update the account balances. The journal and ledger are linked using posting references. This allows an analyst to trace the transaction flow forward or backward, depending upon the need.

SA 2–4

1. The rules of debit and credit must be memorized. Miguel is correct in that the rules of debit and credit could be reversed as long as everyone accepted and abided by the rules. However, the important point is that everyone accepts the rules as the way in which transactions should be recorded. This generates uniformity across the accounting profession and reduces errors and confusion. Since the current rules of debit and credit have been used for centuries, Miguel should adapt to the current rules of debit and credit, rather than devise his own.

   The primary reason that all accounts do not have the same rules for increases and decreases is for control of the recording process. The double-entry accounting system, which includes both (1) the rules of debit and credit and (2) the accounting equation, guarantees that (1) debits always equals credits and (2) assets always equals liabilities plus owner's equity. If all increases in the account were recorded by debits, then the control that debits always equals credits would be removed. In addition, the control that the normal balance of assets is a debit would also be removed. The accounting equation would still hold, but the control over recording transactions would be weakened.

   Miguel is correct that we could call the left and right sides of an account different terms, such as "LE" or "RE." Again, centuries of tradition dictate the current terminology used. One might note, however, that in Latin, *debere* (debit) means left and *credere* (credit) means right.

2. The accounting system may be designed to capture information about the buying habits of various customers or vendors, such as the quantity normally ordered, average amount ordered, number of returns, etc. Thus, in a sense, there can be other "sides" of (information about) a transaction that are recorded by the accounting system. Such information would be viewed as supplemental to the basic double-entry accounting system.

SA 2–5

a. Although the titles and numbers of accounts may differ, depending on how expenses are classified, the following accounts would be adequate for recording transaction data for Birdie Caddy Service:

Balance Sheet Accounts		Income Statement Accounts	
1. Assets		**4. Revenue**	
11	Cash	41	Service Revenue
12	Accounts Receivable		
13	Supplies		**5. Expenses**
		51	Rent Expense
2. Liabilities		52	Supplies Expense
21	Accounts Payable	53	Wages Expense
		54	Utilities Expense
		55	Miscellaneous Expense
3. Owner's Equity			
31	Shane Raburn, Capital		
32	Shane Raburn, Drawing		

b.

BIRDIE CADDY SERVICE
Income Statement
For Month Ended June 30, 2008

Service revenue		$7,200
Expenses:		
Rent expense	$2,000	
Supplies expense	810	
Wages expense	450	
Utilities expense	160	
Miscellaneous expense	180	
Total expenses		3,600
Net income		$3,600

Note to Instructors: Students may have prepared slightly different income statements, depending upon the titles of the major expense classifications chosen. Regardless of the classification of expenses, however, the total sales, total expenses, and net income should be as presented above.

T accounts are not required for the preparation of the income statement of Birdie Caddy Service. The following presentation illustrates one solution using T accounts. Alternative solutions are possible if students used different accounts. In presenting the following T account solution, instructors may wish to emphasize the advantages of using T accounts (or a journal and four-column accounts) when a large number of transactions must be recorded.

SA 2–5   Continued

Cash — 11

2008			2008		
June 1	2,000		June 1	500	
15	3,150		2	650	
30	3,200		3	750	
30	550		17	350	
			20	750	
			28	180	
			30	160	
			30	450	
Bal.	5,110				

Accounts Receivable — 12

2008			2008		
June 25	850		June 30	550	
Bal.	300				

Supplies — 13

2008			2008		
June 2	650		June 30	810	
7	350				
22	200				
Bal.	390				

Accounts Payable — 21

2008			2008		
June 17	350		June 3	750	
20	750		7	350	
			22	200	
			Bal.	200	

Shane Raburn, Capital — 31

			2008		
			June 1	2,000	

Service Revenue — 41

			2008		
			June 15	3,150	
			25	850	
			30	3,200	
			Bal.	7,200	

Rent Expense — 51

2008					
June 1	500				
3	1,500				
Bal.	2,000				

Supplies Expense — 52

2008					
June 30	810				

Wages Expense — 53

2008					
June 30	450				

Utilities Expense — 54

2008					
June 30	160				

Miscellaneous Expense — 55

2008					
June 28	180				

SA 2–5   Concluded

c. $5,110, computed in the following manner:

Cash receipts:

Initial investment	$2,000	
Cash sales..	6,350	
Collections on accounts	550	
Total cash receipts during June		$8,900

Cash disbursements:

Rent expense	$2,000	
Supplies purchased for cash	650	
Wages expense	450	
Payment for supplies on account	350	
Utilities expense...	160	
Miscellaneous expense	180	
Total cash disbursements during June......		3,790

Cash on hand according to records .... | | $5,110*

*If the student used T accounts in completing part (b), or this part, this amount ($5,110) should agree with the balance of the cash account.

d. The difference of $130 between the cash on hand according to records ($5,110) and the cash on hand according to the count ($4,980) could be due to many factors, including errors in the record keeping and withdrawals made by Shane.

SA 2–6

Note to Instructors: The purpose of this activity is to familiarize students with the job opportunities available in accounting or in fields that require (or prefer) the employee to have some knowledge of accounting.

CHAPTER 3
THE ADJUSTING PROCESS

QUESTION INFORMATION

Number	Objective	Description	Difficulty	Time	AACSB	AICPA	SS	GL
Q3-1	3-1		Easy	5 min	Analytic	FN-Measurement		
Q3-2	3-1		Easy	5 min	Analytic	FN-Measurement		
Q3-3	3-1		Easy	5 min	Analytic	FN-Measurement		
Q3-4	3-1		Easy	5 min	Analytic	FN-Measurement		
Q3-5	3-3		Easy	5 min	Analytic	FN-Measurement		
Q3-6	3-3		Easy	5 min	Analytic	FN-Measurement		
Q3-7	3-1		Easy	5 min	Analytic	FN-Measurement		
Q3-8	3-1		Easy	5 min	Analytic	FN-Measurement		
Q3-9	3-2		Easy	5 min	Analytic	FN-Measurement		
Q3-10	3-2		Easy	5 min	Analytic	FN-Measurement		
Q3-11	3-2		Easy	5 min	Analytic	FN-Measurement		
Q3-12	3-3		Easy	5 min	Analytic	FN-Measurement		
Q3-13	3-2		Easy	5 min	Analytic	FN-Measurement		
Q3-14	3-2		Easy	5 min	Analytic	FN-Measurement		
Q3-15	3-2		Easy	5 min	Analytic	FN-Measurement		
PE3-1A	3-1	Accounts requiring adjustment	Easy	5 min	Analytic	FN-Measurement		
PE3-1B	3-1	Accounts requiring adjustment	Easy	5 min	Analytic	FN-Measurement		
PE3-2A	3-1	Type of adjustment	Easy	5 min	Analytic	FN-Measurement		
PE3-2B	3-1	Type of adjustment	Easy	5 min	Analytic	FN-Measurement		
PE3-3A	3-2	Adjustment for supplies used	Easy	5 min	Analytic	FN-Measurement		
PE3-3B	3-2	Adjustment for insurance expired	Easy	5 min	Analytic	FN-Measurement		
PE3-4A	3-2	Adjustment for unearned fees	Easy	5 min	Analytic	FN-Measurement		
PE3-4B	3-2	Adjustment for unearned rent	Easy	5 min	Analytic	FN-Measurement		
PE3-5A	3-2	Adjustment for accrued fees	Easy	5 min	Analytic	FN-Measurement		
PE3-5B	3-2	Adjustment for accrued fees	Easy	5 min	Analytic	FN-Measurement		
PE3-6A	3-2	Adjustment for salaries payable	Easy	5 min	Analytic	FN-Measurement		
PE3-6B	3-2	Adjustment for salaries payable	Easy	5 min	Analytic	FN-Measurement		
PE3-7A	3-2	Adjustment for depreciation	Easy	5 min	Analytic	FN-Measurement		
PE3-7B	3-2	Adjustment for depreciation	Easy	5 min	Analytic	FN-Measurement		
PE3-8A	3-3	Effect of omitting adjustments	Moderate	10 min	Analytic	FN-Measurement		
PE3-8B	3-3	Effect of omitting adjustments	Moderate	10 min	Analytic	FN-Measurement		
PE3-9A	3-4	Effect of errors on adjusted trial balance	Moderate	10 min	Analytic	FN-Measurement		
PE3-9B	3-4	Effect of errors on adjusted trial balance	Moderate	10 min	Analytic	FN-Measurement		
Ex3-1	3-1	Classifying types of adjustments	Easy	5 min	Analytic	FN-Measurement		

Number	Objective	Description	Difficulty	Time	AACSB	AICPA	SS	GL
Ex3-2	3-1	Classifying types of adjustments	Easy	5 min	Analytic	FN-Measurement		
Ex3-3	3-2	Adjusting entry for supplies	Easy	5 min	Analytic	FN-Measurement		
Ex3-4	3-2	Determining supplies purchased	Easy	5 min	Analytic	FN-Measurement		
Ex3-5	3-2	Effect of omitting adjusting entry	Moderate	5 min	Analytic	FN-Measurement		
Ex3-6	3-2	Adjusting entries for prepaid insurance	Easy	5 min	Analytic	FN-Measurement		
Ex3-7	3-2	Adjusting entries for prepaid insurance	Easy	5 min	Analytic	FN-Measurement		
Ex3-8	3-2	Adjusting entries for unearned fees	Easy	5 min	Analytic	FN-Measurement		
Ex3-9	3-2	Effect of omitting adjusting entry	Moderate	5 min	Analytic	FN-Measurement		
Ex3-10	3-2	Adjusting entry for accrued fees	Easy	5 min	Analytic	FN-Measurement		
Ex3-11	3-2	Adjusting entries for unearned and accrued fees	Easy	5 min	Analytic	FN-Measurement		
Ex3-12	3-3	Effect on financial statements of omitting adjusting entry	Moderate	5 min	Analytic	FN-Measurement		
Ex3-13	3-2	Adjusting entries for accrued salaries	Easy	5 min	Analytic	FN-Measurement		
Ex3-14	3-2	Determining wages paid	Easy	5 min	Analytic	FN-Measurement		
Ex3-15	3-2	Effect of omitting adjusting entry	Moderate	5 min	Analytic	FN-Measurement		
Ex3-16	3-2	Effect of omitting adjusting entry	Moderate	5 min	Analytic	FN-Measurement		
Ex3-17	3-2	Adjusting entries for prepaid and accrued taxes	Moderate	10 min	Analytic	FN-Measurement		
Ex3-18	3-2	Adjustment for depreciation	Easy	5 min	Analytic	FN-Measurement		
Ex3-19	3-2	Determining fixed asset's book value	Easy	5 min	Analytic	FN-Measurement		
Ex3-20	3-2	Book value of fixed assets	Easy	5 min	Analytic	FN-Measurement		
Ex3-21	3-2, 3-3	Effects of errors on financial statements	Easy	5 min	Analytic	FN-Measurement		
Ex3-22	3-2, 3-3	Effects of errors on financial statements	Easy	5 min	Analytic	FN-Measurement		
Ex3-23	3-2, 3-3	Effects of errors on financial statements	Moderate	10 min	Analytic	FN-Measurement		
Ex3-24	3-2, 3-3	Effects of errors on financial statements	Moderate	10 min	Analytic	FN-Measurement		
Ex3-25	3-2, 3-3	Adjusting entries for depreciation; effect of error	Easy	5 min	Analytic	FN-Measurement		
Ex3-26	3-4	Adjusting entries from trial balance	Moderate	10 min	Analytic	FN-Measurement		
Ex3-27	3-4	Adjusting entries from trial balance	Difficult	15 min	Analytic	FN-Measurement		
Pr3-1A	3-2	Adjusting entries	Moderate	30 min	Analytic	FN-Measurement		
Pr3-2A	3-2	Adjusting entries	Moderate	45 min	Analytic	FN-Measurement		
Pr3-3A	3-2	Adjusting entries	Moderate	1 hr	Analytic	FN-Measurement		KA

Number	Objective	Description	Difficulty	Time	AACSB	AICPA	SS	GL
Pr3-4A	3-2, 3-3, 3-4	Adjusting entries	Moderate	45 min	Analytic	FN-Measurement		KA
Pr3-5A	3-2, 3-3, 3-4	Adjusting entries and adjusted balances	Difficult	1 hr	Analytic	FN-Measurement	Exl	KA
Pr3-6A	3-3	Adjusting entries and errors	Difficult	1 hr	Analytic	FN-Measurement	Exl	
Pr3-1B	3-2	Adjusting entries	Moderate	30 min	Analytic	FN-Measurement		
Pr3-2B	3-2	Adjusting entries	Moderate	45 min	Analytic	FN-Measurement		
Pr3-3B	3-2	Adjusting errors	Moderate	1 hr	Analytic	FN-Measurement		KA
Pr3-4B	3-2, 3-3, 3-4	Adjusting entries	Moderate	45 min	Analytic	FN-Measurement		KA
Pr3-5B	3-2, 3-3, 3-4	Adjusting entries and adjusted trial balances	Difficult	1 hr	Analytic	FN-Measurement	Exl	KA
Pr3-6B	3-3	Adjusting entries and errors	Difficult	1 hr	Analytic	FN-Measurement	Exl	
DM-3		Continuing Problem						KA
SA3-1	3-1	Ethics and professional conduct in business	Moderate	15 min	Ethics	BB-Industry		
SA3-2	3-1	Accrued expense	Easy	5 min	Analytic	FN-Measurement		
SA3-3	3-1	Accrued revenue	Easy	5 min	Analytic	FN-Measurement		
SA3-4	3-3, 3-4	Adjustments and financial statements	Moderate	15 min	Analytic	FN-Measurement		
SA3-5	1-1	Code of ethics	Easy	15 min	Ethics	BB-Critical Thinking		

EYE OPENERS

1. **a.** Under cash-basis accounting, revenues are reported in the period in which cash is received and expenses are reported in the period in which cash is paid.
   b. Under accrual-basis accounting, revenues are reported in the period in which they are earned and expenses are reported in the same period as the revenues to which they relate.

2. **a.** 2008
   b. 2007

3. **a.** 2008
   b. 2007

4. The matching concept is related to the accrual basis.

5. Yes. The cash amount listed on the trial balance is normally the amount of cash on hand and needs no adjustment at the end of the period.

6. No. The amount listed on the trial balance, before adjustments, normally represents the cost of supplies on hand at the beginning of the period plus the cost of the supplies purchased during the period. Some of the supplies have been used; therefore, an adjustment is necessary for the supplies used before the amount for the balance sheet is determined.

7. Adjusting entries are necessary at the end of an accounting period to bring the ledger up to date.

8. Adjusting entries bring the ledger up to date as a normal part of the accounting cycle. Correcting entries correct errors in the ledger.

9. Four different categories of adjusting entries include prepaid expenses (deferred expenses), unearned revenues (deferred revenues), accrued expenses (accrued liabilities), and accrued revenues (accrued assets).

10. Statement (b): Increases the balance of an expense account.

11. Statement (a): Increases the balance of a revenue account.

12. Yes, because every adjusting entry affects expenses or revenues.

13. **a.** The balance is the sum of the beginning balance and the amount of the insurance premiums paid during the period.
    b. The balance is the unexpired premiums at the end of the period.

14. **a.** The rights acquired represent an asset.
    b. The justification for debiting Rent Expense is that when the ledger is summarized in a trial balance at the end of the month and statements are prepared, the rent will have become an expense. Hence, no adjusting entry will be necessary.

15. **a.** The portion of the cost of a fixed asset deducted from revenue of the period is debited to Depreciation Expense. It is the expired cost for the period. The reduction in the fixed asset account is recorded by a credit to Accumulated Depreciation rather than to the fixed asset account. The use of the contra asset account facilitates the presentation of original cost and accumulated depreciation on the balance sheet.
    b. Depreciation Expense—debit balance; Accumulated Depreciation—credit balance.
    c. No, it is not customary for the balances of the two accounts to be equal in amount.
    d. Depreciation Expense appears in the income statement; Accumulated Depreciation appears on the balance sheet.

PRACTICE EXERCISES

PE 3–1A

a.	Yes	c.	No	e.	Yes
b.	No	d.	Yes	f.	Yes

PE 3–1B

a.	No	c.	Yes	e.	Yes
b.	No	d.	No	f.	No

PE 3–2A

a.	Unearned revenue	c.	Prepaid expense
b.	Accrued expense	d.	Accrued revenue

PE 3–2B

a.	Accrued expense	c.	Prepaid expense
b.	Accrued revenue	d.	Unearned revenue

PE 3–3A

Supplies Expense	2,756	
Supplies		2,756
Supplies used ($1,245 + $2,860 − $1,349).		

PE 3–3B

Insurance Expense	6,525	
Prepaid Insurance		6,525
Insurance expired ($4,800 + $5,850 − $4,125).		

PE 3–4A

Unearned Fees	16,288	
Fees Earned		16,288
Fees earned ($23,676 – $7,388).		

PE 3–4B

Unearned Rent...	2,875	
Rent Revenue		2,875
Rent earned [($6,900/12) × 5 months].		

PE 3–5A

Accounts Receivable	7,234	
Fees Earned		7,234
Accrued fees.		

PE 3–5B

Accounts Receivable	1,772	
Fees Earned		1,772
Accrued fees.		

PE 3–6A

Salaries Expense	4,750	
Salaries Payable		4,750
Accrued salaries [($11,875/5 days) × 2 days].		

PE 3–6B

Salaries Expense	16,560	
Salaries Payable		16,560
Accrued salaries [($24,840/6 days) × 4 days].		

PE 3–7A

Depreciation Expense...	6,450	
Accumulated Depreciation—Equipment................		6,450
Depreciation on equipment.		

PE 3–7B

Depreciation Expense...	1,820	
Accumulated Depreciation—Equipment................		1,820
Depreciation on equipment.		

PE 3–8A

a. Revenues were understated by $9,638.

b. Expenses were understated by $3,056 ($2,276 + $780).

c. Net income was understated by $6,582 ($9,638 – $3,056).

PE 3–8B

a. Revenues were understated by $6,481.

b. Expenses were understated by $8,534 ($1,034 + $7,500).

c. Net income was overstated by $2,053 ($8,534 – $6,481).

PE 3–9A

a. The totals are equal since the adjusting entry was omitted.

b. The totals are unequal. The debit total is higher by $9 ($2,565 – $2,556).

PE 3–9B

a. The totals are unequal. The credit total is higher by $180 ($640 – $460).

b. The totals are equal even though the credit should have been to Wages Payable instead of Accounts Payable.

EXERCISES

Ex. 3–1

1. Accrued revenue
2. Accrued expense
3. Accrued expense
4. Accrued expense

5. Prepaid expense
6. Unearned revenue
7. Prepaid expense
8. Unearned revenue

Ex. 3–2

Account	Answer
Accounts Receivable	Normally requires adjustment (AR).
Cash	Does not normally require adjustment.
Charmaine Hollis, Drawing	Does not normally require adjustment.
Interest Payable	Normally requires adjustment (AE).
Interest Receivable	Normally requires adjustment (AR).
Land	Does not normally require adjustment.
Office Equipment	Does not normally require adjustment.
Prepaid Rent	Normally requires adjustment (PE).
Supplies	Normally requires adjustment (PE).
Unearned Fees	Normally requires adjustment (UR).
Wages Expense	Normally requires adjustment (AE).

Ex. 3–3

Supplies Expense	2,361	
Supplies		2,361
Supplies used ($2,975 – $614).		

Ex. 3–4

$1,540 ($279 + $1,261)

Ex. 3–5

a. Insurance expense (or expenses) will be understated. Net income will be overstated.

b. Prepaid insurance (or assets) will be overstated. Owner's equity will be overstated.

Ex. 3–6

a.	Insurance Expense	4,180	
	Prepaid Insurance..		4,180
	Insurance expired ($6,175 – $1,995).		
b.	Insurance Expense	4,180	
	Prepaid Insurance..		4,180
	Insurance expired ($6,175 – $1,995).		

Ex. 3–7

a.	Insurance Expense	5,450	
	Prepaid Insurance..		5,450
	Insurance expired ($3,600 + $4,800 – $2,950).		
b.	Insurance Expense	5,450	
	Prepaid Insurance..		5,450
	Insurance expired ($3,600 + $4,800 – $2,950).		

Ex. 3–8

Unearned Fees	22,320	
Fees Earned		22,320
Fees earned ($49,500 – $27,180).		

Ex. 3–9

a. Rent revenue (or revenues) will be understated. Net income will be understated.

b. Owner's equity at the end of the period will be understated. Unearned rent (or liabilities) will be overstated.

Ex. 3–10

a.

Accounts Receivable	17,600	
Fees Earned		17,600
Accrued fees.		

b. No. If the cash basis of accounting is used, revenues are recognized only when the cash is received. Therefore, earned but unbilled revenues would not be recognized in the accounts, and no adjusting entry would be necessary.

Ex. 3–11

a.

Unearned Fees	12,300	
Fees Earned		12,300
Unearned fees earned during year.		

b.

Accounts Receivable	7,100	
Fees Earned		7,100
Accrued fees earned.		

Ex. 3–12

a. Fees earned (or revenues) will be understated. Net income will be understated.

b. Accounts (fees) receivable (or assets) will be understated. Owner's equity will be understated.

Ex. 3–13

a.	Salary Expense..	12,375	
	Salaries Payable		12,375
	Accrued salaries [($20,625/5 days) × 3 days].		
b.	Salary Expense..	16,500	
	Salaries Payable		16,500
	Accrued salaries [($20,625/5 days) × 4 days].		

Ex. 3–14

$65,670 ($72,150 – $6,480)

Ex. 3–15

a. Salary expense (or expenses) will be understated. Net income will be overstated.

b. Salaries payable (or liabilities) will be understated. Owner's equity will be overstated.

Ex. 3–16

a. Salary expense (or expenses) will be overstated. Net income will be understated.

b. The balance sheet will be correct. This is because salaries payable has been satisfied, and the net income errors have offset each other. Thus, owner's equity is correct.

Ex. 3–17

a. Taxes Expense 2,250
       Prepaid Taxes   2,250
       Prepaid taxes expired [($3,000/12) × 9 months].

   Taxes Expense 16,425
       Taxes Payable   16,425
       Accrued taxes.

b. $18,675 ($2,250 + $16,425)

Ex. 3–18

   Depreciation Expense 3,275
       Accumulated Depreciation   3,275
       Depreciation on equipment.

Ex. 3–19

a. $416,750 ($678,950 – $262,200)

b. No. Depreciation is an allocation of the cost of the equipment to the periods benefiting from its use. It does not necessarily relate to value or loss of value.

Ex. 3–20

a. $2,223,000,000 ($6,078,000,000 – $3,855,000,000)

b. No. Depreciation is an allocation method, not a valuation method. That is, depreciation allocates the cost of a fixed asset over its useful life. Depreciation does not attempt to measure market values, which may vary significantly from year to year.

Ex. 3–21

$324,755,000 ($95,789,000 + $228,966,000)

Ex. 3–22

a. $606,000,000

b. 58.8% ($606,000,000/$1,030,000,000)

Ex. 3–23

	Error (a)		Error (b)	
	Over-stated	Under-stated	Over-stated	Under-stated
1. Revenue for the year would be	$ 0	$12,450	$ 0	$ 0
2. Expenses for the year would be.............	0	0	0	7,280
3. Net income for the year would be	0	12,450	7,280	0
4. Assets at August 31 would be................	0	0	0	0
5. Liabilities at August 31 would be............	12,450	0	0	7,280
6. Owner's equity at August 31 would be...	0	12,450	7,280	0

Ex. 3–24

$267,970 ($262,800 + $12,450 – $7,280)

Ex. 3–25

a. Depreciation Expense... 18,100
        Accumulated Depreciation.......................................   18,100
            Depreciation on equipment.

b. (1) Depreciation expense would be understated. Net income would be over-stated.

   (2) Accumulated depreciation would be understated, and total assets would be overstated. Owner's equity would be overstated.

Ex. 3–26

1.	Accounts Receivable	12	
	Fees Earned		12
2.	Supplies Expense	9	
	Supplies..		9
3.	Insurance Expense	24	
	Prepaid Insurance..		24
4.	Depreciation Expense...	15	
	Accumulated Depreciation—Equipment.................		15
5.	Wages Expense..	3	
	Wages Payable...		3

Ex. 3–27

1. The accountant debited Accounts Receivable for $3,750, but did not credit Laundry Revenue. This adjusting entry represents accrued laundry revenue.

2. The accountant credited Laundry Equipment for the depreciation expense of $6,000, instead of crediting the accumulated depreciation account.

3. The accountant credited the prepaid insurance account for $3,800, but only debited the insurance expense account for $800.

4. The accountant did not debit Wages Expense for $1,200.

5. The accountant debited rather than credited Laundry Supplies for $1,750.

The corrected adjusted trial balance is shown below.

Sweetwater Laundry
Adjusted Trial Balance
October 31, 2008

	Debit Balances	Credit Balances
Cash	7,500	
Accounts Receivable	22,000	
Laundry Supplies	2,000	
Prepaid Insurance	1,400	
Laundry Equipment	140,000	
Accumulated Depreciation		54,000
Accounts Payable		9,600
Wages Payable		1,200
Mattie Ivy, Capital		60,300
Mattie Ivy, Drawing	28,775	
Laundry Revenue		185,850
Wages Expense	50,400	
Rent Expense	25,575	
Utilities Expense	18,500	
Depreciation Expense	6,000	
Laundry Supplies Expense	1,750	
Insurance Expense	3,800	
Miscellaneous Expense	3,250	
	310,950	310,950

PROBLEMS

Prob. 3–1A

1.

a.	Supplies Expense...	1,350	
	Supplies		1,350
	Supplies used ($1,975 – $625).		
b.	Unearned Rent	1,250	
	Rent Revenue		1,250
	Rent earned ($3,750/3).		
c.	Wages Expense	1,000	
	Wages Payable		1,000
	Accrued wages.		
d.	Accounts Receivable....................................	12,275	
	Fees Earned...		12,275
	Accrued fees earned.		
e.	Depreciation Expense	850	
	Accumulated Depreciation		850
	Depreciation expense.		

2. Adjusting entries are a planned part of the accounting process to update the accounts. Correcting entries are not planned, but arise only when necessary to correct errors.

Prob. 3–2A

a. Accounts Receivable... 1,650
      Fees Earned... 1,650
        Accrued fees earned.

b. Supplies Expense... 1,850
      Supplies 1,850
        Supplies used ($2,050 – $200).

c. Rent Expense.. 5,000
      Prepaid Rent 5,000
        Prepaid rent expired.

d. Depreciation Expense 1,150
      Accumulated Depreciation 1,150
        Equipment depreciation.

e. Unearned Fees... 7,000
      Fees Earned... 7,000
        Fees earned ($8,500 – $1,500).

f. Wages Expense 3,150
      Wages Payable 3,150
        Accrued wages.

Prob. 3–3A

a. Accounts Receivable 1,775
       Fees Earned 1,775
          Accrued fees earned.

b. Supplies Expense 4,200
       Supplies.. 4,200
          Supplies used ($5,400 – $1,200).

c. Depreciation Expense.. 4,100
       Accumulated Depreciation....................................... 4,100
          Equipment depreciation.

d. Unearned Fees 1,750
       Fees Earned 1,750
          Fees earned.

e. Wages Expense... 600
       Wages Payable... 600
          Accrued wages.

Prob. 3–4A

2008

Apr.	30	Supplies Expense..	2,850	
		Supplies..		2,850
		Supplies used ($3,750 – $900).		
	30	Insurance Expense...	3,250	
		Prepaid Insurance...		3,250
		Insurance expired ($4,750 – $1,500).		
	30	Depreciation Expense—Equipment..................	2,500	
		Accumulated Depreciation—Equipment......		2,500
		Equipment depreciation		
		($34,000 – $31,500).		
	30	Depreciation Expense—Automobiles...............	2,150	
		Accumulated Depreciation—Automobiles		2,150
		Automobile depreciation		
		($20,400 – $18,250).		
	30	Utilities Expense..	490	
		Accounts Payable		490
		Accrued utilities expense		
		($8,800 – $8,310).		
	30	Salary Expense..	2,000	
		Salaries Payable...		2,000
		Accrued salary ($174,300 – $172,300).		
	30	Unearned Service Fees.......................................	3,100	
		Service Fees Earned......................................		3,100
		Service fees earned ($6,000 – $2,900).		

Prob. 3–5A

1.

a.	Insurance Expense	4,500	
	Prepaid Insurance		4,500
	Insurance expired ($7,200 – $2,700).		
b.	Supplies Expense	1,500	
	Supplies...		1,500
	Supplies used ($1,980 – $480).		
c.	Depreciation Expense—Building.........................	1,600	
	Accumulated Depreciation—Building.............		1,600
	Building depreciation.		
d.	Depreciation Expense—Equipment	4,400	
	Accumulated Depreciation—Equipment		4,400
	Equipment depreciation.		
e.	Unearned Rent	3,500	
	Rent Revenue..		3,500
	Rent revenue earned ($6,750 – $3,250).		
f.	Salaries and Wages Expense	2,800	
	Salaries and Wages Payable		2,800
	Accrued salaries and wages.		
g.	Accounts Receivable	6,200	
	Fees Earned		6,200
	Accrued fees earned.		

Prob. 3–5A   Concluded

2.

CAMBRIDGE COMPANY
Adjusted Trial Balance
December 31, 2008

	Debit Balances	Credit Balances
Cash	5,550	
Accounts Receivable	34,550	
Prepaid Insurance	2,700	
Supplies	480	
Land	112,500	
Building	212,250	
Accumulated Depreciation—Building		139,150
Equipment	135,300	
Accumulated Depreciation—Equipment		102,350
Accounts Payable		12,150
Salaries and Wages Payable		2,800
Unearned Rent		3,250
Dave Maier, Capital		201,000
Dave Maier, Drawing	15,000	
Fees Earned		300,800
Rent Revenue		3,500
Salaries and Wages Expense	146,170	
Utilities Expense	42,375	
Advertising Expense	22,800	
Repairs Expense	17,250	
Depreciation Expense—Equipment	4,400	
Insurance Expense	4,500	
Depreciation Expense—Building	1,600	
Supplies Expense	1,500	
Miscellaneous Expense	6,075	
	765,000	765,000

Prob. 3–6A

1. a. Supplies Expense 1,800
      Supplies 1,800
         Supplies used.

   b. Accounts Receivable 11,600
      Fees Earned 11,600
         Accrued fees earned.

   c. Depreciation Expense 4,950
      Accumulated Depreciation 4,950
         Equipment depreciation.

   d. Wages Expense 2,250
      Wages Payable 2,250
         Accrued wages.

2.

	Net Income	Total Assets	Total Liabilities	Total Owner's Equity
Reported amounts	$155,000	$350,000	$120,000	$230,000
Corrections:				
Adjustment (a)	– 1,800	– 1,800	0	– 1,800
Adjustment (b)	+ 11,600	+ 11,600	0	+ 11,600
Adjustment (c)	– 4,950	– 4,950	0	– 4,950
Adjustment (d)	– 2,250	0	+ 2,250	– 2,250
Corrected amounts	$157,600	$354,850	$122,250	$232,600

Prob. 3–1B

1. a. Accounts Receivable 11,385
        Fees Earned 11,385
            Accrued fees earned.

    b. Supplies Expense 2,233
        Supplies.. 2,233
            Supplies used ($2,973 – $740).

    c. Wages Expense... 1,500
        Wages Payable.. 1,500
            Accrued wages.

    d. Unearned Rent.. 3,150
        Rent Revenue 3,150
            Rent earned ($9,450/3).

    e. Depreciation Expense... 2,650
        Accumulated Depreciation................................... 2,650
            Depreciation expense.

2. Adjusting entries are a planned part of the accounting process to update the accounts. Correcting entries are not planned, but arise only when necessary to correct errors.

Prob. 3–2B

a. Supplies Expense 1,645

   Supplies 1,645

      Supplies used ($2,145 – $500).

b. Depreciation Expense 1,375

   Accumulated Depreciation 1,375

      Depreciation for year.

c. Rent Expense 4,525

   Prepaid Rent 4,525

      Rent expired.

d. Wages Expense 2,200

   Wages Payable 2,200

      Accrued wages.

e. Unearned Fees 4,675

   Fees Earned 4,675

      Fees earned ($6,175 – $1,500).

f. Accounts Receivable 6,780

   Fees Earned 6,780

      Accrued fees.

Prob. 3–3B

a.	Supplies Expense	1,520	
	Supplies		1,520
	($1,820 – $300).		
b.	Accounts Receivable..	2,310	
	Fees Earned		2,310
c.	Depreciation Expense	1,500	
	Accumulated Depreciation		1,500
d.	Wages Expense	475	
	Wages Payable		475
e.	Unearned Fees	1,000	
	Fees Earned		1,000

Prob. 3–4B

2008				
July 31	Supplies Expense...	2,625	
	Supplies..		2,625
	Supplies used ($3,600 – $975).		
31	Insurance Expense.......................................	4,450	
	Prepaid Insurance		4,450
	Insurance expired ($5,650 – $1,200).		
31	Depreciation Expense—Buildings	3,600	
	Accumulated Depreciation—Buildings.......		3,600
	Depreciation ($53,100 – $49,500).		
31	Depreciation Expense—Trucks	1,500	
	Accumulated Depreciation—Trucks		1,500
	Depreciation ($13,300 – $11,800).		
31	Utilities Expense..	600	
	Accounts Payable		600
	Accrued utilities expense ($7,520 – $6,920).		
31	Salary Expense...	1,180	
	Salaries Payable		1,180
	Accrued salaries ($74,780 – $73,600).		
31	Unearned Service Fees.....................................	2,300	
	Service Fees Earned...................................		2,300
	Service fees earned ($154,980 – $152,680).		

Prob. 3–5B

1.

a.	Depreciation Expense—Building...........................	3,500	
	Accumulated Depreciation—Building.............		3,500
	Building depreciation.		
b.	Depreciation Expense—Equipment	2,300	
	Accumulated Depreciation—Equipment		2,300
	Equipment depreciation.		
c.	Salaries and Wages Expense	1,100	
	Salaries and Wages Payable		1,100
	Accrued salaries and wages.		
d.	Insurance Expense	2,250	
	Prepaid Insurance		2,250
	Insurance expired ($3,000 – $750).		
e.	Accounts Receivable	3,250	
	Fees Earned		3,250
	Accrued fees earned.		
f.	Supplies Expense	1,200	
	Supplies...		1,200
	Supplies used ($1,725 – $525).		
g.	Unearned Rent	2,100	
	Rent Revenue..		2,100
	Rent earned ($3,600 – $1,500).		

2.

LINCOLN SERVICE CO.
Adjusted Trial Balance
December 31, 2008

	Debit Balances	Credit Balances
Cash	2,100	
Accounts Receivable	13,550	
Prepaid Insurance	750	
Supplies	525	
Land	50,000	
Building	80,750	
Accumulated Depreciation—Building		41,350
Equipment	44,000	
Accumulated Depreciation—Equipment		19,950
Accounts Payable		3,750
Salaries and Wages Payable		1,100
Unearned Rent		1,500
Molly Jordan, Capital		83,550
Molly Jordan, Drawing	2,500	
Fees Earned		131,850
Rent Revenue		2,100
Salaries and Wages Expense	52,000	
Utilities Expense	14,100	
Advertising Expense	7,500	
Repairs Expense	6,100	
Depreciation Expense—Equipment	2,300	
Insurance Expense	2,250	
Depreciation Expense—Building	3,500	
Supplies Expense	1,200	
Miscellaneous Expense	2,025	
	285,150	285,150

Prob. 3–6B

1. a. Accounts Receivable.. 8,000
        Fees Earned 8,000
            Accrued fees earned.

    b. Depreciation Expense 5,500
        Accumulated Depreciation 5,500
            Depreciation for October.

    c. Wages Expense 2,500
        Wages Payable 2,500
            Accrued wages.

    d. Supplies Expense.. 1,725
        Supplies 1,725
            Supplies used.

2.

	Net Income	Total Assets	Total Liabilities	Total Owner's Equity
Reported amounts	$ 99,480	$400,000	$100,000	$300,000
Corrections:				
Adjustment (a)	+ 8,000	+ 8,000	0	+ 8,000
Adjustment (b)	– 5,500	– 5,500	0	– 5,500
Adjustment (c)	– 2,500	0	+ 2,500	– 2,500
Adjustment (d)	– 1,725	– 1,725	0	– 1,725
Corrected amounts	$ 97,755	$400,775	$102,500	$298,275

CONTINUING PROBLEM

1.

	JOURNAL			Page 3

Date	Description	Post. Ref.	Debit	Credit
2008				
May 31	Accounts Receivable	12	1,400	
	Fees Earned.................................	41		1,400
	Accrued fees earned			
	(35 hours × $40 = $1,400).			
31	Supplies Expense..............................	56	760	
	Supplies	14		760
	Supplies used ($920 – $160).			
31	Insurance Expense.............................	57	280	
	Prepaid Insurance..........................	15		280
	Insurance expired			
	($3,360/12 months =			
	$280 per month).			
31	Depreciation Expense.........................	58	100	
	Accum. Depr.—Office Equipment.	18		100
	Office equipment depreciation.			
31	Unearned Revenue.............................	23	2,400	
	Fees Earned.................................	41		2,400
	Fees earned ($4,800/2).			
31	Wages Expense..............................	50	200	
	Wages Payable...........................	22		200
	Accrued wages.			

Continuing Problem   Continued

2.

Cash   11

Date	Item	Post. Ref.	Dr.	Cr.	Balance Dr.	Balance Cr.
2008						
May 1	Balance...................	✓	....	....	9,160	....
1	....	1	2,500	....	11,660	....
1	....	1	....	1,600	10,060	....
1	....	1	....	3,360	6,700	....
2	....	1	1,350	....	8,050	....
3	....	1	4,800	....	12,850	....
3	....	1	....	250	12,600	....
4	....	1	....	300	12,300	....
8	....	1	....	180	12,120	....
11	....	1	750	....	12,870	....
13	....	1	....	500	12,370	....
14	....	1	....	1,000	11,370	....
16	....	2	1,500	....	12,870	....
21	....	2	....	325	12,545	....
22	....	2	....	800	11,745	....
23	....	2	750	....	12,495	....
27	....	2	....	560	11,935	....
28	....	2	....	1,000	10,935	....
29	....	2	....	150	10,785	....
30	....	2	400	....	11,185	....
31	....	2	2,800	....	13,985	....
31	....	2	....	900	13,085	....
31	....	2	....	1,000	12,085	....

Accounts Receivable   12

Date	Item	Post. Ref.	Dr.	Cr.	Balance Dr.	Balance Cr.
2008						
May 1	Balance...................	✓	....	....	1,350	....
2	....	1	....	1,350	—	—
23	....	2	1,750	....	1,750	....
30	....	2	1,100	....	2,850	....
31	Adjusting	3	1,400	....	4,250	....

Continuing Problem   Continued

Supplies   14

Date	Item	Post. Ref.	Dr.	Cr.	Balance Dr.	Balance Cr.
2008						
May 1	Balance..................	✓	....	....	170	....
18	....	2	750	....	920	....
31	Adjusting	3	....	760	160	....

Prepaid Insurance   15

2008						
May 1	....	1	3,360	....	3,360	....
31	Adjusting	3	....	280	3,080	....

Office Equipment   17

2008						
May 5	....	1	5,000	....	5,000	....

Accumulated Depreciation—Office Equipment   18

2008						
May 31	Adjusting	3	....	100	....	100

Accounts Payable   21

2008						
May 1	Balance..................	✓	....	....	....	250
3	....	1	250	....	—	—
5	....	1	....	5,000	....	5,000
18	....	2	....	750	....	5,750

Wages Payable   22

2008						
May 31	Adjusting	3	....	200	....	200

Unearned Revenue   23

2008						
May 3	....	1	....	4,800	....	4,800
31	Adjusting	3	2,400	....	....	2,400

Continuing Problem   Continued

Kris Payne, Capital
31

Date	Item	Post. Ref.	Dr.	Cr.	Balance Dr.	Balance Cr.
2008						
May 1	Balance..................	✓	....	....	....	10,000
1	....	1	....	2,500	....	12,500

Kris Payne, Drawing
32

Date	Item	Post. Ref.	Dr.	Cr.	Balance Dr.	Balance Cr.
2008						
May 1	Balance..................	✓	....	....	300	....
31	....	2	1,000	....	1,300	....

Income Summary
33

This account is not used in Chapter 3.

Fees Earned
41

Date	Item	Post. Ref.	Dr.	Cr.	Balance Dr.	Balance Cr.
2008						
May 1	Balance..................	✓	....	....	....	5,700
11	....	1	....	750	....	6,450
16	....	2	....	1,500	....	7,950
23	....	2	....	2,500	....	10,450
30	....	2	....	1,500	....	11,950
31	....	2	....	2,800	....	14,750
31	Adjusting	3	....	1,400	....	16,150
31	Adjusting	3	....	2,400	....	18,550

Wages Expense
50

Date	Item	Post. Ref.	Dr.	Cr.	Balance Dr.	Balance Cr.
2008						
May 1	Balance..................	✓	....	....	400	....
14	....	1	1,000	....	1,400	....
28	....	2	1,000	....	2,400	....
31	Adjusting	3	200	....	2,600	....

Office Rent Expense
51

Date	Item	Post. Ref.	Dr.	Cr.	Balance Dr.	Balance Cr.
2008						
May 1	Balance..................	✓	....	....	1,000	....
1	....	1	1,600	....	2,600	....

Equipment Rent Expense 52

Date	Item	Post. Ref.	Dr.	Cr.	Balance Dr.	Balance Cr.
2008						
May 1	Balance..................	✓	....	....	800	....
13	....	1	500	....	1,300	....

Utilities Expense 53

Date	Item	Post. Ref.	Dr.	Cr.	Balance Dr.	Balance Cr.
2008						
May 1	Balance..................	✓	....	....	350	....
27	....	2	560	....	910	....

Music Expense 54

Date	Item	Post. Ref.	Dr.	Cr.	Balance Dr.	Balance Cr.
2008						
May 1	Balance..................	✓	....	....	1,340	....
21	....	2	325	....	1,665	....
31	....	2	900	....	2,565	....

Advertising Expense 55

Date	Item	Post. Ref.	Dr.	Cr.	Balance Dr.	Balance Cr.
2008						
May 1	Balance..................	✓	....	....	750	....
8	....	1	180	....	930	....
22	....	2	800	....	1,730	....

Supplies Expense 56

Date	Item	Post. Ref.	Dr.	Cr.	Balance Dr.	Balance Cr.
2008						
May 1	Balance..................	✓	....	....	180	....
31	Adjusting	3	760	....	940	....

Insurance Expense 57

Date	Item	Post. Ref.	Dr.	Cr.	Balance Dr.	Balance Cr.
2008						
May 31	Adjusting	3	280	....	280	....

Depreciation Expense 58

Date	Item	Post. Ref.	Dr.	Cr.	Balance Dr.	Balance Cr.
2008						
May 31	Adjusting	3	100	....	100	....

Continuing Problem   Concluded

Miscellaneous Expense   59

Date		Item	Post. Ref.	Dr.	Cr.	Balance	
						Dr.	Cr.
2008							
May	1	Balance..................	✓	....	....	150	....
	4	....	1	300	....	450	....
	29	....	2	150	....	600	....

3.

DANCIN MUSIC
Adjusted Trial Balance
May 31, 2008

	Debit Balances	Credit Balances
Cash..	12,085	
Accounts Receivable...	4,250	
Supplies...	160	
Prepaid Insurance...	3,080	
Office Equipment...	5,000	
Accumulated Depreciation—Office Equipment		100
Accounts Payable..		5,750
Wages Payable..		200
Unearned Revenue		2,400
Kris Payne, Capital		12,500
Kris Payne, Drawing	1,300	
Fees Earned		18,550
Wages Expense	2,600	
Office Rent Expense..	2,600	
Equipment Rent Expense...	1,300	
Utilities Expense	910	
Music Expense..	2,565	
Advertising Expense	1,730	
Supplies Expense	940	
Insurance Expense	280	
Depreciation Expense	100	
Miscellaneous Expense	600	
	39,500	39,500

SPECIAL ACTIVITIES

Activity 3–1

It is acceptable for Annette to prepare the financial statements for Harre Real Estate on an accrual basis. The revision of the financial statements to include the accrual of the $10,000 commissions as of December 31, 2007, is proper if there remain no contingencies related to the signed, unconditional contract of sale. That is, if the closing and title transfer is not contingent upon an appraisal, obtaining a loan, etc., then the earnings process has been completed from the perspective of Harre Real Estate and the commissions have been earned. If contingencies remain, then the commission should not be accrued as of December 31, 2007. Indicating on the loan application to First National Bank that Harre Real Estate has not been rejected previously for credit is unethical and unprofessional. In addition, intentionally filing false loan documents is illegal.

Activity 3–2

The cost of the warranty repairs, $1,560, should be recognized as an expense of 2008 in order to properly match revenues from the sale of the Expedition with the related expenses. Since the cost of the actual repairs will not be known at the time of sale (2008), Ford Motor Company would estimate warranty costs and expenses at the end of 2008. This estimate would be recorded in the accounts through use of an adjusting entry. The adjusting entry would debit Warranty Expense and credit Estimated Warranty Payable, a liability account.

Activity 3–3

Revenue is normally recorded when the services are provided or when the goods are delivered (title passes) to the buyer. By waiting until after the services are provided, the expenses of providing the services can be more accurately measured and matched against the related revenues. Also, at this point, the provider of the services has a right to demand payment for the services if payment hasn't already been received.

Airlines, such as American Airlines, normally record revenue from ticket sales after completing a flight. At this point, the boarding passes, which have been collected from the passengers, represent revenue to the airline. In addition, the expenses related to each flight, such as landing fees and fuel, would have been incurred and would be accurately measured.

Note to Instructors: You might point out to students the following points related to the discussion of the adjusting process in this chapter.

(1) The receipt of revenue from customers in advance of a flight represents unearned revenues to the airline. For example, the purchase of discount tickets, which often requires prepayment months in advance of the actual flight, is unearned revenue to the airline.

(2) At the end of the airline's accounting period, it would have adjusting entries related to such items as the following:

- Accrued wages for employees
- Depreciation on airplanes, terminal buildings, etc.
- Unearned revenues (described above)
- Accrued income from transporting freight, etc.
- Accrued income from other airlines
  (When a flight is delayed or canceled, airlines often accept passengers from other airlines and then later collect the revenue from the other airline.)
- Prepaid expenses related to insurance, etc.

Activity 3–4

a. There are several indications that adjusting entries were not recorded before the financial statements were prepared, including:

1. All expenses on the income statement are identified as "paid" items and not as "expenses."

2. No expense is reported on the income statement for depreciation, and no accumulated depreciation is reported on the balance sheet.

3. No supplies, accounts payable, or wages payable are reported on the balance sheet.

b. Likely accounts requiring adjustment include:

1. Truck (for depreciation).

2. Supplies (paid) expense for supplies on hand.

3. Insurance (paid) expense for unexpired insurance.

4. Wages accrued.

5. Utilities accrued.

Activity 3–5

Note to Instructors: The purpose of this activity is to familiarize students with behaviors that are common in codes of conduct. In addition, this activity addresses an actual ethical dilemma for students.

CHAPTER 4
COMPLETING THE ACCOUNTING CYCLE

QUESTION INFORMATION

Number	Objective	Description	Difficulty	Time	AACSB	AICPA	SS	GL
Q4-1	4-1		Easy	5 min	Analytic	FN-Measurement		
Q4-2	4-1		Easy	5 min	Analytic	FN-Measurement		
Q4-3	4-2		Easy	5 min	Analytic	FN-Measurement		
Q4-4	4-2		Easy	5 min	Analytic	FN-Measurement		
Q4-5	4-2		Easy	5 min	Analytic	FN-Measurement		
Q4-6	4-3		Easy	5 min	Analytic	FN-Measurement		
Q4-7	4-3		Easy	5 min	Analytic	FN-Measurement		
Q4-8	4-3		Easy	5 min	Analytic	FN-Measurement		
Q4-9	4-3		Easy	5 min	Analytic	FN-Measurement		
Q4-10	4-4		Easy	5 min	Analytic	FN-Measurement		
Q4-11	4-4		Easy	5 min	Analytic	FN-Measurement		
Q4-12	4-6		Easy	5 min	Analytic	BB-Industry		
Q4-13	4-6		Easy	5 min	Analytic	BB-Industry		
Q4-14	4-6		Easy	5 min	Analytic	BB-Industry		
PE4-1A	4-1	Flow of accounts into financial statements	Easy	5 min	Analytic	FN-Measurement		
PE4-1B	4-1	Flow of accounts into financial statements	Easy	5 min	Analytic	FN-Measurement		
PE4-2A	4-2	Determining net income from the end-of-period spreadsheet	Easy	5 min	Analytic	FN-Measurement		
PE4-2B	4-2	Determining net income from the end-of-period spreadsheet	Easy	5 min	Analytic	FN-Measurement		
PE4-3A	4-2	Statement of owner's equity	Easy	5 min	Analytic	FN-Measurement		
PE4-3B	4-2	Statement of owner's equity	Easy	5 min	Analytic	FN-Measurement		
PE4-4A	4-2	Reporting accounts on classified balance sheet	Easy	5 min	Analytic	FN-Measurement		
PE4-4B	4-4	Reporting accounts on classified balance sheet	Easy	5 min	Analytic	FN-Measurement		
PE4-5A	4-3	Closing entries with net loss	Easy	5 min	Analytic	FN-Measurement		
PE4-5B	4-3	Closing entries with net income	Easy	5 min	Analytic	FN-Measurement		
PE4-6A	4-4	Missing steps in the accounting cycle	Easy	5 min	Analytic	FN-Measurement		
PE4-6B	4-4	Missing steps in the accounting cycle	Easy	5 min	Analytic	FN-Measurement		
Ex4-1	4-1, 4-2	Extending account balances in an end-of-period spreadsheet	Easy	5 min	Analytic	FN-Measurement		
Ex4-2	4-1, 4-2	Classifying accounts	Easy	5 min	Analytic	FN-Measurement		
Ex4-3	4-1, 4-2	Financial statements from end-of-period spreadsheet	Moderate	15 min	Analytic	FN-Measurement	Exl	

Number	Objective	Description	Difficulty	Time	AACSB	AICPA	SS	GL
Ex4-4	4-1, 4-2	Financial statements from end-of-period spreadsheet	Moderate	15 min	Analytic	FN-Measurement	Exl	
Ex4-5	4-2	Income statement	Easy	10 min	Analytic	FN-Measurement		
Ex4-6	4-2	Income statement; net loss	Easy	10 min	Analytic	FN-Measurement		
Ex4-7	4-2	Income statement	Easy	10 min	Analytic	FN-Measurement		
Ex4-8	4-2	Statement of owner's equity	Moderate	10 min	Analytic	FN-Measurement		
Ex4-9	4-2	Statement of owner's equity; net loss	Moderate	10 min	Analytic	FN-Measurement		
Ex4-10	4-2	Classifying assets	Easy	5 min	Analytic	FN-Measurement		
Ex4-11	4-2	Balance sheet classification	Easy	5 min	Analytic	FN-Measurement		
Ex4-12	4-2	Balance sheet	Moderate	10 min	Analytic	FN-Measurement		
Ex4-13	4-2	Balance sheet	Moderate	15 mn	Analytic	FN-Measurement		
Ex4-14	4-3	Identifying accounts to be closed	Easy	5 min	Analytic	FN-Measurement		
Ex4-15	4-3	Closing entries	Easy	5 min	Analytic	FN-Measurement		
Ex4-16	4-3	Closing entries with net income	Moderate	10 min	Analytic	FN-Measurement		
Ex4-17	4-3	Closing entries with net loss	Easy	10 min	Analytic	FN-Measurement		
Ex4-18	4-3	Identifying permanent accounts	Easy	5 min	Analytic	FN-Measurement		
Ex4-19	4-3	Post-closing trial balance	Moderate	10 min	Analytic	FN-Measurement		
Ex4-20	4-4	Steps in the accounting cycle	Moderate	10 min	Analytic	FN-Measurement		
Ex4-21	Appendix	Steps in completing an end-of-period spreadsheet	Moderate	10 min	Analytic	FN-Measurement		
Ex4-22	Appendix	Adjustment data on an end-of-period spreadsheet	Moderate	15 min	Analytic	FN-Measurement	Exl	
Ex4-23	Appendix	Completing an end-of-period spreadsheet	Moderate	15 min	Analytic	FN-Measurement	Exl	
Ex4-24	Appendix	Financial statements from an end-of-period spreadsheet	Moderate	15 min	Analytic	FN-Measurement	Exl	
Ex4-25	Appendix	Adjusting entries from an end-of-period spreadsheet	Easy	10 min	Analytic	FN-Measurement		
Ex4-26	Appendix	Closing entries from an end-of-period spreadsheet	Moderate	10 min	Analytic	FN-Measurement		
Pr4-1A	4-1, 4-2, 4-3	Financial statements and closing entries	Moderate	1 hr	Analytic	FN-Measurement	Exl	KA
Pr4-2A	4-2, 4-3	Financial statements and closing entries	Moderate	1 hr	Analytic	FN-Measurement	Exl	
Pr4-3A	4-2, 4-3	T accounts, adjusting entries, financial statements, and closing entries; optional end-of-period spreadsheet	Moderate	2 1/4 hr	Analytic	FN-Measurement	Exl	KA

Number	Objective	Description	Difficulty	Time	AACSB	AICPA	SS	GL
Pr4-4A	4-2, 4-3	Ledger accounts, adjusting entries, financial statements, and closing entries; optional end-of-period spreadsheet	Difficult	2 1/2 hr	Analytic	FN-Measurement	Exl	
Pr4-5A	4-2, 4-3	Ledger accounts, adjusting entries, financial statements, and closing entries; optional end-of-period spreadsheet	Difficult	2 1/2 hr	Analytic	FN-Measurement	Exl	KA
Pr4-6A	4-4, 4-5, 4-6	Complete accounting cycle	Difficult	3 hr	Analytic	FN-Measurement	Exl	KA
Pr4-1B	4-1, 4-2, 4-3	Financial statements and closing entries	Moderate	1 hr	Analytic	FN-Measurement	Exl	KA
Pr4-2B	4-2, 4-3	Financial statements and closing entries	Moderate	1 hr	Analytic	FN-Measurement	Exl	
Pr4-3B	4-2, 4-3	T accounts, adjusting entries, financial statements, and closing entries; optional end-of-period spreadsheet	Moderate	2 1/4 hr	Analytic	FN-Measurement	Exl	KA
Pr4-4B	4-2, 4-3	Ledger accounts, adjusting entries, financial statements, and closing entries; optional end-of-period spreadsheet	Difficult	2 1/2 hr	Analytic	FN-Measurement	Exl	
Pr4-5B	4-2, 4-3	Ledger accounts, adjusting entries, financial statements, and closing entries; optional end-of-period spreadsheet	Difficult	2 1/2 hr	Analytic	FN-Measurement	Exl	KA
Pr4-6B	4-4, 4-5, 4-6	Complete accounting cycle	Difficult	3 hr	Analytic	FN-Measurement	Exl	KA
DM-4		Continuing Problem						KA
SA4-1	4-2	Ethics and professional conduct in business	Easy	5 min	Ethics	BB-Industry		
SA4-2	4-4	Financial statements	Moderate	10 min	Technology	BB-Leveraging Technology		
SA4-3	4-1, 4-4	Financial statements	Moderate	15 min	Reflective Thinking	BB-Critical Thinking		
SA4-4	4-2	Compare balance sheets	Moderate	30 min	Reflective Thinking	BB-Critical Thinking		
Comp Problem 1	4-1, 4-2, 4-3, 4-4	Transactions, adjustments, financial statements, closing entries, post-closing trial balance	Difficult	3 hr	Analytic	FN-Measurement		KA

EYE OPENERS

1. The end-of-period spreadsheet (work sheet) illustrates flow of accounting information from the unadjusted trial balance into the adjusted trial balance and into the financial statements. In doing so, the spreadsheet (work sheet) illustrates the impact of the adjustments on the financial statements.

2. No. The end-of-period spreadsheet (work sheet) is a device used by the accountant to facilitate the preparation of statements.

3. A net income of $61,250 ($323,500 – $262,250) would be reported. When the Credit column exceeds the Debit column, net income is reported. If the Debit column of the Income Statement columns is more than the Credit column, a net loss is reported.

4. a. Current assets are composed of cash and other assets that may reasonably be expected to be realized in cash or sold or consumed in the near future through the normal operations of the business.

   b. Property, plant, and equipment is composed of assets used in the business that are of a permanent or relatively fixed nature.

5. Current liabilities are liabilities that will be due within a short time (usually one year or less) and that are to be paid out of current assets. Liabilities that will not be due for a comparatively long time (usually more than one year) are called long-term liabilities.

6. Revenue, expense, and drawing accounts are generally referred to as temporary accounts.

7. Closing entries are necessary at the end of an accounting period (1) to transfer the balances in temporary accounts to permanent accounts and (2) to prepare the temporary accounts for use in accumulating data for the following accounting period.

8. Adjusting entries bring the accounts up to date, while closing entries reduce the revenue, expense, and drawing accounts to zero balances for use in accumulating data for the following accounting period.

9. (1) The first entry closes all income statement accounts with credit balances by transferring the total to the credit side of Income Summary.

   (2) The second entry closes all income statement accounts with debit balances by transferring the total to the debit side of Income Summary.

   (3) The third entry closes Income Summary by transferring its balance, the net income or net loss for the year, to the owner's capital account.

   (4) The fourth entry closes the drawing account by transferring its balance to the owner's capital account.

10. The purpose of the post-closing trial balance is to make sure that the ledger is in balance at the beginning of the next period.

11. a. The financial statements are the most important output of the accounting cycle.

    b. Yes, all companies have an accounting cycle that begins with analyzing and journalizing transactions and ends with a post-closing trial balance. However, companies may differ in how they implement the steps in the accounting cycle. For example, while most companies use computerized accounting systems, some companies may use manual systems.

12. The natural business year is the fiscal year that ends when business activities have reached the lowest point in the annual operating cycle.

13. January is more likely to have a lower level of business activity than is December for a department store. Therefore, the additional work to adjust and close the accounts and prepare the financial statements can more easily be performed at the end of January than at the end of December.

14. All the companies listed are general merchandisers whose busiest time of the year is during the holiday season, which extends through most of December. Traditionally, the lowest point of business activity for general merchandisers will be near the end of January and the beginning of February. Thus, these companies have chosen their natural business year for their fiscal years.

PRACTICE EXERCISES

PE 4–1A

1. Income Statement column
2. Balance Sheet column
3. Balance Sheet column
4. Income Statement column
5. Balance Sheet column
6. Balance Sheet column
7. Income Statement column
8. Balance Sheet column

PE 4–1B

1. Balance Sheet column
2. Income Statement column
3. Balance Sheet column
4. Balance Sheet column
5. Income Statement column
6. Balance Sheet column
7. Balance Sheet column
8. Income Statement column

PE 4–2A

A net loss of $30,410 ($278,100 – $247,690) would be reported. When the Credit column exceeds the Debit column, a net loss is reported. If the Debit column of the Balance Sheet columns is more than the Credit column, a net income is reported.

PE 4–2B

A net income of $86,850 ($523,550 – $436,700) would be reported. When the Credit column exceeds the Debit column, net income is reported. If the Debit column of the Income Statement columns is more than the Credit column, a net loss is reported.

PE 4–3A

Padget Advertising Services
Statement of Owner's Equity
For the Year Ended December 31, 2007

Jody Padget, capital, January 1, 2007	$550,600	
Additional investment during 2007	50,000	
Total		$600,600
Net income	$ 68,150	
Less withdrawals	40,000	
Increase in owner's equity		28,150
Jody Padget, capital, December 31, 2007		$628,750

PE 4–3B

AAA Delivery Services
Statement of Owner's Equity
For the Year Ended December 31, 2007

Ali Khalid, capital, January 1, 2007		$854,450
Net loss	$11,875	
Add withdrawals	38,400	
Decrease in owner's equity		50,275
Ali Khalid, capital, December 31, 2007		$804,175

PE 4–4A

1. Current liability
2. Property, plant, and equipment
3. Current asset
4. Long-term liability
5. Current asset
6. Current liability
7. Current liability
8. Owner's equity

PE 4–4B

1. Current liability
2. Current asset
3. Owner's equity
4. Current liability
5. Long-term liability
6. Current asset
7. Current asset
8. Property, plant, and equipment

PE 4–5A

Oct.	31	Fees Earned..	475,150	
		Income Summary		475,150
	31	Income Summary	526,025	
		Wages Expense...		390,000
		Rent Expense		85,000
		Supplies Expense		38,350
		Miscellaneous Expense................................		12,675
	31	Lisa Jordon, Capital..	50,875	
		Income Summary		50,875
	31	Lisa Jordon, Capital..	36,000	
		Lisa Jordon, Drawing		36,000

PE 4–5B

Apr.	30	Fees Earned..	690,500	
		Income Summary		690,500
	30	Income Summary	553,350	
		Wages Expense...		410,000
		Rent Expense		75,000
		Supplies Expense		48,650
		Miscellaneous Expense................................		19,700
	30	Income Summary	137,150	
		Jayme Carmichael, Capital...........................		137,150
	30	Jayme Carmichael, Capital.................................	60,000	
		Jayme Carmichael, Drawing		60,000

PE 4–6A

The following two steps are missing: (1) posting the transactions to the ledger and (2) the preparation of the financial statements. Transactions should be posted to the ledger after step (a). The financial statements should be prepared after step (f).

PE 4–6B

The following two steps are missing: (1) assembling and analyzing adjustment data and (2) journalizing and posting the closing entries. The adjustment data should be assembled and analyzed after step (c). The closing entries should be journalized and posted to the ledger after step (g).

EXERCISES

Ex. 4–1

    a. Income statement: 5, 8, 9

    b. Balance sheet: 1, 2, 3, 4, 6, 7, 10

Ex. 4–2

    a. Asset: 1, 4, 5, 6, 10

    b. Liability: 9, 12

    c. Revenue: 2, 7

    d. Expense: 3, 8, 11

Ex. 4–3

SANDY BOTTOM CONSULTING
Income Statement
For the Year Ended August 31, 2008

Fees earned...		$32,000
Expenses:		
Salary expense	$17,050	
Supplies expense...	1,750	
Depreciation expense	1,200	
Miscellaneous expense	1,850	
Total expenses		21,850
Net income		$10,150

SANDY BOTTOM CONSULTING
Statement of Owner's Equity
For the Year Ended August 31, 2008

Dee Schofield, capital, September 1, 2007		$19,400
Net income	$10,150	
Less withdrawals..	2,700	
Increase in owner's equity..		7,450
Dee Schofield, capital, August 31, 2008		$26,850

SANDY BOTTOM CONSULTING
Balance Sheet
August 31, 2008

Assets			Liabilities		
Current assets:			Current liabilities:		
Cash	$10,000		Accounts payable....	$6,100	
Accounts receivable ..	12,500		Salaries payable......	800	
Supplies	450		Total liabilities............		$ 6,900
Total current assets		$22,950			
Property, plant, and					
equipment:					
Office equipment........	$14,500				
Less accum. depr.......	3,700		Owner's Equity		
Total property, plant,			D. Schofield, capital...		26,850
and equipment....		10,800	Total liabilities and		
Total assets		$33,750	owner's equity.........		$33,750

Ex. 4–4

RECTIFIER CONSULTING
Income Statement
For the Year Ended June 30, 2008

Fees earned..		$51,750
Expenses:		
Salary expense	$31,150	
Supplies expense	1,850	
Depreciation expense	900	
Miscellaneous expense	1,500	
Total expenses		35,400
Net income		$16,350

RECTIFIER CONSULTING
Statement of Owner's Equity
For the Year Ended June 30, 2008

Adam Beauchamp, capital, July 1, 2007		$25,200
Net income	$16,350	
Less withdrawals...	2,000	
Increase in owner's equity..		14,350
Adam Beauchamp, capital, June 30, 2008.........................		$39,550

RECTIFIER CONSULTING
Balance Sheet
June 30, 2008

Assets			Liabilities		
Current assets:			Current liabilities:		
Cash	$ 8,000		Accounts payable....	$3,300	
Accounts receivable ..	15,500		Salaries payable	400	
Supplies	650		Total liabilities............		$ 3,700
Total current assets		$24,150			
Property, plant, and					
equipment:					
Office equipment........	$24,500		Owner's Equity		
Less accum. depr.......	5,400		Adam Beauchamp,		
Total property, plant,			capital......................		39,550
and equipment		19,100	Total liabilities and		
Total assets		$43,250	owner's equity.........		$43,250

Ex. 4–5

ADMIRAL MESSENGER SERVICE
Income Statement
For the Year Ended April 30, 2008

Fees earned..		$375,500
Expenses:		
Salaries expense	$125,600	
Rent expense	43,400	
Utilities expense	11,500	
Depreciation expense...	5,000	
Supplies expense	2,750	
Insurance expense	1,500	
Miscellaneous expense.......................................	1,250	
Total expenses		191,000
Net income		$184,500

Ex. 4–6

CUPCAKE SERVICES CO.
Income Statement
For the Year Ended October 31, 2008

Service revenue		$163,375
Expenses:		
Wages expense..	$92,800	
Rent expense	51,500	
Utilities expense	18,750	
Depreciation expense...	10,000	
Insurance expense	6,000	
Supplies expense	2,875	
Miscellaneous expense.......................................	4,750	
Total expenses		186,675
Net loss...		$ 23,300

Ex. 4–7

a.

FEDEX CORPORATION
Income Statement
For the Year Ended May 31, 2005
(in millions)

Revenues..		$29,363
Expenses:		
Salaries and employee benefits	$11,963	
Purchased transportation	2,935	
Fuel	2,317	
Rentals and landing fees	2,314	
Maintenance and repairs..	1,680	
Depreciation...	1,462	
Provision for income taxes	864	
Other expenses..	4,379	
Total expenses		27,914
Net income		$ 1,449

b. The income statements are very similar. The actual statement includes some additional expense and income classifications. For example, the actual statement reports Income Before Income Taxes and Provision for Income Taxes separately. In addition, the Other Expenses in the text are a summary of several items from the website, including Other Interest Expense and Other Interest Income.

Ex. 4–8

ICON SYSTEMS CO.
Statement of Owner's Equity
For the Year Ended August 31, 2008

Josh Winfrey, capital, September 1, 2007		$573,750
Net income for year	$95,000	
Less withdrawals..	16,000	
Increase in owner's equity...		79,000
Josh Winfrey, capital, August 31, 2008...........................		$652,750

Ex. 4–9

ASPEN SPORTS
Statement of Owner's Equity
For the Year Ended June 30, 2008

Tammy Eddy, capital, July 1, 2007		$190,800
Net loss for year..	$32,550	
Plus withdrawals	30,000	
Decrease in owner's equity		62,550
Tammy Eddy, capital, June 30, 2008...............................		$128,250

Ex. 4–10

a. Current asset: 1, 3, 5, 6

b. Property, plant, and equipment: 2, 4

Ex. 4–11

Since current liabilities are usually due within one year, $180,000 ($15,000 × 12 months) would be reported as a current liability on the balance sheet. The remainder of $570,000 ($750,000 − $180,000) would be reported as a long-term liability on the balance sheet.

Ex. 4–12

HEALTHY & TRIM CO.
Balance Sheet
November 30, 2008

Assets		
Current assets:		
Cash	$18,750	
Accounts receivable	41,560	
Supplies	1,040	
Prepaid insurance	9,600	
Prepaid rent	6,000	
Total current assets		$ 76,950
Property, plant, and equipment:		
Equipment	$350,000	
Less accumulated depreciation	51,950	
Total property, plant, and		
equipment		298,050
Total assets		$375,000

Liabilities		
Current liabilities:		
Accounts payable	$17,250	
Salaries payable	6,750	
Unearned fees	5,000	
Total liabilities		$ 29,000
Owner's Equity		
Cindy DeLoach, capital ...		346,000
Total liabilities and		
owner's equity		$375,000

Ex. 4–13

1. The date of the statement should be "July 31, 2008" and not "For the Year Ended July 31, 2008."

2. Accounts payable should be a current liability.

3. Land should be classified as property, plant, and equipment.

4. "Accumulated depreciation" should be deducted from the related fixed asset.

5. An adding error was made in determining the amount of the total property, plant, and equipment.

6. Accounts receivable should be a current asset.

7. Net income should be reported on the income statement.

8. Wages payable should be a current liability.

A corrected balance sheet would be as follows:

Ex. 4–13   Concluded

EUCALYPTUS SERVICES CO.
Balance Sheet
July 31, 2008

Assets

Current assets:

Cash	$ 5,280	
Accounts receivable	13,750	
Supplies	1,650	
Prepaid insurance	4,800	
Total current assets		$ 25,480

Property, plant, and equipment:

Land		$60,000	
Building	$156,700		
Less accumulated depreciation	86,700	70,000	
Equipment	$ 43,000		
Less accumulated depreciation	18,480	24,520	
Total property, plant, and equipment			154,520
Total assets			$180,000

Liabilities

Current liabilities:

Accounts payable	$6,790	
Wages payable	1,340	
Total liabilities		$ 8,130

Owner's Equity

Sydney Kitchel, capital	171,870
Total liabilities and owner's equity	$180,000

Ex. 4–14

c. Depreciation Expense—Equipment

e. Fees Earned

j. Supplies Expense

k. Wages Expense

Note: Keri Upshaw, Drawing is closed to Keri Upshaw, Capital rather than to Income Summary.

Ex. 4–15

The income summary account is used to close the revenue and expense accounts, and it aids in detecting and correcting errors. The $279,615 represents expense account balances, and the $392,750 represents revenue account balances that have been closed.

Ex. 4–16

a. Income Summary 156,620

    Rachel Bray, Capital 156,620

        ($375,000 – $218,380).

    Rachel Bray, Capital 18,000

       Rachel Bray, Drawing... 18,000

b. $617,720 ($479,100 + $156,620 – $18,000)

Ex. 4–17

Date	Account	Debit	Credit
Oct. 31	Fees Earned	293,300	
	Income Summary		293,300
31	Income Summary	325,250	
	Wages Expense		250,000
	Rent Expense		65,000
	Supplies Expense		3,150
	Miscellaneous Expense		7,100
31	Natalie Wilson, Capital	31,950	
	Income Summary		31,950
31	Natalie Wilson, Capital	20,000	
	Natalie Wilson, Drawing		20,000

Ex. 4–18

a. Accounts Payable

b. Accumulated Depreciation

c. Cash

f. Office Equipment

h. Salaries Payable

i. Stephanie Hamm, Capital

k. Supplies

Ex. 4–19

HONEST SAM'S REPAIR CO.
Post-Closing Trial Balance
July 31, 2008

	Debit Balances	Credit Balances
Cash	12,915	
Accounts Receivable	46,620	
Supplies	2,770	
Equipment	88,200	
Accumulated Depreciation—Equipment		27,970
Accounts Payable		15,750
Salaries Payable		3,780
Unearned Rent		7,560
Samantha Marcus, Capital		95,445
	150,505	150,505

Ex. 4–20

1.	d	6.	j
2.	g	7.	a
3.	i	8.	b
4.	f	9.	h
5.	e	10.	c

Appendix Ex. 4–21

1.	f	6.	j
2.	c	7.	a
3.	b	8.	i
4.	h	9.	d
5.	g	10.	e

Appendix Ex. 4–22

DAKOTA SERVICES CO.
End-of-Period Spreadsheet (Work Sheet)
For the Year Ended July 31, 2008

	Account Title	Unadjusted Trial Balance Dr.	Cr.	Adjustments Dr.	Cr.	Adjusted Trial Balance Dr.	Cr.	
1	Cash	4				4		1
2	Accounts Receivable	25		(a) 5		30		2
3	Supplies	4			(b) 3	1		3
4	Prepaid Insurance	6			(c) 4	2		4
5	Land	25				25		5
6	Equipment	16				16		6
7	Accum. Depr.—Equip.		1		(d) 2		3	7
8	Accounts Payable		13				13	8
9	Wages Payable		0		(e) 1		1	9
10	Christina Keene, Capital		56				56	10
11	Christina Keene, Drawing	4				4		11
12	Fees Earned		30		(a) 5		35	12
13	Wages Expense	8		(e) 1		9		13
14	Rent Expense	4				4		14
15	Insurance Expense	0		(c) 4		4		15
16	Utilities Expense	3				3		16
17	Depreciation Expense	0		(d) 2		2		17
18	Supplies Expense	0		(b) 3		3		18
19	Miscellaneous Expense	1				1		19
20	Totals	100	100	15	15	108	108	20

Appendix Ex. 4–23

DAKOTA SERVICES CO.
End-of-Period Spreadsheet (Work Sheet)
For the Year Ended July 31, 2008

	Account Title	Adjusted Trial Balance Dr.	Adjusted Trial Balance Cr.	Income Statement Dr.	Income Statement Cr.	Balance Sheet Dr.	Balance Sheet Cr.	
1	Cash	4				4		1
2	Accounts Receivable	30				30		2
3	Supplies	1				1		3
4	Prepaid Insurance	2				2		4
5	Land	25				25		5
6	Equipment	16				16		6
7	Accum. Depr.—Equip.		3				3	7
8	Accounts Payable		13				13	8
9	Wages Payable		1				1	9
10	Christine Keene, Capital		56				56	10
11	Christine Keene, Drawing	4				4		11
12	Fees Earned		35		35			12
13	Wages Expense	9		9				13
14	Rent Expense	4		4				14
15	Insurance Expense	4		4				15
16	Utilities Expense	3		3				16
17	Depreciation Expense	2		2				17
18	Supplies Expense	3		3				18
19	Miscellaneous Expense	1		1				19
20	Totals	108	108	26	35	82	73	20
21	Net income (loss)			9			9	21
22				35	35	82	82	22

Appendix Ex. 4–24

DAKOTA SERVICES CO.
Income Statement
For the Year Ended July 31, 2008

Fees earned...		$35
Expenses:		
Wages expense..	$9	
Rent expense	4	
Insurance expense	4	
Utilities expense	3	
Supplies expense	3	
Depreciation expense...	2	
Miscellaneous expense......................................	1	
Total expenses		26
Net income		$ 9

DAKOTA SERVICES CO.
Statement of Owner's Equity
For the Year Ended July 31, 2008

Christina Keene, capital, August 1, 2007		$56
Net income for the year..	$9	
Less withdrawals..	4	
Increase in owner's equity...		5
Christina Keene, capital, July 31, 2008		$61

DAKOTA SERVICES CO.
Balance Sheet
July 31, 2008

Assets			Liabilities		
Current assets:			Current liabilities:		
Cash...............................	$ 4		Accounts payable.........	$13	
Accounts receivable.....	30		Wages payable	1	
Supplies........................	1		Total liabilities		$14
Prepaid insurance.........	2				
Total current assets...		$37			
Property, plant, and			Owner's Equity		
equipment:			Christina Keene, capital ..		61
Land	$25				
Equipment $16					
Less accum. depr. 3	13				
Total property, plant,					
and equipment		38	Total liabilities and		
Total assets		$75	owner's equity............		$75

Appendix Ex. 4–25

2008
July	31	Accounts Receivable		5	
		Fees Earned...			5
		Accrued fees.			
	31	Supplies Expense..		3	
		Supplies			3
		Supplies used ($4 – $1).			
	31	Insurance Expense..		4	
		Prepaid Insurance..................................			4
		Insurance expired.			
	31	Depreciation Expense......................................		2	
		Accumulated Depreciation—Equipment......			2
		Equipment depreciation.			
	31	Wages Expense...		1	
		Wages Payable.......................................			1
		Accrued wages.			

Appendix Ex. 4–26

2008
July	31	Fees Earned..		35	
		Income Summary			35
	31	Income Summary		26	
		Wages Expense......................................			9
		Rent Expense			4
		Insurance Expense			4
		Utilities Expense			3
		Depreciation Expense			2
		Supplies Expense			3
		Miscellaneous Expense...........................			1
	31	Income Summary		9	
		Christina Keene, Capital..........................			9
	31	Christina Keene, Capital		4	
		Christina Keene, Drawing			4

PROBLEMS

Prob. 4–1A

1.

BLINK-ON COMPANY
Income Statement
For the Year Ended March 31, 2008

Revenues:		
Fees revenue...	$257,200	
Rent revenue	1,200	
Total revenues...		$258,400
Expenses:		
Salaries and wages expense	$104,300	
Advertising expense...	21,700	
Utilities expense	11,400	
Repairs expense	8,850	
Depreciation expense—equipment...........................	3,200	
Insurance expense	2,800	
Supplies expense	1,600	
Depreciation expense—building	1,400	
Miscellaneous expense...	4,320	
Total expenses		159,570
Net income		$ 98,830

2.

BLINK-ON COMPANY
Statement of Owner's Equity
For the Year Ended March 31, 2008

Amanda Ayers, capital, April 1, 2007...............................		$ 78,100
Net income for the year..	$98,830	
Less withdrawals...	5,600	
Increase in owner's capital		93,230
Amanda Ayers, capital, March 31, 2008		$171,330

Prob. 4–1A Continued

3.

BLINK-ON COMPANY
Balance Sheet
March 31, 2008

Assets

Current assets:

Cash		$ 6,300	
Accounts receivable		22,400	
Prepaid insurance		1,400	
Supplies		1,130	
Total current assets			$ 31,230

Property, plant, and equipment:

Land			$98,000
Building	$140,000		
Less accum. depreciation	101,700	38,300	
Equipment	$100,500		
Less accum. depreciation	88,300	12,200	
Total property, plant, and equipment			148,500
Total assets			$179,730

Liabilities

Current liabilities:

Accounts payable	$5,700	
Salaries and wages payable	1,800	
Unearned rent	900	
Total liabilities		$ 8,400

Owner's Equity

Amanda Ayers, capital		171,330
Total liabilities and owner's equity		$179,730

Prob. 4–1A   Continued

4.

2008

Mar.	31	Fees Revenue	257,200	
		Rent Revenue	1,200	
		Income Summary		258,400
	31	Income Summary	159,570	
		Salaries & Wages Expense		104,300
		Advertising Expense......................................		21,700
		Utilities Expense		11,400
		Repairs Expense		8,850
		Miscellaneous Expense.................................		4,320
		Insurance Expense		2,800
		Supplies Expense		1,600
		Depreciation Expense—Building...................		1,400
		Depreciation Expense—Equipment		3,200
	31	Income Summary	98,830	
		Amanda Ayers, Capital		98,830
	31	Amanda Ayers, Capital...	5,600	
		Amanda Ayers, Drawing		5,600

5.

BLINK-ON COMPANY
Post-Closing Trial Balance
March 31, 2008

	Debit Balances	Credit Balances
Cash..	6,300	
Accounts Receivable...	22,400	
Prepaid Insurance...	1,400	
Supplies...	1,130	
Land..	98,000	
Building	140,000	
Accumulated Depreciation—Building..........................		101,700
Equipment	100,500	
Accumulated Depreciation—Equipment.........................		88,300
Accounts Payable...		5,700
Salaries & Wages Payable		1,800
Unearned Rent		900
Amanda Ayers, Capital...		171,330
	369,730	369,730

Prob. 4–2A

1.

NEVUS COMPANY
Income Statement
For the Year Ended April 30, 2008

Revenues:		
Service fees...	$363,000	
Rent revenue	7,000	
Total revenues..		$370,000
Expenses:		
Salary expense...	$270,000	
Rent expense	37,000	
Supplies expense	8,000	
Depreciation expense—equipment..........................	7,000	
Utilities expense	6,400	
Repairs expense	6,200	
Insurance expense	4,800	
Miscellaneous expense...	4,600	
Total expenses		344,000
Net income		$ 26,000

NEVUS COMPANY
Statement of Owner's Equity
For the Year Ended April 30, 2008

Stacey Vargas, capital, May 1, 2007		$142,800
Net income for the year..	$26,000	
Less withdrawals..	16,000	
Increase in owner's capital		10,000
Stacey Vargas, capital, April 30, 2008............................		$152,800

Prob. 4–2A Continued

NEVUS COMPANY
Balance Sheet
April 30, 2008

Assets

Current assets:
Cash .... $ 9,000
Accounts receivable 37,200
Supplies 3,500
Prepaid insurance 4,800
Total current assets .... $ 54,500
Property, plant, and equipment:
Equipment $169,500
Less accum. depreciation............... 55,200
Total property, plant, and
equipment 114,300
Total assets $168,800

Liabilities

Current liabilities:
Accounts payable $10,500
Salary payable................. 2,500
Unearned rent.................. 3,000
Total liabilities.............. $ 16,000

Owner's Equity
Stacey Vargas, capital........ 152,800
Total liabilities and
owner's equity.................. $168,800

Prob. 4–2A   Concluded

2.

2008				
Apr.	30	Service Fees	363,000	
		Rent Revenue	7,000	
		Income Summary		370,000
	30	Income Summary	344,000	
		Salary Expense		270,000
		Rent Expense		37,000
		Supplies Expense		8,000
		Depreciation Expense—Equipment		7,000
		Utilities Expense		6,400
		Repairs Expense		6,200
		Insurance Expense		4,800
		Miscellaneous Expense.................................		4,600
	30	Income Summary	26,000	
		Stacey Vargas, Capital..................................		26,000
	30	Stacey Vargas, Capital...	16,000	
		Stacey Vargas, Drawing		16,000

3. $19,000 net loss. The $35,000 decrease is caused by the $16,000 withdrawals and a $19,000 net loss.

Prob. 4–3A

1, 3, 6.

Cash

June 30 Bal.	5,500		

Laundry Supplies

June 30 Bal.	9,450	June 30 Adj.	7,950
30 Adj. Bal.	1,500		

Prepaid Insurance

June 30 Bal.	4,300	June 30 Adj.	3,200
30 Adj. Bal.	1,100		

Laundry Equipment

June 30 Bal.	142,000		

Accumulated Depreciation

		June 30 Bal.	75,200
		30 Adj.	6,000
		30 Adj. Bal.	81,200

Accounts Payable

		June 30 Bal.	4,900

Wages Payable

		June 30 Adj.	750

Scott Mathis, Capital

Clos.	4,200	June 30 Bal.	53,800
		June 30 Clos.	13,650
		June 30 Bal.	63,250

Scott Mathis, Drawing

June 30 Bal.		4,200	June 30 Clos.		4,200

Income Summary

June 30 Clos.		102,450	June 30 Clos.		116,100
June 30 Clos.		13,650			

Laundry Revenue

June 30 Clos.		116,100	June 30 Bal.		116,100

Wages Expense

June 30 Bal.		52,000	June 30 Clos.		52,750
30 Adj.		750			
30 Adj. Bal.		52,750			

Rent Expense

June 30 Bal.		19,650	June 30 Clos.		19,650

Utilities Expense

June 30 Bal.		10,200	June 30 Clos.		10,200

Laundry Supplies Expense

June 30 Adj.		7,950	June 30 Clos.		7,950

Depreciation Expense

June 30 Adj.		6,000	June 30 Clos.		6,000

Insurance Expense

June 30 Adj.		3,200	June 30 Clos.		3,200

Miscellaneous Expense

June 30 Bal.		2,700	June 30 Clos.		2,700

Prob. 4–3A   Continued

2. Optional (Appendix)

IGUANA LAUNDROMAT
End-of-Period Spreadsheet (Work Sheet)
For the Year Ended June 30, 2008

Account Title	Unadjusted Trial Balance Dr.	Cr.	Adjustments Dr.	Cr.	Adjusted Trial Balance Dr.	Cr.	Income Statement Dr.	Cr.	Balance Sheet Dr.	Cr.	
1 Cash	5,500				5,500				5,500		1
2 Laundry Supplies	9,450			(a) 7,950	1,500				1,500		2
3 Prepaid Insurance	4,300			(b) 3,200	1,100				1,100		3
4 Laundry Equipment	142,000				142,000				142,000		4
5 Accumulated Depr.		75,200		(c) 6,000		81,200				81,200	5
6 Accounts Payable		4,900				4,900				4,900	6
7 Scott Mathis, Capital		53,800				53,800				53,800	7
8 Scott Mathis, Drawing	4,200				4,200				4,200		8
9 Laundry Revenue		116,100				116,100		116,100			9
10 Wages Expense	52,000		(d) 750		52,750		52,750				10
11 Rent Expense	19,650				19,650		19,650				11
12 Utilities Expense	10,200				10,200		10,200				12
13 Misc. Expense	2,700				2,700		2,700				13
14	250,000	250,000									14
15 Laundry Supplies Exp.			(a) 7,950		7,950		7,950				15
16 Insurance Expense			(b) 3,200		3,200		3,200				16
17 Depreciation Expense			(c) 6,000		6,000		6,000				17
18 Wages Payable				(d) 750		750				750	18
19			17,900	17,900	256,750	256,750	102,450	116,100	154,300	140,650	19
20 Net income							13,650			13,650	20
21							116,100	116,100	154,300	154,300	21

Prob. 4–3A   Continued

3.

Adjusting Entries

2008

			Debit	Credit
June 30	Laundry Supplies Expense		7,950	
	Laundry Supplies..................................			7,950
	Supplies used ($9,450 – $1,500).			
30	Insurance Expense		3,200	
	Prepaid Insurance			3,200
	Insurance expired.			
30	Depreciation Expense		6,000	
	Accumulated Depreciation...........................			6,000
	Equipment depreciation.			
30	Wages Expense..		750	
	Wages Payable......................................			750
	Accrued wages.			

4.

IGUANA LAUNDROMAT
Adjusted Trial Balance
June 30, 2008

	Debit Balances	Credit Balances
Cash...	5,500	
Laundry Supplies..	1,500	
Prepaid Insurance..	1,100	
Laundry Equipment	142,000	
Accumulated Depreciation......................................		81,200
Accounts Payable		4,900
Wages Payable...		750
Scott Mathis, Capital		53,800
Scott Mathis, Drawing	4,200	
Laundry Revenue..		116,100
Wages Expense	52,750	
Rent Expense	19,650	
Utilities Expense	10,200	
Laundry Supplies Expense	7,950	
Depreciation Expense	6,000	
Insurance Expense..	3,200	
Miscellaneous Expense	2,700	
	256,750	256,750

5.

IGUANA LAUNDROMAT
Income Statement
For the Year Ended June 30, 2008

Laundry revenue		$116,100
Expenses:		
Wages expense...	$52,750	
Rent expense	19,650	
Utilities expense	10,200	
Laundry supplies expense...	7,950	
Depreciation expense...	6,000	
Insurance expense	3,200	
Miscellaneous expense..	2,700	
Total expenses		102,450
Net income		$ 13,650

IGUANA LAUNDROMAT
Statement of Owner's Equity
For the Year Ended June 30, 2008

Scott Mathis, capital, July 1, 2007		$53,800
Net income for the year..	$13,650	
Less withdrawals...	4,200	
Increase in owner's equity..		9,450
Scott Mathis, capital, June 30, 2008..................................		$63,250

IGUANA LAUNDROMAT
Balance Sheet
June 30, 2008

Assets			Liabilities		
Current assets:			Current liabilities:		
Cash	$ 5,500		Accounts payable....	$4,900	
Laundry supplies	1,500		Wages payable	750	
Prepaid insurance....	1,100		Total liabilities............		$ 5,650
Total current assets		$ 8,100			
Property, plant, and					
equipment:			Owner's Equity		
Laundry equipment..	$142,000		Scott Mathis, capital ..		63,250
Less accum. depr.....	81,200				
Total property, plant,					
and equipment		60,800	Total liabilities and		
Total assets		$68,900	owner's equity.........		$68,900

Prob. 4–3A   Concluded

6.

Closing Entries

2008

June	30	Laundry Revenue	116,100	
		Income Summary		116,100
	30	Income Summary	102,450	
		Wages Expense		52,750
		Rent Expense...		19,650
		Utilities Expense.......................................		10,200
		Miscellaneous Expense		2,700
		Laundry Supplies Expense........................		7,950
		Insurance Expense...................................		3,200
		Depreciation Expense		6,000
	30	Income Summary	13,650	
		Scott Mathis, Capital		13,650
	30	Scott Mathis, Capital.....................................	4,200	
		Scott Mathis, Drawing		4,200

7.

IGUANA LAUNDROMAT
Post-Closing Trial Balance
June 30, 2008

	Debit Balances	Credit Balances
Cash...	5,500	
Laundry Supplies..	1,500	
Prepaid Insurance..	1,100	
Laundry Equipment	142,000	
Accumulated Depreciation......................................		81,200
Accounts Payable		4,900
Wages Payable..		750
Scott Mathis, Capital		63,250
	150,100	**150,100**

Prob. 4–4A

1. Optional (Appendix)

WAINSCOT SERVICES CO.
End-of-Period Spreadsheet (Work Sheet)
For the Month Ended March 31, 2008

Account Title	Unadjusted Trial Balance Dr.	Cr.	Adjustments Dr.	Cr.	Adjusted Trial Balance Dr.	Cr.	Income Statement Dr.	Cr.	Balance Sheet Dr.	Cr.
1 Cash	3,509				3,509				3,509	
2 Accounts Receivable	6,550		(a) 1,750		8,300				8,300	
3 Supplies	1,647			(b) 1,247	400				400	
4 Prepaid Insurance	1,800			(c) 250	1,550				1,550	
5 Land	30,000				30,000				30,000	
6 Building	57,500				57,500				57,500	
7 Acc. Depr.—Building		23,400		(d) 400		23,800				23,800
8 Equipment	30,000				30,000				30,000	
9 Acc. Depr.—Equipment		10,200		(e) 200		10,400				10,400
10 Accounts Payable		5,141				5,141				5,141
11 Unearned Rent		2,200	(f) 1,200			1,000				1,000
12 So Young Lee, Capital		67,825				67,825				67,825
13 So Young Lee, Drawing	2,000				2,000				2,000	
14 Service Revenue		46,984		(a) 1,750		48,734		48,734		
15 Wages Expense	14,799		(g) 500		15,299		15,299			
16 Rent Expense	3,910				3,910		3,910			
17 Utilities Expense	1,728				1,728		1,728			
18 Misc. Expense	2,307				2,307		2,307			
19	155,750	155,750								
20 Supplies Expense			(b) 1,247		1,247		1,247			
21 Insurance Expense			(c) 250		250		250			
22 Depr. Exp.—Building			(d) 400		400		400			
23 Depr. Exp.—Equipment			(e) 200		200		200			
24 Rent Revenue				(f) 1,200		1,200		1,200		
25 Wages Payable				(g) 500		500				500
26			5,547	5,547	158,600	158,600	25,341	49,934	133,259	108,666
27 Net income							24,593			24,593
28							49,934	49,934	133,259	133,259

Prob. 4–4A   Continued

2.

	JOURNAL			Page 26
Date		**Post. Ref.**	**Debit**	**Credit**
2008	**Adjusting Entries**			
Mar. 31	Accounts Receivable.................................	12	1,750	
	Service Revenue	41		1,750
	Accrued revenue.			
31	Supplies Expense.....................................	52	1,247	
	Supplies..	13		1,247
	Supplies used ($1,647 – $400).			
31	Insurance Expense...................................	57	250	
	Prepaid Insurance...............................	14		250
	Insurance expired.			
31	Depreciation Expense—Building	54	400	
	Accum. Depreciation—Building............	17		400
	Building depreciation.			
31	Depreciation Expense—Equipment	56	200	
	Accum. Depreciation—Equipment	19		200
	Equipment depreciation.			
31	Unearned Rent	23	1,200	
	Rent Revenue	42		1,200
	Rent revenue earned ($2,200 – $1,000).			
31	Wages Expense	51	500	
	Wages Payable.....................................	22		500
	Accrued wages.			

Prob. 4–4A   Continued

3.

WAINSCOT SERVICES CO.
Adjusted Trial Balance
March 31, 2008

	Debit Balances	Credit Balances
Cash	3,509	
Accounts Receivable	8,300	
Supplies	400	
Prepaid Insurance	1,550	
Land	30,000	
Building	57,500	
Accumulated Depreciation—Building		23,800
Equipment	30,000	
Accumulated Depreciation—Equipment		10,400
Accounts Payable		5,141
Wages Payable		500
Unearned Rent		1,000
So Young Lee, Capital		67,825
So Young Lee, Drawing	2,000	
Service Revenue		48,734
Rent Revenue		1,200
Wages Expense	15,299	
Supplies Expense	1,247	
Rent Expense	3,910	
Depreciation Expense—Building	400	
Utilities Expense	1,728	
Depreciation Expense—Equipment	200	
Insurance Expense	250	
Miscellaneous Expense	2,307	
	158,600	158,600

Prob. 4–4A   Continued

4.

WAINSCOT SERVICES CO.
Income Statement
For the Month Ended March 31, 2008

Revenues:		
Service revenue	$48,734	
Rent revenue	1,200	
Total revenues		$49,934
Expenses:		
Wages expense	$15,299	
Rent expense	3,910	
Utilities expense	1,728	
Supplies expense	1,247	
Depreciation expense—building	400	
Insurance expense	250	
Depreciation expense—equipment	200	
Miscellaneous expense	2,307	
Total expenses		25,341
Net income		$24,593

WAINSCOT SERVICES CO.
Statement of Owner's Equity
For the Month Ended March 31, 2008

So Young Lee, capital, March 1, 2008		$62,825
Additional investment during the month		5,000
Total		$67,825
Net income for the month	$24,593	
Less withdrawals	2,000	
Increase in owner's equity		22,593
So Young Lee, capital, March 31, 2008		$90,418

Prob. 4–4A   Continued

WAINSCOT SERVICES CO.
Balance Sheet
March 31, 2008

Assets			
Current assets:			
Cash		$ 3,509	
Accounts receivable		8,300	
Supplies		400	
Prepaid insurance		1,550	
Total current assets			$13,759
Property, plant, and equipment:			
Land		$30,000	
Building	$57,500		
Less accum. depreciation	23,800	33,700	
Equipment	$30,000		
Less accum. depreciation	10,400	19,600	
Total property, plant, and equipment			83,300
Total assets			$97,059

Liabilities		
Current liabilities:		
Accounts payable	$5,141	
Wages payable	500	
Unearned rent	1,000	
Total liabilities		$ 6,641
Owner's Equity		
So Young Lee, capital		90,418
Total liabilities and owner's equity		$97,059

Prob. 4–4A   Continued

5.

Date		Post. Ref.	Debit	Credit
2008	**Closing Entries**			
Mar. 31	Service Revenue..	41	48,734	
	Rent Revenue..	42	1,200	
	Income Summary	33		49,934
31	Income Summary..	33	25,341	
	Wages Expense..	51		15,299
	Rent Expense	53		3,910
	Utilities Expense	55		1,728
	Miscellaneous Expense.........................	59		2,307
	Supplies Expense	52		1,247
	Insurance Expense	57		250
	Depreciation Expense—Building..........	54		400
	Depreciation Expense—Equipment	56		200
31	Income Summary..	33	24,593	
	So Young Lee, Capital	31		24,593
31	So Young Lee, Capital................................	31	2,000	
	So Young Lee, Drawing........................	32		2,000

Prob. 4–4A   Continued

2. and 5.

Cash

Date		Item	Post. Ref.	Dr.	Cr.	Balance Dr.	Balance Cr.
2008							
Mar.	1	Balance................	✓	....	....	1,259	....
	3	....	23	....	910	349	....
	4	....	23	5,000	....	5,349	....
	5	....	23	....	86	5,263	....
	7	....	23	800	....	6,063	....
	8	....	23	400	....	6,463	....
	8	....	23	....	2,584	3,879	....
	8	....	23	1,695	....	5,574	....
	10	....	24	....	510	5,064	....
	12	....	24	....	2,319	2,745	....
	15	....	24	2,718	....	5,463	....
	16	....	24	....	1,000	4,463	....
	19	....	24	....	2,135	2,328	....
	22	....	24	....	370	1,958	....
	22	....	24	3,992	....	5,950	....
	24	....	25	....	527	5,423	....
	26	....	25	....	2,480	2,943	....
	30	....	25	....	156	2,787	....
	30	....	25	....	26	2,761	....
	31	....	25	....	1,000	1,761	....
	31	....	25	2,029	....	3,790	....
	31	....	25	....	281	3,509	....

Accounts Receivable

Date		Item	Post. Ref.	Dr.	Cr.	Balance Dr.	Balance Cr.
2008							
Mar.	1	Balance................	✓	....	....	6,200	....
	7	....	23	....	800	5,400	....
	8	....	23	....	400	5,000	....
	22	....	24	1,550	....	6,550	....
	31	Adjusting	26	1,750	....	8,300	....

Prob. 4–4A   Continued

Supplies   13

Date	Item	Post. Ref.	Dr.	Cr.	Balance Dr.	Cr.
2008						
Mar. 1	Balance...............	✓	....	....	610	....
10	....	24	510	....	1,120	....
27	....	25	527	....	1,647	....
31	Adjusting	26	....	1,247	400	....

Prepaid Insurance   14

Date	Item	Post. Ref.	Dr.	Cr.	Balance Dr.	Cr.
2008						
Mar. 1	Balance...............	✓	....	....	420	....
22	....	24	1,380	....	1,800	....
31	Adjusting	26	....	250	1,550	....

Land   15

Date	Item	Post. Ref.	Dr.	Cr.	Balance Dr.	Cr.
2008						
Mar. 1	Balance...............	✓	....	....	30,000	....

Building   16

Date	Item	Post. Ref.	Dr.	Cr.	Balance Dr.	Cr.
2008						
Mar. 1	Balance...............	✓	....	....	57,500	....

Accumulated Depreciation—Building   17

Date	Item	Post. Ref.	Dr.	Cr.	Balance Dr.	Cr.
2008						
Mar. 1	Balance...............	✓	....	....	....	23,400
31	Adjusting	26	....	400	....	23,800

Equipment   18

Date	Item	Post. Ref.	Dr.	Cr.	Balance Dr.	Cr.
2008						
Mar. 1	Balance...............	✓	....	....	29,250	....
3	....	23	750	....	30,000	....

Prob. 4–4A   Continued

Accumulated Depreciation—Equipment   19

Date		Item	Post. Ref.	Dr.	Cr.	Balance Dr.	Balance Cr.
2008							
Mar.	1	Balance..................	✓	....	....	....	10,200
	31	Adjusting	26	....	200	....	10,400

Accounts Payable   21

Date		Item	Post. Ref.	Dr.	Cr.	Balance Dr.	Balance Cr.
2008							
Mar.	1	Balance..................	✓	....	....	....	8,625
	3	....	23	....	750	....	9,375
	8	....	23	2,584	....	....	6,791
	19	....	24	2,135	....	....	4,656
	31	....	25	....	485	....	5,141

Wages Payable   22

Date		Item	Post. Ref.	Dr.	Cr.	Balance Dr.	Balance Cr.
2008							
Mar.	31	Adjusting	26	....	500	....	500

Unearned Rent   23

Date		Item	Post. Ref.	Dr.	Cr.	Balance Dr.	Balance Cr.
2008							
Mar.	1	Balance..................	✓	....	....	....	2,200
	31	Adjusting	26	1,200	....	....	1,000

So Young Lee, Capital   31

Date		Item	Post. Ref.	Dr.	Cr.	Balance Dr.	Balance Cr.
2008							
Mar.	1	Balance..................	✓	....	....	....	62,825
	4	....	23	....	5,000	....	67,825
	31	Closing	27	....	24,593	....	92,418
	31	Closing	27	2,000	....	....	90,418

So Young Lee, Drawing   32

Date		Item	Post. Ref.	Dr.	Cr.	Balance Dr.	Balance Cr.
2008							
Mar.	16	....	24	1,000	....	1,000	....
	31	....	25	1,000	....	2,000	....
	31	Closing	27	....	2,000	—	—

Prob. 4–4A   Continued

Income Summary   33

Date		Item	Post. Ref.	Dr.	Cr.	Balance	
						Dr.	Cr.
2008							
Mar.	31	Closing	27	....	49,934	....	49,934
	31	Closing	27	25,341	....	....	24,593
	31	Closing	27	24,593	....	—	—

Service Revenue   41

Date		Item	Post. Ref.	Dr.	Cr.	Balance	
						Dr.	Cr.
2008							
Mar.	8	....	23	....	14,695	....	14,695
	15	....	24	....	7,718	....	22,413
	22	....	24	....	8,992	....	31,405
	22	....	24	....	7,550	....	38,955
	31	....	25	....	8,029	....	46,984
	31	Adjusting	26	....	1,750	....	48,734
	31	Closing	27	48,734	....	—	—

Rent Revenue   42

Date		Item	Post. Ref.	Dr.	Cr.	Balance	
						Dr.	Cr.
2008							
Mar.	1	Adjusting	26	....	1,200	....	1,200
	31	Closing	27	1,200	....	—	—

Wages Expense   51

Date		Item	Post. Ref.	Dr.	Cr.	Balance	
						Dr.	Cr.
2008							
Mar.	12	....	24	7,319	....	7,319	....
	26	....	25	7,480	....	14,799	....
	31	Adjusting	26	500	....	15,299	....
	31	Closing	27	....	15,299	—	—

Supplies Expense   52

Date		Item	Post. Ref.	Dr.	Cr.	Balance	
						Dr.	Cr.
2008							
Mar.	31	Adjusting	26	1,247	....	1,247	....
	31	Closing	27	....	1,247	—	—

Prob. 4–4A   Continued

Rent Expense   53

Date	Item	Post. Ref.	Dr.	Cr.	Balance Dr.	Balance Cr.
2008						
Mar. 3	....	23	3,910	....	3,910	....
31	Closing	27	....	3,910	—	—

Depreciation Expense—Building   54

Date	Item	Post. Ref.	Dr.	Cr.	Balance Dr.	Balance Cr.
2008						
Mar. 31	Adjusting	26	400	....	400	....
31	Closing	27	....	400	—	—

Utilities Expense   55

Date	Item	Post. Ref.	Dr.	Cr.	Balance Dr.	Balance Cr.
2008						
Mar. 5	....	24	586	....	586	....
30	....	25	456	....	1,042	....
31	....	25	686	....	1,728	....
31	Closing	27	....	1,728	—	—

Depreciation Expense—Equipment   56

Date	Item	Post. Ref.	Dr.	Cr.	Balance Dr.	Balance Cr.
2008						
Mar. 31	Adjusting	26	200	....	200	....
31	Closing	27	....	200	—	—

Insurance Expense   57

Date	Item	Post. Ref.	Dr.	Cr.	Balance Dr.	Balance Cr.
2008						
Mar. 31	Adjusting	26	250	....	250	....
31	Closing	27	....	250	—	—

Miscellaneous Expense   59

Date	Item	Post. Ref.	Dr.	Cr.	Balance Dr.	Balance Cr.
2008						
Mar. 30	....	25	1,026	....	1,026	....
31	....	25	1,281	....	2,307	....
31	Closing	27	....	2,307	—	—

Prob. 4–4A   Concluded

6.

WAINSCOT SERVICES CO.
Post-Closing Trial Balance
March 31, 2008

	Debit Balances	Credit Balances
Cash	3,509	
Accounts Receivable	8,300	
Supplies	400	
Prepaid Insurance	1,550	
Land	30,000	
Building	57,500	
Accumulated Depreciation—Building		23,800
Equipment	30,000	
Accumulated Depreciation—Equipment		10,400
Accounts Payable		5,141
Wages Payable		500
Unearned Rent		1,000
So Young Lee, Capital		90,418
	131,259	131,259

Prob. 4–5A

1., 3., and 6.

Cash   11

Date	Item	Post. Ref.	Dr.	Cr.	Balance Dr.	Balance Cr.
2008						
Oct. 31	Balance..................	✓	....	....	2,950	....

Supplies   13

Date	Item	Post. Ref.	Dr.	Cr.	Balance Dr.	Balance Cr.
2008						
Oct. 31	Balance..................	✓	....	....	12,295	....
31	Adjusting	26	....	5,175	7,120	....

Prepaid Insurance   14

Date	Item	Post. Ref.	Dr.	Cr.	Balance Dr.	Balance Cr.
2008						
Oct. 31	Balance..................	✓	....	....	2,735	....
31	Adjusting	26	....	2,000	735	....

Equipment   16

Date	Item	Post. Ref.	Dr.	Cr.	Balance Dr.	Balance Cr.
2008						
Oct. 31	Balance..................	✓	....	....	95,650	....

Accumulated Depreciation—Equipment   17

Date	Item	Post. Ref.	Dr.	Cr.	Balance Dr.	Balance Cr.
2008						
Oct. 31	Balance..................	✓	....	....	....	21,209
31	Adjusting	26	....	4,200	....	25,409

Trucks   18

Date	Item	Post. Ref.	Dr.	Cr.	Balance Dr.	Balance Cr.
2008						
Oct. 31	Balance..................	✓	....	....	36,300	....

Accumulated Depreciation—Trucks   19

Date	Item	Post. Ref.	Dr.	Cr.	Balance Dr.	Balance Cr.
2008						
Oct. 31	Balance..................	✓	....	....	....	7,400
31	Adjusting	26	....	2,200	....	9,600

Prob. 4–5A   Continued

Accounts Payable   21

Date	Item	Post. Ref.	Dr.	Cr.	Balance Dr.	Balance Cr.
2008						
Oct. 31	Balance.................	✓	....	....	....	4,015

Wages Payable   22

Date	Item	Post. Ref.	Dr.	Cr.	Balance Dr.	Balance Cr.
2008						
Oct. 31	Adjusting	26	....	600	....	600

Rhonda Salter, Capital   31

Date	Item	Post. Ref.	Dr.	Cr.	Balance Dr.	Balance Cr.
2008						
Oct. 31	Balance.................	✓	....	....	....	67,426
31	Closing	27	....	41,705	....	109,131
31	Closing	27	6,000	....	....	103,131

Rhonda Salter, Drawing   32

Date	Item	Post. Ref.	Dr.	Cr.	Balance Dr.	Balance Cr.
2008						
Oct. 31	Balance.................	✓	....	....	6,000	....
31	Closing	27	....	6,000	—	—

Income Summary   33

Date	Item	Post. Ref.	Dr.	Cr.	Balance Dr.	Balance Cr.
2008						
Oct. 31	Closing	27	....	99,950	....	99,950
31	Closing	27	58,245	....	....	41,705
31	Closing	27	41,705	....	—	—

Service Revenue   41

Date	Item	Post. Ref.	Dr.	Cr.	Balance Dr.	Balance Cr.
2008						
Oct. 31	Balance.................	✓	....	....	....	99,950
	Closing	27	99,950	....	—	—

Wages Expense   51

Date	Item	Post. Ref.	Dr.	Cr.	Balance Dr.	Balance Cr.
2008						
Oct. 31	Balance.................	✓	....	....	26,925	....
31	Adjusting	26	600	....	27,525	....
31	Closing	27	....	27,525	—	—

Prob. 4–5A Continued

Supplies Expense   52

Date	Item	Post. Ref.	Dr.	Cr.	Balance Dr.	Balance Cr.
2008						
Oct. 31	Adjusting	26	5,175	....	5,175	....
31	Closing	27	....	5,175	—	—

Rent Expense   53

Date	Item	Post. Ref.	Dr.	Cr.	Balance Dr.	Balance Cr.
2008						
Oct. 31	Balance..................	✓	....	....	9,600	....
31	Closing	27	....	9,600	—	—

Depreciation Expense—Equipment   54

Date	Item	Post. Ref.	Dr.	Cr.	Balance Dr.	Balance Cr.
2008						
Oct. 31	Adjusting	26	4,200	....	4,200	....
31	Closing	27	....	4,200	—	—

Truck Expense   55

Date	Item	Post. Ref.	Dr.	Cr.	Balance Dr.	Balance Cr.
2008						
Oct. 31	Balance..................	✓	....	....	5,350	....
31	Closing	27	....	5,350	—	—

Depreciation Expense—Trucks   56

Date	Item	Post. Ref.	Dr.	Cr.	Balance Dr.	Balance Cr.
2008						
Oct. 31	Adjusting	26	2,200	....	2,200	....
31	Closing	27	....	2,200	—	—

Insurance Expense   57

Date	Item	Post. Ref.	Dr.	Cr.	Balance Dr.	Balance Cr.
2008						
Oct. 31	Adjusting	26	2,000	....	2,000	....
31	Closing	27	....	2,000	—	—

Miscellaneous Expense   59

Date	Item	Post. Ref.	Dr.	Cr.	Balance Dr.	Balance Cr.
2008						
Oct. 31	Balance..................	✓	....	....	2,195	....
31	Closing	27	....	2,195	—	—

Prob. 4–5A Continued

2. Optional (Appendix)

QUICK REPAIRS
End-of-Period Spreadsheet (Work Sheet)
For the Year Ended October 31, 2008

#	Account Title	Unadjusted Trial Balance Dr.	Cr.	Adjustments Dr.	Cr.	Adjusted Trial Balance Dr.	Cr.	Income Statement Dr.	Cr.	Balance Sheet Dr.	Cr.
1	Cash	2,950				2,950				2,950	
2	Supplies	12,295			(a) 5,175	7,120				7,120	
3	Prepaid Insurance	2,735			(b) 2,000	735				735	
4	Equipment	95,650				95,650				95,650	
5	Accum. Depr.—Equip.		21,209		(c) 4,200		25,409				25,409
6	Trucks	36,300				36,300				36,300	
7	Accum. Depr.—Trucks		7,400		(d) 2,200		9,600				9,600
8	Accounts Payable		4,015				4,015				4,015
9	Rhonda Salter, Capital		67,426				67,426				67,426
10	Rhonda Salter, Drawing	6,000				6,000				6,000	
11	Service Revenue		99,950				99,950		99,950		
12	Wages Expense	26,925		(e) 600		27,525		27,525			
13	Rent Expense	9,600				9,600		9,600			
14	Truck Expense	5,350				5,350		5,350			
15	Misc. Expense	2,195				2,195		2,195			
16		200,000	200,000								
17	Supplies Expense			(a) 5,175		5,175		5,175			
18	Insurance Expense			(b) 2,000		2,000		2,000			
19	Depr. Exp.—Equipment			(c) 4,200		4,200		4,200			
20	Depr. Exp.—Trucks			(d) 2,200		2,200		2,200			
21	Wages Payable				(e) 600		600				600
22				14,175	14,175	207,000	207,000	58,245	99,950	148,755	107,050
23	Net income							41,705			41,705
24								99,950	99,950	148,755	148,755

3. JOURNAL Page 26

Date			Post. Ref.	Debit	Credit
		Adjusting Entries			
2008					
Oct.	31	Supplies Expense...................................	52	5,175	
		Supplies..	13		5,175
		Supplies used ($12,295 – $7,120).			
	31	Insurance Expense..................................	57	2,000	
		Prepaid Insurance..............................	14		2,000
		Insurance expired.			
	31	Depreciation Expense—Equipment	54	4,200	
		Accumulated Depr.—Equipment	17		4,200
		Equipment depreciation.			
	31	Depreciation Expense—Trucks..................	56	2,200	
		Accumulated Depr.—Trucks	19		2,200
		Truck depreciation.			
	31	Wages Expense	51	600	
		Wages Payable.....................................	22		600
		Accrued wages.			

Prob. 4–5A   Continued

4.

QUICK REPAIRS
Adjusted Trial Balance
October 31, 2008

	Debit Balances	Credit Balances
Cash	2,950	
Supplies	7,120	
Prepaid Insurance	735	
Equipment	95,650	
Accumulated Depreciation—Equipment		25,409
Trucks	36,300	
Accumulated Depreciation—Trucks		9,600
Accounts Payable		4,015
Wages Payable		600
Rhonda Salter, Capital		67,426
Rhonda Salter, Drawing	6,000	
Service Revenue		99,950
Wages Expense	27,525	
Supplies Expense	5,175	
Rent Expense	9,600	
Depreciation Expense—Equipment	4,200	
Truck Expense	5,350	
Depreciation Expense—Trucks	2,200	
Insurance Expense	2,000	
Miscellaneous Expense	2,195	
	207,000	207,000

5.

QUICK REPAIRS
Income Statement
For the Year Ended October 31, 2008

Service revenue		$99,950
Expenses:		
Wages expense...	$27,525	
Rent expense	9,600	
Truck expense	5,350	
Supplies expense	5,175	
Depreciation expense—equipment...........................	4,200	
Depreciation expense—trucks	2,200	
Insurance expense	2,000	
Miscellaneous expense...	2,195	
Total expenses		58,245
Net income		$41,705

QUICK REPAIRS
Statement of Owner's Equity
For the Year Ended October 31, 2008

Rhonda Salter, capital, November 1, 2007........................		$ 67,426
Net income for the year...	$41,705	
Less withdrawals...	6,000	
Increase in owner's capital...		35,705
Rhonda Salter, capital, October 31, 2008		$103,131

Prob. 4–5A   Continued

QUICK REPAIRS
Balance Sheet
October 31, 2008

Assets			
Current assets:			
Cash	$ 2,950		
Supplies	7,120		
Prepaid insurance	735		
Total current assets		$ 10,805	
Property, plant, and equipment:			
Equipment	$95,650		
Less accum. depreciation	25,409	$70,241	
Trucks	$36,300		
Less accum. depreciation	9,600	26,700	
Total property, plant, and equipment		96,941	
Total assets		$107,746	

Liabilities			
Current liabilities:			
Accounts payable	$4,015		
Wages payable	600		
Total liabilities		$ 4,615	
Owner's Equity			
Rhonda Salter, capital		103,131	
Total liabilities and owner's equity		$107,746	

Prob. 4–5A   Concluded

6.

Date		Post. Ref.	Debit	Credit
	Closing Entries			
2008				
Oct. 31	Service Revenue..	41	99,950	
	Income Summary	33		99,950
31	Income Summary......................................	33	58,245	
	Wages Expense....................................	51		27,525
	Supplies Expense	52		5,175
	Rent Expense	53		9,600
	Depreciation Expense—Equipment	54		4,200
	Truck Expense	55		5,350
	Depreciation Expense—Trucks	56		2,200
	Insurance Expense	57		2,000
	Miscellaneous Expense........................	59		2,195
31	Income Summary......................................	33	41,705	
	Rhonda Salter, Capital..........................	31		41,705
31	Rhonda Salter, Capital	31	6,000	
	Rhonda Salter, Drawing	32		6,000

7.

QUICK REPAIRS
Post-Closing Trial Balance
October 31, 2008

	Debit Balances	Credit Balances
Cash...	2,950	
Supplies..	7,120	
Prepaid Insurance..	735	
Equipment	95,650	
Accumulated Depreciation—Equipment.........................		25,409
Trucks..	36,300	
Accumulated Depreciation—Trucks		9,600
Accounts Payable		4,015
Wages Payable...		600
Rhonda Salter, Capital		103,131
	142,755	142,755

Prob. 4–6A

JOURNAL

Pages 1 and 2

Date	Description	Post. Ref.	Debit	Credit
2008				
Oct. 1	Cash	11	12,950	
	Accounts Receivable	12	2,800	
	Supplies	14	1,500	
	Office Equipment	18	18,750	
	Dawn Lytle, Capital	31		36,000
1	Prepaid Rent	15	3,600	
	Cash	11		3,600
2	Prepaid Insurance	16	2,400	
	Cash	11		2,400
4	Cash	11	4,150	
	Unearned Fees	23		4,150
5	Office Equipment	18	2,500	
	Accounts Payable	21		2,500
6	Cash	11	1,900	
	Accounts Receivable	12		1,900
10	Miscellaneous Expense	59	325	
	Cash	11		325
12	Accounts Payable	21	1,250	
	Cash	11		1,250
12	Accounts Receivable	12	3,750	
	Fees Earned	41		3,750
14	Salary Expense	51	750	
	Cash	11		750
17	Cash	11	6,250	
	Fees Earned	41		6,250
18	Supplies	14	600	
	Cash	11		600
20	Accounts Receivable	12	2,100	
	Fees Earned	41		2,100
24	Cash	11	3,850	
	Fees Earned	41		3,850

Prob. 4–6A Continued

1. and 2.		**JOURNAL**			**Pages 1 and 2**

Date	Description	Post. Ref.	Debit	Credit
2008				
Oct. 26	Cash...	11	4,450	
	Accounts Receivable	12		4,450
27	Salary Expense	51	750	
	Cash	11		750
29	Miscellaneous Expense	59	250	
	Cash	11		250
31	Miscellaneous Expense	59	300	
	Cash	11		300
31	Cash...	11	2,975	
	Fees Earned..	41		2,975
31	Accounts Receivable..................................	12	1,500	
	Fees Earned..	41		1,500
31	Dawn Lytle, Drawing	32	5,000	
	Cash	11		5,000

Prob. 4–6A Continued

2., 6., and 9.

Cash

11

Date	Item	Post. Ref.	Dr.	Cr.	Balance Dr.	Balance Cr.
2008						
Oct. 1	....	1	12,950	....	12,950	....
1	....	1	....	3,600	9,350	....
2	....	1	....	2,400	6,950	....
4	....	1	4,150	....	11,100	....
6	....	1	1,900	....	13,000	....
10	....	1	....	325	12,675	....
12	....	1	....	1,250	11,425	....
14	....	1	....	750	10,675	....
17	....	2	6,250	....	16,925	....
18	....	2	....	600	16,325	....
24	....	2	3,850	....	20,175	....
26	....	2	4,450	....	24,625	....
27	....	2	....	750	23,875	....
29	....	2	....	250	23,625	....
31	....	2	....	300	23,325	....
31	....	2	2,975	....	26,300	....
31	....	2	....	5,000	21,300	....

Accounts Receivable

12

Date	Item	Post. Ref.	Dr.	Cr.	Balance Dr.	Balance Cr.
2008						
Oct. 1	....	1	2,800	....	2,800	....
6	....	1	....	1,900	900	....
12	....	1	3,750	....	4,650	....
20	....	2	2,100	....	6,750	....
26	....	2	....	4,450	2,300	....
31	....	2	1,500	....	3,800	....

Supplies

14

Date	Item	Post. Ref.	Dr.	Cr.	Balance Dr.	Balance Cr.
2008						
Oct. 1	....	1	1,500	....	1,500	....
18	....	2	600	....	2,100	....
31	Adjusting	3	....	1,225	875	....

Prob. 4–6A   Continued

Prepaid Rent   15

Date	Item	Post. Ref.	Dr.	Cr.	Balance Dr.	Balance Cr.
2008						
Oct. 1	....	1	3,600	....	3,600	....
31	Adjusting	3	....	1,550	2,050	....

Prepaid Insurance   16

Date	Item	Post. Ref.	Dr.	Cr.	Balance Dr.	Balance Cr.
2008						
Oct. 2	....	1	2,400	....	2,400	....
31	Adjusting	3	....	200	2,200	....

Office Equipment   18

Date	Item	Post. Ref.	Dr.	Cr.	Balance Dr.	Balance Cr.
2008						
Oct. 1	....	1	18,750	....	18,750	....
5	....	1	2,500	....	21,250	....

Accumulated Depreciation   19

Date	Item	Post. Ref.	Dr.	Cr.	Balance Dr.	Balance Cr.
2008						
Oct. 31	Adjusting	3	....	675	....	675

Accounts Payable   21

Date	Item	Post. Ref.	Dr.	Cr.	Balance Dr.	Balance Cr.
2008						
Oct. 5	....	1	....	2,500	....	2,500
12	....	1	1,250	....	....	1,250

Salaries Payable   22

Date	Item	Post. Ref.	Dr.	Cr.	Balance Dr.	Balance Cr.
2008						
Oct. 31	Adjusting	3	....	150	....	150

Unearned Fees   23

Date	Item	Post. Ref.	Dr.	Cr.	Balance Dr.	Balance Cr.
2008						
Oct. 4	....	1	....	4,150	....	4,150
31	Adjusting	3	3,000	....	....	1,150

Prob. 4–6A   Continued

Dawn Lytle, Capital   31

Date	Item	Post. Ref.	Dr.	Cr.	Balance Dr.	Balance Cr.
2008						
Oct. 1	....	1	....	36,000	....	36,000
31	Closing	4	....	17,250	....	53,250
31	Closing	4	5,000	....	....	48,250

Dawn Lytle, Drawing   32

Date	Item	Post. Ref.	Dr.	Cr.	Balance Dr.	Balance Cr.
2008						
Oct. 31	....	2	5,000	....	5,000	....
31	Closing	4	....	5,000	—	—

Income Summary   33

Date	Item	Post. Ref.	Dr.	Cr.	Balance Dr.	Balance Cr.
2008						
Oct. 31	Closing	4	....	23,425	....	23,425
31	Closing	4	6,175	....	....	17,250
31	Closing	4	17,250	....	—	—

Fees Earned   41

Date	Item	Post. Ref.	Dr.	Cr.	Balance Dr.	Balance Cr.
2008						
Oct. 12	....	1	....	3,750	....	3,750
17	....	2	....	6,250	....	10,000
20	....	2	....	2,100	....	12,100
24	....	2	....	3,850	....	15,950
31	....	2	....	2,975	....	18,925
31	....	2	....	1,500	....	20,425
31	Adjusting	3	....	3,000	....	23,425
31	Closing	4	23,425	....	—	—

Salary Expense   51

Date	Item	Post. Ref.	Dr.	Cr.	Balance Dr.	Balance Cr.
2008						
Oct. 14	....	1	750	....	750	....
27	....	2	750	....	1,500	....
31	Adjusting	3	150	....	1,650	....
31	Closing	4	....	1,650	—	—

Prob. 4–6A   Continued

Rent Expense   52

Date		Item	Post. Ref.	Dr.	Cr.	Balance Dr.	Cr.
2008							
Oct.	31	Adjusting	3	1,550	....	1,550	....
	31	Closing	4	....	1,550	—	—

Supplies Expense   53

Date		Item	Post. Ref.	Dr.	Cr.	Balance Dr.	Cr.
2008							
Oct.	31	Adjusting	3	1,225	....	1,225	....
	31	Closing	4	....	1,225	—	—

Depreciation Expense   54

Date		Item	Post. Ref.	Dr.	Cr.	Balance Dr.	Cr.
2008							
Oct.	31	Adjusting	3	675	....	675	....
	31	Closing	4	....	675	—	—

Insurance Expense   55

Date		Item	Post. Ref.	Dr.	Cr.	Balance Dr.	Cr.
2008							
Oct.	31	Adjusting	3	200	....	200	....
	31	Closing	4	....	200	—	—

Miscellaneous Expense   59

Date		Item	Post. Ref.	Dr.	Cr.	Balance Dr.	Cr.
2008							
Oct.	10	....	1	325	....	325	....
	29	....	2	250	....	575	....
	31	....	2	300	....	875	....
	31	Closing	4	....	875	—	—

Prob. 4–6A Continued

3.

SKY'S THE LIMIT CONSULTING
Unadjusted Trial Balance
October 31, 2008

	Debit Balances	Credit Balances
Cash	21,300	
Accounts Receivable	3,800	
Supplies	2,100	
Prepaid Rent	3,600	
Prepaid Insurance	2,400	
Office Equipment	21,250	
Accumulated Depreciation		
Accounts Payable		1,250
Salaries Payable		
Unearned Fees		4,150
Dawn Lytle, Capital		36,000
Dawn Lytle, Drawing	5,000	
Fees Earned		20,425
Salary Expense	1,500	
Rent Expense		
Supplies Expense		
Depreciation Expense		
Insurance Expense		
Miscellaneous Expense	875	
	61,825	61,825

Prob. 4–6A   Continued

5. Optional (Appendix)

SKY'S-THE-LIMIT CONSULTING
End-of-Period Spreadsheet (Work Sheet)
For the Month Ended October 31, 2008

	Unadjusted Trial Balance		Adjustments		Adjusted Trial Balance		Income Statement		Balance Sheet		
Account Title	Dr.	Cr.	Dr.	Cr.	Dr.	Cr.	Dr.	Cr.	Dr.	Cr.	
1 Cash	21,300				21,300				21,300		1
2 Accounts Receivable	3,800				3,800				3,800		2
3 Supplies	2,100			(b) 1,225	875				875		3
4 Prepaid Rent	3,600			(e) 1,550	2,050				2,050		4
5 Prepaid Insurance	2,400			(a) 200	2,200				2,200		5
6 Office Equipment	21,250				21,250				21,250		6
7 Accum. Depreciation				(c) 675		675				675	7
8 Accounts Payable		1,250				1,250				1,250	8
9 Salaries Payable				(d) 150		150				150	9
10 Unearned Fees		4,150	(f) 3,000			1,150				1,150	10
11 Dawn Lytle, Capital		36,000				36,000				36,000	11
12 Dawn Lytle, Drawing	5,000				5,000				5,000		12
13 Fees Earned		20,425		(f) 3,000		23,425		23,425			13
14 Salary Expense	1,500		(d) 150		1,650		1,650				14
15 Rent Expense			(e) 1,550		1,550		1,550				15
16 Supplies Expense			(b) 1,225		1,225		1,225				16
17 Depreciation Expense			(c) 675		675		675				17
18 Insurance Expense			(a) 200		200		200				18
19 Miscellaneous Expense	875				875		875				19
20	61,825	61,825	6,800	6,800	62,650	62,650	6,175	23,425	56,475	39,225	20
21 Net income							17,250			17,250	21
22							23,425	23,425	56,475	56,475	22

Prob. 4–6A   Continued

6.

Date		Post. Ref.	Debit	Credit
	Adjusting Entries			
2008				
Oct. 31	Insurance Expense............................	55	200	
	Prepaid Insurance..........................	16		200
	Insurance expired.			
31	Supplies Expense.............................	53	1,225	
	Supplies.......................................	14		1,225
	Supplies used ($2,100 – $875).			
31	Depreciation Expense	54	675	
	Accumulated Depreciation....................	19		675
	Equipment depreciation.			
31	Salary Expense	51	150	
	Salaries Payable............................	22		150
	Accrued salaries.			
31	Rent Expense.................................	52	1,550	
	Prepaid Rent.................................	15		1,550
	Rent expired.			
31	Unearned Fees...............................	23	3,000	
	Fees Earned.................................	41		3,000
	Unearned fees earned ($4,150 – $1,150).			

7.

SKY'S THE LIMIT CONSULTING
Adjusted Trial Balance
October 31, 2008

	Debit Balances	Credit Balances
Cash	21,300	
Accounts Receivable	3,800	
Supplies	875	
Prepaid Rent	2,050	
Prepaid Insurance	2,200	
Office Equipment	21,250	
Accumulated Depreciation		675
Accounts Payable		1,250
Salaries Payable		150
Unearned Fees		1,150
Dawn Lytle, Capital		36,000
Dawn Lytle, Drawing	5,000	
Fees Earned		23,425
Salary Expense	1,650	
Rent Expense	1,550	
Supplies Expense	1,225	
Depreciation Expense	675	
Insurance Expense	200	
Miscellaneous Expense	875	
	62,650	62,650

Prob. 4–6A   Continued

8.

SKY'S-THE-LIMIT CONSULTING
Income Statement
For the Month Ended October 31, 2008

Fees earned...		$23,425
Expenses:		
Salary expense...	$1,650	
Rent expense	1,550	
Supplies expense	1,225	
Depreciation expense......................................	675	
Insurance expense	200	
Miscellaneous expense...................................	875	
Total expenses		6,175
Net income		$17,250

SKY'S-THE-LIMIT CONSULTING
Statement of Owner's Equity
For the Month Ended October 31, 2008

Dawn Lytle, capital, October 1, 2008...............................		$ 0
Additional investments during the month		36,000
Total		$36,000
Net income for the month	$17,250	
Less withdrawals..	5,000	
Increase in owner's equity..		12,250
Dawn Lytle, capital, October 31, 2008............................		$48,250

Prob. 4–6A   Continued

SKY'S-THE-LIMIT CONSULTING
Balance Sheet
October 31, 2008

Assets			Liabilities		
Current assets:			Current liabilities:		
Cash	$21,300		Accounts payable....	$1,250	
Accounts receivable ..	3,800		Salaries payable......	150	
Supplies	875		Unearned fees	1,150	
Prepaid rent	2,050		Total liabilities............		$ 2,550
Prepaid insurance......	2,200				
Total current assets		$30,225			
Property, plant, and equipment:..................			Owner's Equity		
Office equipment........	$21,250		Dawn Lytle, capital		48,250
Less accum. depr.......	675				
Total Property, plant, and equipment.........		20,575	Total liabilities and		
Total assets...................		$50,800	owner's equity.........		$50,800

Prob. 4–6A   Concluded

9.

Date		Post. Ref.	Debit	Credit
	Closing Entries			
2008				
Oct. 31	Fees Earned	41	23,425	
	Income Summary	33		23,425
31	Income Summary....................................	33	6,175	
	Salary Expense	51		1,650
	Rent Expense	52		1,550
	Supplies Expense	53		1,225
	Depreciation Expense	54		675
	Insurance Expense	55		200
	Miscellaneous Expense........................	59		875
31	Income Summary....................................	33	17,250	
	Dawn Lytle, Capital	31		17,250
31	Dawn Lytle, Capital.................................	31	5,000	
	Dawn Lytle, Drawing.............................	32		5,000

10.

SKY'S-THE-LIMIT CONSULTING
Post-Closing Trial Balance
October 31, 2008

	Debit Balances	Credit Balances
Cash..	21,300	
Accounts Receivable...	3,800	
Supplies..	875	
Prepaid Rent..	2,050	
Prepaid Insurance..	2,200	
Office Equipment	21,250	
Accumulated Depreciation.....................................		675
Accounts Payable		1,250
Salaries Payable		150
Unearned Fees..		1,150
Dawn Lytle, Capital..		48,250
	51,475	51,475

Prob. 4–1B

1.

LAST-CHANCE COMPANY
Income Statement
For the Year Ended November 30, 2008

Revenues:		
Fees revenue	$290,700	
Rent revenue	2,000	
Total revenues		$292,700
Expenses:		
Salaries & wages expense	$147,000	
Advertising expense	94,800	
Utilities expense	27,000	
Travel expense	18,750	
Depreciation expense—equipment	5,200	
Depreciation expense—building	2,000	
Supplies expense	1,525	
Insurance expense	1,450	
Miscellaneous expense	5,875	
Total expenses		303,600
Net loss		$ 10,900

2.

LAST-CHANCE COMPANY
Statement of Owner's Equity
For the Year Ended November 30, 2008

Corey Evans, capital, December 1, 2007		$318,800
Net loss for the year	$10,900	
Add withdrawals	15,000	
Decrease in owner's equity		25,900
Corey Evans, capital, November 30, 2008		$292,900

3.

LAST-CHANCE COMPANY
Balance Sheet
November 30, 2008

Assets			
Current assets:			
Cash		$ 4,800	
Accounts receivable		19,950	
Prepaid insurance		1,250	
Supplies		500	
Total current assets			$ 26,500
Property, plant, and equipment:			
Land		$ 75,000	
Building	$205,000		
Less accum. depreciation	78,000	127,000	
Equipment	$139,000		
Less accum. depreciation	59,650	79,350	
Total property, plant, and equipment			281,350
Total assets			$307,850

Liabilities		
Current liabilities:		
Accounts payable	$9,750	
Salaries & wages payable	2,700	
Unearned rent	2,500	
Total liabilities		$ 14,950
Owner's Equity		
Corey Evans, capital		292,900
Total liabilities and owner's equity		$307,850

Prob. 4–1B   Continued

4.

2008				
Nov. 30	Fees Revenue		290,700	
	Rent Revenue		2,000	
	Income Summary			292,700
30	Income Summary		303,600	
	Salaries & Wages Expense			147,000
	Advertising Expense			94,800
	Utilities Expense			27,000
	Travel Expense			18,750
	Miscellaneous Expense			5,875
	Insurance Expense			1,450
	Supplies Expense			1,525
	Depreciation Expense—Building			2,000
	Depreciation Expense—Equipment			5,200
30	Corey Evans, Capital		10,900	
	Income Summary			10,900
30	Corey Evans, Capital		15,000	
	Corey Evans, Drawing			15,000

Prob. 4–1B   Concluded

5.

LAST-CHANCE COMPANY
Post-Closing Trial Balance
November 30, 2008

	Debit Balances	Credit Balances
Cash	4,800	
Accounts Receivable	19,950	
Prepaid Insurance	1,250	
Supplies	500	
Land	75,000	
Building	205,000	
Accumulated Depreciation—Building		78,000
Equipment	139,000	
Accumulated Depreciation—Equipment		59,650
Accounts Payable		9,750
Salaries & Wages Payable		2,700
Unearned Rent		2,500
Corey Evans, Capital		292,900
	445,500	445,500

Prob. 4–2B

1.

THE ULTRA SERVICES COMPANY
Income Statement
For the Year Ended July 31, 2008

Revenues:		
Service fees...	$525,000	
Rent revenue	4,500	
Total revenues..		$529,500
Expenses:		
Salary expense...	$219,000	
Depreciation expense—equipment...........................	28,500	
Rent expense	25,500	
Supplies expense	22,950	
Utilities expense	15,900	
Depreciation expense—buildings	15,600	
Repairs expense	12,450	
Insurance expense	3,000	
Miscellaneous expense...	5,100	
Total expenses		348,000
Net income		$181,500

THE ULTRA SERVICES COMPANY
Statement of Owner's Equity
For the Year Ended July 31, 2008

Chad Tillman, capital, August 1, 2007............................		$340,500
Net income for the year..	$181,500	
Less withdrawals...	30,000	
Increase in owner's equity..		151,500
Chad Tillman, capital, July 31, 2008................................		$492,000

THE ULTRA SERVICES COMPANY
Balance Sheet
July 31, 2008

Assets			
Current assets:			
Cash		$ 13,950	
Accounts receivable		41,880	
Supplies		8,400	
Prepaid insurance.........................		7,500	
Total current assets			$ 71,730
Property, plant, and equipment:			
Land		$180,000	
Buildings..	$360,000		
Less accum. depreciation.............	217,200	142,800	
Equipment	$258,270		
Less accum. depreciation.............	122,700	135,570	
Total property, plant, and			
equipment			458,370
Total assets			$530,100

Liabilities		
Current liabilities:		
Accounts payable	$33,300	
Salaries payable...............	3,300	
Unearned rent...................	1,500	
Total liabilities.............		$ 38,100
Owner's Equity		
Chad Tillman, capital.........		492,000
Total liabilities and		
owner's equity...............		$530,100

Prob. 4–2B Concluded

2.

2008

July 31	Service Fees	525,000	
	Rent Revenue	4,500	
	Income Summary		529,500
31	Income Summary	348,000	
	Salary Expense		219,000
	Depreciation Expense—Equipment		28,500
	Rent Expense		25,500
	Supplies Expense		22,950
	Utilities Expense		15,900
	Depreciation Expense—Buildings		15,600
	Repairs Expense		12,450
	Insurance Expense		3,000
	Miscellaneous Expense		5,100
31	Income Summary	181,500	
	Chad Tillman, Capital		181,500
31	Chad Tillman, Capital	30,000	
	Chad Tillman, Drawing		30,000

3. $10,000 net loss. The $40,000 decrease is caused by the $30,000 withdrawals and a $10,000 net loss.

Prob. 4–3B

1, 3, 6.

Cash

Mar. 31 Bal.	1,450	

Laundry Supplies

Mar. 31 Bal.	3,750	Mar. 31 Adj.	2,800
31 Adj. Bal.	950		

Prepaid Insurance

Mar. 31 Bal.	2,400	Mar. 31 Adj.	2,000
31 Adj. Bal.	400		

Laundry Equipment

Mar. 31 Bal.	54,500	

Accumulated Depreciation

		Mar. 31 Bal.	20,500
		31 Adj.	2,900
		31 Adj. Bal.	23,400

Accounts Payable

		Mar. 31 Bal.	3,100

Wages Payable

		Mar. 31 Adj.	600

Ryan Boyle, Capital

Mar. 31 Clos.	1,000	Mar. 31 Bal.	18,900
		31 Clos.	12,300
		31 Bal.	30,200

Ryan Boyle, Drawing

Mar. 31 Bal.	1,000	Mar. 31 Clos.	1,000

Income Summary

Mar.	31 Clos.	70,200	Mar.	31 Clos.	82,500
	31 Clos.	12,300			

Laundry Revenue

Mar.	31 Clos.	82,500	Mar.	31 Bal.	82,500

Wages Expense

Mar.	31 Bal.	35,750	Mar.	31 Clos.	36,350
	31 Adj.	600			
	31 Adj. Bal.	36,350			

Rent Expense

Mar.	31 Bal.	18,000	Mar.	31 Clos.	18,000

Utilities Expense

Mar.	31 Bal.	6,800	Mar.	31 Clos.	6,800

Depreciation Expense

Mar.	31 Adj.	2,900	Mar.	31 Clos.	2,900

Laundry Supplies Expense

Mar.	31 Adj.	2,800	Mar.	31 Clos.	2,800

Insurance Expense

Mar.	31 Adj.	2,000	Mar.	31 Clos.	2,000

Miscellaneous Expense

Mar.	31 Bal.	1,350	Mar.	31 Clos.	1,350

Prob. 4–3B Continued

2. Optional (Appendix)

BEST LAUNDRY
End-of-Period Spreadsheet (Work Sheet)
For the Year Ended March 31, 2008

	Unadjusted Trial Balance		Adjustments		Adjusted Trial Balance		Income Statement		Balance Sheet		
Account Title	Dr.	Cr.	Dr.	Cr.	Dr.	Cr.	Dr.	Cr.	Dr.	Cr.	
1 Cash	1,450				1,450				1,450		1
2 Laundry Supplies	3,750			(c) 2,800	950				950		2
3 Prepaid Insurance	2,400			(d) 2,000	400				400		3
4 Laundry Equipment	54,500				54,500				54,500		4
5 Accum. Depreciation		20,500		(b) 2,900		23,400				23,400	5
6 Accounts Payable		3,100				3,100				3,100	6
7 Ryan Boyle, Capital		18,900				18,900				18,900	7
8 Ryan Boyle, Drawing	1,000				1,000				1,000		8
9 Laundry Revenue		82,500				82,500		82,500			9
10 Wages Expense	35,750		(a) 600		36,350		36,350				10
11 Rent Expense	18,000				18,000		18,000				11
12 Utilities Expense	6,800				6,800		6,800				12
13 Misc. Expense	1,350				1,350		1,350				13
14	125,000	125,000									14
15 Wages Payable				(a) 600		600				600	15
16 Depreciation Expense			(b) 2,900		2,900		2,900				16
17 Laundry Supp. Expense			(c) 2,800		2,800		2,800				17
18 Insurance Expense			(d) 2,000		2,000		2,000				18
19			8,300	8,300	128,500	128,500	70,200	82,500	58,300	46,000	19
20 Net income							12,300			12,300	20
21							82,500	82,500	58,300	58,300	21

Prob. 4–3B Continued

3.

Adjusting Entries

2008

Mar. 31	Wages Expense..	600	
	Wages Payable..		600
	Accrued wages.		
31	Depreciation Expense	2,900	
	Accumulated Depreciation...........................		2,900
	Equipment depreciation.		
31	Laundry Supplies Expense	2,800	
	Laundry Supplies..		2,800
	Supplies used ($3,750 – $950).		
31	Insurance Expense	2,000	
	Prepaid Insurance		2,000
	Insurance expired.		

4.

BEST LAUNDRY
Adjusted Trial Balance
March 31, 2008

	Debit Balances	Credit Balances
Cash..	1,450	
Laundry Supplies..	950	
Prepaid Insurance..	400	
Laundry Equipment	54,500	
Accumulated Depreciation..		23,400
Accounts Payable		3,100
Wages Payable...		600
Ryan Boyle, Capital		18,900
Ryan Boyle, Drawing	1,000	
Laundry Revenue...		82,500
Wages Expense	36,350	
Rent Expense	18,000	
Utilities Expense	6,800	
Depreciation Expense	2,900	
Laundry Supplies Expense	2,800	
Insurance Expense..	2,000	
Miscellaneous Expense	1,350	
	128,500	128,500

Prob. 4–3B Continued

5.

BEST LAUNDRY
Income Statement
For the Year Ended March 31, 2008

Laundry revenue		$82,500
Expenses:		
Wages expense	$36,350	
Rent expense	18,000	
Utilities expense	6,800	
Depreciation expense	2,900	
Laundry supplies expense	2,800	
Insurance expense	2,000	
Miscellaneous expense	1,350	
Total expenses		70,200
Net income		$12,300

BEST LAUNDRY
Statement of Owner's Equity
For the Year Ended March 31, 2008

Ryan Boyle, capital, April 1, 2007		$18,900
Net income for the year	$12,300	
Less withdrawals	1,000	
Increase in owner's equity		11,300
Ryan Boyle, capital, March 31, 2008		$30,200

BEST LAUNDRY
Balance Sheet
March 31, 2008

Assets			Liabilities		
Current assets:			Current liabilities:		
Cash	$ 1,450		Accounts payable	$3,100	
Laundry supplies	950		Wages payable	600	
Prepaid insurance	400		Total liabilities		$ 3,700
Total current assets		$ 2,800			
Property, plant, and equipment:					
			Owner's Equity		
Laundry equipment	$54,500		Ryan Boyle, capital		30,200
Less accum. depr.	23,400				
Total property, plant, and equipment		31,100	Total liabilities and		
Total assets		$33,900	owner's equity		$33,900

239

Prob. 4–3B Concluded

6.

Closing Entries

2008

			Debit	Credit
Mar.	31	Laundry Revenue	82,500	
		Income Summary		82,500
	31	Income Summary	70,200	
		Wages Expense		36,350
		Rent Expense		18,000
		Utilities Expense		6,800
		Miscellaneous Expense		1,350
		Depreciation Expense		2,900
		Laundry Supplies Expense		2,800
		Insurance Expense		2,000
	31	Income Summary	12,300	
		Ryan Boyle, Capital		12,300
	31	Ryan Boyle, Capital	1,000	
		Ryan Boyle, Drawing		1,000

7.

BEST LAUNDRY
Post-Closing Trial Balance
March 31, 2008

	Debit Balances	Credit Balances
Cash	1,450	
Laundry Supplies	950	
Prepaid Insurance	400	
Laundry Equipment	54,500	
Accumulated Depreciation		23,400
Accounts Payable		3,100
Wages Payable		600
Ryan Boyle, Capital		30,200
	57,300	57,300

Prob. 4-4B

1. Optional (Appendix)

WAINSCOT SERVICES CO.
End-of-Period Spreadsheet (Work Sheet)
For the Month Ended March 31, 2008

	Unadjusted Trial Balance		Adjustments		Adjusted Trial Balance		Income Statement		Balance Sheet	
Account Title	Dr.	Cr.	Dr.	Cr.	Dr.	Cr.	Dr.	Cr.	Dr.	Cr.
1 Cash	3,509				3,509				3,509	
2 Accounts Receivable	6,550		(a) 2,000		8,550				8,550	
3 Supplies	1,647			(b) 1,247	400				400	
4 Prepaid Insurance	1,800			(c) 150	1,650				1,650	
5 Land	30,000				30,000				30,000	
6 Building	57,500				57,500				57,500	
7 Acc. Depr.—Building		23,400		(d) 625		24,025				24,025
8 Equipment	30,000				30,000				30,000	
9 Acc. Depr.—Equipment		10,200		(e) 200		10,400				10,400
10 Accounts Payable		5,141				5,141				5,141
11 Unearned Rent		2,200	(f) 400			1,800				1,800
12 So Young Lee, Capital		67,825				67,825				67,825
13 So Young Lee, Drawing	2,000				2,000				2,000	
14 Service Revenue		46,984		(a) 2,000		48,984		48,984		
15 Wages Expense	14,799		(g) 600		15,399		15,399			
16 Rent Expense	3,910				3,910		3,910			
17 Utilities Expense	1,728				1,728		1,728			
18 Misc. Expense	2,307				2,307		2,307			
19	155,750	155,750								
20 Supplies Expense			(b) 1,247		1,247		1,247			
21 Insurance Expense			(c) 150		150		150			
22 Depr. Exp.—Building			(d) 625		625		625			
23 Depr. Exp.—Equipment			(e) 200		200		200			
24 Rent Revenue				(f) 400		400		400		
25 Wages Payable				(g) 600		600				600
26			5,222	5,222	159,175	159,175	25,566	49,384	133,609	109,791
27 Net income							23,818			23,818
28							49,384	49,384	133,609	133,609

Prob. 4–4B   Continued

2.

Date		Post. Ref.	Debit	Credit
2008	**Adjusting Entries**			
Mar. 31	Accounts Receivable...................................	12	2,000	
	Service Revenue	41		2,000
	Accrued revenue.			
31	Supplies Expense.......................................	52	1,247	
	Supplies..	13		1,247
	Supplies used ($1,647 – $400).			
31	Insurance Expense.....................................	57	150	
	Prepaid Insurance...............................	14		150
	Insurance expired.			
31	Depreciation Expense—Building	54	625	
	Accumulated Depreciation—Building..	17		625
	Building depreciation.			
31	Depreciation Expense—Equipment	56	200	
	Accum. Depreciation—Equipment	19		200
	Equipment depreciation.			
31	Unearned Rent..	23	400	
	Rent Revenue	42		400
	Rent revenue earned ($2,200 – $1,800).			
31	Wages Expense	51	600	
	Wages Payable.....................................	22		600
	Accrued wages.			

3.

WAINSCOT SERVICES CO.
Adjusted Trial Balance
March 31, 2008

	Debit Balances	Credit Balances
Cash	3,509	
Accounts Receivable	8,550	
Supplies	400	
Prepaid Insurance	1,650	
Land	30,000	
Building	57,500	
Accumulated Depreciation—Building		24,025
Equipment	30,000	
Accumulated Depreciation—Equipment		10,400
Accounts Payable		5,141
Wages Payable		600
Unearned Rent		1,800
So Young Lee, Capital		67,825
So Young Lee, Drawing	2,000	
Service Revenue		48,984
Rent Revenue		400
Wages Expense	15,399	
Supplies Expense	1,247	
Rent Expense	3,910	
Depreciation Expense—Building	625	
Utilities Expense	1,728	
Depreciation Expense—Equipment	200	
Insurance Expense	150	
Miscellaneous Expense	2,307	
	159,175	159,175

4.

WAINSCOT SERVICES CO.
Income Statement
For the Month Ended March 31, 2008

Revenues:		
Service revenue	$48,984	
Rent revenue	400	
Total revenues		$49,384
Expenses:		
Wages expense	$15,399	
Rent expense	3,910	
Utilities expense	1,728	
Supplies expense	1,247	
Depreciation expense—building	625	
Depreciation expense—equipment	200	
Insurance expense	150	
Miscellaneous expense	2,307	
Total expenses		25,566
Net income		$23,818

WAINSCOT SERVICES CO.
Statement of Owner's Equity
For the Month Ended March 31, 2008

So Young Lee, capital, March 1, 2008		$62,825
Additional investment during the month		5,000
Total		$67,825
Net income for the month	$23,818	
Less withdrawals	2,000	
Increase in owner's equity		21,818
So Young Lee, capital, March 31, 2008		$89,643

WAINSCOT SERVICES CO.
Balance Sheet
March 31, 2008

Assets		
Current assets:		
Cash	$ 3,509	
Accounts receivable	8,550	
Supplies	400	
Prepaid insurance	1,650	
Total current assets		$14,109
Property, plant, and equipment:		
Land		$30,000
Building	$57,500	
Less accum. depreciation	24,025	33,475
Equipment	$30,000	
Less accum. depreciation	10,400	19,600
Total property, plant, and equipment		83,075
Total assets		$97,184

Liabilities		
Current liabilities:		
Accounts payable	$5,141	
Wages payable	600	
Unearned rent	1,800	
Total liabilities		$ 7,541
Owner's Equity		
So Young Lee, capital		89,643
Total liabilities and owner's equity		$97,184

Prob. 4–4B   Continued

5.

Date		Post. Ref.	Debit	Credit
2008	**Closing Entries**			
Mar. 31	Service Revenue..	41	48,984	
	Rent Revenue..	42	400	
	Income Summary	33		49,384
31	Income Summary..	33	25,566	
	Wages Expense...................................	51		15,399
	Rent Expense	53		3,910
	Utilities Expense	55		1,728
	Miscellaneous Expense.........................	59		2,307
	Supplies Expense	52		1,247
	Insurance Expense	57		150
	Depreciation Expense—Building..........	54		625
	Depreciation Expense—Equipment	56		200
31	Income Summary..	33	23,818	
	So Young Lee, Capital	31		23,818
31	So Young Lee, Capital.................................	31	2,000	
	So Young Lee, Drawing.........................	32		2,000

Prob. 4–4B Continued

2. and 5.

Cash

Date		Item	Post. Ref.	Dr.	Cr.	Balance Dr.	Balance Cr.
2008							
Mar.	1	Balance..................	✓	....	....	1,259	....
	3	....	23	....	910	349	....
	4	....	23	5,000	....	5,349	....
	5	....	23	....	86	5,263	....
	7	....	23	800	....	6,063	....
	8	....	23	400	....	6,463	....
	8	....	23	....	2,584	3,879	....
	8	....	23	1,695	....	5,574	....
	10	....	24	....	510	5,064	....
	12	....	24	....	2,319	2,745	....
	15	....	24	2,718	....	5,463	....
	16	....	24	....	1,000	4,463	....
	19	....	24	....	2,135	2,328	....
	22	....	24	....	370	1,958	....
	22	....	24	3,992	....	5,950	....
	24	....	25	....	527	5,423	....
	26	....	25	....	2,480	2,943	....
	30	....	25	....	156	2,787	....
	30	....	25	....	26	2,761	....
	31	....	25	....	1,000	1,761	....
	31	....	25	2,029	....	3,790	....
	31	....	25	....	281	3,509	....

Accounts Receivable

Date		Item	Post. Ref.	Dr.	Cr.	Balance Dr.	Balance Cr.
2008							
Mar.	1	Balance..................	✓	....	....	6,200	....
	7	....	23	....	800	5,400	....
	8	....	23	....	400	5,000	....
	22	....	24	1,550	....	6,550	....
	31	Adjusting	26	2,000	....	8,550	....

Prob. 4–4B   Continued

Supplies 13

Date	Item	Post. Ref.	Dr.	Cr.	Balance Dr.	Balance Cr.
2008						
Mar. 1	Balance...............	✓	....	....	610	....
10	....	24	510	....	1,120	....
27	....	25	527	....	1,647	....
31	Adjusting	26	....	1,247	400	....

Prepaid Insurance 14

Date	Item	Post. Ref.	Dr.	Cr.	Balance Dr.	Balance Cr.
2008						
Mar. 1	Balance...............	✓	....	....	420	....
22	....	24	1,380	....	1,800	....
31	Adjusting	26	....	150	1,650	....

Land 15

Date	Item	Post. Ref.	Dr.	Cr.	Balance Dr.	Balance Cr.
2008						
Mar. 1	Balance...............	✓	....	....	30,000	....

Building 16

Date	Item	Post. Ref.	Dr.	Cr.	Balance Dr.	Balance Cr.
2008						
Mar. 1	Balance...............	✓	....	....	57,500	....

Accumulated Depreciation—Building 17

Date	Item	Post. Ref.	Dr.	Cr.	Balance Dr.	Balance Cr.
2008						
Mar. 1	Balance...............	✓	....	....	....	23,400
31	Adjusting	26	....	625	....	24,025

Equipment 18

Date	Item	Post. Ref.	Dr.	Cr.	Balance Dr.	Balance Cr.
2008						
Mar. 1	Balance...............	✓	....	....	29,250	....
3	....	23	750	....	30,000	....

Accumulated Depreciation—Equipment 19

Date	Item	Post. Ref.	Dr.	Cr.	Balance Dr.	Balance Cr.
2008						
Mar. 1	Balance...............	✓	....	....	....	10,200
31	Adjusting	26	....	200	....	10,400

Prob. 4–4B Continued

Accounts Payable
21

Date	Item	Post. Ref.	Dr.	Cr.	Balance Dr.	Balance Cr.
2008						
Mar. 1	Balance...............	✓	....	....	....	8,625
3	....	23	....	750	....	9,375
8	....	23	2,584	....	....	6,791
19	....	24	2,135	....	....	4,656
31	....	25	....	485	....	5,141

Wages Payable
22

Date	Item	Post. Ref.	Dr.	Cr.	Balance Dr.	Balance Cr.
2008						
Mar. 31	Adjusting	26	....	600	....	600

Unearned Rent
23

Date	Item	Post. Ref.	Dr.	Cr.	Balance Dr.	Balance Cr.
2008						
Mar. 1	Balance...............	✓	....	....	....	2,200
31	Adjusting	26	400	....	....	1,800

So Young Lee, Capital
31

Date	Item	Post. Ref.	Dr.	Cr.	Balance Dr.	Balance Cr.
2008						
Mar. 1	Balance...............	✓	....	....	....	62,825
4	....	23	....	5,000	....	67,825
31	Closing	27	....	23,818	....	91,643
31	Closing	27	2,000	....	....	89,643

So Young Lee, Drawing
32

Date	Item	Post. Ref.	Dr.	Cr.	Balance Dr.	Balance Cr.
2008						
Mar. 16	....	24	1,000	....	1,000	....
31	....	25	1,000	....	2,000	....
31	Closing	27	....	2,000	—	—

Income Summary
33

Date	Item	Post. Ref.	Dr.	Cr.	Balance Dr.	Balance Cr.
2008						
Mar. 31	Closing	27	....	49,384	....	49,384
31	Closing	27	25,566	....	....	23,818
31	Closing	27	23,818	....	—	—

Prob. 4–4B Continued

Service Revenue 41

Date	Item	Post. Ref.	Dr.	Cr.	Balance Dr.	Balance Cr.
2008						
Mar. 8	....	23	....	14,695	....	14,695
15	....	24	....	7,718	....	22,413
22	....	24	....	8,992	....	31,405
22	....	24	....	7,550	....	38,955
31	....	25	....	8,029	....	46,984
31	Adjusting	26	....	2,000	....	48,984
31	Closing	27	48,984	....	—	—

Rent Revenue 42

Date	Item	Post. Ref.	Dr.	Cr.	Balance Dr.	Balance Cr.
2008						
Mar. 31	Adjusting	26	....	400	....	400
31	Closing	27	400	....	—	—

Wages Expense 51

Date	Item	Post. Ref.	Dr.	Cr.	Balance Dr.	Balance Cr.
2008						
Mar. 12	....	24	7,319	....	7,319	....
26	....	25	7,480	....	14,799	....
31	Adjusting	26	600	....	15,399	....
31	Closing	27	....	15,399	—	—

Supplies Expense 52

Date	Item	Post. Ref.	Dr.	Cr.	Balance Dr.	Balance Cr.
2008						
Mar. 31	Adjusting	26	1,247	....	1,247	....
31	Closing	27	....	1,247	—	—

Rent Expense 53

Date	Item	Post. Ref.	Dr.	Cr.	Balance Dr.	Balance Cr.
2008						
Mar. 3	....	23	3,910	....	3,910	....
31	Closing	27	....	3,910	—	—

Prob. 4–4B   Continued

Depreciation Expense—Building   54

Date		Item	Post. Ref.	Dr.	Cr.	Balance	
						Dr.	Cr.
2008							
Mar.	31	Adjusting	26	625	....	625	....
	31	Closing	27	....	625	—	—

Utilities Expense   55

Date		Item	Post. Ref.	Dr.	Cr.	Balance	
						Dr.	Cr.
2008							
Mar.	5	....	24	586	....	586	....
	30	....	25	456	....	1,042	....
	31	....	25	686	....	1,728	....
	31	Closing	27	....	1,728	—	—

Depreciation Expense—Equipment   56

Date		Item	Post. Ref.	Dr.	Cr.	Balance	
						Dr.	Cr.
2008							
Mar.	31	Adjusting	26	200	....	200	....
	31	Closing	27	....	200	—	—

Insurance Expense   57

Date		Item	Post. Ref.	Dr.	Cr.	Balance	
						Dr.	Cr.
2008							
Mar.	31	Adjusting	26	150	....	150	....
	31	Closing	27	....	150	—	—

Miscellaneous Expense   59

Date		Item	Post. Ref.	Dr.	Cr.	Balance	
						Dr.	Cr.
2008							
Mar.	30	....	25	1,026	....	1,026	....
	31	....	25	1,281	....	2,307	....
	31	Closing	27	....	2,307	—	—

6.

WAINSCOT SERVICES CO.
Post-Closing Trial Balance
March 31, 2008

	Debit Balances	Credit Balances
Cash	3,509	
Accounts Receivable	8,550	
Supplies	400	
Prepaid Insurance	1,650	
Land	30,000	
Building	57,500	
Accumulated Depreciation—Building		24,025
Equipment	30,000	
Accumulated Depreciation—Equipment		10,400
Accounts Payable		5,141
Wages Payable		600
Unearned Rent		1,800
So Young Lee, Capital		89,643
	131,609	131,609

Prob. 4–5B

1., 3., and 6.

Cash   11

Date	Item	Post. Ref.	Dr.	Cr.	Balance Dr.	Balance Cr.
2008						
Dec. 31	Balance..................	✓	....	....	2,825	....

Supplies   13

Date	Item	Post. Ref.	Dr.	Cr.	Balance Dr.	Balance Cr.
2008						
Dec. 31	Balance..................	✓	....	....	10,820	....
31	Adjusting	26	....	4,320	6,500	....

Prepaid Insurance   14

Date	Item	Post. Ref.	Dr.	Cr.	Balance Dr.	Balance Cr.
2008						
Dec. 31	Balance..................	✓	....	....	7,500	....
31	Adjusting	26	....	2,500	5,000	....

Equipment   16

Date	Item	Post. Ref.	Dr.	Cr.	Balance Dr.	Balance Cr.
2008						
Dec. 31	Balance..................	✓	....	....	54,200	....

Accumulated Depreciation—Equipment   17

Date	Item	Post. Ref.	Dr.	Cr.	Balance Dr.	Balance Cr.
2008						
Dec. 31	Balance..................	✓	....	....	....	12,050
31	Adjusting	26	....	4,800	....	16,850

Trucks   18

Date	Item	Post. Ref.	Dr.	Cr.	Balance Dr.	Balance Cr.
2008						
Dec. 31	Balance..................	✓	....	....	50,000	....

Accumulated Depreciation—Trucks   19

Date	Item	Post. Ref.	Dr.	Cr.	Balance Dr.	Balance Cr.
2008						
Dec. 31	Balance..................	✓	....	....	....	27,100
31	Adjusting	26	....	3,500	....	30,600

Prob. 4–5B Continued

Accounts Payable 21

Date	Item	Post. Ref.	Dr.	Cr.	Balance Dr.	Balance Cr.
2008 Dec. 31	Balance..................	✓	....	....	....	12,015

Wages Payable 22

Date	Item	Post. Ref.	Dr.	Cr.	Balance Dr.	Balance Cr.
2008 Dec. 31	Adjusting	26	....	1,000	....	1,000

Lee Mendoza, Capital 31

Date	Item	Post. Ref.	Dr.	Cr.	Balance Dr.	Balance Cr.
2008 Dec. 31	Balance..................	✓	....	....	....	32,885
31	Closing	27	....	30,175	....	63,060
31	Closing	27	5,000	....	....	58,060

Lee Mendoza, Drawing 32

Date	Item	Post. Ref.	Dr.	Cr.	Balance Dr.	Balance Cr.
2008 Dec. 31	Balance..................	✓	....	....	5,000	....
31	Closing	27	....	5,000	—	—

Income Summary 33

Date	Item	Post. Ref.	Dr.	Cr.	Balance Dr.	Balance Cr.
2008 Dec. 31	Closing	27	....	90,950	....	90,950
31	Closing	27	60,775	....	....	30,175
31	Closing	27	30,175	....	—	—

Service Revenue 41

Date	Item	Post. Ref.	Dr.	Cr.	Balance Dr.	Balance Cr.
2008 Dec. 31	Balance..................	✓	....	....	....	90,950
31	Closing	27	90,950	....	—	—

Wages Expense 51

Date	Item	Post. Ref.	Dr.	Cr.	Balance Dr.	Balance Cr.
2008 Dec. 31	Balance..................	✓	....	....	28,010	....
31	Adjusting	26	1,000	....	29,010	....
31	Closing	27	....	29,010	—	—

Prob. 4–5B   Continued

Supplies Expense   52

Date	Item	Post. Ref.	Dr.	Cr.	Balance Dr.	Balance Cr.
2008						
Dec. 31	Adjusting	26	4,320	....	4,320	....
31	Closing	27	....	4,320	—	—

Rent Expense   53

Date	Item	Post. Ref.	Dr.	Cr.	Balance Dr.	Balance Cr.
2008						
Dec. 31	Balance...................	✓	....	....	8,100	....
31	Closing	27	....	8,100	—	—

Depreciation Expense—Equipment   54

Date	Item	Post. Ref.	Dr.	Cr.	Balance Dr.	Balance Cr.
2008						
Dec. 31	Adjusting	26	4,800	....	4,800	....
31	Closing	27	....	4,800	—	—

Truck Expense   55

Date	Item	Post. Ref.	Dr.	Cr.	Balance Dr.	Balance Cr.
2008						
Dec. 31	Balance...................	✓	....	....	6,350	....
31	Closing	27	....	6,350	—	—

Depreciation Expense—Trucks   56

Date	Item	Post. Ref.	Dr.	Cr.	Balance Dr.	Balance Cr.
2008						
Dec. 31	Adjusting	26	3,500	....	3,500	....
31	Closing	27	....	3,500	—	—

Insurance Expense   57

Date	Item	Post. Ref.	Dr.	Cr.	Balance Dr.	Balance Cr.
2008						
Dec. 31	Adjusting	26	2,500	....	2,500	....
31	Closing	27	....	2,500	—	—

Miscellaneous Expense   59

Date	Item	Post. Ref.	Dr.	Cr.	Balance Dr.	Balance Cr.
2008						
Dec. 31	Balance...................	✓	....	....	2,195	....
31	Closing	27	....	2,195	—	—

Prob. 4–5B Continued
2. Optional (Appendix)

RELIABLE REPAIRS
End-of-Period Spreadsheet (Work Sheet)
For the Year Ended December 31, 2008

Account Title	Unadjusted Trial Balance Dr.	Cr.	Adjustments Dr.	Cr.	Adjusted Trial Balance Dr.	Cr.	Income Statement Dr.	Cr.	Balance Sheet Dr.	Cr.
1 Cash	2,825				2,825				2,825	
2 Supplies	10,820			(a) 4,320	6,500				6,500	
3 Prepaid Insurance	7,500			(b) 2,500	5,000				5,000	
4 Equipment	54,200				54,200				54,200	
5 Accum. Depr.—Equip.		12,050		(c) 4,800		16,850				16,850
6 Trucks	50,000				50,000				50,000	
7 Accum. Depr.—Trucks		27,100		(d) 3,500		30,600				30,600
8 Accounts Payable		12,015				12,015				12,015
9 Lee Mendoza, Capital		32,885				32,885				32,885
10 Lee Mendoza, Drawing	5,000				5,000				5,000	
11 Service Revenue		90,950				90,950		90,950		
12 Wages Expense	28,010		(e) 1,000		29,010		29,010			
13 Rent Expense	8,100				8,100		8,100			
14 Truck Expense	6,350				6,350		6,350			
15 Misc. Expense	2,195				2,195		2,195			
16	175,000	175,000								
17 Supplies Expense			(a) 4,320		4,320		4,320			
18 Insurance Expense			(b) 2,500		2,500		2,500			
19 Depr. Exp.—Equipment			(c) 4,800		4,800		4,800			
20 Depr. Exp.—Trucks			(d) 3,500		3,500		3,500			
21 Wages Payable				(e) 1,000		1,000				1,000
22			16,120	16,120	184,300	184,300	60,775	90,950	123,525	93,350
23 Net income							30,175			30,175
24							90,950	90,950	123,525	123,525

Prob. 4–5B   Continued

3.

Date		Post. Ref.	Debit	Credit
	Adjusting Entries			
2008				
Dec. 31	Supplies Expense...............................	52	4,320	
	Supplies..................................	13		4,320
	Supplies used ($10,820 – $6,500).			
31	Insurance Expense............................	57	2,500	
	Prepaid Insurance..............................	14		2,500
	Insurance expired.			
31	Depreciation Expense—Equipment...........	54	4,800	
	Accumulated Depreciation—Equip.	17		4,800
	Equipment depreciation.			
31	Depreciation Expense—Trucks..................	56	3,500	
	Accumulated Depreciation—Trucks.....	19		3,500
	Truck depreciation.			
31	Wages Expense	51	1,000	
	Wages Payable.......................................	22		1,000
	Accrued wages.			

Prob. 4–5B Continued

4.

RELIABLE REPAIRS
Adjusted Trial Balance
December 31, 2008

	Debit Balances	Credit Balances
Cash	2,825	
Supplies	6,500	
Prepaid Insurance	5,000	
Equipment	54,200	
Accumulated Depreciation—Equipment		16,850
Trucks	50,000	
Accumulated Depreciation—Trucks		30,600
Accounts Payable		12,015
Wages Payable		1,000
Lee Mendoza, Capital		32,885
Lee Mendoza, Drawing	5,000	
Service Revenue		90,950
Wages Expense	29,010	
Supplies Expense	4,320	
Rent Expense	8,100	
Depreciation Expense—Equipment	4,800	
Truck Expense	6,350	
Depreciation Expense—Trucks	3,500	
Insurance Expense	2,500	
Miscellaneous Expense	2,195	
	184,300	184,300

5.

RELIABLE REPAIRS
Income Statement
For the Year Ended December 31, 2008

Service revenue		$90,950
Expenses:		
Wages expense..	$29,010	
Rent expense	8,100	
Truck expense	6,350	
Depreciation expense—equipment...........................	4,800	
Supplies expense	4,320	
Depreciation expense—trucks	3,500	
Insurance expense	2,500	
Miscellaneous expense...	2,195	
Total expenses		60,775
Net income		$30,175

RELIABLE REPAIRS
Statement of Owner's Equity
For the Year Ended December 31, 2008

Lee Mendoza, capital, January 1, 2008		$32,885
Net income for the year...	$30,175	
Less withdrawals..	5,000	
Increase in owner's equity..		25,175
Lee Mendoza, capital, December 31, 2008.........................		$58,060

Prob. 4–5B   Continued

RELIABLE REPAIRS
Balance Sheet
December 31, 2008

Assets

Current assets:

Cash	$ 2,825	
Supplies	6,500	
Prepaid insurance	5,000	
Total current assets		$14,325

Property, plant, and equipment:

Equipment	$54,200		
Less accumulated depr.	16,850	$37,350	
Trucks	$50,000		
Less accumulated depr.	30,600	19,400	
Total property, plant, and equipment			56,750
Total assets			$71,075

Liabilities

Current liabilities:

Accounts payable	$12,015	
Wages payable	1,000	
Total liabilities		$13,015

Owner's Equity

Lee Mendoza, capital	58,060
Total liabilities and owner's equity	$71,075

Prob. 4–5B   Concluded

6.

Date		Post. Ref.	Debit	Credit
	Closing Entries			
2008				
Dec. 31	Service Revenue	41	90,950	
	Income Summary	33		90,950
31	Income Summary	33	60,775	
	Wages Expense	51		29,010
	Supplies Expense	52		4,320
	Rent Expense	53		8,100
	Depreciation Expense—Equipment	54		4,800
	Truck Expense	55		6,350
	Depreciation Expense—Trucks	56		3,500
	Insurance Expense	57		2,500
	Miscellaneous Expense	59		2,195
31	Income Summary	33	30,175	
	Lee Mendoza, Capital	31		30,175
31	Lee Mendoza, Capital	31	5,000	
	Lee Mendoza, Drawing	32		5,000

7.

RELIABLE REPAIRS
Post-Closing Trial Balance
December 31, 2008

	Debit Balances	Credit Balances
Cash	2,825	
Supplies	6,500	
Prepaid Insurance	5,000	
Equipment	54,200	
Accumulated Depreciation—Equipment		16,850
Trucks	50,000	
Accumulated Depreciation—Trucks		30,600
Accounts Payable		12,015
Wages Payable		1,000
Lee Mendoza, Capital		58,060
	118,525	118,525

Prob. 4–6B

1. and 2.   JOURNAL   Pages 1 and 2

Date		Description	Post. Ref.	Debit	Credit
2008					
June	1	Cash..	11	26,200	
		Accounts Receivable....................................	12	6,000	
		Supplies...	14	2,800	
		Office Equipment..	18	25,000	
		Derrick Epstein, Capital........................	31		60,000
	1	Prepaid Rent	15	5,250	
		Cash...	11		5,250
	2	Prepaid Insurance	16	2,100	
		Cash...	11		2,100
	4	Cash..	11	2,700	
		Unearned Fees	23		2,700
	5	Office Equipment..	18	5,000	
		Accounts Payable	21		5,000
	6	Cash..	11	3,000	
		Accounts Receivable	12		3,000
	10	Miscellaneous Expense	59	200	
		Cash...	11		200
	12	Accounts Payable...	21	1,000	
		Cash...	11		1,000
	12	Accounts Receivable....................................	12	5,100	
		Fees Earned..	41		5,100
	14	Salary Expense	51	800	
		Cash...	11		800
	17	Cash..	11	3,500	
		Fees Earned..	41		3,500
	18	Supplies..	14	750	
		Cash...	11		750
	20	Accounts Receivable....................................	12	1,100	
		Fees Earned..	41		1,100
	24	Cash..	11	4,150	
		Fees Earned..	41		4,150

Prob. 4–6B   Continued

JOURNAL   Pages 1 and 2

Date	Description	Post. Ref.	Debit	Credit
2008				
June 26	Cash..	11	4,900	
	Accounts Receivable	12		4,900
27	Salary Expense	51	800	
	Cash	11		800
29	Miscellaneous Expense	59	150	
	Cash	11		150
30	Miscellaneous Expense	59	400	
	Cash	11		400
30	Cash..	11	1,500	
	Fees Earned..	41		1,500
30	Accounts Receivable................................	12	1,000	
	Fees Earned..	41		1,000
30	Derrick Epstein, Drawing	32	8,000	
	Cash	11		8,000

Prob. 4–6B Continued

2., 6., and 9.

Cash   11

Date	Item	Post. Ref.	Dr.	Cr.	Balance Dr.	Balance Cr.
2008						
June 1	....	1	26,200	....	26,200	....
1	....	1	....	5,250	20,950	....
2	....	1	....	2,100	18,850	....
4	....	1	2,700	....	21,550	....
6	....	1	3,000	....	24,550	....
10	....	1	....	200	24,350	....
12	....	1	....	1,000	23,350	....
14	....	1	....	800	22,550	....
17	....	2	3,500	....	26,050	....
18	....	2	....	750	25,300	....
24	....	2	4,150	....	29,450	....
26	....	2	4,900	....	34,350	....
27	....	2	....	800	33,550	....
29	....	2	....	150	33,400	....
30	....	2	....	400	33,000	....
30	....	2	1,500	....	34,500	....
30	....	2	....	8,000	26,500	....

Accounts Receivable   12

Date	Item	Post. Ref.	Dr.	Cr.	Balance Dr.	Balance Cr.
2008						
June 1	....	1	6,000	....	6,000	....
6	....	1	....	3,000	3,000	....
12	....	1	5,100	....	8,100	....
20	....	2	1,100	....	9,200	....
26	....	2	....	4,900	4,300	....
30	....	2	1,000	....	5,300	....

Supplies   14

Date	Item	Post. Ref.	Dr.	Cr.	Balance Dr.	Balance Cr.
2008						
June 1	....	1	2,800	....	2,800	....
18	....	2	750	....	3,550	....
30	Adjusting	3	....	1,550	2,000	....

Prob. 4–6B Continued

Prepaid Rent   15

Date	Item	Post. Ref.	Dr.	Cr.	Balance Dr.	Balance Cr.
2008						
June 1	....	1	5,250	....	5,250	....
30	Adjusting	3	....	1,500	3,750	....

Prepaid Insurance   16

Date	Item	Post. Ref.	Dr.	Cr.	Balance Dr.	Balance Cr.
2008						
June 2	....	1	2,100	....	2,100	....
30	Adjusting	3	....	175	1,925	....

Office Equipment   18

Date	Item	Post. Ref.	Dr.	Cr.	Balance Dr.	Balance Cr.
2008						
June 1	....	1	25,000	....	25,000	....
5	....	1	5,000	....	30,000	....

Accumulated Depreciation   19

Date	Item	Post. Ref.	Dr.	Cr.	Balance Dr.	Balance Cr.
2008						
June 30	Adjusting	3	....	500	....	500

Accounts Payable   21

Date	Item	Post. Ref.	Dr.	Cr.	Balance Dr.	Balance Cr.
2008						
June 5	....	1	....	5,000	....	5,000
12	....	1	1,000	....	....	4,000

Salaries Payable   22

Date	Item	Post. Ref.	Dr.	Cr.	Balance Dr.	Balance Cr.
2008						
June 30	Adjusting	3	....	120	....	120

Unearned Fees   23

Date	Item	Post. Ref.	Dr.	Cr.	Balance Dr.	Balance Cr.
2008						
June 4	....	1	....	2,700	....	2,700
30	Adjusting	3	825	....	....	1,875

Prob. 4–6B Continued

Derrick Epstein, Capital 31

Date	Item	Post. Ref.	Dr.	Cr.	Balance Dr.	Balance Cr.
2008						
June 1	....	1	....	60,000	....	60,000
30	Closing	4	....	10,980	....	70,980
30	Closing	4	8,000	....	....	62,980

Derrick Epstein, Drawing 32

Date	Item	Post. Ref.	Dr.	Cr.	Balance Dr.	Balance Cr.
2008						
June 30	....	2	8,000	....	8,000	....
30	Closing	4	....	8,000	—	—

Income Summary 33

Date	Item	Post. Ref.	Dr.	Cr.	Balance Dr.	Balance Cr.
2008						
June 30	Closing	4	....	17,175	....	17,175
30	Closing	4	6,195	....	....	10,980
30	Closing	4	10,980	....	—	—

Fees Earned 41

Date	Item	Post. Ref.	Dr.	Cr.	Balance Dr.	Balance Cr.
2008						
June 12	....	1	....	5,100	....	5,100
17	....	2	....	3,500	....	8,600
20	....	2	....	1,100	....	9,700
24	....	2	....	4,150	....	13,850
30	....	2	....	1,500	....	15,350
30	....	2	....	1,000	....	16,350
30	Adjusting	3	....	825	....	17,175
30	Closing	4	17,175	....	—	—

Salary Expense 51

Date	Item	Post. Ref.	Dr.	Cr.	Balance Dr.	Balance Cr.
2008						
June 14	....	1	800	....	800	....
27	....	2	800	....	1,600	....
30	Adjusting	3	120	....	1,720	....
30	Closing	4	....	1,720	—	—

Prob. 4–6B   Continued

Rent Expense 52

Date	Item	Post. Ref.	Dr.	Cr.	Balance Dr.	Balance Cr.
2008						
June 30	Adjusting	3	1,500	....	1,500	....
30	Closing	4	....	1,500	—	—

Supplies Expense 53

Date	Item	Post. Ref.	Dr.	Cr.	Balance Dr.	Balance Cr.
2008						
June 30	Adjusting	3	1,550	....	1,550	....
30	Closing	4	....	1,550	—	—

Depreciation Expense 54

Date	Item	Post. Ref.	Dr.	Cr.	Balance Dr.	Balance Cr.
2008						
June 30	Adjusting	3	500	....	500	....
30	Closing	4	....	500	—	—

Insurance Expense 55

Date	Item	Post. Ref.	Dr.	Cr.	Balance Dr.	Balance Cr.
2008						
June 30	Adjusting	3	175	....	175	....
30	Closing	4	....	175	—	—

Miscellaneous Expense 59

Date	Item	Post. Ref.	Dr.	Cr.	Balance Dr.	Balance Cr.
2008						
June 10	....	1	200	....	200	....
29	....	2	150	....	350	....
30	....	2	400	....	750	....
30	Closing	4	....	750	—	—

Prob. 4–6B Continued

3.

LUMINARY CONSULTING
Unadjusted Trial Balance
June 30, 2008

	Debit Balances	Credit Balances
Cash	26,500	
Accounts Receivable	5,300	
Supplies	3,550	
Prepaid Rent	5,250	
Prepaid Insurance	2,100	
Office Equipment	30,000	
Accumulated Depreciation		
Accounts Payable		4,000
Salaries Payable		
Unearned Fees		2,700
Derrick Epstein, Capital		60,000
Derrick Epstein, Drawing	8,000	
Fees Earned		16,350
Salary Expense	1,600	
Rent Expense		
Supplies Expense		
Depreciation Expense		
Insurance Expense		
Miscellaneous Expense	750	
	83,050	83,050

Prob. 4–6B Continued

5. Optional (Appendix)

LUMINARY CONSULTING
End-of-Period Spreadsheet (Work Sheet)
For the Month Ended June 30, 2008

	Account Title	Unadjusted Trial Balance Dr.	Unadjusted Trial Balance Cr.	Adjustments Dr.	Adjustments Cr.	Adjusted Trial Balance Dr.	Adjusted Trial Balance Cr.	Income Statement Dr.	Income Statement Cr.	Balance Sheet Dr.	Balance Sheet Cr.	
1	Cash	26,500				26,500				26,500		1
2	Accounts Receivable	5,300				5,300				5,300		2
3	Supplies	3,550			(b) 1,550	2,000				2,000		3
4	Prepaid Rent	5,250			(e) 1,500	3,750				3,750		4
5	Prepaid Insurance	2,100			(a) 175	1,925				1,925		5
6	Office Equipment	30,000				30,000				30,000		6
7	Accum. Depreciation				(c) 500		500				500	7
8	Accounts Payable		4,000				4,000				4,000	8
9	Salaries Payable				(d) 120		120				120	9
10	Unearned Fees		2,700	(f) 825			1,875				1,875	10
11	Derrick Epstein, Capital		60,000				60,000				60,000	11
12	Derrick Epstein, Drawing	8,000				8,000				8,000		12
13	Fees Earned		16,350		(f) 825		17,175		17,175			13
14	Salary Expense	1,600		(d) 120		1,720		1,720				14
15	Rent Expense			(e) 1,500		1,500		1,500				15
16	Supplies Expense			(b) 1,550		1,550		1,550				16
17	Depreciation Expense			(c) 500		500		500				17
18	Insurance Expense			(a) 175		175		175				18
19	Miscellaneous Expense	750				750		750				19
20		83,050	83,050	4,670	4,670	83,670	83,670	6,195	17,175	77,475	66,495	20
21	Net income							10,980			10,980	21
22								17,175	17,175	77,475	77,475	22

6.   JOURNAL   Page 3

Date		Post. Ref.	Debit	Credit
	Adjusting Entries			
2008				
June 30	Insurance Expense.....................................	55	175	
	Prepaid Insurance.................................	16		175
	Insurance expired.			
30	Supplies Expense.....................................	53	1,550	
	Supplies...	14		1,550
	Supplies used ($3,550 – $2,000).			
30	Depreciation Expense	54	500	
	Accumulated Depreciation....................	19		500
	Equipment depreciation.			
30	Salary Expense	51	120	
	Salaries Payable...................................	22		120
	Accrued salaries.			
30	Rent Expense...	52	1,500	
	Prepaid Rent...	15		1,500
	Rent expired.			
30	Unearned Fees..	23	825	
	Fees Earned...	41		825
	Unearned fees earned ($2,700 – $1,875).			

Prob. 4–6B   Continued

7.

LUMINARY CONSULTING
Adjusted Trial Balance
June 30, 2008

	Debit Balances	Credit Balances
Cash	26,500	
Accounts Receivable	5,300	
Supplies	2,000	
Prepaid Rent	3,750	
Prepaid Insurance	1,925	
Office Equipment	30,000	
Accumulated Depreciation		500
Accounts Payable		4,000
Salaries Payable		120
Unearned Fees		1,875
Derrick Epstein, Capital		60,000
Derrick Epstein, Drawing	8,000	
Fees Earned		17,175
Salary Expense	1,720	
Supplies Expense	1,550	
Rent Expense	1,500	
Depreciation Expense	500	
Insurance Expense	175	
Miscellaneous Expense	750	
	83,670	83,670

Prob. 4–6B   Continued

8.

LUMINARY CONSULTING
Income Statement
For the Month Ended June 30, 2008

Fees earned...		$17,175
Expenses:		
Salary expense..	$1,720	
Supplies expense	1,550	
Rent expense	1,500	
Depreciation expense...	500	
Insurance expense	175	
Miscellaneous expense......................................	750	
Total expenses		6,195
Net income		$10,980

LUMINARY CONSULTING
Statement of Owner's Equity
For the Month Ended June 30, 2008

Derrick Epstein, capital, June 1, 2008.............................		$ 0
Additional investments during the month		60,000
Total		$60,000
Net income for the month	$10,980	
Less withdrawals...	8,000	
Increase in owner's equity..		2,980
Derrick Epstein, capital, June 30, 2008...........................		$62,980

Prob. 4–6B   Continued

LUMINARY CONSULTING
Balance Sheet
June 30, 2008

Assets			
Current assets:			
Cash	$26,500		
Accounts receivable ..	5,300		
Supplies	2,000		
Prepaid rent	3,750		
Prepaid insurance......	1,925		
Total current assets		$39,475	
Property, plant, and equipment:			
Office equipment........	$30,000		
Less accum. depr.	500		
Total property, plant, and equipment		29,500	
Total assets		$68,975	

Liabilities		
Current liabilities:		
Accounts payable....	$4,000	
Salaries payable......	120	
Unearned fees	1,875	
Total liabilities............		$ 5,995
Owner's Equity		
Derrick Epstein, capital......................		62,980
Total liabilities and owner's equity.........		$68,975

9.

Date		Post. Ref.	Debit	Credit
	JOURNAL			**Page 4**
	Closing Entries			
2008				
June 30	Fees Earned	41	17,175	
	Income Summary	33		17,175
30	Income Summary	33	6,195	
	Salary Expense	51		1,720
	Rent Expense	52		1,500
	Supplies Expense	53		1,550
	Depreciation Expense	54		500
	Insurance Expense	55		175
	Miscellaneous Expense	59		750
30	Income Summary	33	10,980	
	Derrick Epstein, Capital	31		10,980
30	Derrick Epstein, Capital	31	8,000	
	Derrick Epstein, Drawing	32		8,000

10.

LUMINARY CONSULTING
Post-Closing Trial Balance
June 30, 2008

	Debit Balances	Credit Balances
Cash	26,500	
Accounts Receivable	5,300	
Supplies	2,000	
Prepaid Rent	3,750	
Prepaid Insurance	1,925	
Office Equipment	30,000	
Accumulated Depreciation		500
Accounts Payable		4,000
Salaries Payable		120
Unearned Fees		1,875
Derrick Epstein, Capital		62,980
	69,475	69,475

CONTINUING PROBLEM

1. Optional (Appendix)

DANCIN MUSING
End-of-Period Spreadsheet (Work Sheet)
For the Two Months Ended May 31, 2008

Account Title	Unadjusted Trial Balance Dr.	Cr.	Adjustments Dr.	Cr.	Adjusted Trial Balance Dr.	Cr.	Income Statement Dr.	Cr.	Balance Sheet Dr.	Cr.
1 Cash	12,085				12,085				12,085	
2 Accounts Receivable	2,850		(a) 1,400		4,250				4,250	
3 Supplies	920			(b) 760	160				160	
4 Prepaid Insurance	3,360			(c) 280	3,080,				3,080	
5 Office Equipment	5,000				5,000				5,000	
6 Acc. Depr.—Office Equip.				(d) 100		100				100
7 Accounts Payable		5,750				5,750				5,750
8 Wages Payable				(f) 200		200				200
9 Unearned Revenue		4,800	(e) 2,400			2,400				2,400
10 Kris Payne, Capital		12,500				12,500				12,500
11 Kris Payne, Drawing	1,300				1,300				1,300	
12 Fees Earned		14,750		(a) 1,400 (e) 2,400		18,550		18,550		
13										
14 Wages Expense	2,400		(f) 200		2,600		2,600			
15 Office Rent Expense	2,600				2,600		2,600			
16 Equip. Rent Expense	1,300				1,300		1,300			
17 Utilities Expense	910				910		910			
18 Music Expense	2,565				2,565		2,565			
19 Advertising Expense	1,730				1,730		1,730			
20 Supplies Expense	180		(b) 760		940		940			
21 Insurance Expense			(c) 280		280		280			
22 Depreciation Expense			(d) 100		100		100			
23 Miscellaneous Expense	600				600		600			
24	37,800	37,800	5,140	5,140	39,500	39,500	13,625	18,550	25,875	20,950
25 Net income							4,925			4,925
26							18,550	18,550	25,875	25,875

275

Continuing Problem   Continued

2.

DANCIN MUSIC
Income Statement
For the Two Months Ended May 31, 2008

Fees earned..		$18,550
Expenses:		
Wages expense...	$2,600	
Office rent expense	2,600	
Music expense	2,565	
Advertising expense.......................................	1,730	
Equipment rent expense	1,300	
Supplies expense	940	
Utilities expense	910	
Insurance expense	280	
Depreciation expense....................................	100	
Miscellaneous expense..................................	600	
Total expenses		13,625
Net income		$ 4,925

DANCIN MUSIC
Statement of Owner's Equity
For the Two Months Ended May 31, 2008

Kris Payne, capital, April 1, 2008......................................		$ 0
Additional investments during the period		12,500
Total		$12,500
Net income for the period	$4,925	
Less withdrawals...	1,300	
Increase in owner's equity...		3,625
Kris Payne, capital, May 31, 2008		$16,125

DANCIN MUSIC
Balance Sheet
May 31, 2008

Assets			Liabilities		
Current assets:			**Current liabilities:**		
Cash	$12,085		Accounts payable....	$5,750	
Accounts receivable	4,250		Wages payable	200	
Supplies	160		Unearned revenue...	2,400	
Prepaid insurance........	3,080		Total liabilities...........		$ 8,350
Total current assets ..		$19,575			
Property, plant, and equipment:			**Owner's Equity**		
Office equipment..........	$5,000		Kris Payne,		
Less accum. depr.........	100		capital......................		16,125
Total property, plant, and equipment		4,900	**Total liabilities and**		
Total assets.....................		$24,475	owner's equity.........		$24,475

Continuing Problem   Continued

3.

Date		Post. Ref.	Debit	Credit
	Closing Entries			
2006				
May 31	Fees Earned	41	18,550	
	Income Summary	33		18,550
31	Income Summary...	33	13,625	
	Wages Expense.......................................	50		2,600
	Office Rent Expense	51		2,600
	Equipment Rent Expense......................	52		1,300
	Utilities Expense	53		910
	Music Expense	54		2,565
	Advertising Expense.............................	55		1,730
	Supplies Expense	56		940
	Insurance Expense	57		280
	Depreciation Expense	58		100
	Miscellaneous Expense........................	59		600
31	Income Summary...	33	4,925	
	Kris Payne, Capital................................	31		4,925
31	Kris Payne, Capital	31	1,300	
	Kris Payne, Drawing	32		1,300

Continuing Problem   Continued

Cash 11

Date		Item	Post. Ref.	Dr.	Cr.	Balance Dr.	Balance Cr.
2008							
May	1	Balance..................	✓	....	....	9,160	....
	1	....	1	2,500	....	11,660	....
	1	....	1	....	1,600	10,060	....
	1	....	1	....	3,360	6,700	....
	2	....	1	1,350	....	8,050	....
	3	....	1	4,800	....	12,850	....
	3	....	1	....	250	12,600	....
	4	....	1	....	300	12,300	....
	8	....	1	....	180	12,120	....
	11	....	1	750	....	12,870	....
	13	....	1	....	500	12,370	....
	14	....	1	....	1,000	11,370	....
	16	....	2	1,500	....	12,870	....
	21	....	2	....	325	12,545	....
	22	....	2	....	800	11,745	....
	23	....	2	750	....	12,495	....
	27	....	2	....	560	11,935	....
	28	....	2	....	1,000	10,935	....
	29	....	2	....	150	10,785	....
	30	....	2	400	....	11,185	....
	31	....	2	2,800	....	13,985	....
	31	....	2	....	900	13,085	....
	31	....	2	....	1,000	12,085	....

Accounts Receivable 12

Date		Item	Post. Ref.	Dr.	Cr.	Balance Dr.	Balance Cr.
2008							
May	1	Balance..................	✓	....	....	1,350	....
	2	....	1	....	1,350	—	—
	23	....	2	1,750	....	1,750	....
	30	....	2	1,100	....	2,850	....
	31	Adjusting	3	1,400	....	4,250	....

Continuing Problem   Continued

Supplies

14

Date	Item	Post. Ref.	Dr.	Cr.	Balance Dr.	Balance Cr.
2008						
May 1	Balance.................	✓	....	....	170	....
18	....	2	750	....	920	....
31	Adjusting	3	....	760	160	....

Prepaid Insurance

15

Date	Item	Post. Ref.	Dr.	Cr.	Balance Dr.	Balance Cr.
2008						
May 1	....	1	3,360	....	3,360	....
31	Adjusting	3	....	280	3,080	....

Office Equipment

17

Date	Item	Post. Ref.	Dr.	Cr.	Balance Dr.	Balance Cr.
2008						
May 5	....	1	5,000	....	5,000	....

Accumulated Depreciation—Office Equipment

18

Date	Item	Post. Ref.	Dr.	Cr.	Balance Dr.	Balance Cr.
2008						
May 31	Adjusting	3	....	100	....	100

Accounts Payable

21

Date	Item	Post. Ref.	Dr.	Cr.	Balance Dr.	Balance Cr.
2008						
May 1	Balance.................	✓	....	....	....	250
3	....	1	250	....	—	—
5	....	1	....	5,000	....	5,000
18	....	2	....	750	....	5,750

Wages Payable

22

Date	Item	Post. Ref.	Dr.	Cr.	Balance Dr.	Balance Cr.
2008						
May 31	Adjusting	3	....	200	....	200

Unearned Revenue

23

Date	Item	Post. Ref.	Dr.	Cr.	Balance Dr.	Balance Cr.
2008						
May 3	....	1	....	4,800	....	4,800
31	Adjusting	3	2,400	....	....	2,400

Continuing Problem   Continued

Kris Payne, Capital

31

Date		Item	Post. Ref.	Dr.	Cr.	Balance Dr.	Balance Cr.
2008							
May	1	Balance..................	✓	....	....	....	10,000
	1	....	1	....	2,500	....	12,500
	31	Closing	4	....	4,925	....	17,425
	31	Closing	4	1,300	....	....	16,125

Kris Payne, Drawing

32

Date		Item	Post. Ref.	Dr.	Cr.	Balance Dr.	Balance Cr.
2008							
May	1	Balance..................	✓	....	....	300	....
	31	....	2	1,000	....	1,300	....
	31	Closing	4	....	1,300	—	—

Income Summary

33

Date		Item	Post. Ref.	Dr.	Cr.	Balance Dr.	Balance Cr.
2008							
May	31	Closing	4	....	18,550	....	18,550
	31	Closing	4	13,625	....	....	4,925
	31	Closing	4	4,925	....	—	—

Fees Earned

41

Date		Item	Post. Ref.	Dr.	Cr.	Balance Dr.	Balance Cr.
2008							
May	1	Balance..................	✓	....	....	....	5,700
	11	....	1	....	750	....	6,450
	16	....	2	....	1,500	....	7,950
	23	....	2	....	2,500	....	10,450
	30	....	2	....	1,500	....	11,950
	31	....	2	....	2,800	....	14,750
	31	Adjusting	3	....	1,400	....	16,150
	31	Adjusting	3	....	2,400	....	18,550
	31	Closing	4	18,550	....	—	—

Wages Expense

50

Date		Item	Post. Ref.	Dr.	Cr.	Balance Dr.	Balance Cr.
2008							
May	1	Balance..................	✓	....	....	400	....
	14	....	1	1,000	....	1,400	....
	28	....	2	1,000	....	2,400	....
	31	Adjusting	3	200	....	2,600	....
	31	Closing	4	....	2,600	—	—

Continuing Problem   Continued

Office Rent Expense

51

Date	Item	Post. Ref.	Dr.	Cr.	Balance Dr.	Balance Cr.
2008						
May 1	Balance	✓	....	....	1,000	....
1	....	1	1,600	....	2,600	....
31	Closing	4	....	2,600	—	—

Equipment Rent Expense

52

Date	Item	Post. Ref.	Dr.	Cr.	Balance Dr.	Balance Cr.
2008						
May 1	Balance	✓	....	....	800	....
13	....	1	500	....	1,300	....
31	Closing	4	....	1,300	—	—

Utilities Expense

53

Date	Item	Post. Ref.	Dr.	Cr.	Balance Dr.	Balance Cr.
2008						
May 1	Balance	✓	....	....	350	....
27	....	2	560	....	910	....
31	Closing	4	....	910	—	—

Music Expense

54

Date	Item	Post. Ref.	Dr.	Cr.	Balance Dr.	Balance Cr.
2008						
May 1	Balance	✓	....	....	1,340	....
21	....	2	325	....	1,665	....
31	....	2	900	....	2,565	....
31	Closing	4	....	2,565	—	—

Advertising Expense

55

Date	Item	Post. Ref.	Dr.	Cr.	Balance Dr.	Balance Cr.
2008						
May 1	Balance	✓	....	....	750	....
8	....	1	180	....	930	....
22	....	2	800	....	1,730	....
31	Closing	4	....	1,730	—	—

Supplies Expense

56

Date	Item	Post. Ref.	Dr.	Cr.	Balance Dr.	Balance Cr.
2008						
May 1	Balance	✓	....	....	180	....
31	Adjusting	3	760	....	940	....
31	Closing	4	....	940	—	—

Continuing Problem   Concluded

Insurance Expense
57

Date	Item	Post. Ref.	Dr.	Cr.	Balance Dr.	Balance Cr.
2008						
May 31	Adjusting	3	280	....	280	....
31	Closing	4	....	280	—	—

Depreciation Expense
58

Date	Item	Post. Ref.	Dr.	Cr.	Balance Dr.	Balance Cr.
2008						
May 31	Adjusting	3	100	....	100	....
31	Closing	4	....	100	—	—

Miscellaneous Expense
59

Date	Item	Post. Ref.	Dr.	Cr.	Balance Dr.	Balance Cr.
2008						
May 1	Balance...................	✓	....	....	150	....
4	....	1	300	....	450	....
29	....	2	150	....	600	....
31	Closing	4	....	600	—	—

4.

DANCIN MUSIC
Post-Closing Trial Balance
May 31, 2008

	Debit Balances	Credit Balances
Cash...	12,085	
Accounts Receivable..	4,250	
Supplies...	160	
Prepaid Insurance...	3,080	
Office Equipment	5,000	
Accumulated Depreciation—Office Equipment		100
Accounts Payable...		5,750
Wages Payable...		200
Unearned Revenue		2,400
Kris Payne, Capital		16,125
	24,575	**24,575**

Activity 4–1

It is unacceptable to prepare financial statements in such a way that users of the statements would be misled. The January 31, 2008, balance sheet of Fantasy Graphics Co. could be misleading in two ways. First, the account receivable from Kent should be segregated and reported separately from trade (customer) receivables. Such receivables are normally reported as "officer receivables" or "other receivables" and accompanied by a note disclosing the nature of the receivable. Such disclosure is required for what are termed "related-party transactions." Second, given that the receivable has been outstanding since November 2007, it is questionable whether the receivable from Kent should be classified as a current asset. Terri could justify the classification as "current" if Kent has agreed to a written schedule for repaying within the next year. Alternatively, the receivable could be classified as current if it has been converted to a note receivable with a specific due date within the next year.

In summary, because of the preceding issues, it appears that Terri is not behaving in a professional manner. *Note:* It is a criminal offense to submit false or misleading documents to a bank in applying for a loan.

Activity 4–2

1. (a) With the decreasing cost of computers and related software, Cupboard Supplies Co. may find it desirable to computerize its financial reporting system. In many cases, the computerization of a manual accounting system reduces the overall cost of the accounting function.

   (b) A computerized accounting system would allow for eliminating the end-of-period spreadsheet (work sheet), and thus, financial statements could be prepared with "a push of a button." However, adjustment data would still need to be recorded at the end of the accounting period before the financial statements could be prepared.

   (c) In designing a computerized financial reporting (accounting) system, it is essential that proper accounting principles, concepts, and procedures be followed. At a minimum, basic controls such as the use of the double-entry accounting system should be included. For example, debits must equal credits for all transactions, and assets must equal liabilities plus owner's equity. In addition, the system should be designed to detect obvious errors, such as a credit (minus) balance for supplies or prepaid insurance. In other words, to design an adequate financial reporting system, a computer programmer must have a thorough understanding of accounting and the accounting cycle.

   Note: Numerous accounting software packages, similar to the Klooster and Allen General Ledger Software package accompanying this text, are available. Therefore, it would probably be better for Cupboard Supplies Co. to purchase an existing accounting software package rather than trying to design its own.

2. Supplies cannot have a credit balance, since the supplies account is an asset account. A business cannot have a "negative" asset. Thus, the only way that a credit balance could have occurred in supplies is the result of an error in recording one or more transactions.

Activity 4–3

1. A set of financial statements provides useful information concerning the economic condition of a company. For example, the balance sheet describes the financial condition of the company as of a given date and is useful in assessing the company's financial soundness and liquidity. The income statement describes the results of operations for a period and indicates the profitability of the company. The statement of owner's equity describes the changes in the owner's interest in the company for a period. Each of these statements is useful in evaluating whether to extend credit to the company.

2. The following adjustments might be necessary before an accurate set of financial statements could be prepared:

   - No supplies expense is shown. The supplies account should be adjusted for the supplies used during the year.

   - No depreciation expense is shown for the trucks or equipment accounts. An adjusting entry should be prepared for depreciation expense on each of these assets.

   - An inquiry should be made as to whether any accrued expenses, such as wages or utilities, exist at the end of the year.

   - An inquiry should be made as to whether any prepaid expenses, such as rent or insurance, exist at the end of the year.

   - An inquiry should be made as to whether the owner withdrew any funds from the company during the year. No drawing account is shown in the "Statement of Accounts."

   - The following items should be relabeled for greater clarity:

        Billings Due from Others—Accounts Receivable

        Amounts Owed to Others—Accounts Payable

        Investment in Business—Marion Zastrow, Capital

        Other Expenses—Miscellaneous Expense

Note to Instructors: The preceding items are not intended to include all adjustments that might exist in the Statement of Accounts. The possible adjustments listed include only items that have been covered in Chapters 1–4. For example, uncollectible accounts expense (discussed in a later chapter) is not mentioned.

Activity 4–3 Concluded

3. In general, the decision to extend a loan is based upon an assessment of the profitability and riskiness of the loan. Although the financial statements provide useful data for this purpose, other factors such as the following might also be significant:

- The due date and payment terms of the loan.

- Security for the loan. For example, whether Marion Zastrow is willing to pledge personal assets in support of the loan will affect the riskiness of the loan.

- The intended use of the loan. For example, if the loan is to purchase real estate (possibly for a future building site), the real estate could be used as security for the loan.

- The projected profitability of the company.

Activity 4–4

Note to Instructors: The purpose of this activity is to familiarize students with the information that a balance sheet provides about a company.

COMPREHENSIVE PROBLEM 1

JOURNAL

Date	Description	Post. Ref.	Debit	Credit
2008				
May 3	Cash	11	1,550	
	Unearned Fees	23		1,550
5	Cash	11	1,750	
	Accounts Receivable	12		1,750
9	Miscellaneous Expense	59	100	
	Cash	11		100
13	Accounts Payable	21	400	
	Cash	11		400
15	Accounts Receivable	12	5,100	
	Fees Earned	41		5,100
16	Salary Expense	51	630	
	Salaries Payable	22	120	
	Cash	11		750
17	Cash	11	7,380	
	Fees Earned	41		7,380
20	Supplies	14	500	
	Accounts Payable	21		500
21	Accounts Receivable	12	2,900	
	Fees Earned	41		2,900
25	Cash	11	4,200	
	Fees Earned	41		4,200
27	Cash	11	6,600	
	Accounts Receivable	12		6,600
28	Salary Expense	51	750	
	Cash	11		750
30	Miscellaneous Expense	59	150	
	Cash	11		150
31	Miscellaneous Expense	59	225	
	Cash	11		225
31	Cash	11	2,875	
	Fees Earned	41		2,875

Comp. Prob. 1   Continued

JOURNAL   **Pages 5 and 6**

Date	Description	Post. Ref.	Debit	Credit
2008				
May 31	Accounts Receivable................................	12	2,200	
	Fees Earned...	41		2,200
31	Kelly Pitney, Drawing	32	7,500	
	Cash	11		7,500

Comp. Prob. 1   Continued

2., 6., and 9.

Cash

Date	Item	Post. Ref.	Dr.	Cr.	Balance Dr.	Balance Cr.
2008						
May 1	Balance..................	✓	....	....	22,100	....
3	....	5	1,550	....	23,650	....
5	....	5	1,750	....	25,400	....
9	....	5	....	100	25,300	....
13	....	5	....	400	24,900	....
16	....	5	....	750	24,150	....
17	....	6	7,380	....	31,530	....
25	....	6	4,200	....	35,730	....
27	....	6	6,600	....	42,330	....
28	....	6	....	750	41,580	....
30	....	6	....	150	41,430	....
31	....	6	....	225	41,205	....
31	....	6	2,875	....	44,080	....
31	....	6	....	7,500	36,580	....

Accounts Receivable

Date	Item	Post. Ref.	Dr.	Cr.	Balance Dr.	Balance Cr.
2008						
May 1	Balance..................	✓	....	....	3,400	....
5	....	5	....	1,750	1,650	....
15	....	5	5,100	....	6,750	....
21	....	6	2,900	....	9,650	....
27	....	6	....	6,600	3,050	....
31	....	6	2,200	....	5,250	....

Supplies

Date	Item	Post. Ref.	Dr.	Cr.	Balance Dr.	Balance Cr.
2008						
May 1	Balance..................	✓	....	....	1,350	....
20	....	6	500	....	1,850	....
31	Adjusting	7	....	900	950	....

290

Comp. Prob. 1   Continued

Prepaid Rent

Date	Item	Post. Ref.	Dr.	Cr.	Balance Dr.	Balance Cr.
2008						
May 1	Balance..................	✓	....	....	3,200	....
31	Adjusting	7	....	1,600	1,600	....

Prepaid Insurance

Date	Item	Post. Ref.	Dr.	Cr.	Balance Dr.	Balance Cr.
2008						
May 1	Balance..................	✓	....	....	1,500	....
31	Adjusting	7	....	300	1,200	....

Office Equipment

Date	Item	Post. Ref.	Dr.	Cr.	Balance Dr.	Balance Cr.
2008						
May 1	Balance..................	5	....	....	14,500	....

Accumulated Depreciation

Date	Item	Post. Ref.	Dr.	Cr.	Balance Dr.	Balance Cr.
2008						
May 1	Balance..................	✓	....	....	....	330
31	Adjusting	7	....	330	....	660

Accounts Payable

Date	Item	Post. Ref.	Dr.	Cr.	Balance Dr.	Balance Cr.
2008						
May 1	Balance..................	✓	....	....	....	800
13	....	5	400	....	....	400
20	....	6	....	500	....	900

Salaries Payable

Date	Item	Post. Ref.	Dr.	Cr.	Balance Dr.	Balance Cr.
2008						
May 1	Balance..................	✓	....	....	....	120
16	....	5	120	....	....	—
31	Adjusting	7	....	260	....	260

Unearned Fees

Date	Item	Post. Ref.	Dr.	Cr.	Balance Dr.	Balance Cr.
2008						
May 1	Balance..................	✓	....	....	....	2,500
3	....	5	....	1,550	....	4,050
31	Adjusting	7	2,750	....	....	1,300

Comp. Prob. 1   Continued

Kelly Pitney, Capital   31

Date		Item	Post. Ref.	Dr.	Cr.	Balance Dr.	Balance Cr.
2008							
May	1	Balance...............	✓	....	....	....	42,300
	31	Closing	8	....	22,160	....	64,460
	31	Closing	8	7,500	....	....	56,960

Kelly Pitney, Drawing   32

Date		Item	Post. Ref.	Dr.	Cr.	Balance Dr.	Balance Cr.
2008							
May	31	....	6	7,500	....	7,500	....
	31	Closing	8	....	7,500	—	—

Income Summary   33

Date		Item	Post. Ref.	Dr.	Cr.	Balance Dr.	Balance Cr.
2008							
May	31	Closing	8	....	27,405	....	27,405
	31	Closing	8	5,245	....	....	22,160
	31	Closing	8	22,160	....	—	—

Fees Earned   41

Date		Item	Post. Ref.	Dr.	Cr.	Balance Dr.	Balance Cr.
2008							
May	15	....	5	....	5,100	....	5,100
	17	....	6	....	7,380	....	12,480
	21	....	6	....	2,900	....	15,380
	25	....	6	....	4,200	....	19,580
	31	....	6	....	2,875	....	22,455
	31	....	6	....	2,200	....	24,655
	31	Adjusting	7	....	2,750	....	27,405
	31	Closing	8	27,405	....	—	—

Salary Expense   51

Date		Item	Post. Ref.	Dr.	Cr.	Balance Dr.	Balance Cr.
2008							
May	16	....	5	630	....	630	....
	28	....	6	750	....	1,380	....
	31	Adjusting	7	260	....	1,640	....
	31	Closing	8	....	1,640	—	—

Rent Expense   52

Date	Item	Post. Ref.	Dr.	Cr.	Balance Dr.	Balance Cr.
2008						
May 31	Adjusting	7	1,600	....	1,600	....
31	Closing	8	....	1,600	—	—

Supplies Expense   53

Date	Item	Post. Ref.	Dr.	Cr.	Balance Dr.	Balance Cr.
2008						
May 31	Adjusting	7	900	....	900	....
31	Closing	8	....	900	—	—

Depreciation Expense   54

Date	Item	Post. Ref.	Dr.	Cr.	Balance Dr.	Balance Cr.
2008						
May 31	Adjusting	7	330	....	330	....
31	Closing	8	....	330	—	—

Insurance Expense   55

Date	Item	Post. Ref.	Dr.	Cr.	Balance Dr.	Balance Cr.
2008						
May 31	Adjusting	7	300	....	300	....
31	Closing	8	....	300	—	—

Miscellaneous Expense   59

Date	Item	Post. Ref.	Dr.	Cr.	Balance Dr.	Balance Cr.
2008						
May 9	....	5	100	....	100	....
30	....	6	150	....	250	....
31	....	6	225	....	475	....
31	Closing	8	....	475	—	—

3.

KELLY CONSULTING
Unadjusted Trial Balance
May 31, 2008

	Debit Balances	Credit Balances
Cash	36,580	
Accounts Receivable	5,250	
Supplies	1,850	
Prepaid Rent	3,200	
Prepaid Insurance	1,500	
Office Equipment	14,500	
Accumulated Depreciation		330
Accounts Payable		900
Salaries Payable		
Unearned Fees		4,050
Kelly Pitney, Capital		42,300
Kelly Pitney, Drawing	7,500	
Fees Earned		24,655
Salary Expense	1,380	
Rent Expense		
Supplies Expense		
Depreciation Expense		
Insurance Expense		
Miscellaneous Expense	475	
	72,235	72,235

Comp. Prob. 1   Continued

5. Optional (Appendix)

KELLY CONSULTING
End-of-Period Spreadsheet (Work Sheet)
For the Month Ended May 31, 2008

Account Title	Unadjusted Trial Balance Dr.	Cr.	Adjustments Dr.	Cr.	Adjusted Trial Balance Dr.	Cr.	Income Statement Dr.	Cr.	Balance Sheet Dr.	Cr.	
Cash	36,580				36,580				36,580		1
Accounts Receivable	5,250				5,250				5,250		2
Supplies	1,850			(b) 900	950				950		3
Prepaid Rent	3,200			(e) 1,600	1,600				1,600		4
Prepaid Insurance	1,500			(a) 300	1,200				1,200		5
Office Equipment	14,500				14,500				14,500		6
Accum. Depreciation		330		(c) 330		660				660	7
Accounts Payable		900				900				900	8
Salaries Payable				(d) 260		260				260	9
Unearned Fees		4,050	(f) 2,750			1,300				1,300	10
Kelly Pitney, Capital		42,300				42,300				42,300	11
Kelly Pitney, Drawing	7,500				7,500				7,500		12
Fees Earned		24,655		(f) 2,750		27,405		27,405			13
Salary Expense	1,380		(d) 260		1,640		1,640				14
Rent Expense			(e) 1,600		1,600		1,600				15
Supplies Expense			(b) 900		900		900				16
Depreciation Expense			(c) 330		330		330				17
Insurance Expense			(a) 300		300		300				18
Miscellaneous Expense	475				475		475				19
	72,235	72,235	6,140	6,140	72,825	72,825	5,245	27,405	67,580	45,420	20
Net income							22,160			22,160	21
							27,405	27,405	67,580	67,580	22

6.   JOURNAL   Page 7

Date			Post. Ref.	Debit	Credit
		Adjusting Entries			
2008					
May	31	Insurance Expense...............................	55	300	
		Prepaid Insurance...............................	16		300
		Insurance expired.			
	31	Supplies Expense.................................	53	900	
		Supplies..	14		900
		Supplies used ($1,850 – $950).			
	31	Depreciation Expense...........................	54	330	
		Accumulated Depreciation...................	19		330
		Equipment depreciation.			
	31	Salary Expense...................................	51	260	
		Salaries Payable.................................	22		260
		Accrued salaries.			
	31	Rent Expense......................................	52	1,600	
		Prepaid Rent.......................................	15		1,600
		Rent expired.			
	31	Unearned Fees....................................	23	2,750	
		Fees Earned..	41		2,750
		Unearned fees ($4,050 – $1,300).			

7.

KELLY CONSULTING
Adjusted Trial Balance
May 31, 2008

	Debit Balances	Credit Balances
Cash	36,580	
Accounts Receivable	5,250	
Supplies	950	
Prepaid Rent	1,600	
Prepaid Insurance	1,200	
Office Equipment	14,500	
Accumulated Depreciation		660
Accounts Payable		900
Salaries Payable		260
Unearned Fees		1,300
Kelly Pitney, Capital		42,300
Kelly Pitney, Drawing	7,500	
Fees Earned		27,405
Salary Expense	1,640	
Rent Expense	1,600	
Supplies Expense	900	
Depreciation Expense	330	
Insurance Expense	300	
Miscellaneous Expense	475	
	72,825	72,825

Comp. Prob. 1   Continued

8.

KELLY CONSULTING
Income Statement
For the Month Ended May 31, 2008

Fees earned..		$27,405
Expenses:		
Salary expense..	$1,640	
Rent expense	1,600	
Supplies expense	900	
Depreciation expense......................................	330	
Insurance expense	300	
Miscellaneous expense...................................	475	
Total expenses		5,245
Net income		$22,160

KELLY CONSULTING
Statement of Owner's Equity
For the Month Ended May 31, 2008

Kelly Pitney, capital, May 1, 2008		$42,300
Net income for the month	$22,160	
Less withdrawals..	7,500	
Increase in owner's equity..................................		14,660
Kelly Pitney, capital, May 31, 2008		$56,960

KELLY CONSULTING
Balance Sheet
May 31, 2008

<u>Assets</u>			<u>Liabilities</u>		
Current assets:			**Current liabilities:**		
Cash	$36,580		Accounts payable....	$ 900	
Accounts receivable ..	5,250		Salaries payable	260	
Supplies	950		Unearned fees	1,300	
Prepaid rent	1,600		Total liabilities		$ 2,460
Prepaid insurance	1,200				
Total current assets		$45,580			
Property, plant, and			**<u>Owner's Equity</u>**		
equipment:.................			Kelly Pitney,		
Office equipment........	$14,500		capital.......................		56,960
Less accum. depr.	660	13,840	**Total liabilities and**		
Total assets		$59,420	owner's equity.........		$59,420

Comp. Prob. 1   Concluded

JOURNAL   Page 8

Date		Post. Ref.	Debit	Credit
	Closing Entries			
2008				
May 31	Fees Earned	41	27,405	
	Income Summary	33		27,405
31	Income Summary..	33	5,245	
	Salary Expense	51		1,640
	Rent Expense	52		1,600
	Supplies Expense	53		900
	Depreciation Expense	54		330
	Insurance Expense	55		300
	Miscellaneous Expense........................	59		475
31	Income Summary..	33	22,160	
	Kelly Pitney, Capital.............................	31		22,160
31	Kelly Pitney, Capital	31	7,500	
	Kelly Pitney, Drawing............................	32		7,500

10.

KELLY CONSULTING
Post-Closing Trial Balance
May 31, 2008

	Debit Balances	Credit Balances
Cash...	36,580	
Accounts Receivable...	5,250	
Supplies...	950	
Prepaid Rent..	1,600	
Prepaid Insurance..	1,200	
Office Equipment	14,500	
Accumulated Depreciation..		660
Accounts Payable...		900
Salaries Payable		260
Unearned Fees...		1,300
Kelly Pitney, Capital...		56,960
Totals	60,080	60,080

CHAPTER 5
ACCOUNTING SYSTEMS

QUESTION INFORMATION

Number	Objective	Description	Difficulty	Time	AACSB	AICPA	SS	GL
Q5-1	5-2		Easy	5 min	Analytic	FN-Measurement		
Q5-2	5-2		Easy	5 min	Analytic	FN-Measurement		
Q5-3	5-2		Easy	5 min	Analytic	FN-Measurement		
Q5-4	5-2		Easy	5 min	Analytic	FN-Measurement		
Q5-5	5-2		Easy	5 min	Analytic	FN-Measurement		
Q5-6	5-2		Easy	5 min	Analytic	FN-Measurement		
Q5-7	5-2		Easy	5 min	Analytic	FN-Measurement		
Q5-8	5-4		Easy	5 min	Technology	BB-Leveraging Technology		
Q5-9	5-4		Easy	5 min	Technology	BB-Leveraging Technology		
Q5-10	5-4		Easy	5 min	Technology	BB-Leveraging Technology		
Q5-11	5-4		Easy	5 min	Technology	BB-Leveraging Technology		
Q5-12	5-5		Easy	5 min	Technology	BB-Leveraging Technology		
PE5-1A	5-2	Prepare journal entries in a revenue journal	Easy	5 min	Analytic	FN-Measurement		
PE5-1B	5-2	Prepare journal entries in a revenue journal	Easy	10 min	Analytic	FN-Measurement		
PE5-2A	5-2	Identify transactions in an accounts receivable ledger	Easy	10 min	Analytic	FN-Measurement		
PE5-2B	5-2	Identify transactions in an accounts receivable ledger	Easy	5 min	Analytic	FN-Measurement		
PE5-3A	5-2	Prepare journal entries in a purchases journal	Easy	5 min	Analytic	FN-Measurement		
PE5-3B	5-2	Prepare journal entries in a purchases journal	Easy	10 min	Analytic	FN-Measurement		
PE5-4A	5-2	Prepare journal entries in an accounts payable ledger	Easy	10 min	Analytic	FN-Measurement		
PE5-4B	5-2	Identify transactions in an accounts payable ledger	Easy	5 min	Analytic	FN-Measurement		
PE5-5A	5-3	Prepare journal entries in a modified revenue journal	Easy	5 min	Analytic	FN-Measurement		
PE5-5B	5-3	Prepare journal entries in a modified revenue journal	Easy	5 min	Analytic	FN-Measurement		
Ex5-1	5-2	Identify postings from revenue journal	Easy	5 min	Analytic	FN-Measurement		
Ex5-2	5-2	Accounts receivable ledger	Easy	15 min	Analytic	FN-Measurement	Exl	

Number	Objective	Description	Difficulty	Time	AACSB	AICPA	SS	GL
Ex5-3	5-2	Identify journals	Easy	10 min	Analytic	FN-Measurement		
Ex5-4	5-2	Identify journals	Easy	10 min	Analytic	FN-Measurement		
Ex5-5	5-2	Identify transactions in accounts receivable ledger	Easy	5 min	Analytic	FN-Measurement		
Ex5-6	5-2	Prepare journal entries in a revenue journal	Moderate	15 min	Analytic	FN-Measurement		
Ex5-7	5-2	Posting a revenue journal	Moderate	15 min	Analytic	FN-Measurement		
Ex5-8	5-2	Schedule of accounts receivable	Moderate	15 min	Analytic	FN-Measurement	Exl	
Ex5-9	5-2	Revenue and cash receipts journals	Moderate	20 min	Analytic	FN-Measurement		
Ex5-10	5-2	Revenue and cash receipts journals	Moderate	25 min	Analytic	FN-Measurement		
Ex5-11	5-2	Identify postings from purchases journal	Easy	10 min	Analytic	FN-Measurement		
Ex5-12	5-2	Identify postings from cash payments journal	Easy	10 min	Analytic	FN-Measurement		
Ex5-13	5-2	Identify transactions in accounts payable ledger account	Easy	5 min	Analytic	FN-Measurement		
Ex5-14	5-2	Prepare journal entries in a purchases journal	Easy	15 min	Analytic	FN-Measurement		
Ex5-15	5-2	Posting a purchases journal	Moderate	20 min	Analytic	FN-Measurement		
Ex5-16	5-2	Schedule of accounts payable	Moderate	15 min	Analytic	FN-Measurement	Exl	
Ex5-17	5-2	Purchases and cash payments journals	Moderate	20 min	Analytic	FN-Measurement		
Ex5-18	5-2	Purchases and cash payments journal	Moderate	25 min	Analytic	FN-Measurement		
Ex5-19	5-2	Error in accounts payable ledger and schedule of accounts payable	Difficult	25 min	Analytic	FN-Measurement		
Ex5-20	5-2	Identify postings from special journals	Moderate	20 min	Analytic	FN-Measurement		
Ex5-21	5-2	Cash receipts journal	Easy	10 min	Analytic	FN-Measurement		
Ex5-22	5-2, 5-3	Modified special journals	Moderate	20 min	Analytic	FN-Measurement		
Ex5-23	5-4	Computerized accounting systems	Easy	10 min	Technology	BB-Leveraging Technology		
Ex5-24	5-5	E-commerce	Easy	20 min	Technology	BB-Leveraging Technology		
Pr5-1A	5-2	Revenue journal; accounts receivable and general ledgers	Moderate	1 hr	Analytic	FN-Measurement	Exl	
Pr5-2A	5-2	Revenue and cash receipts journals; accounts receivable and general ledgers	Moderate	1 3/4 hr	Analytic	FN-Measurement		KA
Pr5-3A	5-2, 5-3	Purchases, accounts payable accounts, and accounts payable ledger	Moderate	1 hr	Analytic	FN-Measurement		KA

Number	Objective	Description	Difficulty	Time	AACSB	AICPA	SS	GL
Pr5-4A	5-2, 5-3	Purchases and cash payments journals; accounts payable and general ledgers	Moderate	1 3/4 hr	Analytic	FN-Measurement		KA
Pr5-5A	5-2, 5-3	All journals and general ledger; trial balance	Difficult	2 1/4 hr	Analytic	FN-Measurement		KA
Pr5-1B	5-2	Revenue journal; accounts receivable and general ledgers	Moderate	1 hr	Analytic	FN-Measurement	Exl	
Pr5-2B	5-2	Revenue and cash receipts journals; accounts receivable and general ledgers	Moderate	1 3/4 hr	Analytic	FN-Measurement		KA
Pr5-3B	5-2, 5-3	Purchases, accounts payable accounts, and accounts payable ledger	Moderate	1 hr	Analytic	FN-Measurement		KA
Pr5-4B	5-2, 5-3	Purchases and cash payments journals; accounts payable and general ledgers	Moderate	1 3/4 hr	Analytic	FN-Measurement		KA
Pr5-5B	5-2, 5-3	All journals and general ledger; trial balance	Difficult	2 1/4 hr	Analytic	FN-Measurement		KA
SA5-1	5-1	Ethics and professional ;conduct in business	Moderate	15 min	Ethics	BB-Industry		
SA5-2	5-4	Manual vs. computerized accounting systems	Easy	10 min	Technology	BB-Leveraging Technology		
SA5-3	5-2	Accounts receivable and accounts payable	Easy	10 min	Analytic	FN-Measurement		
SA5-4	5-5	The virtual close	Moderate	15 min	Reflective Thinking	BB-Critical Thinking		
SA5-5	5-1	Design of accounting systems	Moderate	20 min	Reflective Thinking	BB-Critical Thinking		
SA5-6	5-5	Web-based accounting systems	Moderate	45 min	Reflective Thinking	BB-Critical Thinking		
SA5-7	5-5	SCM and CRM	Moderate	45 min	Analytic	FN-Measurement		

EYE OPENERS

1. The individual accounts receivable ledger accounts provide business managers information on the status of individual customer accounts, which is necessary for managing collections. Managers need to know which customers owe money, how much they owe, and how long the amount owed has been outstanding.

2. The major advantages of the use of special journals are substantial savings in record-keeping expenses and a reduction of record-keeping errors.

3. **a.** 250
   b. None

4. **a.** 250
   b. 1

5. **a.** Sometime following the end of the current month, one of two things may happen: (1) an overdue notice will be received from Collins Co., and/or (2) a letter will be received from Collings Co., informing the buyer of the overpayment. (It is also possible that the error will be discovered at the time of making payment if the original invoice is inspected at the time the check is being written.)
   b. The schedule of accounts payable would not agree with the balance of the accounts payable account. The error might also be discovered at the time the invoice is paid.
   c. The creditor will call the attention of the debtor to the unpaid balance of $1,000.
   d. The error will become evident during the verification process at the end of the month. The total debits in the purchases journal will be less than the total credits by $2,000.

6. **a.** No, the error will not cause the trial balance totals to be unequal.
   b. No, the sum of the balances in the creditors ledger will not agree with the balance of the accounts payable account in the general ledger.

7. **a.** Purchases journal
   b. Cash payments journal

c. Purchases journal
d. Cash payments journal
e. Cash payments journal

8. A database is used to collect, store, and organize accounting transaction information so it can be quickly retrieved. Reports can be requested from a database to help managers direct the business.

9. An electronic form is a software window that provides the inputs for a particular transaction. For example, a check form provides the inputs (payee, amount, date) for a cash payment transaction. An electronic invoice provides the inputs (customer, amount sold, item sold) for recording revenues earned on account.

10. The use of controlling accounts to verify the accuracy of subsidiary accounts is used in a manual system. In a computerized system, it is assumed that the computer will accurately sum the individual transactions in the subsidiary accounts in determining the aggregate balance.

11. For automated systems that use electronic forms, the special journals are not used to record original transactions. Rather, electronic forms capture the original transaction detail from an invoice, for example, and automatically post the transaction details to the appropriate ledger accounts.

12. E-commerce can be used by a business to conduct transactions directly with customers. Thus, an order can be received directly from the customer's Internet input and cash can be received from the credit card. Many times, the cash is received prior to actually shipping the product, resulting in a faster revenue/collection cycle. Reducing paperwork throughout the cycle also improves the efficiency of the process. For example, all of the accounting transactions can be fed automatically from the initial Web-based inputs.

PRACTICE EXERCISES

PE 5–1A

REVENUE JOURNAL

Date		Invoice No.	Account Debited	Post. Ref.	Accounts Rec. Dr. Fees Earned Cr.
Mar.	3	78	Langley Co.		450
	12	79	Hitchcock Inc.		215
	28	80	Sunshine Inc.		685

PE 5–1B

REVENUE JOURNAL

Date		Invoice No.	Account Debited	Post. Ref.	Accounts Rec. Dr. Fees Earned Cr.
Sept.	9	121	Barney Co.		6,780
	20	122	Triple A Inc.		5,240
	24	123	Connors Co.		2,890

PE 5–2A

Jan. 10. Provided $895 services on account to New Generation Products Inc., itemized on Invoice No. 345. Amount posted from page 45 of the revenue journal.

19. Collected cash of $1,080 from New Generation Products Inc. (Invoice No. 329). Amount posted from page 78 of the cash receipts journal.

PE 5–2B

Apr. 14. Collected cash of $140 from Hopewell Communications Inc. (Invoice No. 962). Amount posted from page 315 of the cash receipts journal.

25. Provided $85 of services on account to Hopewell Communications Inc., itemized on Invoice No. 976. Amount posted from page 240 of the revenue journal.

PE 5–3A

PURCHASES JOURNAL

Date	Account Credited	Post. Ref.	Accounts Payable Cr.	Office Supplies Dr.	Other Accounts Dr. — Account	Post. Ref.	Amount	
June 4	Office-to-Go Inc.	✓	85	85	....		....	1
19	Bell Computer Inc.	✓	3,890	....	Office Equipment		3,890	2
23	Paper Warehouse Inc.	✓	145	145	....		....	3

PE 5–3B

PURCHASES JOURNAL

Date	Account Credited	Post. Ref.	Accounts Payable Cr.	Party Supplies Dr.	Other Accounts Dr. — Account	Post. Ref.	Amount	
Oct. 11	Celebration Supplies Inc.		445	445	....		....	1
19	Party Time Supplies Inc.		230	230	....		....	2
24	Office Space Inc.		2,570	....	Office Furniture		2,570	3

PE 5–4A

Dec. 9. Paid $54 to Xavier Inc. on account (Invoice 456). Amount posted from page 55 of the cash payments journal.

18. Purchased $94 services on account from Xavier Inc., itemized on Invoice 475. Amount posted from page 89 of the purchases journal.

PE 5–4B

Feb. 19. Purchased $4,250 of services on account from Bonitelli Computer Services Inc., itemized on Invoice 45. Amount posted from page 16 of the purchases journal.

26. Paid $6,700 to Bonitelli Computer Services Inc. on account (Invoice 39). Amount posted from page 36 of the cash payments journal.

PE 5–5A

REVENUE JOURNAL

	Date	Invoice No.	Account Debited	Post. Ref.	Accts. Rec. Dr.	Fees Earned Cr.	Sales Tax Payable Cr.	
1	May 8	112	Howerton Inc.		4,410	4,200	210	1
2	20	113	Tel Optics Inc.		6,069	5,780	289	2

PE 5–5B

REVENUE JOURNAL

	Date	Invoice No.	Account Debited	Post. Ref.	Accts. Rec. Dr.	Fees Earned Commercial Cr.	Fees Earned- Residential Cr.	
1	Mar. 1	919	Matrix Inc.		350	350		1
2	1	920	James King		75		75	2

307

EXERCISES

Ex. 5–1

1. General ledger accounts: (e)
2. Subsidiary ledger accounts: (a), (b), (c), (d)

Ex. 5–2

a., b., and c.

Accounts Receivable

Sept. 1 Bal.	540		
Sept. 30	6,040		
Sept. 30 Bal.	6,580		

Eco-Systems

Sept. 20	1,400	
Sept. 30 Bal.	1,400	

Environmental Safety Co.

Sept. 1	2,625	
Sept. 30 Bal.	2,625	

Greenberg Co.

Sept. 10	1,050	
Sept. 30 Bal.	1,050	

SSC Corp.

Sept. 1 Bal.	540	
Sept. 27	965	
Sept. 30 Bal.	1,505	

d.

OMEGA SERVICES INC.
Customer Balance Summary
September 30, 2008

Eco-Systems	$1,400
Environmental Safety Co.	2,625
Greenberg Co.	1,050
SSC Corp.	1,505
Total accounts receivable	$6,580

Ex. 5–3

a. Cash receipts journal
b. Cash receipts journal
c. General journal
d. General journal (not a revenue transaction)
e. Cash receipts journal

f. Cash receipts journal
g. General journal
h. Cash receipts journal
i. Revenue journal
j. Cash receipts journal

Ex. 5–4

a. General journal
b. General journal
c. Cash payments journal
d. Purchases journal
e. Cash payments journal
f. Purchases journal

g. General journal
h. General journal
i. Cash payments journal
j. Purchases journal
k. Cash payments journal

Ex. 5–5

Dec. 3. Provided service on account; posted from revenue journal page 50.
9. Granted allowance or corrected error related to sale of December 3; posted from general journal page 9.
13. Received cash for balance due; posted from cash receipts journal page 38.

Ex. 5–6

a.

REVENUE JOURNAL

Date		Invoice No.	Account Debited	Post. Ref.	Accounts Rec. Dr. Fees Earned Cr.
May	2	201	Townley Corp.		320
	3	202	Mid States Inc.		450
	12	203	Townley Corp.		165
	24	204	Parker Co.		665
	31				1,600

b. $1,600   Debit to Accounts Receivable [from revenue journal column total in (a)].

   $1,600   Credit to Fees Earned [from revenue journal column total in (a)].

c. $165   ($0 + $320 + $165 – $320)

Ex. 5–7

a. and b.

Accounts Receivable—Ayres Co.			Accounts Receivable—Brown Co.		
May 1 Bal.	1,200		May 4	2,250	
14	1,890		22	2,820	
Bal.	3,090		Bal.	5,070	

Accounts Receivable—Life Star Inc.		
May 9	3,640	
Bal.	3,640	

c.

Accounts Receivable—Control			Fees Earned		
May 1 Bal.	1,200			May 30	10,600
30	10,600			Bal.	10,600
Bal.	11,800				

d.

TRI STAR CONSULTING, INC.
Customer Balance Summary
May 31, 2008

Ayres Co.	$ 3,090
Brown Co.	5,070
Life Star Inc.	3,640
Total accounts receivable..	$11,800

The total in the schedule above agrees with the T account balance for the accounts receivable control account in part (c).

Ex. 5–8

STAR PRODUCTIONS INC.
Customer Balance Summary
September 30, 2008

Alpha Communications Inc.	$2,440
Blockbuster Studios Inc.	1,410
Central States Broadcasting Co.	2,450
Gold Coast Media	0
Total accounts receivable..	$6,300

Accounts Receivable
(Control)

Balance, September 1, 2008	$ 5,060
Total debits (from revenue journal)...	13,900
Total credits (from cash receipts journal)	(12,660)
Balance, September 30, 2008	$ 6,300

Ex. 5–9

REVENUE JOURNAL   PAGE 8

	Date	Invoice No.	Account Debited	Post. Ref.	Accounts Rec. Dr. Fees Earned Cr.	
	2008					
1	Oct. 2	512	Bellows Co............................	✓	870	1
2	8	513	Gabriel Co.	✓	275	2
3	12	514	Drake Inc.	✓	730	3
4	22	515	Electronic Central Inc.	✓	180	4
5	31		Total.....................................		2,055	5

CASH RECEIPTS JOURNAL   PAGE 12

	Date	Account Credited	Post. Ref.	Fees Earned Cr.	Accts. Rec. Cr.	Cash Dr.	
	2008						
1	Oct. 4	CMI Inc.	✓	....	210	210	1
2	19	Drake Inc......................	✓	....	670	670	2
3	27	Fees Earned................		105	....	105	3
4	29	Bellows Co..................	✓	....	870	870	4
5	31	Fees Earned...............		80	....	80	5
6	31	Total		185	1,750	1,935	6

Ex. 5–10

a.

		REVENUE JOURNAL		Page 19
Date	Invoice No.	Account Debited	Post. Ref.	Accounts Rec. Dr. Fees Earned Cr.
2008				
Aug. 3	622	Phillips Corp.........................	✓	2,340
10	623	Sunstream Aviation Inc.	✓	4,260
18	624	Amex Services Inc.	✓	2,900
28	625	Townley Co..........................	✓	2,380
31		Total		11,880

	CASH RECEIPTS JOURNAL				PAGE 25
Date	Account Credited	Post. Ref.	Fees Earned Cr.	Accts. Rec. Cr.	Cash Dr.
2008					
Aug. 5	Dunn Co.	✓		1,030	1,030
15	Townley Co.......................	✓		1,460	1,460
23	Phillips Corp....................	✓		2,340	2,340
30	Fees Earned....................	✓	60		60
31	Total		60	4,830	4,890

b.

ORION CORP.
Customer Balance Summary
August 31, 2008

Amex Services Inc.	$2,900
Sunstream Aviation Inc.	4,260
Townley Co...	2,380
Total accounts receivable...	$9,540

The total of the customer accounts on August 31, 2008, $9,540, equals the balance of the accounts receivable control account, shown as follows:

Accounts Receivable—Control

Aug. 1 Bal.	2,490	Aug. 31	4,830
31	11,880		
Aug. 31 Bal.	9,540		

Ex. 5–11

1. General ledger account: (c), (e), (h), (j), (k), (l)
2. Subsidiary ledger account: (a), (b), (d), (f), (g), (i)
3. No posting required: (m)

Ex. 5–12

1. General ledger account: (b), (c), (d), (f), (g), (i), (k), (l)
2. Subsidiary ledger account: (a), (e), (h)
3. No posting required: (j)

Ex. 5–13

Mar. 6.   Purchased services, supplies, equipment, or other commodities on account; posted from purchases journal page 34.

    10.   Received allowance or corrected error related to purchase of March 6; posted from general journal page 10.

    16.   Paid balance owed; posted from cash payments journal page 37.

Ex. 3–14

a.

PURCHASES JOURNAL

Date	Account Credited	Post. Ref.	Accounts Payable Cr.	Office Supplies Dr.	Other Accounts Dr. Account	Post Ref.	Amount
Apr. 4	Office Helper Inc.		420	420			
8	Best Equipment, Inc.		1,800	......	Office Equipment		1,800
12	Office Helper Inc.		120	120			......
21	Paper-to-Go Inc.		185	185			......
30	....		2,525	725			......

b. $2,525 Credit to Accounts Payable [from purchases journal column total in (a)].

 $725 Debit to Office Supplies [from purchases journal column total in (a)].

c. $120 ($0 + $420 + $120 – $420)

315

Ex. 5–15

a. and b.

Accounts Payable—Best Cleaning Supplies Inc.

	Jan. 4	345
	26	310
	Bal.	655

Accounts Payable—Lawson Co.

	Jan. 1 Bal.	265
	15	285
	Bal.	550

Accounts Payable—Office Mate Inc.

	Jan. 21	3,400
	Bal.	3,400

c.

Accounts Payable—Control

	Jan. 1 Bal.	265
	31	4,340
	Bal.	4,605

Cleaning Supplies

Jan. 31	940	
Bal.	940	

d.

KEEP WINDOWS CLEANER INC.
Supplier Balance Summary
January 31, 2008

Best Cleaning Supplies Inc.	$ 655
Lawson Co.	550
Office Mate Inc.	3,400
Total supplier account balances	$ 4,605

The total in the schedule above agrees with the T account balance for the accounts payable control account in (c).

Ex. 5–16

SILVER SPRING LANDSCAPING CO.
Supplier Balance Summary
June 30, 2008

Augusta Sod Co.	$ 6,310
Gibraltar Insurance Co.	1,100
Kimble Lumber Co.	3,650
Schott's Fertilizer..	0
Total accounts payable	$11,060

Accounts Payable
(Control)

Balance, June 1, 2008..	$ 2,940
Total credits (from purchases journal)	17,950
Total debits (from cash payments journal)..............................	(9,830)
Balance, June 30, 2008..	$11,060

Ex. 5–17

PURCHASES JOURNAL
PAGE 36

Date	Account Credited	Post. Ref.	Accounts Payable Cr.	Cleaning Supplies Dr.	Other Accounts Dr. Account	Post. Ref.	Amount	
2008								
Dec. 3	Industrial Products Inc.	✓	130	130	....		....	1
12	Purcell Products Inc.	✓	190	190	....		....	2
17	Liquid Klean Supplies...........	✓	245	245	....		....	3
20	Maryville Laundry Service	✓	95	......	Laundry Service Expense	53	95	4
31	Total		660	565	....		95	5

CASH PAYMENTS JOURNAL
PAGE 41

Date	Ck. No.	Account Debited	Post. Ref.	Other Accounts Dr.	Accounts Payable Dr.	Cash Cr.	
2008							
Dec. 1	57	Liquid Klean Supplies, Inc.	✓	....	205	205	1
8	58	Equipment	18	2,600	....	2,600	2
15	59	Maryville Laundry Service..	✓	....	100	100	4
25	60	Industrial Products Inc.	✓	....	130	130	5
31	61	Salary Expense	51	4,100	....	4,100	6
31		Total		6,700	435	7,135	7

a.

PURCHASES JOURNAL

Date	Account Credited	Post. Ref.	Accounts Payable Cr.	Pet Supplies Dr.	Other Accounts Dr. Account	Post. Ref.	Amount	
2008								
May 4	Best Friend Supplies Inc.	✓	265	265			......	1
11	Poodle Pals Inc.	✓	675	675			......	2
19	Office Helper, Inc.	✓	2,400		Office Equipment	13	2,400	3
27	Pets Mart Inc.	✓	410	410			......	4
31			3,750	1,350			2,400	5

CASH PAYMENTS JOURNAL

Date	Ck. No.	Account Debited	Post. Ref.	Other Accounts Dr.	Accounts Payable Dr.	Cash Cr.	
2008							
May 6	345	Larrimore Inc.		......	455	455	1
18	346	Pets Mart Inc.		......	230	230	2
23	347	Best Friend Supplies Inc.		......	265	265	3
30	348	Cleaning Expense	54	45		45	4
31				45	950	995	5

Ex. 5–18   Concluded

b.

PET GROOM INC.
Supplier Balance Summary
May 31, 2008

Pets Mart Inc.	$ 410
Poodle Pals Inc.	675
Office Helper Inc.	2,400
Total supplier (creditor) accounts..	$3,485

The total of the creditor accounts on May 31, 2008, $3,485, equals the balance of the accounts payable control account, shown as follows:

Accounts Payable—Control

May 31	950	May 1 Bal.	685
		31	3,750
		Bal.	3,485

Ex. 5–19

a. Two errors were made in balancing the accounts in the subsidiary ledger:

   (1) The Martinez Mining Co. transaction of October 25 should have resulted in a balance of $3,050 instead of $2,050.

   (2) The Cheyenne Minerals Inc. transaction of October 7 should have resulted in a balance of $14,200 instead of $14,300, and the account balance at October 31 should have been $8,400 instead of $8,500.

b.

WESTERN ASSAY SERVICES INC.
Supplier Balance Summary Report
October 31, 2008

C. D. Greer and Son..	$13,750
Cheyenne Minerals Inc..	8,400
Cutler and Powell...	9,100
Martinez Mining Co.	3,050
Valley Power..	3,150
Total accounts payable	$37,450

Ex. 5–20

Revenue journal: (d), (i)

Cash receipts journal: (a), (e)

Purchases journal: (g), (h)

Cash payments journal: (b), (f)

General journal: (c), (j)

Ex. 5–21

1. The Cash column is for debits (not credits).
2. The Other Accounts column is for credits (not debits).
3. A better order of columns would be to place the Other Accounts Cr. column to the left of the Fees Earned Cr. column.

A recommended and corrected cash receipts journal is as follows:

CASH RECEIPTS JOURNAL   PAGE 12

Date	Account Credited	Post. Ref.	Other Accounts Cr.	Fees Earned Cr.	Accounts Rec. Cr.	Cash Dr.

Ex. 5–22

a.

REVENUE JOURNAL   PAGE 1

	Date	Invoice No.	Account Debited	Post. Ref.	Accts. Rec. Dr.	Fees Earned Cr.	Sales Tax Payable Cr.	
1	June 16	1	A. Sommerfeld	✓	420	400	20	1
2	19	2	R. Mendoza	✓	189	180	9	2
3	21	3	J. Koss	✓	105	100	5	3
4	22	4	D. Jeffries	✓	168	160	8	4
5	26	5	J. Koss	✓	294	280	14	5
6	28	6	R. Mendoza	✓	42	40	2	6
7	30				1,218	1,160	58	7
8					(12)	(41)	(22)	8

Ex. 5–22   Continued

JOURNAL

PAGE 1

Date	Description	Post. Ref.	Debit	Credit
2008				
June 24	Office Supplies	14	105	
	Fees Earned..	41		100
	Sales Tax Payable	22		5

ACCOUNTS RECEIVABLE SUBSIDIARY LEDGER

D. Jeffries

Date	Item	Post. Ref.	Dr.	Cr.	Balance
2008					
June 22	....	R1	168	....	168

J. Koss

Date	Item	Post. Ref.	Dr.	Cr.	Balance
2008					
June 21	....	R1	105	....	105
26	....	R1	294	....	399

R. Mendoza

Date	Item	Post. Ref.	Dr.	Cr.	Balance
2008					
June 19	....	R1	189	....	189
28	....	R1	42	....	231

A. Sommerfeld

Date	Item	Post. Ref.	Dr.	Cr.	Balance
2008					
June 16	....	R1	420	....	420

Ex. 5–22   Concluded

b.

GENERAL LEDGER

Accounts Receivable   **12**

Date	Item	Post. Ref.	Dr.	Cr.	Balance Dr.	Balance Cr.
2008						
June 30	....	R1	1,218	....	1,218	....

Office Supplies   **14**

Date	Item	Post. Ref.	Dr.	Cr.	Balance Dr.	Balance Cr.
2008						
June 24	....	J1	105	....	105	....

Sales Tax Payable   **22**

Date	Item	Post. Ref.	Dr.	Cr.	Balance Dr.	Balance Cr.
2008						
June 24	....	J1	....	5	....	5
30	....	R1	....	58	....	63

Fees Earned   **41**

Date	Item	Post. Ref.	Dr.	Cr.	Balance Dr.	Balance Cr.
2008						
June 24	....	J1	....	100	....	100
30	....	R1	....	1,160	....	1,260

c. 1. $1,218 ($168 + $399 + $231 + $420)
    2. $1,218

Ex. 5–23

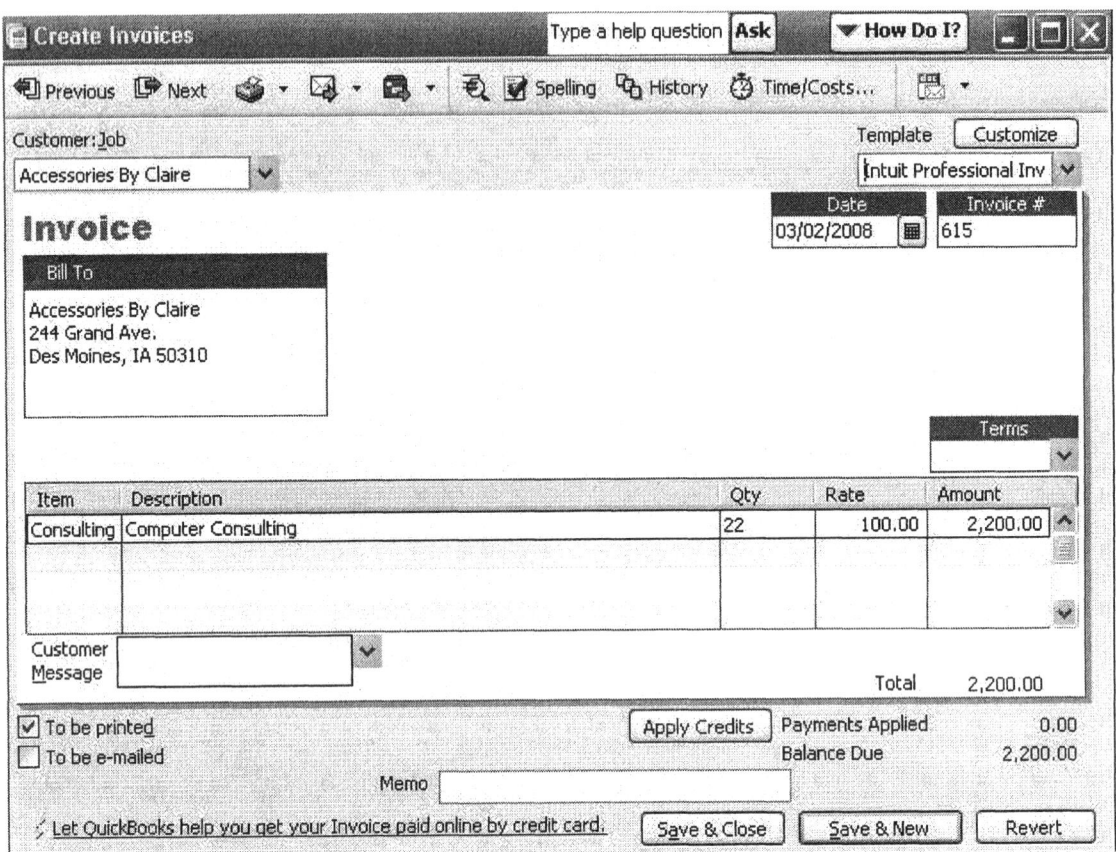

a. In the electronic invoice form from QuickBooks® shown above, typical fields for data input can be identified:
   1. Customer name and address
   2. Date and invoice number
   3. Description of item sold
   4. Amount of revenue

b. The customer Accounts Receivable is debited, and Fees Earned is credited. A computerized accounting system does not require posting to a separate accounts receivable control account. In this case, the total accounts receivable reported on the balance sheet is merely the sum of the balances of the individual customer account balances.

Ex. 5–23   Concluded

c. Controlling accounts are not posted at the end of the month in a computer-ized accounting system. In addition, special journals are not normally used to accumulate transactions. Transactions are recorded through data input into electronic forms (or for infrequent transactions, by an electronic general journal). Balances of affected accounts are automatically posted and updated from the information recorded on the form. If desired, the computer can pro-vide a printout of the monthly transaction history for a particular account, which provides the same information as a journal. In addition, the controlling account is not separately posted. In a manual system, separate posting to the controlling account provides additional control by reconciling the controlling account balance against the sum of the individual customer account bal-ances. However, in a computerized accounting system, there are no separate postings to a controlling account because the computer is not going to make posting or mathematical errors. Therefore, there is no need for the additional control provided by posting a journal total to a controlling account.

Ex. 5–24

a. Amazon.com   B2C. Sells books, DVDs, and other products to individual consumers.

b. Dell Inc.   B2C and B2B. Sells computer products to both individu-als and corporations. Its site separates individual and corporate sales.

c. W.W. Grainger, Inc.   B2B. Sells maintenance, repair, and operating supplies to manufacturing companies.

d. L.L. Bean, Inc.   B2C. Consumer clothes e-retailer.

e. Smurfit-Stone Container Corporation   B2B. One of the largest providers of corrugated contain-ers and boxes.

f. Intuit Inc.   B2C and B2B. Arranges its site for both individuals and businesses, since its products are divided this way.

PROBLEMS

Prob. 5–1A

1. and 2.

			REVENUE JOURNAL		PAGE 1

Date	Invoice No.	Account Debited	Post. Ref.	Accounts Rec. Dr. Fees Earned Cr.	
2008					
1 Mar. 21	1	J. Dunlop	✓	70	1
2 22	2	K. Thorne	✓	310	2
3 24	3	T. Morris	✓	95	3
4 27	4	F. Mintz	✓	190	4
5 28	5	D. Bennett	✓	175	5
6 30	6	K. Thorne	✓	105	6
7 31	7	T. Morris	✓	115	7
8 31				1,060	8
9				(12) (41)	9

			JOURNAL		PAGE 1

Date	Description	Post. Ref.	Debit	Credit
2008				
Mar. 25	Supplies...	13	125	
	Fees Earned	41		125

Prob. 5–1A   Continued

ACCOUNTS RECEIVABLE LEDGER

D. Bennett

Date	Item	Post. Ref.	Dr.	Cr.	Balance
2008					
Mar. 28	....	R1	175	....	175

J. Dunlop

Date	Item	Post. Ref.	Dr.	Cr.	Balance
2008					
Mar. 21	....	R1	70	....	70

F. Mintz

Date	Item	Post. Ref.	Dr.	Cr.	Balance
2008					
Mar. 27	....	R1	190	....	190

T. Morris

Date	Item	Post. Ref.	Dr.	Cr.	Balance
2008					
Mar. 24	....	R1	95	....	95
31	....	R1	115	....	210

K. Thorne

Date	Item	Post. Ref.	Dr.	Cr.	Balance
2008					
Mar. 22	....	R1	310	....	310
30	....	R1	105	....	415

Prob. 5–1A   Concluded

2.

GENERAL LEDGER

Accounts Receivable   12

Date	Item	Post. Ref.	Dr.	Cr.	Balance Dr.	Balance Cr.
2008						
Mar. 31	....	R1	1,060	....	1,060	....

Supplies   13

Date	Item	Post. Ref.	Dr.	Cr.	Balance Dr.	Balance Cr.
2008						
Mar. 25	....	J1	125	....	125	....

Fees Earned   41

Date	Item	Post. Ref.	Dr.	Cr.	Balance Dr.	Balance Cr.
2008						
Mar. 25	....	J1	....	125	....	125
31	....	R1	....	1,060	....	1,185

3. a. $1,060 ($175 + $70 + $190 + $210 + $415)

    b. $1,060

4. The single money column in the revenue journal can be replaced with three columns for (1) Accounts Receivable Dr., (2) Fees Earned Cr., and (3) Sales Tax Payable Cr.

Prob. 5–2A

1. and 5.

GENERAL LEDGER

Cash 11

Date		Item	Post. Ref.	Dr.	Cr.	Balance Dr.	Balance Cr.
2008							
Sept.	1	Balance	✓	....	....	13,650	....
	30	....	CR36	34,680	....	48,330	....

Accounts Receivable 12

Date		Item	Post. Ref.	Dr.	Cr.	Balance Dr.	Balance Cr.
2008							
Sept.	1	Balance	✓	....	....	15,370	....
	25	....	J1	....	2,000	13,370	....
	30	....	R40	24,450	....	37,820	....
	30	....	CR36	....	22,750	15,070	....

Notes Receivable 14

Date		Item	Post. Ref.	Dr.	Cr.	Balance Dr.	Balance Cr.
2008							
Sept.	1	Balance	✓	....	....	5,000	....
	25	....	J1	2,000	....	7,000	....

Fees Earned 41

Date		Item	Post. Ref.	Dr.	Cr.	Balance Dr.	Balance Cr.
2008							
Sept.	30	....	R40	....	24,450	....	24,450
	30	....	CR36	....	11,930	....	36,380

Prob. 5–2A   Continued

2. and 4.

ACCOUNTS RECEIVABLE SUBSIDIARY LEDGER

Mendez Co.

Date	Item	Post. Ref.	Dr.	Cr.	Balance
2008					
Sept. 1	Balance	✓	....	....	8,960
5	....	CR36	....	8,960	—
22	....	R40	8,020	....	8,020

Morton Co.

Date	Item	Post. Ref.	Dr.	Cr.	Balance
2008					
Sept. 2	....	R40	5,400	....	5,400
19	....	CR36	....	5,400	—

Quest Co.

Date	Item	Post. Ref.	Dr.	Cr.	Balance
2008					
Sept. 1	Balance	✓	....	....	6,410
6	....	R40	1,980	....	8,390
15	....	CR36	....	6,410	1,980
16	....	R40	6,100	....	8,080
20	....	CR36	....	1,980	6,100

Shilo Co.

Date	Item	Post. Ref.	Dr.	Cr.	Balance
2008					
Sept. 13	....	R40	2,950	....	2,950
25	....	J1	....	2,000	950

Prob. 5–2A   Concluded

3., 4., and 5.

REVENUE JOURNAL

	Date	Invoice No.	Account Debited	Post. Ref.	Accounts Rec. Dr. Fees Earned Cr.	
	2008					
1	Sept. 2	793	Morton Co.	✓	5,400	1
2	6	794	Quest Co.	✓	1,980	2
3	13	795	Shilo Co................................	✓	2,950	3
4	16	796	Quest Co.	✓	6,100	4
5	22	797	Mendez Co.	✓	8,020	5
6	30				24,450	6
7					(12) (41)	7

CASH RECEIPTS JOURNAL

	Date	Account Credited	Post. Ref.	Fees Earned Cr.	Accts. Rec. Cr.	Cash Dr.	
	2008						
1	Sept. 5	Mendez Co.	✓	....	8,960	8,960	1
2	15	Quest Co.	✓	....	6,410	6,410	2
3	19	Morton Co.	✓	....	5,400	5,400	3
4	20	Quest Co.	✓	....	1,980	1,980	4
5	30	Fees Earned................	✓	11,930	....	11,930	5
6	30			11,930	22,750	34,680	6
7				(41)	(12)	(11)	7

JOURNAL

Date	Description	Post. Ref.	Debit	Credit
2008				
Sept. 25	Notes Receivable	14	2,000	
	Accounts Receivable—Shilo Co.	12/✓		2,000

The subsidiary account of Shilo Co. must also be posted for a $2,000 credit.

6. The subsidiary ledger is in agreement with the controlling account. Both have balances of $15,070 ($8,020 + $6,100 + $950).

Prob. 5–3A

1. and 4.

GENERAL LEDGER

Field Supplies — 14

Date	Item	Post. Ref.	Dr.	Cr.	Balance Dr.	Balance Cr.
2008						
May 1	Balance	✓	....	....	6,310	....
31	....	P30	10,460	....	16,770	....

Office Supplies — 15

Date	Item	Post. Ref.	Dr.	Cr.	Balance Dr.	Balance Cr.
2008						
May 1	Balance	✓	....	....	830	....
31	....	P30	890	....	1,720	....

Office Equipment — 18

Date	Item	Post. Ref.	Dr.	Cr.	Balance Dr.	Balance Cr.
2008						
May 1	Balance	✓	....	....	14,300	....
5	....	P30	5,150	....	19,450	....

Accounts Payable — 21

Date	Item	Post. Ref.	Dr.	Cr.	Balance Dr.	Balance Cr.
2008						
May 1	Balance	✓	....	....	....	1,105
31	....	P30	....	16,500	....	17,605

Prob. 5–3A   Continued

2. and 3.

ACCOUNTS PAYABLE SUBSIDIARY LEDGER

Executive Office Supply Co.

Date		Item	Post. Ref.	Dr.	Cr.	Balance
2008						
May	1	Balance	✓	....	....	365
	9	....	P30	....	305	670
	29	....	P30	....	225	895

Lawson Co.

Date		Item	Post. Ref.	Dr.	Cr.	Balance
2008						
May	1	Balance	✓	....	....	740
	2	....	P30	....	360	1,100

Nelson Co.

Date		Item	Post. Ref.	Dr.	Cr.	Balance
2008						
May	14	....	P30	....	2,940	2,940
	24	....	P30	....	3,810	6,750
	31	....	P30	....	1,005	7,755

Peach Computers Co.

Date		Item	Post. Ref.	Dr.	Cr.	Balance
2008						
May	5	....	P30	....	5,150	5,150

Yee Co.

Date		Item	Post. Ref.	Dr.	Cr.	Balance
2008						
May	13	....	P30	....	1,360	1,360
	17	....	P30	....	1,345	2,705

Prob. 5–3A   Concluded

3. and 4.

PURCHASES JOURNAL

PAGE 30

Date	Account Credited	Post. Ref.	Accounts Payable Cr.	Field Supplies Dr.	Office Supplies Dr.	Other Accounts Dr. Account	Post. Ref.	Amount	
2008									
May 2	Lawson Co.	✓	360	....	360	....		....	1
5	Peach Computers Co.	✓	5,150	....		Office Equipment	18	5,150	2
9	Executive Office Supply Co.	✓	305	....	305	....		....	3
13	Yee Co	✓	1,360	1,360		....		....	4
14	Nelson Co	✓	2,940	2,940		....		....	5
17	Yee Co.	✓	1,345	1,345		....		....	6
24	Nelson Co	✓	3,810	3,810		....		....	7
29	Executive Office Supply Co.	✓	225	....	225	....		....	8
31	Nelson Co	✓	1,005	1,005		....		....	9
31	....		16,500	10,460	890	....		5,150	10
			(21)	(14)	(15)			(✓)	11

5. a. $17,605 ($895 + $1,100 + $7,755 + $5,150 + $2,705)

    b. $17,605

Prob. 5—4A

1., 2., and 3.

PURCHASES JOURNAL

	Date	Account Credited	Post. Ref.	Accounts Payable Cr.	Field Supplies Dr.	Office Supplies Dr.	Other Accounts Dr. Account	Post. Ref.	Amount	
	2008									
1	Sept. 16	Heath Supply Co.	✓	4,360	4,360	....	....		....	1
2	16	Test-Rite Equipment Co.	✓	15,900	....	....	Field Equipment	17	15,900	2
3	17	Baker Supply Co.	✓	280	....	280	....		....	3
4	23	Baker Supply Co.	✓	410	....	410	....		....	4
5	30	Heath Supply Co.	✓	5,300	5,300	....	....		....	5
6	30	Test-Rite Equipment Co.	✓	4,300	700	....	Field Equipment	17	3,600	6
7	30			30,550	10,360	690			19,500	7
8				(21)	(14)	(15)			(✓)	8

335

Prob. 5–4A   Continued

Date	Ck. No.	Account Debited	Post. Ref.	Other Accounts Dr.	Accounts Payable Dr.	Cash Cr.	
2008							
Sept. 16	1	Rent Expense	71	1,500	....	1,500	1
19	2	Field Supplies	14	2,420	....	2,420	2
		Office Supplies	15	300	....	300	3
23	3	Land.	19	35,000	....	35,000	4
24	4	Heath Supply Co.	✓	....	4,360	4,360	5
26	5	Test-Rite Equipment Co...	✓	....	15,900	15,900	6
30	6	Baker Supply Co.	✓	....	280	280	7
30	7	Salary Expense	61	21,400	....	21,400	8
30		Total		60,620	20,540	81,160	9
				(✓)	(21)	(11)	10

1. and 2.

Date	Description	Post. Ref.	Debit	Credit
2008				
Sept. 30	Land	19	7,000	
	Field Equipment	17		7,000

Prob. 5–4A   Continued

1.

ACCOUNTS PAYABLE SUBSIDIARY LEDGER

Baker Supply Co.

Date		Item	Post. Ref.	Dr.	Cr.	Balance
2008						
Sept.	17	....	P1	....	280	280
	23	....	P1	....	410	690
	30	....	CP1	280	....	410

Heath Supply Co.

Date		Item	Post. Ref.	Dr.	Cr.	Balance
2008						
Sept.	16	....	P1	....	4,360	4,360
	24	....	CP1	4,360	....	—
	30	....	P1	....	5,300	5,300

Test-Rite Equipment Co.

Date		Item	Post. Ref.	Dr.	Cr.	Balance
2008						
Sept.	16	....	P1	....	15,900	15,900
	26	....	CP1	15,900	....	—
	30	....	P1	....	4,300	4,300

Prob. 5–4A   Continued

2. and 3.

GENERAL LEDGER

Cash   11

Date	Item	Post. Ref.	Dr.	Cr.	Balance Dr.	Balance Cr.
2008						
Sept. 30	....	CP1	....	81,160	....	81,160

Field Supplies   14

Date	Item	Post. Ref.	Dr.	Cr.	Balance Dr.	Balance Cr.
2008						
Sept. 19	....	CP1	2,420	....	2,420	....
30	....	P1	10,360	....	12,780	....

Office Supplies   15

Date	Item	Post. Ref.	Dr.	Cr.	Balance Dr.	Balance Cr.
2008						
Sept. 19	....	CP1	300	....	300	....
30	....	P1	690	....	990	....

Field Equipment   17

Date	Item	Post. Ref.	Dr.	Cr.	Balance Dr.	Balance Cr.
2008						
Sept. 16	....	P1	15,900	....	15,900	....
30	....	P1	3,600	....	19,500	....
30	....	J1	....	7,000	12,500	....

Land   19

Date	Item	Post. Ref.	Dr.	Cr.	Balance Dr.	Balance Cr.
2008						
Sept. 23	....	CP1	35,000	....	35,000	....
30	....	J1	7,000	....	42,000	....

Accounts Payable   21

Date	Item	Post. Ref.	Dr.	Cr.	Balance Dr.	Balance Cr.
2008						
Sept. 30	....	P1	....	30,550	....	30,550
30	....	CP1	20,540	....	....	10,010

Prob. 5–4A   Concluded

GENERAL LEDGER

Salary Expense   61

Date	Item	Post. Ref.	Dr.	Cr.	Balance Dr.	Cr.
2008						
Sept. 30	....	CP1	21,400	....	21,400	....

Rent Expense   71

Date	Item	Post. Ref.	Dr.	Cr.	Balance Dr.	Cr.
2008						
Sept. 16	....	CP1	1,500	....	1,500	....

4.

ARTESIAN SPRINGS WATER TESTING SERVICE
Supplier Balance Summary
September 30, 2008

Baker Supply Co.	$ 410
Heath Supply Co.	5,300
Test-Rite Equipment Co.	4,300
Total accounts payable	$10,010*

*The total of the schedule of accounts payable is equal to the balance of the accounts payable control account.

Prob. 5–5A

1., 3., and 4.

GENERAL LEDGER

Cash   11

| | | Post. | | | Balance | |
Date	Item	Ref.	Dr.	Cr.	Dr.	Cr.
2008						
July 1	Balance	✓	....	....	158,965	....
31		CR31	52,560	....	211,525	....
31		CP34	....	117,725	93,800	....

Accounts Receivable   12

2008						
July 1	Balance	✓	....	....	13,400	....
31		R35	20,870	....	34,270	....
31		CR31	....	15,820	18,450	....

Maintenance Supplies   14

2008						
July 1	Balance	✓	....	....	9,300	....
20		J1	....	3,500	5,800	....
31		P37	3,710	....	9,510	....

Office Supplies   15

2008						
July 1	Balance	✓	....	....	4,500	....
31		CP34	800	....	5,300	....
31		P37	1,030	....	6,330	....

Office Equipment   16

2008						
July 1	Balance	✓	....	....	24,300	....
6		P37	4,200	....	28,500	....

Accumulated Depreciation—Office Equipment   17

2008						
July 1	Balance	✓	....	....	....	4,500

Prob. 5–5A   Continued

GENERAL LEDGER

Vehicles   18

Date		Item	Post. Ref.	Dr.	Cr.	Balance Dr.	Balance Cr.
2008							
July	1	Balance	✓	....	....	84,600	....
	5	....	P37	31,600	....	116,200	....
	16	....	CP34	38,900	....	155,100	....

Accumulated Depreciation—Vehicles   19

Date		Item	Post. Ref.	Dr.	Cr.	Balance Dr.	Balance Cr.
2008							
July	1	Balance	✓	....	....	....	12,300

Accounts Payable   21

Date		Item	Post. Ref.	Dr.	Cr.	Balance Dr.	Balance Cr.
2008							
July	1	Balance	✓	....	....	....	5,315
	31	....	P37	....	40,540	....	45,855
	31	....	CP34	41,115	....	....	4,740

K. Rivera, Capital   31

Date		Item	Post. Ref.	Dr.	Cr.	Balance Dr.	Balance Cr.
2008							
July	1	Balance	✓	....	....	....	272,950

K. Rivera, Drawing   32

Date		Item	Post. Ref.	Dr.	Cr.	Balance Dr.	Balance Cr.
2008							
July	24	....	CP34	3,000	....	3,000	....

Fees Earned   41

Date		Item	Post. Ref.	Dr.	Cr.	Balance Dr.	Balance Cr.
2008							
July	16	....	CR31	....	17,800	....	17,800
	31	....	CR31	....	18,940	....	36,740
	31	....	R35	....	20,870	....	57,610

GENERAL LEDGER

Driver Salaries Expense   51

Date	Item	Post. Ref.	Dr.	Cr.	Balance Dr.	Balance Cr.
2008 July 30	....	CP34	16,500	....	16,500	....

Maintenance Supplies Expense   52

Date	Item	Post. Ref.	Dr.	Cr.	Balance Dr.	Balance Cr.
2008 July 20	....	J1	3,500	....	3,500	....

Fuel Expense   53

Date	Item	Post. Ref.	Dr.	Cr.	Balance Dr.	Balance Cr.
2008 July 9	....	CP34	850	....	850	....

Office Salaries Expense   61

Date	Item	Post. Ref.	Dr.	Cr.	Balance Dr.	Balance Cr.
2008 July 30	....	CP34	8,200	....	8,200	....

Rent Expense   62

Date	Item	Post. Ref.	Dr.	Cr.	Balance Dr.	Balance Cr.
2008 July 1	....	CP34	6,400	....	6,400	....

Advertising Expense   63

Date	Item	Post. Ref.	Dr.	Cr.	Balance Dr.	Balance Cr.
2008 July 20	....	CP34	1,700	....	1,700	....

Miscellaneous Administrative Expense   64

Date	Item	Post. Ref.	Dr.	Cr.	Balance Dr.	Balance Cr.
2008 July 17	....	CP34	260	....	260	....

Prob. 5-5A   Continued

2., 3., and 4.

PURCHASES JOURNAL

Date	Account Credited	Post. Ref.	Accounts Payable Cr.	Maintenance Supplies Dr.	Office Supplies Dr.	Other Accounts Dr. Account	Post. Ref.	Amount	
2008									
July 5	Browning Trans.	✓	31,600	....	....	Vehicles	18	31,600	1
6	Bell Computer Co.	✓	4,200	....	....	Office Equipment	16	4,200	2
18	Crowne Supply Co.	✓	1,730	1,730	....				3
19	McClain Co.	✓	2,410	1,980	430				4
23	Office To Go Inc.	✓	600	....	600	....			5
31			40,540	3,710	1,030	....		35,800	6
			(21)	(14)	(15)			(✓)	7

CASH RECEIPTS JOURNAL

Date	Account Credited	Post. Ref.	Other Accounts Cr.	Accounts Receivable Cr.	Cash Dr.	
2008						
July 3	Perkins Co.	✓	....	5,400	5,400	1
10	Shingo Co.	✓	....	4,050	4,050	2
12	Capps Co.	✓	....	2,420	2,420	3
16	Fees Earned	41	17,800	....	17,800	4
25	Perkins Co.	✓	....	3,950	3,950	5
31	Fees Earned	41	18,940	....	18,940	6
31	Total		36,740	15,820	52,560	7
			(✓)	(12)	(11)	8

Prob. 5–5A Continued

2. and 4.

REVENUE JOURNAL

PAGE 35

	Date		Invoice No.	Account Debited	Post. Ref.	Accounts Rec. Dr. Fees Earned Cr.	
	2008						
1	July	2	940	Capps Co.	✓	2,420	1
2		6	941	Darr Co.	✓	5,920	2
3		10	942	Joy Co.	✓	1,260	3
4		24	943	Shingo Co.	✓	5,070	4
5		25	944	Darr Co.	✓	6,200	5
6		31				20,870	6
7						(12) (41)	7

2., 3., and 4.

CASH PAYMENTS JOURNAL

PAGE 34

	Date		Ck. No.	Account Debited	Post. Ref.	Other Accounts Dr.	Accounts Payable Dr.	Cash Cr.	
	2008								
1	July	1	610	Rent Expense	62	6,400		6,400	1
2		9	611	Fuel Expense	53	850		850	2
3		10	612	Office To Go Inc.	✓		905	905	3
4		11	613	Crowne Supply Co.	✓		3,605	3,605	4
5		11	614	Porter Co.	✓		805	805	5
6		13	615	Browning Trans.	✓		31,600	31,600	6
7		16	616	Vehicles	18	38,900		38,900	7
8		17	617	Misc. Admin. Exp.	64	260		260	8
9		20	618	Advertising Exp.	63	1,700		1,700	9
10		24	619	K. Rivera, Drawing	32	3,000		3,000	10
11		26	620	Bell Computer Co.	✓		4,200	4,200	11
12		30	621	Driver Salaries Exp.	51	16,500		16,500	12
13				Office Salaries Exp.	61	8,200		8,200	13
14		31	622	Office Supplies	15	800		800	14
15		31				76,610	41,115	117,725	15
16						(✓)	(21)	(11)	16

Prob. 5–5A   Concluded

2. and 3.

		Post.		
Date	Description	Ref.	Debit	Credit

JOURNAL   PAGE 1

2008
July 20   Maintenance Supplies Expense   52   3,500
              Maintenance Supplies.......................   14   3,500

5.

LIGHTENING EXPRESS DELIVERY COMPANY
Unadjusted Trial Balance
July 31, 2008

	Debit Balances	Credit Balances
Cash..	93,800	
Accounts Receivable..	18,450	
Maintenance Supplies	9,510	
Office Supplies...	6,330	
Office Equipment	28,500	
Accumulated Depreciation—Office Equipment		4,500
Vehicles	155,100	
Accumulated Depreciation—Vehicles		12,300
Accounts Payable...		4,740
K. Rivera, Capital		272,950
K. Rivera, Drawing	3,000	
Fees Earned		57,610
Driver Salaries Expense....................................	16,500	
Maintenance Supplies Expense	3,500	
Fuel Expense..	850	
Office Salaries Expense	8,200	
Rent Expense...	6,400	
Advertising Expense	1,700	
Miscellaneous Administrative Expense........................	260	
	352,100	352,100

6.   Balance of accounts receivable control account, $18,450.

    Balance of accounts payable control account, $4,740.

Prob. 5–1B

1. and 2.

				REVENUE JOURNAL			PAGE 1	

	Date	Invoice No.		Account Debited	Post. Ref.	Accounts Rec. Dr. Fees Earned Cr.	
	2008						
1	Aug. 18	1		Jacob Co.	✓	340	1
2	20	2		Qwik-Mart Co.	✓	275	2
3	22	3		Great Northern Co.	✓	580	3
4	27	4		Carson Co.	✓	465	4
5	28	5		Bower Co.	✓	105	5
6	30	6		Qwik-Mart Co.	✓	135	6
7	31	7		Great Northern Co.	✓	240	7
8	31					2,140	8
9						(12) (41)	9

	JOURNAL			PAGE 1

Date	Description	Post. Ref.	Debit	Credit
2008				
Aug. 28	Supplies..	14	90	
	Fees Earned	41		90

Prob. 5–1B   Continued

1.

ACCOUNTS RECEIVABLE LEDGER

Bower Co.

Date	Item	Post. Ref.	Dr.	Cr.	Balance
2008					
Aug. 28	....	R1	105	....	105

Carson Co.

Date	Item	Post. Ref.	Dr.	Cr.	Balance
2008					
Aug. 27	....	R1	465	....	465

Great Northern Co.

Date	Item	Post. Ref.	Dr.	Cr.	Balance
2008					
Aug. 22	....	R1	580	....	580
31	....	R1	240	....	820

Jacob Co.

Date	Item	Post. Ref.	Dr.	Cr.	Balance
2008					
Aug. 18	....	R1	340	....	340

Qwik-Mart Co.

Date	Item	Post. Ref.	Dr.	Cr.	Balance
2008					
Aug. 20	....	R1	275	....	275
30	....	R1	135	....	410

2.

GENERAL LEDGER

Accounts Receivable 12

Date	Item	Post. Ref.	Dr.	Cr.	Balance Dr.	Balance Cr.
2008 Aug. 31	....	R1	2,140	....	2,140	....

Supplies 14

Date	Item	Post. Ref.	Dr.	Cr.	Balance Dr.	Balance Cr.
2008 Aug. 28	....	J1	90	....	90	....

Fees Earned 41

Date	Item	Post. Ref.	Dr.	Cr.	Balance Dr.	Balance Cr.
2008 Aug. 28	....	J1	....	90	....	90
31	....	R1	....	2,140	....	2,230

3. a. $2,140 ($105 + $465 + $820 + $340 + $410)

   b. $2,140

4. The single money column in the revenue journal can be replaced with three columns for (1) Accounts Receivable Dr., (2) Fees Earned Cr., and (3) Sales Tax Payable Cr.

Prob. 5–2B

1. and 5.

GENERAL LEDGER

Cash 11

Date		Item	Post. Ref.	Dr.	Cr.	Balance Dr.	Balance Cr.
2008							
Nov.	1	Balance	✓	....	....	18,940	....
	30	....	CR36	7,040	....	25,980	....

Accounts Receivable 12

Date		Item	Post. Ref.	Dr.	Cr.	Balance Dr.	Balance Cr.
2008							
Nov.	1	Balance	✓	....	....	2,250	....
	30	....	J1	....	1,600	650	....
	30	....	R40	4,280	....	4,930	....
	30	....	CR36	....	3,530	1,400	....

Office Equipment 18

Date		Item	Post. Ref.	Dr.	Cr.	Balance Dr.	Balance Cr.
2008							
Nov.	1	Balance	✓	....	....	32,600	....
	30	....	J1	1,600	....	34,200	....

Fees Earned 41

Date		Item	Post. Ref.	Dr.	Cr.	Balance Dr.	Balance Cr.
2008							
Nov.	30	....	R40	....	4,280	....	4,280
	30	....	CR36	....	3,510	....	7,790

Prob. 5–2B   Continued

2. and 4.

ACCOUNTS RECEIVABLE SUBSIDIARY LEDGER

AGI Co.

Date	Item	Post. Ref.	Dr.	Cr.	Balance
2008					
Nov. 1	Balance	✓	....	....	1,490
3	....	CR36	....	1,490	—
23	....	R40	695	....	695

Phoenix Development Co.

Date	Item	Post. Ref.	Dr.	Cr.	Balance
2008					
Nov. 1	Balance	✓	....	....	760
7	....	R40	430	....	1,190
14	....	CR36	....	760	430
16	....	R40	295	....	725
20	....	CR36	....	430	295

Ross and Son

Date	Item	Post. Ref.	Dr.	Cr.	Balance
2008					
Nov. 10	....	R40	2,010	....	2,010
30	....	J1	....	1,600	410

Yamura Co.

Date	Item	Post. Ref.	Dr.	Cr.	Balance
2008					
Nov. 2	....	R40	850	....	850
19	....	CR36	....	850	—

Prob. 5–2B   Concluded

3., 4., and 5.

REVENUE JOURNAL   PAGE 40

	Date	Invoice No.	Account Debited	Post. Ref.	Accounts Rec. Dr. Fees Earned Cr.	
	2008					
1	Nov. 2	717	Yamura Co.	✓	850	1
2	7	718	Phoenix Development Co. ...	✓	430	2
3	10	719	Ross and Son	✓	2,010	3
4	16	720	Phoenix Development Co. ...	✓	295	4
5	23	721	AGI Co.	✓	695	5
6	30				4,280	6
7					(12) (41)	7

CASH RECEIPTS JOURNAL   PAGE 36

	Date	Account Credited	Post. Ref.	Fees Earned Cr.	Accts. Rec. Cr.	Cash Dr.	
	2008						
1	Nov. 3	AGI Co.	✓	....	1,490	1,490	1
2	14	Phoenix Development Co.	✓	....	760	760	2
3	19	Yamura Co.	✓	....	850	850	3
4	20	Phoenix Development Co.	✓	....	430	430	4
5	30	Fees Earned...............	✓	3,510	....	3,510	5
6	30			3,510	3,530	7,040	6
7				(41)	(12)	(11)	7

JOURNAL   PAGE 1

Date	Description	Post. Ref.	Debit	Credit
2008				
Nov. 30	Office Equipment...	18	1,600	
	Accounts Receivable—Ross and Son...	12/✓		1,600

The subsidiary account for Ross and Son must also be posted for a $1,600 credit.

6. The subsidiary ledger is in agreement with the controlling account. Both have balances of $1,400 ($695 + $295 + $410).

Prob. 5–3B

1. and 4.

GENERAL LEDGER

Field Supplies   14

Date		Item	Post. Ref.	Dr.	Cr.	Balance Dr.	Balance Cr.
2008							
Oct.	1	Balance	✓	....	....	5,300	....
	31	....	P30	13,770	....	19,070	....

Office Supplies   15

Date		Item	Post. Ref.	Dr.	Cr.	Balance Dr.	Balance Cr.
2008							
Oct.	1	Balance	✓	....	....	1,230	....
	31	....	P30	855	....	2,085	....

Office Equipment   18

Date		Item	Post. Ref.	Dr.	Cr.	Balance Dr.	Balance Cr.
2008							
Oct.	1	Balance	✓	....	....	18,400	....
	19	....	P30	7,000	....	25,400	....

Accounts Payable   21

Date		Item	Post. Ref.	Dr.	Cr.	Balance Dr.	Balance Cr.
2008							
Oct.	1	Balance	✓	....	....	....	4,540
	31	....	P30	....	21,625	....	26,165

Prob. 5–3B   Continued

2. and 3.

ACCOUNTS PAYABLE SUBSIDIARY LEDGER

Eskew Co.

Date		Item	Post. Ref.	Dr.	Cr.	Balance
2008						
Oct.	1	Balance	✓	....	....	3,500
	19	....	P30	....	7,000	10,500

J-Mart Co.

Date		Item	Post. Ref.	Dr.	Cr.	Balance
2008						
Oct.	1	Balance	✓	....	....	620
	15	....	P30	....	390	1,010
	26	....	P30	....	185	1,195

Lassiter Co.

Date		Item	Post. Ref.	Dr.	Cr.	Balance
2008						
Oct.	1	Balance	✓	....	....	420
	3	....	P30	....	280	700

Precision Supplies

Date		Item	Post. Ref.	Dr.	Cr.	Balance
2008						
Oct.	8	....	P30	....	3,640	3,640
	23	....	P30	....	1,940	5,580
	30	....	P30	....	2,650	8,230

Wendell Co.

Date		Item	Post. Ref.	Dr.	Cr.	Balance
2008						
Oct.	1	....	P30	....	2,540	2,540
	12	....	P30	....	3,000	5,540

Prob. 5-3B   Concluded

3. and 4.

PURCHASES JOURNAL

Date	Account Credited	Post. Ref.	Accounts Payable Cr.	Field Supplies Dr.	Office Supplies Dr.	Other Accounts Dr. Account	Other Accounts Dr. Post. Ref.	Other Accounts Dr. Amount	
2008									
Oct. 1	Wendell Co.	✓	2,540	2,540	....	....		....	1
3	Lassiter Co.	✓	280	....	280	....		....	2
8	Precision Supplies	✓	3,640	3,640	....	....		....	3
12	Wendell Co.	✓	3,000	3,000	....	....		....	4
15	J-Mart Co.	✓	390	....	390	....		....	5
19	Eskew Co.	✓	7,000	....	....	Office Equipment	18	7,000	6
23	Precision Supplies.	✓	1,940	1,940	....	....		....	7
26	J-Mart Co.	✓	185	....	185	....		....	8
30	Precision Supplies	✓	2,650	2,650	....	....		....	9
31			21,625	13,770	855			7,000	10
			(21)	(14)	(15)			(✓)	11

5. a. $26,165 ($10,500 + $1,195 + $700 + $8,230 + $5,540)

   b. $26,165

Prob. 5—4B

1., 2., and 3.

PURCHASES JOURNAL

	Date	Account Credited	Post. Ref.	Accounts Payable Cr.	Field Supplies Dr.	Office Supplies Dr.	Other Accounts Dr. Account	Post. Ref.	Amount	
1	2008 Mar. 16	PMI Sales Inc.	✓	28,500	....	....	Field Equipment	17	28,500	1
2	17	Culver Supply Co.	✓	8,740	8,740	....	....		....	2
3	20	Castle Office Supply Co.	✓	1,060	....	1,060	....		....	3
4	28	Castle Office Supply Co.	✓	2,570	....	2,570	....		....	4
5	30	PMI Sales Inc.	✓	33,580	21,380	....	Office Equipment	18	12,200	5
6	30	Culver Supply Co.	✓	11,100	11,100	....	....		....	6
7	31			85,550	41,220	3,630			40,700	7
8				(21)	(14)	(15)			(✓)	8

Prob. 5–4B   Continued

1. and 2.

JOURNAL

Date	Description	Post. Ref.	Debit	Credit
2008				
Mar. 31	Prepaid Rent	16	12,400	
	Field Equipment	17		12,400

1., 2., and 3.

CASH PAYMENTS JOURNAL

	Date	Ck. No.	Account Debited	Post. Ref.	Other Accounts Dr.	Accounts Payable Dr.	Cash Cr.	
	2008							
1	Mar. 16	1	Rent Expense....................	71	4,800	....	4,800	1
2	18	2	Field Supplies	14	2,150	....	2,150	2
3			Office Supplies	15	390	....	390	3
4	24	3	PMI Sales Inc....................	✓	....	28,500	28,500	4
5	26	4	Culver Supply Co.............	✓	....	8,740	8,740	5
6	28	5	Land................................	19	165,000	....	165,000	6
7	30	6	Castle Office Supply Co...	✓	....	1,060	1,060	7
8	31	7	Salary Expense	61	24,500	....	24,500	8
9	31		Total................................		196,840	38,300	235,140	9
10					(✓)	(21)	(11)	10

Prob. 5–4B   Continued

1.

ACCOUNTS PAYABLE LEDGER

Castle Office Supply Co.

Date	Item	Post. Ref.	Dr.	Cr.	Balance
2008					
Mar. 20	....	P1	....	1,060	1,060
28	....	P1	....	2,570	3,630
30	....	CP1	1,060	....	2,570

Culver Supply Co.

Date	Item	Post. Ref.	Dr.	Cr.	Balance
2008					
Mar. 17	....	P1	....	8,740	8,740
26	....	CP1	8,740	....	—
30	....	P1	....	11,100	11,100

PMI Sales Inc.

Date	Item	Post. Ref.	Dr.	Cr.	Balance
2008					
Mar. 16	....	P1	....	28,500	28,500
24	....	CP1	28,500	....	—
30	....	P1	....	33,580	33,580

Prob. 5–4B   Continued

2. and 3.

GENERAL LEDGER

Cash   11

Date	Item	Post. Ref.	Dr.	Cr.	Balance Dr.	Balance Cr.
2008						
Mar. 31	....	CP1	....	235,140	....	235,140

Field Supplies   14

Date	Item	Post. Ref.	Dr.	Cr.	Balance Dr.	Balance Cr.
2008						
Mar. 18	....	CP1	2,150	....	2,150	....
31	....	P1	41,220	....	43,370	....

Office Supplies   15

Date	Item	Post. Ref.	Dr.	Cr.	Balance Dr.	Balance Cr.
2008						
Mar. 18	....	CP1	390	....	390	....
31	....	P1	3,630	....	4,020	....

Prepaid Rent   16

Date	Item	Post. Ref.	Dr.	Cr.	Balance Dr.	Balance Cr.
2008						
Mar. 31	....	J1	12,400	....	12,400	....

Field Equipment   17

Date	Item	Post. Ref.	Dr.	Cr.	Balance Dr.	Balance Cr.
2008						
Mar. 16	....	P1	28,500	....	28,500	....
31	....	J1	....	12,400	16,100	....

Office Equipment   18

Date	Item	Post. Ref.	Dr.	Cr.	Balance Dr.	Balance Cr.
2008						
Mar. 30	....	P1	12,200	....	12,200	....

Land   19

Date	Item	Post. Ref.	Dr.	Cr.	Balance Dr.	Balance Cr.
2008						
Mar. 28	....	CP1	165,000	....	165,000	....

Prob. 5–4B   Concluded

GENERAL LEDGER

Accounts Payable   21

Date	Item	Post. Ref.	Dr.	Cr.	Balance Dr.	Balance Cr.
2008						
Mar. 31	....	P1	....	85,550	....	85,550
31	....	CP1	38,300	....	....	47,250

Salary Expense   61

Date	Item	Post. Ref.	Dr.	Cr.	Balance Dr.	Balance Cr.
2008						
Mar. 31	....	CP1	24,500	....	24,500	....

Rent Expense   71

Date	Item	Post. Ref.	Dr.	Cr.	Balance Dr.	Balance Cr.
2008						
Mar. 16	....	CP1	4,800	....	4,800	....

4.

TEXAS TEA EXPLORATION CO.
Supplier Balance Summary
March 31, 2008

Castle Office Supply Co.	$ 2,570
Culver Supply Co.	11,100
PMI Sales Inc.	33,580
Total accounts payable	$47,250*

*The total of the schedule of accounts payable is equal to the balance of the accounts payable control account.

Prob. 5–5B

1., 3., and 4.

GENERAL LEDGER

Cash   11

Date	Item	Post. Ref.	Dr.	Cr.	Balance Dr.	Balance Cr.
2008						
May 1	Balance	✓	....	....	57,900	....
31		CR31	65,430	....	123,330	....
31		CP34	....	104,940	18,390	....

Accounts Receivable   12

Date	Item	Post. Ref.	Dr.	Cr.	Balance Dr.	Balance Cr.
2008						
May 1	Balance	✓	....	....	24,430	....
31		R35	31,360	....	55,790	....
31		CR31	....	29,130	26,660	....

Maintenance Supplies   14

Date	Item	Post. Ref.	Dr.	Cr.	Balance Dr.	Balance Cr.
2008						
May 1	Balance	✓	....	....	6,150	....
20		J1	....	2,200	3,950	....
31		P37	3,540	....	7,490	....

Office Supplies   15

Date	Item	Post. Ref.	Dr.	Cr.	Balance Dr.	Balance Cr.
2008						
May 1	Balance	✓	....	....	2,580	....
31		CP34	300	....	2,880	....
31		P37	2,180	....	5,060	....

Office Equipment   16

Date	Item	Post. Ref.	Dr.	Cr.	Balance Dr.	Balance Cr.
2008						
May 1	Balance	✓	....	....	14,370	....
3		P37	470	....	14,840	....

Accumulated Depreciation—Office Equipment   17

Date	Item	Post. Ref.	Dr.	Cr.	Balance Dr.	Balance Cr.
2008						
May 1	Balance	✓	....	....	....	2,580

GENERAL LEDGER

Vehicles   18

Date		Item	Post. Ref.	Dr.	Cr.	Balance Dr.	Balance Cr.
2008							
May	1	Balance	✓	....	....	48,000	....
	2	....	P37	21,700	....	69,700	....
	16	....	CP34	21,800	....	91,500	....

Accumulated Depreciation—Vehicles   19

Date		Item	Post. Ref.	Dr.	Cr.	Balance Dr.	Balance Cr.
2008							
May	1	Balance	✓	....	....	....	13,590

Accounts Payable   21

Date		Item	Post. Ref.	Dr.	Cr.	Balance Dr.	Balance Cr.
2008							
May	1	Balance	✓	....	....	....	1,980
	31	....	P37	....	27,890	....	29,870
	31	....	CP34	24,150	....	....	5,720

F. Desai, Capital   31

Date		Item	Post. Ref.	Dr.	Cr.	Balance Dr.	Balance Cr.
2008							
May	1	Balance	✓	....	....	....	135,280

F. Desai, Drawing   32

Date		Item	Post. Ref.	Dr.	Cr.	Balance Dr.	Balance Cr.
2008							
May	27	....	CP34	3,000	....	3,000	....

Fees Earned   41

Date		Item	Post. Ref.	Dr.	Cr.	Balance Dr.	Balance Cr.
2008							
May	16	....	CR31	....	16,800	....	16,800
	31	....	CR31	....	18,500	....	35,300
	31	....	R35	....	31,360	....	66,660

Rent Revenue   42

Date		Item	Post. Ref.	Dr.	Cr.	Balance Dr.	Balance Cr.
2008							
May	18	....	CR31	....	1,000	....	1,000

Prob. 5–5B   Continued

GENERAL LEDGER

Driver Salaries Expense 51

Date	Item	Post. Ref.	Dr.	Cr.	Balance Dr.	Balance Cr.
2008						
May 30	....	CP34	26,900	....	26,900	....

Maintenance Supplies Expense 52

Date	Item	Post. Ref.	Dr.	Cr.	Balance Dr.	Balance Cr.
2008						
May 20	....	J1	2,200	....	2,200	....

Fuel Expense 53

Date	Item	Post. Ref.	Dr.	Cr.	Balance Dr.	Balance Cr.
2008						
May 9	....	CP34	590	....	590	....

Office Salaries Expense 61

Date	Item	Post. Ref.	Dr.	Cr.	Balance Dr.	Balance Cr.
2008						
May 31	....	CP34	16,800	....	16,800	....

Rent Expense 62

Date	Item	Post. Ref.	Dr.	Cr.	Balance Dr.	Balance Cr.
2008						
May 1	....	CP34	800	....	800	....

Advertising Expense 63

Date	Item	Post. Ref.	Dr.	Cr.	Balance Dr.	Balance Cr.
2008						
May 20	....	CP34	6,900	....	6,900	....

Miscellaneous Administrative Expense 64

Date	Item	Post. Ref.	Dr.	Cr.	Balance Dr.	Balance Cr.
2008						
May 17	....	CP34	3,700	....	3,700	....

Prob. 5–5B Continued

2., 4.

PURCHASES JOURNAL

Date	Account Credited	Post. Ref.	Accounts Payable Cr.	Maintenance Supplies Dr.	Office Supplies Dr.	Other Accounts Dr. — Account	Post. Ref.	Amount
2008								
May 2	McIntyre Sales Co.	✓	21,700			Vehicles	18	21,700
3	Office Mate Inc.	✓	470			Office Equipment	16	470
18	Bastille Co.	✓	1,590	1,590				
19	Master Supply Co.	✓	3,500	1,950	1,550			
21	Office City	✓	630		630			
31	Total		27,890	3,540	2,180			22,170
			(21)	(14)	(15)			(✓)

CASH RECEIPTS JOURNAL

PAGE 31

Date	Account Credited	Post. Ref.	Other Accounts Cr.	Accounts Receivable Cr.	Cash Dr.
2008					
May 6	Baker Co.	✓		5,240	5,240
10	Sing Co.	✓		7,490	7,490
12	Martin Co.	✓		4,700	4,700
16	Fees Earned	41	16,800		16,800
18	Rent Revenue	42	1,000		1,000
25	Baker Co.	✓		11,700	11,700
31	Fees Earned	41	18,500		18,500
	Total		36,300	29,130	65,430
			(✓)	(12)	(11)

Prob. 5–5B   Continued

2., 4.

REVENUE JOURNAL   PAGE 35

Date	Invoice No.	Account Debited	Post. Ref.	Accounts Rec. Dr. Fees Earned Cr.	
2008					
1 May 5	91	Martin Co.	✓	4,700	1
2	7 92	Trent Co.	✓	7,900	2
3	11 93	Jarvis Co.	✓	6,300	3
4	24 94	Sing Co.	✓	7,590	4
5	25 95	Trent Co.	✓	4,870	5
6	31	Total.......................................		31,360	6
7				(41) (12)	7

CASH PAYMENTS JOURNAL   PAGE 34

Date	Ck. No.	Account Debited	Post. Ref.	Other Accounts Dr.	Accounts Payable Dr.	Cash Cr.	
2008							
1 May 1	205	Rent Expense....................	62	800	....	800	1
2	9 206	Fuel Expense	53	590	....	590	2
3	10 207	Office City.........................	✓	....	440	440	3
4	10 208	Bastille Co.	✓	....	1,250	1,250	4
5	11 209	Porter Co.	✓	....	290	290	5
6	13 210	McIntyre Sales Co.............	✓	....	21,700	21,700	6
7	16 211	Vehicles...........................	18	21,800	....	21,800	7
8	17 212	Misc. Admin. Expense......	64	3,700	....	3,700	8
9	20 213	Advertising Expense	63	6,900	....	6,900	9
10	26 214	Office Mate Inc.	✓	....	470	470	10
11	27 215	F. Desai, Drawing.............	32	3,000	....	3,000	11
12	30 216	Driver Salaries Expense...	51	26,900	....	26,900	12
13	31 217	Office Salaries Expense...	61	16,800	....	16,800	13
14	31 218	Office Supplies	15	300	....	300	14
15	31	Total		80,790	24,150	104,940	15
16				(✓)	(21)	(11)	16

JOURNAL   PAGE 1

Date	Description	Post. Ref.	Debit	Credit
2008				
May 20	Maintenance Supplies Expense	52	2,200	
	Maintenance Supplies.......................	14		2,200

Prob. 5–5B   Concluded

5.

ONE DAY COURIER COMPANY
Unadjusted Trial Balance
May 31, 2008

	Debit Balances	Credit Balances
Cash	18,390	
Accounts Receivable	26,660	
Maintenance Supplies	7,490	
Office Supplies	5,060	
Office Equipment	14,840	
Accumulated Depreciation—Office Equipment		2,580
Vehicles	91,500	
Accumulated Depreciation—Vehicles		13,590
Accounts Payable		5,720
F. Desai, Capital		135,280
F. Desai, Drawing	3,000	
Fees Earned		66,660
Rent Revenue		1,000
Driver Salaries Expense	26,900	
Maintenance Supplies Expense	2,200	
Fuel Expense	590	
Office Salaries Expense	16,800	
Rent Expense	800	
Advertising Expense	6,900	
Miscellaneous Administrative Expense	3,700	
	224,830	224,830

6.   Balance of accounts receivable control account, $26,660.

Balance of accounts payable control account, $5,720.

SPECIAL ACTIVITIES

SA 5–1

a. Based on Els's knowledge of the situation, she was not acting in the best interests of her employer but was acting in her own short-term best interests. Thus, Els was not acting in an ethical manner. Els could still have had the sale by insisting on cash up front, rather than performing the service on account. Moreover, this contract may come back to haunt Els in the long term, once the company determines that the account cannot be collected after the security system has been installed. Els may have to answer for this decision.

b. Guardsman management has placed Els in a short-term dilemma by requiring her to act contrary to her own short-term best interests. Guardsman Security Co. could avoid this scenario by establishing a separate credit department. All potential contracts could be referred from the field salesperson to the credit office. If credit is approved, then the sale is credited to the salesperson for purposes of quota determination. If credit is not approved, then a contract is not signed. This is an example of separation of duties (sales are separated from credit authorization). Another approach would be to determine the quota on the basis of collections, rather than sales. In this way, the salesperson would be more concerned about the eventual collection of a sale.

SA 5–2

Todd is missing some of the principal benefits of the computerized system. There are three primary advantages of a computerized system. First, the computerized system is much more efficient and accurate at transaction processing. In the computerized system, once the transaction data have been input, the information is simultaneously recorded in the electronic journal (file) and posted to the ledger accounts. This saves a significant amount of time in recording and posting transactions. Second, the computerized environment is less prone to mathematical, posting, and recording errors. The computer does not make these types of mistakes. Thus, the computerized environment should require less time correcting errors. Third, the computerized system provides more timely information to management because account balances are always kept current. Under the manual system, ledger accounts will only be as current as the latest posting date, but the computerized system posts every transaction when it is journalized or recorded on a form. Thus, management has more current information with which to make decisions.

As an additional note, Todd may be reacting out of some fear of the unknown. This is a common reaction to change. Thus, Todd may be overreacting to the new computer environment because it will require significant change in the way the job is done as compared to the manual approach.

SA 5–3

One of the major reasons businesses have transactions "on account" is to control the disbursement and receipt of cash. The cash of the business does not belong to the employees. Thus, the cash transaction is separated from the decision to purchase or sell. This provides for separation of duties between the sale (or purchase) event and the cash receipt (or payment) event. This prevents possible embezzlement and fraud by employees. As an example, if an employee selling the service also received the cash, then it would be possible to hide the sale event by not reporting it and then pocketing the cash. However, with a sale on account, the person providing the service invoices the customer. The customer then remits payment to a different function in the firm according to the terms of the invoice. In this case, there is very little possibility that a single person would be able to defraud Eagle Company. These issues do not arise with individuals because the person controlling the cash also owns the cash in the checking account. Thus, there is no control problem because it is not possible to embezzle cash from oneself.

SA 5–4

a. Cisco uses Internet technology to link its accounting information continually to its underlying business events. As a result, Cisco practices what is termed a "virtual close." A virtual close continually updates the financial records as transactions are completed. Under more typical scenarios, the computer systems are like a set of leaky pipes. At the end of each period, the financial "leaks" must be cleaned up and reconciled, causing a delay in the close cycle. Using Internet technology, Cisco has tightened up the financial "pipeline," so that there are few information leaks and minimal corrections required.

b. A virtual close means that the financial records are available for management decision making on a real-time basis. No more does Cisco management need to wait until the end of an accounting period and closing cycle to receive financial information for decision making. Day-by-day financial information is accumulated and summarized for management so that managers are able to plan and react to business conditions as required. Cisco uses database technology so that its corporate data may be sorted and queried on demand by management's need of the moment.

SA 5–5

1. Special journals are used to reduce the processing time and expense to record transactions. A special journal is usually created when a specific type of transaction occurs frequently enough so that the use of the traditional two-column journal becomes cumbersome. The frequency of transactions for FMG would probably justify the following special journals:

    > Purchases Journal
    >
    > Cash Payments Journal
    >
    > Revenue Journal
    >
    > Cash Receipts Journal

    Note to Instructors: The number and nature of the special journals to be established for FMG involve judgment. Differences of opinion may exist as to whether all the preceding special journals are necessary or cost-efficient. You may wish to use this time to comment further on the costs of establishing special journals and the potential benefits of reducing the processing time to record transactions.

2.

PURCHASES JOURNAL

Date	Account Credited	Post. Ref.	Accounts Payable Cr.	Medical Supplies Dr.	Office Supplies Dr.	Other Accounts Dr.		
						Account	Post. Ref.	Amount

REVENUE JOURNAL

Date	Invoice No.	Account Debited	Post. Ref.	Accounts Receivable Dr.	Fees Earned Cr.	Sales Tax Payable Cr.

Note: The Sales Tax Payable Cr. column is included because fees earned are subject to a sales tax, which is collected by the business. The sales tax must then be periodically remitted to the state or local government. Many states do not charge sales tax on services.

3. The business should maintain subsidiary ledgers for customer accounts receivable, supplier accounts payable, and medical equipment.

SA 5–6

To: **Senior Management**

From: **Student**

Re: **Web-based accounting software**

A new approach to automating our accounting processing is now available. It is called Web-based accounting using an application service provider (ASP). Rather than purchasing our accounting software and loading it on our own computers, Web-based accounting software is rented and resides on the provider's computers. Our data, along with the accounting software, stay with the provider. There are several advantages to this approach:

1. We don't need to administer the application or data on our own computers. This becomes the job of the service provider, thus saving us computer system personnel costs. All we need is a desktop computer and browser to use the software.

2. Our people can work with our data anytime or anyplace. We don't need to rely on our own internal computer network for accounting-related work. Instead, the Web-based product is available on the Internet. This means that we can enter transactions and access our accounting data from anywhere in the world, rather than having to be plugged into our corporate network. This also will save us network support costs.

3. We never need to purchase and load software upgrades. All upgrades are provided on the provider's server when they are available. Thus, we are always using the latest version.

4. Providers promise a highly secure environment for our data.

5. An Internet-based accounting system should help us when passing data, such as orders, between ourselves and our customers and suppliers.

There are also a number of disadvantages we need to consider:

1. The cost of the software is recurring. Thus, we are trading off the recurring costs of maintaining our system infrastructure for the recurring cost of the service. A financial analysis should be conducted to determine if the service is cost effective.

2. The Internet can be slow. During busy times, we may experience slow response times.

3. Our data physically reside with the service provider. Thus, we don't control the security of our own data; the provider does. Our data are our lifeblood, so confidence in the provider's controls is paramount.

4. Once we begin, we will become "locked in" to the provider. It will be hard to change our mind at a later date. However, this is also true for purchased software to some extent.

SA 5–7

Note to Instructors: While the list of functions can be quite large, the key functions are identified below. The purpose of these functions will be fairly advanced for most students. The activity asks for a listing rather than an explanation because most students would have very limited experience by which to provide much explanation. Use this case to demonstrate the scope and basic nature of these application tools.

Manugistics' Supply Chain Management Solution

- Collaborate with customers, distribution partners, transportation providers, and suppliers in order to plan, order, move, and receive materials from suppliers and deliver finished goods to customers.
- Provide trading platforms for conducting Internet auctions.
- Design optimal supply chain networks (finding the optimal location for plants and warehouses).
- Optimize manufacturing planning and scheduling for a given set of demand and capacity constraints.
- Support sales and operations planning (which is a process for coordinating the demand plan with the plant capacity).
- Optimize inventory levels across the supply chain.

Salesforce.com Customer Relationship Management Solution

- Provide the sales force with real-time information about all customer contacts with the firm in order to improve the effectiveness of the sales call.
- Provide real-time forecast estimation and accumulation tools.
- Support promotion plans and integrate the plans with forecasting and manufacturing.
- Decision tools for evaluating marketing campaign effectiveness.
- Tools to support call center responsiveness.

CHAPTER 6
ACCOUNTING FOR MERCHANDISING BUSINESSES

QUESTION INFORMATION

Number	Objective	Description	Difficulty	Time	AACSB	AICPA	SS	GL
Q6-1	6-1		Easy	5 min	Analytic	FN-Measurement		
Q6-2	6-1		Easy	5 min	Analytic	FN-Measurement		
Q6-3	6-2		Easy	5 min	Analytic	FN-Measurement		
Q6-4	6-2		Easy	5 min	Analytic	FN-Measurement		
Q6-5	6-2		Easy	5 min	Analytic	FN-Measurement		
Q6-6	6-2		Easy	5 min	Analytic	FN-Measurement		
Q6-7	6-2		Easy	5 min	Analytic	FN-Measurement		
Q6-8	6-3		Easy	5 min	Analytic	FN-Measurement		
Q6-9	6-3		Easy	5 min	Analytic	FN-Measurement		
Q6-10	6-3		Easy	5 min	Analytic	FN-Measurement		
Q6-11	6-3		Easy	5 min	Analytic	FN-Measurement		
Q6-12	6-3		Easy	5 min	Analytic	FN-Measurement		
Q6-13	6-3		Easy	5 min	Analytic	FN-Measurement		
Q6-14	6-3		Easy	5 min	Analytic	FN-Measurement		
Q6-15	6-4		Easy	5 min	Analytic	FN-Measurement		
PE6-1A	6-1	Determine gross profit	Easy	5 min	Analytic	FN-Measurement		
PE6-1B	6-1	Determine gross profit	Easy	5 min	Analytic	FN-Measurement		
PE6-2A	6-2	Computing cost of merchandise sold	Easy	5 min	Analytic	FN-Measurement		
PE6-2B	6-2	Computing cost of merchandise sold	Easy	5 min	Analytic	FN-Measurement		
PE6-3A	6-3	Entries for sales transaction	Easy	5 min	Analytic	FN-Measurement		
PE6-3B	6-3	Entries for sales transactions	Easy	5 min	Analytic	FN-Measurement		
PE6-4A	6-3	Entries for purchase transactions	Easy	5 min	Analytic	FN-Measurement		
PE6-4B	6-3	Entries for purchase transactions	Easy	5 min	Analytic	FN-Measurement		
PE6-5A	6-3	Payments under different transportation terms	Easy	5 min	Analytic	FN-Measurement		
PE6-5B	6-3	Payments under different transportation terms	Easy	5 min	Analytic	FN-Measurement		
PE6-6A	6-3	Recording transactions for buyer and seller	Easy	5 min	Analytic	FN-Measurement		
PE6-6B	6-3	Recording transactions for buyer and seller	Easy	5 min	Analytic	FN-Measurement		
PE6-7A	6-4	Entry of inventory shrinkage	Easy	5 min	Analytic	FN-Measurement		
PE6-7B	6-4	Entry of inventory shrinkage	Easy	5 min	Analytic	FN-Measurement		
Ex6-1	6-1	Determining gross profit	Easy	5 min	Analytic	FN-Measurement		
Ex6-2	6-1	Determining cost of merchandise sold	Easy	5 min	Analytic	FN-Measurement		

Number	Objective	Description	Difficulty	Time	AACSB	AICPA	SS	GL
Ex6-3	6-2	Identify items missing in determine cost of merchandise sold	Moderate	10 min	Analytic	FN-Measurement		
Ex6-4	6-2	Cost of merchandise sold and related items	Moderate	10 min	Analytic	FN-Measurement		
Ex6-5	6-2	Cost of merchandise sold	Moderate	15 min	Analytic	FN-Measurement		
Ex6-6	6-2	Income statement of merchandiser	Easy	5 min	Analytic	FN-Measurement		
Ex6-7	6-2	Income statement of merchandiser	Easy	5 min	Analytic	FN-Measurement		
Ex6-8	6-2	Single-step income statement	Easy	10 min	Analytic	FN-Measurement		
Ex6-9	6-2	Multiple-step income statement	Moderate	15 min	Analytic	FN-Measurement		
Ex6-10	6-2	Determining amounts for items omitted from income statement	Moderate	15 min	Analytic	FN-Measurement		
Ex6-11	6-2	Multiple-step income statement	Moderate	30 min	Analytic	FN-Measurement	Exl	
Ex6-12	6-3	Chart of accounts	Easy	20 min	Analytic	FN-Measurement		
Ex6-13	6-3	Sales-related transactions, including the use of credit cards	Easy	20 min	Analytic	FN-Measurement		
Ex6-14	6-3	Sales returns and allowances	Easy	10 min	Analytic	FN-Measurement		
Ex6-15	6-3	Sales-related transactions	Easy	10 min	Analytic	FN-Measurement		
Ex6-16	6-3	Sales-related transactions	Easy	10 min	Analytic	FN-Measurement		
Ex6-17	6-3	Sales-related transactions	Easy	10 min	Analytic	FN-Measurement		
Ex6-18	6-3	Purchase-related transactions	Easy	10 min	Analytic	FN-Measurement		
Ex6-19	6-3	Purchase-related transactions	Easy	5 min	Analytic	FN-Measurement		
Ex6-20	6-3	Purchase-related transactions	Easy	10 min	Analytic	FN-Measurement		
Ex6-21	6-3	Purchase-related transactions	Easy	10 min	Analytic	FN-Measurement		
Ex6-22	6-3	Purchase-related transactions	Moderate	15 min	Analytic	FN-Measurement		
Ex6-23	6-3	Determining amounts to be paid on invoices	Moderate	15 min	Analytic	FN-Measurement		
Ex6-24	6-3	Sales tax	Easy	10 min	Analytic	FN-Measurement		
Ex6-25	6-3	Sales tax transactions	Easy	10 min	Analytic	FN-Measurement		
Ex6-26	6-3	Sales-related transactions	Easy	10 min	Analytic	FN-Measurement		
Ex6-27	6-3	Purchase-related transactions	Easy	10 min	Analytic	FN-Measurement		
Ex6-28	6-3	Normal balances of merchandise accounts	Easy	5 min	Analytic	FN-Measurement		
Ex6-29	6-4	Adjusting entry for merchandise inventory shrinkage	Easy	5 min	Analytic	FN-Measurement		
Ex6-30	6-4	Closing the accounts of a merchandiser	Easy	5 min	Analytic	FN-Measurement		
Ex6-31	6-4	Closing entries; net income	Easy	10 min	Analytic	FN-Measurement		

Number	Objective	Description	Difficulty	Time	AACSB	AICPA	SS	GL
Ex6-32	6-4	Closing entries	Moderate	20 min	Analytic	FN-Measurement		
Ex6-33	FAI	Ratio of net sales to total assets	Moderate	15 min	Analytic	FN-Measurement		
Ex6-34	FAI	Ratio of net sales to total assets	Moderate	15 min	Analytic	FN-Measurement		
Ex6-35	Appendix 1	Merchandising special journals	Moderate	30 min	Analytic	FN-Measurement	Exl	
Ex6-36	Appendix 2	Accounts for periodic and perpetual inventory methods	Easy	10 min	Analytic	FN-Measurement		
Ex6-37	Appendix 2	Rules of debit and credit for periodic inventory accounts	Easy	5 min	Analytic	FN-Measurement		
Ex6-38	Appendix 2	Journal entries using the periodic inventory method	Moderate	15 min	Analytic	FN-Measurement		
Ex6-39	Appendix 2	Journal entries using perpetual inventory methods	Moderate	15 min	Analytic	FN-Measurement		
Ex6-40	Appendix 2	Closing entries using periodic inventory method	Moderate	15 min	Analytic	FN-Measurement		
Pr6-1A	6-2	Multiple-step income statement and report from balance sheet	Moderate	1 1/2 hr	Analytic	FN-Measurement	Exl	KA
Pr6-2A	6-2, 6-4	Single-step income statement and account form of balance sheet	Moderate	1 hr	Analytic	FN-Measurement	Exl	
Pr6-3A	6-3	Sales-related transactions	Moderate	45 min	Analytic	FN-Measurement		KA
Pr6-4A	6-3	Purchase-related transactions	Moderate	45 min	Analytic	FN-Measurement		KA
Pr6-5A	6-3	Sales-related and purchase related transactions	Difficult	1 1/4 hr	Analytic	FN-Measurement		KA
Pr6-6A	6-3	Sales-related and purchase related transactions for buyer and seller	Difficult	2 hr	Analytic	FN-Measurement		
Pr6-7A	Appendix 2	Purchase-related transactions using periodic inventory method	Moderate	45 min	Analytic	FN-Measurement		
Pr6-8A	Appendix 2	Sales-related and purchase-related transactions using periodic inventory method	Difficult	1 1/4 hr	Analytic	FN-Measurement		
Pr6-9A	Appendix 2	Sales-related and purchase related transactions for buyer and seller using periodic inventory method	Difficult	2 hr	Analytic	FN-Measurement		
Pr6-10A	Appendix 2	Periodic inventory accounts, multiple-step income statement, closing entries	Difficult	2 hr	Analytic	FN-Measurement	Exl	
Pr6-1B	6-2	Multiple-step income statement and report from balance sheet	Moderate	1 1/2 hr	Analytic	FN-Measurement	Exl	KA

Number	Objective	Description	Difficulty	Time	AACSB	AICPA	SS	GL
Pr6-2B	6-2, 6-4	Single-step income statement and account form of balance sheet	Moderate	1 hr	Analytic	FN-Measurement	Exl	
Pr6-3B	6-3	Sales-related transactions	Moderate	45 min	Analytic	FN-Measurement		KA
Pr6-4B	6-3	Purchase-related transactions	Moderate	45 min	Analytic	FN-Measurement		KA
Pr6-5B	6-3	Sales-related and purchase related transactions	Difficult	1 1/4 hr	Analytic	FN-Measurement		KA
Pr6-6B	6-3	Sales-related and purchase related transactions for buyer and seller	Difficult	2 hr	Analytic	FN-Measurement		
Pr6-7B	Appendix 2	Purchase-related transactions using periodic inventory method	Moderate	45 min	Analytic	FN-Measurement		
Pr6-8B	Appendix 2	Sales-related and purchase-related transactions using periodic inventory method	Difficult	1 1/4 hr	Analytic	FN-Measurement		
Pr6-9B	Appendix 2	Sales-related and purchase related transactions for buyer and seller using periodic inventory method	Difficult	2 hr	Analytic	FN-Measurement		
Pr6-10B	Appendix 2	Periodic inventory accounts, multiple-step income statement, closing entries	Difficult	2 hr	Analytic	FN-Measurement	Exl	
Comp Problem 2	6-2, 6-3, 6-4	Journalize entries, adjusted trial balance, financial statements, closing entries, post-closing trial balance	Difficult	3 hr	Analytic	FN-Measurement		KA
SA6-1	6-3	Ethics and professional conduct in business	Easy	5 min	Ethics	BB-Industry		
SA6-2	6-3	Purchases discounts and accounts payable	Easy	10 min	Analytic	FN-Measurement		
SA6-3	6-3	Determining cost pf purchases	Moderate	15 min	Analytic	FN-Measurement		
SA6-4	6-3	Sales discounts	Difficult	30 min	Analytic	FN-Measurement		
SA6-5	6-3	Shopping for a television	Moderate	30 min	Analytic	FN-Measurement		

EYE OPENERS

1. Merchandising businesses acquire merchandise for resale to customers. It is the selling of merchandise, instead of a service, that makes the activities of a merchandising business different from the activities of a service business.

2. Yes. Gross profit is the excess of (net) sales over cost of merchandise sold. A net loss arises when operating expenses exceed gross profit. Therefore, a business can earn a gross profit but incur operating expenses in excess of this gross profit and end up with a net loss.

3. a. Increase   c. Decrease
   b. Increase   d. Decrease

4. Under the *periodic system*, the inventory records do not show the amount available for sale or the amount sold during the period. In contrast, under the *perpetual system* of accounting for merchandise inventory, each purchase and sale of merchandise is recorded in the inventory and the cost of merchandise sold accounts. As a result, the amount of merchandise available for sale and the amount sold are continuously (perpetually) disclosed in the inventory records.

5. The multiple-step form of income statement contains conventional groupings for revenues and expenses, with intermediate balances, before concluding with the net income balance. In the single-step form, the total of all expenses is deducted from the total of all revenues, without intermediate balances.

6. The major advantages of the single-step form of income statement are its simplicity and its emphasis on total revenues and total expenses as the determinants of net income. The major objection to the form is that such relationships as gross profit to sales and income from operations to sales are not as readily determinable as when the multiple-step form is used.

7. Revenues from sources other than the principal activity of the business are classified as other income. Examples would include rent, revenue, and interest.

8. Examples of such accounts include the following: Sales, Sales Discounts, Sales Returns and Allowances, Cost of Merchandise Sold, Merchandise Inventory.

9. Sales to customers who use MasterCard or VISA cards are recorded as cash sales.

10. The date of sale as shown by the date of the invoice or bill.

11. a. 2% discount allowed if paid within 10 days of date of invoice; entire amount of invoice due within 60 days of date of invoice.
    b. Payment due within 30 days of date of invoice.
    c. Payment due by the end of the month in which the sale was made.

12. a. A credit memorandum issued by the seller of merchandise indicates the amount for which the buyer's account is to be credited (credit to Accounts Receivable) and the reason for the sales return or allowance.
    b. A debit memorandum issued by the buyer of merchandise indicates the amount for which the seller's account is to be debited (debit to Accounts Payable) and the reason for the purchases return or allowance.

13. a. The buyer
    b. The seller

14. Cost of Merchandise Sold would be debited; Merchandise Inventory would be credited.

15. Loss from Merchandise Inventory Shrinkage would be debited.

PRACTICE EXERCISES

PE 6–1A

$140,775 ($127,500 + $435,600 – $422,325)

PE 6–1B

$31,850 ($17,500 + $141,750 – $127,400)

PE 6–2A

Cost of merchandise sold:			
Merchandise inventory, July 1			$ 88,370
Purchases		$681,400	
Less: Purchases returns and allowances..	$9,250		
Purchases discounts.........................	7,000	16,250	
Net purchases..		$665,150	
Add transportation in		3,180	
Cost of merchandise purchased			668,330
Merchandise available for sale....................			$756,700
Less merchandise inventory, July 31			92,120
Cost of merchandise sold...........................			$664,580

PE 6–2B

Cost of merchandise sold:			
Merchandise inventory, April 1			$ 128,120
Purchases		$983,400	
Less: Purchases returns and allowances..	$10,250		
Purchases discounts.........................	8,000	18,250	
Net purchases..		$965,150	
Add transportation in		5,680	
Cost of merchandise purchased			970,830
Merchandise available for sale....................			$ 1,098,950
Less merchandise inventory, April 30			140,500
Cost of merchandise sold...........................			$ 958,450

PE 6–3A

a.

Accounts Receivable		12,250	
Sales			12,250
Cost of Merchandise Sold		7,400	
Merchandise Inventory			7,400

b.

Cash	12,005	
Sales Discounts	245	
Accounts Receivable		12,250

PE 6–3B

a.

Accounts Receivable	22,500	
Sales		22,500
Cost of Merchandise Sold	14,150	
Merchandise Inventory		14,150

b.

Cash	22,275	
Sales Discounts	225	
Accounts Receivable		22,500

PE 6–4A

a. $5,880. Purchase of $7,500 less the return of $1,500 less the discount of $120 [($7,500 – $1,500) × 2%)].

b. Merchandise Inventory

PE 6–4B

a. $11,385. Purchase of $13,200 less the return of $1,700 less the discount of $115 [($13,200 – $1,700) × 1%].

b. Accounts Payable

PE 6–5A

a. $5,350. Purchase of $6,000 less return of $1,000 less the discount of $50 [($6,000 – $1,000) × 1%] plus $400 of shipping.

b. $1,568. Purchase of $2,500 less return of $900 less the discount of $32 [($2,500 – $900) × 2%].

PE 6–5B

a. $6,713. Purchase of $8,150 less return of $1,300 less the discount of $137 [($8,150 – $1,300) × 2%].

b. $10,180. Purchase of $12,750 less return of $3,000 less the discount of $195 [($12,750 – $3,000) × 2%] plus $625 of shipping.

PE 6–6A

Stuckey Co. journal entries:

Cash ($5,250 – $650 – $92)	4,508	
Sales Discounts [($5,250 – $650) × 2%]............................	92	
Accounts Receivable—Bullock Co. ($5,250 – $650)		4,600

Bullock Co. journal entries:

Accounts Payable—Stuckey Co. ($5,250 – $650)	4,600	
Merchandise Inventory [($5,250 – $650) × 2%]		92
Cash ($5,250 – $650 – $92)..		4,508

PE 6–6B

Sparks Co. journal entries:

Cash ($8,500 – $170 + $225)...	8,555	
Sales Discounts ($8,500 × 2%)...	170	
Accounts Receivable—Boyt Co. ($8,500 + $225)..........		8,725

Boyt Co. journal entries:

Accounts Payable—Sparks Co. ($8,500 + $225)................	8,725	
Merchandise Inventory ($8,500 × 2%)...........................		170
Cash ($8,500 – $170 + $225)...		8,555

PE 6–7A

Sept. 30 Cost of Merchandise Sold 4,100
        Merchandise Inventory   4,100
            Inventory shrinkage ($111,500 – $107,400).

PE 6–7B

Aug. 31 Cost of Merchandise Sold 23,485
        Merchandise Inventory   23,485
            Inventory shrinkage ($543,735 – $520,250).

EXERCISES

Ex. 6–1

a. $855,225 ($2,850,750 – $1,995,525)

b. 30% ($855,225/$2,850,750)

c. No. If operating expenses are less than gross profit, there will be a net income. On the other hand, if operating expenses exceed gross profit, there will be a net loss.

Ex. 6–2

$20,938 million ($27,433 million – $6,495 million)

Ex. 6–3

a. Purchases discounts, purchases returns and allowances
b. Transportation in
c. Merchandise available for sale
d. Merchandise inventory (ending)

Ex. 6–4

a. Cost of merchandise sold:

Merchandise inventory, July 1, 2007			$ 183,250
Purchases		$1,279,600	
Less: Purchases returns and allowances	$41,200		
Purchases discounts	20,500	61,700	
Net purchases		$1,217,900	
Add transportation in		17,250	
Cost of merchandise purchased			1,235,150
Merchandise available for sale			$1,418,400
Less merchandise inventory, June 30, 2008			200,100
Cost of merchandise sold			$1,218,300

b. $581,700 ($1,800,000 – $1,218,300)

Ex. 6–5

1. The schedule should begin with the April 1, 2007, not the March 31, 2008, merchandise inventory.
2. Purchases returns and allowances and purchases discounts should be deducted from (not added to) purchases.
3. The result of subtracting purchases returns and allowances and purchases discounts from purchases should be labeled "net purchases."
4. Transportation in should be added to net purchases to yield cost of merchandise purchased.
5. The merchandise inventory at March 31, 2008, should be deducted from merchandise available for sale to yield cost of merchandise sold.

A correct cost of merchandise sold section is as follows:

Cost of merchandise sold:

Merchandise inventory, April 1, 2007			$115,150
Purchases		$852,100	
Less: Purchases returns and allowances	$10,500		
Purchases discounts......................	8,000	18,500	
Net purchases..		$833,600	
Add transportation in		7,500	
Cost of merchandise purchased			841,100
Merchandise available for sale.................			$956,250
Less merchandise inventory,			
March 31, 2008			135,750
Cost of merchandise sold.........................			$820,500

Ex. 6–6

a. Net sales: $3,559,050 ($4,125,800 – $380,000 – $186,750)
b. Gross profit: $1,083,550 ($3,559,050 – $2,475,500)

Ex. 6–7

a. Selling expense, (1), (2), (7), (8)
b. Administrative expense, (3), (5), (6)
c. Other expense, (4)

Ex. 6–8

THE VOODOO COMPANY
Income Statement
For the Year Ended November 30, 2008

Revenues:

Net sales		$4,000,000
Rent revenue		30,000
Total revenues		$4,030,000
Expenses:		
Cost of merchandise sold	$2,175,350	
Selling expenses	880,000	
Administrative expenses	500,000	
Interest expense	23,200	
Total expenses		3,578,550
Net income		$ 451,450

Ex. 6–9

1. Sales returns and allowances and sales discounts should be deducted from (not added to) sales.

2. Sales returns and allowances and sales discounts should be deducted from sales to yield "net sales" (not gross sales).

3. Deducting the cost of merchandise sold from net sales yields gross profit.

4. Deducting the total expenses from gross profit would yield income from operations (or operating income).

5. Interest revenue should be reported under the caption "Other income" and should be added to income from operations to arrive at net income.

6. The final amount on the income statement should be labeled net income, not gross profit.

A correct income statement would be as follows:

THE EUCLIDIAN COMPANY
Income Statement
For the Year Ended March 31, 2008

Revenue from sales:			
Sales		$7,127,500	
Less: Sales returns and allowances	$112,300		
Sales discounts	60,000	172,300	
Net sales			$6,955,200
Cost of merchandise sold			4,175,100
Gross profit			$2,780,100
Expenses:			
Selling expenses		$ 710,000	
Administrative expenses		525,000	
Delivery expense		18,100	
Total expenses			1,253,100
Income from operations			$1,527,000
Other income:			
Interest revenue			80,000
Net income			$1,607,000

Ex. 6–10

a. $30,000 ($400,000 − $20,000 − $350,000)

b. $150,000 ($350,000 − $200,000)

c. $477,000 ($500,000 − $15,000 − $8,000)

d. $192,000 ($477,000 − $285,000)

e. $50,000 ($1,000,000 − $40,000 − $910,000)

f. $623,500 ($910,000 − $286,500)

g. $757,500 ($690,000 + $37,000 + $30,500)

h. $690,000 ($540,000 + $150,000)

Ex. 6–11

a.

THE BENT NEEDLE COMPANY
Income Statement
For the Year Ended August 31, 2008

Revenue from sales:			
Sales		$1,275,000	
Less: Sales returns and allowances	$80,000		
Sales discounts	20,000	100,000	
Net sales			$1,175,000
Cost of merchandise sold.............................			700,000
Gross profit			$ 475,000
Expenses:			
Selling expenses		$ 205,000	
Administrative expenses		125,000	
Total expenses			330,000
Income from operations...............................			$ 145,000
Other expense:			
Interest expense			7,500
Net income			$ 137,500

b. The major advantage of the multiple-step form of income statement is that relationships such as gross profit to sales are indicated. The major disadvantages are that it is more complex and the total revenues and expenses are not indicated, as is the case in the single-step income statement.

Ex. 6–12

Balance Sheet Accounts

100   **Assets**
- 110   **Cash**
- 112   **Accounts Receivable**
- 114   **Merchandise Inventory**
- 115   **Store Supplies**
- 116   **Office Supplies**
- 117   **Prepaid Insurance**
- 120   **Land**
- 123   **Store Equipment**
- 124   **Accumulated Depreciation— Store Equipment**
- 125   **Office Equipment**
- 126   **Accumulated Depreciation— Office Equipment**

200   **Liabilities**
- 210   **Accounts Payable**
- 211   **Salaries Payable**
- 212   **Notes Payable**

300   **Owner's Equity**
- 310   **Jung Qiang, Capital**
- 311   **Jung Qiang, Drawing**
- 312   **Income Summary**

Income Statement Accounts

400   **Revenues**
- 410   **Sales**
- 411   **Sales Returns and Allowances**
- 412   **Sales Discounts**

500   **Expenses**
- 510   **Cost of Merchandise Sold**
- 520   **Sales Salaries Expense**
- 521   **Advertising Expense**
- 522   **Depreciation Expense— Store Equipment**
- 523   **Store Supplies Expense**
- 524   **Delivery Expense**
- 529   **Miscellaneous Selling Expense**
- 530   **Office Salaries Expense**
- 531   **Rent Expense**
- 532   **Depreciation Expense— Office Equipment**
- 533   **Insurance Expense**
- 534   **Office Supplies Expense**
- 539   **Miscellaneous Administrative Expense**

600   **Other Expense**
- 610   **Interest Expense**

Note: The order of some of the accounts within subclassifications is somewhat arbitrary, as in accounts 115–117 and accounts 521–524. In a new business, the order of magnitude of balances in such accounts is not determinable in advance. The magnitude may also vary from period to period.

Ex. 6–13

a.	Cash...	12,150	
	Sales...		12,150
	Cost of Merchandise Sold..	9,100	
	Merchandise Inventory		9,100
b.	Accounts Receivable..	6,000	
	Sales...		6,000
	Cost of Merchandise Sold..	4,000	
	Merchandise Inventory		4,000
c.	Cash...	30,780	
	Sales...		30,780
	Cost of Merchandise Sold..	20,000	
	Merchandise Inventory		20,000
d.	Cash...	17,650	
	Sales...		17,650
	Cost of Merchandise Sold..	10,500	
	Merchandise Inventory		10,500
e.	Credit Card Expense	1,900	
	Cash..		1,900

Ex. 6–14

It was acceptable to debit Sales for the $172,100. However, using Sales Returns and Allowances assists management in monitoring the amount of returns so that quick action can be taken if returns become excessive.

Accounts Receivable should also have been credited for $172,100. In addition, Cost of Merchandise Sold should only have been credited for the cost of the merchandise sold, not the selling price. Merchandise Inventory should also have been debited for the cost of the merchandise returned. The entries to correctly record the returns would have been as follows:

Sales (or Sales Returns and Allowances)	172,100	
Accounts Receivable		172,100
Merchandise Inventory...	100,300	
Cost of Merchandise Sold		100,300

Ex. 6–15

a. $18,130 [$18,500 – $370 ($18,500 × 2%)]

b.

Sales Returns and Allowances....................................	18,500	
Sales Discounts...		370
Cash..		18,130
Merchandise Inventory..	11,100	
Cost of Merchandise Sold		11,100

Ex. 6–16

(1) Sold merchandise on account, $11,750.

(2) Recorded the cost of the merchandise sold and reduced the merchandise inventory account, $6,900.

(3) Accepted a return of merchandise and granted an allowance, $2,250.

(4) Updated the merchandise inventory account for the cost of the merchandise returned, $1,350.

(5) Received the balance due within the discount period, $9,310. [Sale of $11,750, less return of $2,250, less discount of $190 (2% × $9,500).]

Ex. 6–17

a. $9,200

b. $9,838

c. $184 ($9,200 × 2%)

d. $9,654 ($9,838 – $184)

Ex. 6–18

a. $5,145 [Purchase of $6,750, less return of $1,500, less discount of $105 [($6,750 – $1,500) × 2%)]

b. Merchandise Inventory

Ex. 6–19

Offer B is lower than offer A. Details are as follows:

	A	B
List price	$37,500	$38,000
Less discount	750	380
	$36,750	$37,620
Transportation	1,050	
	$37,800	$37,620

Ex. 6–20

(1) Purchased merchandise on account at a net cost of $11,500.

(2) Paid transportation costs, $450.

(3) An allowance or return of merchandise was granted by the creditor, $500.

(4) Paid the balance due within the discount period: debited Accounts Payable, $11,000, and credited Merchandise Inventory for the amount of the discount, $220, and Cash, $10,780.

Ex. 6–21

a.	Merchandise Inventory	10,000	
	Accounts Payable		10,000
b.	Accounts Payable	2,500	
	Merchandise Inventory		2,500
c.	Accounts Payable	7,500	
	Cash		7,350
	Merchandise Inventory		150

Ex. 6–22

a.	Merchandise Inventory..	18,400	
	Accounts Payable—Harbin Co.		18,400
b.	Accounts Payable—Harbin Co.	18,400	
	Cash..		18,032
	Merchandise Inventory		368
c.	Accounts Payable*—Harbin Co.	4,410	
	Merchandise Inventory		4,410
d.	Merchandise Inventory..	3,000	
	Accounts Payable—Harbin Co.		3,000
e.	Cash...	1,410	
	Accounts Payable—Harbin Co.		1,410

*Note: The debit of $4,410 to Accounts Payable in entry (c) is the amount of cash refund due from Harbin Co. It is computed as the amount that was paid for the returned merchandise, $4,500, less the purchase discount of $90 ($4,500 × 2%). The credit to Accounts Payable of $3,000 in entry (d) reduces the debit balance in the account to $1,410, which is the amount of the cash refund in entry (e). The alternative entries below yield the same final results.

c.	Accounts Receivable—Harbin Co.	4,410	
	Merchandise Inventory		4,410
d.	Merchandise Inventory..	3,000	
	Accounts Payable—Harbin Co.		3,000
e.	Cash...	1,410	
	Accounts Payable—Harbin Co.	3,000	
	Accounts Receivable—Harbin Co.		4,410

Ex. 6–23

a. $6,435 [($8,000 – $1,500) – ($6,500 × 1%)]

b. $2,575 [($2,900 – $400) – ($2,500 × 2%) + $125]

c. $3,773 [$3,850 – ($3,850 × 2%)]

d. $12,500 ($15,000 – $2,500)

e. $4,195 [($5,000 – $1,000) – ($4,000 × 2%) + $275]

Ex. 6–24

a. At the time of sale

b. $12,200

c. $12,932 ($12,200 + $732)

d. Sales Tax Payable

Ex. 6–25

a.	Accounts Receivable	17,010	
	Sales		15,750
	Sales Tax Payable		1,260
	Cost of Merchandise Sold	9,450	
	Merchandise Inventory		9,450
b.	Sales Tax Payable	29,183	
	Cash		29,183

Ex. 6–26

a.	Accounts Receivable—Beyer Co.	14,500	
	Sales		14,500
	Cost of Merchandise Sold	8,800	
	Merchandise Inventory		8,800
b.	Sales Returns and Allowances	3,750	
	Accounts Receivable—Beyer Co.		3,750
	Merchandise Inventory	2,100	
	Cost of Merchandise Sold		2,100
c.	Cash	10,535	
	Sales Discounts	215	
	Accounts Receivable—Beyer Co.		10,750

Ex. 6–27

a.	Merchandise Inventory...	14,500	
	Accounts Payable—Sellers Co.		14,500
b.	Accounts Payable—Sellers Co.	3,750	
	Merchandise Inventory		3,750
c.	Accounts Payable—Sellers Co.	10,750	
	Cash...		10,535
	Merchandise Inventory		215

Ex. 6–28

a. credit

b. debit

c. debit

d. debit

e. debit

f. debit

g. credit

Ex. 6–29

Cost of Merchandise Sold..	17,125	
Merchandise Inventory		17,125
Inventory shrinkage ($715,275 – $698,150).		

Ex. 6–30

(b) Advertising Expense

(c) Cost of Merchandise Sold

(e) Sales

(f) Sales Discounts

(g) Sales Returns and Allowances

(i) Supplies Expense

Note: (j) Terry Weaver, Drawing is closed to Terry Weaver, Capital *not* Income Summary.

Ex. 6–31

Sales	1,275,000	
Income Summary...		1,275,000
Income Summary...	1,137,500	
Sales Discounts..		20,000
Sales Returns and Allowances		80,000
Cost of Merchandise Sold		700,000
Selling Expenses...		205,000
Administrative Expenses.............................		125,000
Interest Expense...		7,500
Income Summary...	137,500	
Jason Ritchie, Capital		137,500
Jason Ritchie, Capital	25,000	
Jason Ritchie, Drawing...............................		25,000

Ex. 6–32

2008				
Oct.	31	Sales..	1,567,700	
		Income Summary		1,567,700
	31	Income Summary	2,058,425	
		Administrative Expenses		326,500
		Cost of Merchandise Sold		940,000
		Interest Expense		9,600
		Sales Discounts		90,000
		Sales Returns and Allowances		60,000
		Selling Expenses		620,000
		Store Supplies Expense		12,325
	31	Lillian Kavanaugh, Capital.................................	490,725	
		Income Summary		490,725
	31	Lillian Kavanaugh, Capital.................................	39,750	
		Lillian Kavanaugh, Drawing		39,750

Ex. 6–33

a. 2005:   1.99 [$73,094 / ($38,907 + $34,437)/2]
    2004:   2.01 [$64,816 / ($34,437 + $30,011)/2]

b. These analyses indicate a slight decrease in the effectiveness in the use of the assets to generate profits. However, a comparison with similar companies or industry averages would be helpful in making a more definitive statement on the effectiveness of the use of the assets.

Ex. 6–34

a. 2.74 [$56,434 / ($20,491 + $20,763)/2]

b. Although Kroger and Tiffany are both retail stores, Tiffany sells jewelry at a much slower velocity than Kroger sells groceries. Thus, Kroger is able to generate $2.74 of sales for every dollar of assets. Tiffany, however, is only able to generate $0.87 in sales per dollar of assets. This difference is reasonable when one considers the sales rate for jewelry and the relative cost of holding jewelry inventory, relative to groceries. Fortunately, Tiffany is able to offset its slow sales velocity, relative to groceries, with higher gross profits, relative to groceries.

Note to Instructors: For 2005, Kroger's gross profit percentage (gross profit divided by revenues) was 25.3%, while Tiffany's gross profit percentage was 55.8%. Kroger's ratio of operating income to revenues was 1.5%, while Tiffany's ratio of operating income to revenues was 13.8%.

Appendix 1—Ex. 6-35

a. and c.

SALES JOURNAL

Date	Invoice No.	Account Debited	Post. Ref.	Accts. Rec. Dr. Sales Cr.	Cost of Merchandise Sold Dr. Merchandise Inventory Cr.
2008					
Mar. 3	80	Samantha McGill............	✓	14,750	7,500
8	81	L. Smith	✓	10,000	5,500
19	82	Paula Larkin	✓	11,500	6,000
26	83	Amy Pugh	✓	21,000	16,500
				57,250	35,500
				(11)(41)	(51)(12)

b. and c.

PURCHASES JOURNAL

Date	Account Credited	Post. Ref.	Accounts Payable Cr.	Merchandise Inventory Dr.	Other Accounts Dr.	Post. Ref.	Amount
2008							
Mar. 10	Lee Rug Importers.................	✓	12,000	12,000			
12	Lee Rug Importers.................	✓	10,500	10,500			
21	Lee Rug Importers.................	✓	49,500	49,500			
			72,000	72,000			
			(21)	(12)			

d.

Merchandise inventory, March 1	$26,000
Plus: March purchases	72,000
Less: Cost of merchandise sold......................................	(35,500)
Merchandise inventory, March 31	$62,500

OR

Quantity	Rug Style	Cost
2	10 by 8 Chinese*	$18,000
1	8 by 12 Persian	5,500
1	8 by 10 Indian	6,000
2	10 by 12 Persian	33,000
		$62,500

*($7,500 + $10,500)

Appendix 2—Ex. 6–36

(1)   (b)   perpetual inventory system
(2)   (a)   periodic inventory system
(3)   (c)   both
(4)   (c)   both
(5)   (c)   both
(6)   (a)   periodic inventory system
(7)   (c)   both
(8)   (c)   both
(9)   (a)   periodic inventory system
(10) (a)   periodic inventory system

Appendix 2—Ex. 6–37

(a) debit
(b) debit
(c) credit
(d) credit
(e) debit
(f) debit
(g) debit

Appendix 2—Ex. 6–38

Aug.	3	Purchases	24,500	
		Accounts Payable		24,500
	4	Transportation In..................................	475	
		Cash		475
	7	Accounts Payable.................................	4,000	
		Purchases Returns and Allowances		4,000
	11	Accounts Receivable	12,700	
		Sales		12,700
	12	Delivery Expense..................................	300	
		Cash		300
	13	Accounts Payable.................................	20,500	
		Purchases Discounts		410
		Cash		20,090
	26	Cash	12,446	
		Sales Discounts....................................	254	
		Accounts Receivable		12,700

Appendix 2—Ex. 6–39

Aug.	3	Merchandise Inventory	24,500	
		Accounts Payable		24,500
	4	Merchandise Inventory	475	
		Cash		475
	7	Accounts Payable.................................	4,000	
		Merchandise Inventory		4,000
	11	Accounts Receivable	12,700	
		Sales		12,700
	11	Cost of Merchandise Sold	7,600	
		Merchandise Inventory		7,600
	12	Delivery Expense..................................	300	
		Cash		300
	13	Accounts Payable.................................	20,500	
		Merchandise Inventory		410
		Cash		20,090
	26	Cash	12,446	
		Sales Discounts....................................	254	
		Accounts Receivable		12,700

Appendix 2—Ex. 6–40

Mar.	31	Merchandise Inventory	42,150	
		Sales	925,000	
		Purchases Discounts	2,000	
		Purchases Returns and Allowances	9,000	
		Income Summary		978,150
	31	Income Summary	655,450	
		Merchandise Inventory		34,500
		Sales Discounts		4,000
		Sales Returns and Allowances		8,000
		Purchases		480,000
		Transportation In		15,400
		Salaries Expense		76,300
		Advertising Expense		25,800
		Depreciation Expense		5,100
		Miscellaneous Expense		6,350
	31	Income Summary	322,700	
		Lorene Greenway, Capital		322,700
	31	Lorene Greenway, Capital	50,000	
		Lorene Greenway, Drawing		50,000

PROBLEMS

Prob. 6–1A

1.

MAGIC VINYL CO.
Income Statement
For the Year Ended March 31, 2008

Revenue from sales:			
Sales		$1,542,000	
Less: Sales returns and allowances	$ 27,720		
Sales discounts	26,280	54,000	
Net sales			$1,488,000
Cost of merchandise sold			930,000
Gross profit			$ 558,000
Expenses:			
Selling expenses:			
Sales salaries expense	$207,840		
Advertising expense	52,560		
Depreciation expense—store equipment	7,680		
Miscellaneous selling expense	1,920		
Total selling expenses		$ 270,000	
Administrative expenses:			
Office salaries expense	$100,980		
Rent expense	37,620		
Depreciation expense—office equipment	15,240		
Insurance expense	4,680		
Office supplies expense	1,560		
Miscellaneous administrative expense	1,920		
Total administrative expenses		162,000	
Total expenses			432,000
Income from operations			$ 126,000
Other expense:			
Interest expense			6,000
Net income			$ 120,000

Prob. 6–1A   Continued

2.

MAGIC VINYL CO.
Statement of Owner's Equity
For the Year Ended March 31, 2008

Tiffany Garland, capital, April 1, 2007		$564,900
Net income for the year.......................................	$120,000	
Less withdrawals..	42,000	
Increase in owner's equity..		78,000
Tiffany Garland, capital, March 31, 2008........................		$642,900

Prob. 6–1A   Continued

3.

MAGIC VINYL CO.
Balance Sheet
March 31, 2008

Assets

Current assets:

Cash..		$184,500
Accounts receivable.................................		145,200
Merchandise inventory		210,000
Office supplies.....................................		6,720
Prepaid insurance		4,080
Total current assets...............................			$550,500

Property, plant, and equipment:

Office equipment	$102,000	
Less accumulated depreciation	15,360	$ 86,640
Store equipment	$183,600	
Less accumulated depreciation	41,040	142,560
Total property, plant, and equipment...................................		229,200
Total assets		$779,700

Liabilities

Current liabilities:

Accounts payable	$ 66,720	
Note payable (current portion)	9,000	
Salaries payable	2,880	
Total current liabilities		$ 78,600

Long-term liabilities:

Note payable (final payment due 2018) ...	58,200
Total liabilities..	$136,800

Owner's Equity

Tiffany Garland, capital	642,900
Total liabilities and owner's equity	$779,700

Prob. 6–1A   Concluded

4. a. The multiple-step form of income statement contains various sections for revenues and expenses, with intermediate balances, and concludes with net income. In the single-step form, the total of all expenses is deducted from the total of all revenues. There are no intermediate balances.

    b. In the report form of balance sheet, the assets, liabilities, and owner's equity are presented in that order in a downward sequence. In the account form, the assets are listed on the left-hand side, and the liabilities and owner's equity are listed on the right-hand side.

Prob. 6–2A

1.

MAGIC VINYL CO.
Income Statement
For the Year Ended March 31, 2008

Revenues:		
Net sales		$1,488,000
Expenses:		
Cost of merchandise sold	$930,000	
Selling expenses	270,000	
Administrative expenses	162,000	
Interest expense	6,000	
Total expenses		1,368,000
Net income		$ 120,000

2.

MAGIC VINYL CO.
Statement of Owner's Equity
For the Year Ended March 31, 2008

Tiffany Garland, capital, April 1, 2007		$564,900
Net income for the year	$120,000	
Less withdrawals	42,000	
Increase in owner's equity		78,000
Tiffany Garland, capital, March 31, 2008		$642,900

3.

MAGIC VINYL CO.
Balance Sheet
March 31, 2008

Assets

Current assets:			
Cash		$184,500	
Accounts receivable		145,200	
Merchandise inventory		210,000	
Office supplies		6,720	
Prepaid insurance		4,080	
Total current assets			$550,500
Property, plant, and equipment:			
Office equipment	$102,000		
Less accumulated depreciation	15,360	$ 86,640	
Store equipment	$183,600		
Less accumulated depreciation	41,040	142,560	
Total property, plant, and equipment			229,200
Total assets			$779,700

Liabilities

Current liabilities:			
Accounts payable	$66,720		
Note payable (current portion)	9,000		
Salaries payable	2,880		
Total current liabilities		$ 78,600	
Long-term liabilities:			
Note payable (final payment due 2018)		58,200	
Total liabilities		$136,800	
Owner's Equity			
Tiffany Garland, capital		642,900	
Total liabilities and owner's equity		$779,700	

405

Prob. 6–2A   Concluded

4.

2008				
Mar.	31	Sales	1,542,000	
		Income Summary		1,542,000
	31	Income Summary	1,422,000	
		Sales Returns and Allowances		27,720
		Sales Discounts		26,280
		Cost of Merchandise Sold		930,000
		Sales Salaries Expense		207,840
		Advertising Expense		52,560
		Depreciation Expense—Store Equipment		7,680
		Miscellaneous Selling Expense		1,920
		Office Salaries Expense		100,980
		Rent Expense		37,620
		Depreciation Expense—Office Equipment		15,240
		Insurance Expense		4,680
		Office Supplies Expense		1,560
		Miscellaneous Administrative Expense		1,920
		Interest Expense		6,000
	31	Income Summary	120,000	
		Tiffany Garland, Capital		120,000
	31	Tiffany Garland, Capital	42,000	
		Tiffany Garland, Drawing		42,000

Prob. 6–3A

Jan.	2	Accounts Receivable—Kibler Co.	10,000	
		Sales		10,000
	2	Cost of Merchandise Sold	6,500	
		Merchandise Inventory		6,500
	3	Cash	12,960	
		Sales		12,000
		Sales Tax Payable		960
	3	Cost of Merchandise Sold	9,000	
		Merchandise Inventory		9,000
	4	Accounts Receivable—Glickman Co.	5,600	
		Sales		5,600
	4	Cost of Merchandise Sold	3,100	
		Merchandise Inventory		3,100
	5	Cash	8,640	
		Sales		8,000
		Sales Tax Payable		640
	5	Cost of Merchandise Sold	6,000	
		Merchandise Inventory		6,000
	12	Cash	9,900	
		Sales Discounts.....................................	100	
		Accounts Receivable—Kibler Co.		10,000
	14	Cash	15,000	
		Sales		15,000
	14	Cost of Merchandise Sold	9,200	
		Merchandise Inventory		9,200
	16	Accounts Receivable—Bryan Co.	12,000	
		Sales		12,000
	16	Cost of Merchandise Sold	7,200	
		Merchandise Inventory		7,200
	18	Sales Returns and Allowances	3,000	
		Accounts Receivable—Bryan Co.		3,000
	18	Merchandise Inventory	1,800	
		Cost of Merchandise Sold............................		1,800

Prob. 6–3A   Concluded

Jan.	19	Accounts Receivable—Cooney Co.	15,750	
		Sales		15,750
	19	Accounts Receivable—Cooney Co.	400	
		Cash		400
	19	Cost of Merchandise Sold	9,500	
		Merchandise Inventory		9,500
	26	Cash	8,910	
		Sales Discounts...	90	
		Accounts Receivable—Bryan Co.		9,000
	28	Cash	15,835	
		Sales Discounts...	315	
		Accounts Receivable—Cooney Co.		16,150
	31	Cash	5,600	
		Accounts Receivable—Glickman Co.		5,600
	31	Delivery Expense..	1,875	
		Cash		1,875
Feb.	3	Credit Card Expense	1,150	
		Cash		1,150
	15	Sales Tax Payable	1,600	
		Cash		1,600

Prob. 6–4A

July	1	Merchandise Inventory	18,750	
		Accounts Payable—Kermit Co.		18,750
	3	Merchandise Inventory	12,330	
		Accounts Payable—Basaway Co.		12,330
	4	Merchandise Inventory	13,800	
		Accounts Payable—Phillips Co.		13,800
	6	Accounts Payable—Phillips Co.	1,900	
		Merchandise Inventory		1,900
	13	Accounts Payable—Basaway Co.	12,330	
		Cash		12,087
		Merchandise Inventory		243
	14	Accounts Payable—Phillips Co.	11,900	
		Cash		11,662
		Merchandise Inventory		238
	19	Merchandise Inventory	18,000	
		Accounts Payable—Cleghorne Co.		18,000
	19	Merchandise Inventory	500	
		Cash		500
	20	Merchandise Inventory	9,000	
		Accounts Payable—Graham Co.		9,000
	30	Accounts Payable—Graham Co.	9,000	
		Cash		8,910
		Merchandise Inventory		90
	31	Accounts Payable—Kermit Co.	18,750	
		Cash		18,750
	31	Accounts Payable—Cleghorne Co.	18,000	
		Cash		18,000

Prob. 6–5A

Apr.	3	Merchandise Inventory	18,000	
		Accounts Payable—Mandell Co.		18,000
		[$30,000 – ($30,000 × 40%)] = $18,000.		
	4	Cash	12,800	
		Sales		12,800
	4	Cost of Merchandise Sold	7,600	
		Merchandise Inventory		7,600
	5	Merchandise Inventory	19,465	
		Accounts Payable—Quinn Co.		19,465
	6	Accounts Payable—Mandell Co.	3,500	
		Merchandise Inventory		3,500
	11	Accounts Receivable—Campo Co.	4,800	
		Sales		4,800
		[$6,000 – ($6,000 × 20%)] = $4,800.		
	11	Cost of Merchandise Sold	3,200	
		Merchandise Inventory		3,200
	13	Accounts Payable—Mandell Co.	14,500	
		Cash		14,210
		Merchandise Inventory		290
	14	Cash	52,700	
		Sales		52,700
	14	Cost of Merchandise Sold	31,500	
		Merchandise Inventory		31,500
	15	Accounts Payable—Quinn Co.	19,465	
		Cash		19,090
		Merchandise Inventory		375
	21	Cash	4,752	
		Sales Discounts...	48	
		Accounts Receivable—Campo Co.		4,800
	24	Accounts Receivable—Elkins Co.	8,150	
		Sales		8,150

Prob. 6–5A   Continued

Apr.	24	Cost of Merchandise Sold	4,500	
		Merchandise Inventory		4,500
	28	Credit Card Expense	1,500	
		Cash		1,500
	30	Sales Returns and Allowances	1,200	
		Accounts Receivable—Elkins Co.		1,200
	30	Merchandise Inventory	900	
		Cost of Merchandise Sold		900

Prob. 6–6A

1.

Aug.				
	1	Accounts Receivable—Beyer Co.	17,850	
		Sales		17,850
	1	Cost of Merchandise Sold	10,700	
		Merchandise Inventory		10,700
	2	Delivery Expense..	140	
		Cash		140
	5	Accounts Receivable—Beyer Co.	27,550	
		Sales		27,550
	5	Cost of Merchandise Sold	16,500	
		Merchandise Inventory		16,500
	6	Sales Returns and Allowances	1,800	
		Accounts Receivable—Beyer Co.		1,800
	6	Merchandise Inventory	1,050	
		Cost of Merchandise Sold.............................		1,050
	15	Accounts Receivable—Beyer Co.	32,000	
		Sales		32,000
	15	Accounts Receivable—Beyer Co.	1,243	
		Cash		1,243
	15	Cost of Merchandise Sold	19,200	
		Merchandise Inventory		19,200
	16	Cash	15,729	
		Sales Discounts..	321	
		Accounts Receivable—Beyer Co.		16,050
	25	Cash	32,923	
		Sales Discounts..	320	
		Accounts Receivable—Beyer Co.		33,243
	31	Cash	27,550	
		Accounts Receivable—Beyer Co.		27,550

Prob. 6–6A   Concluded

2.

			Debit	Credit
Aug.	1	Merchandise Inventory	17,850	
		Accounts Payable—Sellars Company..........		17,850
	5	Merchandise Inventory	27,550	
		Accounts Payable—Sellars Company..........		27,550
	6	Accounts Payable—Sellars Company	1,800	
		Merchandise Inventory		1,800
	9	Merchandise Inventory	165	
		Cash		165
	15	Merchandise Inventory	33,243	
		Accounts Payable—Sellars Company..........		33,243
		$32,000 + $1,243 = $33,243.		
	16	Accounts Payable—Sellars Company	16,050	
		Cash		15,729
		Merchandise Inventory		321
	25	Accounts Payable—Sellars Company	33,243	
		Cash		32,923
		Merchandise Inventory		320
	31	Accounts Payable—Sellars Company	27,550	
		Cash		27,550

July	1	Purchases	18,750	
		Accounts Payable—Kermit Co.		18,750
	3	Purchases	12,150	
		Transportation In	180	
		Accounts Payable—Basaway Co.		12,330
	4	Purchases	13,800	
		Accounts Payable—Phillips Co.		13,800
	6	Accounts Payable—Phillips Co.	1,900	
		Purchases Returns and Allowances		1,900
	13	Accounts Payable—Basaway Co.	12,330	
		Cash		12,087
		Purchases Discounts		243
	14	Accounts Payable—Phillips Co.	11,900	
		Cash		11,662
		Purchases Discounts		238
	19	Purchases	18,000	
		Accounts Payable—Cleghorne Co.		18,000
	19	Transportation In	500	
		Cash		500
	20	Purchases	9,000	
		Accounts Payable—Graham Co.		9,000
	30	Accounts Payable—Graham Co.	9,000	
		Cash		8,910
		Purchases Discounts		90
	31	Accounts Payable—Kermit Co.	18,750	
		Cash		18,750
	31	Accounts Payable—Cleghorne Co.	18,000	
		Cash		18,000

Appendix 2—Prob. 6–8A

Apr.	3	Purchases	18,000	
		Accounts Payable—Mandell Co.		18,000
		[$30,000 − ($30,000 × 40%)] = $18,000.		
	4	Cash	12,800	
		Sales		12,800
	5	Purchases	18,750	
		Transportation In......................................	715	
		Accounts Payable—Quinn Co.		19,465
	6	Accounts Payable—Mandell Co.	3,500	
		Purchases Returns and Allowances		3,500
	11	Accounts Receivable—Campo Co.	4,800	
		Sales		4,800
		[$6,000 − ($6,000 × 20%)] = $4,800.		
	13	Accounts Payable—Mandell Co.	14,500	
		Cash		14,210
		Purchases Discounts		290
	14	Cash	52,700	
		Sales		52,700
	15	Accounts Payable—Quinn Co.	19,465	
		Cash		19,090
		Purchases Discounts		375
	21	Cash	4,752	
		Sales Discounts.......................................	48	
		Accounts Receivable—Campo Co.		4,800
	24	Accounts Receivable—Elkins Co.	8,150	
		Sales		8,150
	28	Credit Card Expense	1,500	
		Cash		1,500
	30	Sales Returns and Allowances	1,200	
		Accounts Receivable—Elkins Co.		1,200

Appendix 2—Prob. 6–9A

1.

Aug.	1	Accounts Receivable—Beyer Co.	17,850	
		Sales		17,850
	2	Delivery Expense..	140	
		Cash		140
	5	Accounts Receivable—Beyer Co.	27,550	
		Sales		27,550
	6	Sales Returns and Allowances	1,800	
		Accounts Receivable—Beyer Co.		1,800
	15	Accounts Receivable—Beyer Co.	32,000	
		Sales		32,000
	15	Accounts Receivable—Beyer Co.	1,243	
		Cash		1,243
	16	Cash	15,729	
		Sales Discounts...	321	
		Accounts Receivable—Beyer Co.		16,050
	25	Cash	32,923	
		Sales Discounts...	320	
		Accounts Receivable—Beyer Co.		33,243
	31	Cash	27,550	
		Accounts Receivable—Beyer Co.		27,550

Appendix 2—Prob. 6–9A   Concluded

2.

Aug.				
1	Purchases		17,850	
	Accounts Payable—Sellars Company			17,850
5	Purchases		27,550	
	Accounts Payable—Sellars Company			27,550
6	Accounts Payable—Sellars Company		1,800	
	Purchases Returns and Allowances			1,800
9	Transportation In		165	
	Cash			165
15	Purchases		32,000	
	Transportation In		1,243	
	Accounts Payable—Sellars Company			33,243
16	Accounts Payable—Sellars Company		16,050	
	Cash			15,729
	Purchases Discounts			321
25	Accounts Payable—Sellars Company		33,243	
	Cash			32,923
	Purchases Discounts			320
31	Accounts Payable—Sellars Company		27,550	
	Cash			27,550

Appendix 2—Prob. 6-10A

1. **Periodic inventory system. Odell Company uses a periodic inventory system since it maintains accounts for purchases, purchases returns and allowances, purchases discounts, and transportation in.**

2. **See page 419.**

2.

ODELL COMPANY
Income Statement
For the Year Ended July 31, 2008

Revenue from sales:			
Sales			$4,425,800
Less: Sales returns and allowances		$ 40,000	
Sales discounts		37,500	77,500
Net sales			$4,348,300
Cost of merchandise sold:			
Merchandise inventory, August 1, 2007 ..		$ 350,900	
Purchases	$2,146,000		
Less: Purchases returns and allows.......	24,000		
Purchases discounts......................	18,000		
Net purchases	$2,104,000		
Add transportation in	43,600		
Cost of merchandise purchased		2,147,600	
Cost of merchandise available for sale ...		$2,498,500	
Less merchandise inventory, July 31, 2008		376,400	
Cost of merchandise sold			2,122,100
Gross profit			$2,226,200
Expenses:			
Selling expenses:			
Sales salaries expense........................	$ 625,000		
Advertising expense	220,000		
Delivery expense..................................	36,000		
Depreciation expense—store equip.	23,600		
Miscellaneous selling expense...........	42,800		
Total selling expenses		$ 947,400	
Administrative expenses:			
Office salaries expense	$ 400,000		
Rent expense..	125,000		
Insurance expense...............................	12,000		
Office supplies expense.......................	9,200		
Depreciation expense—office equip.	6,000		
Miscellaneous administrative expense	23,400		
Total administrative expenses		575,600	
Total expenses			1,523,000
Income from operations..............................			$ 703,200
Other income and expense:			
Rent revenue...		$ 25,000	
Less interest expense.............................		3,000	22,000
Net income			$ 725,200

419

3.

Merchandise Inventory	376,400	
Sales	4,425,800	
Purchases Returns and Allowances	24,000	
Purchases Discounts	18,000	
Rent Revenue	25,000	
Income Summary		4,869,200
Income Summary	4,144,000	
Merchandise Inventory		350,900
Sales Returns and Allowances		40,000
Sales Discounts		37,500
Purchases		2,146,000
Transportation In		43,600
Sales Salaries Expense		625,000
Advertising Expense		220,000
Delivery Expense		36,000
Depreciation Expense—Store Equipment		23,600
Miscellaneous Selling Expense		42,800
Office Salaries Expense		400,000
Rent Expense		125,000
Insurance Expense		12,000
Office Supplies Expense		9,200
Depreciation Expense—Office Equipment		6,000
Miscellaneous Administrative Expense		23,400
Interest Expense		3,000
Income Summary	725,200	
Marcus Odell, Capital		725,200
Marcus Odell, Capital	75,000	
Marcus Odell, Drawing		75,000

Prob. 6–1B

1.

HOBBS' CO.
Income Statement
For the Year Ended June 30, 2008

Revenue from sales:			
Sales		$1,351,800	
Less: Sales returns and allowances	$ 18,900		
Sales discounts	9,900	28,800	
Net sales			$1,323,000
Cost of merchandise sold			963,000
Gross profit			$ 360,000
Expenses:			
Selling expenses:			
Sales salaries expense	$189,000		
Advertising expense	25,470		
Depreciation expense—store			
equipment	4,140		
Miscellaneous selling expense	990		
Total selling expenses		$ 219,600	
Administrative expenses:			
Office salaries expense	$ 36,900		
Rent expense	19,935		
Insurance expense	11,475		
Depreciation expense—office			
equipment	8,100		
Office supplies expense	810		
Miscellaneous administrative expense	1,080		
Total administrative expenses		78,300	
Total expenses			297,900
Income from operations			$ 62,100
Other expense:			
Interest expense			900
Net income			$ 61,200

Prob. 6–1B   Continued

2.

HOBBS' CO.
Statement of Owner's Equity
For the Year Ended June 30, 2008

Jeremiah Hobbs, capital, July 1, 2007		$241,200
Net income for the year	$61,200	
Less withdrawals	22,500	
Increase in owner's equity		38,700
Jeremiah Hobbs, capital, June 30, 2008		$279,900

Prob. 6–1B   Continued

3.

HOBBS' CO.
Balance Sheet
June 30, 2008

Assets

Current assets:			
Cash..		$ 68,850	
Accounts receivable................................		55,800	
Merchandise inventory		90,000	
Office supplies...		2,340	
Prepaid insurance		6,120	
Total current assets............................			$223,110
Property, plant, and equipment:			
Office equipment	$ 57,600		
Less accumulated depreciation	9,720	$ 47,880	
Store equipment......................................	$105,750		
Less accumulated depreciation	43,740	62,010	
Total property, plant, and equipment...			109,890
Total assets			$333,000

Liabilities

Current liabilities:		
Accounts payable.....................................	$ 24,300	
Note payable (current portion)	2,250	
Salaries payable	1,800	
Total current liabilities		$ 28,350
Long-term liabilities:		
Note payable (final payment due 2018) ...		24,750
Total liabilities...		$ 53,100

Owner's Equity

Jeremiah Hobbs, capital	279,900
Total liabilities and owner's equity	$333,000

Prob. 6–1B   Concluded

4. a. The multiple-step form of income statement contains various sections for revenues and expenses, with intermediate balances, and concludes with net income. In the single-step form, the total of all expenses is deducted from the total of all revenues. There are no intermediate balances.

    b. In the report form of balance sheet, the assets, liabilities, and owner's equity are presented in that order in a downward sequence. In the account form, the assets are listed on the left-hand side, and the liabilities and owner's equity are listed on the right-hand side.

Prob. 6–2B

1.

HOBBS' CO.
Income Statement
For the Year Ended June 30, 2008

Revenues:		
Net sales..		$1,323,000
Expenses:		
Cost of merchandise sold.........................	$963,000	
Selling expenses	219,600	
Administrative expenses...........................	78,300	
Interest expense	900	
Total expenses		1,261,800
Net income		$ 61,200

2.

HOBBS' CO.
Statement of Owner's Equity
For the Year Ended June 30, 2008

Jeremiah Hobbs, capital, July 1, 2007		$241,200
Net income for the year......................................	$61,200	
Less withdrawals..	22,500	
Increase in owner's equity...............................		38,700
Jeremiah Hobbs, capital, June 30, 2008		$279,900

Prob. 6–2B   Continued

3.

HOBBS' CO.
Balance Sheet
June 30, 2008

Assets			
Current assets:			
Cash		$68,850	
Accounts receivable		55,800	
Merchandise inventory		90,000	
Office supplies		2,340	
Prepaid insurance		6,120	
Total current assets			$223,110
Property, plant, and equipment:			
Office equipment	$ 57,600		
Less accum. depreciation	9,720	$47,880	
Store equipment	$105,750		
Less accum. depreciation	43,740	62,010	
Total property, plant, and equipment			109,890
Total assets			$333,000

Liabilities		
Current liabilities:		
Accounts payable	$24,300	
Note payable (current portion)	2,250	
Salaries payable	1,800	
Total current liabilities		$ 28,350
Long-term liabilities:		
Note payable (final payment due 2018)		24,750
Total liabilities		$ 53,100
Owner's Equity		
Jeremiah Hobbs, capital		279,900
Total liabilities and owner's equity		$333,000

Prob. 6–2B   Concluded

4.

2008

June	30	Sales...	1,351,800	
		Income Summary		1,351,800
	30	Income Summary	1,290,600	
		Sales Returns and Allowances		18,900
		Sales Discounts		9,900
		Cost of Merchandise Sold............................		963,000
		Sales Salaries Expense..................................		189,000
		Advertising Expense.......................................		25,470
		Depreciation Expense—Store Equipment ...		4,140
		Miscellaneous Selling Expense....................		990
		Office Salaries Expense		36,900
		Rent Expense		19,935
		Insurance Expense		11,475
		Depreciation Expense—Office Equipment ..		8,100
		Office Supplies Expense		810
		Miscellaneous Administrative Expense.......		1,080
		Interest Expense		900
	30	Income Summary	61,200	
		Jeremiah Hobbs, Capital		61,200
	30	Jeremiah Hobbs, Capital	22,500	
		Jeremiah Hobbs, Drawing.............................		22,500

Prob. 6–3B

July	1	Accounts Receivable—Upshaw Co.	8,000	
		Sales		8,000
	1	Cost of Merchandise Sold	4,800	
		Merchandise Inventory		4,800
	2	Cash	16,050	
		Sales		15,000
		Sales Tax Payable		1,050
	2	Cost of Merchandise Sold	8,800	
		Merchandise Inventory		8,800
	5	Accounts Receivable—Westone Company.......	16,000	
		Sales		16,000
	5	Cost of Merchandise Sold	10,500	
		Merchandise Inventory		10,500
	8	Cash	12,305	
		Sales		11,500
		Sales Tax Payable		805
	8	Cost of Merchandise Sold	7,000	
		Merchandise Inventory		7,000
	13	Cash	8,000	
		Sales		8,000
	13	Cost of Merchandise Sold	4,750	
		Merchandise Inventory		4,750
	14	Accounts Receivable—Tyler Co.	7,500	
		Sales		7,500
	14	Cost of Merchandise Sold	4,000	
		Merchandise Inventory		4,000
	15	Cash	15,840	
		Sales Discounts..	160	
		Accounts Receivable—Westone Company		16,000

Prob. 6–3B   Continued

July	16	Sales Returns and Allowances	800	
		Accounts Receivable—Tyler Co.		800
	16	Merchandise Inventory	360	
		Cost of Merchandise Sold		360
	18	Accounts Receivable—Horton Company	6,850	
		Sales		6,850
	18	Accounts Receivable—Horton Company	210	
		Cash		210
	18	Cost of Merchandise Sold	4,100	
		Merchandise Inventory		4,100
	24	Cash	6,633	
		Sales Discounts..	67	
		Accounts Receivable—Tyler Co.		6,700
	28	Cash	6,923	
		Sales Discounts..	137	
		Accounts Receivable—Horton Company.....		7,060
	31	Delivery Expense...	3,100	
		Cash		3,100
	31	Cash	8,000	
		Accounts Receivable—Upshaw Co.		8,000
Aug.	3	Credit Card Expense	780	
		Cash		780
	10	Sales Tax Payable	1,855	
		Cash		1,855

Prob. 6–4B

Oct.	1	Merchandise Inventory	12,125	
		Accounts Payable—Mantooth Co.		12,125
	5	Merchandise Inventory	17,500	
		Accounts Payable—Hauck Co.		17,500
	10	Accounts Payable—Mantooth Co.	12,125	
		Cash		11,889
		Merchandise Inventory		236
	13	Merchandise Inventory	7,500	
		Accounts Payable—Lieu Co.		7,500
	14	Accounts Payable—Lieu Co.	2,500	
		Merchandise Inventory		2,500
	18	Merchandise Inventory	9,600	
		Accounts Payable—Fowler Company..........		9,600
	18	Merchandise Inventory	150	
		Cash		150
	19	Merchandise Inventory	9,750	
		Accounts Payable—Hatcher Co.		9,750
	23	Accounts Payable—Lieu Co.	5,000	
		Cash		4,950
		Merchandise Inventory		50
	29	Accounts Payable—Hatcher Co.	9,750	
		Cash		9,555
		Merchandise Inventory		195
	31	Accounts Payable—Fowler Company	9,600	
		Cash		9,600
	31	Accounts Payable—Hauck Co.	17,500	
		Cash		17,500

Prob. 6–5B

Dec.	3	Merchandise Inventory	18,615	
		Accounts Payable—Shipley Co.		18,615
		[$24,000 − ($24,000 × 25%)] = $18,000;		
		$18,000 + $615 = $18,615.		
	5	Merchandise Inventory	10,250	
		Accounts Payable—Kirch Co.		10,250
	6	Accounts Receivable—Murdock Co.	11,700	
		Sales		11,700
		[$18,000 − ($18,000 × 35%)] = $11,700.		
	6	Cost of Merchandise Sold	8,250	
		Merchandise Inventory		8,250
	7	Accounts Payable—Kirch Co.	1,800	
		Merchandise Inventory		1,800
	13	Accounts Payable—Shipley Co.	18,615	
		Cash		18,255
		Merchandise Inventory		360
	15	Accounts Payable—Kirch Co.	8,450	
		Cash		8,281
		Merchandise Inventory		169
	16	Cash	11,466	
		Sales Discounts..	234	
		Accounts Receivable—Murdock Co.		11,700
	19	Cash	39,500	
		Sales		39,500
	19	Cost of Merchandise Sold	23,700	
		Merchandise Inventory		23,700
	22	Accounts Receivable—Milk River Co.	11,300	
		Sales		11,300
	22	Cost of Merchandise Sold	6,700	
		Merchandise Inventory		6,700
	23	Cash	17,680	
		Sales		17,680

Dec.	23	Cost of Merchandise Sold	9,100	
		Merchandise Inventory		9,100
	28	Sales Returns and Allowances	2,000	
		Accounts Receivable—Milk River Co.		2,000
	28	Merchandise Inventory	1,100	
		Cost of Merchandise Sold		1,100
	31	Credit Card Expense	1,050	
		Cash		1,050

Prob. 6–6B

1.

Nov.	2	Accounts Receivable—Byce Company	12,500	
		Sales		12,500
	2	Accounts Receivable—Byce Company	425	
		Cash		425
	2	Cost of Merchandise Sold	7,500	
		Merchandise Inventory		7,500
	8	Accounts Receivable—Byce Company	21,600	
		Sales		21,600
	8	Cost of Merchandise Sold	13,000	
		Merchandise Inventory		13,000
	8	Delivery Expense...	879	
		Cash		879
	12	Sales Returns and Allowances	5,000	
		Accounts Receivable—Byce Company........		5,000
	12	Merchandise Inventory	2,900	
		Cost of Merchandise Sold............................		2,900
	12	Cash	12,675	
		Sales Discounts..	250	
		Accounts Receivable—Byce Company........		12,925
	23	Cash	16,434	
		Sales Discounts..	166	
		Accounts Receivable—Byce Company........		16,600
	24	Accounts Receivable—Byce Company	15,000	
		Sales		15,000
	24	Cost of Merchandise Sold	9,000	
		Merchandise Inventory		9,000
	30	Cash	15,000	
		Accounts Receivable—Byce Company........		15,000

2.

Nov.	2	Merchandise Inventory	12,925	
		Accounts Payable—Sallis Company		12,925
		$12,500 + $425 = $12,925.		
	8	Merchandise Inventory	21,600	
		Accounts Payable—Sallis Company		21,600
	12	Accounts Payable—Sallis Company	5,000	
		Merchandise Inventory		5,000
	12	Accounts Payable—Sallis Company	12,925	
		Cash		12,675
		Merchandise Inventory		250
	23	Accounts Payable—Sallis Company	16,600	
		Cash		16,434
		Merchandise Inventory		166
	24	Merchandise Inventory	15,000	
		Accounts Payable—Sallis Company		15,000
	26	Merchandise Inventory	400	
		Cash		400
	30	Accounts Payable—Sallis Company	15,000	
		Cash		15,000

Appendix 2—Prob. 6–7B

Oct.	1	Purchases	11,800	
		Transportation In	325	
		Accounts Payable—Mantooth Co.		12,125
	5	Purchases	17,500	
		Accounts Payable—Hauck Co.		17,500
	10	Accounts Payable—Mantooth Co.	12,125	
		Cash		11,889
		Purchases Discounts		236
	13	Purchases	7,500	
		Accounts Payable—Lieu Co.		7,500
	14	Accounts Payable—Lieu Co.	2,500	
		Purchases Returns and Allowances		2,500
	18	Purchases	9,600	
		Accounts Payable—Fowler Co.		9,600
	18	Transportation In	150	
		Cash		150
	19	Purchases	9,750	
		Accounts Payable—Hatcher Co.		9,750
	23	Accounts Payable—Lieu Co.	5,000	
		Cash		4,950
		Purchases Discounts		50
	29	Accounts Payable—Hatcher Co.	9,750	
		Cash		9,555
		Purchases Discounts		195
	31	Accounts Payable—Fowler Co.	9,600	
		Cash		9,600
	31	Accounts Payable—Hauck Co.	17,500	
		Cash		17,500

Dec.	3	Purchases	18,000	
		Transportation In..	615	
		Accounts Payable—Shipley Co.		18,615
		[$24,000 – ($24,000 × 25\%)] = $18,000.		
	5	Purchases	10,250	
		Accounts Payable—Kirch Co.		10,250
	6	Accounts Receivable—Murdock Co.	11,700	
		Sales		11,700
		[$18,000 – ($18,000 × 35\%)] = $11,700.		
	7	Accounts Payable—Kirch Co.	1,800	
		Purchases Returns and Allowances		1,800
	13	Accounts Payable—Shipley Co.	18,615	
		Cash		18,255
		Purchases Discounts		360
	15	Accounts Payable—Kirch Co.	8,450	
		Cash		8,281
		Purchases Discounts		169
	16	Cash	11,466	
		Sales Discounts..	234	
		Accounts Receivable—Murdock Co.		11,700
	19	Cash	39,500	
		Sales		39,500
	22	Accounts Receivable—Milk River Co.	11,300	
		Sales		11,300
	23	Cash	17,680	
		Sales		17,680
	28	Sales Returns and Allowances	2,000	
		Accounts Receivable—Milk River Co.		2,000
	31	Credit Card Expense	1,050	
		Cash		1,050

Appendix 2—Prob. 6–9B

1.

			Debit	Credit
Nov.	2	Accounts Receivable—Byce Company	12,500	
		Sales		12,500
	2	Accounts Receivable—Byce Company	425	
		Cash		425
	8	Accounts Receivable—Byce Company	21,600	
		Sales		21,600
	8	Delivery Expense..	879	
		Cash		879
	12	Sales Returns and Allowances	5,000	
		Accounts Receivable—Byce Company........		5,000
	12	Cash	12,675	
		Sales Discounts...	250	
		Accounts Receivable—Byce Company........		12,925
	23	Cash	16,434	
		Sales Discounts...	166	
		Accounts Receivable—Byce Company........		16,600
	24	Accounts Receivable—Byce Company	15,000	
		Sales		15,000
	30	Cash	15,000	
		Accounts Receivable—Byce Company........		15,000

2.

Nov. 2	Purchases	12,500	
	Transportation In	425	
	Accounts Payable—Sallis Company		12,925
8	Purchases	21,600	
	Accounts Payable—Sallis Company		21,600
12	Accounts Payable—Sallis Company	5,000	
	Purchases Returns and Allowances		5,000
12	Accounts Payable—Sallis Company	12,925	
	Cash		12,675
	Purchases Discounts		250
23	Accounts Payable—Sallis Company	16,600	
	Cash		16,434
	Purchases Discounts		166
24	Purchases	15,000	
	Accounts Payable—Sallis Company		15,000
26	Transportation In	400	
	Cash		400
30	Accounts Payable—Sallis Company	15,000	
	Cash		15,000

Appendix 2—Prob. 6–10B

1. **Periodic inventory system.** Headwinds Company uses a periodic inventory system since it maintains accounts for purchases, purchases returns and allowances, purchases discounts, and transportation in.

2. **See page 440.**

2.

HEADWINDS COMPANY
Income Statement
For the Year Ended April 30, 2008

Revenue from sales:			
Sales			$1,106,450
Less: Sales returns and allowances		$ 10,000	
Sales discounts		9,375	19,375
Net sales			$1,087,075
Cost of merchandise sold:			
Merchandise inventory, May 1, 2007		$ 87,725	
Purchases	$536,500		
Less: Purchases returns and allows.	6,000		
Purchases discounts	4,500		
Net purchases	$526,000		
Add transportation in	10,900		
Cost of merchandise purchased		536,900	
Cost of merchandise available for sale		$624,625	
Less merchandise inventory, Apr. 30, 2008		94,100	
Cost of merchandise sold			530,525
Gross profit			$ 556,550
Expenses:			
Selling expenses:			
Sales salaries expense	$156,250		
Advertising expense	55,000		
Delivery expense	9,000		
Depreciation expense—store equip.	5,900		
Miscellaneous selling expense	10,700		
Total selling expenses		$236,850	
Administrative expenses:			
Office salaries expense	$100,000		
Rent expense	31,250		
Insurance expense	3,000		
Office supplies expense	2,300		
Depreciation expense—office equip.	1,500		
Miscellaneous administrative expense	5,850		
Total administrative expenses		143,900	
Total expenses			380,750
Income from operations			$ 175,800
Other income and expense:			
Rent revenue		$ 6,250	
Less interest expense		750	5,500
Net income			$ 181,300

3.

Merchandise Inventory	94,100	
Sales	1,106,450	
Purchases Returns and Allowances	6,000	
Purchases Discounts	4,500	
Rent Revenue	6,250	
Income Summary		1,217,300
Income Summary	1,036,000	
Merchandise Inventory		87,725
Sales Returns and Allowances		10,000
Sales Discounts		9,375
Purchases		536,500
Transportation In		10,900
Sales Salaries Expense		156,250
Advertising Expense		55,000
Delivery Expense		9,000
Depreciation Expense—Store Equipment		5,900
Miscellaneous Selling Expense		10,700
Office Salaries Expense		100,000
Rent Expense		31,250
Insurance Expense		3,000
Office Supplies Expense		2,300
Depreciation Expense—Office Equipment		1,500
Miscellaneous Administrative Expense		5,850
Interest Expense		750
Income Summary	181,300	
Kasey Kurtz, Capital		181,300
Kasey Kurtz, Capital	18,750	
Kasey Kurtz, Drawing		18,750

COMPREHENSIVE PROBLEM 2

1., 2., 6., and 9.

Cash   110

Date	Item	Post. Ref.	Dr.	Cr.	Balance Dr.	Balance Cr.
2008						
Mar. 1	Balance..................	✓	....	....	21,200	....
1	....	20	....	2,400	....	....
4	....	20	....	500	....	....
7	....	20	8,900	....	....	....
10	....	20	27,200	....	....	....
13	....	20	....	21,168	....	....
15	....	20	....	2,600	....	....
16	....	20	6,860	....	....	....
19	....	20	....	11,800	....	....
19	....	20	....	9,000	....	....
21	....	21	....	1,100	....	....
21	....	21	17,600	....	....	....
26	....	21	....	1,200	....	....
28	....	21	....	12,400	....	....
29	....	21	....	800	....	....
30	....	21	23,177	....	....	....
31	....	21	....	17,721	24,248	....

Accounts Receivable   112

Date	Item	Post. Ref.	Dr.	Cr.	Balance Dr.	Balance Cr.
2008						
Mar. 1	Balance..................	✓	....	....	51,300	....
6	....	20	8,500	....	....	....
7	....	20	....	8,900	....	....
14	....	20	....	1,500	....	....
16	....	20	....	7,000	....	....
20	....	21	22,300	....	....	....
21	....	21	1,100	....	....	....
21	....	21	....	17,600	....	....
30	....	21	18,750	....	....	....
30	....	21	....	23,400	43,550	....

Comp. Prob. 2   Continued

Merchandise Inventory
115

Date	Item	Post. Ref.	Dr.	Cr.	Balance Dr.	Balance Cr.
2008						
Mar. 1	Balance..................	✓	....	....	200,800	....
3	....	20	21,600	....	....	....
4	....	20	500	....	....	....
6	....	20	....	5,000	....	....
10	....	20	....	16,000	....	....
13	....	20	....	432	....	....
14	....	20	900	....	....	....
19	....	20	11,800	....	....	....
20	....	21	....	13,200	....	....
21	....	21	19,900	....	....	....
24	....	21	....	2,000	....	....
26	....	21	700	....	....	....
30	....	21	....	11,250	....	....
31	....	21	....	179	208,139	....
31	Adjusting	22	....	12,000	196,139	....

Prepaid Insurance
116

Date	Item	Post. Ref.	Dr.	Cr.	Balance Dr.	Balance Cr.
2008						
Mar. 1	Balance..................	✓	....	....	5,600	....
31	Adjusting	22	....	1,875	3,725	....

Store Supplies
117

Date	Item	Post. Ref.	Dr.	Cr.	Balance Dr.	Balance Cr.
2008						
Mar. 1	Balance..................	✓	....	....	3,800	....
29	....	21	800	....	4,600	....
31	Adjusting	22	....	3,100	1,500	....

Store Equipment
123

Date	Item	Post. Ref.	Dr.	Cr.	Balance Dr.	Balance Cr.
2008						
Mar. 1	Balance..................	✓	....	....	156,500	....

Comp. Prob. 2   Continued

Accumulated Depreciation—Store Equipment   124

Date		Item	Post. Ref.	Dr.	Cr.	Balance Dr.	Balance Cr.
2008							
Mar.	1	Balance..................	✓	....	....	....	18,900
	31	Adjusting	22	....	9,500	....	28,400

Accounts Payable   210

Date		Item	Post. Ref.	Dr.	Cr.	Balance Dr.	Balance Cr.
2008							
Mar.	1	Balance..................	✓	....	....	....	32,200
	3	....	20	....	21,600	....	....
	13	....	20	21,600	....	....	....
	19	....	20	9,000	....	....	....
	21	....	21	....	19,900	....	....
	24	....	21	2,000	....	....	....
	31	....	21	17,900	....	....	23,200

Salaries Payable   211

Date		Item	Post. Ref.	Dr.	Cr.	Balance Dr.	Balance Cr.
2008							
Mar.	31	Adjusting	22	....	2,000	....	2,000

Evan Raskind, Capital   310

Date		Item	Post. Ref.	Dr.	Cr.	Balance Dr.	Balance Cr.
2007							
Apr.	1	Balance..................	✓	....	....	....	185,100
2008							
Mar.	31	Closing	23	....	231,962	....	....
	31	Closing	23	45,000	....	....	372,062

Evan Raskind, Drawing   311

Date		Item	Post. Ref.	Dr.	Cr.	Balance Dr.	Balance Cr.
2008							
Mar.	1	Balance..................	✓	....	....	45,000	....
	31	Closing	23	....	45,000	—	—

Comp. Prob. 2   Continued

Income Summary   312

Date	Item	Post. Ref.	Dr.	Cr.	Balance Dr.	Balance Cr.
2008						
Mar. 31	Closing	23	....	1,150,450	....	....
31	Closing	23	918,488	....	....	....
31	Closing	23	231,962	....	—	—

Sales   410

Date	Item	Post. Ref.	Dr.	Cr.	Balance Dr.	Balance Cr.
2008						
Mar. 1	Balance..................	✓	....	....	....	1,073,700
6	....	20	....	8,500	....	....
10	....	20	....	27,200	....	....
20	....	21	....	22,300	....	....
30	....	21	....	18,750	....	1,150,450
31	Closing	23	1,150,450	....	—	—

Sales Returns and Allowances   411

Date	Item	Post. Ref.	Dr.	Cr.	Balance Dr.	Balance Cr.
2008						
Mar. 1	Balance..................	✓	....	....	30,900	....
14	....	20	1,500	....	....	....
26	....	21	1,200	....	33,600	....
31	Closing	23	....	33,600	—	—

Sales Discounts   412

Date	Item	Post. Ref.	Dr.	Cr.	Balance Dr.	Balance Cr.
2008						
Mar. 1	Balance..................	✓	....	....	19,800	....
16	....	20	140	....	....	....
30	....	21	223	....	20,163	....
31	Closing	23	....	20,163	—	—

Cost of Merchandise Sold   510

Date	Item	Post. Ref.	Dr.	Cr.	Balance Dr.	Balance Cr.
2008						
Mar. 1	Balance..................	✓	....	....	541,000	....
6	....	20	5,000	....	....	....
10	....	20	16,000	....	....	....
14	....	20	....	900	....	....
20	....	21	13,200	....	....	....
26	....	21	....	700	....	....
30	....	21	11,250	....	584,850	....
31	Adjusting	22	12,000	....	596,850	....
31	Closing	23	....	596,850	—	—

Sales Salaries Expense   520

Date	Item	Post. Ref.	Dr.	Cr.	Balance Dr.	Balance Cr.
2008						
Mar. 1	Balance..................	✓	....	....	111,600	....
28	....	21	7,600	....	119,200	....
31	Adjusting	22	1,200	....	120,400	....
31	Closing	23	....	120,400	—	—

Advertising Expense   521

Date	Item	Post. Ref.	Dr.	Cr.	Balance Dr.	Balance Cr.
2008						
Mar. 1	Balance..................	✓	....	....	27,000	....
15	....	20	2,600	....	29,600	....
31	Closing	23	....	29,600	—	—

Depreciation Expense   522

Date	Item	Post. Ref.	Dr.	Cr.	Balance Dr.	Balance Cr.
2008						
Mar. 31	Adjusting	22	9,500	....	9,500	....
31	Closing	23	....	9,500	—	—

Store Supplies Expense   523

Date	Item	Post. Ref.	Dr.	Cr.	Balance Dr.	Balance Cr.
2008						
Mar. 31	Adjusting	22	3,100	....	3,100	....
31	Closing	23	....	3,100	—	—

Comp. Prob. 2   Continued

Miscellaneous Selling Expense
529

Date		Item	Post. Ref.	Dr.	Cr.	Balance Dr.	Balance Cr.
2008							
Mar.	1	Balance...................	✓	....	....	4,200	....
	31	Closing	23	....	4,200	—	—

Office Salaries Expense
530

Date		Item	Post. Ref.	Dr.	Cr.	Balance Dr.	Balance Cr.
2008							
Mar.	1	Balance...................	✓	....	....	60,700	....
	28	....	21	4,800	....	65,500	....
	31	Adjusting	22	800	....	66,300	....
	31	Closing	23	....	66,300	—	—

Rent Expense
531

Date		Item	Post. Ref.	Dr.	Cr.	Balance Dr.	Balance Cr.
2008							
Mar.	1	Balance...................	✓	....	....	27,900	....
	1	....	20	2,400	....	30,300	....
	31	Closing	23	....	30,300	—	—

Insurance Expense
532

Date		Item	Post. Ref.	Dr.	Cr.	Balance Dr.	Balance Cr.
2008							
Mar.	31	Adjusting	22	1,875	....	1,875	....
	31	Closing	23	....	1,875	—	—

Miscellaneous Administrative Expense
539

Date		Item	Post. Ref.	Dr.	Cr.	Balance Dr.	Balance Cr.
2008							
Mar.	1	Balance...................	✓	....	....	2,600	....
	31	Closing	23	....	2,600	—	—

Comp. Prob. 2   Continued

1. and 2.

Date		Description	Post. Ref.	Debit	Credit
2008					
Mar.	1	Rent Expense	531	2,400	
		Cash...	110		2,400
	3	Merchandise Inventory	115	21,600	
		Accounts Payable—Huisman Co. ...	210		21,600
	4	Merchandise Inventory	115	500	
		Cash...	110		500
	6	Accounts Receivable—Hillcrest Co.	112	8,500	
		Sales	410		8,500
	6	Cost of Merchandise Sold	510	5,000	
		Merchandise Inventory......................	115		5,000
	7	Cash	110	8,900	
		Accounts Receivable—Foley Co.	112		8,900
	10	Cash	110	27,200	
		Sales	410		27,200
	10	Cost of Merchandise Sold	510	16,000	
		Merchandise Inventory......................	115		16,000
	13	Accounts Payable—Huisman Co.	210	21,600	
		Cash...	110		21,168
		Merchandise Inventory......................	115		432
	14	Sales Returns and Allowances	411	1,500	
		Accounts Receivable—Hillcrest Co.	112		1,500
	14	Merchandise Inventory	115	900	
		Cost of Merchandise Sold.................	510		900
	15	Advertising Expense.............................	521	2,600	
		Cash...	110		2,600
	16	Cash	110	6,860	
		Sales Discounts	412	140	
		Accounts Receivable—Hillcrest Co.	112		7,000
	19	Merchandise Inventory	115	11,800	
		Cash...	110		11,800
	19	Accounts Payable—Bakke Co.	210	9,000	
		Cash...	110		9,000

JOURNAL

Date		Description	Post. Ref.	Debit	Credit
2008					
Mar.	20	Accounts Receivable—Wilts Co.	112	22,300	
		Sales	410		22,300
	20	Cost of Merchandise Sold	510	13,200	
		Merchandise Inventory.......................	115		13,200
	21	Accounts Receivable—Wilts Co.	112	1,100	
		Cash..	110		1,100
	21	Cash	110	17,600	
		Accounts Receivable—Owen Co.	112		17,600
	21	Merchandise Inventory	115	19,900	
		Accounts Payable—Nye Co.	210		19,900
	24	Accounts Payable—Nye Co.	210	2,000	
		Merchandise Inventory.......................	115		2,000
	26	Sales Returns and Allowances	411	1,200	
		Cash..	110		1,200
	26	Merchandise Inventory	115	700	
		Cost of Merchandise Sold.................	510		700
	28	Sales Salaries Expense	520	7,600	
		Office Salaries Expense	530	4,800	
		Cash..	110		12,400
	29	Store Supplies.......................................	117	800	
		Cash..	110		800
	30	Accounts Receivable—Whitetail Co.	112	18,750	
		Sales	410		18,750
	30	Cost of Merchandise Sold	510	11,250	
		Merchandise Inventory.......................	115		11,250
	30	Cash...	110	23,177	
		Sales Discounts	412	223	
		Accounts Receivable—Wilts Co.	112		23,400
	31	Accounts Payable—Nye Co.	210	17,900	
		Cash..	110		17,721
		Merchandise Inventory.......................	115		179

Comp. Prob. 2   Continued

3.

WORLD BOARDS CO.
Unadjusted Trial Balance
March 31, 2008

	Debit Balances	Credit Balances
Cash..	24,248	
Accounts Receivable...	43,550	
Merchandise Inventory..	208,139	
Prepaid Insurance...	5,600	
Store Supplies..	4,600	
Store Equipment...	156,500	
Accumulated Depreciation—Store Equipment		18,900
Accounts Payable		23,200
Salaries Payable		
Evan Raskind, Capital		185,100
Evan Raskind, Drawing	45,000	
Sales		1,150,450
Sales Returns and Allowances................................	33,600	
Sales Discounts	20,163	
Cost of Merchandise Sold.......................................	584,850	
Sales Salaries Expense..	119,200	
Advertising Expense	29,600	
Depreciation Expense		
Store Supplies Expense..		
Miscellaneous Selling Expense...............................	4,200	
Office Salaries Expense..	65,500	
Rent Expense...	30,300	
Insurance Expense...		
Miscellaneous Administrative Expense...................	2,600	
	1,377,650	1,377,650

Comp. Prob. 2   Continued

Date	Description	Post. Ref.	Debit	Credit
	Adjusting Entries			
2008				
Mar. 31	Cost of Merchandise Sold......................	510	12,000	
	Merchandise Inventory......................	115		12,000
	Inventory shrinkage ($208,139 –$196,139).			
31	Insurance Expense	532	1,875	
	Prepaid Insurance	116		1,875
	Insurance expired.			
31	Store Supplies Expense	523	3,100	
	Store Supplies	117		3,100
	Supplies used ($4,600 – $1,500).			
31	Depreciation Expense	522	9,500	
	Accum. Depr.—Store Equipment	124		9,500
	Store equipment depreciation.			
31	Sales Salaries Expense	520	1,200	
	Office Salaries Expense	530	800	
	Salaries Payable	211		2,000
	Accrued salaries.			

Comp. Prob. 2   Continued

7.

WORLD BOARDS CO.
Adjusted Trial Balance
March 31, 2008

	Debit Balances	Credit Balances
Cash	24,248	
Accounts Receivable	43,550	
Merchandise Inventory	196,139	
Prepaid Insurance	3,725	
Store Supplies	1,500	
Store Equipment	156,500	
Accumulated Depreciation—Store Equipment		28,400
Accounts Payable		23,200
Salaries Payable		2,000
Evan Raskind, Capital		185,100
Evan Raskind, Drawing	45,000	
Sales		1,150,450
Sales Returns and Allowances	33,600	
Sales Discounts	20,163	
Cost of Merchandise Sold	596,850	
Sales Salaries Expense	120,400	
Advertising Expense	29,600	
Depreciation Expense	9,500	
Store Supplies Expense	3,100	
Miscellaneous Selling Expense	4,200	
Office Salaries Expense	66,300	
Rent Expense	30,300	
Insurance Expense	1,875	
Miscellaneous Administrative Expense	2,600	
	1,389,150	1,389,150

452

Comp. Prob. 2   Continued

8.

WORLD BOARDS CO.
Income Statement
For the Year Ended March 31, 2008

Revenue from sales:			
Sales			$1,150,450
Less: Sales returns and allowances	$ 33,600		
Sales discounts	20,163	$53,763	
Net sales			$1,096,687
Cost of merchandise sold			596,850
Gross profit			$ 499,837
Expenses:			
Selling expenses:			
Sales salaries expense	$120,400		
Advertising expense	29,600		
Depreciation expense	9,500		
Store supplies expense	3,100		
Miscellaneous selling expense	4,200		
Total selling expenses		$ 166,800	
Administrative expenses:			
Office salaries expense	$ 66,300		
Rent expense	30,300		
Insurance expense	1,875		
Miscellaneous administrative expense	2,600		
Total administrative expenses		101,075	
Total expenses			267,875
Net income			$ 231,962

WORLD BOARDS CO.
Statement of Owner's Equity
For the Year Ended March 31, 2008

Evan Raskind, capital, April 1, 2007		$185,100
Net income for the year	$231,962	
Less withdrawals	45,000	
Increase in owner's equity		186,962
Evan Raskind, capital, March 31, 2008		$372,062

WORLD BOARDS CO.
Balance Sheet
March 31, 2008

Assets

Current assets:

Cash...	$ 24,248	
Accounts receivable...	43,550	
Merchandise inventory	196,139	
Prepaid insurance	3,725	
Store supplies...	1,500	
Total current assets		$269,162
Property, plant, and equipment:		
Store equipment	$156,500	
Less accumulated depreciation...........................	28,400	
Total property, plant, and equipment..................		128,100
Total assets		$397,262

Liabilities

Current liabilities:

Accounts payable...	$ 23,200	
Salaries payable	2,000	
Total liabilities		$ 25,200

Owner's Equity

Evan Raskind, capital...		372,062
Total liabilities and owner's equity		$397,262

Comp. Prob. 2   Continued

9.

Date	Description	Post. Ref.	Debit	Credit
	Closing Entries			
2008				
Mar. 31	Sales..	410	1,150,450	
	Income Summary...............................	312		1,150,450
31	Income Summary	312	918,488	
	Sales Returns and Allowances.........	411		33,600
	Sales Discounts..............................	412		20,163
	Cost of Merchandise Sold.................	510		596,850
	Sales Salaries Expense....................	520		120,400
	Advertising Expense	521		29,600
	Depreciation Expense	522		9,500
	Store Supplies Expense....................	523		3,100
	Miscellaneous Selling Expense........	529		4,200
	Office Salaries Expense....................	530		66,300
	Rent Expense....................................	531		30,300
	Insurance Expense............................	532		1,875
	Miscellaneous Administrative Exp...	539		2,600
31	Income Summary	312	231,962	
	Evan Raskind, Capital	310		231,962
31	Evan Raskind, Capital............................	310	45,000	
	Evan Raskind, Drawing.....................	311		45,000

Comp. Prob. 2   Continued

10.

WORLD BOARDS CO.
Post-Closing Trial Balance
March 31, 2008

	Debit Balances	Credit Balances
Cash	24,248	
Accounts Receivable	43,550	
Merchandise Inventory	196,139	
Prepaid Insurance	3,725	
Store Supplies	1,500	
Store Equipment	156,500	
Accumulated Depreciation		28,400
Accounts Payable		23,200
Salaries Payable		2,000
Evan Raskind, Capital		372,062
	425,662	425,662

Comp. Prob. 2 Concluded

5. Optional.

This solution is applicable only if the end-of-period spreadsheet (work sheet) is used.

WORLD BOARDS CO.
End-of-Period Spreadsheet (Work Sheet)
For the Year Ended March 31, 2008

#	Account Title	Unadjusted Trial Balance Dr.	Unadjusted Trial Balance Cr.	Adjustments Dr.	Adjustments Cr.	Adjusted Trial Balance Dr.	Adjusted Trial Balance Cr.	Income Statement Dr.	Income Statement Cr.	Balance Sheet Dr.	Balance Sheet Cr.
1	Cash	24,248				24,248				24,248	
2	Accounts Receivable	43,550				43,550				43,550	
3	Merchandise Inventory	208,139			(a) 12,000	196,139				196,139	
4	Prepaid Insurance	5,600			(b) 1,875	3,725				3,725	
5	Store Supplies	4,600			(c) 3,100	1,500				1,500	
6	Store Equipment	156,500				156,500				156,500	
7	Acc. Depr.—Store Equipment		18,900		(d) 9,500		28,400				28,400
8	Accounts Payable		23,200				23,200				23,200
9	Salaries Payable				(e) 2,000		2,000				2,000
10	Evan Raskind, Capital		185,100				185,100				185,100
11	Evan Raskind, Drawing	45,000				45,000				45,000	
12	Sales		1,150,450				1,150,450		1,150,450		
13	Sales Returns and Allow.	33,600				33,600		33,600			
14	Sales Discounts	20,163				20,163		20,163			
15	Cost of Merchandise Sold	584,850		(a) 12,000		596,850		596,850			
16	Sales Salaries Expense	119,200		(e) 1,200		120,400		120,400			
17	Advertising Expense	29,600				29,600		29,600			
18	Depreciation Expense			(d) 9,500		9,500		9,500			
19	Store Supplies Expense			(c) 3,100		3,100		3,100			
20	Misc. Selling Expense	4,200				4,200		4,200			
21	Office Salaries Expense	65,500		(e) 800		66,300		66,300			
22	Rent Expense	30,300				30,300		30,300			
23	Insurance Expense			(b) 1,875		1,875		1,875			
24	Misc. Admin. Expense	2,600				2,600		2,600			
25		1,377,650	1,377,650	28,475	28,475	1,389,150	1,389,150	918,488	1,150,450	470,662	238,700
26	Net income							231,962			231,962
27								1,150,450	1,150,450	470,662	470,662

457

SPECIAL ACTIVITIES

SA 6–1

Standards of Ethical Conduct for Management Accountants requires management accountants to perform in a competent manner and to comply with relevant laws, regulations, and technical standards. If Corey Gilbert intentionally subtracted the discount with knowledge that the discount period had expired, he would have behaved in an unprofessional manner. Such behavior could eventually jeopardize Lawn Ranger Company's buyer/supplier relationship with Nebraska Farm Co.

SA 6–2

Jared Helms is correct. The accounts payable due suppliers could be included on the balance sheet at an amount of $83,440 ($76,440 + $7,000). This is the amount that will be expected to be paid to satisfy the obligation (liability) to suppliers. However, this is proper only if The Eclipse Video Store Co. has a history of taking all purchases discounts, has a properly designed accounting system to identify available discounts, and has sufficient liquidity (cash) to pay the accounts payable within the discount period. In this case, The Eclipse Video Store Co. apparently meets these criteria, since it has a history of taking all available discounts, as indicated by Allison Fain. Thus, The Eclipse Video Store Co. could report total accounts payable of $83,440 on its balance sheet. Merchandise Inventory would also need to be reduced by the discount of $1,560 in order to maintain consistency in approach.

SA 6–3

1. If Kate doesn't need the stereo immediately (by the next day), Big Sound Electronics offers the best buy, as shown below.

Big Sound Electronics:

List price	$599.99
Shipping and handling (not including next-day air)	18.99
Total	$618.98

Design Sound:

List price	$580.00
Sales tax (8%)	46.40
Total	$626.40

Even if the 1% cash discount offered by Design Sound is considered, Big Sound Electronics still offers the best buy, as shown below.

List price	$580.00
Less 1% cash discount	5.80
Subtotal	$574.20
Sales tax (8%)	45.94
Total	$620.14

If Kate needs the stereo immediately (the next day), then Design Sound has the best price. This is because a shipping and handling charge of $24.99 would be added to the Big Sound Electronics price, as shown below.

Big Sound Electronics list price	$599.99
Next-day freight charge	24.99
Total	$624.98

Since both Big Sound Electronics and Design Sound will accept Kate's VISA, the ability to use a credit card would not affect the buying decision. Design Sound will, however, allow Kate to pay her bill in three installments (the first due immediately). This would allow Kate to save some interest charges on her VISA for two months. If we assume that Kate would have otherwise used her VISA and that Kate's VISA carries an interest of 1.5% per month on the unpaid balance, the potential interest savings would be calculated as follows:

Design Sound price (see previous page)............................	$626.40
Less first installment (down payment)................................	208.80
Remaining balance	$417.60
Interest for first month at 1.5%	$ 6.26
($417.60 × 1.5%)	
Remaining balance ($417.60 + $6.26).................................	$423.86
Less second installment	208.80
Remaining balance	$215.06
Interest for second month at 1.5%	$ 3.23
($215.06 × 1.5%)	

The total interest savings would be $9.49 ($6.26 + $3.23). This interest savings would be enough to just offset the price advantage of Big Sound Electronics, as shown below, resulting in a $2.07 price advantage ($618.98 − $616.91) to Design Sound.

Design Sound price (see above)...	$626.40
Less interest savings..	9.49
Total	$616.91

2. Other considerations in buying the stereo include the ability to have the stereo repaired locally by Design Sound. In addition, Design Sound employees would presumably be available to answer questions on the operation and installation of the stereo. In addition, if Kate purchased the stereo from Design Sound, she would have the stereo the same day rather than the next day, which is the earliest that Big Sound Electronics could deliver the stereo.

SA 6–4

1.

EMIGRANT PARTS COMPANY
Projected Income Statement
For the Year Ended July 31, 2009

Revenues:		
Net sales (a)		$ 920,000
Interest revenue		10,000
Total revenues...		$ 930,000
Expenses:		
Cost of merchandise sold (b)	$598,000	
Selling expenses (c)..	73,500	
Administrative expenses (d)......................................	49,000	
Interest expense	15,000	
Total expenses		735,500
Net income		$ 194,500

Notes:

(a) Projected net sales
    [$800,000 + (15% × $800,000)].............................. $ 920,000

(b) Projected cost of merchandise sold
    ($920,000 × 65%) .... $ 598,000

(c) Total selling expenses for year ended
    July 31, 2008.. $ 90,000
    Add: Increase in store supplies expense
          ($12,000 × 15%)... $1,800
        Increase in miscellaneous selling expense
          ($3,000 × 15%).. 450   2,250
    Less delivery expenses..   (18,750)
    Projected total selling expenses .... $ 73,500

(d) Total administrative expenses for year ended
    July 31, 2008.. $ 48,550
    Add: Increase in office supplies expense
          ($2,000 × 15%).. $ 300
        Increase in miscellaneous administrative
          expense ($1,000 × 15%)............................. 150   450
    Projected total administrative expenses .... $ 49,000

SA 6–4   Concluded

2. a. Yes. The proposed change will increase net income from $136,450 to $194,500, a change of $58,050.

   b. Possible concerns related to the proposed changes include the following:

   The primary concern is with the accuracy of the estimates used for projecting the effects of the proposed changes. If the increase in sales does not materialize, Emigrant Parts Company could incur significant costs of carrying excess inventory stocked in anticipation of increasing sales. At the same time it is incurring these additional inventory costs, cash collections from customers will be reduced by the amount of the discounts. This could create a liquidity problem for Emigrant Parts Company.

   Another concern arises from the proposed change in shipping terms so as to eliminate all shipments of merchandise FOB destination, thereby eliminating delivery expenses. Emigrant Parts Company assumes that this change will have no effect on sales. However, some (perhaps a significant number) customers may object to this change and may seek other vendors with more favorable shipping terms. Hence, an unanticipated decline in sales could occur because of this change.

   As with any business decision, risks (concerns) such as those mentioned above must be thoroughly considered before final action is taken.

SA 6–5

Note to Instructors: The purpose of this activity is to familiarize students with the variety of possible purchase prices for a fairly common household item. Students should report several alternative prices when they consider the source of the purchase and the other factors that affect the purchase, e.g., delivery, financing, warranties, etc.

CHAPTER 7
INVENTORIES

QUESTION INFORMATION

Number	Objective	Description	Difficulty	Time	AACSB	AICPA	SS	GL
Q7-1	7-1		Easy	5 min	Analytic	FN-Measurement		
Q7-2	7-1		Easy	5 min	Analytic	FN-Measurement		
Q7-3	7-1		Easy	5 min	Analytic	FN-Measurement		
Q7-4	7-1		Easy	5 min	Analytic	FN-Measurement		
Q7-5	7-2		Easy	5 min	Analytic	FN-Measurement		
Q7-6	7-2		Easy	5 min	Analytic	FN-Measurement		
Q7-7	7-5		Easy	5 min	Analytic	FN-Measurement		
Q7-8	7-5		Easy	5 min	Analytic	FN-Measurement		
Q7-9	7-5		Easy	5 min	Analytic	FN-Measurement		
Q7-10	7-5		Easy	5 min	Analytic	FN-Measurement		
Q7-11	7-6		Easy	5 min	Analytic	FN-Measurement		
Q7-12	7-6		Easy	5 min	Analytic	FN-Measurement		
Q7-13	7-6		Easy	5 min	Analytic	FN-Measurement		
Q7-14	7-6		Easy	5 min	Analytic	FN-Measurement		
Q7-15	7-6		Easy	5 min	Analytic	FN-Measurement		
Q7-16	7-7		Easy	5 min	Analytic	FN-Measurement		
PE7-1A	7-2	Cost flows, gross profit, and ending inventory	Easy	15 min	Analytic	FN-Measurement		
PE7-1B	7-2	Cost flows, gross profit, and ending inventory	Easy	15 min	Analytic	FN-Measurement		
PE7-2A	7-3	Perpetual inventory using FIFO method	Easy	10 min	Analytic	FN-Measurement		
PE7-2B	7-3	Perpetual inventory using FIFO method	Easy	10 min	Analytic	FN-Measurement		
PE7-3A	7-3	Perpetual inventory using LIFO method	Easy	10 min	Analytic	FN-Measurement		
PE7-3B	7-3	Perpetual inventory using LIFO method	Easy	10 min	Analytic	FN-Measurement		
PE7-4A	7-4	Periodic inventory using FIFO, LIFO, average cost methods	Easy	15 min	Analytic	FN-Measurement		
PE7-4B	7-4	Periodic inventory using FIFO, LIFO, average cost methods	Easy	15 min	Analytic	FN-Measurement		
PE7-5A	7-6	Lower of cost or market	Easy	5 min	Analytic	FN-Measurement		
PE7-5B	7-6	Lower of cost or market	Easy	5 min	Analytic	FN-Measurement		
PE7-6A	7-6	Effect of inventory errors	Easy	5 min	Analytic	FN-Measurement		
PE7-6B	7-6	Effect of inventory errors	Easy	5 min	Analytic	FN-Measurement		
PE7-7A	7-7	Retail inventory method	Easy	5 min	Analytic	FN-Measurement		
PE7-7B	7-7	Retail inventory method	Easy	5 min	Analytic	FN-Measurement		
PE7-8A	7-7	Gross profit method	Easy	5 min	Analytic	FN-Measurement		
PE7-8B	7-7	Gross profit method	Easy	5 min	Analytic	FN-Measurement		

Number	Objective	Description	Difficulty	Time	AACSB	AICPA	SS	GL
Ex7-1	7-1	Control of inventories	Easy	5 min	Analytic	FN-Measurement		
Ex7-2	7-1	Control of inventories	Easy	10 min	Analytic	FN-Measurement		
Ex7-3	7-2, 7-3	Perpetual inventory using FIFO	Easy	15 min	Analytic	FN-Measurement	Exl	
Ex7-4	7-2, 7-3	Perpetual inventory using LIFO	Easy	15 min	Analytic	FN-Measurement	Exl	
Ex7-5	7-2, 7-3	Perpetual inventory using LIFO	Easy	15 min	Analytic	FN-Measurement	Exl	
Ex7-6	7-2, 7-3	Perpetual inventory using FIFO	Easy	15 min	Analytic	FN-Measurement	Exl	
Ex7-7	7-2, 7-3	FIFO, LIFO costs under perpetual inventory system	Easy	15 min	Analytic	FN-Measurement		
Ex7-8	7-2, 7-4	Periodic inventory by three methods	Easy	15 min	Analytic	FN-Measurement		
Ex7-9	7-2, 7-4	Periodic inventory by three methods; cost of merchandise sold	Easy	20 min	Analytic	FN-Measurement	Exl	
Ex7-10	7-5	Comparing inventory methods	Easy	5 min	Analytic	FN-Measurement		
Ex7-11	7-6	Lower-of-cost- or-market	Easy	10 min	Analytic	FN-Measurement	Exl	
Ex7-12	7-6	Merchandise inventory on the balance sheet	Easy	5 min	Analytic	FN-Measurement		
Ex7-13	7-6	Effect of errors in physical inventory	Easy	5 min	Analytic	FN-Measurement		
Ex7-14	7-6	Effect of errors in physical inventory	Easy	5 min	Analytic	FN-Measurement		
Ex7-15	7-6	Error in inventory	Moderate	5 min	Analytic	FN-Measurement		
Ex7-16	7-7	Retail inventory method	Easy	5 min	Analytic	FN-Measurement		
Ex7-17	7-7	Retail inventory method	Easy	10 min	Analytic	FN-Measurement	Exl	
Ex7-18	7-7	Gross profit inventory method	Easy	10 min	Analytic	FN-Measurement		
Ex7-19	FAI	Inventory turnover	Moderate	10 min	Analytic	FN-Measurement		
Ex7-20	FAI	Inventory turnover and number of days' sales in inventory	Moderate	15 min	Analytic	FN-Measurement		
Pr7-1A	7-2, 7-3	FIFO perpetual inventory	Moderate	45 min	Analytic	FN-Measurement	Exl	
Pr7-2A	7-2, 7-3	LIFO perpetual inventory	Moderate	45 min	Analytic	FN-Measurement	Exl	
Pr7-3A	7-2, 7-4	Periodic inventory by three methods	Difficult	1 1/2 hr	Analytic	FN-Measurement	Exl	
Pr7-4A	7-6	Lower-of-cost-or-market inventory	Difficult	1 1/2 hr	Analytic	FN-Measurement		
Pr7-5A	7-7	Retail method; gross profit method	Difficult	1 1/4 hr	Analytic	FN-Measurement		
Pr7-1B	7-2, 7-3	FIFO perpetual inventory	Moderate	45 min	Analytic	FN-Measurement	Exl	
Pr7-2B	7-2, 7-3	LIFO perpetual inventory	Moderate	45 min	Analytic	FN-Measurement	Exl	
Pr7-3B	7-2, 7-4	Periodic inventory by three methods	Difficult	1 1/2 hr	Analytic	FN-Measurement	Exl	
Pr7-4B	7-6	Lower-of-cost-or-market inventory	Difficult	1 1/2 hr	Analytic	FN-Measurement		
Pr7-5B	7-7	Retail method; gross profit method	Difficult	1 1/4 hr	Analytic	FN-Measurement		

Number	Objective	Description	Difficulty	Time	AACSB	AICPA	SS	GL
SA7-1	7-1	Ethics and professional conduct in business	Easy	5 min	Ethics	BB-Industry		
SA7-2	7-3, 7-4	LIFO and inventory flow	Easy	10 min	Analytic	FN-Measurement		
SA7-3	7-3, 7-4	Costing inventory	Difficult	1 hr	Analytic	FN-Measurement		
SA7-4	FAI	Inventory ratios for Dell and HP	Moderate	30 min	Analytic	FN-Measurement		
SA7-5	FAI	Comparing inventory ratios for two companies	Easy	10 min	Analytic	FN-Measurement		
SA7-6	FAI	Comparing inventory ratios for three companies	Moderate	15 min	Analytic	FN-Measurement		

EYE OPENERS

1. The receiving report should be reconciled to the initial purchase order and the vendor's invoice before recording or paying for inventory purchases. This procedure will verify that the inventory received matches the type and quantity of inventory ordered. It also verifies that the vendor's invoice is charging the company for the actual quantity of inventory received at the agreed-upon price.

2. To protect inventory from customer theft, retailers use two-way mirrors, cameras, security guards, locked display cabinets, and inventory tags that set off an alarm if the inventory is removed from the store.

3. Perpetual. The perpetual inventory system provides the more effective means of controlling inventories, since the inventory account is updated for each purchase and sale. This also assists managers in determining when to reorder inventory items.

4. A physical inventory should be taken periodically to test the accuracy of the perpetual records. In addition, a physical inventory will identify inventory shortages or shrinkage.

5. No, they are not techniques for determining physical quantities. The terms refer to cost flow assumptions, which affect the determination of the cost prices assigned to items in the inventory.

6. No, the term refers to the flow of costs rather than the items remaining in the inventory. The inventory cost is composed of the earliest acquisitions costs rather than the most recent acquisitions costs.

7. a. FIFO   c. FIFO
   b. LIFO   d. LIFO

8. FIFO

9. LIFO. In periods of rising prices, the use of LIFO will result in the lowest net income and thus the lowest income tax expense.

10. Yes. The inventory method may be changed for a valid reason. The effect of any change in method and the reason for the change should be fully disclosed in the financial statements for the period in which the change occurred.

11. Net realizable value (estimated selling price less any direct cost of disposition, such as sales commissions).

12. By a notation next to "Merchandise inventory" on the balance sheet or in a note to the financial statements.

13. a. Gross profit for the year was understated by $8,750.
    b. Merchandise inventory and owner's equity were understated by $8,750.

14. Keepsakes Company. Since the merchandise was shipped FOB shipping point, title passed to Keepsakes Company when it was shipped and should be reported in Keepsakes Company's financial statements at December 31, the end of the fiscal year.

15. Manufacturer's

16. Inventories estimated by the gross profit method are useful in preparing interim statements and in establishing an estimate of the cost of merchandise destroyed by fire or other disasters.

PRACTICE EXERCISES

PE 7–1A

		Gross Profit	Ending Inventory
a.	First-in, first-out (FIFO)	$35 ($150 – $115)	$239 ($118 + $121)
b.	Last-in, first-out (LIFO)	$29 ($150 – $121)	$233 ($115 + $118)
c.	Average cost	$32 ($150 – $118)	$236 ($118 × 2)

PE 7–1B

		Gross Profit	Ending Inventory
a.	First-in, first-out (FIFO)	$12 ($100 – $88)	$167 ($85 + $82)
b.	Last-in, first-out (LIFO)	$18 ($100 – $82)	$173 ($88 + $85)
c.	Average cost	$15 ($100 – $85)	$170 ($85 × 2)

PE 7–2A

a. Cost of merchandise sold (August 30):

13 units @ $34	$442
7 units @ $38	266
20	$708

b. Inventory, August 31:

$570 = (15 units × $38)

PE 7–2B

a. Cost of merchandise sold (March 29):

5 units @ $10	$ 50
35 units @ $14	490
40	$540

b. Inventory, March 31:

$308 = (22 units × $ 14)

PE 7–3A

a. Cost of merchandise sold (August 30):

$760 = (20 units × $38)

b. Inventory, August 31:

13 units @ $34	$442
2 units @ $38	76
15	$518

PE 7–3B

a. Cost of merchandise sold (March 29):

$560 = (40 units × $14)

b. Inventory, March 31:

5 units @ $10	$ 50
17 units @ $14	238
22	$288

PE 7–4A

a. First-in, first-out (FIFO) method: $720 = (20 units × $36)

b. Last-in, first-out (LIFO) method: $540 = (12 units × $25) + (8 units × $30)

c. Average cost method: $645 (20 units × $32.25), where average cost = $32.25 = $2,580/80 units

PE 7–4B

a. First-in, first-out (FIFO) method: $9,550 = (36 units × $250) + (2 units × $275)

b. Last-in, first-out (LIFO) method: $10,900 = (18 units × $300) + (20 units × $275)

c. Average cost method: $10,279 (38 units × $270.50), where average cost = $270.50 = $27,050/100 units

PE 7–5A

	A	B	C	D	E	F	G	
			Unit	Unit	Total			
		Inventory	Cost	Market			Lower	
	Commodity	Quantity	Price	Price	Cost	Market	of C or M	
1	TRP4	96	$29	18	$2,784	$1,728	$1,728	1
2	V555	200	13	14	2,600	2,800	2,600	2
3	Total				$5,384	$4,528	$4,328	3

PE 7–5B

	A	B	C	D	E	F	G	
			Unit	Unit	Total			
		Inventory	Cost	Market			Lower	
	Commodity	Quantity	Price	Price	Cost	Market	of C or M	
1	E662	215	$30	$28	$ 6,450	$ 6,020	$ 6,020	1
2	C11R	741	22	26	16,302	19,266	16,302	2
3	Total				$22,752	$25,286	$22,322	3

PE 7–6A

	Amount of Misstatement Overstatement (Understatement)
Balance Sheet:	
Merchandise inventory understated	$(9,000)
Current assets understated	(9,000)
Total assets understated	(9,000)
Owner's equity understated	(9,000)
Income Statement:	
Cost of merchandise sold overstated..........	$ 9,000
Gross profit understated..............................	(9,000)
Net income understated...............................	(9,000)

PE 7–6B

	Amount of Misstatement Overstatement (Understatement)
Balance Sheet:	
Merchandise inventory overstated..............	$29,000
Current assets overstated	29,000
Total assets overstated................................	29,000
Owner's equity overstated...........................	29,000
Income Statement:	
Cost of merchandise sold understated	$(29,000)
Gross profit overstated	29,000
Net income overstated	29,000

PE 7–7A

$540,000 ($675,000 × 80%)

PE 7–7B

$182,000 ($280,000 × 65%)

PE 7–8A

Merchandise available for sale..	$1,380,000
Less cost of merchandise sold [$1,500,000 × (100% – 35%)]	975,000
Estimated ending merchandise inventory...	$ 405,000

PE 7–8B

Merchandise available for sale..	$700,000
Less cost of merchandise sold [$800,000 × (100% – 36%)]	512,000
Estimated ending merchandise inventory...	$188,000

EXERCISES

Ex. 7–1

Switching to a perpetual inventory system will strengthen Handy Hardware's internal controls over inventory, since the store managers will be able to keep track of how much of each item is on hand. This should minimize shortages of good-selling items and excess inventories of poor-selling items.

On the other hand, switching to a perpetual inventory system will not eliminate the need to take a physical inventory count. A physical inventory must be taken to verify the accuracy of the inventory records in a perpetual inventory system. In addition, a physical inventory count is needed to detect shortages of inventory due to damage or theft.

Ex. 7–2

a. Inappropriate. The control of using security measures to protect the inventory is violated if the stockroom is not locked.

b. Inappropriate. Good controls include a receiving report, prepared after all inventory items received have been counted and inspected. Inventory purchased should only be recorded and paid for after reconciling the receiving report, the initial purchase order, and the vendor's invoice.

c. Appropriate. The inventory tags will protect the inventory from customer theft.

Ex. 7-3

Portable MP3 Players

Date	Purchases			Cost of Merchandise Sold			Inventory		
	Quantity	Unit Cost	Total Cost	Quantity	Unit Cost	Total Cost	Quantity	Unit Cost	Total Cost
Nov. 1							70	40	2,800
5				52	40	2,080	18	40	720
16	30	42	1,260				18	40	720
							30	42	1,260
21				18	40	720	24	42	1,008
				6	42	252			
24				8	42	336	16	42	672
30	14	45	630				16	42	672
							14	45	630
30 Balances						3,388			1,302

472

Ex. 7–4

Portable MP3 Players

Date	Purchases			Cost of Merchandise Sold			Inventory		
	Quantity	Unit Cost	Total Cost	Quantity	Unit Cost	Total Cost	Quantity	Unit Cost	Total Cost
Nov. 1							70	40	2,800
5				52	40	2,080	18	40	720
16	30	42	1,260				18	40	720
							30	42	1,260
21				24	42	1,008	18	40	720
							6	42	252
24				6	42	252	16	40	640
				2	40	80			
30	14	45	630				16	40	640
							14	45	630
30	Balances					3,420			1,270

473

Ex. 7–5

Cell Phones

Date	Purchases			Cost of Merchandise Sold			Inventory		
	Quantity	Unit Cost	Total Cost	Quantity	Unit Cost	Total Cost	Quantity	Unit Cost	Total Cost
July 1							100	30	3,000
3	80	32	2,560				100	30	3,000
							80	32	2,560
7				72	32	2,304	100	30	3,000
							8	32	256
13				8	32	256	28	30	840
				72	30	2,160			
21	60	33	1,980				28	30	840
							60	33	1,980
31				32	33	1,056	28	30	840
							28	33	924
31	Balances					5,776			1,764

Ex. 7-6

Cell Phones

Date	Purchases			Cost of Merchandise Sold			Inventory		
	Quantity	Unit Cost	Total Cost	Quantity	Unit Cost	Total Cost	Quantity	Unit Cost	Total Cost
July 1							100	30	3,000
3	80	32	2,560				100	30	3,000
							80	32	2,560
7				72	30	2,160	28	30	840
							80	32	2,560
13				28	30	840			
				52	32	1,664	28	32	896
21	60	33	1,980				28	32	896
							60	33	1,980
31				28	32	896			
				4	33	132	56	33	1,848
31 Balances						5,692			1,848

Ex. 7–7

a. $5,040 ($72 × 70 units)

b. $4,600 [($60 × 25 units) + ($65 × 20 units) + ($72 × 25 units)] = $1,500 + $1,300 + $1,800

Ex. 7–8

a. $1,788 (24 units at $55 plus 9 units at $52) = $1,320 + $468

b. $1,410 (18 units at $40 plus 15 units at $46) = $720 + $690

c. $1,617 (33 units at $49; $5,880 / 120 units = $49)

Cost of merchandise available for sale:

18 units at $40...	$ 720
36 units at $46...	1,656
42 units at $52...	2,184
24 units at $55...	1,320
120 units (at average cost of $49).............................	$5,880

Ex. 7–9

Inventory Method	Cost	
	Merchandise Inventory	**Merchandise Sold**
a. FIFO......................	$9,760	$29,240
b. LIFO......................	8,400	30,600
c. Average cost........	9,100	29,900

Cost of merchandise available for sale:

168 units at $60..	$10,080
232 units at $65..	15,080
80 units at $68..	5,440
120 units at $70..	8,400
600 units (at average cost of $65)............................	$39,000

a. First-in, first-out:

Merchandise inventory:

120 units at $70..	$8,400
20 units at $68..	1,360
140 units...	$9,760

Merchandise sold:

$39,000 – $9,760...	$29,240

b. Last-in, first-out:

Merchandise inventory:

140 units at $60..	$8,400

Merchandise sold:

$39,000 – $8,400...	$30,600

c. Average cost:

Merchandise inventory:

140 units at $65 ($39,000 / 600 units).......................	$9,100

Merchandise sold:

$39,000 – $9,100...	$29,900

Ex. 7–10

1. a. FIFO inventory   > (greater than)   LIFO inventory
   b. FIFO cost of goods sold < (less than)   LIFO cost of goods sold
   c. FIFO net income   > (greater than)   LIFO net income
   d. FIFO income tax   > (greater than)   LIFO income tax

2. In periods of rising prices, the income shown on the company's tax return would be lower than if FIFO were used; thus, there is a tax advantage of using LIFO.

Note to Instructors: The federal tax laws require that if LIFO is used for tax purposes, LIFO must also be used for financial reporting purposes. This is known as the LIFO conformity rule. Thus, selecting LIFO for tax purposes means that the company's reported income will also be lower than if FIFO had been used. Company's using LIFO believe the tax advantages from using LIFO outweighs any negative impact of reporting a lower income to shareholders.

Ex. 7–11

	A	B	C	D	E	F	G	
			Unit	Unit		Total		
		Inventory	Cost	Market			Lower	
	Commodity	Quantity	Price	Price	Cost	Market	of C or M	
1	62CF3	10	$120	$131	$ 1,200	$ 1,310	$ 1,200	1
2	41DH2	35	80	75	2,800	2,625	2,625	2
3	03MQ3	10	275	260	2,750	2,600	2,600	3
4	23FH6	16	40	28	640	448	448	4
5	10KT4	40	90	94	3,600	3,760	3,600	5
6	Total				$10,990	$10,743	$10,473	6

Ex. 7–12

The merchandise inventory would appear in the Current Assets section, as follows:

Merchandise inventory—at lower of cost, FIFO, or market $10,473

Alternatively, the details of the method of determining cost and the method of valuation could be presented in a note.

Ex. 7–13

a.

	Balance Sheet
Merchandise inventory	$6,630 ($285,780 – $279,150) understated
Current assets	$6,630 ($285,780 – $279,150) understated
Total assets	$6,630 ($285,780 – $279,150) understated
Owner's equity	$6,630 ($285,780 – $279,150) understated

b.

	Income Statement
Cost of merchandise sold	$6,630 ($285,780 – $279,150) overstated
Gross profit	$6,630 ($285,780 – $279,150) understated
Net income	$6,630 ($285,780 – $279,150) understated

Ex. 7–14

a.

	Balance Sheet
Merchandise inventory	$14,450 ($315,200 – $300,750) overstated
Current assets	$14,450 ($315,200 – $300,750) overstated
Total assets	$14,450 ($315,200 – $300,750) overstated
Owner's equity	$14,450 ($315,200 – $300,750) overstated

b.

	Income Statement
Cost of merchandise sold	$14,450 ($315,200 – $300,750) understated
Gross profit	$14,450 ($315,200 – $300,750) overstated
Net income	$14,450 ($315,200 – $300,750) overstated

Ex. 7–15

When an error is discovered affecting the prior period, it should be corrected. In this case, the merchandise inventory account should be debited and the owner's capital account credited for $8,175.

Failure to correct the error for 2007 and purposely misstating the inventory and the cost of merchandise sold in 2008 would cause the balance sheets and the income statements for the two years to not be comparable.

Ex. 7–16

$932,400 ($1,260,000 × 74%)

Ex. 7–17

	A	B	C	
		Cost	Retail	
1	Merchandise inventory, September 1	$ 220,000	$ 320,000	1
2	Purchases in September (net)	1,718,000	2,530,000	2
3	Merchandise available for sale	$ 1,938,000	$ 2,850,000	3
4	Ratio of cost to retail price: $\dfrac{\$1,938,000}{\$2,850,000} = 68\%$			4
5	Sales for September (net)		2,595,000	5
6	Merchandise inventory, September 30, at retail price		$ 255,000	6
7	Merchandise inventory, September 30, at estimated cost ($255,000 × 68%)		$ 173,400	7

Ex. 7–18

a.

	A	B	C	
		Cost	Retail	
1	Merchandise inventory, January 1		$ 360,000	1
2	Purchases (net), January 1–August 19		3,200,000	2
3	Merchandise available for sale		$ 3,560,000	3
4	Sales (net), January 1–August 19	$5,200,000		4
5	Less estimated gross profit ($5,200,000 × 36%)	1,872,000		5
6	Estimated cost of merchandise sold		3,328,000	6
7	Estimated merchandise inventory, August 19		$ 232,000	7

b. The gross profit method is useful for estimating inventories for monthly or quarterly financial statements. It is also useful in estimating the cost of merchandise destroyed by fire or other disasters.

Ex. 7–19

a. Apple: 74.3 {$9,888,000,000 / [($165,000,000 + $101,000,000) / 2]}

American Greetings: 3.9 {$905,201,000 / [($222,874,000 + $246,171,000) / 2]}

b. Lower. Although American Greetings' business is seasonal in nature, with most of its revenue generated during the major holidays, much of its nonholiday inventory may turn over very slowly. Apple, on the other hand, turns its inventory over very fast because it maintains a low inventory, which allows it to respond quickly to customer needs. Additionally, Apple's computer products can quickly become obsolete, so it cannot risk building large inventories.

Ex. 7–20

a. Number of Days' Sales in Inventory $= \dfrac{\text{Average Inventory}}{\text{Cost of Goods Sold}/365}$

Albertson's, $\dfrac{[(\$3,162 + \$3,104)/2]}{\$28,711/365} = \dfrac{\$3,133}{78.7} = 40$ days

Kroger, $\dfrac{[(\$4,356 + \$4,169)/2]}{\$42,140/365} = \dfrac{\$4,262.5}{115.5} = 37$ days

Safeway, $\dfrac{[(\$2,741 + \$2,642)/2]}{\$25,228/365} = \dfrac{\$2,691.5}{69.1} = 39$ days

Inventory Turnover $= \dfrac{\text{Cost of Goods Sold}}{\text{Average Inventory}}$

Albertson's, $\dfrac{\$28,711}{(\$3,162 + \$3,104)/2} = 9.2$

Kroger, $\dfrac{\$42,140}{(\$4,356 + \$4,169)/2} = 9.9$

Safeway, $\dfrac{\$25,228}{(\$2,741 + \$2,642)/2} = 9.4$

b. The number of days' sales in inventory and inventory turnover ratios are consistent. Albertson's has slightly more inventory than does Safeway. Kroger has relatively less inventory (2–3 days) than does Albertson's and Safeway.

Ex. 7–20   Concluded

c. If Albertson's matched Kroger's days' sales in inventory, then its hypothetical ending inventory would be determined as follows,

$$\text{Number of Days' Sales in Inventory} = \frac{\text{Average Inventory}}{\text{Cost of Goods Sold}/365}$$

$$37 \text{ days} = \frac{X}{\$28{,}711/365}$$

$X = 37 \times (\$28{,}711/365) = 37 \times \$78.7 \text{ per day}$

$X = \$2{,}912$

Thus, the additional cash flow that would have been generated is the difference between the actual average inventory and the hypothetical average inventory, as follows:

Actual average inventory..........................	$ 3,133 million
Hypothetical average inventory	2,912
Positive cash flow potential....................	$ 221 million

That is, a lower average inventory amount would have required less cash than actually was required.

PROBLEMS

Prob. 7–1A

1.

Date	Purchases Quantity	Purchases Unit Cost	Purchases Total Cost	Cost of Merchandise Sold Quantity	Cost of Merchandise Sold Unit Cost	Cost of Merchandise Sold Total Cost	Inventory Quantity	Inventory Unit Cost	Inventory Total Cost
Jan. 1							50	20	1,000
7	200	22	4,400				50	20	1,000
							200	22	4,400
20				50	20	1,000	160	22	3,520
				40	22	880			
30				110	22	2,420	50	22	1,100
Feb. 8				20	22	440	30	22	660
10	130	23	2,990				30	22	660
							130	23	2,990
27				30	22	660	70	23	1,610
				60	23	1,380			
28				50	23	1,150	20	23	460
Mar. 5	180	24	4,320				20	23	460
							180	24	4,320
13				20	23	460	110	24	2,640
				70	24	1,680			
23	100	26	2,600				110	24	2,640
							100	26	2,600
30				80	24	1,920	30	24	720
							100	26	2,600
31 Balances						11,990			3,320

483

Prob. 7–1A   Concluded

2. Accounts Receivable	23,410	
Sales..		23,410
Cost of Merchandise Sold	11,990	
Merchandise Inventory		11,990

3. $11,420 ($23,410 − $11,990)

4. $3,320 = [(30 units × $24) + (100 units × $26)] = $720 + $2,600

Prob. 7-2A

1.

Date	Purchases			Cost of Merchandise Sold			Inventory		
	Quantity	Unit Cost	Total Cost	Quantity	Unit Cost	Total Cost	Quantity	Unit Cost	Total Cost
Jan. 1							50	20	1,000
7	200	22	4,400				50	20	1,000
							200	22	4,400
20				90	22	1,980	50	20	1,000
							110	22	2,420
30				110	22	2,420	50	20	1,000
Feb. 8				20	20	400	30	20	600
10	130	23	2,990				30	20	600
							130	23	2,990
27				90	23	2,070	30	20	600
							40	23	920
28				40	23	920	20	20	400
				10	20	200			
Mar. 5	180	24	4,320				20	20	400
							180	24	4,320
13				90	24	2,160	20	20	400
							90	24	2,160
23	100	26	2,600				20	20	400
							90	24	2,160
							100	26	2,600
30				80	26	2,080	20	20	400
							90	24	2,160
							20	26	520
31 Balances						12,230			3,080

Prob. 7–2A   Concluded

2. Total sales... $23,410
   Total cost of merchandise sold.................................... <u>12,230</u>
   Gross profit... <u>$11,180</u>

3. $3,080 = [(20 units × $20) + (90 units × $24) + (20 units × $26)] = $400 + $2,160 + $520

Prob. 7–3A

1. First-In, First-Out Method

Model	Quantity	Unit Cost	Total Cost
T742	2	$140	$ 280
	3	135	405
PM18	9	259	2,331
K21G	6	90	540
H60W	3	130	390
	2	128	256
B153Z	6	92	552
	2	85	170
J600T	7	180	1,260
	1	175	175
C273W	4	101	404
	1	100	100
Total...			$6,863

2. Last-In, First-Out Method

Model	Quantity	Unit Cost	Total Cost
T742	2	$125	$ 250
	2	130	260
	1	135	135
PM18	7	242	1,694
	2	250	500
K21G	6	80	480
H60W	2	108	216
	2	110	220
	1	128	128
B153Z	8	88	704
J600T	5	160	800
	3	170	510
C273W	4	75	300
	1	100	100
Total...			$6,297

Prob. 7–3A   Concluded

3. Average Cost Method

Model	Quantity	Unit Cost*	Total Cost
T742	5	$133	$ 665
PM18	9	253	2,277
K21G	6	86	516
H60W	5	121	605
B153Z	8	87	696
J600T	8	172	1,376
C273W	5	92	460
Total...			$6,595

*Computations of unit costs:

T742: $133 = [(2 × $125) + (2 × $130) + (4 × $135) + (2 × $140)] / (2 + 2 + 4 + 2)

PM18: $253 = [(7 × $242) + (6 × $250) + (5 × $260) + (10 × $259)] / (7 + 6 + 5 + 10)

K21G: $86 = [(6 × $80) + (5 × $82) + (8 × $89) + (8 × $90)] / (6 + 5 + 8 + 8)

H60W: $121 = [(2 × $108) + (2 × $110) + (3 × $128) + (3 × $130)] / (2 + 2 + 3 + 3)

B153Z: $87 = [(8 × $88) + (4 × $79) + (3 × $85) + (6 × $92)] / (8 + 4 + 3 + 6)

J600T: $172 = [(5 × $160) + (4 × $170) + (4 × $175) + (7 × $180)] / (5 + 4 + 4 + 7)

C273W: $92 = [(4 × $75) + (4 × $100) + (4 × $101)] / (4 + 4 + 4)

4. a. During periods of rising prices, the LIFO method will result in a lesser amount of inventory, a greater amount of cost of merchandise sold, and a lesser amount of net income than the other two methods. For Del Mar Appliances, the LIFO method would be preferred for the current year, since it would result in a lesser amount of income tax.

   b. During periods of declining prices, the FIFO method will result in a lesser amount of net income and would be preferred for income tax purposes.

Prob. 7–4A

	A	B		C	D	E	F	G	
				Inventory Sheet **December 31, 2008**					
	Description	**Inventory Quantity**		**Unit Cost Price**	**Unit Market Price**	**Total Cost**	**Market**	**Lower of C or M**	
1	AC172	~~38~~	25	$ 60	$ 56	$ 1,500	$ 1,400		1
2			13	58		754	728		2
3						2,254	2,128	$ 2,128	3
4	BE43	18		175	180	3,150	3,240	3,150	4
5	CJ9	~~30~~	18	130	120	2,340	2,160		5
6			12	128		1,536	1,440		6
7						3,876	3,600	3,600	7
8	E34	125		25	26	3,125	3,250	3,125	8
9	F17	~~18~~	10	565	550	5,650	5,500		9
10			8	560		4,480	4,400		10
11						10,130	9,900	9,900	11
12	G68	60		15	15	900	900	900	12
13	K41	5		385	390	1,925	1,950	1,925	13
14	Q79	375		6	6	2,250	2,250	2,250	14
15	RZ13	~~90~~	80	22	18	1,760	1,440		15
16			10	21		210	180		16
17						1,970	1,620	1,620	17
18	S60	~~6~~	5	250	235	1,250	1,175		18
19			1	260		260	235		19
20						1,510	1,410	1,410	20
21	W21	~~140~~	100	20	18	2,000	1,800		21
22			40	19		760	720		22
23						2,760	2,520	2,520	23
24	XR90	~~15~~	9	750	745	6,750	6,705		24
25			6	740		4,440	4,470		25
26						11,190	11,175	11,175	26
27	Total					$45,040	$43,943	$ 43,703	27

Prob. 7–5A

1.

A	B	C	
HACIENDA CO.			
	Cost	Retail	
1 Merchandise inventory, June 1	$ 200,000	$ 290,000	1
2 Net purchases	2,086,000	2,885,000	2
3 Merchandise available for sale	$ 2,286,000	$ 3,175,000	3
4 Ratio of cost to retail price: $\dfrac{\$2,286,000}{\$3,175,000} = 72\%$			4
5 Sales	$ 2,780,000		5
6 Less sales returns and allowances	30,000		6
7 Net sales		2,750,000	7
8 Merchandise inventory, June 30, at retail		$ 425,000	8
9 Merchandise inventory, at estimated cost ($425,000 × 72%)		$ 306,000	9

2.

A	B	C	
SAN LUCAS CO.			
a.	Cost	Retail	
1 Merchandise inventory, November 1		$ 225,000	1
2 Net purchases		1,685,000	2
3 Merchandise available for sale		$ 1,910,000	3
4 Sales	$ 2,815,000		4
5 Less sales returns and allowances	85,000		5
6 Net sales	$ 2,730,000		6
7 Less estimated gross profit ($2,730,000 × 40%)	1,092,000		7
8 Estimated cost of merchandise sold		1,638,000	8
9 Estimated merchandise inventory, December 31		$ 272,000	9
b.			
10 Estimated merchandise inventory, December 31		$ 272,000	10
11 Physical inventory count, December 31		269,250	11
12 Estimated loss due to theft or damage, November 1– December 31		$ 2,750	12

Prob. 7-1B

1.

Date	Purchases			Cost of Merchandise Sold			Inventory		
	Quantity	Unit Cost	Total Cost	Quantity	Unit Cost	Total Cost	Quantity	Unit Cost	Total Cost
Mar. 1							132	1,500	198,000
8	108	2,000	216,000				132	1,500	198,000
							108	2,000	216,000
11				72	1,500	108,000	60	1,500	90,000
							108	2,000	216,000
22				60	1,500	90,000	102	2,000	204,000
				6	2,000	12,000			
Apr. 3	96	2,300	220,800				102	2,000	204,000
							96	2,300	220,800
10				60	2,000	120,000	42	2,000	84,000
							96	2,300	220,800
21				30	2,000	60,000	12	2,000	24,000
							96	2,300	220,800
30	120	2,350	282,000				12	2,000	24,000
							96	2,300	220,800
							120	2,350	282,000

Continued

Prob. 7–1B   Concluded

Date	Purchases			Cost of Merchandise Sold			Inventory		
	Quantity	Unit Cost	Total Cost	Quantity	Unit Cost	Total Cost	Quantity	Unit Cost	Total Cost
May 5				12	2,000	24,000			
				96	2,300	220,800			
				12	2,350	28,200	108	2,350	253,800
13				72	2,350	169,200	36	2,350	84,600
21	180	2,400	432,000				36	2,350	84,600
							180	2,400	432,000
28				36	2,350	84,600			
				54	2,400	129,600	126	2,400	302,400
31	Balances					1,046,400			302,400

2. Accounts Receivable............................   2,606,400
   Sales...   2,606,400

   Cost of Merchandise Sold.....................   1,046,400
   Merchandise Inventory........................   1,046,400

3. $1,560,000 ($2,606,400 – $1,046,400)

4. $302,400 (126 units × $2,400)

492

Prob. 7-2B

1.

Date	Purchases			Cost of Merchandise Sold			Inventory		
	Quantity	Unit Cost	Total Cost	Quantity	Unit Cost	Total Cost	Quantity	Unit Cost	Total Cost
Mar. 1							132	1,500	198,000
8	108	2,000	216,000				132	1,500	198,000
							108	2,000	216,000
11				72	2,000	144,000	132	1,500	198,000
							36	2,000	72,000
22				36	2,000	72,000	102	1,500	153,000
				30	1,500	45,000			
Apr. 3	96	2,300	220,800				102	1,500	153,000
							96	2,300	220,800
10				60	2,300	138,000	102	1,500	153,000
							36	2,300	82,800
21				30	2,300	69,000	102	1,500	153,000
							6	2,300	13,800
30	120	2,350	282,000				102	1,500	153,000
							6	2,300	13,800
							120	2,350	282,000

Continued

Prob. 7–2B   Concluded

Date	Purchases			Cost of Merchandise Sold			Inventory		
	Quantity	Unit Cost	Total Cost	Quantity	Unit Cost	Total Cost	Quantity	Unit Cost	Total Cost
May 5				120	2,350	282,000	102	1,500	153,000
							6	2,300	13,800
13				6	2,300	13,800	36	1,500	54,000
				66	1,500	99,000			
21	180	2,400	432,000				36	1,500	54,000
							180	2,400	432,000
28				90	2,400	216,000	36	1,500	54,000
							90	2,400	216,000
31 Balances						1,078,800			270,000

2. Total sales $2,606,400
    Total cost of merchandise sold 1,078,800
    Gross profit $1,527,600

3. $270,000 = [(36 \text{ units} \times \$1,500) + (90 \text{ units} \times \$2,400)] = \$54,000 + \$216,000$

Prob. 7–3B

1. First-In, First-Out Method

Model	Quantity	Unit Cost	Total Cost
F10	2	$ 70	$ 140
	1	65	65
J64	4	317	1,268
M13	2	535	1,070
	2	530	1,060
Q73	6	542	3,252
	1	549	549
144Z	6	225	1,350
	5	222	1,110
Z120	2	232	464
W941	5	156	780
Total..			$11,108

2. Last-In, First-Out Method

Model	Quantity	Unit Cost	Total Cost
F10	3	$ 60	$ 180
J64	4	305	1,220
M13	2	520	1,040
	2	527	1,054
Q73	6	520	3,120
	1	531	531
144Z	9	213	1,917
	2	215	430
Z120	2	222	444
W941	4	140	560
	1	144	144
Total..			$10,640

Prob. 7–3B   Concluded

3. Average Cost Method

Model	Quantity	Unit Cost*	Total Cost
F10	3	$ 64	$ 192
J64	4	311	1,244
M13	4	528	2,112
Q73	7	534	3,738
144Z	11	218	2,398
Z120	2	227	454
W941	5	148	740
Total..			$10,878

*Computations of unit costs:

F10: $64 = [(5 × $60) + (6 × $65) + (2 × $65) + (2 × $70)] / (5 + 6 + 2 + 2)

J64: $311 = [(6 × $305) + (3 × $310) + (3 × $316) + (4 × $317)] / (6 + 3 + 3 + 4)

M13: $528 = [(2 × $520) + (2 × $527) + (2 × $530) + (2 × $535)] / (2 + 2 + 2 + 2)

Q73: $534 = [(6 × $520) + (8 × $531) + (4 × $549) + (6 × $542)] / (6 + 8 + 4 + 6)

144Z: $218 = [(9 × $213) + (7 × $215) + (6 × $222) + (6 × $225)] / (9 + 7 + 6 + 6)

Z120: $227 = [(4 × $222) + (4 × $232)] / (4 + 4)

W941: $148 = [(4 × $140) + (6 × $144) + (8 × $148) + (7 × $156)] / (4 + 6 + 8 + 7)

4. a. During periods of rising prices, the LIFO method will result in a lesser amount of inventory, a greater amount of the cost of merchandise sold, and a lesser amount of net income than the other two methods. For Concord Appliances, the LIFO method would be preferred for the current year, since it would result in a lesser amount of income tax.

   b. During periods of declining prices, the FIFO method will result in a lesser amount of net income and would be preferred for income tax purposes.

Prob. 7–4B

	A	B		C	D	E	F	G	
							Inventory Sheet December 31, 2008		
				Unit	Unit	Total			
		Inventory		Cost	Market			Lower	
	Description	Quantity		Price	Price	Cost	Market	of C or M	
1	AC172	38	30	$ 60	$ 56	$ 1,800	$ 1,680		1
2			8	59		472	448		2
3						2,272	2,128	$ 2,128	3
4	BE43	18		175	180	3,150	3,240	3,150	4
5	CJ9	30	20	130	120	2,600	2,400		5
6			10	128		1,280	1,200		6
7						3,880	3,600	3,600	7
8	E34	125		25	26	3,125	3,250	3,125	8
9	F17	18	6	550	550	3,300	3,300		9
10			12	540		6,480	6,600		10
11						9,780	9,900	9,780	11
12	G68	60		14	15	840	900	840	12
13	K41	5		400	390	2,000	1,950	1,950	13
14	Q79	375		6	6	2,250	2,250	2,250	14
15	RZ13	90	65	22	18	1,430	1,170		15
16			25	21		525	450		16
17						1,955	1,620	1,620	17
18	S60	6	5	250	235	1,250	1,175		18
19			1	260		260	235		19
20						1,510	1,410	1,410	20
21	W21	140	120	20	18	2,400	2,160		21
22			20	17		340	360		22
23						2,740	2,520	2,520	23
24	XR90	15	10	750	745	7,500	7,450		24
25			5	740		3,700	3,725		25
26						11,200	11,175	11,175	26
27	Total					$44,702	$43,943	$ 43,548	27

Prob. 7–5B

1.

	A	B	C	
	MIRAMAR CO.			
		Cost	**Retail**	
1	Merchandise inventory, March 1	$ 185,000	$ 280,000	1
2	Net purchases	2,246,000	3,295,000	2
3	Merchandise available for sale	$ 2,431,000	$ 3,575,000	3
4	Ratio of cost to retail price: $\dfrac{\$2,431,000}{\$3,575,000} = 68\%$			4
5	Sales	$ 3,360,000		5
6	Less sales returns and allowances	60,000		6
7	Net sales		3,300,000	7
8	Merchandise inventory, March 31, at retail		$ 275,000	8
9	Merchandise inventory, at estimated cost ($275,000 × 68%)		$ 187,000	9

2.

	A	B	C	
	BOYAR'S CO.			
a.		**Cost**	**Retail**	
1	Merchandise inventory, August 1		$ 425,000	1
2	Net purchases		2,980,000	2
3	Merchandise available for sale		$ 3,405,000	3
4	Sales	$ 5,075,000		4
5	Less sales returns and allowances	75,000		5
6	Net sales	$ 5,000,000		6
7	Less estimated gross profit ($5,000,000 × 40%)	2,000,000		7
8	Estimated cost of merchandise sold		3,000,000	8
9	Estimated merchandise inventory, September 30		$ 405,000	9
b.				
10	Estimated merchandise inventory, September 30		$ 405,000	10
11	Physical inventory count, September 30		398,250	11
12	Estimated loss due to theft or damage, August 1– September 30		$ 6,750	12

SPECIAL ACTIVITIES

SA 7–1

Since the title to merchandise shipped FOB shipping point passes to the buyer when the merchandise is shipped, the shipments made before midnight, December 31, 2008, should properly be recorded as sales for the fiscal year ending December 31, 2008. Hence, Julia Faure is behaving in a professional manner. However, Julia should realize that recording these sales in 2008 precludes them from being recognized as sales in 2009. Thus, accelerating the shipment of orders to increase sales of one period will have the effect of decreasing sales of the next period.

SA 7–2

In developing a response to Jack's concerns, you should probably first emphasize the practical need for an assumption concerning the flow of cost of goods purchased and sold. That is, when identical goods are frequently purchased, it may not be practical to specifically identify each item of inventory. If all the identical goods were purchased at the same price, it wouldn't make any difference for financial reporting purposes which goods we assumed were sold first, second, etc. However, in most cases, goods are purchased over time at different prices, and, hence, a need arises to determine which goods are sold so that the price (cost) of those goods can be matched against the revenues to determine operating income.

Next, you should emphasize that accounting principles allow for the fact that the physical flow of the goods may differ from the flow of costs. Specifically, accounting principles allow for three cost flow assumptions: first-in, first-out; last-in, first-out; and average. Each of these methods has advantages and disadvantages. One primary advantage of the last-in, first-out method is that it better matches current costs (the cost of goods purchased last) with current revenues. Therefore, the reported operating income is more reflective of current operations and what might be expected in the future. Another reason that the last-in, first-out method is often used is that it tends to minimize taxes during periods of price increases. Since for most businesses prices tend to increase, the LIFO method will generate lower taxes than will the alternative cost flow methods.

The preceding explanation should help Jack better understand LIFO and its impact on the financial statements and taxes.

SA 7–3

1. a. First-in, first-out method:

1,000 units at $16.00	$ 16,000
1,000 units at $14.95	14,950
1,600 units at $14.50	23,200
400 units at $14.25	5,700
4,000 units..	$ 59,850

b. Last-in, first-out method:

3,875 units at $12.20	$ 47,275
125 units at $13.00	1,625
4,000 units..	$ 48,900

c. Average cost method:

4,000 units at $13.58*	$ 54,320

*($339,500 / 25,000) = $13.58

2.

	FIFO	LIFO	Average Cost
Sales..	$325,000	$325,000	$325,000
Cost of merchandise sold*..................	279,650	290,600	285,180
Gross profit..	$ 45,350	$ 34,400	$ 39,820
*Cost of merchandise available			
for sale	$339,500	$339,500	$339,500
Less ending inventory.........................	59,850	48,900	54,320
Cost of merchandise sold..................	$279,650	$290,600	$285,180

3. a. The LIFO method is often viewed as the best basis for reflecting income from operations. This is because the LIFO method matches the most current cost of merchandise purchases against current sales. The matching of current costs with current sales results in a gross profit amount that many consider to best reflect the results of current operations. For Kowalski Company, the gross profit of $34,400 reflects the matching of the most current costs of the product of $290,600 against the current period sales of $325,000. This matching of current costs with current sales also tends to minimize the effects of price trends on the results of operations.

The LIFO method will not match current sales and the current cost of merchandise sold if the current period quantity of sales exceeds the current period quantity of purchases. In this case, the cost of merchandise sold will include a portion of the cost of the beginning inventory, which may have a unit cost from purchases made several years prior to the current period. The results of operations may then be distorted in the sense of the current matching concept. This situation occurs rarely in most businesses because of consistently increasing quantities of year-end inventory from year to year.

While the LIFO method is often viewed as the best method for matching revenues and expenses, the FIFO method is often consistent with the physical movement of merchandise in a business, since most businesses tend to dispose of commodities in the order of their acquisition. To the extent that this is the case, the FIFO method approximates the results that will be attained by a specific identification of costs.

The average cost method is, in a sense, a compromise between LIFO and FIFO. The effect of price trends is averaged, both in determining net income and in determining inventory cost.

Which inventory costing method best reflects the results of operations for Kowalski Company depends upon whether one emphasizes the importance of matching revenues and expenses (the LIFO method) or whether one emphasizes the physical flow of merchandise (the FIFO method). The average cost method might be considered best if one emphasizes the matching and physical flow of goods concepts equally.

b.   The FIFO method provides the best reflection of the replacement cost of the ending inventory for the balance sheet. This is because the amount reported on the balance sheet for merchandise inventory will be assigned costs from the most recent purchases. For most businesses, these costs will reflect purchases made near the end of the period. For example, Kowalski Company's ending inventory on December 31, 2007, is assigned costs totaling $59,850 under the FIFO method. These costs represent purchases made during the period of August through December. This FIFO inventory amount ($59,850) more closely approximates the replacement cost of the ending inventory than either the LIFO ($48,900) or the average cost ($54,320) figures.

c. During periods of rising prices, such as shown for Kowalski Company, the LIFO method will result in a lesser amount of net income than the other two methods. Hence, for Kowalski Company, the LIFO method would be preferred for the current year, since it would result in a lesser amount of income tax.

During periods of declining prices, the FIFO method will result in a lesser amount of net income and would be preferred for income tax purposes.

d. The advantages of the perpetual inventory system include the following:

1. A perpetual inventory system provides an effective means of control over inventory. A comparison of the amount of inventory on hand with the balance of the subsidiary account can be used to determine the existence and seriousness of any inventory shortages.

2. A perpetual inventory system provides an accurate method for determining inventories used in the preparation of interim statements.

3. A perpetual inventory system provides an aid for maintaining inventories at optimum levels. Frequent review of the perpetual inventory records helps management in the timely reordering of merchandise, so that loss of sales and excessive accumulation of inventory are avoided. An analysis of Kowalski Company's purchases and sales, as shown below, indicates that the company may have accumulated excess inventory from May through August because the amount of month-end inventory increased materially, while sales remained relatively constant for the period.

Month	Purchases	Sales	Increase (Decrease) in Inventory	Inventory at End of Month	Next Month's Sales
April	3,875 units	2,000 units	1,875 units	1,875 units	2,000 units
May	4,125	2,000	2,125	4,000	2,500
June	5,000	2,500	2,500	6,500	3,000
July	5,000	3,000	2,000	8,500	3,500
August	3,400	3,500	(100)	8,400	3,500
September	—	3,500	(3,500)	4,900	2,250
October	1,600	2,250	(650)	4,250	1,250
November	1,000	1,250	(250)	4,000	1,000
December	1,000	1,000	0	4,000	—

SA 7–3   Concluded

It appears that during April through July, the company ordered inventory without regard to the accumulation of excess inventory. A perpetual inventory system might have prevented this excess accumulation from occurring.

The primary disadvantage of the perpetual inventory system is the cost of maintaining the necessary inventory records. However, computers may be used to reduce this cost.

SA 7–4

a. $\text{Inventory Turnover} = \dfrac{\text{Cost of Goods Sold}}{\text{Average Inventory}}$

$\text{Number of Days' Sales in Inventory} = \dfrac{\text{Average Inventory}}{\text{Cost of Goods Sold}/365}$

Dell

Inventory Turnover: $\dfrac{\$40{,}190}{(\$327 + \$459)/2} = \dfrac{\$40{,}190}{\$393} = 102.3$

Days' Sales in Inventory: $\dfrac{(\$327 + \$459)/2}{\$40{,}190/365} = \dfrac{\$393}{110.1} = 3.6 \text{ days}$

Hewlett-Packard

Inventory Turnover : $\dfrac{\$66{,}224}{(\$7{,}071 + \$6{,}877)/2} = \dfrac{\$66{,}224}{\$6{,}974} = 9.5$

Days' Sales in Inventory: $\dfrac{(\$7{,}071 + \$6{,}877)/2}{\$66{,}224/365} = \dfrac{\$6{,}974}{181.4} = 38.4 \text{ days}$

b. Dell builds its computers to a customer order, called a build-to-order strategy. That is, Dell doesn't make a computer until it has an order from a customer. Customers place their orders on the Internet. Dell then builds and delivers the computer, usually in a matter of days. HP, in contrast, builds computers before actual orders are received. This is called a build-to-stock strategy. HP must forecast the type of computers customers want before it receives the orders. This strategy results in greater inventory for HP, since the computers are built before there is a sale. HP has significant finished goods inventory, while Dell has little finished goods. This difference in strategy is why you see HP computers at a retail store, but not a Dell computer. It also explains the difference in their inventory efficiency ratios.

SA 7–5

a.

	Inventory Turnover	Number of Days' Sales in Inventory
Neiman Marcus	3.30	110.7
Amazon.com	13.8	26.5

Calculations:

Neiman Marcus

$$\text{Inventory Turnover} = \frac{\text{Cost of Goods Sold}}{\text{Average Inventory}}$$

$$\text{Inventory Turnover} = \frac{\$2,321,110,000}{(\$720,277,000 + \$687,062,000)/2}, \text{ or } 3.30$$

$$\text{Number of Days' Sales in Inventory} = \frac{\text{Average Inventory}}{\text{Cost of Goods Sold}/365}$$

$$\text{Number of Days' Sales in Inventory} = \frac{[(\$720,277,000 + \$687,062,000)/2]}{\$2,321,110,000/365},$$

or 110.7 days

SA 7–5   Concluded

<u>Amazon.com</u>

$$\text{Inventory Turnover} = \frac{\text{Cost of Goods Sold}}{\text{Average Inventory}}$$

$$\text{Inventory Turnover} = \frac{\$5,319,127,000}{(\$479,709,000 + \$293,917,000)/2}, \text{ or } 13.8$$

$$\text{Number of Days' Sales in Inventory} = \frac{\text{Average Inventory}}{\text{Cost of Goods Sold}/365}$$

$$\text{Number of Days' Sales in Inventory} = \frac{[(\$479,709,000 + \$293,917,000)/2]}{\$5,319,127,000/365},$$

or 26.5 days

b. Amazon.com has a smaller investment in inventory for its volume than does Neiman Marcus. Amazon.com's inventory turnover is faster (larger) and the number of days' sales in inventory is shorter (smaller). This is because Amazon.com uses a different business model than Neiman Marcus. That is, Amazon.com sells through the Internet, while Neiman Marcus uses the traditional department store model which requires Neiman Marcus to stock more inventory.

SA 7–6

a.

	Costco	Wal-Mart	JCPenney
a. Cost of merchandise sold	$42,092	$219,793	$11,285
Merchandise inventory, beginning	$ 3,339	$ 26,612	$ 3,156
Merchandise inventory, ending	3,644	29,447	3,169
Total	$ 6,983	$ 56,059	$ 6,325
b. Average merchandise inventory (Total / 2)	$3,491.50	$28,029.50	$3,162.50
Inventory turnover (a / b)	12.1	7.8	3.6

b.

	Costco	Wal-Mart	JCPenney
a. Average merchandise inventory [from part (a)]..	$3,491.50	$28,029.50	$3,162.50
Cost of merchandise sold	$ 42,092	$ 219,793	$ 11,285
b. Average daily cost of merchandise sold (COMS / 365)..............................	$115.32	$602.17	$30.92
Number of day's sales in inventory (a / b)	30.3	46.5	102.3

c. Both the inventory turnover ratio and the number of day's sales in inventory reflect the merchandising approaches of the three companies. Costco is a club warehouse. Its approach is to hold only mass appeal items that are sold quickly off the shelf. Most items are sold in bulk quantities at very attractive prices. Costco couples thin margins with very fast inventory turnover. Wal-Mart has a traditional discounter approach. It has attractive pricing, but the inventory moves slower than would be the case of a club warehouse. For example, many purchases made at Wal-Mart would not be packaged in the same bulk as would be the case at Costco. JCPenney is a traditional department store with a wider assortment of goods that will not necessarily appeal to the mass market. That is, some of the merchandise items will be more specialized and unique. As such, its inventory moves slower, but at a higher price (and margin).

CHAPTER 8
SARBANES-OXLEY, INTERNAL CONTROL, AND CASH

QUESTION INFORMATION

Number	Objective	Description	Difficulty	Time	AACSB	AICPA	SS	GL
Q8-1	8-1		Easy	5 min	Analytic	FN-Measurement		
Q8-2	8-1		Easy	5 min	Analytic	FN-Measurement		
Q8-3	8-2		Easy	5 min	Analytic	FN-Measurement		
Q8-4	8-3		Easy	5 min	Analytic	FN-Measurement		
Q8-5	8-3		Easy	5 min	Analytic	FN-Measurement		
Q8-6	8-3		Easy	5 min	Analytic	FN-Measurement		
Q8-7	8-3		Easy	5 min	Analytic	FN-Measurement		
Q8-8	8-3		Easy	5 min	Analytic	FN-Measurement		
Q8-9	8-3		Easy	5 min	Analytic	FN-Measurement		
Q8-10	8-3		Easy	5 min	Analytic	FN-Measurement		
Q8-11	8-3		Easy	5 min	Analytic	FN-Measurement		
Q8-12	8-3		Easy	5 min	Analytic	FN-Measurement		
Q8-13	8-4		Easy	5 min	Analytic	FN-Measurement		
Q8-14	8-5		Easy	5 min	Analytic	FN-Measurement		
Q8-15	8-5		Easy	5 min	Analytic	FN-Measurement		
Q8-16	8-6		Easy	5 min	Analytic	FN-Measurement		
Q8-17	8-7		Easy	5 min	Analytic	FN-Measurement		
PE8-1A	8-2	Internal control elements	Easy	5 min	Analytic	FN-Measurement		
PE8-1B	8-2	Internal control elements	Easy	5 min	Analytic	FN-Measurement		
PE8-2A	8-4	Effect of items on depositor's bank account	Easy	5 min	Analytic	FN-Measurement		
PE8-2B	8-4	Effect of items on depositor's bank account	Easy	5 min	Analytic	FN-Measurement		
PE8-3A	8-5	Adjusted balance and entries from bank account reconciliation	Easy	10 min	Analytic	FN-Measurement		
PE8-3B	8-5	Adjusted balance and entries from bank account reconciliation	Easy	10 min	Analytic	FN-Measurement		
PE8-4A	8-6	Entries for petty cash fund	Easy	10 min	Analytic	FN-Measurement		
PE8-4B	8-6	Entries for petty cash fund	Easy	10 min	Analytic	FN-Measurement		
Ex8-1	8-1	Sarbanes-Oxley internal control report	Easy	15 min	Analytic	FN-Measurement		
Ex8-2	8-2, 8-3	Internal controls	Easy	15 min	Analytic	FN-Measurement		
Ex8-3	8-2, 8-3	Internal controls	Easy	15 min	Analytic	FN-Measurement		
Ex8-4	8-2, 8-3	Internal controls for bank lending	Easy	5 min	Analytic	FN-Measurement		
Ex8-5	8-2, 8-3	Internal controls	Easy	5 min	Analytic	FN-Measurement		
Ex8-6	8-2, 8-3	Internal controls	Easy	5 min	Analytic	FN-Measurement		
Ex8-7	8-2, 8-3	Internal controls	Easy	5 min	Analytic	FN-Measurement		
Ex8-8	8-2, 8-3	Financial statement fraud	Easy	10 min	Analytic	FN-Measurement		

Number	Objective	Description	Difficulty	Time	AACSB	AICPA	SS	GL
Ex8-9	8-2, 8-3	Internal control of cash receipts	Easy	5 min	Analytic	FN-Measurement		
Ex8-10	8-1, 8-2, 8-3	Internal control of cash receipts	Easy	5 min	Analytic	FN-Measurement		
Ex8-11	8-2, 8-3	Internal control of cash receipts	Easy	5 min	Analytic	FN-Measurement		
Ex8-12	8-2, 8-3	Entry for cash sales; cash short	Easy	5 min	Analytic	FN-Measurement		
Ex8-13	8-2, 8-3	Entry for cash sales; cash over	Easy	5 min	Analytic	FN-Measurement		
Ex8-14	8-2, 8-3	Internal control of cash payments	Easy	5 min	Analytic	FN-Measurement		
Ex8-15	8-2, 8-3	Internal control of cash payments	Easy	10 min	Analytic	FN-Measurement		
Ex8-16	8-5	Bank reconciliation	Easy	10 min	Analytic	FN-Measurement		
Ex8-17	8-5	Entries based on bank reconciliation	Easy	5 min	Analytic	FN-Measurement		
Ex8-18	8-5	Bank reconciliation	Easy	15 min	Analytic	FN-Measurement		
Ex8-19	8-5	Entries for bank reconciliation	Easy	10 min	Analytic	FN-Measurement		
Ex8-20	8-5	Entries for note collected by bank	Easy	5 min	Analytic	FN-Measurement		
Ex8-21	8-5	Bank reconciliation	Moderate	15 min	Analytic	FN-Measurement		
Ex8-22	8-5	Bank reconciliation	Moderate	15 min	Analytic	FN-Measurement		
Ex8-23	8-5	Using bank reconciliation to determine cash receipts stolen	Moderate	10 min	Analytic	FN-Measurement		
Ex8-24	8-6	Petty cash fund entries	Easy	10 min	Analytic	FN-Measurement		
Ex8-25	8-7	Variation in cash flows	Easy	10 min	Analytic	FN-Measurement		
Ex8-26	FAI	Cash to monthly expenses ratio	Moderate	10 min	Analytic	FN-Measurement		
Ex8-27	FAI	Cash to monthly expenses ratio	Moderate	10 min	Analytic	FN-Measurement		
Ex8-28	FAI	Cash to monthly expenses ratio	Moderate	10 min	Analytic	FN-Measurement		
Pr8-1A	8-2, 8-3	Evaluating internal control of cash	Moderate	30 min	Analytic	FN-Measurement		
Pr8-2A	8-3, 8-6	Transactions for petty cash, cash short and over	Moderate	45 min	Analytic	FN-Measurement	Exl	
Pr8-3A	8-5	Bank reconciliation and entries	Moderate	45 min	Analytic	FN-Measurement	Exl	KA
Pr8-4A	8-5	Bank reconciliation and entries	Moderate	45 min	Analytic	FN-Measurement	Exl	KA
Pr8-5A	8-5	Bank reconciliation and entries	Difficult	1 3/4 hr	Analytic	FN-Measurement	Exl	
Pr8-1B	8-2, 8-3	Evaluating internal control of cash	Moderate	30 min	Analytic	FN-Measurement		
Pr8-2B	8-3, 8-6	Transactions for petty cash, cash short and over	Moderate	45 min	Analytic	FN-Measurement	Exl	
Pr8-3B	8-5	Bank reconciliation and entries	Moderate	45 min	Analytic	FN-Measurement	Exl	KA
Pr8-4B	8-5	Bank reconciliation and entries	Moderate	45 min	Analytic	FN-Measurement	Exl	KA
Pr8-5B	8-5	Bank reconciliation and entries	Difficult	1 3/4 hr	Analytic	FN-Measurement	Exl	

Number	Objective	Description	Difficulty	Time	AACSB	AICPA	SS	GL
SA8-1	8-2, 8-4	Ethics and professional conduct in business	Easy	5 min	Ethics	BB-Industry		
SA8-2	8-2, 8-3	Internal controls	Moderate	15 min	Analytic	FN-Measurement		
SA8-3	8-2, 8-4	Internal controls	Moderate	15 min	Analytic	FN-Measurement		
SA8-4	8-2, 8-3	Ethics and professional conduct in business	Moderate	10 min	Ethics	BB-Industry		
SA8-5	8-3, 8-5	Bank reconciliation and internal control	Difficult	45 min	Analytic	FN-Measurement		
SA8-6	8-3	Observe internal control over cash	Difficult	1 hr	Reflective Thinking	BB-Critical Thinking		
SA8-7	FAI	Cash to monthly expenses ratio	Moderate	15 min	Analytic	FN-Measurement		
SA8-8	FAI	Cash to monthly expenses ratio	Moderate	15 min	Analytic	FN-Measurement		

EYE OPENERS

1. a. Congress passed the Sarbanes-Oxley Act of 2002 because of the Enron, Worldcom, Tyco, Adelphia, and other financial scandals of the early 2000s that caused stockholders, creditors, and other investors to lose millions and in some cases billions of dollars.

   b. The purpose of Sarbanes-Oxley was to restore public confidence and trust in the financial statements of companies.

2. Internal control is broadly defined as the procedures and processes used by a company to safeguard its assets, process information accurately, and ensure compliance with laws and regulations.

3. a. The five elements of internal control are the control environment, risk assessment, control procedures, monitoring, and information and communication. The control environment is the overall attitude of management and employees about the importance of controls. Risk assessment includes evaluating various risks facing the business, including competitive threats, regulatory changes, and changes in economic factors. Control procedures are established to provide reasonable assurance that business goals will be achieved. Monitoring is the evaluation of the internal control system. Information and communication provide management with feedback about internal control.

   b. No. One element of internal control is not more important than another element. All five elements are necessary for effective internal control. The accounting system is an information system because it provides information for management's use in conducting the affairs of the business and in reporting to owners, creditors, and other stakeholders. It includes the entire network of communications used by the business.

4. The knowledge that job rotation is practiced and that one employee may perform another's job at a later date tends to discourage deviations from prescribed procedures. Also, rotation helps to disclose any irregularities that may occur.

5. Authorizing complete control over a sequence of related operations by one individual presents opportunities for inefficiency, errors, and fraud. The control over a sequence of operations should be divided so that the work of each employee is automatically checked by another employee in the normal course of work. A system functioning in this manner helps prevent errors and inefficiency. Fraud is unlikely without collusion between two or more employees.

6. To reduce the possibility of errors and embezzlement, the functions of operations and accounting should be separated. Thus, one employee should not be responsible for handling cash receipts (operations) and maintaining the accounts receivable records (accounting).

7. No. Combining the responsibility for related operations, such as combining the functions of purchasing, receiving, and storing of supplies, increases the possibility of errors and fraud.

8. The control procedure requiring that responsibility for a sequence of related operations be divided among different persons is violated in this situation. This weakness in the internal control may permit irregularities. For example, the ticket seller, while acting as ticket taker, could admit friends without a ticket.

9. The responsibility for maintaining the accounting records should be separated from the responsibility for operations so that the accounting records can serve as an independent check on operations.

10. Controls that could have prevented or detected the fraud include (1) requiring supporting documentation such as receiving reports and purchase orders of all payments, (2) requiring approval by an independent party, and (3) allowing payments to only vendors who have been previously approved by upper management.

11. The three documents supporting the liability are vendor's invoice, purchase order, and receiving report. The invoice should be compared with the receiving report to determine that the items billed have been received and with the purchase order to verify quantities, prices, and terms.

12. The prenumbering of checks and the paying of obligations by check are desirable elements of internal control. The fundamental weakness in internal control is the failure to separate the responsibility for the maintenance of the accounting records (bookkeep-

ing) from the responsibility for operations (payment of obligations).

13. The Cash balance and the bank statement balance are likely to differ because of (1) a delay by the bank or company in recording transactions or (2) errors by the bank or company in recording transactions.

14. The purpose of a bank reconciliation is to determine the reasons for the difference between the balance according to the company's records and the balance according to the bank statement and to correct those items representing errors in recording that may have been made by the bank or by the company.

15. (a) Additions made by the bank to the company's balance. This is because on the bank's records the company's account represents a liability; thus, a credit to the company's account increases the account on the bank's records.

16. a. Yes. Even though the petty cash fund is only $2,000, if the fund is replenished frequently, a significant amount of cash could be stolen. For example, if the fund is replenished weekly, then $104,000 ($2,000 × 52 weeks) could be subject to theft.

b. Controls for petty cash include (1) designating one person who is responsible for the fund, (2) maintaining a written record of all payments, (3) requiring support (receipts) for payments from the fund, and (4) periodic review of the funds on hand and the payments by an independent person.

17. a. Cash and cash equivalents are usually reported as one amount in the Current Assets section of the balance sheet.

b. Examples of cash equivalents include certificates of deposit, U.S. government securities, corporate notes and bonds, and commercial paper.

PRACTICE EXERCISES

PE 8–1A

1. (b) control procedures
2. (c) information and communication
3. (a) the control environment

PE 8–1B

1. (a) the control environment
2. (b) control procedures
3. (c) monitoring

PE 8–2A

Item No.	Appears on the Bank Statement as a Debit or Credit Memorandum	Increases or Decreases the Balance of the Depositor's Bank Account
1	debit memorandum	decreases
2	credit memorandum	increases
3	credit memorandum	increases
4	debit memorandum	decreases

PE 8–2B

Item No.	Appears on the Bank Statement as a Debit or Credit Memorandum	Increases or Decreases the Balance of the Depositor's Bank Account
1	credit memorandum	increases
2	credit memorandum	increases
3	debit memorandum	decreases
4	credit memorandum	increases

PE 8–3A

a. $8,820 as shown below.

Bank section of reconciliation: $9,200 + $2,800 – $3,180 = $8,820
Company section of reconciliation: $9,335 – $40 – $475 = $8,820

b.	Accounts Receivable	475	
	Miscellaneous Expense	40	
	Cash		515

PE 8–3B

a. $24,300 as shown below.

Bank section of reconciliation: $28,100 + $3,100 – $6,900 = $24,300
Company section of reconciliation: $9,155 + $15,225 – $80 = $24,300

b.	Miscellaneous Expense	80	
	Cash		80
	Cash	15,225	
	Notes Receivable		15,000
	Interest Revenue		225

PE 8–4A

a.	Petty Cash	600	
	Cash		600
b.	Repairs Expense	350	
	Miscellaneous Selling Expense	55	
	Cash Short and Over	20	
	Cash		425

PE 8–4B

a.	Petty Cash	400	
	Cash		400
b.	Store Supplies	180	
	Miscellaneous Selling Expense	110	
	Cash Short and Over	25	
	Cash		315

EXERCISES

Ex. 8–1

Section 404 requires management's internal control report to:

(1) state the responsibility of management for establishing and maintaining an adequate internal control structure and procedures for financial reporting; and

(2) contain an assessment, as of the end of the issuer's fiscal year, of the effectiveness of the internal control structure and procedures of the issuer for financial reporting.

The complete AICPA summary of Section 404 of Sarbanes-Oxley is as follows:

Section 404: Management Assessment of Internal Controls.

Requires each annual report of an issuer to contain an "internal control report," which shall:

(1) state the responsibility of management for establishing and maintaining an adequate internal control structure and procedures for financial reporting; and

(2) contain an assessment, as of the end of the issuer's fiscal year, of the effectiveness of the internal control structure and procedures of the issuer for financial reporting.

Each issuer's auditor shall attest to, and report on, the assessment made by the management of the issuer. An attestation made under this section shall be in accordance with standards for attestation engagements issued or adopted by the Board. An attestation engagement shall not be the subject of a separate engagement.

The language in the report of the Committee which accompanies the bill to explain the legislative intent states, "...the Committee does not intend that the auditor's evaluation be the subject of a separate engagement or the basis for increased charges or fees."

Directs the SEC to require each issuer to disclose whether it has adopted a code of ethics for its senior financial officers and the contents of that code.

Directs the SEC to revise its regulations concerning prompt disclosure on Form 8-K to require immediate disclosure "of any change in, or waiver of," an issuer's code of ethics.

Ex. 8–2

a. Agree. Tyler has made one employee responsible for the cash drawer in accordance with the internal control principle of assignment of responsibility. In addition, Tyler has segregated the operations (preparing the orders) from the accounting (taking orders and payments).

b. Disagree. It is commendable that Tyler has given the employee a specific responsibility and is holding that employee accountable for it. However, after the cashier has counted the cash, another employee (or perhaps Tyler) should remove the cash register tape and compare the amount on the tape with the cash in the drawer. Also, Tyler's standard of no mistakes may encourage the cashiers to overcharge a few customers in order to cover any possible shortages in the cash drawer.

c. Disagree. Stealing is a serious issue. An employee who can justify taking a box of tea bags can probably justify "borrowing" cash from the cash register.

Ex. 8–3

a. The sales clerks could steal money by writing phony refunds and pocketing the cash supposedly refunded to these fictitious customers.

b. Rare Earth Clothing suffers from inadequate separation of responsibilities for related operations since the clerks issue refunds and restock all merchandise. In addition, there is a lack of proofs and security measures since the supervisors authorize returns two hours after they are issued.

c. A store credit for any merchandise returned without a receipt would reduce the possibility of theft of cash. In this case, a clerk could only issue a phony store credit rather than taking money from the cash register. A store credit is not as tempting as cash. In addition, sales clerks could only use a few store credits to purchase merchandise for themselves without management getting suspicious.

An advantage of issuing a store credit for returns without a receipt is that the possibility of stealing cash is reduced. The store will also lose less revenue if customers must choose other store merchandise instead of getting a cash refund. The overall level of returns/exchanges may be reduced, since customers will not return an acceptable gift simply because they need cash more than the gift. The policy will also reduce the "cash drain" during the weeks immediately following the holidays, allowing Rare Earth Clothing to keep more of its money earning interest or use that cash to purchase spring merchandise or pay creditors.

Ex. 8–3   Concluded

A disadvantage of issuing a store credit for returns without a receipt is that preholiday sales might drop as gift-givers realize that the return policy has tightened. After the holidays, customers wishing to return items for cash refunds may be frustrated when they learn the store policy has changed. The ill will may reduce future sales. It may take longer to explain the new policy and fill out the paperwork for a store credit, lengthening lines at the return counter after the holidays. Sales clerks will need to be trained to apply the new policy and write up a store credit. Sales clerks also will need to be trained to handle the redemption of the store credit on future merchandise purchases.

d. The potential for abuse in the cash refund system could be eliminated if clerks were required to get a supervisor's authorization for a refund before giving the customer the cash. The supervisor should only authorize the refund after seeing both the customer and the merchandise that is being returned.

An alternative would be to use security measures that would detect a sales clerk attempting to ring up a refund and remove cash when a customer is not present at the sales desk. These security measures could include cameras or additional security personnel discreetly monitoring the sales desk.

Ex. 8–4

As an internal auditor, you would probably disagree with the change in policy. First Capone Bank has some normal business risk associated with default on bank loans. One way to help minimize this is to carefully evaluate loan applications. Large loans present greater risk in the event of default than do smaller loans. Thus, it is reasonable to have more than one person involved in making the decision to grant a large loan. In addition, loans should be granted on their merits, not on the basis of favoritism or mere association with the bank president. Allowing the bank president to have sole authority to grant large loans can lead to the president granting loans to friends and business associates, without the required due diligence. This can result in a bank becoming exposed to very poor credit risks. Indeed, this scenario is one of the causes of the savings and loan failures of the past.

Ex. 8–5

The Barings Bank fraud shows how small lapses in internal control can have huge consequences. In this case, the "rogue trader" was able to accumulate and hide huge losses. When the losses became so large that they could no longer be hidden, it was too late. This fraud could have been avoided with a number of internal controls. First, and most obvious, the execution and recording of trades should have been separate duties. The trader makes the trades but should never have access to accounting for them. In this way, the actual performance of the trader could not be disguised by "fixing the books." Second, the trader should be under managerial oversight. For example, trades that exceed a certain amount of exposure should require management approval. In this way, a trader would be forced to slow down or stop once trades reached a certain limit. This would avoid the trader's tendency to try to "make up" losses with even larger bets. Third, there should be no possibility for unauthorized accounts. All accounts should require formal approval and be set up by individuals other than the trader. Once the account is set up, the accounting should also be separated from the trader. In this way, the trader would not be able to set up a "private" account that goes undetected.

Ex. 8–6

This is an example of a fraud with significant collusion. Frauds that are perpetrated with multiple parties in different positions of control make detecting fraud more difficult. In this case, the fraud began with an employee responsible for authorizing claim payments. This is a sensitive position because his decisions would initiate payments. However, claims would need to be authorized and verified before payment would be made. Knowing this, the employee made sure each claim has a phony "victim." Thus, there was a verifiable story behind each claim. Only by tracking physical evidence of the accident could it be discovered that the claim was fictitious. However, the very nature of the process was to resolve small claims quickly without excessive control. Lastly, corrupt lawyers were brought into the fraud to act as attorneys for the claimants. This gave the claims even more credibility. In actuality, the lawyers had done legitimate business with the trucking company, so all appeared normal. This fraud was discovered when the fraudulent employee's bank noticed irregularities in his bank account and notified authorities. As the saying goes, "Follow the money!" As a side note, the corrupt claims administrator fell into this behavior due to gambling problems.

Ex. 8–7

Quality Sound Co. should not have relied on the unusual nature of the vendors and delivery frequency to uncover this fraud. The purchase and payment cycle is one of the most critical business cycles to control, because the potential for abuse is so great. Purchases should be initiated by a requisition document. This document should be countersigned by a superior so that two people agree as to what is being purchased. The requisition should initiate a purchase order to a vendor for goods or services. The vendor responds to the purchase order by delivering the goods. The goods should be formally received using a receiving document. An accounts payable clerk matches the requisition, purchase order, and invoice before any payment is made. Such "triple matching" prevents unauthorized requests and payments. In this case, the requests were unauthorized, suggesting that the employee has sole authority to make a request. Second, this employee had access to the invoices. This access allowed the employee to change critical characteristics of the invoice to hide the true nature of the goods being received. The invoice should have been delivered directly to the accounts payable clerk to avoid corrupting the document. There apparently was no receiving document (common for smaller companies); thus, only the invoice provided proof of what was received and needed to be paid. If there had been a receiving report, the invoice could not have been doctored and gone undetected, because it would not have matched the receiving report.

Note to Instructors: This exercise is based on an actual fraud.

Ex. 8–8

a. The most difficult frauds to detect are those that involve the senior management of a company that is in a conspiracy to commit the fraud. The senior managers have the power to access many parts of the accounting system, while the normal separation of duties is subverted by involving many people in the fraud. In addition, the authorization control is subverted because most of the authorization power resides in the senior management.

b. Overall, this type of fraud can be stopped if there is a strong oversight of senior management, such as an audit committee of the board of directors. Individual "whistle blowers" in the company can make their concerns known to the independent or internal auditors who, in turn, can inform the audit committee. The audit committee should be independent of management and have the power to monitor the actions of management.

Ex. 8–9

a. The sales clerks should not have access to the cash register tapes.

b. The cash register tapes should be locked in the cash register and the key retained by the cashier. An employee of the cashier's office should remove the cash register tape, record the total on the memorandum form, and note discrepancies.

Ex. 8–10

Jackpot Burgers suffers from a failure to separate responsibilities for related operations.

Jackpot Burgers could stop this theft by limiting the drive-through clerk to taking customer orders, entering them on the cash register, accepting the customers' payments, returning customers' change, and handing customers their orders that another employee has assembled. By making another employee responsible for assembling orders, the drive-through clerk must enter the orders on the cash register. This will produce a printed receipt or an entry on a computer screen at the food bin area, specifying the items that must be assembled to fill each order. Once the drive-through clerk has entered the sale on the cash register, the clerk cannot steal the customer's payment because the clerk's cash drawer will not balance at the end of the shift. This change also makes the drive-through more efficient and could reduce the time it takes to service a drive-through customer.

If another employee cannot be added, the weakness in internal control could be improved with more thorough supervision. The restaurant manager should be directed to keep a watchful eye on the drive-through area in order to detect when a clerk takes an order without ringing up the sale.

Ex. 8–11

a. The remittance advices should not be sent to the cashier.

b. The remittance advices should be sent directly to the Accounting Department by the mailroom.

Ex. 8–12

Cash	21,099.75	
Cash Short and Over	14.51	
Sales		21,114.26

Ex. 8–13

Cash	8,374.58	
Sales		8,351.14
Cash Short and Over		23.44

Ex. 8–14

The use of the voucher system is appropriate, the essentials of which are outlined below. (Although invoices could be used instead of vouchers, the latter more satisfactorily provide for account distribution, signatures, and other significant data.)

1. Each voucher should be approved for payment by a designated official only after completion of the following verifications: (a) that prices, quantities, terms, etc., on the invoice are in accordance with the provisions of the purchase order, (b) that all quantities billed have been received in good condition, as indicated on a receiving report, and (c) that all arithmetic details are correct.

2. The file for unpaid vouchers should be composed of 31 compartments, one for each day of the month. Each voucher should be filed in the compartment representing the last day of the discount period or the due date if the invoice is not subject to a cash discount.

3. Each day, the vouchers should be removed from the appropriate section of the file and checks issued by the disbursing official. If the bank balance is insufficient to pay all of the vouchers, those that remain unpaid should be refiled according to the date when payment should next be considered.

4. At the time of payment, all vouchers and supporting documents should be stamped or perforated "Paid" to prevent their resubmission for payment. They should then be filed in numerical sequence for future reference. The implementation and use of a computerized system would also reduce the chance that any available cash discounts are missed. For example, when invoices are received and approved for payment, they would automatically be scheduled for payment within the discount period. However, even in a computerized system, the use of an approval process that requires supporting documents and indicating "paid" on these supporting documents is an important control for avoiding duplicate payments.

Ex. 8–15

To prevent the fraud scheme described, Clear Voice must separate responsibilities for related operations. As in the past, all service requisitions should be submitted to the Purchasing Department. After receiving the service request, Purchasing should complete a Service Verification form, stating what service has been ordered and the name of the company that will provide the service. This form should be delivered via intercompany mail to the person responsible for verifying that the service was performed. This person should be someone who has firsthand knowledge of whether the service has been performed. This person, who must be someone other than the manager requesting the service, should fill in the date and time the service was received and sign the form. In addition, the vendor providing the service should sign the form before leaving the premises. When completed, the Service Verification form should be forwarded to the Accounting Department. Accounting will authorize payment of the vendor's invoice after the Service Verification form has been compared with the invoice.

Ex. 8–16

a. Addition to the balance per bank: (3), (6)
b. Deduction from the balance per bank: (2)
c. Addition to the balance per company's records: (4), (5)
d. Deduction from the balance per company's records: (1), (7)

Ex. 8–17

(1), (4), (5), (7)

Ex. 8–18

SPECTRUM CO.
Bank Reconciliation
July 31, 20—

Cash balance according to bank statement	$ 9,066.35
Add deposit in transit, not recorded by bank..............................	2,615.40
	$11,681.75
Deduct outstanding checks	3,175.25
Adjusted balance	$ 8,506.50
Cash balance according to company's records	$ 8,346.50
Add error in recording check...	180.00
	$ 8,526.50
Deduct bank service charge	20.00
Adjusted balance	$ 8,506.50

Ex. 8–19

Cash	180.00	
Accounts Payable		180.00
Miscellaneous Administrative Expense	20.00	
Cash		20.00

Ex. 8–20

Cash	17,750	
Notes Receivable		15,000
Interest Revenue		2,750

Ex. 8–21

a.

LOCK-IT CO.
Bank Reconciliation
October 31, 2008

Cash balance according to bank statement....................		$ 8,600.50
Add: Deposit in transit on October 31		13,690.45
		$22,290.95
Deduct: Outstanding checks		7,115.35
Adjusted balance		$15,175.60
Cash balance according to company's records		$ 9,305.60
Add: Error in recording Check No. 1007 as $4,715		
instead of $4,175...	$ 540.00	
Note for $5,000 collected by bank, including		
interest..	5,375.00	5,915.00
		$15,220.60
Deduct: Bank service charges...		45.00
Adjusted balance		$15,175.60

b. $15,175.60

Ex. 8–22

1. The heading should be for June 30, 2008, and not For the Month Ended June 30, 2008.

2. The outstanding checks should be deducted from the balance per bank.

3. The deposit of June 30, not recorded by the bank, should be added to the balance per bank.

4. In deducting the deposit of June 30, not recorded by the bank, the adjusted balance of $7,120.28 is mathematically incorrect. It should be $6,120.28.

5. Service charges should be deducted from the balance per company's records.

6. The error in recording the June 15 deposit of $3,960 as $3,690 should be added to the balance per company's records.

A correct bank reconciliation would be as follows:

MKABE CO.
Bank Reconciliation
June 30, 2008

Cash balance according to bank statement.			$ 7,560.14
Add deposit of June 30, not recorded by bank			5,182.04
			$12,742.18
Deduct outstanding checks:			
No. 315..		$ 717.42	
360..		617.11	
364..		906.15	
365..		1,501.50	3,742.18
Adjusted balance			$ 9,000.00
Cash balance according to company's			
records..			$ 3,735.70
Add: Proceeds of note collected by bank:			
Principal...	$6,000.00		
Interest...	180.00	$6,180.00	
Error in recording June 15 deposit as			
$3,690 instead of $3,960.................		270.00	6,450.00
			$10,185.70
Deduct: Check returned because			
of insufficient funds..................		$1,158.70	
Service charges		27.00	1,185.70
Adjusted balance			$ 9,000.00

Ex. 8–23

a. The amount of cash receipts stolen by the sales clerk can be determined by attempting to reconcile the bank account. The bank reconciliation will not reconcile by the amount of cash receipts stolen. The amount stolen by the sales clerk is $3,936.22, determined as shown below.

ARGONAUT CO.
Bank Reconciliation
November 30, 2008

Cash balance according to bank statement.................................	$22,060.65
Deduct: Outstanding checks...	6,381.42
Adjusted balance..	$15,679.23
Cash balance according to company's records	$12,510.45
Add: Note collected by bank, including interest..........................	7,140.00
	$19,650.45
Deduct: Bank service charges...	35.00
Adjusted balance..	$19,615.45

Amount stolen: $3,936.22 ($19,615.45 – $15,679.23)

b. The theft of the cash receipts might have been prevented by having more than one person make the daily deposit. Collusion between two individuals would then have been necessary to steal cash receipts. In addition, two employees making the daily cash deposits would tend to discourage theft of the cash receipts from the employees on the way to the bank.

Daily reconciliation of the amount of cash receipts, comparing the cash register tapes to a receipt from the bank as to the amount deposited (a duplicate deposit ticket), would also discourage theft of the cash receipts. In this latter case, if the reconciliation were prepared by an employee independent of the cash function, any theft of cash receipts from the daily deposit would be discovered immediately. That is, the daily deposit would not reconcile against the daily cash receipts.

Ex. 8–24

a.	Petty Cash	1,000.00	
	Cash		1,000.00
b.	Office Supplies..	379.10	
	Miscellaneous Selling Expense.............................	216.25	
	Miscellaneous Administrative Expense.................	143.06	
	Cash Short and Over	22.43	
	Cash		760.84

Ex. 8–25

Toy manufacturers and retailers experience a seasonal trend in cash flows from operating activities. Mattel, Inc., experiences negative cash flows during the periods when merchandise is ordered for the holiday season. Mattel, Inc., generates positive cash flows during the holiday season, November–December. As a result, Mattel, Inc., reports overall positive net cash flows from operating activities for the year.

Ex. 8–26

a. 9 months ($1,575,000/$175,000)

b. At the current rate of operations, Kinetic has 9 months of cash remaining. Kinetic should either restructure its operations or begin planning on raising additional financing in order to continue in business.

Ex. 8–27

a. $93.6 ($1,123/12)

b. 19.3 months ($1,811/$93.6)

c. During 2004, Delta suffered from rising fuel prices and increasing competition from discount airlines. Delta was able to negotiate wage concessions from its pilots and employees. However, Delta declared bankruptcy in fall 2005. Eventually, Delta hopes to reorganize its operations and emerge from bankruptcy.

Ex. 8–28

a.   2005: $652.3 ($7,827/12) per month
       2004: $213.2 ($2,558/12) per month

b.   2005:   6.0 ($3,897/$652.3) months
       2004:   27.6 ($5,875/$213.2) months

c.   During 2005, Hyperspace's monthly cash expenses (also called monthly cash burn) has increased threefold from $213.2 to $652.3. As a result, the ratio of cash to monthly cash expenses has decreased from 27.6 months to 6.0 months. Unless Hyperspace changes its operations or raises additional financing, it will run out of cash in approximately six months.

PROBLEMS

Prob. 8–1A

Strengths: a, b, f, and g

Weaknesses:

c. Employees should not be allowed to use the petty cash fund to cash personal checks. In any case, post-dated checks should not be accepted. In effect, post-dated checks represent a receivable from the employees.

d. Requiring cash register clerks to make up any cash shortages from their own funds gives the clerks an incentive to short-change customers. That is, the clerks will want to make sure that they don't have a shortage at the end of the day. In addition, one might also assume that the clerks can keep any overages. This would again encourage clerks to short-change customers. The short-changing of customers will create customer complaints, etc. The best policy is to report any cash shortages or overages at the end of each day. If a clerk is consistently short or over, then corrective action (training, removal, etc.) could be taken.

e. The mail clerk should prepare an initial listing of cash remittances before forwarding the cash receipts to the cashier. This establishes initial accountability for the cash receipts. The mail clerk should forward a copy of the listing of remittances to the accounts receivable clerk for recording in the accounts.

h. The bank reconciliation should be prepared by someone not involved with the handling or recording of cash.

Prob. 8–2A

2008

Oct.	1	Petty Cash...	750.00	
		Cash		750.00
	15	Cash..	9,752.38	
		Cash Short and Over......................................		50.00
		Sales...		9,702.38
	31	Store Supplies	217.30	
		Delivery Expense..	315.00	
		Office Supplies	80.10	
		Miscellaneous Administrative Expense	71.95	
		Cash Short and Over......................................	24.90	
		Cash		709.25
	31	Cash..	10,123.05	
		Cash Short and Over......................................	2.90	
		Sales...		10,125.95
	31	Petty Cash...	150.00	
		Cash		150.00

Prob. 8–3A

1.

BONITA MEDICAL CO.
Bank Reconciliation
September 30, 2008

Cash balance according to bank statement.....................			$ 5,604.60
Add: Deposit of September 30, not recorded by bank		$9,226.15	
Bank error in charging check as $2,300 instead			
of $230		2,070.00	11,296.15
			$16,900.75
Deduct outstanding checks...			4,790.45
Adjusted balance..			$12,110.30
Cash balance according to company's records			$ 5,335.30
Add proceeds of note collected by bank, including			
$225 interest			7,725.00
			$13,060.30
Deduct: Error in recording check...................................		$ 900.00	
Bank service charges		50.00	950.00
Adjusted balance..			$12,110.30

2.
Cash...	7,725.00	
Notes Receivable		7,500.00
Interest Revenue		225.00
Accounts Payable—Rowe Co.	900.00	
Miscellaneous Administrative Expense	50.00	
Cash		950.00

Prob. 8–4A

1.

CABRILLO CO.
Bank Reconciliation
March 31, 2008

Balance per bank statement....................................		$10,960.06
Add: Deposit of March 31, not recorded by bank.........	$ 8,773.34	
Bank error in charging check as $830 instead		
of $380..	450.00	9,223.34
		$20,183.40
Deduct outstanding checks.....................................		11,008.25
Adjusted balance..		$ 9,175.15
Balance per company's records		$ 6,904.65*
Add proceeds of note collected by bank,		
including $210 interest		3,710.00
		$10,614.65
Deduct: Check returned because of insufficient funds	$ 1,129.50	
Bank service charges.......................................	40.00	
Error in recording check.................................	270.00	1,439.50
Adjusted balance..		$ 9,175.15

*Cash balance, March 1	$10,676.67	
Plus cash deposited in March.................................	39,146.38	
Less checks written in March	(42,918.40)	
Balance per company's books, March 31	$ 6,904.65	

2. Cash...	3,710.00	
Notes Receivable		3,500.00
Interest Revenue		210.00
Accounts Payable—Graven Co.	270.00	
Accounts Receivable—Kane-Miller Co.	1,129.50	
Miscellaneous Administrative Expense	40.00	
Cash		1,439.50

Prob. 8–5A

1.

PACIFIC FURNITURE COMPANY
Bank Reconciliation
June 30, 20—

Cash balance according to bank statement...		$13,091.76
Add deposit of June 30, not recorded		
by bank		1,510.06
		$14,601.82
Deduct outstanding checks:		
No. 736..	$ 345.95	
755..	272.75	
758..	259.60	
759..	901.50	1,779.80
Adjusted balance...		$12,822.02

Cash balance according to company's			
records			$10,576.87*
Add: Proceeds of note collected by bank:			
Principal	$2,500.00		
Interest	125.00	$2,625.00	
Error in recording Check No. 749.........		0.18	2,625.18
			$13,202.05
Deduct: Check returned because of			
insufficient funds		$ 291.90	
Error in recording June 17 deposit		53.73	
Service charges...............................		34.40	380.03
Adjusted balance...			$12,822.02
*Balance per cash account, June 1			$ 9,317.40
Add June receipts.......................................			9,565.31
Deduct June disbursements			(8,305.84)
Balance per cash account, June 30...........			$10,576.87

Prob. 8–5A Concluded

2. Cash 2,625.18
    Notes Receivable 2,500.00
    Interest Revenue 125.00
    Accounts Payable 0.18

  Sales.. 53.73
  Accounts Receivable 291.90
  Miscellaneous Administrative Expense 34.40
    Cash 380.03

3. $12,822.02

4. The error of $540 in the canceled check should be added to the "balance according to bank statement" on the bank reconciliation. The canceled check should be presented to the bank with a request that the bank balance be corrected.

Prob. 8–1B

Strengths: a, b, e, and f

Weaknesses:

c. Cash receipts should not be handled by the accounts receivable clerk. This violates the segregation of duties between the handling of cash receipts and the recording of cash receipts.

d. An independent person (for example, a supervisor) should count the cash in each cashier's cash register, unlock the record, and compare the amount of cash with the amount on the record to determine cash shortages or overages.

g. The bank reconciliation should be prepared by someone not involved with the handling or recording of cash.

Prob. 8–2B

2008

Apr.	1	Petty Cash	900.00	
		Cash		900.00
	4	Cash	12,115.42	
		Cash Short and Over		15.73
		Sales		12,099.69
	30	Store Supplies	62.18	
		Merchandise Inventory	191.70	
		Office Supplies	240.62	
		Miscellaneous Administrative Expense	280.60	
		Cash Short and Over	6.50	
		Cash		781.60
	30	Cash	13,774.90	
		Cash Short and Over	25.70	
		Sales		13,800.60
	30	Cash	100.00	
		Petty Cash		100.00

Prob. 8–3B

1.

TURBOCHARGED SYSTEMS
Bank Reconciliation
February 29, 2008

Cash balance according to bank statement..................		$17,877.63
Add deposit of February 29, not recorded by bank......		11,322.90
		$29,200.53
Deduct: Outstanding checks..	$ 9,652.40	
Bank error in charging check as $690		
instead of $960......................................	270.00	9,922.40
Adjusted balance..		$19,278.13
Cash balance according to company's records...........		$ 8,608.13
Add: Proceeds of note collected by bank, including		
$250 interest..	$10,250.00	
Error in recording check......................................	450.00	10,700.00
		$19,308.13
Deduct bank service charges...		30.00
Adjusted balance..		$19,278.13

2.

Cash	10,700.00	
Notes Receivable..		10,000.00
Interest Revenue...		250.00
Accounts Payable—Yanni Co.		450.00
Miscellaneous Administrative Expense	30.00	
Cash..		30.00

Prob. 8–4B

1.

BLACK DIAMOND SPORTS CO.
Bank Reconciliation
November 30, 2008

Balance per bank statement..		$24,226.75
Add deposit of November 30, not recorded by bank		18,332.15
		$42,558.90
Deduct: Outstanding checks	$ 12,673.40	
Bank error in charging check as $580		
instead of $850	270.00	12,943.40
Adjusted balance...		$29,615.50
Balance per company's records		$25,802.00*
Add: Proceeds of note collected by bank,		
including $90 interest.....................................	$ 4,590.00	
Error in recording check	353.70	4,943.70
		$30,745.70
Deduct: Check returned because of insufficient		
funds	$ 1,080.20	
Bank service charges	50.00	1,130.20
Adjusted balance...		$29,615.50
*Cash balance, November 1	$ 23,326.69	
Plus cash deposited in November..........................	118,125.41	
Less checks written in November	(115,650.10)	
Balance per company's records, November 30....	$ 25,802.00	

2.

Cash	4,943.70	
Notes Receivable		4,500.00
Interest Revenue...		90.00
Accounts Payable—Locke & Son...........................		353.70
Accounts Receivable—Kalina Co.	1,080.20	
Miscellaneous Administrative Expense	50.00	
Cash..		1,130.20

Prob. 8–5B

1.

VINTAGE INTERIORS
Bank Reconciliation
July 31, 20—

Cash balance according to bank statement..................		$13,145.54
Add deposit of July 31, not recorded by bank..............		925.05
		$14,070.59
Deduct outstanding checks:		
No. 602..	$ 85.50	
628...	837.70	
634...	503.30	1,426.50
Adjusted balance..		$12,644.09
Cash balance according to company's records		$ 7,133.09*
Add proceeds of note collected by bank:		
Principal..	$ 5,000.00	
Interest...	400.00	
Add error in recording deposit of $601.50	0.50	
Add error in recording Check No. 625......................	360.00	5,760.50
		$12,893.59
Deduct: Check returned because of insufficient funds	$ 225.40	
Service charges	24.10	249.50
Adjusted balance..		$12,644.09
*Balance per cash in bank account, July 1	$ 9,578.00	
Add July receipts	6,230.10	
Deduct July disbursements	(8,675.01)	
Balance per cash in bank account, July 31	$ 7,133.09	

2.

Cash	5,760.50	
Notes Receivable..		5,000.00
Interest Revenue...		400.00
Accounts Payable..		360.00
Sales		0.50
Accounts Receivable	225.40	
Miscellaneous Administrative Expense	24.10	
Cash...		249.50

3. $12,644.09

4. The error of $3,600 in the canceled check should be added to the "balance according to bank statement" on the bank reconciliation. The canceled check should be presented to the bank, with a request that the bank balance be corrected.

SPECIAL ACTIVITIES

SA 8–1

Acceptable business and professional conduct requires Javier Frailey to notify the bank of the error. *Note to Instructors:* Individuals may be criminally prosecuted for knowingly using funds that are erroneously credited to their bank accounts.

SA 8–2

Several control procedures could be implemented to prevent or detect the theft of cash from fictitious returns.

One procedure would be to establish a policy of "no cash refunds." That is, returns could only be exchanged for other merchandise. However, such a policy might not be popular with customers, and Wireless Electronics might lose sales from customers who would shop at other stores with a more liberal return policy.

Another procedure would be to allow returns only through a centralized location, such as a customer service desk. The customer service desk clerk would issue an approved refund slip, which the customer could then take to a cash register to receive a cash refund. Since the customer service clerk does not have access to cash, the customer service clerk could not steal cash through fictitious returns.

Yet another procedure would be to allow returns at the individual cash registers but require that all returns be approved by a supervisor. In this way, cash could be stolen through fictitious returns only with collusion of the supervisor and the cash register clerk.

SA 8–3

Several possible procedures for preventing or detecting the theft of grocery items by failing to scan their prices include the following:

a. Most scanning systems are designed so that an audible beep is heard each time an item is rung up on the cash register. This is intended to alert the cashier that the item has been properly rung up. Thus, observing whether a cashier is ringing up all merchandise can be accomplished by standing near the cash register and listening for the beeps. Such observations might be done on a periodic, surprise basis by supervisors.

b. Some grocery stores have their cash registers networked so that a monitor in a centralized office, usually high above the floor, can monitor any cash register's activity. In this way, a supervisor could monitor cash register activity on a periodic basis.

c. Although this detection procedure would probably not be used in a grocery store, it is used by Sam's Clubs to detect this activity. Specifically, an employee is stationed at the exit to the store and checks each cash register receipt against the items with which the customer is leaving the store. This would not work well for a grocery store because of the large number of items that are usually placed in grocery bags at the checkout counter.

SA 8–4

Sara is clearly behaving in an unprofessional manner in intentionally short-changing her customers.

At this point, Pete is in a difficult position. He is apparently adhering to Farmers' Markets' policy of making up shortages out of his own pocket, but he is obviously upset about it. If Pete accepts Sara's advice, he will be engaging in unprofessional behavior. Pete is also faced with the dilemma of whether he should report Sara's behavior. If Pete continues to work for Farmers' Markets, his best course of action is simply to try to do the best job possible in not making errors in ringing up sales and providing customers change.

One could argue that Majed is also acting in an unprofessional manner. First, allowing Sara to keep overages will simply encourage her to continue to short-change customers. Second, since Sara has had no shortages in over a year, it should be obvious to Majed that Sara is short-changing customers. Therefore, as store manager, Majed should take action to stop Sara's behavior. Better yet, Majed should consider revising Farmers' Markets' control policy on shortages and overages. The cash register clerks should be required to report all shortages and overages without having to make up shortages from their own pockets. The cash register clerks could then be monitored for their effectiveness in making change for customers. Unusual amounts or trends could be investigated and corrective action taken, such as training, reassigning employees to other duties, etc. In any case, employees should not be allowed to keep overages at the end of each day.

SA 8–5

1. There are several methods that could be used to determine how much the cashier has stolen. The method described below is based on preparing a bank reconciliation as illustrated in this chapter. Because of the theft of the undeposited receipts, the bank reconciliation adjusted balances will not agree. The difference between the adjusted balances is the estimate of the amount stolen by the cashier.

FILIPPI'S COMPANY
Bank Reconciliation
March 31, 20—

Balance according to bank statement		$ 7,004.95
Add undeposited cash receipts on hand		5,000.00
		$12,004.95
Deduct outstanding checks:		
No. 670	$1,129.16	
679	830.00	
690	525.90	
2148	127.40	
2149	520.00	
2157	851.50	3,983.96
Adjusted balance		$ 8,020.99
Balance according to company's records		$10,806.05
Add note collected by bank, with interest		3,120.00
Adjusted balance		$13,926.05
Adjusted balance according to company's records		$13,926.05
Adjusted balance according to bank statement		8,020.99
Amount stolen by cashier		$ 5,905.06

Note to Instructors: The amount stolen by the cashier could also be computed directly from the cashier-prepared bank reconciliation as follows:

Outstanding checks omitted from the bank reconciliation prepared by the cashier:		
No. 670	$1,129.16	
679	830.00	
690	525.90	$ 2,485.06
Unrecorded note plus interest incorrectly recorded on the bank reconciliation prepared by the cashier		3,120.00
Addition error in the total of the outstanding checks in the bank reconciliation prepared by the cashier*		300.00
		$ 5,905.06

Note: The cashier has altered the adding machine tape so that the total is not correct.

SA 8–5   Concluded

2. The cashier attempted to conceal the theft by preparing an incorrect bank reconciliation. Specifically, the cashier (1) omitted outstanding checks on March 31 totaling $2,485.06, (2) added the list of outstanding checks shown on the bank reconciliation incorrectly so that the total is misstated by $300, and (3) incorrectly handled the treatment of the note and interest collected by the bank.

3. a. Two major weaknesses in internal controls, which allowed the cashier to steal the undeposited cash receipts, are as follows:

   • Undeposited cash receipts were kept on hand for a two-day period, March 30 and 31. This large amount of undeposited cash receipts allowed the cashier to steal the cash without arousing suspicion that any cash was missing.

   • The cashier prepared the bank reconciliation. This allowed the cashier to conceal the theft temporarily.

   b. Two recommendations that would improve internal controls so that similar types of thefts of undeposited cash receipts could be prevented are as follows:

   • All cash receipts should be deposited daily. This would reduce the risk of significant cash losses. In addition, any missing cash would be more easily detected.

   • The bank reconciliation should be prepared by an independent individual who does not handle cash or the accounting records. One possibility would be for the owner of Filippi's Company to prepare the reconciliation.

Note to Instructors: In addition to the above recommendations, Filippi's Company should be counseled that it is standard practice for any disgruntled employees, fired employees, or employees who have announced quitting dates to be removed from sensitive positions (such as the cashier position) so that company assets or records will not be jeopardized. Finally, checks which have been outstanding for long periods of time (such as Nos. 670, 679, and 690) should be voided (with stop payment instructions given to the bank) and reentered in the cash records. This establishes control over these items and prevents their misuse.

SA 8–6

Note to Instructors: The purpose of this activity is to familiarize students with the internal controls used by specific businesses.

SA 8–7

1. 2005: $1,559.2 ($18,710/12) per month
   2004: $448.5 ($5,382/12) per month
   2003: $197.9 ($2,375/12) per month

2. 2005: 26.5 ($41,268/1,559.2) months
   2004: 133.9 ($60,040/$448.5) months
   2003: 6.3 ($1,239/$197.9) months

3. At the end of 2003, OccuLogix had just over six months of cash left to run its operations. However, in 2004 the company was able to raise over $60 million by issuing stock. Thus, at the end of 2004, the company had 133.9 months of available cash to run its operations. Unfortunately, during 2005 OccuLogix's monthly cash expenses increased over threefold from $448.5 to $1,559.2 per month. As a result, the ratio of cash to monthly cash expenses has decreased from 133.9 months at the end of 2004 to 26.5 months at the end of 2005. Unless OccuLogix changes its operations or raises additional financing, it will run out of cash in just over two years.

SA 8–8

1. 2005: $2,556.9 ($30,683/12) per month
   2004: $1,609.9 ($19,319/12) per month
   2003: $1,292.3 ($15,507/12) per month

2. 2005: 20.0 ($51,112/2,556.9) months
   2004: 28.1 ($45,180/$1,609.9) months
   2003: 42.2 ($54,562/$1,292.3) months

3. Since 2003, Acusphere's monthly cash expenses have increased from $1,292.3 in 2003, to $1,609.9 in 2004, to $2,556.9 in 2005. At the same time, the ratio of cash to monthly cash expenses has decreased from 42.2 months at the end of 2003, to 28.1 months at the end of 2004, to 20.0 months at the end of 2005. Thus, at the end of 2005, Acusphere will run out of cash in less than two years unless it changes its operations or raises additional financing. Unless the company improves its cash flows, it may have difficulty raising sufficient cash from investors or creditors to continue operations beyond the next two years.

CHAPTER 9
RECEIVABLES

QUESTION INFORMATION

Number	Objective	Description	Difficulty	Time	AACSB	AICPA	SS	GL
Q9-1	9-1		Easy	5 min	Analytic	FN-Measurement		
Q9-2	9-1		Easy	5 min	Analytic	FN-Measurement		
Q9-3	9-1		Easy	5 min	Analytic	FN-Measurement		
Q9-4	9-1		Easy	5 min	Analytic	FN-Measurement		
Q9-5	9-2		Easy	5 min	Analytic	FN-Measurement		
Q9-6	9-2		Easy	5 min	Analytic	FN-Measurement		
Q9-7	9-4		Easy	5 min	Analytic	FN-Measurement		
Q9-8	9-7		Easy	5 min	Analytic	FN-Measurement		
Q9-9	9-4		Easy	5 min	Analytic	FN-Measurement		
Q9-10	9-5		Easy	5 min	Analytic	FN-Measurement		
Q9-11	9-6		Easy	5 min	Analytic	FN-Measurement		
Q9-12	9-6		Easy	5 min	Analytic	FN-Measurement		
Q9-13	9-6		Easy	5 min	Analytic	FN-Measurement		
Q9-14	9-6		Easy	5 min	Analytic	FN-Measurement		
Q9-15	9-6		Easy	5 min	Analytic	FN-Measurement		
Q9-16	9-7		Easy	5 min	Analytic	FN-Measurement		
PE9-1A	9-3	Entries for uncollect- ible accounts using the direct write-off method	Easy	5 min	Analytic	FN-Measurement		
PE9-1B	9-3	Entries for uncollect- ible accounts using the direct write-off method	Easy	5 min	Analytic	FN-Measurement		
PE9-2A	9-3	Entries for uncollect- ible accounts using the allowance method	Easy	5 min	Analytic	FN-Measurement		
PE9-2B	9-3	Entries for uncollect- ible accounts using the allowance method	Easy	5 min	Analytic	FN-Measurement		
PE9-3A	9-4	Percent of sales method of estimating uncollectible accounts	Easy	10 min	Analytic	FN-Measurement		
PE9-3B	9-4	Percent of sales method of estimating uncollectible accounts	Easy	10 min	Analytic	FN-Measurement		
PE9-4A	9-4	Aging method of es- timating uncollectible accounts	Easy	10 min	Analytic	FN-Measurement		
PE9-4B	9-4	Aging method of es- timating uncollectible accounts	Easy	10 min	Analytic	FN-Measurement		
PE9-5A	9-6	Notes receivable due date, maturity value, and entry	Easy	10 min	Analytic	FN-Measurement		
PE9-5B	9-6	Notes receivable due date, maturity value, and entry	Easy	10 min	Analytic	FN-Measurement		
Ex9-1	9-1	Classification of re- ceivables	Easy	5 min	Analytic	FN-Measurement		

Number	Objective	Description	Difficulty	Time	AACSB	AICPA	SS	GL
Ex9-2	9-2	Nature of uncollectible accounts	Easy	10 min	Analytic	FN-Measurement		
Ex9-3	9-3	Entries for uncollectible accounts, using direct write-off method	Easy	10 min	Analytic	FN-Measurement		
Ex9-4	9-3	Entries for uncollectible accounts, using allowance method	Easy	10 min	Analytic	FN-Measurement		
Ex9-5	9-3, 9-4	Entries to write off accounts receivable	Easy	10 min	Analytic	FN-Measurement		
Ex9-6	9-4	Providing for doubtful accounts	Moderate	15 min	Analytic	FN-Measurement		
Ex9-7	9-4	Number of days past due	Easy	15 min	Analytic	FN-Measurement		
Ex9-8	9-4	Aging-of-receivable schedule	Moderate	20 min	Analytic	FN-Measurement	Exl	
Ex9-9	9-4	Estimating allowance for doubtful accounts	Moderate	20 min	Analytic	FN-Measurement	Exl	
Ex9-10	9-4	Adjustment for uncollectible accounts	Easy	5 min	Analytic	FN-Measurement		
Ex9-11	9-4	Estimating doubtful accounts	Moderate	15 min	Analytic	FN-Measurement		
Ex9-12	9-4	Entry for uncollectible accounts	Easy	5 min	Analytic	FN-Measurement		
Ex9-13	9-5	Entries for bad debt expense under the direct write-off and allowance methods	Moderate	30 min	Analytic	FN-Measurement		
Ex9-14	9-5	Entries for bad debt expense under the direct write-off and allowance methods	Moderate	30 min	Analytic	FN-Measurement		
Ex9-15	9-5	Effect of doubtful accounts on net income	Easy	10 min	Analytic	FN-Measurement		
Ex9-16	9-5	Effect of doubtful accounts on net income	Moderate	15 min	Analytic	FN-Measurement		
Ex9-17	9-5	Entries for bad debt expense under direct write-off and allowance methods	Moderate	30 min	Analytic	FN-Measurement		
Ex9-18	9-5	Entries for bad debt expense under direct write-off and allowance methods	Moderate	30 min	Analytic	FN-Measurement		
Ex9-19	9-6	Determine due date and interest on notes	Easy	15 min	Analytic	FN-Measurement	Exl	
Ex9-20	9-6	Entries for notes receivable	Easy	10 min	Analytic	FN-Measurement		
Ex9-21	9-6	Entries for notes receivable	Moderate	15 min	Analytic	FN-Measurement		
Ex9-22	9-6	Entries for notes receivable, including year-end entries	Easy	10 min	Analytic	FN-Measurement		
Ex9-23	9-6	Entries for receipt and dishonor of note receivable	Easy	10 min	Analytic	FN-Measurement		
Ex9-24	9-4, 9-6	Entries for receipt and dishonor of note receivable	Moderate	15 min	Analytic	FN-Measurement		

Number	Objective	Description	Difficulty	Time	AACSB	AICPA	SS	GL
Ex9-25	9-7	Receivable on the balance sheet	Easy	5 min	Analytic	FN-Measurement		
Ex9-26	FAI	Accounts receivable turnover and days' sales in receivable	Moderate	15 min	Analytic	FN-Measurement		
Ex9-27	FAI	Accounts receivable turnover and days' sales in receivable	Moderate	15 min	Analytic	FN-Measurement		
Ex9-28	FAI	Accounts receivable turnover and days' sales in receivable	Moderate	15 min	Analytic	FN-Measurement		
Ex9-29	FAI	Accounts receivable turnover	Moderate	15 min	Analytic	FN-Measurement		
Ex9-30	Appendix	Discounting notes receivable	Moderate	15 min	Analytic	FN-Measurement		
Ex9-31	Appendix	Entries for discounting of note receivable and dishonored notes	Moderate	15 min	Analytic	FN-Measurement		
Pr9-1A	9-4	Entries related to uncollectible accounts	Difficult	1 hr	Analytic	FN-Measurement		KA
Pr9-2A	9-4	Aging of receivables; estimating allowance for doubtful accounts	Difficult	1 hr	Analytic	FN-Measurement	Exl	
Pr9-3A	9-3, 9-4, 9-5	Compare two methods of accounting for uncollectible receivables	Difficult	1 hr	Analytic	FN-Measurement		
Pr9-4A	9-6	Details of notes receivable and related entries	Moderate	30 min	Analytic	FN-Measurement		
Pr9-5A	9-6	Notes receivable entries	Moderate	1 hr	Analytic	FN-Measurement		
Pr9-6A	9-6	Sales and notes receivable transactions	Moderate	1 hr	Analytic	FN-Measurement		KA
Pr9-1B	9-4	Entries related to uncollectible accounts	Difficult	1 hr	Analytic	FN-Measurement		KA
Pr9-2B	9-4	Aging of receivables; estimating allowance for doubtful accounts	Difficult	1 hr	Analytic	FN-Measurement	Exl	
Pr9-3B	9-3, 9-4, 9-5	Compare two methods of accounting for uncollectible receivables	Difficult	1 hr	Analytic	FN-Measurement		
Pr9-4B	9-6	Details of notes receivable and related entries	Moderate	30 min	Analytic	FN-Measurement		
Pr9-5B	9-6	Notes receivable entries	Moderate	1 hr	Analytic	FN-Measurement		
Pr9-6B	9-6	Sales and notes receivable transactions	Moderate	1 hr	Analytic	FN-Measurement		KA
SA9-1	9-6	Ethics and professional conduct in business	Easy	5 min	Ethics	BB-Industry		
SA9-2	9-4	Estimate uncollectible accounts	Moderate	30 min	Analytic	FN-Measurement		
SA9-3	FAI	Accounts receivable turnover and days' sales in receivables	Difficult	30 min	Reflective Thinking	BB-Critical Thinking		

Number	Objective	Description	Difficulty	Time	AACSB	AICPA	SS	GL
SA9-4	FAI	Accounts receivable turnover and days' sales in receivables	Difficult	1 hr	Reflective Thinking	BB-Critical Thinking		
SA9-5	FAI	Accounts receivable turnover and days' sales in receivables	Moderate	30 min	Reflective Thinking	BB-Critical Thinking		
SA9-6	FAI	Accounts receivable turnover	Difficult	1 hr	Reflective Thinking	BB-Critical Thinking		

EYE OPENERS

1. Receivables are normally classified as (1) accounts receivable, (2) notes receivable, or (3) other receivables.

2. Transactions in which merchandise is sold or services are provided on credit generate accounts receivable.

3. **a.** Current Assets
   b. Investments

4. Examples of other receivables include interest receivable, taxes receivable, and receivables from officers or employees.

5. Wilson's should use the direct write-off method because it is a small business that has a relatively small number and volume of accounts receivable.

6. The allowance method

7. Contra asset, credit balance

8. The accounts receivable and allowance for doubtful accounts may be reported at a net amount of $741,456 ($783,150 – $41,694) in the Current Assets section of the balance sheet. In this case, the amount of the allowance for doubtful accounts should be shown separately in a note to the financial statements or in parentheses on the balance sheet. Alternatively, the accounts receivable may be shown at the gross amount of $783,150 less the amount of the allowance for doubtful accounts of $41,694, thus yielding net accounts receivable of $741,456.

9. **(1)** The percentage rate used is excessive in relationship to the volume of accounts written off as uncollectible; hence, the balance in the allowance is excessive.
   (2) A substantial volume of old uncollectible accounts is still being carried in the accounts receivable account.

10. An estimate based on analysis of receivables provides the most accurate estimate of the current net realizable value.

11. The advantages of a claim evidenced by a note are that (1) the debt is acknowledged, (2) the payment terms are specified, (3) it is a stronger claim in the event of court action, and (4) it is usually more readily transferable to a creditor in settlement of a debt or to a bank for cash.

12. **a.** Bauer Company
    b. Notes Receivable

13. The interest will amount to $6,000 only if the note is payable one year from the date it was created. The usual practice is to state the interest rate in terms of an annual rate, rather than in terms of the period covered by the note.

14. Debit Accounts Receivable
    Credit Notes Receivable
    Credit Interest Revenue

15. Cash 6,246.50
    Accounts Receivable ..   6,200.00
    Interest Revenue 46.50
    ($6,200 × 30/360 × 9% = $46.50)

16. Current Assets

PRACTICE EXERCISES

PE 9–1A

Feb.	12	Cash	750	
		Bad Debt Expense..	2,000	
		Accounts Receivable—Manning Wingard ..		2,750
June	30	Accounts Receivable—Manning Wingard	2,000	
		Bad Debt Expense		2,000
	30	Cash	2,000	
		Accounts Receivable—Manning Wingard ..		2,000

PE 9–1B

Aug.	7	Cash	175	
		Bad Debt Expense..	400	
		Accounts Receivable—Roosevelt McLair ..		575
Nov.	23	Accounts Receivable—Roosevelt McLair........	400	
		Bad Debt Expense		400
	23	Cash	400	
		Accounts Receivable—Roosevelt McLair ..		400

PE 9–2A

Feb.	12	Cash	750	
		Allowance for Doubtful Accounts.....................	2,000	
		Accounts Receivable—Manning Wingard ..		2,750
June	30	Accounts Receivable—Manning Wingard	2,000	
		Allowance for Doubtful Accounts		2,000
	30	Cash	2,000	
		Accounts Receivable—Manning Wingard ..		2,000

PE 9–2B

Aug.	7	Cash	175	
		Allowance for Doubtful Accounts....................	400	
		Accounts Receivable—Roosevelt McLair ..		575
Nov.	23	Accounts Receivable—Roosevelt McLair........	400	
		Allowance for Doubtful Accounts		400
	23	Cash	400	
		Accounts Receivable—Roosevelt McLair ..		400

PE 9–3A

1. $7,000 ($2,800,000 × 0.0025)

		Adjusted Balance
2.	Accounts Receivable	$500,000
	Allowance for Doubtful Accounts ($4,000 + $7,000) ...	11,000
	Bad Debt Expense...	7,000
3.	Net realizable value ($500,000 – $11,000).....................	$489,000

PE 9–3B

1. $31,000 ($6,200,000 × 0.005)

		Adjusted Balance
2.	Accounts Receivable	$1,200,000
	Allowance for Doubtful Accounts ($31,000 – $5,000)	26,000
	Bad Debt Expense...	31,000
3.	Net realizable value ($1,200,000 – $26,000)..................	$1,174,000

PE 9–4A

1. $12,000 ($16,000 – $4,000)

	Adjusted Balance
2. Accounts Receivable	$500,000
Allowance for Doubtful Accounts...............................	16,000
Bad Debt Expense..	12,000
3. Net realizable value ($500,000 – $16,000).....................	$484,000

PE 9–4B

1. $39,500 ($34,500 + $5,000)

	Adjusted Balance
2. Accounts Receivable	$1,200,000
Allowance for Doubtful Accounts...............................	34,500
Bad Debt Expense..	39,500
3. Net realizable value ($1,200,000 – $34,500)...................	$1,165,500

PE 9–5A

1. The due date for the note is November 8, determined as follows:

August...	21 days (31 – 10)
September	30 days
October	31 days
November	8 days
Total	90 days

2. $25,500 [$25,000 + ($25,000 × 8% × 90/360)]

3. Nov. 8 Cash	25,500	
Note Receivable		25,000
Interest Revenue		500

552

PE 9–5B

1. The due date for the note is June 1, determined as follows:

April	28 days (30 – 2)
May	31 days
June	1 days
Total	60 days

2. $121,400 [$120,000 + ($120,000 × 7% × 60/360)]

3.

June 1	Cash		121,400	
	Note Receivable			120,000
	Interest Revenue			1,400

EXERCISES

Ex. 9–1

Accounts receivable from the U.S. government are significantly different from receivables from commercial aircraft carriers such as Delta and United. Thus, Boeing should report each type of receivable separately. In the December 31, 2005, filing with the Securities and Exchange Commission, Boeing reports the receivables together on the balance sheet, but discloses each receivable separately in a note to the financial statements.

Ex. 9–2

a. Hotel accounts and notes receivable: $1,699/$31,724 = 5.4%

b. Casino accounts receivable: $12,300/$44,139 = 27.9%

c. Casino operations experience greater bad debt risk than do hotel operations, since it is difficult to control the creditworthiness of customers entering the casino. In addition, individuals who may have adequate creditworthiness could overextend themselves and lose more than they can afford if they get caught up in the excitement of gambling.

Ex. 9–3

Feb.	10	Accounts Receivable—Dr. Pete Baker..............	21,400	
		Sales		21,400
	10	Cost of Merchandise Sold	12,600	
		Merchandise Inventory.................................		12,600
July	9	Cash	13,000	
		Bad Debt Expense...	8,400	
		Accounts Receivable—Dr. Pete Baker........		21,400
Oct.	27	Accounts Receivable—Dr. Pete Baker..............	8,400	
		Bad Debt Expense		8,400
	27	Cash	8,400	
		Accounts Receivable—Dr. Pete Baker........		8,400

554

Ex. 9–4

June	2	Accounts Receivable—Lynn Berry..................	16,000	
		Sales		16,000
	2	Cost of Merchandise Sold	9,400	
		Merchandise Inventory..............................		9,400
Oct.	15	Cash	4,000	
		Allowance for Doubtful Accounts....................	12,000	
		Accounts Receivable—Lynn Berry		16,000
Dec.	30	Accounts Receivable—Lynn Berry..................	12,000	
		Allowance for Doubtful Accounts		12,000
	30	Cash	12,000	
		Accounts Receivable—Lynn Berry		12,000

Ex. 9–5

a.	Bad Debt Expense...	12,500	
	Accounts Receivable—Jadelis Resources.............		12,500
b.	Allowance for Doubtful Accounts................................	12,500	
	Accounts Receivable—Jadelis Resources.............		12,500

Ex. 9–6

a. $13,750 ($5,500,000 × 0.0025)   c. $27,500 ($5,500,000 × 0.005)

b. $12,900 ($17,500 − $4,600)   d. $32,750 ($24,650 + $8,100)

Ex. 9–7

Account	Due Date	Number of Days Past Due
Ben's Pickup Shop	June 9	52 (21 + 31)
Bumper Auto	July 10	21
Downtown Repair	March 18	135 (13 + 30 + 31 + 30 + 31)
Jake's Auto Repair	May 19	73 (12 + 30 + 31)
Like New	June 18	43 (12 + 31)
Sally's	April 12	110 (18 + 31 + 30 + 31)
Uptown Auto	May 8	84 (23 + 30 + 31)
Yellowstone Repair & Tow	April 15	107 (15 + 31 + 30 + 31)

Ex. 9–8

a.

Customer	Due Date	Number of Days Past Due
Tamika Industries	August 24	98 days (7 + 30 + 31 + 30)
Ruppert Company	September 3	88 days (27 + 31 + 30)
Welborne Inc.	October 17	44 days (14 + 30)
Kristi Company	November 5	25 days
Simrill Company	December 3	Not past due

b.

	A	B	C	D	E	F	G	
			Aging-of-Receivables Schedule					
			November 30					
					Days Past Due			
	Customer	Balance	Not Past Due	1–30	31–60	61–90	Over 90	
1	Aaron Brothers Inc.	2,000	2,000					1
2	Abell Company	1,500		1,500				2
21	Zollo Company	5,000			5,000			21
22	Subtotals	772,500	440,000	180,000	78,500	42,300	31,700	22
23	Tamika Industries	25,000					25,000	23
24	Ruppert Company	8,500				8,500		24
25	Welborne Inc.	35,000			35,000			25
26	Kristi Company	6,500		6,500				26
27	Simrill Company	12,000	12,000					27
28	Totals	859,500	452,000	186,500	113,500	50,800	56,700	28

Ex. 9–9

	Balance	Not Past Due	Days Past Due			
			1–30	31–60	61–90	Over 90
Total receivables	859,500	452,000	186,500	113,500	50,800	56,700
Percentage uncollectible		3%	5%	15%	25%	40%
Allowance for Doubtful Accounts	75,290	13,560	9,325	17,025	12,700	22,680

Ex. 9–10

Nov.	30	Bad Debt Expense...	69,140	
		Allowance for Doubtful Accounts		69,140
		Uncollectible accounts estimate.		
		($75,290 – $6,150)		

Ex. 9–11

Age Interval	Estimated Uncollectible Accounts		
	Balance	Percent	Amount
Not past due..	$400,000	1%	$ 4,000
1–30 days past due...................................	80,000	2	1,600
31–60 days past due.................................	18,000	5	900
61–90 days past due.................................	12,500	10	1,250
91–180 days past due...............................	6,000	70	4,200
Over 180 days past due.............................	2,500	90	2,250
Total..	$519,000		$14,200

Ex. 9–12

2008

Dec.	31	Bad Debt Expense...	17,700	
		Allowance for Doubtful Accounts		17,700
		Uncollectible accounts estimate.		
		($14,200 + $3,500)		

Ex. 9–13

a. Jan. 31   Bad Debt Expense 2,400

                Accounts Receivable—B. Roberts.................   2,400

Mar. 26   Cash... 1,500

        Bad Debt Expense 2,000

                Accounts Receivable—Carol Castellino........   3,500

July 7   Accounts Receivable—B. Roberts 2,400

                Bad Debt Expense..   2,400

7   Cash... 2,400

                Accounts Receivable—B. Roberts.................   2,400

Oct. 12   Bad Debt Expense 4,675

                Accounts Receivable—Julie Lindley   1,350

                Accounts Receivable—Mark Black...............   950

                Accounts Receivable—Jennifer Kerlin..........   525

                Accounts Receivable—Beth Chalhoub   1,125

                Accounts Receivable—Allison Fain   725

Dec. 31   No entry

b. Jan. 31   Allowance for Doubtful Accounts 2,400

                Accounts Receivable—B. Roberts.................   2,400

Mar. 26   Cash... 1,500

        Allowance for Doubtful Accounts 2,000

                Accounts Receivable—Carol Castellino........   3,500

July 7   Accounts Receivable—B. Roberts 2,400

                Allowance for Doubtful Accounts   2,400

7   Cash... 2,400

                Accounts Receivable—B. Roberts.................   2,400

Oct. 12   Allowance for Doubtful Accounts 4,675

                Accounts Receivable—Julie Lindley   1,350

                Accounts Receivable—Mark Black...............   950

                Accounts Receivable—Jennifer Kerlin..........   525

                Accounts Receivable—Beth Chalhoub   1,125

                Accounts Receivable—Allison Fain   725

Dec. 31   Bad Debt Expense 15,000

                Allowance for Doubtful Accounts.................   15,000

                Uncollectible accounts estimate.

                ($750,000 × 2% = $15,000)

Ex. 9–13   Concluded

c. **Bad debt expense under:**

Allowance method 15,000

Direct write-off method ($2,400 + $2,000 – $2,400 + $4,675) ...... $ 6,675

Difference ($15,000 – $6,675) .... $ 8,325

Shaw's income would be $8,325 higher under the direct write-off method than under the allowance method.

Ex. 9–14

a.	Feb.	2	Bad Debt Expense	7,250	
			Accounts Receivable—L. Armstrong		7,250
	May	10	Cash..	4,150	
			Bad Debt Expense	4,350	
			Accounts Receivable—Jill Knapp..........		8,500
	Aug.	12	Accounts Receivable—L. Armstrong..........	7,250	
			Bad Debts Expense		7,250
		12	Cash..	7,250	
			Accounts Receivable—L. Armstrong		7,250
	Sept.	27	Bad Debt Expense	12,525	
			Accounts Receivable—Kim Whalen		4,400
			Accounts Receivable—Brad Johnson...		2,210
			Accounts Receivable—Angelina Quan		1,375
			Accounts Receivable—Tammy Newsome		2,850
			Accounts Receivable—Donna Short		1,690
	Dec.	31	No entry		

Ex. 9–14   Continued

b. Feb.   2 Allowance for Doubtful Accounts 7,250
                  Accounts Receivable—L. Armstrong   7,250

    May 10 Cash... 4,150
                  Allowance for Doubtful Accounts 4,350
                  Accounts Receivable—Jill Knapp..........   8,500

    Aug. 12 Accounts Receivable—L. Armstrong.......... 7,250
                  Allowance for Doubtful Accounts..........   7,250

          12 Cash... 7,250
                  Accounts Receivable—L. Armstrong   7,250

    Sept. 27 Allowance for Doubtful Accounts 12,525
                  Accounts Receivable—Kim Whalen   4,400
                  Accounts Receivable—Brad Johnson...   2,210
                  Accounts Receivable—Angelina Quan   1,375
                  Accounts Receivable—Tammy Newsome   2,850
                  Accounts Receivable—Donna Short   1,690

    Dec. 31 Bad Debt Expense 20,550
                  Allowance for Doubtful Accounts..........   20,550
                  Uncollectible accounts estimate.
                  ($21,675 – $1,125)

Computations

Aging Class (Number of Days Past Due)	Receivables Balance on December 31	Estimated Doubtful Accounts	
		Percent	Amount
0–30 days	$160,000	3%	$ 4,800
31–60 days	40,000	10	4,000
61–90 days	18,000	20	3,600
91–120 days	11,000	40	4,400
More than 120 days	6,500	75	4,875
Total receivables	$235,500		$21,675

Estimated balance of allowance account from aging schedule...... $21,675
Unadjusted credit balance of allowance account 1,125*
Adjustment $20,550

*$18,000 – $7,250 – $4,350 + $7,250 – $12,525 = $1,125

Ex. 9–14 Concluded

c. Bad debt expense under:
    Allowance method $20,550
    Direct write-off method ($7,250 + $4,350 – $7,250 + $12,525) 16,875
    Difference ($20,550 – $16,875) .... $ 3,675

Kemper's income would be $3,675 higher under the direct method than under the allowance method.

Ex. 9–15

$122,000 [$125,000 + $51,000 – ($1,800,000 × 3%)]

Ex. 9–16

a. $139,000 [$143,500 + $61,500 – ($2,200,000 × 3%)]

b. $7,500 [($54,000 – $51,000) + ($66,000 – $61,500)]

Ex. 9–17

a. Bad Debt Expense.. 45,000
   Accounts Receivable—Skip Simon........................... 20,000
   Accounts Receivable—Clarence Watson 13,500
   Accounts Receivable—Bill Jacks.............................. 7,300
   Accounts Receivable—Matt Putnam........................ 4,200

b. Allowance for Doubtful Accounts................................. 45,000
   Accounts Receivable—Skip Simon........................... 20,000
   Accounts Receivable—Clarence Watson 13,500
   Accounts Receivable—Bill Jacks.............................. 7,300
   Accounts Receivable—Matt Putnam........................ 4,200

   Bad Debt Expense.. 60,000
   Allowance for Doubtful Accounts 60,000
      Uncollectible accounts estimate.
      ($2,000,000 × 3% = $60,000)

c. Net income would have been $15,000 higher in 2008 under the direct write-off method, because bad debt expense would have been $15,000 higher under the allowance method ($60,000 expense under the allowance method vs. $45,000 expense under the direct write-off method).

Ex. 9–18

a.

Bad Debt Expense	19,000	
Accounts Receivable—Boss Hogg		5,000
Accounts Receivable—Daisy Duke		3,500
Accounts Receivable—Bo Duke		6,300
Accounts Receivable—Luke Duke		4,200

b.

Allowance for Doubtful Accounts	19,000	
Accounts Receivable—Boss Hogg		5,000
Accounts Receivable—Daisy Duke		3,500
Accounts Receivable—Bo Duke		6,300
Accounts Receivable—Luke Duke		4,200
Bad Debt Expense	27,850	
Allowance for Doubtful Accounts		27,850
Uncollectible accounts estimate.		
($26,850 + $1,000)		

Computations

Aging Class (Number of Days Past Due)	Receivables Balance on December 31	Estimated Doubtful Accounts	
		Percent	Amount
0–30 days	$380,000	2%	$ 7,600
31–60 days	70,000	5	3,500
61–90 days	30,000	15	4,500
91–120 days	25,000	25	6,250
More than 120 days	10,000	50	5,000
Total receivables	$515,000		$26,850

Unadjusted debit balance of Allowance for Doubtful Accounts ($18,000 – $19,000)	$ 1,000
Estimated balance of Allowance for Doubtful Accounts from aging schedule	26,850
Adjustment	$27,850

Ex. 9–19

	Due Date	Interest	
a.	May 5	$225.00	[$15,000 × 0.09 × (60/360)]
b.	July 19	133.33	[$8,000 × 0.10 × (60/360)]
c.	Aug. 31	150.00	[$5,000 × 0.12 × (90/360)]
d.	Dec. 28	600.00	[$18,000 × 0.10 × (120/360)]
e.	Nov. 30	210.00	[$10,500 × 0.12 × (60/360)]

Ex. 9–20

a. August 18 (11 + 30 + 31 + 18)

b. $30,675 [($30,000 × 0.09% × 90/360) + $30,000]

c. (1) Notes Receivable... 30,000

        Accounts Rec.—Holsten Interior Decorators ..   30,000

   (2) Cash.. 30,675

        Notes Receivable   30,000

        Interest Revenue   675

Ex. 9–21

1. Sale on account.

2. Cost of merchandise sold for the sale on account.

3. A sale return or allowance.

4. Cost of merchandise returned.

5. Note received from customer on account.

6. Note dishonored and charged maturity value of note to customer's account receivable.

7. Payment received from customer for dishonored note plus interest earned after due date.

Ex. 9–22

2007
Dec.	13	Notes Receivable	60,000	
		Accounts Receivable—Lady Ann's Co.		60,000

	31	Interest Receivable	270	
		Interest Revenue...		270
		Accrued interest		
		($60,000 × 0.09 × 18/360 = $270).		

	31	Interest Revenue	270	
		Income Summary..		270

2008
Mar.	12	Cash	61,350	
		Notes Receivable...		60,000
		Interest Receivable		270
		Interest Revenue...		1,080*

  *$60,000 × 0.09 × 72/360

Ex. 9–23

May	3	Notes Receivable	150,000	
		Accounts Receivable—Xpedx Company		150,000

Aug.	1	Accounts Receivable—Xpedx Company	153,000	
		Notes Receivable...		150,000
		Interest Revenue...		3,000

	31	Cash	154,275	
		Accounts Receivable—Xpedx Company		153,000
		Interest Revenue...		1,275*

  *$153,000 × 0.10 × 30/360 = $1,275

Ex. 9–24

Mar.	1	Notes Receivable	45,000	
		Accounts Receivable—Pynn Co.		45,000
	18	Notes Receivable	24,000	
		Accounts Receivable—Abode Co.		24,000
Apr.	30	Accounts Receivable—Pynn Co.	45,450	
		Notes Receivable		45,000
		Interest Revenue		450*
		*($45,000 × 6% × 60/360)		
May	17	Accounts Receivable—Abode Co.	24,360	
		Notes Receivable		24,000
		Interest Revenue		360*
		*($24,000 × 9% × 60/360)		
July	29	Cash	46,359	
		Accounts Receivable—Pynn Co.		45,450
		Interest Revenue		909*
		*45,450 × 0.08 × 90/360 = $909		
Aug.	23	Allowance for Doubtful Accounts.....................	24,360	
		Accounts Receivable—Abode Co.		24,360

Ex. 9–25

1. The interest receivable should be reported separately as a current asset. It should not be deducted from notes receivable.

2. The allowance for doubtful accounts should be deducted from accounts receivable.

A corrected partial balance sheet would be as follows:

MISHKIE COMPANY
Balance Sheet
December 31, 2008

Assets

Current assets:		
Cash		$127,500
Notes receivable...		400,000
Accounts receivable	$529,200	
Less allowance for doubtful accounts...............	42,000	487,200
Interest receivable..		24,000

Ex. 9–26

a. and b.

	2005		2004	
Net sales	$3,305,415		$2,649,654	
Accounts receivable	$530,503		$463,289	
Average accounts receivable	$496,896	[($530,503 + $463,289)/2]	$427,423.5	[($463,289 + $391,558)/2]
Accounts receivable turnover	6.7	($3,305,415/$496,896)	6.2	($2,649,654/$427,423.5)
Average daily sales	$9,055.9	($3,305,415/365)	7,259.3	($2,649,654/365)
Days' sales in receivables	54.9	($496,896/$9,055.9)	58.9	($427,423.5/$7,259.3)

c. The accounts receivable turnover indicates an increase in the efficiency of collecting accounts receivable by increasing from 6.2 to 6.7, a favorable trend. The days' sales in receivables also indicates an increase in the efficiency of collecting accounts receivable by decreasing from 58.9 to 54.9, also indicating a favorable trend. Before reaching a definitive conclusion, the ratios should be compared with industry averages and similar firms.

Ex. 9–27

a. 2005: 8.2 {$8,912,297/[($1,093,155 + $1,092,394)/2]}
    2004: 7.5 {$8,414,538/[($1,093,155 + $1,165,460)/2]}

b. 2005: 44.8 days [($1,093,155 + $1,092,394)/2] = $1,092,774.5; [$1,092,774.5/($8,912,297/365)] = 44.8 days
    2004: 49.0 days [($1,093,155 + $1,165,460)/2] = $1,129,308; [$1,129,308/($8,414,538/365)] = 49.0 days

c. The accounts receivable turnover indicates an increase in the efficiency of collecting accounts receivable by increasing from 7.5 to 8.2, a favorable trend. The number of days' sales in receivables decreased from 49.0 to 44.8 days, also indicating a favorable trend in collections of receivables. Before reaching a more definitive conclusion, both ratios should be compared with those of past years, industry averages, and similar firms.

Ex. 9–28

a. and b.

For the Period Ending

	Jan. 31, 2006		Jan. 29, 2005	
Net sales	$9,699		$9,408	
Accounts receivable	$182		$128	
Average accounts receivable	$155	[($182 + $128)/2]	$119	[($128 + $110)/2]
Accounts receivable turnover	62.6	($9,699/$155)	79.1	($9,408/$119)
Average daily sales	$26.6	($9,699/365)	$25.8	($9,408/365)
Days' sales in receivables	5.8	($155/$26.6)	4.6	($119/$25.8)

c. The accounts receivable turnover indicates a decrease in the efficiency of collecting accounts receivable by decreasing from 79.1 to 62.6, an unfavorable trend. The days' sales in receivables indicates a decrease in the efficiency of collecting accounts receivable by increasing from 4.6 to 5.8, also indicating an unfavorable trend. Before reaching a definitive conclusion, the ratios should be compared with industry averages and similar firms.

Ex. 9–29

a. The average accounts receivable turnover ratios are as follows:

The Limited, Inc.: 70.9 [(79.1 + 62.6)/2]

H.J. Heinz Company: 7.9 [(8.2 + 7.5)/2]

Note: For computations of the individual ratios, see Ex. 9–27 and Ex. 9–28.

b. The Limited has the higher average accounts receivable turnover ratio.

c. The Limited operates a specialty retail chain of stores that sell directly to in-dividual consumers. Many of these consumers (retail customers) pay with MasterCards or VISAs that are recorded as cash sales. In contrast, H.J. Heinz manufactures processed foods that are sold to food wholesalers, grocery store chains, and other food distributors who eventually sell Heinz products to individual consumers. Accordingly, because of the extended distribution chain we would expect Heinz's business customers to take a longer period to pay their receivables. Accordingly, we would expect Heinz's average ac-counts receivable turnover ratio to be lower than The Limited as shown in (a).

Appendix Ex. 9–30

a. $82,400 [$80,000 + ($80,000 × 9% × 120/360)]

b. 60 days (8 + 31 + 21)

c. $1,648 ($82,400 × 12% × 60/360)

d. $80,752 ($82,400 – $1,648)

e.

Cash...	80,752	
Interest Revenue		752
Notes Receivable		80,000

Appendix Ex. 9–31

Aug.	1	Notes Receivable	100,000	
		Accounts Receivable—Elk Horn Co.		100,000
Sept.	1	Cash	100,300*	
		Notes Receivable		100,000
		Interest Revenue		300

*Computations
Maturity value

$100,000 + ($100,000 × 8% × 90/360)	$102,000
Discount ($102,000 × 10% × 60/360)	1,700
Proceeds	$100,300

Oct.	30	Accounts Receivable—Elk Horn	102,500	
		Cash		102,500
Nov.	29	Cash	103,525*	
		Accounts Receivable—Elk Horn		102,500
		Interest Revenue		1,025

*$102,500 + ($102,500 × 0.12 × 30/360) = $103,525

PROBLEMS

Prob. 9–1A

2. 20—

			Debit	Credit
July	5	Cash..	14,700	
		Allowance for Doubtful Accounts	6,300	
		Accounts Receivable—Dockins Co.		21,000
Sept.	21	Accounts Receivable—Bart Tiffany	4,875	
		Allowance for Doubtful Accounts.................		4,875
	21	Cash..	4,875	
		Accounts Receivable—Bart Tiffany..............		4,875
Oct.	19	Allowance for Doubtful Accounts	6,275	
		Accounts Receivable—Ski Time Co.		6,275
Nov.	6	Accounts Receivable—Kirby Co.	4,750	
		Allowance for Doubtful Accounts.................		4,750
	6	Cash..	4,750	
		Accounts Receivable—Kirby Co.		4,750
Dec.	31	Allowance for Doubtful Accounts	13,000	
		Accounts Receivable—Maxie Co.		2,150
		Accounts Receivable—Kommers Co.		3,600
		Accounts Receivable—Helena Distributors..		5,500
		Accounts Receivable—Ed Ballantyne		1,750
	31	Bad Debt Expense	20,150	
		Allowance for Doubtful Accounts.................		20,150
		Uncollectible accounts estimate.		
		($16,750 + $3,400)		

Prob. 9–1A   **Concluded**

1. and 2.

Allowance for Doubtful Accounts

July	5		6,300	Jan.	1 Balance	12,550
Oct.	19		6,275	Sept.	21	4,875
Dec.	31		13,000	Nov.	6	4,750
Dec.	31	Unadjusted Balance	3,400			
				Dec.	31 Adjusting Entry	20,150
				Dec.	31 Adj. Balance	16,750

Bad Debt Expense

Dec.	31	Adjusting Entry	20,150

3. $798,490 ($815,240 – $16,750)

4. a. $17,815 ($7,126,000 × 0.0025)
    b. $14,415 ($17,815 – $3,400)
    c. $800,825 ($815,240 – $14,415)

Prob. 9–2A

1.

Customer	Due Date	Number of Days Past Due
Baitfish Sports & Flies	June 21, 2007	193 days (9 + 31 + 31 + 30 + 31 + 30 + 31)
Kiwi Flies	Sept. 9, 2007	113 days (21 + 31 + 30 + 31)
Adams Co.	Sept. 30, 2007	92 days (31 + 30 + 31)
Bailey Sports	Oct. 17, 2007	75 days (14 + 30 + 31)
Prince Sports	Nov. 18, 2007	43 days (12 + 31)
Cahill Co.	Nov. 28, 2007	33 days (2 + 31)
Wintson Company	Dec. 1, 2007	30 days
Goofus Bug Sports	Jan. 6, 2008	Not past due

Prob. 9–2A   Concluded

2. and 3.

	A	B	C	D	E	F	G	H	
				Aging-of-Receivables Schedule					
				December 31, 2007					
						Days Past Due			
	Customer	Balance	Not Past Due	1–30	31–60	61–90	91–120	Over 120	
1	Alexandra Fishery	15,000	15,000						1
2	Cutthroat Sports	5,500			5,500				2
30	Yellowstone Sports	2,900		2,900					30
31	Subtotals	880,000	448,600	247,250	98,750	33,300	29,950	22,150	31
32	Baitfish Sports & Flies	1,750						1,750	32
33	Kiwi Flies	650					650		33
34	Adams Co.	1,500					1,500		34
35	Bailey Sports	600				600			35
36	Prince Sports	950			950				36
37	Cahill Co.	2,000			2,000				37
38	Wintson Company	2,250		2,250					38
39	Goofus Bug Sports	6,200	6,200						39
40	Totals	895,900	454,800	249,500	101,700	33,900	32,100	23,900	40
41	Percent uncollectible		2%	5%	10%	25%	45%	90%	41
42	Estimate of doubtful accounts	76,171	9,096	12,475	10,170	8,475	14,445	21,510	42

4. Bad Debt Expense..   79,370

      Allowance for Doubtful Accounts   79,370

        Uncollectible accounts estimate. ($76,171 + $3,199)

Prob. 9–3A

1.

| Year | Bad Debt Expense | | | Balance of Allowance Account, End of Year |
	Expense Actually Reported	Expense Based on Estimate	Increase (Decrease) in Amount of Expense	
1st	$ 3,500	$ 6,825	$3,325	$ 3,325
2nd	4,130	7,980	3,850	7,175
3rd	7,980	9,975	1,995	9,170
4th	10,920	18,900	7,980	17,150

2. Yes. The actual write-offs of accounts originating in the first two years are reasonably close to the expense that would have been charged to those years on the basis of 3/4% of sales. The total write-off of receivables originating in the first year amounted to $7,140 ($3,500 + $2,660 + $980), as compared with bad debt expense, based on the percentage of sales, of $6,825. For the second year, the comparable amounts were $8,750 ($1,470 + $5,600 + $1,680) and $7,980.

Prob. 9–4A

1.

Note	(a) Due Date	(b) Interest Due at Maturity
1.	May 2	$360 ($27,000 × 60/360 × 8%)
2.	July 15	190 ($19,000 × 30/360 × 12%)
3.	Dec. 18	216 ($10,800 × 120/360 × 6%)
4.	Dec. 30	540 ($36,000 × 60/360 × 9%)
5.	Jan. 22	150 ($15,000 × 60/360 × 6%)
6.	Jan. 26	270 ($27,000 × 30/360 × 12%)

2. Dec. 18 Accounts Receivable...................................... 11,016
     Notes Receivable..   10,800
     Interest Revenue   216

3. Dec. 31 Interest Receivable.. 131
     Interest Revenue   131
    Accrued interest.

    $15,000 × 0.06 × 38/360 = $ 95
    $27,000 × 0.12 × 4/360 = 36
    Total $131

4. Jan. 22 Cash.. 15,150
     Notes Receivable..   15,000
     Interest Receivable.....................................   95
     Interest Revenue 55*

    *$15,000 × 0.06 × 22/360

    26 Cash.. 27,270
     Notes Receivable..   27,000
     Interest Receivable.....................................   36
     Interest Revenue 234**

    **$27,000 × 0.12 × 26/360

Prob. 9–5A

June	12	Notes Receivable		20,000	
		Accounts Receivable.....................................			20,000
July	13	Notes Receivable		36,000	
		Accounts Receivable.....................................			36,000
Aug.	11	Cash		20,300	
		Notes Receivable...			20,000
		Interest Revenue...			300
Sept.	4	Notes Receivable		15,000	
		Accounts Receivable.....................................			15,000
Nov.	3	Cash		15,225	
		Notes Receivable...			15,000
		Interest Revenue...			225
	5	Notes Receivable		24,000	
		Accounts Receivable.....................................			24,000
	10	Cash		37,200	
		Notes Receivable...			36,000
		Interest Revenue...			1,200
	30	Notes Receivable		15,000	
		Accounts Receivable.....................................			15,000
Dec.	5	Cash		24,140	
		Notes Receivable...			24,000
		Interest Revenue...			140
	30	Cash		15,125	
		Notes Receivable...			15,000
		Interest Revenue...			125

Prob. 9–6A

Jan.	15	Notes Receivable	6,000	
		Cash...		6,000
Feb.	6	Accounts Receivable—Kent and Son	16,000	
		Sales		16,000
	6	Cost of Merchandise Sold	9,000	
		Merchandise Inventory....................................		9,000
	13	Accounts Receivable—Centennial Co.	30,000	
		Sales		30,000
	13	Cost of Merchandise Sold	15,750	
		Merchandise Inventory....................................		15,750
Mar.	5	Notes Receivable	16,000	
		Accounts Receivable—Kent and Son		16,000
	14	Notes Receivable	30,000	
		Accounts Receivable—Centennial Co.		30,000
Apr.	15	Notes Receivable	6,000	
		Cash	120	
		Notes Receivable.......................................		6,000
		Interest Revenue.......................................		120*
		*($6,000 × 8% × 90/360)		
May	4	Cash	16,160	
		Notes Receivable.......................................		16,000
		Interest Revenue.......................................		160*
		*($16,000 × 6% × 60/360)		
	13	Accounts Receivable—Centennial Co.	30,600	
		Notes Receivable.......................................		30,000
		Interest Revenue.......................................		600*
		*($30,000 × 12% × 60/360)		
June	12	Cash	30,906	
		Accounts Receivable—Centennial Co.		30,600
		Interest Revenue.......................................		306*
		*($30,600 × 12% × 30/360 = $306)		
July	14	Cash	6,150	
		Notes Receivable.......................................		6,000
		Interest Revenue.......................................		150*
		*($6,000 × 10% × 90/360)		

Prob. 9–6A   Concluded

Aug.	10	Accounts Receivable—Conover Co.	10,000	
		Sales		10,000
	10	Cost of Merchandise Sold	6,500	
		Merchandise Inventory..		6,500
	20	Cash	9,900	
		Sales Discounts	100	
		Accounts Receivable—Conover Co.		10,000

Prob. 9–1B

2. 20—

Mar.	21	Accounts Receivable—Tony Marshal	4,050	
		Allowance for Doubtful Accounts		4,050
	21	Cash..	4,050	
		Accounts Receivable—Tony Marshal...........		4,050
Apr.	18	Allowance for Doubtful Accounts	5,500	
		Accounts Receivable—Crossroads Co.		5,500
Aug.	17	Cash..	2,500	
		Allowance for Doubtful Accounts	7,500	
		Accounts Receivable—Raven Co.		10,000
Oct.	10	Accounts Receivable—Elden Hickman	2,400	
		Allowance for Doubtful Accounts		2,400
	10	Cash..	2,400	
		Accounts Receivable—Elden Hickman		2,400
Dec.	31	Allowance for Doubtful Accounts	25,145	
		Accounts Receivable—Buffalo Co.		13,275
		Accounts Receivable—Combs Co.		4,000
		Accounts Receivable—Nash Furniture		6,150
		Accounts Receivable—Tony DePuy		1,720
	31	Bad Debt Expense	48,195	
		Allowance for Doubtful Accounts		48,195
		Uncollectible accounts estimate.		
		($58,000 – $9,805)		

Prob. 9–1B   Concluded

1. and 2.

Allowance for Doubtful Accounts

Apr.	18	5,500	Jan.	1 Balance	41,500
Aug.	17	7,500	Mar.	21	4,050
Dec.	31	25,145	Oct.	10	2,400
			Dec.	31 Unadjusted Balance	9,805
			Dec.	31 Adjusting Entry	48,195
			Dec.	31 Adjusted Balance	58,000

Bad Debt Expense

Dec.	31 Adjusting Entry	48,195	

3. $842,750 ($900,750 – $58,000)

4. a. $51,900 ($10,380,000 × 0.005)
    b. $61,705 ($51,900 + $9,805)
    c. $839,045 ($900,750 – $61,705)

Prob. 9–2B

1.

Customer	Due Date	Number of Days Past Due
Uniquely Yours	July 1, 2007	183 days (30 + 31 + 30 + 31 + 30 + 31)
Paradise Beauty Store	Sept. 29, 2007	93 days (1 + 31 + 30 + 31)
Morgan's Hair Products	Oct. 17, 2007	75 days (14 + 30 + 31)
Hairy's Hair Care	Oct. 31, 2007	61 days (30 + 31)
Superior Images	Nov. 18, 2007	43 days (12 + 31)
Oh The Hair	Nov. 30, 2007	31 days
Mountain Coatings	Dec. 1, 2007	30 days
Theatrical Images	Jan. 3, 2008	Not past due

Prob. 9–2B   Concluded

2. and 3.

	A	B	C	D	E	F	G	H	
	Aging-of-Receivables Schedule								
	December 31, 2007								
					Days Past Due				
	Customer	Balance	Not Past Due	1–30	31–60	61–90	91–120	Over 120	
1	Daytime Beauty	20,000	20,000						1
2	Blount Wigs	11,000			11,000				2
30	Zabka's	2,900		2,900					30
31	Subtotals	780,000	398,600	197,250	98,750	33,300	29,950	22,150	31
32	Uniquely Yours	1,200						1,200	32
33	Paradise Beauty Store	1,050					1,050		33
34	Morgan's Hair Products	800				800			34
35	Hairy's Hair Care	2,000				2,000			35
36	Superior Images	700			700				36
37	Oh The Hair	3,500			3,500				37
38	Mountain Coatings	1,000		1,000					38
39	Theatrical Images	6,200	6,200						39
40	Totals	796,450	404,800	198,250	102,950	36,100	31,000	23,350	40
41	Percent uncollectible		2%	4%	10%	15%	35%	80%	41
42	Estimate of doubtful accounts	61,266	8,096	7,930	10,295	5,415	10,850	18,680	42

4. Bad Debt Expense..   51,716
      Allowance for Doubtful Accounts   51,716
      Uncollectible accounts estimate.
         ($61,266 – $9,550)

Prob. 9–3B

1.

| Year | Bad Debt Expense | | | Balance of Allowance Account, End of Year |
	Expense Actually Reported	Expense Based on Estimate	Increase (Decrease) in Amount of Expense	
1st	$ 600	$ 2,500	$1,900	$1,900
2nd	1,500	3,750	2,250	4,150
3rd	6,500	5,750	(750)	3,400
4th	8,850	10,500	1,650	5,050

2. Yes. The actual write-offs of accounts originating in the first two years are reasonably close to the expense that would have been charged to those years on the basis of 1/2% of sales. The total write-off of receivables originating in the first year amounted to $3,200 ($600 + $700 + $1,900), as compared with bad debt expense, based on the percentage of sales, of $2,500. For the second year, the comparable amounts were $4,300 ($800 + $1,500 + $2,000) and $3,750.

Prob. 9–4B

1.

Note	(a) Due Date	(b) Interest Due at Maturity
1.	July 1	$135 ($12,000 × 45/360 × 9%)
2.	Sept. 7	200 ($15,000 × 60/360 × 8%)
3.	Oct. 30	315 ($18,000 × 90/360 × 7%)
4.	Dec. 3	300 ($20,000 × 90/360 × 6%)
5.	Jan. 25	720 ($54,000 × 60/360 × 8%)
6.	Feb. 14	780 ($36,000 × 60/360 × 13%)

2. Oct. 30 Accounts Receivable.................................. 18,315
                Notes Receivable..................................... 18,000
                Interest Revenue 315

3. Dec. 31 Interest Receivable.................................... 615
                Interest Revenue 615
                Accrued interest.

        $54,000 × 0.08 × 35/360 = $420
        $36,000 × 0.13 × 15/360 = 195
        Total $615

4. Jan. 25 Cash... 54,720
                Notes Receivable..................................... 54,000
                Interest Receivable................................. 420
                Interest Revenue 300*

        *$54,000 × 0.08 × 25/360

     Feb. 14 Cash... 36,780
                Notes Receivable..................................... 36,000
                Interest Receivable................................. 195
                Interest Revenue 585**

        **$36,000 × 0.13 × 45/360

Prob. 9–5B

Mar.	6	Notes Receivable	18,000	
		Accounts Receivable..................................		18,000
	25	Notes Receivable	10,000	
		Accounts Receivable..................................		10,000
May	5	Cash	18,270	
		Notes Receivable.......................................		18,000
		Interest Revenue.......................................		270
	16	Notes Receivable	40,000	
		Accounts Receivable..................................		40,000
	31	Notes Receivable	12,000	
		Accounts Receivable..................................		12,000
June	23	Cash	10,200	
		Notes Receivable.......................................		10,000
		Interest Revenue.......................................		200
	30	Cash	12,080	
		Notes Receivable.......................................		12,000
		Interest Revenue.......................................		80
July	1	Notes Receivable	5,000	
		Accounts Receivable..................................		5,000
	31	Cash	5,050	
		Notes Receivable.......................................		5,000
		Interest Revenue.......................................		50
Aug.	14	Cash	40,700	
		Notes Receivable.......................................		40,000
		Interest Revenue.......................................		700

Prob. 9–6B

20—

Date		Account	Debit	Credit
Jan.	12	Accounts Receivable—Dewit Co.	12,300.00	
		Sales		12,300.00
	12	Cost of Merchandise Sold	6,800.00	
		Merchandise Inventory...............................		6,800.00
Mar.	12	Notes Receivable	12,300.00	
		Accounts Receivable—Dewit Co.		12,300.00
May	11	Cash	12,464.00	
		Notes Receivable		12,300.00
		Interest Revenue..		164.00
June	3	Accounts Receivable—Kihl's...........................	15,000.00	
		Sales		15,000.00
	3	Cost of Merchandise Sold	10,750.00	
		Merchandise Inventory...............................		10,750.00
	5	Notes Receivable	18,000.00	
		Cash..		18,000.00
	13	Cash	14,700.00	
		Sales Discounts	300.00	
		Accounts Receivable—Kihl's		15,000.00
July	5	Notes Receivable	18,000.00	
		Cash..	90.00	
		Notes Receivable		18,000.00
		Interest Revenue..		90.00
Sept.	3	Cash..	18,270.00	
		Notes Receivable		18,000.00
		Interest Revenue..		270.00
	17	Accounts Receivable—Wood Co.	9,000.00	
		Sales		9,000.00
	17	Cost of Merchandise Sold	6,250.00	
		Merchandise Inventory...............................		6,250.00

Prob. 9–6B   Concluded

Oct.	4	Notes Receivable	9,000.00	
		Accounts Receivable—Wood Co.		9,000.00
Dec.	3	Accounts Receivable—Wood Co.	9,090.00	
		Notes Receivable		9,000.00
		Interest Revenue		90.00
	29	Cash	9,129.39	
		Accounts Receivable—Wood Co.		9,090.00
		Interest Revenue		39.39
		($9,090 × 0.06 × 26/360 = $39.39).		

SPECIAL ACTIVITIES

SA 9–1

By computing interest using a 365-day year for depository accounts (payables), Neka is minimizing interest expense to the bank. By computing interest using a 360-day year for loans (receivables), Neka is maximizing interest revenue to the bank. However, federal legislation (Truth in Lending Act) requires banks to compute interest on a 365-day year. Hence, Neka is behaving in an unprofessional manner.

SA 9–2

1.

Year	a. Addition to Allowance for Doubtful Accounts	b. Accounts Written Off During Year
2005	$20,400	$11,880 ($20,400 – $8,520)
2006	21,000	13,680 ($8,520 + $21,000 – $15,840)
2007	21,300	14,460 ($15,840 + $21,300 – $22,680)
2008	21,750	11,610 ($22,680 + $21,750 – $32,820)

2. a. The estimate of 1/4 of 1% of credit sales may be too large, since the allowance for doubtful accounts has steadily increased each year. The increasing balance of the allowance for doubtful accounts may also be due to the failure to write off a large number of uncollectible accounts. These possibilities could be evaluated by examining the accounts in the subsidiary ledger for collectibility and comparing the result with the balance in the allowance for doubtful accounts.

Note to Instructors: Since the amount of credit sales has been fairly uniform over the years, the increase cannot be explained by an expanding volume of sales.

b. The balance of Allowance for Doubtful Accounts that should exist at December 31, 2008, can only be determined after all attempts have been made to collect the receivables on hand at December 31, 2008. However, the account balances at December 31, 2008, could be analyzed, perhaps using an aging schedule, to determine a reasonable amount of allowance and to determine accounts that should be written off. Also, past write-offs of uncollectible accounts could be analyzed in depth in order to develop a reasonable percentage for future adjusting entries, based on past history. Caution, however, must be exercised in using historical percentages. Specifically, inquiries should be made to determine whether any significant changes between prior years and the current year may have occurred, which might reduce the accuracy of the historical data. For example, a recent change in credit-granting policies or changes in the general economy (entering a recessionary period, for example) could reduce the usefulness of analyzing historical data.

Based on the preceding analyses, a recommendation to decrease the annual rate charged as an expense may be in order (perhaps Litespeed Co. is experiencing a lower rate of uncollectibles than is the industry average), or perhaps a change to the "estimate based on analysis of receivables" method may be appropriate.

SA 9–3

1. and 2.

	2005		2004	
Net sales	$27,433		$24,548	
Accounts receivable	$375		$343	
Average accounts receivable	$359	[($375 + $343)/2]	$327.5	[($343 + $312)/2]
Accounts receivable turnover	76.4	($27,433/$359)	75.0	($24,548/$327.5)
Average daily sales	$75.2	($27,433/365)	$67.3	($24,548/365)
Days' sales in receivables	4.8	($359/$75.2)	4.9	($327.5/$67.3)

3. The accounts receivable turnover indicates a slight increase in the efficiency of collecting accounts receivable by increasing from 75.0 to 76.4, a favorable trend. The days' sales in receivables decreased from 4.9 days to 4.8, a favorable trend. Thus, based upon (1) and (2), Best Buy has slightly improved its efficiency in the collection of receivables.

4. Based upon accounts receivable turnover ratios, Best Buy is more efficient in collection of receivables than is Circuit City during 2005 and 2004. Comparing 2005 and 2004 ratios also reveals favorable trends for Best Buy in contrast to unfavorable trends for Circuit City.

5. We assumed that the percentage of credit sales to total sales remains constant from one period to the next and is similar for both companies. For example, if the percentage of credit sales to total sales is not similar or if the percentage changes between periods, then the ratios would be distorted and, thus, not comparable.

SA 9–4

1. 2005: 16.7 {$13,931/ [($895 + $774)/2]}
    2004: 10.8 {$8,279/[($774 + $766)/2]}

2. 2005: 21.9 days [($895 + $774)/2] = $834.5; [$834.5/ (13,931/365)] = 21.9 days
    2004: 33.9 days [($774 + $766)/2] = $770; [$770/($8,279/365)] = 33.9 days

3. The accounts receivable turnover indicates an increase in the efficiency of collecting accounts receivable by increasing from 10.8 to 16.7, a favorable trend. The days' sales in receivables decreased from 33.9 days to 21.9, a favorable trend. Before reaching a more definitive conclusion, the ratios should be compared with industry averages and similar firms.

4. The company with receivables is Ingram Micro, Inc., as described in Apple's 10-K filing.

SA 9–5

1. and 2.

	2005		2004	
Net sales	$1,290,072		$1,382,202	
Accounts receivable	$36,033		$30,733	
Average accounts receivable	$33,383	[($36,033 + $30,733)/2]	$33,159	[($30,733 + $35,585)/2]
Accounts receivable turnover	38.6	($1,290,072/$33,383)	41.7	($1,382,202/$33,159)
Average daily sales	$3,534.4	($1,290,072/365)	$3,786.9	($1,382,202/365)
Days' sales in receivables	9.4	($33,383/$3,534.4)	8.8	($33,159/$3,786.9)

3. The accounts receivable turnover indicates a decrease in the efficiency of collecting accounts receivable by decreasing from 41.7 to 38.6, an unfavorable trend. The days' sales in receivables increased from 8.8 days to 9.4 days, an unfavorable trend. Before reaching a more definitive conclusion, the ratios should be compared with industry averages and similar firms.

4. EarthLink's accounts receivable turnover would normally be higher than that of a typical manufacturing company such as Boeing or Kellogg Company. This is because most of EarthLink's customers usually charge their monthly bill to MasterCards or VISAs. In contrast, the customers of Boeing and Kellogg are other businesses who pay their accounts receivable on a less timely basis. For a recent year, the accounts receivable turnover ratio for H.J. Heinz was 8.2 (see Exercise 9–27).

SA 9–6

1. *Note to Instructors:* The turnover ratios will vary over time. As of April 2005, the various turnover ratios (rounded to one decimal place) were as follows:

Alcoa Inc.	7.99
AutoZone, Inc.	100.6
Barnes & Noble, Inc.	65.1
Caterpillar	6.2
The Coca-Cola Company	10.1
Delta Air Lines	20.9
The Home Depot	59.8
IBM	3.2
Kroger	76
Procter & Gamble	13.6
Wal-Mart	153.0
Whirlpool Corporation	6.6

2. Based upon (1), the companies can be categorized as follows:

Accounts Receivable Turnover Ratio

Below 15	Above 15
Alcoa Inc.	AutoZone, Inc.
Caterpillar	Barnes & Noble, Inc.
The Coca-Cola Company	Delta Air Lines
IBM	The Home Depot
Procter & Gamble	Kroger
Whirlpool Corporation	Wal-Mart

3. The companies with accounts receivable turnover ratios above 15 are all companies selling directly to individual consumers. In contrast, companies with turnover ratios below 15 all sell to other businesses. Generally, we would expect companies selling directly to consumers to have higher turnover ratios since many customers will charge their purchases on credit cards. In contrast, companies selling to other businesses normally allow a credit period of at least 30 days or longer.

CHAPTER 10
FIXED ASSETS AND INTANGIBLE ASSETS

QUESTION INFORMATION

Number	Objective	Description	Difficulty	Time	AACSB	AICPA	SS	GL
Q10-1	10-1		Easy	5 min	Analytic	FN-Measurement		
Q10-2	10-1		Easy	5 min	Analytic	FN-Measurement		
Q10-3	10-1		Easy	5 min	Analytic	FN-Measurement		
Q10-4	10-1		Easy	5 min	Analytic	FN-Measurement		
Q10-5	10-1		Easy	5 min	Analytic	FN-Measurement		
Q10-6	10-1		Easy	5 min	Analytic	FN-Measurement		
Q10-7	10-1		Easy	5 min	Analytic	FN-Measurement		
Q10-8	10-6		Easy	5 min	Analytic	FN-Measurement		
Q10-9	10-2		Easy	5 min	Analytic	FN-Measurement		
Q10-10	10-2		Easy	5 min	Analytic	FN-Measurement		
Q10-11	10-2		Easy	5 min	Analytic	FN-Measurement		
Q10-12	10-2		Easy	5 min	Analytic	FN-Measurement		
Q10-13	10-2		Easy	5 min	Analytic	FN-Measurement		
Q10-14	10-2		Easy	5 min	Analytic	FN-Measurement		
Q10-15	10-5		Easy	5 min	Analytic	FN-Measurement		
PE10-1A	10-1	Capital and revenue expenditure entries	Easy	5 min	Analytic	FN-Measurement		
PE10-1B	10-1	Capital and revenue expenditure entries	Easy	5 min	Analytic	FN-Measurement		
PE10-2A	10-2	Straight-line depreciation	Easy	10 min	Analytic	FN-Measurement		
PE10-2B	10-2	Straight-line depreciation	Easy	10 min	Analytic	FN-Measurement		
PE10-3A	10-2	Units-of-production depreciation	Easy	10 min	Analytic	FN-Measurement		
PE10-3B	10-2	Units-of-production depreciation	Easy	10 min	Analytic	FN-Measurement		
PE10-4A	10-2	Double declining balance depreciation	Easy	10 min	Analytic	FN-Measurement		
PE10-4B	10-2	Double declining balance depreciation	Easy	10 min	Analytic	FN-Measurement		
PE10-5A	10-2	Revisions of depreciation estimates	Easy	10 min	Analytic	FN-Measurement		
PE10-5B	10-2	Revisions of depreciation estimates	Easy	10 min	Analytic	FN-Measurement		
PE10-6A	10-3	Sale of equipment	Easy	10 min	Analytic	FN-Measurement		
PE10-6B	10-3	Sale of equipment	Easy	10 min	Analytic	FN-Measurement		
PE10-7A	10-3	Exchange of similar fixed assets	Easy	10 min	Analytic	FN-Measurement		
PE10-7B	10-3	Exchange of similar fixed assets	Easy	10 min	Analytic	FN-Measurement		
PE10-8A	10-4	Entry for depletion of mineral rights	Easy	10 min	Analytic	FN-Measurement		
PE10-8B	10-4	Entry for depletion of mineral rights	Easy	10 min	Analytic	FN-Measurement		
PE10-9A	10-5	Entries for impaired goodwill and amortization of patent	Easy	10 min	Analytic	FN-Measurement		
PE10-9B	10-5	Entries for impaired goodwill and amortization of patent	Easy	10 min	Analytic	FN-Measurement		

Number	Objective	Description	Difficulty	Time	AACSB	AICPA	SS	GL
Ex10-1	10-1	Costs of acquiring fixed assets	Easy	10 min	Analytic	FN-Measurement		
Ex10-2	10-1	Determine cost of land	Easy	5 min	Analytic	FN-Measurement		
Ex10-3	10-1	Determine cost of land	Easy	5 min	Analytic	FN-Measurement		
Ex10-4	10-1	Capital and revenue expenditures	Easy	10 min	Analytic	FN-Measurement		
Ex10-5	10-1	Capital and revenue expenditures	Easy	10 min	Analytic	FN-Measurement		
Ex10-6	10-1	Capital and revenue expenditures	Easy	15 min	Analytic	FN-Measurement		
Ex10-7	10-2	Nature of depreciation	Easy	5 min	Analytic	FN-Measurement		
Ex10-8	10-2	Straight-line depreciation rates	Easy	10 min	Analytic	FN-Measurement		
Ex10-9	10-2	Straight-line depreciation	Easy	5 min	Analytic	FN-Measurement		
Ex10-10	10-2	Depreciation by units-of-production method	Easy	5 min	Analytic	FN-Measurement		
Ex10-11	10-2	Depreciation by units-of-production method	Moderate	20 min	Analytic	FN-Measurement		
Ex10-12	10-2	Depreciation by two methods	Easy	10 min	Analytic	FN-Measurement		
Ex10-13	10-2	Depreciation by two methods	Easy	10 min	Analytic	FN-Measurement		
Ex10-14	10-2	Partial-year depreciation	Moderate	10 min	Analytic	FN-Measurement		
Ex10-15	10-2	Revision of depreciation	Moderate	15 min	Analytic	FN-Measurement		
Ex10-16	10-1, 10-2	Capital expenditures and depreciation	Easy	10 min	Analytic	FN-Measurement		
Ex10-17	10-3	Entries for sale of fixed asset	Easy	10 min	Analytic	FN-Measurement		
Ex10-18	10-3	Disposal of fixed asset	Moderate	20 min	Analytic	FN-Measurement		
Ex10-19	10-3	Asset traded for similar asset	Easy	5 min	Analytic	FN-Measurement		
Ex10-20	10-3	Asset traded for similar asset	Easy	5 min	Analytic	FN-Measurement		
Ex10-21	10-3	Entries for trade of fixed asset	Moderate	15 min	Analytic	FN-Measurement		
Ex10-22	10-3	Entries for trade of fixed asset	Moderate	15 min	Analytic	FN-Measurement		
Ex10-23	10-3	Depreciable cost of asset acquired by exchange	Easy	10 min	Analytic	FN-Measurement		
Ex10-24	10-4	Depletion entries	Easy	10 min	Analytic	FN-Measurement		
Ex10-25	10-5	Amortization entries	Easy	10 min	Analytic	FN-Measurement		
Ex10-26	10-6	Book value of fixed assets	Moderate	15 min	Analytic	FN-Measurement		
Ex10-27	10-6	Balance sheet presentation	Moderate	10 min	Analytic	FN-Measurement		
Ex10-28	FAI	Fixed asset turnover ratio	Easy	10 min	Analytic	FN-Measurement		
Ex10-29	FAI	Fixed asset turnover ratio	Easy	10 min	Analytic	FN-Measurement		
Ex10-30	Appendix	Sum-of-the-years-digits depreciation	Easy	10 min	Analytic	FN-Measurement		
Ex10-31	Appendix	Sum-of-the-years-digits depreciation	Easy	10 min	Analytic	FN-Measurement		

Number	Objective	Description	Difficulty	Time	AACSB	AICPA	SS	GL
Ex10-32	Appendix	Partial-year deprecia-tion	Moderate	10 min	Analytic	FN-Measurement		
Pr10-1A	10-1	Allocate payments and receipts to fixed asset accounts	Moderate	1 hr	Analytic	FN-Measurement	Exl	
Pr10-2A	10-2	Compare three de-preciation methods	Moderate	1 hr	Analytic	FN-Measurement		
Pr10-3A	10-2	Depreciation by three methods; partial years	Moderate	1 hr	Analytic	FN-Measurement		
Pr10-4A	10-2, 10-3	Depreciation by two methods; trade of fixed asset	Difficult	1 1/4 hr	Analytic	FN-Measurement	Exl	KA
Pr10-5A	10-1, 10-2, 10-3	Transactions for fixed assets, including trade	Difficult	1 1/2 hr	Analytic	FN-Measurement		KA
Pr10-6A	10-4, 10-5	Amortization and de-pletion entries	Moderate	45 min	Analytic	FN-Measurement		
Pr10-1B	10-1	Allocate payments and receipts to fixed asset accounts	Moderate	1 hr	Analytic	FN-Measurement	Exl	
Pr10-2B	10-2	Compare three de-preciation methods	Moderate	1 hr	Analytic	FN-Measurement		
Pr10-3B	10-2	Depreciation by three methods; partial years	Moderate	1 hr	Analytic	FN-Measurement		
Pr10-4B	10-2, 10-3	Depreciation by two methods; trade of fixed asset	Difficult	1 1/4 hr	Analytic	FN-Measurement	Exl	KA
Pr10-5B	10-1, 10-2, 10-3	Transactions for fixed assets, including trade	Difficult	1 1/2 hr	Analytic	FN-Measurement		KA
Pr10-6B	10-4, 10-5	Amortization and de-pletion entries	Moderate	45 min	Analytic	FN-Measurement		
SA10-1	10-1	Ethics and profes-sional conduct in business	Easy	10 min	Ethics	BB-Industry		
SA10-2	10-2	Financial vs. tax de-preciation	Easy	10 min	Analytic	FN-Measurement		
SA10-3	10-2	Effect of depreciation on net income	Moderate	20 min	Analytic	FN-Measurement		
SA10-4	10-1	Shopping for a deliv-ery truck	Moderate	1 hr	Reflective Thinking	BB-Critical Thinking		
SA10-5	10-5	Applying for patents, copyrights and trademarks	Moderate	1 hr	Reflective Thinking	BB-Critical Thinking		
SA10-6	FAI	Fixed asset turnover; three industries	Moderate	15 min	Analytic	FN-Measurement		

EYE OPENERS

1. **a.** Tangible
   b. Capable of repeated use in the operations of the business
   e. Long-lived

2. **a.** Property, plant, and equipment
   b. Current assets (merchandise inventory)

3. Real estate acquired as speculation should be listed in the balance sheet under the caption "Investments," below the Current Assets section.

4. $590,000

5. Capital expenditures include the cost of acquiring fixed assets and the cost of improving an asset. These costs are recorded by increasing (debiting) the fixed asset account. Capital expenditures also include the costs of extraordinary repairs, which are recorded by decreasing (debiting) the asset's accumulated depreciation account. Revenue expenditures are recorded as expenses and are costs that benefit only the current period and are incurred for normal maintenance and repairs of fixed assets.

6. Capital expenditure

7. A capital lease is accounted for as if the lessee has purchased the asset and the asset is written off over its useful life. An operating lease is accounted for as a current period expense (rent expense).

8. Ordinarily not; if the book values closely approximate the market values of fixed assets, it is coincidental.

9. **a.** No, it does not provide a special cash fund for the replacement of assets. Unlike most expenses, however, depreciation expense does not require an equivalent outlay of cash in the period to which the expense is allocated.
   b. Depreciation is the cost of fixed assets periodically charged to revenue over their expected useful lives.

10. 13 years

11. **a.** No
    b. No

12. **a.** An accelerated depreciation method is most appropriate for situations in which the decline in productivity or earning power of the asset is proportionately greater in the early years of use than in later years, and the repairs tend to increase with the age of the asset.
    b. An accelerated depreciation method reduces income tax payable to the IRS in the earlier periods of an asset's life. Thus, cash is freed up in the earlier periods to be used for other business purposes.
    c. MACRS was enacted by the Tax Reform Act of 1986 and provides for depreciation for fixed assets acquired after 1986.

13. No. *Financial Accounting Standard No. 154*, "Accounting Changes and Error Corrections," is quite specific about the treatment of changes in depreciable assets' estimated service lives. Such changes should be reflected in the amounts for depreciation expense in the current and future periods. The amounts recorded for depreciation expense in the past are not affected.

14. **a.** No, the accumulated depreciation for an asset cannot exceed the cost of the asset. To do so would create a negative book value, which is meaningless.
    b. The cost and accumulated depreciation should be removed from the accounts when the asset is no longer useful and is removed from service. Presumably, the asset will then be sold, traded in, or discarded.

15. **a.** Over the shorter of its legal life or years of usefulness.
    b. Expense as incurred.
    c. Goodwill should not be amortized, but written down when impaired.

PRACTICE EXERCISES

PE 10–1A

Feb. 13 Delivery Truck...	1,650	
Cash		1,650
13 Repairs and Maintenance Expense	25	
Cash		25

PE 10–1B

Aug. 30 Accumulated Depreciation—Delivery Van	1,325	
Cash		1,325
30 Delivery Van...	1,100	
Cash		1,100

PE 10–2A

a. $82,000 ($88,000 – $6,000)
b. 20% = (1/5)
c. $16,400 ($82,000 × 20%), or ($82,000/5 years)

PE 10–2B

a. $268,000 ($316,000 – $48,000)
b. 2.5% = (1/40)
c. $6,700 ($268,000 × 2.5%), or ($268,000/40 years)

PE 10–3A

a. $115,000 ($120,000 – $5,000)
b. $2.30 per hour ($115,000/50,000 hours)
c. $9,660 (4,200 hours × $2.30)

PE 10–3B

a. $72,000 ($90,000 – $18,000)

b. $0.36 per mile ($72,000/200,000 miles)

c. $14,400 (40,000 miles × $0.36)

PE 10–4A

a. $82,000 ($88,000 – $6,000)

b. 40% = [(1/5) × 2]

c. $35,200 ($88,000 × 40%)

PE 10–4B

a. $268,000 ($316,000 – $48,000)

b. 5% = [(1/40) × 2]

c. $15,800 ($316,000 × 5%)

PE 10–5A

a. $9,375 [($90,000 – $15,000)/8]

b. $52,500 [$90,000 – ($9,375 × 4)]

c. $8,000 [($52,500 – $12,500)/5]

PE 10–5B

a. $11,000 [($189,000 – $24,000)/15]

b. $90,000 [$189,000 – ($11,000 × 9)]

c. $10,500 [($90,000 – $6,000)/8]

PE 10–6A

a. $13,000 [($158,000 – $28,000)/10]

b. $7,000 loss {$86,000 – [$158,000 – ($13,000 × 5)]}

c.
Cash	86,000	
Accumulated Depreciation—Equipment	65,000	
Loss on Sale of Equipment	7,000	
Equipment		158,000

PE 10–6B

a. $50,000 = $250,000 × [(1/10) × 2)] = $250,000 × 20%

b. $18,000 loss, computed as follows:

Cost	$250,000	
Less: First year depreciation	(50,000)	
Second year depreciation	(40,000)	[($250,000 – $50,000) × 20%]
Book value at end of second year	$160,000	

Loss on sale ($160,000 – $142,000) = $18,000

c.
Cash	142,000	
Accumulated Depreciation—Equipment	90,000	
Loss on Sale of Equipment	18,000	
Equipment		250,000

PE 10–7A

a. $156,000

List price of new equipment		$160,000
Trade-in allowance on old equipment		
($160,000 – $136,000)	$24,000	
Book value of old truck ($99,000 – $79,000)	20,000	
Unrecognized gain on exchange...................................		(4,000)
Cost of new equipment		$156,000

or

Book value of old equipment ($99,000 – $79,000)	$ 20,000
Plus cash paid at date of exchange	136,000
Cost of new equipment	$156,000

b.

Equipment (new)..	156,000	
Accumulated Depreciation—Equipment (old)............	79,000	
Equipment (old)		99,000
Cash..		136,000

PE 10–7B

a. $90,000

List price of new truck...	$90,000
Book value of old truck ($60,000 – $42,000)...............	$18,000
Trade-in allowance on old truck ($90,000 – $74,500)	15,500
Loss on exchange	$ 2,500

Note to Instructors: In exchanges of similar assets where there is a loss, the loss is recorded and the new asset is recorded at its list price.

b.

Truck (new)	90,000	
Accumulated Depreciation—Truck (old)....................	42,000	
Loss of Exchange of Truck...	2,500	
Truck (old)..		60,000
Cash..		74,500

PE 10–8A

a. $0.48 per ton = $36,000,000/75,000,000 tons

b. $14,088,000 = (29,350,000 tons × $0.48 per ton)

c. Dec. 31 Depletion Expense.. 14,088,000
            Accumulated Depletion............................   14,088,000
            Depletion of mineral deposit.

PE 10–8B

a. $0.80 per ton = $88,000,000/110,000,000 tons

b. $27,040,000 = (33,800,000 tons × $0.80 per ton)

c. Dec. 31 Depletion Expense.. 27,040,000
            Accumulated Depletion............................   27,040,000
            Depletion of mineral deposit.

PE 10–9A

a. Dec. 31 Loss from Impaired Goodwill 100,000
            Goodwill   100,000
            Impaired goodwill.

b. Dec. 31 Amortization Expense—Patents.................. 21,875
            Patents   21,875
            Amortized patent rights
            [($450,000/12) × 7/12].

PE 10–9B

a. Dec. 31 Loss from Impaired Goodwill 375,000
            Goodwill   375,000
            Impaired goodwill.

b. Dec. 31 Amortization Expense—Patents.................. 15,000
            Patents   15,000
            Amortized patent rights
            [($600,000/10) × 3/12].

EXERCISES

Ex. 10–1

a. New printing press: 1, 2, 3, 4, 5

b. Used printing press: 7, 8, 10, 11

Ex. 10–2

a. Yes. All expenditures incurred for the purpose of making the land suitable for its intended use should be debited to the land account.

b. No. Land is not depreciated.

Ex. 10–3

Initial cost of land ($25,000 + $175,000).....................		$200,000
Plus: Legal fees...	$ 1,200	
Delinquent taxes..	10,850	
Demolition of building..	15,000	27,050
		$227,050
Less: Salvage of materials...		2,400
Cost of land..		$224,650

Ex. 10–4

Capital expenditures: 2, 4, 5, 6, 7, 9, 10

Revenue expenditures: 1, 3, 8

Ex. 10–5

Capital expenditures: 3, 4, 6, 7, 9, 10

Revenue expenditures: 1, 2, 5, 8

Ex. 10–6

Feb.	22	Accumulated Depreciation—Delivery Truck	2,300	
		Cash		2,300
Mar.	20	Delivery Truck	900	
		Cash		900
Nov.	2	Repairs and Maintenance Expense	67	
		Cash		67

Ex. 10–7

a. No. The $975,600 represents the original cost of the equipment. Its replacement cost, which may be more or less than $975,600, is not reported in the financial statements.

b. No. The $600,000 is the accumulation of the past depreciation charges on the equipment. The recognition of depreciation expense has no relationship to the cash account or accumulation of cash funds.

Ex. 10–8

(a) 50% (1/2), (b) 12.5% (1/8), (c) 10% (1/10), (d) 5% (1/20), (e) 4% (1/25), (f) 2.5% (1/40), (g) 2% (1/50)

Ex. 10–9

$11,200 [($198,500 – $30,500)/15]

Ex. 10–10

$$\frac{\$215,000 - \$27,000}{80,000 \text{ hours}} = \$2.35 \text{ depreciation per hour}$$

380 hours at $2.35 = $893 depreciation for October

Ex. 10–11

a.

Truck No.	Rate per Mile	Miles Operated	Credit to Accumulated Depreciation
1	42.0 cents	36,000	$15,120
2	21.0	18,000	3,150*
3	17.5	36,000	6,300
4	30.0	16,000	4,800
Total...			$29,370

* Mileage depreciation of $3,780 (21 cents × 18,000) is limited to $3,150, which reduces the book value of the truck to $9,900, its residual value.

b. Depreciation Expense—Trucks 29,370
     Accumulated Depreciation—Trucks   29,370

Ex. 10–12

First Year	Second Year
a. 6 1/4% of $44,800 = $2,800	6 1/4% of $44,800 = $2,800
or	or
($44,800/16) = $2,800	($44,800/16) = $2,800
b. 12 1/2% of $44,800 = $5,600	12 1/2% of ($44,800 – $5,600) = $4,900

Ex. 10–13

a. 12 1/2% of ($86,000 – $10,000) = $9,500 or [($86,000 – $10,000)/8]

b. Year 1: 25% of $86,000 = $21,500
Year 2: 25% of ($86,000 – $21,500) = $16,125

Ex. 10–14

a. Year 1: 3/12 × [($68,000 – $18,000)/10] = $1,250
Year 2: ($68,000 – $18,000)/10 = $5,000

b. Year 1: 3/12 × 20% of $68,000 = $3,400
Year 2: 20% of ($68,000 – $3,400) = $12,920

Ex. 10–15

a. $12,500 [($750,000 – $300,000)/36]

b. $500,000 [$750,000 – ($12,500 × 20 yrs.)]

c. $15,000 [($500,000 – $200,000)/20 yrs.]

Ex. 10–16

| a. | Mar. | 29 | Carpet | 48,000 | |
| | | | Cash | | 48,000 |

b.	Dec.	31	Depreciation Expense	2,400	
			Accumulated Depreciation		2,400
			Carpet depreciation [($48,000/15 years) × 9/12].		

Ex. 10–17

a.	Cost of equipment	$360,000
	Accumulated depreciation at December 31, 2008 (4 years at $27,500* per year)	110,000
	Book value at December 31, 2008	$250,000

*($360,000 – $30,000)/12 = $27,500

| b. | (1) | Depreciation Expense—Equipment | 6,875 | |
| | | Accumulated Depreciation—Equipment | | 6,875 |

	(2)	Cash	220,000	
		Accumulated Depreciation—Equipment	116,875	
		Loss on Disposal of Fixed Assets	23,125	
		Equipment		360,000

Ex. 10–18

a. 2005 depreciation expense: $16,250 [($147,500 – $17,500)/8]

   2006 depreciation expense: $16,250

   2007 depreciation expense: $16,250

b. $98,750 [$147,500 – ($16,250 × 3)]

c.

Cash	95,000	
Accumulated Depreciation—Equipment	48,750	
Loss on Disposal of Fixed Assets	3,750	
Equipment		147,500

d.

Cash	100,000	
Accumulated Depreciation—Equipment	48,750	
Equipment		147,500
Gain on Disposal of Fixed Assets		1,250

Ex. 10–19

a. $200,000 ($280,000 – $80,000)

b. $278,750 [$280,000 – ($80,000 – $78,750)], or

   $278,750 ($200,000 + $78,750)

Ex. 10–20

a. $200,000 ($280,000 – $80,000)

b. $280,000. The new printing press's cost cannot exceed $280,000 on a similar exchange. The $23,250 loss on disposal ($103,250 book value – $80,000 trade-in allowance) must be recognized.

Ex. 10–21

a. Depreciation Expense—Equipment...............................	9,375	
Accumulated Depreciation—Equipment................		9,375
Equipment depreciation ($12,500 × 9/12).		

b. Accumulated Depreciation—Equipment......................	146,875	
Equipment..	288,750	
Loss on Disposal of Fixed Assets	3,125	
Equipment		210,000
Cash..		28,750
Notes Payable		200,000*

*$288,750 – $60,000 – $28,750

Ex. 10–22

a. Depreciation Expense—Trucks	2,000	
Accumulated Depreciation—Trucks		2,000
Truck depreciation ($8,000 × 3/12).		

b. Accumulated Depreciation—Trucks............................	34,000	
Trucks	74,000	
Trucks...		48,000
Cash..		10,000
Notes Payable		50,000*

*$75,000 – $15,000 – $10,000

Ex. 10–23

a. $86,500. The new truck's cost cannot exceed $86,500 in a similar exchange.

b. $81,000 [$86,500 – ($11,500 – $6,000)] or
$81,000 ($75,000 + $6,000)

Ex. 10–24

a. $30,000,000/75,000,000 tons = $0.40 depletion per ton
11,250,000 × $0.40 = $4,500,000 depletion expense

b. Depletion Expense	4,500,000	
Accumulated Depletion...		4,500,000
Depletion of mineral deposit.		

Ex. 10–25

a. ($661,500/15) + ($105,000/12) = $52,850 total patent expense

b.
Amortization Expense—Patents	52,850	
Patents..		52,850

Amortized patent rights ($44,100 + $8,750).

Ex. 10–26

a. Property, Plant, and Equipment (in millions):

	Current Year	Preceding Year
Land and buildings	$ 361	$ 351
Machinery, equipment, and internal-use software..	494	422
Office furniture and equipment................................	81	79
Other fixed assets related to leases........................	545	446
	$1,481	$1,298
Less accumulated depreciation...............................	664	591
Book value...	$ 817	$ 707

A comparison of the book values of the current and preceding years indicates that they increased. A comparison of the total cost and accumulated depreciation reveals that Apple purchased $183 million ($1,481 – $1,298) of additional fixed assets, which was offset by the additional depreciation expense of $73 million ($664 – $591) taken during the current year.

b. The book value of fixed assets should normally increase during the year. Although additional depreciation expense will reduce the book value, most companies invest in new assets in an amount that is at least equal to the depreciation expense. However, during periods of economic downturn, companies purchase fewer fixed assets, and the book value of their fixed assets may decline.

Ex. 10–27

1. Fixed assets should be reported at cost and not replacement cost.

2. Land does not depreciate.

3. Patents and goodwill are intangible assets that should be listed in a separate section following the Fixed Assets section. Patents should be reported at their net book values (cost less amortization to date). Goodwill should not be amortized, but should be only written down upon impairment.

Ex. 10–28

a. Fixed Asset Turnover Ratio $= \dfrac{\text{Revenue}}{\text{Average Book Value of Fixed Assets}}$

Fixed Asset Turnover Ratio $= \dfrac{\$75,112}{(\$74,124 + \$75,305)/2}$

Fixed Asset Turnover Ratio = 1.01

b. Verizon earns $1.01 revenue for every dollar of fixed assets. This is a low fixed asset turnover ratio, reflecting the high fixed asset intensity in a telecommunications company. The industry average fixed turnover ratio is slightly higher at 1.10. Thus, Verizon is using its fixed assets slightly less efficiently than the industry as a whole.

Ex. 10–29

a. Best Buy: 11.65 ($27,433/$2,354)

Circuit City Stores, Inc.: 15.82 ($10,472/$662)

b. Circuit City's fixed asset turnover ratio of 15.82 is higher than Best Buy's fixed asset turnover ratio of 11.65. Thus, Circuit City is generating $4.17 ($15.82 – $11.65) more revenue for each dollar of fixed assets than is Best Buy. On this basis, Circuit City is managing its fixed assets more efficiently than is Best Buy.

Appendix Ex. 10–30

First year: 16/136 × $44,800 = $5,271

Second year: 15/136 × $44,800 = $4,941

Appendix Ex. 10–31

First year: 8/36 × ($86,000 − $10,000) = $16,889

Second year: 7/36 × ($86,000 − $10,000) = $14,778

Appendix Ex. 10–32

First year: 3/12 × 10/55 × ($68,000 − $18,000) = $2,273

Second year:

[(9/12 × 10/55 × ($68,000 − $18,000)] + [(3/12 × 9/55 × ($68,000 − $18,000)] =
$6,818 + $2,045 = $8,863

PROBLEMS

Prob. 10–1A

1.

Item	Land	Land Improvements	Building	Other Accounts
a.	$ 3,000			
b.	400,000			
c.	10,000			
d.	12,800			
e.	3,900			
f.	(4,000)*			
g.	17,500			
h.			$ 40,000	
i.			4,800	
j.		$ 9,000		
k.				$(800,000)*
l.		15,000		
m.				2,000
n.				2,500
o.		1,100		
p.			42,000	
q.			915,000	
r.				(4,000)*
s.			(400)*	
2.	$443,200	$25,100	$1,001,400	

*Receipt

3. Since land used as a plant site does not lose its ability to provide services, it is not depreciated. However, land improvements do lose their ability to provide services as time passes and are therefore depreciated.

Prob. 10–2A

Depreciation Expense

Year	a. Straight-Line Method	b. Units-of-Production Method	c. Double-Declining-Balance Method
2006	$28,000	$32,000	$60,000
2007	28,000	30,000	20,000
2008	28,000	22,000	4,000
Total	$84,000	$84,000	$84,000

Calculations:

Straight-line method:

($90,000 – $6,000)/3 = $28,000 each year

Units-of-production method:

($90,000 – $6,000)/21,000 hours = $4.00 per hour

2006: 8,000 hours @ $4.00 = $32,000
2007: 7,500 hours @ $4.00 = $30,000
2008: 5,500 hours @ $4.00 = $22,000

Double-declining-balance method:

2006: $90,000 × 2/3 = $60,000
2007: ($90,000 – $60,000) × 2/3 = $20,000
2008: ($90,000 – $60,000 – $20,000 – $6,000*) = $4,000

*Book value should not be reduced below the residual value of $6,000.

Prob. 10–3A

a. **Straight-line method:**

2006:	[($7,830 – $300)/3] × 1/2	$1,255
2007:	($7,830 – $300)/3	2,510
2008:	($7,830 – $300)/3	2,510
2009:	[($7,830 – $300)/3] × 1/2	1,255

b. **Units-of-production method:**

2006:	1,600 hours @ $0.75*	$1,200
2007:	3,800 hours @ $0.75...	2,850
2008:	3,400 hours @ $0.75...	2,550
2009:	1,240 hours @ $0.75...	930

*($7,830 – $300)/10,040 hours = $0.75 per hour

c. **Double-declining-balance method:**

2006:	$7,830 × 2/3 × 1/2	$2,610
2007:	($7,830 – $2,610) × 2/3...	3,480
2008:	($7,830 – $2,610 – $3,480) × 2/3..	1,160
2009:	($7,830 – $2,610 – $3,480 – $1,160 – $300*)	280

*Book value should not be reduced below $300, the residual value.

Prob. 10–4A

1.

	Year	Depreciation Expense	Accumulated Depreciation, End of Year	Book Value, End of Year
a.	1	$32,000*	$ 32,000	$143,000
	2	32,000	64,000	111,000
	3	32,000	96,000	79,000
	4	32,000	128,000	47,000
	5	32,000	160,000	15,000

*[($175,000 – $15,000)/5]

	Year	Depreciation Expense	Accumulated Depreciation, End of Year	Book Value, End of Year
b.	1	$70,000 [$175,000 × (1/5) × 2]	$ 70,000	$105,000
	2	42,000 [$105,000 × (1/5) × 2]	112,000	63,000
	3	25,200 [$63,000 × (1/5) × 2]	137,200	37,800
	4	15,120 [$37,800 × (1/5) × 2]	152,320	22,680
	5	7,680 [$175,000 – $152,320 – $15,000]	160,000	15,000

2. Book value of old equipment .... $ 22,680
   Boot given (cash and notes payable) 215,000
   Cost of new equipment.. $237,680

or

   Price of new equipment.. $240,000
   Less unrecognized gain on exchange ($25,000 – $22,680) 2,320
   Cost of new equipment.. $237,680

3. Accumulated Depreciation—Equipment....................... 152,320
   Equipment.. 237,680
      Equipment 175,000
      Cash... 15,000
      Notes Payable 200,000

4. Accumulated Depreciation—Equipment....................... 152,320
   Equipment.. 240,000
   Loss on Disposal of Fixed Assets 4,680*
      Equipment 175,000
      Cash... 15,000
      Notes Payable 207,000

*($22,680 – $18,000)

Prob. 10–5A

2006

Jan.	9	Delivery Equipment...	32,000	
		Cash..		32,000
Sept.	24	Truck Repair Expense	470	
		Cash..		470
Dec.	31	Depreciation Expense—Delivery Equipment..............	16,000	
		Acc. Depr.—Delivery Equipment		16,000
		Delivery equipment depreciation [$32,000 × (1/4 × 2)].		

2007

Jan.	1	Delivery Equipment...	57,500	
		Cash..		57,500
June	30	Depreciation Expense—Delivery Equipment..............	4,000	
		Acc. Depr.—Delivery Equipment		4,000
		Delivery equipment depreciation [50% × ($32,000 – $16,000) × 6/12].		
	30	Accumulated Depreciation—Delivery Equipment	20,000	
		Cash	13,500	
		Delivery Equipment		32,000
		Gain on Disposal of Fixed Assets		1,500
Nov.	23	Truck Repair Expense	550	
		Cash..		550
Dec.	31	Depreciation Expense—Delivery Equipment..............	23,000	
		Accumulated Depreciation—Delivery Equipment		23,000
		Delivery equipment depreciation [$57,500 × (1/5 × 2)].		

617

2008

July	1	Delivery Equipment...	60,000	
		Cash...		60,000
Oct.	1	Depreciation Expense—Delivery Equipment..............	10,350	
		Accumulated Depreciation—Delivery Equipment		10,350
		Delivery equipment depreciation		
		[9/12 × 40% × ($57,500 – $23,000)].		
	1	Cash	22,000	
		Accumulated Depreciation—Delivery Equipment	33,350	
		Loss on Disposal of Fixed Assets	2,150	
		Delivery Equipment		57,500
Dec.	31	Depreciation Expense—Delivery Equipment..............	7,500	
		Accumulated Depreciation—Delivery Equipment		7,500
		Delivery equipment depreciation		
		[$60,000 × (1/8 × 2) × 1/2].		

Prob. 10–6A

1. a. $648,000/3,600,000$ board feet = $0.18 per board foot; 1,200,000 board feet × $0.18 per board foot = $216,000

    b. Goodwill is not amortized.

    c. $780,000/12 years = $65,000; 1/4 of $65,000 = $16,250

2. a. Depletion Expense.. 216,000
        Accumulated Depletion....................................... 216,000
            Depletion of timber rights.

    b. No entry for goodwill amortization.

    c. Amortization Expense—Patents............................. 16,250
        Patents 16,250
            Patent amortization.

Prob. 10–1B

1.

Item	Land	Land Improvements	Building	Other Accounts
a.	$ 7,500			
b.	260,000			
c.	2,500			
d.	20,650			
e.	16,250			
f.	12,500			
g.	(5,000)*			
h.			$ 36,000	
i.	8,000			
j.			3,600	
k.				$(900,000)*
l.		$18,000		
m.				3,000
n.				4,200
o.		15,000		
p.				(7,000)*
q.			54,000	
r.			1,000,000	
s.			(600)*	
2.	$322,400	$33,000	$1,093,000	

*Receipt

3. Since land used as a plant site does not lose its ability to provide services, it is not depreciated. However, land improvements do lose their ability to provide services as time passes and are therefore depreciated.

620

Prob. 10–2B

Depreciation Expense

Year	a. Straight-Line Method	b. Units-of-Production Method	c. Double-Declining-Balance Method
2007	$107,500	$152,000	$237,500
2008	107,500	136,000	118,750
2009	107,500	102,000	59,375
2010	107,500	40,000	14,375*
Total	$430,000	$430,000	$430,000

Calculations:

Straight-line method:

($475,000 − $45,000)/4 = $107,500 each year

Units-of-production method:

($475,000 − $45,000)/21,500 hours = $20 per hour

2007: 7,600 hours @ $20 = $152,000
2008: 6,800 hours @ $20 = $136,000
2009: 5,100 hours @ $20 = $102,000
2010: 2,000 hours @ $20 = $40,000

Double-declining-balance method:

2007: $475,000 × 50% = $237,500
2008: ($475,000 − $237,500) × 50% = $118,750
2009: ($475,000 − $237,500 − $118,750) × 50% = $59,375
2010: ($475,000 − $237,500 − $118,750 − $59,375 − $45,000*) = $14,375

*Book value should not be reduced below the residual value of $45,000.

Prob. 10–3B

a. **Straight-line method:**

2006: [($97,200 – $6,000)/3] × 1/2	$15,200
2007: ($97,200 – $6,000)/3	30,400
2008: ($97,200 – $6,000)/3	30,400
2009: [($97,200 – $6,000)/3] × 1/2	15,200

b. **Units-of-production method:**

2006: 3,650 hours @ $4*	$14,600
2007: 8,000 hours @ $4	32,000
2008: 7,850 hours @ $4	31,400
2009: 3,300 hours @ $4	13,200

*($97,200 – $6,000)/22,800 hours = $4 per hour

c. **Double-declining-balance method:**

2006: $97,200 × 2/3 × 1/2	$32,400
2007: ($97,200 – $32,400) × 2/3	43,200
2008: ($97,200 – $32,400 – $43,200) × 2/3	14,400
2009: ($97,200 – $32,400 – $43,200 – $14,400 – $6,000*)	1,200

*Book value should not be reduced below $6,000, the residual value.

Prob. 10–4B

1.

	Year	Depreciation Expense	Accumulated Depreciation, End of Year	Book Value, End of Year
a.	1	$55,500*	$ 55,500	$184,500
	2	55,500	111,000	129,000
	3	55,500	166,500	73,500
	4	55,500	222,000	18,000

*[($240,000 – $18,000)/4]

	Year	Depreciation Expense	Accumulated Depreciation, End of Year	Book Value, End of Year
b.	1	$120,000 [$240,000 × (1/4) × 2]	$120,000	$120,000
	2	60,000 [$120,000 × (1/4) × 2]	180,000	60,000
	3	30,000 [$60,000 × (1/4) × 2]	210,000	30,000
	4	12,000 [$240,000 – $210,000 – $18,000]	222,000	18,000

2.

Book value of old equipment	$ 30,000
Boot given (cash and notes payable)	280,000
Cost of new equipment..	$ 310,000

or

Price of new equipment..	$ 325,000
Less unrecognized gain on exchange ($45,000 – $30,000)	15,000
Cost of new equipment..	$ 310,000

3.

Accumulated Depreciation—Equipment......................	210,000	
Equipment...	310,000	
Equipment		240,000
Cash..		10,000
Notes Payable		270,000

4.

Accumulated Depreciation—Equipment......................	210,000	
Equipment...	325,000	
Loss on Disposal of Fixed Assets	5,000*	
Equipment		240,000
Cash..		10,000
Notes Payable		290,000

*($30,000 – $25,000)

Prob. 10–5B

2006

Jan. 9 Delivery Equipment... 38,000
            Cash... 38,000

Mar. 15 Truck Repair Expense 180
            Cash... 180

Dec. 31 Depreciation Expense—Delivery Equipment.............. 9,500
            Accumulated Depreciation—Delivery Equipment 9,500
            Delivery equipment depreciation
                [$38,000 × (1/8 × 2)].

2007

Jan. 3 Delivery Equipment... 62,500
            Cash... 62,500

Feb. 20 Truck Repair Expense 150
            Cash... 150

Apr. 30 Depreciation Expense—Delivery Equipment.... 2,375
            Acc. Depr.—Delivery Equipment 2,375
            Delivery equipment depreciation
                [25% × ($38,000 – $9,500) × 1/3].

       30 Acc. Depr.—Delivery Equipment 11,875
            Cash 25,000
            Loss on Disposal of Fixed Assets..................... 1,125
            Delivery Equipment 38,000

Dec. 31 Depreciation Expense—Delivery Equipment.... 12,500
            Acc. Depr.—Delivery Equipment 12,500
            Delivery equipment depreciation
                ($62,500 × (1/10 × 2)].

Prob. 10–5B   Concluded

2008

July	1	Delivery Equipment...	70,000	
		Cash..		70,000

Oct.	6	Depreciation Expense—Delivery Equipment....	7,500	
		Acc. Depr.—Delivery Equipment		7,500
		Delivery equipment depreciation		
		[9/12 × 20% ($62,500 – $12,500)].		

	6	Cash	43,900	
		Acc. Depr.—Delivery Equipment	20,000	
		Delivery Equipment		62,500
		Gain on Disposal of Fixed Assets		1,400

Dec.	31	Depreciation Expense—Delivery Equipment....	7,000	
		Acc. Depr.—Delivery Equipment		7,000
		Delivery equipment depreciation		
		(1/2 × 20% × $70,000).		

Prob. 10–6B

1. a. Goodwill is not amortized.

   b. $475,000/10 years = $47,500; 1/2 of $47,500 = $23,750

   c. $900,000/6,000,000 board feet = $0.15 per board foot; 800,000 board feet × $0.15 per board foot = $120,000

2. a. No entry for goodwill amortization.

   b. Amortization Expense—Patents............................. 23,750
          Patents 23,750
            Patent amortization.

   c. Depletion Expense.. 120,000
          Accumulated Depletion...................................... 120,000
            Depletion of timber rights.

SPECIAL ACTIVITIES

SA 10–1

It is considered unprofessional for employees to use company assets for personal reasons, because such use reduces the useful life of the assets for normal business purposes. Thus, it is unethical for Leah Corbin to use Beartooth Consulting Co.'s computers and laser printers to service her part-time accounting business, even on an after-hours basis. In addition, it is improper for Leah's clients to call her during regular working hours. Such calls may interrupt or interfere with Leah's ability to carry out her assigned duties for Beartooth Consulting Co.

SA 10–2

You should explain to Clay and Haley that it is acceptable to maintain two sets of records for tax and financial reporting purposes. This can happen when a company uses one method for financial statement purposes, such as straight-line depreciation, and another method for tax purposes, such as MACRS depreciation. This should not be surprising, since the methods for taxes and financial statements are established by two different groups with different objectives. That is, tax laws and related accounting methods are established by Congress. The Internal Revenue Service then applies the laws and, in some cases, issues interpretations of the law and congressional intent. The primary objective of the tax laws is to generate revenue in an equitable manner for government use. Generally accepted accounting principles, on the other hand, are established primarily by the Financial Accounting Standards Board. The objective of generally accepted accounting principles is the preparation and reporting of true economic conditions and results of operations of business entities.

You might note, however, that companies are required in their tax returns to reconcile differences in accounting methods. For example, income reported on the company's financial statements must be reconciled with taxable income.

Finally, you might also indicate to Clay and Haley that even generally accepted accounting principles allow for alternative methods of accounting for the same transactions or economic events. For example, a company could use straight-line depreciation for some assets and double-declining-balance depreciation for other assets.

SA 10–3

1. a. **Straight-line method:**

2006: ($150,000/5) × 1/2	$15,000
2007: ($150,000/5)	30,000
2008: ($150,000/5)	30,000
2009: ($150,000/5)	30,000
2010: ($150,000/5)	30,000
2011: ($150,000/5) × 1/2	15,000

b. **MACRS:**

2006: ($150,000 × 20%)	$30,000
2007: ($150,000 × 32%)	48,000
2008: ($150,000 × 19.2%)	28,800
2009: ($150,000 × 11.5%)	17,250
2010: ($150,000 × 11.5%)	17,250
2011: ($150,000 × 5.8%)	8,700

2.

a. Straight-line method

			Year			
	2006	2007	2008	2009	2010	2011
Income before depreciation	$300,000	$300,000	$300,000	$300,000	$300,000	$300,000
Depreciation expense	15,000	30,000	30,000	30,000	30,000	15,000
Income before income tax	$285,000	$270,000	$270,000	$270,000	$270,000	$285,000
Income tax	85,500	81,000	81,000	81,000	81,000	85,500
Net income	$199,500	$189,000	$189,000	$189,000	$189,000	$199,500

b. MACRS

			Year			
	2006	2007	2008	2009	2010	2011
Income before depreciation	$300,000	$300,000	$300,000	$300,000	$300,000	$300,000
Depreciation expense	30,000	48,000	28,800	17,250	17,250	8,700
Income before income tax	$270,000	$252,000	$271,200	$282,750	$282,750	$291,300
Income tax	81,000	75,600	81,360	84,825	84,825	87,390
Net income	$189,000	$176,400	$189,840	$197,925	$197,925	$203,910

SA 10–3 Concluded

3. For financial reporting purposes, Tom should select the method that provides the net income figure that best represents the results of operations. (*Note to Instructors:* The concept of matching revenues and expenses is discussed in Chapter 3.) However, for income tax purposes, Tom should consider selecting the method that will minimize taxes. Based upon the analyses in (2), both methods of depreciation will yield the same total amount of taxes over the useful life of the equipment. MACRS results in fewer taxes paid in the early years of useful life and more in the later years. For example, in 2006 the income tax expense using MACRS is $81,000, which is $4,500 ($85,500 – $81,000) less than the income tax expense using the straight-line depreciation of $85,500. Cowboy Construction Co. can invest such differences in the early years and earn income.

In some situations, it may be more beneficial for a taxpayer not to choose MACRS. These situations usually occur when a taxpayer is expected to be subject to a low tax rate in the early years of use of an asset and a higher tax rate in the later years of the asset's useful life. In this case, the taxpayer may be better off to defer the larger deductions to offset the higher tax rate.

SA 10–4

Note to Instructors: The purpose of this activity is to familiarize students with the differences in cost and other factors in leasing and buying a business vehicle.

SA 10–5

Note to Instructors: The purpose of this activity is to familiarize students with the procedures involved in acquiring a patent, a copyright, and a trademark.

SA 10–6

a. Fixed Asset Turnover = $\dfrac{\text{Revenue}}{\text{Average Book Value of Fixed Assets}}$

Wal-Mart: $\dfrac{\$258,681}{\$51,686} = 5.00$

Alcoa Inc.: $\dfrac{\$21,504}{\$12,333} = 1.74$

Comcast Corporation: $\dfrac{\$18,348}{\$18,427} = 1.00$

b. The fixed asset turnover measures the amount of revenue earned per dollar of fixed assets. Wal-Mart earns $5.00 of revenue for every dollar of fixed assets, while Alcoa only earns $1.74 and Comcast Corporation only earns $1.00 in revenue for every dollar of fixed assets. This says that Alcoa and Comcast require more fixed assets to operate their businesses than does Wal-Mart, for a given level of revenue volume. Does this mean that Wal-Mart is a better company? Not necessarily. Revenue is not the same as earnings. More likely, Wal-Mart has a smaller profit margin than do Alcoa and Comcast. Although not required by the exercise, the income from operations before tax as a percent of sales (operating margin) for the three companies is: Comcast, 10.6%, Alcoa, 7.8%, and Wal-Mart, 5.5%. Thus, the difference between the fixed asset turnovers seems reasonable. Generally, companies with very low fixed asset turnovers, such as aluminum making and cable communications, must be compensated with higher operating margins.

Note to Instructors: You may wish to consider the impact of different fixed asset turnover ratios across industries and the implications of these differences. This is a conceptual question designed to have students think about how competitive markets would likely reward the low fixed asset turnover companies for embracing high fixed asset commitments.

QUESTION INFORMATION

Number	Objective	Description	Difficulty	Time	AACSB	AICPA	SS	GL
Q11-1	11-1		Easy	5 min	Analytic	FN-Measurement		
Q11-2	11-1		Easy	5 min	Analytic	FN-Measurement		
Q11-3	11-2		Easy	5 min	Analytic	FN-Measurement		
Q11-4	11-2		Easy	5 min	Analytic	FN-Measurement		
Q11-5	11-2		Easy	5 min	Analytic	FN-Measurement		
Q11-6	11-2		Easy	5 min	Analytic	FN-Measurement		
Q11-7	11-3		Easy	5 min	Analytic	FN-Measurement		
Q11-8	11-3		Easy	5 min	Analytic	FN-Measurement		
Q11-9	11-3		Easy	5 min	Analytic	FN-Measurement		
Q11-10	11-4		Easy	5 min	Analytic	FN-Measurement		
Q11-11	11-4		Easy	5 min	Analytic	FN-Measurement		
Q11-12	11-5		Easy	5 min	Analytic	FN-Measurement		
Q11-13	11-5		Easy	5 min	Analytic	FN-Measurement		
Q11-14	11-5		Easy	5 min	Analytic	FN-Measurement		
PE11-1A	11-1	Calculate proceeds from notes payable	Easy	5 min	Analytic	FN-Measurement		
PE11-1B	11-1	Calculate proceeds from notes payable	Easy	5 min	Analytic	FN-Measurement		
PE11-2A	11-2	Calculate federal income tax withholding	Easy	5 min	Analytic	FN-Measurement		
PE11-2B	11-2	Calculate federal income tax withholding	Easy	5 min	Analytic	FN-Measurement		
PE11-3A	11-2	Calculate employee net pay	Easy	5 min	Analytic	FN-Measurement		
PE11-3B	11-2	Calculate employee net pay	Easy	5 min	Analytic	FN-Measurement		
PE11-4A	11-3	Journalize period payroll	Easy	5 min	Analytic	FN-Measurement		
PE11-4B	11-3	Journalize period payroll	Easy	5 min	Analytic	FN-Measurement		
PE11-5A	11-3	Journalize period payroll	Easy	5 min	Analytic	FN-Measurement		
PE11-5B	11-3	Journalize period payroll	Easy	5 min	Analytic	FN-Measurement		
PE11-6A	11-4	Journalize vacation pay and pension benefits	Easy	5 min	Analytic	FN-Measurement		
PE11-6B	11-4	Journalize vacation pay and pension benefits	Easy	5 min	Analytic	FN-Measurement		
PE11-7A	11-5	Journalize estimated warranty liability	Easy	10 min	Analytic	FN-Measurement		
PE11-7B	11-5	Journalize estimated warranty liability	Easy	10 min	Analytic	FN-Measurement		
Ex11-1	11-1	Current liabilities	Easy	10 min	Analytic	FN-Measurement		
Ex11-2	11-1	Entries for discounting notes payable	Easy	15 min	Analytic	FN-Measurement		
Ex11-3	11-1	Evaluate alternative notes	Moderate	15 min	Analytic	FN-Measurement		
Ex11-4	11-1	Entries for notes payable	Easy	10 min	Analytic	FN-Measurement		

Number	Objective	Description	Difficulty	Time	AACSB	AICPA	SS	GL
Ex11-5	11-1	Entries for discounted notes payable	Easy	10 min	Analytic	FN-Measurement		
Ex11-6	11-1	Fixed asset purchases with note	Moderate	15 min	Analytic	FN-Measurement		
Ex11-7	11-1	Current portion of long-term debt	Easy	10 min	Analytic	FN-Measurement		
Ex11-8	11-2	Calculate payroll	Easy	10 min	Analytic	FN-Measurement		
Ex11-9	11-2	Calculate payroll	Moderate	15 min	Analytic	FN-Measurement		
Ex11-10	11-2, 11-3	Summary payroll data	Moderate	15 min	Analytic	FN-Measurement		
Ex11-11	11-3	Payroll tax entries	Easy	10 min	Analytic	FN-Measurement		
Ex11-12	11-3	Payroll tax entries	Easy	10 min	Analytic	FN-Measurement		
Ex11-13	11-3	Payroll tax entries	Easy	10 min	Analytic	FN-Measurement		
Ex11-14	11-3	Payroll internal control procedures	Easy	10 min	Analytic	FN-Measurement		
Ex11-15	11-3	Internal control procedures	Moderate	15 min	Analytic	FN-Measurement		
Ex11-16	11-3	Payroll procedures	Easy	5 min	Analytic	FN-Measurement		
Ex11-17	11-4	Accrued vacation pay	Easy	5 min	Analytic	FN-Measurement		
Ex11-18	11-4	Pension plan entries	Easy	10 min	Analytic	FN-Measurement		
Ex11-19	11-4	Defined benefit pension plan	Easy	5 min	Analytic	FN-Measurement		
Ex11-20	11-5	Accrued product warranty	Easy	10 min	Analytic	FN-Measurement		
Ex11-21	11-5	Accrued product warranty	Easy	5 min	Analytic	FN-Measurement		
Ex11-22	11-5	Contingent liabilities	Moderate	15 min	Analytic	FN-Measurement		
Ex11-23	FAI	Quick ratio	Easy	10 min	Analytic	FN-Measurement		
Ex11-24	FAI	Quick ratio	Easy	10 min	Analytic	FN-Measurement		
Pr11-1A	11-1, 11-5	Liability transactions	Moderate	45 min	Analytic	FN-Measurement		KA
Pr11-2A	11-2, 11-3	Entries for payroll and payroll taxes	Moderate	1 hr	Analytic	FN-Measurement		KA
Pr11-3A	11-2, 11-3	Wage and tax statement data and employer FICA	Difficult	1 1/4 hr	Analytic	FN-Measurement	Exl	
Pr11-4A	11-2, 11-3	Payroll register	Moderate	1 hr	Analytic	FN-Measurement		
Pr11-5A	11-2, 11-3	Payroll register	Difficult	1 1/4 hr	Analytic	FN-Measurement	Exl	
Pr11-6A	11-2, 11-3, 11-4	Payroll accounts and year-end entries	Difficult	2 hr	Analytic	FN-Measurement		KA
Pr11-1B	11-1, 11-5	Liability transactions	Moderate	45 min	Analytic	FN-Measurement		KA
Pr11-2B	11-2, 11-3	Entries for payroll and payroll taxes	Moderate	1 hr	Analytic	FN-Measurement		KA
Pr11-3B	11-2, 11-3	Wage and tax statement data and employer FICA	Difficult	1 1/4 hr	Analytic	FN-Measurement	Exl	
Pr11-4B	11-2, 11-3	Payroll register	Moderate	1 hr	Analytic	FN-Measurement		
Pr11-5B	11-2, 11-3	Payroll register	Difficult	1 1/4 hr	Analytic	FN-Measurement	Exl	
Pr11-6B	11-2 ,11-3, 11-4	Payroll accounts and year-end entries	Difficult	2 hr	Analytic	FN-Measurement		KA
Comp Problem 3	11-1, 11-2, 11-3, 11-4,11-5	Journal entries, bank reconciliation, adjusting entries, balance sheet	Difficult	3 hr	Analytic	FN-Measurement		KA
SA11-1	11-3	Ethics and professional conduct	Easy	15 min	Ethics	BB-Industry		
SA11-2	11-4	Recognizing pension expense	Easy	15 min	Analytic	FN-Measurement		

Number	Objective	Description	Difficulty	Time	AACSB	AICPA	SS	GL
SA11-3	11-3	Executive bonuses and accounting methods	Easy	15 min	Analytic	FN-Measurement		
SA11-4	11-2	Ethics and professional conduct	Easy	15 min	Ethics	BB-Industry		
SA11-5	11-3	Payroll forms	Moderate	30 min	Analytic	FN-Measurement		
SA11-6	11-5	Contingent liabilities	Moderate	30 min	Analytic	FN-Measurement		

EYE OPENERS

1. A discounted note payable has no stated interest rate, but provides interest by discounting the note proceeds. The discount, which is the difference between the proceeds and the face of the note, is the interest and is accounted for as such.

2. **a.** Income or withholding taxes, social security, and Medicare
   b. Employees Federal Income Tax Payable, Social Security Tax Payable, and Medicare Tax Payable.

3. There is a ceiling on (c) the social security portion of the FICA tax and (d) the federal unemployment compensation tax.

4. The deductions from employee earnings are for amounts owed (liabilities) to others for such items as federal taxes, state and local income taxes, and contributions to pension plans.

5. Yes. Unemployment compensation taxes are paid by the employer on the first $7,000 of annual earnings for each employee. Therefore, hiring two employees, each earning $12,500 per year, would require the payment of twice the unemployment tax than if only one employee, earning $25,000, was hired.

6. **1.** a
   2. c
   3. c
   4. b
   5. b

7. The use of special payroll checks relieves the treasurer or other executives of the task of signing a large number of regular checks each payday. Another advantage of this system is that reconciling the regular bank statement is simplified. The paid payroll checks are returned by the bank separately from regular checks and are accompanied by a statement of the special bank account. Any balance shown on the bank's statement will correspond to the sum of the payroll checks outstanding because the amount of each deposit is exactly the same as the total amount of checks drawn.

8. **a.** Input data that remain relatively unchanged from period to period (and therefore do not need to be reintroduced into the system frequently) are called *constants.*
   b. Input data that differ from period to period are called *variables.*

9. **a.** If employees' attendance records are kept and their preparation supervised in such a manner as to prevent errors and abuses, then one can be assured that wages paid are based on hours actually worked. The use of "In" and "Out" cards, whereby employees indicate by punching a time clock their time of arrival and departure, is especially useful. Employee identification cards or badges can be very helpful in giving additional assurance. Employee identification cards and badges can also contain bar codes that can be used by electronic scanners to account for employee time and control access to authorized locations.
   b. The requirement that the addition of names on the payroll be supported by written authorizations from the Personnel Department can help ensure that payroll checks are not being issued to fictitious persons. Endorsements on payroll checks can be compared with other samples of employees' signatures. Many businesses directly deposit payroll checks to employee bank accounts, thereby eliminating the need for endorsement and check disbursement controls.

10. If the vacation payment is probable and can be reasonably estimated, the vacation pay expense should be recorded during the period in which the vacation privilege is earned.

11. Employee life expectancies, expected employee retirement dates, employee turnover, employee compensation levels, and investment income on pension contributions are factors that influence the future pension obligation of an employer.

12. To match revenues and expenses properly, the liability to cover product warranties should be recorded in the period during which the sale of the product is made.

13. When the defective product is repaired, the repair costs would be recorded by debiting Product Warranty Payable and crediting Cash, Supplies, or another appropriate account.

14. Yes. Since the $5,000 is payable within one year, Company A should present it as a current liability at September 30.

PRACTICE EXERCISES

PE 11–1A

a. $120,000.

b. $117,600. [$120,000 – ($120,000 × 90/360 × 8%)]

PE 11–1B

a. $50,000.

b. $49,750. [$50,000 – ($50,000 × 30/360 × 6%)]

PE 11–2A

Total wage payment		$1,680.00
One allowance (provided by IRS)	$63.00	
Multiplied by allowances claimed on Form W-4	× 3	189.00
Amount subject to withholding		$1,491.00
Initial withholding from wage bracket in Exhibit 3		$ 275.55
Plus additional withholding: 28% of excess over $1,409		22.96*
Federal income tax withholding		$ 298.51

*($1,491 – $1,409) × 28%.

PE 11–2B

Total wage payment		$600.00
One allowance (provided by IRS)	$63.00	
Multiplied by allowances claimed on Form W-4	× 1	63.00
Amount subject to withholding		$537.00
Initial withholding from wage bracket in Exhibit 3		$ 14.10
Plus additional withholding: 15% of excess over $192		51.75*
Federal income tax withholding		$ 65.85

*($537 – $192) × 15%.

PE 11–3A

Total wage payment		$1,680.00
Less: Federal income tax withholding		298.51
Earnings subject to social security tax	$1,000.00	
($100,000 – $99,000)		
Social security tax rate	× 6%	
Social security tax		60.00
Medicare tax ($1,680 × 1.5%)		25.20
Net pay		$1,296.29

PE 11–3B

Total wage payment		$ 600.00
Less: Federal income tax withholding		65.85
Earnings subject to social security tax	600.00	
Social security tax rate	× 6%	
Social security tax		36.00
Medicare tax ($600 × 1.5%)		9.00
Net pay		$ 489.15

PE 11–4A

Salaries Expense	21,000	
Social Security Tax Payable		1,260
Medicare Tax Payable		315
Employees Federal Income Tax Payable		3,822
Salaries Payable		15,603

PE 11–4B

Salaries Expense	450,000	
Social Security Tax Payable		25,650
Medicare Tax payable		6,750
Employees Federal Income Tax Payable		89,100
Retirement Savings Deductions Payable		27,000
Salaries Payable		301,500

PE 11–5A

Payroll Tax Expense...	1,980.48	
Social Security Tax Payable		1,260.00
Medicare Tax Payable		315.00
State Unemployment Tax Payable		353.16*
Federal Unemployment Tax Payable		52.32**

*$6,540 × 5.4%
**$6,540 × 0.8%

PE 11–5B

Payroll Tax Expense...	33,178.10	
Social Security Tax Payable		25,650.00
Medicare Tax Payable		6,750.00
State Unemployment Tax Payable		677.70*
Federal Unemployment Tax Payable		100.40**

*$12,550 × 5.4%
**$12,550 × 0.8%

PE 11–6A

a.	Vacation Pay Expense..	17,500	
	Vacation Pay Payable..		17,500
	Vacation pay accrued for the period.		
b.	Pension Expense...	12,600	
	Cash...		12,600
	To record pension contribution, 7% × $180,000.		

PE 11–6B

a.	Vacation Pay Expense..	52,300	
	Vacation Pay Payable..		52,300
	Vacation pay accrued for the period.		
b.	Pension Expense...	123,000	
	Cash...		100,000
	Unfunded Pension Liability		23,000
	To record pension cost and funding.		

PE 11–7A

a.

Mar. 31	Product Warranty Expense..................................		39,150	
	Product Warranty Payable			39,150
	To record warranty expense for March, 4.5% × $870,000.			

b.

Oct. 4	Product Warranty Payable.................................		520	
	Supplies			420
	Wages Payable			100

PE 11–7B

a.

June 30	Product Warranty Expense..................................		24,000	
	Product Warranty Payable			24,000
	To record warranty expense for June, 5% × $480,000.			

b.

Aug. 16	Product Warranty Payable.................................		90	
	Cash			90

EXERCISES

Ex. 11–1

Current liabilities:	
Federal income taxes payable	$ 49,000*
Advances on magazine subscriptions	299,250**
Total current liabilities	$ 348,250

    *$140,000 × 35%
    **11,400 × $35 × 9/12 = $299,250

The nine months of unfilled subscriptions are a current liability because Rock On received payment prior to providing the magazines.

Ex. 11–2

a.	1.	Merchandise Inventory	246,875	
		Interest Expense	3,125*	
		Notes Payable		250,000
	2.	Notes Payable	250,000	
		Cash		250,000
b.	1.	Notes Receivable	250,000	
		Sales		246,875
		Interest Revenue		3,125*
	2.	Cash	250,000	
		Notes Receivable		250,000

*$250,000 × 5% × 90/360

Ex. 11–3

a. $120,000 × 6% × 90/360 = $1,800 for each alternative.

b. (1) $120,000 simple-interest note: $120,000 proceeds

   (2) $120,000 discounted note: $120,000 − $1,800 interest = $118,200 proceeds

c. Alternative (1) is more favorable to the borrower. This can be verified by comparing the effective interest rates for each loan as follows:

   Situation (1): 6% effective interest rate

   ($1,800 × 360/90) / $120,000 = 6%

   Situation (2): 6.09% effective interest rate

   ($1,800 × 360/90) / $118,200 = 6.09%

The effective interest rate is higher for the second loan because the creditor lent only $118,200 in return for $1,800 interest over 90 days. In the simple-interest loan, the creditor must lend $120,000 for 90 days to earn the same $1,800 interest.

Ex. 11–4

a.	Accounts Payable	15,000	
	Notes Payable		15,000
b.	Notes Payable	15,000	
	Interest Expense	175*	
	Cash		15,175

*$15,000 × 7% × 60/360 = $175

Ex. 11–5

a.	Accounts Payable	78,400	
	Interest Expense	1,600*	
	Notes Payable		80,000

*$80,000 × 8% × 90/360

b.	Notes Payable	80,000	
	Cash		80,000

Ex. 11–6

a. June 30
Building	690,000	
Land	250,000	
Note Payable		700,000
Cash		240,000

b. Dec. 31
Note Payable	35,000	
Interest Expense ($700,000 × 8% × 1/2)	28,000	
Cash		63,000

c. June 30
Note Payable	35,000	
Interest Expense ($665,000 × 8% × 1/2)	26,600	
Cash		61,600

Ex. 11–7

a. $10,714,000, or the amount disclosed as the current portion of long-term debt.

b. The current liabilities increased by $714,000 ($10,714,000 – $10,000,000).

c. $64,286,000 ($75,000,000 – $10,714,000)

Ex. 11–8

a.
Regular pay (40 hrs. × $22)	$ 880
Overtime pay (10 hrs. × $33)	330
Gross pay	$1,210

b.
Gross pay		$1,210.00
Less: Social security tax (6.0% × $1,210)	$ 72.60	
Medicare tax (1.5% × $1,210)	18.15	
Federal withholding	236.00	326.75
Net pay		$ 883.25

Ex. 11–9

	Consultant	Computer Programmer	Administrator
Regular earnings	$2,400.00	$1,600.00	$ 880.00
Overtime earnings		480.00	165.00
Gross pay	$2,400.00	$2,080.00	$1,045.00
Less: Social security tax...................	$ 0.00[1]	$ 84.00[2]	$ 62.70[3]
Medicare tax	36.00	31.20	15.68
Federal income tax withheld[4]..	535.39	463.43	137.30
	$ 571.39	$ 578.63	$ 215.68
Net pay..	$1,828.61	$1,501.37	$ 829.32

[1]Gross pay exceeds $100,000, so there is no social security tax withheld.
[2][($100,000 − $98,600) × 6%] = $84.00
[3]$1,045 × 6% = $62.70
[4]The federal income tax withheld is determined from applying the calculation procedure associated with Exhibit 3 in the chapter, as follows:

Withholding supporting calculations:

	Consultant	Computer Programmer	Administrator
Gross weekly pay	$2,400.00	$2,080.00	$1,045.00
Number of withholding allowances	1	0	3
Multiplied by: Value of one allowance .	× $63.00	× $63.00	× $63.00
Amount to be deducted.........................	$ 63.00	$ 0.00	$ 189.00
Amount subject to withholding	$2,337.00	$2,080.00	$ 856.00
Initial withholding from wage bracket in Exhibit 3	$ 275.55	$ 275.55	$ 78.30
Plus: Bracket percentage over bracket excess.................................	259.84[5]	187.88[6]	59.00[7]
Amount withheld....................................	$ 535.39	$ 463.43	$ 137.30

[5]28% × ($2,337 − $1,409)
[6]28% × ($2,080 − $1,409)
[7]25% × ($856 − $620)

Ex. 11–10

a. Summary: (1) $220,520; (3) $260,000; (8) $2,485; (12) $61,900

Details:

	Net amount paid	$184,000
	Total deductions	76,000
(3)	Total earnings	$260,000
	Overtime	39,480
(1)	Regular	$220,520

	Total deductions		$ 76,000
	Social security tax	$ 15,250	
	Medicare tax	3,900	
	Income tax withheld	46,590	
	Medical insurance	7,775	73,515
(8)	Union dues		$ 2,485

	Total earnings		$260,000
	Factory wages	$138,900	
	Office salaries	59,200	198,100
(12)	Sales salaries		$ 61,900

b.

Factory Wages Expense	138,900	
Sales Salaries Expense	61,900	
Office Salaries Expense	59,200	
Social Security Tax Payable		15,250
Medicare Tax Payable		3,900
Employees Income Tax Payable		46,590
Medical Insurance Payable		7,775
Union Dues Payable		2,485
Salaries Payable		184,000

c.

Salaries Payable	184,000	
Cash		184,000

d. The amount of social security tax withheld, $15,250, is $350 less than 6.0% of the total earnings of $260,000. This indicates that the cumulative earnings of some employees exceed $100,000. Therefore, it is unlikely that this payroll was paid during the first few weeks of the calendar year.

Ex. 11–11

a.

Social security tax (6% × $350,000)		$21,000
Medicare tax (1.5% × $420,000)		6,300
State unemployment (4.3% × $14,000)		602
Federal unemployment (0.8% × $14,000)		112
		$28,014

b.

Payroll Tax Expense	28,014	
Social Security Tax Payable		21,000
Medicare Tax Payable		6,300
State Unemployment Tax Payable		602
Federal Unemployment Tax Payable		112

Ex. 11–12

a.

Salaries Expense	690,000	
Social Security Tax Payable		32,700
Medicare Tax Payable		10,350
Employees Federal Income Tax Payable		138,700
Salaries Payable		508,250

b.

Payroll Tax Expense	44,610	
Social Security Tax Payable		32,700
Medicare Tax Payable		10,350
State Unemployment Tax Payable		1,352*
Federal Unemployment Tax Payable		208**

 *5.2% × $26,000
**0.8% × $26,000

Ex. 11–13

a. Wages Expense 356,000
    Social Security Tax Payable   17,100
    Medicare Tax Payable   5,340
    Employees Federal Income Tax Payable...............   66,900
    Wages Payable   266,660
        To record unfunded pension cost for the quarter.

b. Payroll Tax Expense.. 23,556
    Social Security Tax Payable   17,100
    Medicare Tax Payable   5,340
    State Unemployment Tax Payable 972*
    Federal Unemployment Tax Payable 144**

 *5.4% × $18,000
**0.8% × $18,000

Ex. 11–14

Nashville Sounds does have an internal control procedure that should detect the payroll error. Before funds are transferred from the regular bank account to the payroll account, the owner authorizes a voucher for the total amount of the week's payroll. The owner should catch the error, since the extra 360 hours will cause the weekly payroll to be substantially higher than usual.

Ex. 11–15

a. Inappropriate. Each employee should record his or her own time out for lunch. Under the current procedures, one employee could clock in several employees who are still out to lunch. The company would be paying employees for more time than they actually worked.

b. Inappropriate. Payroll should be informed when any employee is terminated. A supervisor or other individual could continue to clock in and out for the terminated employee and collect the extra paycheck.

c. Appropriate. All changes to the payroll system, including wage rate increases, should be authorized by someone outside the Payroll Department.

d. Appropriate. The use of a special payroll account assists in preventing fraud and makes it easier to reconcile the company's bank accounts.

e. Inappropriate. Access to the check-signing machine should be restricted.

Ex. 11–16

Super Sales Stores Inc. should not compute and report payroll taxes according to its fiscal year. Rather, employers are required to compute and report all payroll taxes on the calendar-year basis, regardless of the fiscal year they may use for financial reporting purposes. Thus, social security and FUTA maximum earnings limitations apply to the calendar-year payroll.

Ex. 11–17

Vacation Pay Expense	4,580	
Vacation Pay Payable		4,580
Vacation pay accrued for January, $54,960 × 1/12.		

Ex. 11–18

a.	Dec. 31	Pension Expense..	87,500	
		Unfunded Pension Liability		87,500
		To record quarterly pension cost.		
b.	Jan. 15	Unfunded Pension Liability..........................	87,500	
		Cash		87,500

Ex. 11–19

The $2,096 million unfunded pension liability is the approximate amount of the pension obligation that exceeds the value of the accumulated net assets of the pension plan. Apparently, Procter & Gamble has underfunded its plan relative to the actuarial obligation that has accrued over time. This can occur when the company contributes less to the plan than the annual pension cost.

The obligation grows yearly by the amount of the periodic pension cost. Thus, the periodic pension cost is an actuarial measure of the amount of pension earned by employees during the year. The annual pension cost is determined by making actuarial assumptions about employee life expectancies, employee turnover, expected compensation levels, and interest.

Ex. 11–20

a. Product Warranty Expense 1,700
     Product Warranty Payable 1,700
         To record warranty expense for January,
          2% × $85,000.

b. Product Warranty Payable.. 345
     Supplies.. 210
     Wages Payable.. 135

Ex. 11–21

a. The warranty liability represents estimated outstanding automobile warranty claims. Of these claims, $12,953 million is estimated to be due during 2006, while the remainder ($7,359 million) is expected to be paid after 2006. The distinction between short-term and long-term liabilities is important to creditors in order to accurately evaluate the near-term cash demands on the business, relative to the quick current assets and other longer-term demands.

b. Product Warranty Expense 10,502,000,000
     Product Warranty Payable 10,502,000,000

$$\$21,810 + X - \$12,000 = \$20,312$$
$$X = \$20,312 - \$21,810 + \$12,000$$
$$X = \$10,502 \text{ million}$$

Ex. 11–22

a. Damage Awards and Fines 710,000
     EPA Fines Payable... 560,000
     Litigation Claims Payable 150,000

Note to Instructors: The "damage awards and fines" would be disclosed on the income statement under "Other expenses."

b. The company experienced a hazardous materials spill at one of its plants during the previous period. This spill has resulted in a number of lawsuits to which the company is a party. The Environmental Protection Agency (EPA) has fined the company $560,000, which the company is contesting in court. Although the company does not admit fault, legal counsel believes that the fine payment is probable. In addition, an employee has sued the company. A $150,000 out-of-court settlement has been reached with the employee. The EPA fine and out-of-court settlement have been recognized as an expense for the period. There is one other outstanding lawsuit related to this incident. Counsel does not believe that the lawsuit has merit. Other lawsuits and unknown liabilities may arise from this incident.

Ex. 11–23

a. Quick Ratio = $\dfrac{\text{Quick Assets}}{\text{Current Liabilities}}$

December 31, 2007: $\dfrac{\$205,000 + \$245,000}{\$375,000} = 1.20$

December 31, 2008: $\dfrac{\$140,000 + \$250,000}{\$390,000} = 1.0$

b. The quick ratio decreased between the two balance sheet dates. The major reason is a significant increase in inventory. Cash also declined, possibly to purchase the inventory. As a result, quick assets actually declined, while the current liabilities increased. The quick ratio for December 31, 2008, is not yet at an alarming level. However, the trend suggests that the firm's current asset (working capital) management should be watched closely.

Ex. 11–24

a.

	Apple Computer, Inc.	Dell Inc.
Quick Ratio	2.63	0.83

$$\text{Quick Ratio} = \frac{\text{Quick Assets}}{\text{Current Liabilities}}$$

Apple Computer, Inc.:

$$\text{Quick Ratio} = \frac{\$10,300 - \$165 - \$979}{\$3,484} = 2.63$$

Dell Inc.:

$$\text{Quick Ratio} = \frac{\$17,706 - \$576 - \$3,983}{\$15,927} = 0.83$$

b. It is clear that Apple Computer's short-term liquidity is stronger than Dell's. Apple's quick ratio is 217% [(2.63 − 0.83) / 0.83] higher. Apple has a much stronger relative cash and short-term investment position than does Dell. Apple's cash and short-term investments are over 80% of total current assets (237% of current liabilities), compared to Dell's 51% of total current assets (57% of current liabilities). In addition, Dell's relative accounts payable position is larger than Apple's, indicating the possibility that Dell has longer supplier payment terms than does Apple. A quick ratio of 2.63 for Apple suggests ample flexibility to make strategic investments with its excess cash, while a quick ratio of 0.83 for Dell indicates an efficient but tight quick asset management policy.

PROBLEMS

Prob. 11–1A

1.

Apr.	7	Cash..	36,000	
		Notes Payable..		36,000
May	10	Equipment..	122,500	
		Interest Expense ($125,000 × 120/360 × 6%)	2,500	
		Notes Payable..		125,000
June	6	Notes Payable	36,000	
		Interest Expense ($36,000 × 60/360 × 8%)	480	
		Notes Payable..		36,000
		Cash		480
July	6	Notes Payable	36,000	
		Interest Expense ($36,000 × 30/360 × 9%)	270	
		Cash		36,270
Aug.	3	Merchandise Inventory................................	15,000	
		Accounts Payable—Hamilton Co.		15,000
Sept.	2	Accounts Payable—Hamilton Co.	15,000	
		Notes Payable..		15,000
	7	Notes Payable	125,000	
		Cash		125,000
Nov.	1	Notes Payable	15,000	
		Interest Expense ($15,000 × 60/360 × 6%)	150	
		Cash		15,150
	15	Store Equipment..	150,000	
		Notes Payable..		94,500
		Cash		55,500
Dec.	15	Notes Payable	13,500	
		Interest Expense ($13,500 × 8% × 30/360)	90	
		Cash		13,590
	21	Litigation Loss	30,000	
		Litigation Claims Payable.............................		30,000

Prob. 11–1A   Concluded

2. a. Product Warranty Expense   8,400
        Product Warranty Payable   8,400
            Warranty expense for the current year.

    b. Interest Expense   828
        Interest Payable   828
            Interest on notes, $13,500 × 8% × 46/360 × 6.

Prob. 11–2A

1. a. Dec. 30 Sales Salaries Expense................................. 320,000
                 Warehouse Salaries Expense..................... 84,500
                 Office Salaries Expense............................. 155,500
                     Employees Income Tax Payable   109,760
                     Social Security Tax Payable   28,560
                     Medicare Tax Payable   8,400
                     Bond Deductions Payable   16,400
                     Group Insurance Payable   24,690
                     Salaries Payable   372,190

   b. Dec. 30 Payroll Tax Expense.................................. 37,650
                     Social Security Tax Payable   28,560
                     Medicare Tax Payable   8,400
                     State Unemployment Tax Payable ....   570[1]
                     Federal Unemployment Tax Payable .....   120[2]

           [1]$15,000 × 3.8%
           [2]$15,000 × 0.8%

2. a. Dec. 30 Sales Salaries Expense................................. 320,000
                 Warehouse Salaries Expense..................... 84,500
                 Office Salaries Expense............................. 155,500
                     Employees Income Tax Payable   109,760
                     Social Security Tax Payable ....   33,600[3]
                     Medicare Tax Payable ....   8,400[4]
                     Bond Deductions Payable   16,400
                     Group Insurance Payable   24,690
                     Salaries Payable   367,150

           [3]$560,000 × 6%
           [4]$560,000 × 1.5%

   b. Jan. 4 Payroll Tax Expense.................................. 67,760
                     Social Security Tax Payable   33,600
                     Medicare Tax Payable   8,400
                     State Unemployment Tax Payable ....   21,280[5]
                     Federal Unemployment Tax Payable .....   4,480[6]

           [5]$560,000 × 3.8%
           [6]$560,000 × 0.8%

Prob. 11–3A

1.

Employee	Gross Earnings**	Federal Income Tax Withheld	Social Security Tax Withheld	Medicare Tax Withheld
Arnold	$ 44,800	$ 9,856	$ 2,688	$ 672
Charles	103,200	24,768	6,000*	1,548
Gillam	50,000	9,500	3,000	750
Nelson	45,600	8,208	2,736	684
Quinn	6,600	1,221	396	99
Ramirez	27,200	4,760	1,632	408
Wu	105,800	26,450	6,000*	1,587
			$22,452	$5,748

*$100,000 maximum × 6%

**The gross earnings are determined by multiplying the monthly earnings by the number of months of employment based upon the date of hire.

2. a.   Social security tax paid by employer $22,452.00

   b.   Medicare tax paid by employer 5,748.00

   c.   Earnings subject to unemployment compensation tax, $9,000 for all employees except Quinn, who has only $6,600 in gross earnings. Thus, total earnings subject to SUTA and FUTA are $60,600 [(6 × $9,000) + $6,600]. State unemployment compensation tax: $60,600 × 3.8% 2,302.80

   d.   Federal unemployment compensation tax: $60,600 × 0.8% .. 484.80

   e.   Total payroll tax expense $30,987.60

Prob. 11–4A

1. 2008
Dec. 12 Sales Salaries Expense................................. 3,666.50
Office Salaries Expense............................... 2,600.00
Delivery Salaries Expense 1,959.00
Social Security Tax Payable.................. 493.53
Medicare Tax Payable........................... 123.39
Employees Income Tax Payable 1,402.06
Medical Insurance Payable.................... 469.20
Salaries Payable 5,737.32

2. Dec. 12 Salaries Payable 5,737.32
Cash 5,737.32

3. Dec. 12 Payroll Tax Expense.................................... 664.92
Social Security Tax Payable.................. 493.53
Medicare Tax Payable........................... 123.39
State Unemployment Tax Payable 38.40*
Federal Unemployment Tax Payable 9.60**

*$1,200 × 3.2%
**$1,200 × 0.8%

4. Dec. 15 Employees Income Tax Payable.................. 1,402.06
Social Security Tax Payable 987.06
Medicare Tax Payable 246.78
Cash 2,635.90

Prob. 11-5A

PAYROLL FOR WEEK ENDING *December 7, 2008*

1.

	EARNINGS				DEDUCTIONS					PAID		ACCOUNTS DEBITED	
Name	Total Hours	Regular	Overtime	Total	Social Security Tax	Medicare Tax	Federal Income Tax	U.S. Savings Bonds	Total	Net Amount	Ck. No.	Sales Salaries Expense	Office Salaries Expense
A	38	608		608	36.48	9.12	109.44		155.04	452.96	981	608	
B	44	1,000	150	1,150	69.00	17.25	241.50	20.00	347.75	802.25	982	1,150	
C	46	1,200	270	1,470	88.20	22.05	338.10	20.00	468.35	1,001.65	983	1,470	
D	40	480		480	28.80	7.20	81.60	35.00	152.60	327.40	984	480	
E	30	300		300	18.00	4.50	36.00	10.00	68.50	231.50	985	300	
F				1,100	66.00	16.50	242.00		324.50	775.50	986		1,100
G	41	960	36	996	59.76	14.94	199.20		273.90	722.10	987	996	
H				2,200		33.00	550.00	90.00	673.00	1,527.00	988		2,200
I	48	720	216	936	56.16	14.04	187.20	10.00	267.40	668.60	989	936	
		5,268	672	9,240	422.40	138.60	1,985.04	185.00	2,731.04	6,508.96		5,940	3,300

2.

Sales Salaries Expense	5,940.00
Office Salaries Expense	3,300.00
Social Security Tax Payable	422.40
Medicare Tax Payable	138.60
Employees Federal Income Tax Payable	1,985.04
Bond Deductions Payable	185.00
Salaries Payable	6,508.96

657

Prob. 11–6A

1.

Dec.					
	1	Medical Insurance Payable		2,400	
		Cash			2,400
	2	Social Security Tax Payable		5,888	
		Medicare Tax Payable		1,550	
		Employees Federal Income Tax Payable		9,555	
		Cash			16,993
	3	Bond Deductions Payable		2,000	
		Cash			2,000
	14	Sales Salaries Expense		31,000	
		Officers Salaries Expense		14,800	
		Office Salaries Expense		5,600	
		Social Security Tax Payable			2,827
		Medicare Tax Payable			771
		Employees Federal Income Tax Payable			9,149
		Employees State Income Tax Payable			2,313
		Bond Deductions Payable			1,000
		Medical Insurance Payable			400
		Salaries Payable			34,940
	14	Salaries Payable		34,940	
		Cash			34,940
	14	Payroll Tax Expense		3,903	
		Social Security Tax Payable			2,827
		Medicare Tax Payable			771
		State Unemployment Tax Payable			250
		Federal Unemployment Tax Payable			55
	17	Social Security Tax Payable		5,654	
		Medicare Tax Payable		1,542	
		Employees Federal Income Tax Payable		9,149	
		Cash			16,345

Prob. 11–6A Continued

Dec. 28	Sales Salaries Expense	31,500	
	Officers Salaries Expense	15,000	
	Office Salaries Expense	5,500	
	Social Security Tax Payable		2,808
	Medicare Tax Payable		780
	Employees Federal Income Tax Payable		9,256
	Employees State Income Tax Payable		2,340
	Bond Deductions Payable		1,000
	Salaries Payable		35,816
28	Salaries Payable	35,816	
	Cash		35,816
28	Payroll Tax Expense	3,738	
	Social Security Tax Payable		2,808
	Medicare Tax Payable		780
	State Unemployment Tax Payable		120
	Federal Unemployment Tax Payable		30
30	Employees State Income Tax Payable	13,950	
	Cash		13,950
30	Bond Deductions Payable	2,000	
	Cash		2,000
31	Pension Expense	65,000	
	Cash		55,700
	Unfunded Pension Liability		9,300

2.

Dec. 31	Sales Salaries Expense	3,150	
	Officers Salaries Expense	1,500	
	Office Salaries Expense	550	
	Salaries Payable		5,200
	Accrued wages for the period.		
31	Vacation Pay Expense	13,200	
	Vacation Pay Payable		13,200
	Vacation pay accrued for the period.		

Prob. 11–1B

1.

Feb. 15	Merchandise Inventory..	120,000	
	Accounts Payable—Ranier Co.		120,000
Mar. 17	Accounts Payable—Ranier Co.	120,000	
	Notes Payable..		120,000
Apr. 16	Notes Payable	120,000	
	Interest Expense ($120,000 × 30/360 × 5%)	500	
	Cash		120,500
July 15	Cash..	180,000	
	Notes Payable..		180,000
25	Tools	131,850	
	Interest Expense ($135,000 × 120/360 × 7%)	3,150	
	Notes Payable..		135,000
Oct. 13	Notes Payable	180,000	
	Interest Expense ($180,000 × 90/360 × 6%)	2,700	
	Notes Payable..		180,000
	Cash		2,700
Nov. 12	Notes Payable	180,000	
	Interest Expense ($180,000 × 30/360 × 9%)	1,350	
	Cash		181,350
22	Notes Payable	135,000	
	Cash		135,000
Dec. 1	Office Equipment...	40,000	
	Notes Payable..		30,000
	Cash		10,000
17	Litigation Loss	56,000	
	Litigation Claims Payable		56,000
31	Notes Payable	3,000	
	Interest Expense ($3,000 × 6% × 30/360)	15	
	Cash		3,015

Prob. 11–1B Concluded

2. a. Product Warranty Expense 21,410
        Product Warranty Payable   21,410
        Warranty expense for the current year.

  b. Interest Expense 135
        Interest Payable   135
        Interest on notes, $3,000 × 6% × 30/360 × 9.

Prob. 11–2B

1. a. Dec. 30

Sales Salaries Expense	162,400	
Warehouse Salaries Expense	54,200	
Office Salaries Expense	83,400	
Employees Income Tax Payable		52,800
Social Security Tax Payable		16,200
Medicare Tax Payable		4,500
Bond Deductions Payable		6,500
Group Insurance Payable		5,600
Salaries Payable		214,400

b. Dec. 30

Payroll Tax Expense	21,450	
Social Security Tax Payable		16,200
Medicare Tax Payable		4,500
State Unemployment Tax Payable		630[1]
Federal Unemployment Tax Payable		120[2]

[1]$15,000 × 4.2%
[2]$15,000 × 0.8%

2. a. Dec. 30

Sales Salaries Expense	162,400	
Warehouse Salaries Expense	54,200	
Office Salaries Expense	83,400	
Employees Income Tax Payable		52,800
Social Security Tax Payable		18,000[3]
Medicare Tax Payable		4,500[4]
Bond Deductions Payable		6,500
Group Insurance Payable		5,600
Salaries Payable		212,600

[3]$300,000 × 6%
[4]$300,000 × 1.5%

b. Jan. 5

Payroll Tax Expense	37,500	
Social Security Tax Payable		18,000
Medicare Tax Payable		4,500
State Unemployment Tax Payable		12,600[5]
Federal Unemployment Tax Payable		2,400[6]

[5]$300,000 × 4.2%
[6]$300,000 × 0.8%

Prob. 11–3B

1.

Employee	Gross Earnings	Federal Income Tax Withheld	Social Security Tax Withheld	Medicare Tax Withheld
Alvarez	$110,400	$27,600	$ 6,000*	$1,656
Collins	5,000	750	300	75
Felix	36,000	5,760	2,160	540
Lydall	24,200	4,356	1,452	363
Penn	105,600	25,344	6,000*	1,584
Song	40,800	7,344	2,448	612
Walker	21,000	2,520	1,260	315
			$19,620	$5,145

*$100,000 maximum × 6%

2. a. Social security tax paid by employer... $19,620

    b. Medicare tax paid by employer... 5,145

    c. Earnings subject to unemployment compensation tax,
       $7,000 for all employees except Collins, who has only
       $5,000 in gross earnings. Thus, total earnings subject
       to SUTA and FUTA are $47,000 [(6 × $7,000) + $5,000].
       State unemployment compensation tax: $47,000 × 4.8%........... 2,256

    d. Federal unemployment compensation tax: $47,000 × 0.8%....... 376

    e. Total payroll tax expense... $27,397

Prob. 11–4B

1. 2008
   Dec. 12 Sales Salaries Expense............................... 3,666.50
            Office Salaries Expense.............................. 2,600.00
            Delivery Salaries Expense 1,959.00
                 Social Security Tax Payable...................   493.53
                 Medicare Tax Payable.............................   123.39
                 Employees Income Tax Payable 1,402.06
                 Medical Insurance Payable....................   469.20
                 Salaries Payable 5,737.32

2. Dec. 12 Salaries Payable 5,737.32
                 Cash 5,737.32

3. Dec. 12 Payroll Tax Expense.................................... 654.32
                 Social Security Tax Payable...................   493.53
                 Medicare Tax Payable.............................   123.39
                 State Unemployment Tax Payable 30.60*
                 Federal Unemployment Tax Payable 6.80**

            *$850 × 3.6%
            **$850 × 0.8%

4. Dec. 15 Employees Income Tax Payable.................. 1,402.06
            Social Security Tax Payable 987.06
            Medicare Tax Payable 246.78
                 Cash 2,635.90

Prob. 11–5B

1.

PAYROLL FOR WEEK ENDING December 7, 2008

Name	Total Hours	EARNINGS			DEDUCTIONS					PAID		ACCOUNTS DEBITED	
		Regular	Overtime	Total	Social Security Tax	Medicare Tax	Federal Income Tax	U.S. Savings Bonds	Total	Net Amount	Ck. No.	Sales Salaries Expense	Office Salaries Expense
M	52	1,440	648	2,088	125.28	31.32	480.24	50	686.84	1,401.16	826	2,088	
N		1,200		1,200	72.00	18.00	258.00		348.00	852.00	825		1,200
O	38	608		608	36.48	9.12	115.52	25	186.12	421.88	824	608	
P	44	740	111	851	51.06	12.77	178.71		242.54	608.46	823	851	
Q	40	800		800	48.00	12.00	168.00	15	243.00	557.00	822	800	
R				2,400		36.00	576.00	100	712.00	1,688.00	820		2,400
S	32	704		704	42.24	10.56	105.60		158.40	545.60	819	704	
T	46	1,120	252	1,372	82.32	20.58	301.84	40	444.74	927.26	818	1,372	
U	40	720		720	43.20	10.80	144.00	20	218.00	502.00	821	720	
		6,132	1,011	10,743	500.58	161.15	2,327.91	250	3,239.64	7,503.36		7,143	3,600

2.

Sales Salaries Expense	7,143.00
Office Salaries Expense	3,600.00
Social Security Tax Payable	500.58
Medicare Tax Payable	161.15
Employees Federal Income Tax Payable	2,327.91
Bond Deductions Payable	250.00
Salaries Payable	7,503.36

665

Prob. 11–6B

1.

Dec.	2	Bond Deductions Payable.....................................	3,000	
		Cash		3,000
	3	Social Security Tax Payable	8,032	
		Medicare Tax Payable	2,114	
		Employees Federal Income Tax Payable............	13,035	
		Cash		23,181
	14	Operations Salaries Expense	38,500	
		Officers Salaries Expense..................................	25,500	
		Office Salaries Expense	6,200	
		Social Security Tax Payable		3,931
		Medicare Tax Payable		1,053
		Employees Federal Income Tax Payable		12,496
		Employees State Income Tax Payable		3,159
		Bond Deductions Payable		1,500
		Medical Insurance Payable.............................		4,000
		Salaries Payable		44,061
	14	Salaries Payable	44,061	
		Cash		44,061
	14	Payroll Tax Expense..	5,358	
		Social Security Tax Payable		3,931
		Medicare Tax Payable		1,053
		State Unemployment Tax Payable		290
		Federal Unemployment Tax Payable		84
	17	Social Security Tax Payable	7,862	
		Medicare Tax Payable	2,106	
		Employees Federal Income Tax Payable............	12,496	
		Cash		22,464
	18	Medical Insurance Payable..................................	24,000	
		Cash		24,000

666

Prob. 11–6B   Continued

Dec. 28	Operations Salaries Expense	39,000	
	Officers Salaries Expense..................................	26,000	
	Office Salaries Expense	6,400	
	Social Security Tax Payable		3,856
	Medicare Tax Payable		1,071
	Employees Federal Income Tax Payable		12,709
	Employees State Income Tax Payable		3,213
	Bond Deductions Payable		1,500
	Salaries Payable		49,051
28	Salaries Payable	49,051	
	Cash		49,051
28	Payroll Tax Expense..	5,120	
	Social Security Tax Payable		3,856
	Medicare Tax Payable		1,071
	State Unemployment Tax Payable		155
	Federal Unemployment Tax Payable		38
30	Bond Deductions Payable..................................	3,000	
	Cash		3,000
30	Employees State Income Tax Payable................	19,054	
	Cash		19,054
31	Pension Expense..	45,000	
	Cash		43,000
	Unfunded Pension Liability		2,000

2.

Dec. 31	Operations Salaries Expense	3,900	
	Officers Salaries Expense..................................	2,600	
	Office Salaries Expense	640	
	Salaries Payable		7,140
	Accrued wages for the period.		
31	Vacation Pay Expense..	12,650	
	Vacation Pay Payable.....................................		12,650
	Vacation pay accrued for the period.		

COMPREHENSIVE PROBLEM 3

1.

Jan.	2	Petty Cash	1,400	
		Cash		1,400
Mar.	1	Office Supplies..	678	
		Miscellaneous Selling Expense..........................	389	
		Miscellaneous Administrative Expense.............	245	
		Cash		1,312
Apr.	5	Merchandise Inventory.................................	12,000	
		Accounts Payable.....................................		12,000
May	5	Accounts Payable..	12,000	
		Cash		12,000
	10	Cash...	7,755	
		Cash Short and Over	20	
		Sales...		7,775
June	2	Notes Receivable	60,000	
		Accounts Receivable—Stevens		60,000
Aug.	1	Cash...	60,840	
		Notes Receivable.....................................		60,000
		Interest Revenue		840*

*$60,000 \times 8.4\% \times 60/360 = \$840$

	3	Cash...	2,300	
		Allowance for Doubtful Accounts	200	
		Accounts Receivable—Jacobs		2,500
	28	Accounts Receivable—Jacobs..........................	200	
		Allowance for Doubtful Accounts		200
	28	Cash...	200	
		Accounts Receivable—Jacobs		200

Comp. Prob. 3   Continued

Sept. 2	Land	245,000	
	Interest Expense	5,000*	
	Notes Payable		250,000
	*$250,000 × 8% × 90/360		
Oct. 2	Cash	55,000	
	Notes Receivable	25,000	
	Accumulated Depreciation—Office Equipment .	10,000	
	Loss on Disposal of Fixed Assets	6,000	
	Office Equipment		96,000
Nov. 30	Sales Salaries Expense	58,200	
	Office Salaries Expense	29,600	
	Employees Federal Income Tax Payable		15,804
	Social Security Tax Payable		5,120
	Medicare Tax Payable		1,317
	Salaries Payable		65,559
30	Payroll Tax Expense	6,529	
	Social Security Tax Payable		5,120
	Medicare Tax Payable		1,317
	State Unemployment Tax Payable		76*
	Federal Unemployment Tax Payable		16**
	*$2,000 × 3.8%		
	**$2,000 × 0.8%		
Dec. 1	Notes Payable	250,000	
	Cash		250,000
30	Pension Expense	65,000	
	Cash		57,450
	Unfunded Pension Liability		7,550
	Pension cost of $65,000 funded at $57,450.		

Comp. Prob. 3   Continued

2.

HIRATA COMPANY
Bank Reconciliation
December 31, 2007

Balance according to bank statement		$123,200
Add deposit in transit, not recorded by bank.................		12,450
		$135,650
Deduct outstanding checks..		27,450
Adjusted balance		$108,200
Balance according to company's records......................		$108,680
Deduct:		
Bank service charges...	$280	
Error in recording check	200	480
Adjusted balance		$108,200

3.	Miscellaneous Administrative Expense	280	
	Accounts Payable	200	
	Cash...		480
4.	a. Uncollectible Accounts Expense	7,090	
	Allowance for Doubtful Accounts......................		7,090
	To record estimated uncollectible accounts,		
	$6,490 + $600.		
	b. Cost of Merchandise Sold.......................................	1,320	
	Merchandise Inventory		1,320
	To record inventory shrinkage.		
	c. Insurance Expense...	9,850	
	Prepaid Insurance		9,850
	To record expired insurance.		
	d. Office Supplies Expense...	1,580	
	Office Supplies		1,580
	To record supplies used during the period.		

e. Depreciation Expense—Buildings   7,600
    Depreciation Expense—Office Equipment.............   3,800
    Depreciation Expense—Store Equipment..............   11,250
        Accumulated Depreciation—Buildings   7,600
        Accumulated Depreciation—Office Equipment   3,800
        Accumulated Depreciation—Store Equipment.   11,250
            To record depreciation for the period.

    Computations:
        Buildings ($380,000 × 2%) .... $ 7,600
        Office Equipment
        [1/4 × 20% × ($90,000 – $14,000)]   3,800
        Store Equipment ($45,000 × 25%)......   11,250

f. Amortization Expense—Patents ($18,600 / 6)   3,100
        Patents   3,100
            To record patent amortization, $18,600/6 years.

g. Depletion Expense..   12,500
        Accumulated Depletion.....................................   12,500
            To record depletion,
                ($185,000/333,000 tons) × 22,500 tons

h. Vacation Pay Expense...   4,400
        Vacation Pay Payable...   4,400
            To record vacation pay for the period.

i. Product Warranty Expense....................................   19,900
        Product Warranty Payable..................................   19,900
            To record product warranty for the period,
                $796,000 × 2.5%.

j. Interest Receivable..   375
        Interest Revenue   375
            To record interest earned on note
                receivable, $25,000 × 6% × 90/360.

5.

HIRATA COMPANY
Balance Sheet
December 31, 2007

Assets

Current assets:

Petty cash		$ 1,400
Cash..		108,200
Notes receivable......................................		25,000
Accounts receivable.................................	$202,300	
Less allowance for doubtful accounts	6,490	195,810
Merchandise inventory—at cost		
(last-in, first-out).................................		140,600
Interest receivable...................................		375
Prepaid insurance		19,700
Office supplies...		7,100
Total current assets.............................		$ 498,185

Property, plant, and equipment:

	Cost	Accumulated Depreciation (Depletion)	Book Value	
Land..	$245,000		$245,000	
Buildings	380,000	$ 7,600	372,400	
Office equipment	90,000	3,800	86,200	
Store equipment	45,000	11,250	33,750	
Mineral rights...........................	185,000	12,500	172,500	
Total property, plant, and				
equipment.........................	$945,000	$35,150		909,850

Intangible assets:

Patents	15,500
Total assets	$1,423,535

Comp. Prob. 3   Continued

<u>Liabilities</u>

Current liabilities:

Social security tax payable..........................	$ 9,910	
Medicare tax payable	2,700	
Employees federal income tax payable.......................................	15,887	
State unemployment tax payable.......................................	42	
Federal unemployment tax payable.......................................	9	
Salaries payable	90,000	
Accounts payable.......................................	125,300	
Interest payable	3,000	
Product warranty payable........................	19,900	
Vacation pay payable	3,000	
Notes payable (current portion)	25,000	
Total current liabilities.........................		$ 294,748

Long-term liabilities:

Vacation pay payable	$ 1,400	
Unfunded pension liability........................	7,550	
Notes payable	75,000	
Total long-term liabilities.....................		83,950
Total liabilities..		$ 378,698

<u>Owner's Equity</u>

J. Goll, capital	1,044,837
Total liabilities and owner's equity	$1,423,535

Comp. Prob. 3 Concluded

6. The merchandise inventory destroyed was $137,800, determined as follows:

Merchandise inventory, January 1		$140,600
Purchases, January 1–February 7		38,000
Merchandise available for sale		$178,600
Sales, January 1–February 7..	$68,000	
Less estimated gross profit ($68,000 × 40%)...............	27,200	
Estimated cost of merchandise sold...........................		40,800
Estimated merchandise inventory destroyed..............		$137,800

SPECIAL ACTIVITIES

SA 11–1

The firm has no implicit or explicit contract to pay any bonus. The bonus is discretionary, even if the firm paid a two-week bonus for 10 straight years. The firm is not behaving unethically for reducing the bonus to one week—regardless of the reason. Dan Lanier, on the other hand, has taken things into his own hands. Sensing that he is being cheated, he tries to rectify the situation to his own advantage by working overtime that isn't required. This behavior could be considered fraudulent, even though Dan is actually present on the job during the overtime hours. The point is that the overtime is not required by the firm. Dan is incorrect in thinking that his behavior is justified because he did not receive the full two-week bonus. In fact, this behavior would not be justified even if he had a legitimate claim against the company. If he had a claim or grievance against the firm, then it should be handled by other procedural or legal means.

SA 11–2

Latiffah's interpretation of the pension issue is correct. The employee earns the pension during the working years. The pension is part of the employee's compensation that is deferred until retirement. Thus, Eclipse should record an expense equal to the amount of pension benefit earned by the employee for the period. This gives rise to the rather complex issue of estimating the amount of the pension expense. Greg indicates that the complexity of this calculation makes determining the annual pension expense impossible. This is not so. There are a number of mathematical and statistical approaches (termed "actuarial" approaches) that can reliably estimate the amount of benefits earned by the workforce for a given year.

As a side note, Greg's perspective can be summarized as "pay as you go." In his interpretation, there is no expense until a pension is paid to the retiree. Failing to account for pension promises when they are earned is not considered sound accounting.

SA 11–3

The CEO may have requested the two changes because they would reduce the amount of depreciation expense and increase the amount of reported earnings recorded in a particular year. Thus, the CEO's bonus would be higher due to the larger reported earnings. Straight-line depreciation recognizes lower depreciation expense in the earlier years of a truck's life. As long as the company is replacing trucks, straight-line depreciation will result in a lower depreciation expense and hence a higher income number. Adding 50% to the useful lives of trucks (such as increasing the life from six to nine years) would spread the recognition of depreciation expense over a longer life. Thus, depreciation expense would be lower and income higher in any particular year.

The CEO may request a change from one generally accepted accounting principle to another. Changing from double-declining-balance to straight-line depreciation is such a change. Though the CEO may be suggesting the change in order to influence the bonus, the change is acceptable, if Rogers Trucking Company's auditors agree with the change. The increase in the useful lives of the trucks is another matter. The useful lives of trucks should be based on objective analysis. An arbitrary increase in useful lives for all the trucks cannot be supported. Such a change could be viewed as a violation of generally accepted accounting principles.

SA 11–4

a. The so-called "underground economy" hides transactions from IRS scrutiny by conducting business with cash (not check or credit card, which leaves an audit trail). The intent in many such transactions is to evade income tax illegally. However, just because a transaction is in cash does not exempt it from taxation. McIntyre also appears to perform landscaping services on a cash basis to evade reporting income while paying employees with cash to avoid paying social security and Medicare payroll taxes. The IRS reports that nearly 86% of the persons convicted of evading employment taxes were sentenced to an average of 17 months in prison and ordered to make restitution to the government for the taxes evaded, plus interest and penalties.

b. Connor should respond that he would rather receive a payroll check as a normal employee does. Receiving cash as an employee, rather than a payroll check, subverts the U.S. tax system. That is, such cash payments do not include deductions for payroll taxes, as required by law. That is why, for example, cash tips must be formally reported to the IRS and subjected to payroll tax deductions by the employer. In addition, if Connor followed Jarrod's advice, Connor not only would be avoiding payroll deductions, but would also be underreporting income. This would subject Connor to potential fines and possible criminal prosecution for underreporting income.

Activity 11–5

The purpose of this activity is to familiarize students with retrieving and using IRS forms. Students should be able to find the three required forms without much difficulty. Encourage students to retrieve the forms from the IRS Web site, since this is a useful source for any IRS form or publication that they might need. IRS Web site forms come in *.pdf format*, which means an Adobe Acrobat Reader is necessary to open and print the file. This software is available as a free plug-in on most Internet browser software. However, some students may need to download a free version in order to open the forms. This is also a useful exercise, since many sophisticated forms on the Web require an Acrobat Reader.

The W-2 Form is the Annual Wage and Tax Statement transmitted by the employer to the IRS. The IRS uses this information to reconcile the taxpayer's reported income and withholding taxes with the taxpayer's tax return. Copies of the W-2 are provided for the employee's own records and for submitting with state and federal tax returns.

Form 940 is the Employer's Annual Federal Unemployment Tax Return. The FUTA tax is reported annually, while the 941 payroll taxes are reported quarterly to the IRS.

Form 941 is the Employer's Quarterly Federal Tax Return. This return is used to report federal withholding payroll taxes collected from employees and FICA taxes (both employee and employer portions) for the quarter.

SA 11–6

This activity does not require the student to research the contingency notes for the Altria Group. The contingency disclosure is extensive and complicated. Rather, the student should identify Altria Group's main business, and from this information determine the likely cause of the contingency disclosures.

a. Altria Group is a holding company for a number of businesses including Philip Morris and Kraft Foods, Inc. Thus, Altria's primary business (around 70%) is in the manufacture and distribution of tobacco products.

b. The health concerns surrounding tobacco products give rise to numerous lawsuits and legal actions against Altria. The notes to the financial statements include an extensive section describing the scope and status of these actions. As of December 31, 2005, Altria had over 265 cases pending, including seven class actions and 5 health care recovery actions (by state and federal governments). Altria's Web site provides a section describing some of these actions.

CHAPTER 12
ACCOUNTING FOR PARTNERSHIPS AND
LIMITED LIABILITY COMPANIES

QUESTION INFORMATION

Number	Objective	Description	Difficulty	Time	AACSB	AICPA	SS	GL
Q12-1	12-1		Easy	5 min	Analytic	FN-Measurement		
Q12-2	12-1		Easy	5 min	Analytic	FN-Measurement		
Q12-3	12-1		Easy	5 min	Analytic	FN-Measurement		
Q12-4	12-1		Easy	5 min	Analytic	FN-Measurement		
Q12-5	12-1		Easy	5 min	Analytic	FN-Measurement		
Q12-6	12-2		Easy	5 min	Analytic	FN-Measurement		
Q12-7	12-3		Easy	5 min	Analytic	FN-Measurement		
Q12-8	12-3		Easy	5 min	Analytic	FN-Measurement		
Q12-9	12-3		Easy	5 min	Analytic	FN-Measurement		
Q12-10	12-3		Easy	5 min	Analytic	FN-Measurement		
Q12-11	12-3		Easy	5 min	Analytic	FN-Measurement		
Q12-12	12-3		Easy	5 min	Analytic	FN-Measurement		
Q12-13	12-3		Easy	5 min	Analytic	FN-Measurement		
Q12-14	12-4		Easy	5 min	Analytic	FN-Measurement		
Q12-15	12-5		Easy	5 min	Analytic	FN-Measurement		
PE12-1A	12-2	Journalize partner's original investment	Easy	5 min	Analytic	FN-Measurement		
PE12-1B	12-2	Journalize partner's original investment	Easy	5 min	Analytic	FN-Measurement		
PE12-2A	12-2	Dividing partnership net income	Easy	5 min	Analytic	FN-Measurement		
PE12-2B	12-2	Dividing partnership net loss	Easy	5 min	Analytic	FN-Measurement		
PE12-3A	12-3	Revalue assets and contribute assets to a partnership	Easy	5 min	Analytic	FN-Measurement		
PE12-3B	12-3	Revalue assets and contribute assets to a partnership	Easy	5 min	Analytic	FN-Measurement		
PE12-4A	12-3	Partner bonus	Easy	5 min	Analytic	FN-Measurement		
PE12-4B	12-3	Partner bonus	Easy	5 min	Analytic	FN-Measurement		
PE12-5A	12-4	Liquidating partner-ships-gain	Easy	5 min	Analytic	FN-Measurement		
PE12-5B	12-4	Liquidating partner-ships-gain	Easy	5 min	Analytic	FN-Measurement		
PE12-6A	12-4	Liquidating partner-ships-deficiency	Easy	5 min	Analytic	FN-Measurement		
PE12-6B	12-4	Liquidating partner-ships-deficiency	Easy	5 min	Analytic	FN-Measurement		
Ex12-1	12-2	Record partner's original investment	Easy	10 min	Analytic	FN-Measurement		
Ex12-2	12-2	Record partner's original investment	Easy	10 min	Analytic	FN-Measurement		
Ex12-3	12-2	Dividing partnership income	Easy	15 min	Analytic	FN-Measurement		
Ex12-4	12-2	Dividing partnership income	Easy	15 min	Analytic	FN-Measurement		
Ex12-5	12-2	Dividing partnership net loss	Easy	5 min	Analytic	FN-Measurement		

Number	Objective	Description	Difficulty	Time	AACSB	AICPA	SS	GL
Ex12-6	12-2	Negotiating income-sharing ratio	Moderate	10 min	Analytic	FN-Measurement		
Ex12-7	12-2	Dividing LLC income	Easy	10 min	Analytic	FN-Measurement		
Ex12-8	12-2, 12-5	Dividing LLC net income and statement of member's equity	Moderate	15 min	Analytic	FN-Measurement		
Ex12-9	12-2, 12-3	Partner income and withdrawal journal entries	Moderate	15 min	Analytic	FN-Measurement		
Ex12-10	12-3	Admitting new partners	Easy	5 min	Analytic	FN-Measurement		
Ex12-11	12-3	Admitting new partners	Moderate	15 min	Analytic	FN-Measurement		
Ex12-12	12-3	Admitting new partners who buy an interest and contribute assets	Easy	10 min	Analytic	FN-Measurement		
Ex12-13	12-3	Admitting new partner who contributes assets	Easy	10 min	Analytic	FN-Measurement		
Ex12-14	12-3	Admitting new LLC member	Moderate	15 min	Analytic	FN-Measurement		
Ex12-15	12-3	Admitting new partner with bonus	Moderate	15 min	Analytic	FN-Measurement		
Ex12-16	12-2, 12-3, 12-5	Partner bonuses, statement of partners' equity	Moderate	20 min	Analytic	FN-Measurement	Exl	
Ex12-17	12-3	Withdrawal of partner	Moderate	15 min	Analytic	FN-Measurement		
Ex12-18	12-2, 12-3, 12-5	Statement of members' equity, admitting new member	Difficult	20 min	Analytic	FN-Measurement		
Ex12-19	12-4	Distribution of cash upon liquidation	Easy	5 min	Analytic	FN-Measurement		
Ex12-20	12-4	Distribution of cash upon liquidation	Easy	5 min	Analytic	FN-Measurement		
Ex12-21	12-4	Liquidating partnerships-capital deficiency	Easy	15 min	Analytic	FN-Measurement		
Ex12-22	12-4	Distribution of cash upon liquidation	Easy	10 min	Analytic	FN-Measurement		
Ex12-23	12-4	Liquidating partnerships-capital deficiency	Easy	5 min	Analytic	FN-Measurement		
Ex12-24	12-4	Statement of partnership equity	Moderate	15 min	Analytic	FN-Measurement	Exl	
Ex12-25	12-4	Statement of LLC liquidation	Moderate	15 min	Analytic	FN-Measurement	Exl	
Ex12-26	12-2, 12-5	Partnership entries and statement of partners' equity	Moderate	15 min	Analytic	FN-Measurement	Exl	
Ex12-27	FAI	Financial analysis and interpretation	Easy	10 min	Analytic	FN-Measurement		
Ex12-28	FAI	Financial analysis and interpretation	Easy	10 min	Analytic	FN-Measurement		
Pr12-1A	12-2	Entries and balance sheet for partnership	Moderate	1 hr	Analytic	FN-Measurement	Exl	KA
Pr12-2A	12-2	Dividing partnership income	Moderate	1 hr	Analytic	FN-Measurement		
Pr12-3A	12-2, 12-5	Financial statements for partnership	Difficult	1 1/2 hr	Analytic	FN-Measurement	Exl	

Number	Objective	Description	Difficulty	Time	AACSB	AICPA	SS	GL
Pr12-4A	12-3	Admitting new partner	Difficult	1 1/2 hr	Analytic	FN-Measurement		KA
Pr12-5A	12-4	Statement of partnership liquidation	Moderate	1 hr	Analytic	FN-Measurement	Exl	
Pr12-6A	12-4	Statement of partnership liquidation	Moderate	1 hr	Analytic	FN-Measurement	Exl	
Pr12-1B	12-2	Entries and balance sheet for partnership	Moderate	1 hr	Analytic	FN-Measurement	Exl	KA
Pr12-2B	12-2	Dividing partnership income	Moderate	1 hr	Analytic	FN-Measurement		
Pr12-3B	12-2, 12-5	Financial statements for partnership	Difficult	1 1/2 hr	Analytic	FN-Measurement	Exl	
Pr12-4B	12-3	Admitting new partner	Difficult	1 1/2 hr	Analytic	FN-Measurement		KA
Pr12-5B	12-4	Statement of partnership liquidation	Moderate	1 hr	Analytic	FN-Measurement	Exl	
Pr12-6B	12-4	Statement of partnership liquidation	Moderate	1 hr	Analytic	FN-Measurement	Exl	
SA12-1	12-1	Partnership agreement	Easy	10 min	Ethics	BB-Industry		
SA12-2	12-2	Dividing partnership income	Easy	10 min	Analytic	FN-Measurement		
SA12-3	FAI	Revenue per employee	Moderate	20 min	Analytic	FN-Measurement		
SA12-4	FAI	Revenue per employee	Moderate	20 min	Analytic	FN-Measurement		
SA12-5	12-1	Partnership agreement	Easy	10 min	Analytic	FN-Measurement		

EYE OPENERS

1. Proprietorship: Ease of formation and nontaxable entity.

   Partnership: Expanded owner expertise and capital, nontaxable entity, and ease of formation.

   Limited liability company: Limited liability to owners, expanded access to capital, nontaxable entity, and ease of formation.

2. The disadvantages of a partnership are its life is limited, each partner has unlimited liability, one partner can bind the partnership to contracts, and raising large amounts of capital is more difficult for a partnership than a limited liability company.

3. Yes. A partnership may incur losses in excess of the total investment of all partners. The division of losses among the partners would be made according to their agreement. In addition, because of the unlimited liability of each partner for partnership debts, a particular partner may actually lose a greater amount than his or her capital balance.

4. The partnership agreement (partnership) or operating agreement (LLC) establishes the income-sharing ratio among the partners (members), amounts to be invested, and buy-sell agreements between the partners (members). In addition, for an LLC the operating agreement specifies if the LLC is owner-managed or manager-managed.

5. Equally.

6. No. Maholic would have to bear his share of losses. In the absence of any agreement as to division of net income or net loss, his share would be one-third. In addition, because of the unlimited liability of each partner, Maholic may lose more than one-third of the losses if one partner is unable to absorb his share of the losses.

7. The delivery equipment should be recorded at $10,000, the valuation agreed upon by the partners.

8. The accounts receivable should be recorded by a debit of $150,000 to Accounts Receivable and a credit of $15,000 to Allowance for Doubtful Accounts.

9. Yes. Partnership net income is divided according to the income-sharing ratio, regardless of the amount of the withdrawals by the partners. Therefore, it is very likely that the partners' monthly withdrawals from a partnership will not exactly equal their shares of net income.

10. a. Debit the partner's drawing account and credit Cash.

    b. No. Payments to partners and the division of net income are separate. The amount of one does not affect the amount of the other.

    c. Debit the income summary account for the amount of the net income and credit the partners' capital accounts for their respective shares of the net income.

11. a. By purchase of an interest, the capital interest of the new partner is obtained from the old partner, and neither the total assets nor the total equity of the partnership is affected.

    b. By investment, both the total assets and the total equity of the partnership are increased.

12. It is important to state all partnership assets in terms of current prices at the time of the admission of a new partner because failure to do so might result in participation by the new partner in gains or losses attributable to the period prior to admission to the partnership. To illustrate, assume that A and B share net income and net loss equally and operate a partnership that owns land recorded at and costing $20,000. C is admitted to the partnership, and the three partners share in income equally. The day after C is admitted to the partnership, the land is sold for $35,000 and, since the land was not revalued, C receives one-third distribution of the $15,000 gain. In this case, C participates in the gain attributable to the period prior to admission to the partnership.

13. A new partner who is expected to improve the fortunes (income) of the partnership, through such things as reputation or skill, might be given equity in excess of the amount invested to join the partnership.

14. a. Losses and gains on realization are divided among partners in the income-sharing ratio.

    b. Cash is distributed to the partners according to their ownership claims, as indicated by the credit balances in their capital accounts, after taking into consideration the potential deficiencies that may result from the inability to collect from a deficient partner.

15. The statement of partners' equity (for a partnership) and statement of members' equity (for an LLC) both show the material changes in owner's equity for each ownership person or class for a specified period.

PRACTICE EXERCISES

PE 12–1A

Cash	58,000	
Inventory	45,000	
Land	68,000	
Notes Payable		20,000
Conway Shelton, Capital		151,000

PE 12–1B

Cash	15,000	
Accounts Receivable	22,000	
Patent	280,000	
Accounts Payable		8,000
Allowance for Doubtful Accounts		1,000
Ashley Wells, Capital		308,000

PE 12–2A

Distributed to Adkins:

Annual salary	$ 49,000
Interest (12% × $120,000)	14,400
Remaining income	55,900*
Total distributed to Adkins	$119,300

*[$180,000 – $49,000 – $14,400 – (12% × $40,000)] × 50%

PE 12–2B

Distributed to Lodge:

Annual salary	$ 54,000
Interest (10% × $100,000)	10,000
Deduct excess of allowances over income	(16,000)*
Total distributed to Lodge	$ 48,000

*[$60,000 – $54,000 – $10,000 – (10% × $200,000)] × 2/3

PE 12–3A

a.	Equipment...	15,000	
	Stuart Townley, Capital		10,000
	Ayesha Starr, Capital..		5,000
b.	Cash..	28,000	
	Devin Morris, Capital		28,000

PE 12–3B

a.	Land..	25,000	
	Leon Browne, Capital		12,500
	Craig Little, Capital		12,500
b.	Craig Little, Capital..	15,250	
	Lane Tway, Capital..		15,250*

*($18,000 + $12,500) × 50%

PE 12–4A

Equity of Masterson...	$ 90,000
Nutley contribution	50,000
Total equity after admitting Nutley...	$ 140,000
Nutley's equity interest	× 40%
Nutley's equity after admission	$ 56,000
Nutley's contribution	50,000
Bonus paid to Nutley..	$ 6,000

PE 12–4B

Equity of Porter..	$ 420,000
Billings's contribution	200,000
Total equity after admitting Billings...	$ 620,000
Billings's equity interest	× 30%
Billings's equity after admission	$ 186,000
Billings's contribution	$ 200,000
Billings's equity after admission..	186,000
Bonus paid to Porter	$ 14,000

PE 12–5A

Chow's equity prior to liquidation....................................		$18,000
Realization of asset sales	$46,000	
Book value of assets ($18,000 + $25,000 + $1,000)............	44,000	
Gain on liquidation	$ 2,000	
Chow's share of gain (50% × $2,000)		1,000
Chow's cash distribution		$19,000

PE 12–5B

Dickens's equity prior to liquidation....................................		$ 55,000
Realization of asset sales	$ 75,000	
Book value of assets ($55,000 + $45,000 + $10,000)..........	110,000	
Loss on liquidation...	$ 35,000	
Dickens's share of loss (50% × $35,000)		(17,500)
Dickens's cash distribution		$ 37,500

PE 12–6A

a. Martin's equity prior to liquidation................................		$ 8,000
Realization of asset sales	$ 5,000	
Book value of assets...	28,000	
Loss on liquidation...	$23,000	
Martin's share of loss (50% × $23,000)		(11,500)
Martin's deficiency		$ (3,500)

b. $5,000. $20,000 – $11,500 share of loss – $3,500 Martin deficiency, also equals the amount realized from asset sales.

PE 12–6B

a. Mee's equity prior to liquidation		$ 40,000
Realization of asset sales	$ 50,000	
Book value of assets...	160,000	
Loss on liquidation...	$110,000	
Mee's share of loss (50% x $110,000)		(55,000)
Mee's deficiency		$ (15,000)

b. $50,000. $120,000 – $55,000 share of loss – $15,000 Mee deficiency, also equal to the amount realized from asset sales.

EXERCISES

Ex. 12–1

Cash...	10,000	
Accounts Receivable...	118,000	
Merchandise Inventory..	74,300	
Equipment	67,000	
Allowance for Doubtful Accounts		8,100
Lamar Kline, Capital		261,200

Ex. 12–2

Cash...	30,000	
Accounts Receivable...	65,000	
Land	165,000	
Equipment	10,000	
Allowance for Doubtful Accounts		5,000
Accounts Payable...		18,000
Notes Payable		45,000
Ron Maples, Capital		202,000

Ex. 12–3

	Haley	Manos
a.	$ 75,000	$75,000
b.	112,500	37,500
c.	68,400	81,600
d.	67,500	82,500
e.	73,500	76,500

Details

	Haley	Manos	Total
a. Net income (1:1)..	$ 75,000	$75,000	$150,000
b. Net income (3:1)..	$112,500	$37,500	$150,000
c. Interest allowance	$ 18,000	$ 6,000	$ 24,000
Remaining income (2:3)............................	50,400	75,600	126,000
Net income..	$ 68,400	$81,600	$150,000
d. Salary allowance...	$ 45,000	$60,000	$105,000
Remaining income (1:1)............................	22,500	22,500	45,000
Net income..	$ 67,500	$82,500	$150,000
e. Interest allowance	$ 18,000	$ 6,000	$ 24,000
Salary allowance..	45,000	60,000	105,000
Remaining income (1:1)............................	10,500	10,500	21,000
Net income..	$ 73,500	$76,500	$150,000

Ex. 12–4

		Haley	Manos
a.	....	$120,000	$120,000
b.	....	180,000	60,000
c.	....	104,400	135,600
d.	....	112,500	127,500
e.	....	118,500	121,500

Details

	Haley	Manos	Total
a. Net income (1:1)...	$120,000	$120,000	$240,000
b. Net income (3:1)...	$180,000	$ 60,000	$240,000
c. Interest allowance	$ 18,000	$ 6,000	$ 24,000
Remaining income (2:3).................................	86,400	129,600	216,000
Net income	$104,400	$135,600	$240,000
d. Salary allowance..	$ 45,000	$ 60,000	$105,000
Remaining income (1:1).................................	67,500	67,500	135,000
Net income	$112,500	$127,500	$240,000
e. Interest allowance	$ 18,000	$ 6,000	$ 24,000
Salary allowance..	45,000	60,000	105,000
Remaining income (1:1).................................	55,500	55,500	111,000
Net income	$118,500	$121,500	$240,000

Ex. 12–5

	Curt Kelly	Greg Kaufman	Total
Salary allowances..	$ 45,000	$ 30,000	$ 75,000
Remainder (net loss, $25,000 plus $75,000 salary allowances) divided equally.........	(50,000)	(50,000)	(100,000)
Net loss..	$ (5,000)	$ (20,000)	$ (25,000)

Ex. 12–6

The partners can divide net income in any ratio that they wish. However, in the absence of an agreement, net income is divided equally between the partners. Therefore, Jan's conclusion was correct, but for the wrong reasons. In addition, note that the monthly drawings have no impact on the division of income.

Ex. 12–7

a.

Net income: $132,000

	Gardner	Ross	Total
Salary allowance	$58,000	$42,000	$100,000
Remaining income	19,200	12,800	32,000
Net income	$77,200	$54,800	$132,000

Gardner remaining income: ($132,000 – $100,000) × 3/5
Ross remaining income: ($132,000 – $100,000) × 2/5

b.

(1)

Income Summary	132,000	
L. Gardner, Member Equity		77,200
L. Ross, Member Equity		54,800

(2)

L. Gardner, Member Equity	58,000	
L. Ross, Member Equity	42,000	
L. Gardner, Drawing		58,000
L. Ross, Drawing		42,000

Note: The reduction in members' equity from withdrawals would be disclosed on the statement of members' equity but does not affect the allocation of net income in part (a) of this exercise.

Ex. 12–8

a.

	KXT Radio Partners	Rachel Sizemore	Daily Sun Newspaper, LLC	Total
Salary allowance		$139,800		$139,800
Interest allowance	$ 19,200[1]	3,200[2]	$ 12,800[3]	35,200
Remaining income (4:3:3)	158,000	118,500	118,500	395,000
Net income	$177,200	$261,500	$131,300	$570,000

[1] 8% × $240,000
[2] 8% × $40,000
[3] 8% × $160,000

b.

Date	Account	Debit	Credit
Dec. 31, 2008	Income Summary	570,000	
	KXT Radio Partners, Member Equity		177,200
	Rachel Sizemore, Member Equity		261,500
	Daily Sun Newspaper, LLC, Member Equity		131,300
Dec. 31, 2008	KXT Radio Partners, Member Equity	19,200	
	Rachel Sizemore, Member Equity	143,000	
	Daily Sun Newspaper, LLC, Member Equity	12,800	
	KXT Radio Partners, Drawing		19,200
	Rachel Sizemore, Drawing		143,000
	Daily Sun Newspaper, LLC, Drawing		12,800

c.

MEDIA PROPERTIES, LLC
Statement of Members' Equity
For the Year Ended December 31, 2008

	KXT Radio Partners	Rachel Sizemore	Daily Sun Newspaper, LLC	Total
Members' equity, January 1, 2008	$240,000	$40,000	$160,000	$ 440,000
Additional investment during the year	50,000			50,000
	$290,000	$40,000	$160,000	$ 490,000
Net income for the year	177,200	261,500	131,300	570,000
	$467,200	$301,500	$291,300	$1,060,000
Withdrawals during the year	19,200	143,000	12,800	175,000
Members' equity, December 31, 2008	$448,000	$158,500	$278,500	$ 885,000

Ex 12–9

a.

| Jan. 31 | Partner, Drawing .... | 25,000,000 | |
| | Cash.. | | 25,000,000 |

b.

| Dec. 31 | Income Summary .... | 350,000,000 | |
| | Partner, Capital .... | | 350,000,000 |

c.

| Dec. 31 | Partner, Capital .... | 300,000,000* | |
| | Partner, Drawing........................... | | 300,000,000 |

*12 months × £25,000,000

Ex. 12–10

a. and b.

| Charles Shivers, Capital.. | 40,000 | |
| Theresa Pepin, Capital .... | | 40,000 |

$120,000 × 1/3

Note: The sale to Shivers is not a transaction of the partnership; so, the sales price is not considered in this journal entry.

Ex. 12–11

a. $1,172,000 ($2,450,000,000/2,090), rounded

b. $172,000 ($360,000,000/2,090), rounded

c. A new partner might contribute more than $172,000 because of goodwill attributable to the firm's reputation, future income potential, and a strong client base, etc.

Ex. 12–12

a. (1) Kris Perry, Capital (20% × $100,000)........................ 20,000
        Melvin Newman, Capital (25% × $90,000) 22,500
            Paul Lester, Capital.. 42,500

    (2) Cash.. 40,000
            Steve Hurd, Capital 40,000

b. Kris Perry... 80,000
    Melvin Newman.. 67,500
    Paul Lester 42,500
    Steve Hurd.. 40,000

Ex. 12–13

a. Cash.. 50,000
    Mike Heil, Capital 6,000
    Alan Delong, Capital... 6,000
        Felix Estavez, Capital 62,000

b. Mike Heil 69,000
    Alan Delong.. 79,000
    Felix Estavez 62,000

Ex. 12–14

a.

Medical Equipment	20,000		
Dobbs, Member Equity		8,000[1]	
Fox, Member Equity		12,000[2]	

[1]$20,000 × 2/5 = $8,000
[2]$20,000 × 3/5 = $12,000

b. 1.

Cash	310,000	
Dobbs, Member Equity		9,400
Fox, Member Equity		14,100
Kopp, Member Equity		286,500

Supporting calculations for the bonus:

Equity of Dobbs	$308,000
Equity of Fox	337,000
Contribution by Kopp	310,000
Total equity after admitting Kopp	$955,000
Kopp's equity interest after admission	× 30%
Kopp's equity after admission	$286,500

Contribution by Kopp	$310,000
Kopp's equity after admission	286,500
Bonus paid to Dobbs and Fox	$ 23,500

Dobbs: $23,500 × 2/5 = $9,400
Fox: $23,500 × 3/5 = $14,100

b. 2.

Cash	175,000	
Dobbs, Member Equity	12,000	
Fox, Member Equity	18,000	
Kopp, Member Equity		205,000

Supporting calculations for the bonus:

Equity of Dobbs	$308,000
Equity of Fox	337,000
Contribution by Kopp	175,000
Total equity after admitting Kopp	$820,000
Kopp's equity interest after admission	× 25%
Kopp's equity after admission	$205,000
Contribution by Kopp	175,000
Bonus paid to Kopp	$ 30,000

Dobbs: $30,000 × 2/5 = $12,000
Fox: $30,000 × 3/5 = $18,000

Ex. 12–15

a. J. Trifilio, Capital.. 3,000
    K. Graham, Capital 3,000
        Equipment 6,000

b. 1. Cash 50,000
     J. Trifilio, Capital 3,400
     K. Graham, Capital.. 3,400
        L. Holden, Capital 56,800

Supporting calculations for the bonus:

Equity of Trifilio...	$ 87,000
Equity of Graham	147,000
Contribution by Holden	50,000
Total equity after admitting Holden	$284,000
Holden's equity interest after admission	× 20%
Holden's equity after admission	$ 56,800
Contribution by Holden	50,000
Bonus paid to Holden	$ 6,800

The bonus to Holden is debited equally between Trifilio's and Graham's
capital accounts.

b. 2. Cash 125,000
        J. Trifilio, Capital.. 8,650
        K. Graham, Capital.. 8,650
        L. Holden, Capital 107,700

Supporting calculations for the bonus:

Equity of Trifilio...	$ 87,000
Equity of Graham	147,000
Contribution by Holden	125,000
Total equity after admitting Holden	$359,000
Holden's equity interest after admission	× 30%
Holden's equity after admission	$107,700
Contribution by Holden	$125,000
Holden's equity after admission...	107,700
Bonus paid to Trifilio and Graham	$ 17,300

The bonus to Trifilio and Graham is credited equally between Trifilio's and
Graham's capital accounts.

Ex. 12–16

ANGEL INVESTOR ASSOCIATES
Statement of Partnership Equity
For the Year Ended December 31, 2008

	Jan Strous, Capital	Lisa Lankford, Capital	Sarah Rogers, Capital	Total Partnership Capital
Partnership Capital, January 1, 2008	$ 36,000	$ 84,000		$120,000
Admission of Sarah Rogers......................	—	—	$ 30,000	30,000
Salary allowance.....................................	25,000			25,000
Remaining income..................................	27,600	64,400	23,000	115,000
Less: Partner withdrawals	(13,800)	(32,200)	(11,500)	(57,500)
Partnership Capital, December 31, 2008..	$ 74,800	$116,200	$41,500	$232,500

Admission of Sarah Rogers:

Equity of initial partners prior to admission.................	$120,000
Contribution by Rogers..	30,000
Total	$150,000
Rogers's equity interest after admission......................	× 20%
Rogers's equity after admission	$ 30,000
Contribution by Rogers..	30,000
No bonus	$ 0

Net income distribution:

The income-sharing ratio is equal to the proportion of the capital balances after admitting Rogers according to the partnership agreement:

Jan Strous: $\dfrac{\$36,000}{\$150,000} = 24\%$

Lisa Lankford: $\dfrac{\$84,000}{\$150,000} = 56\%$

Sarah Rogers: $\dfrac{\$30,000}{\$150,000} = 20\%$

These ratios can be multiplied by the $115,000 remaining income ($140,000 – $25,000 salary allowance to Strous) to distribute the earnings to the respective partner capital accounts.

Withdrawals:

Half of the remaining income is distributed to the three partners. Strous need not take the salary allowance as a withdrawal but may allow it to accumulate in the member equity account.

Ex. 12–17

a.

Merchandise Inventory...	30,000	
Allowance for Doubtful Accounts........................		6,200
Glenn Powell, Capital..		10,200[1]
Tammie Sawyer, Capital		6,800[2]
Joe Patel, Capital..		6,800[2]

[1]$23,800 × 3/7
[2]$23,800 × 2/7

b.

Glenn Powell, Capital	270,200[1]	
Cash..		105,200
Notes Payable..		165,000

[1]$260,000 + $10,200

Ex. 12–18

a. The income-sharing ratio is determined by dividing the net income for each member by the total net income. Thus, in 2007, the income-sharing ratio is as follows:

Utah Properties, LLC: $\dfrac{\$70,000}{\$280,000} = 25\%$

Aztec Holdings, Ltd.: $\dfrac{\$210,000}{\$280,000} = 75\%$

Or a 1:3 ratio

b. Following the same procedure as in (a):

Utah Properties, LLC: $\dfrac{\$78,400}{\$392,000} = 20\%$

Aztec Holdings, Ltd.: $\dfrac{\$254,800}{\$392,000} = 65\%$

Cleveland Porter: $\dfrac{\$58,800}{\$392,000} = 15\%$

c. Cleveland Porter provided a $287,500 cash contribution to the business. The amount credited to his member equity account is this amount less a $20,000 bonus paid to the other two members, or $267,500.

Ex. 12–18 Concluded

d. The positive entries to Utah Properties and Aztec Holdings are the result of a bonus paid by Cleveland Porter.

e. Cleveland Porter acquired a 20% interest in the business, computed as follows:

Cleveland Porter's contribution.............................	$ 287,500
Utah Properties, LLC, member equity................	530,000
Aztec Holdings, Ltd., member equity.................	520,000
Total	$1,337,500
Porter's ownership interest after admission ($267,500 ÷ $1,337,500)..	20.00%

Ex. 12–19

a.

Cash balance...	$24,000
Sum of capital accounts..................................	35,000
Loss from sale of noncash assets.................	$11,000

	Pitt	Leon
Capital balances before realization	$ 15,000	$ 20,000
b. Division of loss on sale of noncash assets	5,500[1]	5,500[1]
Balances	$ 9,500	$ 14,500
c. Cash distributed to partners	9,500	14,500
Final balances	$ 0	$ 0

[1] $11,000/2

Ex. 12–20

	Boling	Bishop
Capital balances before realization.....................	$ 43,000	$ 57,000
Division of loss on sale of noncash assets [($100,000 – $76,000)/2]	12,000	12,000
Capital balances after realization	$ 31,000	$ 45,000
Cash distributed to partners...............................	31,000	45,000
Final balances	$ 0	$ 0

Ex. 12–21

a. Deficiency

b. $64,000 ($21,000 + $57,500 – $14,500)

c.
Cash..	14,500	
Shelby, Capital		14,500

	Mawby	White	Shelby
Capital balances after realization	$21,000	$57,500	$(14,500) Dr.
Receipt of partner deficiency.............			14,500
Capital balances after eliminating deficiency	$21,000	$57,500	$ 0

Ex. 12–22

a. Cash should be distributed as indicated in the following tabulation:

	Seth	Kerr	Driver	Total
Capital invested	$ 225	$ 150	$ —	$ 375
Net income	+ 200	+ 200	+ 200	+ 600
Capital balances and cash distribution	$ 425	$ 350	$ 200	$ 975

b. Driver has a capital deficiency of $40, as indicated in the following tabulation:

	Seth	Kerr	Driver	Total
Capital invested	$ 225	$ 150	$ —	$ 375
Net loss...	– 40	– 40	– 40	– 120
Capital balances	$ 185	$ 110	$ 40 Dr.	$ 255

Ex. 12–23

	Heinz	Dicer	Ho
Capital balances after realization	$(18,000)	$70,000	$45,000
Distribution of partner deficiency	18,000	(12,000)[1]	(6,000)[2]
Capital balances after deficiency distribution	$ 0	$58,000	$39,000

[1]$18,000 × 2/3
[2]$18,000 × 1/3

Ex. 12–24

DILLS, GORDON, AND CHAVEZ
Statement of Partnership Liquidation
For the Period Ending July 1–29, 2008

| | Cash | + | Noncash Assets | = | Liabilities | + | Capital | | |
							Dills (3/6)	Gordon (2/6)	Chavez (1/6)
Balances before realization	$ 42,000		$ 90,000		$ 45,000		$ 32,000	$ 40,000	$ 15,000
Sale of assets and division of loss	+ 66,000		– 90,000		—		– 12,000	– 8,000	– 4,000
Balances after realization	$108,000		$ 0		$ 45,000		$ 20,000	$ 32,000	$ 11,000
Payment of liabilities	– 45,000		—		– 45,000		—	—	—
Balances after payment of liabilities	$ 63,000		$ 0		$ 0		$ 20,000	$ 32,000	$ 11,000
Cash distributed to partners	– 63,000		—		—		– 20,000	– 32,000	– 11,000
Final balances	$ 0		$ 0		$ 0		$ 0	$ 0	$ 0

Ex. 12–25

a.

CITY SIGNS, LLC
Statement of LLC Liquidation
For the Period March 1–31, 2008

| | Cash | + | Noncash Assets | = | Liabilities | + | Member Equity | | |
							Gilley (2/5)	+ Hughes (2/5)	+ Moussa (1/5)
Balances before realization	$ 14,000		$ 126,000		$ 35,000		$ 19,000	$ 54,000	$ 32,000
Sale of assets and division of gain	+ 146,000		– 126,000		—		+ 8,000	+ 8,000	+ 4,000
Balances after realization	$ 160,000		$ 0		$ 35,000		$ 27,000	$ 62,000	$ 36,000
Payment of liabilities	– 35,000		—		– 35,000				—
Balances after payment of liabilities	$ 125,000		$ 0		$ 0		$ 27,000	$ 62,000	$ 36,000
Distribution of cash to members	– 125,000		—		—		– 27,000	– 62,000	– 36,000
Final balances	$ 0		$ 0		$ 0		$ 0	$ 0	$ 0

b.

Gilley, Member Equity	27,000	
Hughes, Member Equity	62,000	
Moussa, Member Equity	36,000	
Cash		125,000

Ex. 12–26

a.

(1) Income Summary 180,000
    Dal Polivka, Capital 90,000
    Amanda Pratt, Capital 90,000

(2) Dal Polivka, Capital 65,000
    Amanda Pratt, Capital 76,000
    Dal Polivka, Drawing 65,000
    Amanda Pratt, Drawing 76,000

b.

POLIVKA AND PRATT
Statement of Partners' Equity
For the Year Ended December 31, 2008

	Dal Polivka	Amanda Pratt	Total
Capital, January 1, 2008	$105,000	$135,000	$240,000
Additional investment during the year	15,000	—	15,000
	$120,000	$135,000	$255,000
Net income for the year	90,000	90,000	180,000
	$210,000	$225,000	$435,000
Withdrawals during the year	65,000	76,000	141,000
Capital, December 31, 2008	$145,000	$149,000	$294,000

Ex. 12–27

a. Revenue per professional staff, 2004: $\dfrac{\$6,876,000,000}{22,841} = \$301,000$

   Revenue per professional staff, 2005: $\dfrac{\$7,814,000}{26,401} = \$296,000$

b. The revenues increased between the two years from $6,876 million to $7,814 million, or 13.6% [($7,814 – $6,876)/$6,876]. Revenue growth has been strong, mostly resulting from Sarbanes-Oxley work. However, the number of employees has grown at a faster rate, from 22,841 to 26,401, or 15.6% [(26,401 – 22,841)/22,841]. As a result, the revenue per professional staff employee has dropped from $301,000 to $296,000. This slight loss in efficiency is probably to be expected. Public accounting firms have had difficulty finding employees for the emerging Sarbanes-Oxley work. From 2004 to 2005, they have aggressively hired employees to bring the workforce in line with the demand for work. Prior to this time, the firm was relying heavily on overtime.

Ex. 12–28

a. Revenue per employee, 2007: $\dfrac{\$32,500,000}{260} = \$125,000$

   Revenue per employee, 2008: $\dfrac{\$38,000,000}{380} = \$100,000$

b. Revenues increased between the two years; however, the number of employees has increased at a faster rate. Thus, the revenue per employee declined from $125,000 in 2007 to $100,000 in 2008. This indicates that the efficiency of the firm has declined in the two years. This is likely the result of the expansion. That is, the large increase in the employment base is the likely result of the expansion into the four new cities. These new employees may need to be trained and thus are not as efficient in their jobs as the more experienced employees in the existing cities. Often, a business will suffer productivity losses in the midst of significant expansion because of the inexperience of the new employees.

PROBLEMS

Prob. 12–1A

1.

May	1	Cash	16,500	
		Merchandise Inventory	43,500	
		Crystal Polles, Capital		60,000
	1	Cash	13,000	
		Accounts Receivable	19,100	
		Equipment..	53,300	
		Allowance for Doubtful Accounts..............		1,400
		Accounts Payable		14,000
		Notes Payable		20,000
		Doug Kovac, Capital		50,000

2.

POLLES AND KOVAC
Balance Sheet
May 1, 2007

Assets

Current assets:			
Cash...		$ 29,500	
Accounts receivable.................................	$ 19,100		
Less allowance for doubtful accounts	1,400	17,700	
Merchandise inventory		43,500	
Total current assets			$ 90,700
Plant assets:			
Equipment...			53,300
Total assets			$ 144,000

Liabilities

Current liabilities:		
Accounts payable..	$ 14,000	
Notes payable	20,000	
Total liabilities..		$ 34,000

Partners' Equity

Crystal Polles, capital..	$ 60,000	
Doug Kovac, capital...	50,000	
Total partners' equity		110,000
Total liabilities and partners' equity......................		$ 144,000

3.

Apr. 30	Income Summary		74,000	
	Crystal Polles, Capital			35,000*
	Doug Kovac, Capital			39,000*
30	Crystal Polles, Capital....................................		22,000	
	Doug Kovac, Capital.......................................		28,000	
	Crystal Polles, Drawing			22,000
	Doug Kovac, Drawing			28,000

*Computations:

	Polles	Kovac	Total
Interest allowance	$ 6,000[1]	$ 5,000[2]	$ 11,000
Salary allowance..	20,000	25,000	45,000
Remaining income (1:1)	9,000	9,000	18,000
Net income	$ 35,000	$ 39,000	$ 74,000

[1]10% × $60,000
[2]10% × $50,000

Prob. 12–2A

Plan	(1) $114,000 Lange	(1) $114,000 Lopez	(2) $210,000 Lange	(2) $210,000 Lopez
a.	$57,000	$57,000	$105,000	$105,000
b.	85,500	28,500	157,500	52,500
c.	38,000	76,000	70,000	140,000
d.	66,600	47,400	114,600	95,400
e.	49,100	64,900	97,100	112,900
f.	48,200	65,800	86,600	123,400

Details

		$114,000 Lange	$114,000 Lopez	$210,000 Lange	$210,000 Lopez
a.	Net income (1:1)	$ 57,000	$ 57,000	$ 105,000	$ 105,000
b.	Net income (3:1)	$ 85,500	$ 28,500	$ 157,500	$ 52,500
c.	Net income (1:2)	$ 38,000	$ 76,000	$ 70,000	$ 140,000
d.	Interest allowance	$ 28,800	$ 9,600	$ 28,800	$ 9,600
	Remaining Income (1:1)	37,800	37,800	85,800	85,800
	Net income	$ 66,600	$ 47,400	$ 114,600	$ 95,400
e.	Interest allowance	$ 28,800	$ 9,600	$ 28,800	$ 9,600
	Salary allowance	35,000	70,000	35,000	70,000
	Excess of allowances over income (1:1)	(14,700)	(14,700)		
	Remaining income (1:1)			33,300	33,300
	Net income	$ 49,100	$ 64,900	$ 97,100	$ 112,900
f.	Interest allowance	$ 28,800	$ 9,600	$ 28,800	$ 9,600
	Salary allowance	35,000	70,000	35,000	70,000
	Bonus allowance		1,800[1]		21,000[2]
	Excess of allowances over income (1:1)	(15,600)	(15,600)		
	Remaining income (1:1)			22,800	22,800
	Net income	$ 48,200	$ 65,800	$ 86,600	$ 123,400

[1]20% × ($114,000 − $105,000)
[2]20% × ($210,000 − $105,000)

Prob. 12–3A

1.

SATO AND KOENING
Income Statement
For the Year Ended December 31, 2008

Professional fees		$297,450
Expenses:		
Salary expense	$132,300	
Depreciation expense—building	10,500	
Property tax expense	7,000	
Heating and lighting expense	6,300	
Supplies expense	2,850	
Depreciation expense—office equipment	2,800	
Miscellaneous expense	5,700	
Total expenses		167,450
Net income		$130,000

	Peter Sato	May Koening	Total
Division of net income:			
Salary allowance	$ 40,000	$ 50,000	$ 90,000
Interest allowance	9,500*	5,700**	15,200
Remaining income	12,400	12,400	24,800
Net income	$ 61,900	$ 68,100	$ 130,000

 *$95,000 × 10%
**($65,000 – $8,000) × 10%

2.

SATO AND KOENING
Statement of Partners' Equity
For the Year Ended December 31, 2008

	Peter Sato	May Koening	Total
Capital, January 1, 2008	$ 95,000	$ 57,000	$ 152,000
Additional investment during the year	—	8,000	8,000
	$ 95,000	$ 65,000	$ 160,000
Net income for the year	61,900	68,100	130,000
	$ 156,900	$ 133,100	$ 290,000
Withdrawals during the year	50,000	70,000	120,000
Capital, December 31, 2008	$ 106,900	$ 63,100	$ 170,000

Prob. 12–3A   Concluded

3.

SATO AND KOENING
Balance Sheet
December 31, 2008

Assets

Current assets:			
Cash..		$ 30,000	
Accounts receivable................................		38,900	
Supplies		1,900	
Total current assets			$ 70,800
Plant and equipment:			
Land..		$ 25,000	
Building...	$ 130,000		
Less accumulated depreciation..........	69,200	60,800	
Office equipment	$ 39,000		
Less accumulated depreciation..........	21,500	17,500	
Total plant assets			103,300
Total assets			$ 174,100

Liabilities

Current liabilities:			
Accounts payable....................................		$ 2,100	
Salaries payable		2,000	
Total liabilities...................................			$ 4,100

Partners' Equity

Peter Sato, capital..................................		$ 106,900	
May Koening, capital		63,100	
Total partners' equity			170,000
Total liabilities and partners' equity.............			$ 174,100

Prob. 12–4A

1. Apr. 30   Asset Revaluations   3,080

         Accounts Receivable   2,400

         Allowance for Doubtful Accounts.............   680*

         *[($34,000 − $2,400) × 5%] − $900

       30   Asset Revaluations   3,000

         Merchandise Inventory   3,000

       30   Accumulated Depreciation—Equipment   80,000

         Equipment...   60,080**

         Asset Revaluations   140,080

         **$240,080 − $180,000

       30   Asset Revaluations   134,000

         Prad Kumar, Capital....................................   67,000

         Carol Grigg, Capital   67,000

2. May   1   Carol Grigg, Capital...   55,000

         Sara Culver, Capital   55,000

        1   Cash   25,000

         Sara Culver, Capital   25,000

Prob. 12–4A Concluded

3.

KUMAR, GRIGG, AND CULVER
Balance Sheet
May 1, 2008

Assets

Current assets:		
Cash..		$ 31,800
Accounts receivable...............................	$31,600	
Less allowance for doubtful accounts	1,580	30,020
Merchandise inventory		60,000
Prepaid insurance		2,100
Total current assets		$123,920
Plant assets:		
Equipment..		240,080
Total assets		$364,000

Liabilities

Current liabilities:		
Accounts payable...................................		$ 12,000
Notes payable		20,000
Total liabilities....................................		$ 32,000

Partners' Equity

Prad Kumar, capital	$167,000[1]	
Carol Grigg, capital................................	85,000[2]	
Sara Culver, capital................................	80,000	
Total partners' equity		332,000
Total liabilities and partners' equity.............		$364,000

[1]$100,000 + $67,000
[2]$73,000 + $67,000 – $55,000

Prob. 12–5A

1.

DANIELS, BURTON, AND RAMARIZ
Statement of Partnership Liquidation
For Period July 3–29, 2008

	Cash	+	Noncash Assets	=	Liabilities	+	Daniels (50%)	+	Burton (25%)	+	Ramariz (25%)
									Capital		
Balances before realization	$ 9,500		$ 84,000		$ 30,000		$ 27,000		$ 4,500		$ 32,000
Sale of assets and division of loss	+ 54,000		– 84,000		—		– 15,000		– 7,500		– 7,500
Balances after realization	$ 63,500		$ 0		$ 30,000		$ 12,000		$ (3,000)		$ 24,500
Payment of liabilities	– 30,000		—		– 30,000		—		—		—
Balances after payment of liabilities	$ 33,500		$ 0		$ 0		$ 12,000		$ (3,000)		$ 24,500
Receipt of deficiency	+ 3,000		—		—		—		+ 3,000		—
Balances	$ 36,500		$ 0		$ 0		$ 12,000		$ 0		$ 24,500
Cash distributed to partners	– 36,500		—		—		– 12,000		—		– 24,500
Final balances	$ 0		$ 0		$ 0		$ 0		$ 0		$ 0

2. The $3,000 deficiency of Burton would be divided between the other partners, Daniels and Ramariz, in their income-sharing ratio (2:1, respectively). Therefore, Daniels would absorb 2/3 of the $3,000 deficiency, or $2,000, and Ramariz would absorb 1/3 of the $3,000 deficiency, or $1,000.

1.

ALLEN, DEE, AND ITO
Statement of Partnership Liquidation
For Period October 1–30, 2008

	Cash	+	Noncash Assets	=	Liabilities	+	Allen (2/5)	+	Dee (2/5)	+	Ito (1/5)
									Capital		
Balances before realization...........	$ 13,000		$ 179,000		$ 50,000		$ 55,000		$ 75,000		$ 12,000
Sale of assets and division											
of gain......................	+ 224,000		– 179,000		—		+ 18,000		+ 18,000		+ 9,000
Balances after realization............	$ 237,000		$ 0		$ 50,000		$ 73,000		$ 93,000		$ 21,000
Payment of liabilities	– 50,000		—		– 50,000		—		—		—
Balances after payment											
of liabilities	$ 187,000		$ 0		$ 0		$ 73,000		$ 93,000		$ 21,000
Cash distributed to partners	– 187,000		—		—		– 73,000		– 93,000		– 21,000
Final balances	$ 0		$ 0		$ 0		$ 0		$ 0		$ 0

Prob. 12–6A   Concluded

2.

ALLEN, DEE, AND ITO
Statement of Partnership Liquidation
For Period October 1–30, 2008

	Cash	+	Noncash Assets	=	Liabilities	+	Allen (2/5)	+	Dee (2/5)	+	Ito (1/5)
Balances before realization.......	$ 13,000		$ 179,000		$ 50,000		$ 55,000		$ 75,000		$ 12,000
Sale of assets and division of loss	+ 109,000		– 179,000		—		– 28,000		– 28,000		– 14,000
Balances after realization........	$ 122,000		$ 0		$ 50,000		$ 27,000		$ 47,000		$ (2,000)
Payment of liabilities	– 50,000		—		– 50,000		—		—		—
Balances after payment of liabilities	$ 72,000		$ 0		$ 0		$ 27,000		$ 47,000		$ (2,000)
Receipt of deficiency	+ 2,000		—		—		—		—		+ 2,000
Balances.................................	$ 74,000		$ 0		$ 0		$ 27,000		$ 47,000		$ 0
Cash distributed to partners........	– 74,000		—		—		– 27,000		– 47,000		—
Final balances	$ 0		$ 0		$ 0		$ 0		$ 0		$ 0

Prob. 12–1B

1.

Nov.	1	Cash..	9,000	
		Merchandise Inventory..........................	16,000	
		E. Hoffman, Capital		25,000
	1	Cash..	10,600	
		Accounts Receivable.............................	22,000	
		Merchandise Inventory..........................	31,000	
		Equipment	38,000	
		Allowance for Doubtful Accounts..................		900
		Accounts Payable		7,300
		Notes Payable..		3,400
		Mark Torres, Capital......................................		90,000

2.

HOFFMAN AND TORRES
Balance Sheet
November 1, 2007

Assets

Current assets:			
Cash..		$19,600	
Accounts receivable...............................	$22,000		
Less allowance for doubtful accounts ...	900	21,100	
Merchandise inventory		47,000	
Total current assets			$ 87,700
Plant assets:			
Equipment..			38,000
Total assets			$125,700

Liabilities

Current liabilities:		
Accounts payable.....................................	$ 7,300	
Notes payable	3,400	
Total liabilities...		$ 10,700

Partners' Equity

E. Hoffman, capital...	$25,000	
Mark Torres, capital.......................................	90,000	
Total partners' equity		115,000
Total liabilities and partners' equity............		$125,700

Prob. 12–1B   Concluded

3.

Oct. 31	Income Summary	95,500		
	E. Hoffman, Capital		58,000*	
	Mark Torres, Capital		37,500*	
31	E. Hoffman, Capital	20,000		
	Mark Torres, Capital	12,000		
	E. Hoffman, Drawing		20,000	
	Mark Torres, Drawing		12,000	

*Computations:

	Hoffman	Torres	Total
Interest allowance	$ 2,500[1]	$ 9,000[2]	$11,500
Salary allowance	48,000	21,000	69,000
Remaining income (1:1)	7,500	7,500	15,000
Net income	$58,000	$37,500	$95,500

[1] 10% × $250,000
[2] 10% × $90,000

Prob. 12–2B

Plan	(1) $135,000 LaRue	(1) $135,000 Small	(2) $60,000 LaRue	(2) $60,000 Small
a.	$67,500	$67,500	$30,000	$30,000
b.	54,000	81,000	24,000	36,000
c.	90,000	45,000	40,000	20,000
d.	80,200	54,800	35,200	24,800
e.	74,600	60,400	37,100	22,900
f.	83,600	51,400	38,600	21,400

Details

	$135,000 LaRue	$135,000 Small	$60,000 LaRue	$60,000 Small
a. Net income (1:1).........................	$ 67,500	$ 67,500	$ 30,000	$ 30,000
b. Net income (2:3).........................	$ 54,000	$ 81,000	$ 24,000	$ 36,000
c. Net income (2:1).........................	$ 90,000	$ 45,000	$ 40,000	$ 20,000
d. Interest allowance......................	$ 1,600	$ 2,400	$ 1,600	$ 2,400
Remaining income (3:2)	78,600	52,400	33,600	22,400
Net income	$ 80,200	$ 54,800	$ 35,200	$ 24,800
e. Interest allowance......................	$ 1,600	$ 2,400	$ 1,600	$ 2,400
Salary allowance........................	30,000	15,000	30,000	15,000
Remaining income (1:1)	43,000	43,000	5,500	5,500
Net income	$ 74,600	$ 60,400	$ 37,100	$ 22,900
f. Interest allowance......................	$ 1,600	$ 2,400	$ 1,600	$ 2,400
Salary allowance........................	30,000	15,000	30,000	15,000
Bonus allowance	18,000[1]		3,000[2]	
Remaining income (1:1)	34,000	34,000	4,000	4,000
Net income	$ 83,600	$ 51,400	$ 38,600	$ 21,400

[1] 20% × ($135,000 – $45,000)
[2] 20% × ($60,000 – $45,000)

Prob. 12–3B

1.

WARRICK AND MURPHY
Income Statement
For the Year Ended December 31, 2008

Professional fees		$465,000
Expenses:		
Salary expense	$305,800	
Depreciation expense—building	6,800	
Property tax expense	2,400	
Heating and lighting expense...................................	9,400	
Supplies expense	2,100	
Depreciation expense—office equipment	4,200	
Miscellaneous expense...	4,300	
Total expenses		335,000
Net income		$130,000

	Dan Warrick	Ron Murphy	Total
Division of net income:			
Salary allowance.......................................	$ 40,000	$ 50,000	$ 90,000
Interest allowance	11,400*	14,400**	25,800
Remaining income.....................................	7,100	7,100	14,200
Net income	$ 58,500	$ 71,500	$ 130,000

*$95,000 × 12%
**($140,000 – $20,000) × 12%

2.

WARRICK AND MURPHY
Statement of Partners' Equity
For the Year Ended December 31, 2008

	Dan Warrick	Ron Murphy	Total
Capital, January 1, 2008	$ 95,000	$ 120,000	$ 215,000
Additional investment during the year..........	—	20,000	20,000
	$ 95,000	$ 140,000	$ 235,000
Net income for the year.................................	58,500	71,500	130,000
	$ 153,500	$ 211,500	$ 365,000
Withdrawals during the year..........................	45,000	50,000	95,000
Capital, December 31, 2008...........................	$ 108,500	$ 161,500	$ 270,000

Prob. 12–3B   Concluded

3.

WARRICK AND MURPHY
Balance Sheet
December 31, 2008

Assets

Current assets:		
Cash..	$ 12,500	
Accounts receivable................................	31,800	
Supplies	1,400	
Total current assets		$ 45,700
Plant assets:		
Land..	$140,000	
Building	$110,000	
Less accumulated depreciation..........	46,900	63,100
Office equipment	$ 46,000	
Less accumulated depreciation..........	19,200	26,800
Total plant assets		229,900
Total assets		$275,600

Liabilities

Current liabilities:		
Accounts payable.....................................	$ 1,600	
Salaries payable	4,000	
Total liabilities...		$ 5,600

Partners' Equity

Dan Warrick, capital......................................	$108,500	
Ron Murphy, capital.......................................	161,500	
Total partners' equity		270,000
Total liabilities and partners' equity..............		$275,600

Prob. 12–4B

1. May 31   Asset Revaluations   3,300
       Accounts Receivable............................   2,500
       Allowance for Doubtful Accounts 800*

       *[($26,500 – $2,500) × 5%] – $400

       31   Merchandise Inventory   9,000
       Asset Revaluations..............................   9,000

       31   Accumulated Depreciation—Equipment..   34,200
       Equipment   2,000
       Asset Revaluations..............................   32,200

       31   Asset Revaluations   37,900
       Adrian Knox, Capital   18,950
       Lisa Oaks, Capital...............................   18,950

2. June 1   Lias Oaks, Capital   30,000
       Todd Aguero, Capital   30,000

       1   Cash   40,000
       Todd Aguero, Capital   40,000

Prob. 12–4B   Concluded

3.

KNOX, OAKS, AND AGUERO
Balance Sheet
June 1, 2008

Assets

Current assets:			
Cash...		$ 52,300	
Accounts receivable..................................	$ 24,000		
Less allowance for doubtful accounts	1,200	22,800	
Merchandise inventory		98,000	
Prepaid insurance		4,200	
Total current assets			$177,300
Plant assets:			
Equipment..			124,000
Total assets			$301,300

Liabilities

Current liabilities:		
Accounts payable......................................	$ 34,400	
Notes payable	30,000	
Total liabilities...		$ 64,400

Partners' Equity

Adrian Knox, capital	$103,950[1]	
Lisa Oaks, capital	62,950[2]	
Todd Aguero, capital	70,000	
Total partners' capital....................................		236,900
Total liabilities and partners' capital		$301,300

[1]$85,000 + $18,950
[2]$74,000 + $18,950 – $30,000

Prob. 12–5B

1.

NICHOLS, NEWBY, AND PATEL
Statement of Partnership Liquidation
For the Period September 10–30, 2008

| | Cash | + | Noncash Assets | = | Liabilities | + | Capital | | |
							Nichols (25%)	+ Newby (25%)	+ Patel (50%)
Balances before realization	$ 4,300		$ 73,700		$ 12,000		$ 32,200	$ 5,400	$ 28,400
Sale of assets and division of loss	+ 47,300		– 73,700				– 6,600	– 6,600	– 13,200
Balances after realization	$ 51,600		$ 0		$ 12,000		$ 25,600	$ (1,200)	$ 15,200
Payment of liabilities	– 12,000				– 12,000				—
Balances after payment of liabilities	$ 39,600		$ 0		$ 0		$ 25,600	$ (1,200)	$ 15,200
Receipt of deficiency	+ 1,200							+ 1,200	
Balances	$ 40,800		$ 0		$ 0		$ 25,600	$ 0	$ 15,200
Cash distributed to partners	– 40,800						– 25,600		– 15,200
Final balances	$ 0		$ 0		$ 0		$ 0	$ 0	$ 0

2. The $1,200 deficiency of Newby would be divided between the other partners, Nichols and Patel, in their income-sharing ratio (1:2 respectively). Therefore, Nichols would absorb 1/3 of the $1,200 deficiency, or $400.00, and Patel would absorb 2/3 of the $1,200 deficiency, or $800.00.

1.

STREET, RHODES, AND FLYNN
Statement of Partnership Liquidation
For Period June 3–29, 2008

	Cash	+	Noncash Assets	=	Liabilities	+	Capital		
							Street (1/5)	Rhodes (2/5)	Flynn (2/5)
Balances before realization..........	$ 43,000		$ 234,000		$ 60,000		$ 16,000	$ 78,000	$ 123,000
Sale of assets and division									
of gain	+ 300,000		− 234,000		—		+ 13,200	+ 26,400	+ 26,400
Balances after realization...........	$ 343,000		$ 0		$ 60,000		$ 29,200	$ 104,400	$ 149,400
Payment of liabilities	− 60,000		—		− 60,000		—	—	—
Balances after payment									
of liabilities	$ 283,000		$ 0		$ 0		$ 29,200	$ 104,400	$ 149,400
Cash distributed to partners	− 283,000		—		—		− 29,200	− 104,400	− 149,400
Final balances	$ 0		$ 0		$ 0		$ 0	$ 0	$ 0

721

Prob. 12-6B   Concluded

2.

STREET, RHODES, AND FLYNN
Statement of Partnership Liquidation
For Period June 3–29, 2008

	Cash	+	Noncash Assets	=	Liabilities	+	Street (1/5)	+	Rhodes (2/5)	+	Flynn (2/5)
									Capital			
Balances before realization........	$ 43,000		$ 234,000		$ 60,000		$ 16,000		$ 78,000		$ 123,000
Sale of assets and division											
of loss	+106,000		–234,000		—		– 25,600		– 51,200		– 51,200
Balances after realization.........	$ 149,000		$ 0		$ 60,000		$ (9,600)		$ 26,800		$ 71,800
Payment of liabilities	– 60,000		—		– 60,000		—		—		—
Balances after payment											
of liabilities	$ 89,000		$ 0		$ 0		$ (9,600)		$ 26,800		$ 71,800
Receipt of deficiency	+ 9,600		—		—		+ 9,600		—		—
Balances........	$ 98,600		$ 0		$ 0		$ 0		$ 26,800		$ 71,800
Cash distributed to partners	– 98,600		—		—		—		– 26,800		– 71,800
Final balances	$ 0		$ 0		$ 0		$ 0		$ 0		$ 0

SPECIAL ACTIVITIES

SA 12–1

This scenario highlights one of the problems that arises in partnerships: attempting to align contribution with income division. Often, disagreements are based upon honest differences of opinion. However, in this scenario, there is evidence that Tate was acting unethically. Tate apparently made no mention of his plans to "scale back" once the partnership was consummated. As a result, Crowe agreed to an equal division of income based on the assumption that Tate's past efforts would project into the future, while in fact, Tate had no intention of this. As a result, Crowe is now providing more effort, while receiving the same income as Tate. This is clearly not sustainable in the long term. Tate does not appear to be concerned about this inequity. Thus, the evidence points to some duplicity on Tate's part. Essentially, he knows that he is riding on Crowe's effort and had planned it that way.

Crowe could respond to this situation by either withdrawing from the partnership or changing the partnership agreement. One possible change would be to provide a partner salary based on the amount of patient billings. This salary would be highly associated with the amount of revenue brought into the partnership, thus avoiding disputes associated with unequal contribution to the firm.

SA 12–2

A good solution to this problem would be to divide income in three steps:
1. Provide interest on each partner's capital balance.
2. Provide a monthly salary for each partner.
3. Divide the remainder according to a partnership formula.

With this approach, the return on capital and effort will be separately calculated in the income division formula before applying the percentage formula. Thus, Wise will receive a large interest distribution based on the large capital balance, while Sanchez should receive a large salary distribution based on the larger service contribution. The return on capital and salary allowances should be based on prevailing market rates. If both partners are pleased with their return on capital and effort, then the remaining income could be divided equally among them.

SA 12–3

a.

	Revenue per Partner	Revenue per Professional Staff
Deloitte & Touche...	$2,677,570	$339,170
Ernst & Young	2,755,500	334,223
PricewaterhouseCoopers....................................	2,358,636	244,649
KPMG	2,596,215	346,789

*Revenue per partner is determined by dividing the total revenue by the number of partners for each firm, adjusting the revenues for the fact that they are expressed in millions in the table. Revenue per partner is determined as follows:

$$\text{Deloitte \& Touche revenue per partner: } \frac{\$6,876,000,000}{2,568} = \$2,677,570$$

**Likewise, the revenue per professional staff is determined by dividing the total revenue by the number of professional staff, adjusting the revenues for the fact that they are expressed in millions in the table. Revenue per professional staff is determined as follows:

$$\text{Deloitte \& Touche revenue per professional staff: } \frac{\$6,876,000,000}{20,273} = \$339,170$$

b. The amount earned per partner is not significantly different between the four firms. Ernst & Young has the highest revenue per partner, while PricewaterhouseCoopers (PWC) has the lowest. PWC's revenue per partner is about 14% below the highest revenue per partner firm, Ernst & Young [$2,755,500 – $2,358,636)/$2,755,500]. The revenue per professional staff is significantly lower for PWC. PWC revenue per professional staff member is 29% below the highest revenue per professional firm, KPMG LLP [($346,789 – $244,649)/$346,789]. Indeed, PWC appears to be somewhat of an outlier in its revenue earned per professional staff. Together these data indicate that PWC may not be operating its firm as efficiently as the other three firms. The mix of services offered by the firms does not appear to impact these numbers. It is interesting to note that only Deloitte & Touche is significantly more involved in management advisory services (MAS) than the other three firms. The other three firms have sold their MAS operations in order to better conform to the Sarbanes-Oxley Act, which prohibited audit clients from using MAS services from the same firm. Deloitte & Touche has decided not to sell its consulting practice.

SA 12–4

a. A key distinction between a partnership and a corporation is that all of the partners (owners) are not only investors but also work in the partnership. The partners provide both capital and "sweat equity." This is a key distinction that provides insight about the performance of the firm. The expected income from the partnership is given as the country average, or $260,000.

The following is what each partner actually earned from the partnership.

Allocation of partnership income ($44,000,000 ÷ 200 partners) = $220,000 per partner

Note that the partners' earnings are less than what might be expected from the expected, or average, income. Thus, the partnership has performed below the partners' expectations.

b. The income statement indicates some large litigation losses. These losses appear to be the major reason for the partnership's poor performance. Without the losses, the partnership net income allocation would have been $295,000 [($44,000,000 + $15,000,000) ÷ 200]. The $295,000 exceeds the market-based compensation of $260,000 per year. In addition, the staff professional salaries of $80,000 per year ($120,000,000 ÷ 1,500) is slightly higher than average ($75,000). This would also have led to a smaller income to the partners than might have been expected.

SA 12–5

When developing an LLC (or partnership), the operating (or partnership) agreement is a critical part of establishing a business. Each party must consider the various incentives of each individual in the LLC. For example, in this case, one party, Dave Lester, is providing all of the funding, while the other two parties are providing expertise and talent. This type of arrangement can create some natural conflicts because the interests of an investor might not be exactly the same as those operating the LLC. Specifically, you would want to advise Lester that not all matters should be settled by majority vote. Such a provision would allow the two noninvesting members to vote as a block to the detriment of Lester. For example, the salaries for the two working members could be set by their vote, so that little profit would be left to be distributed. This would essentially keep Lester's return limited to the 10% preferred return. Lester should insist that salary allowances require unanimous approval of all members.

A second issue is the division of partnership income. The suggested agreement is for all the partners to share the remaining income, after the 10% preferred return, equally. Lester should be counseled to consider all aspects of the LLC contribution to determine if this division is equitable. There are many considerations including the amount of investment, risk of the venture, degree of expertise of noninvesting partners, and degree of exclusivity of noninvesting members' effort contribution (unique skills or business connections, for example). Often, the simple assumption of equal division is not appropriate.

In addition, it is sometimes best to require even working members to have an investment in the LLC, even if it is small, so that they are sensitive to the perspective of financial loss.

CHAPTER 13
CORPORATIONS: ORGANIZATION, STOCK TRANSACTIONS, AND DIVIDENDS

QUESTION INFORMATION

Number	Objective	Description	Difficulty	Time	AACSB	AICPA	SS	GL
Q13-1	13-1		Easy	5 min	Analytic	FN-Measurement		
Q13-2	13-1		Easy	5 min	Analytic	FN-Measurement		
Q13-3	13-3		Easy	5 min	Analytic	FN-Measurement		
Q13-4	13-3		Easy	5 min	Analytic	FN-Measurement		
Q13-5	13-3		Easy	5 min	Analytic	FN-Measurement		
Q13-6	13-3		Easy	5 min	Analytic	FN-Measurement		
Q13-7	13-4		Easy	5 min	Analytic	FN-Measurement		
Q13-8	13-4		Easy	5 min	Analytic	FN-Measurement		
Q13-9	13-4		Easy	5 min	Analytic	FN-Measurement		
Q13-10	13-4		Easy	5 min	Analytic	FN-Measurement		
Q13-11	13-5		Easy	5 min	Analytic	FN-Measurement		
Q13-12	13-5		Easy	5 min	Analytic	FN-Measurement		
Q13-13	13-5		Easy	5 min	Analytic	FN-Measurement		
Q13-14	13-6		Easy	5 min	Analytic	FN-Measurement		
Q13-15	13-6		Easy	5 min	Analytic	FN-Measurement		
Q13-16	13-6		Easy	5 min	Analytic	FN-Measurement		
Q13-17	13-6		Easy	5 min	Analytic	FN-Measurement		
Q13-18	13-7		Easy	5 min	Analytic	FN-Measurement		
PE13-1A	13-3	Dividends per share	Easy	10 min	Analytic	FN-Measurement		
PE13-1B	13-3	Dividends per share	Easy	10 min	Analytic	FN-Measurement		
PE13-2A	13-3	Entries for issuing stock	Easy	5 min	Analytic	FN-Measurement		
PE13-2B	13-3	Entries for issuing stock	Easy	5 min	Analytic	FN-Measurement		
PE13-3A	13-4	Entries for cash dividends	Easy	5 min	Analytic	FN-Measurement		
PE13-3B	13-4	Entries for cash dividends	Easy	5 min	Analytic	FN-Measurement		
PE13-4A	13-4	Entries for stock dividends	Easy	10 min	Analytic	FN-Measurement		
PE13-4B	13-4	Entries for stock dividends	Easy	10 min	Analytic	FN-Measurement		
PE13-5A	13-5	Entries for treasury stock	Easy	10 min	Analytic	FN-Measurement		
PE13-5B	13-5	Entries for treasury stock	Easy	10 min	Analytic	FN-Measurement		
PE13-6A	13-6	Stockholders' equity section of balance sheet	Easy	5 min	Analytic	FN-Measurement		
PE13-6B	13-6	Stockholders' equity section of balance sheet	Easy	5 min	Analytic	FN-Measurement		
PE13-7A	13-6	Retained earnings statement	Easy	5 min	Analytic	FN-Measurement		
PE13-7B	13-6	Retained earnings statement	Easy	5 min	Analytic	FN-Measurement		
Ex13-1	13-3	Dividends per share	Easy	10 min	Analytic	FN-Measurement		
Ex13-2	13-3	Dividends per share	Easy	10 min	Analytic	FN-Measurement		

Number	Objective	Description	Difficulty	Time	AACSB	AICPA	SS	GL
Ex13-3	13-3	Entries for issuing par stock	Easy	10 min	Analytic	FN-Measurement		
Ex13-4	13-3	Entries for issuing no-par stock	Easy	10 min	Analytic	FN-Measurement		
Ex13-5	13-3	Issuing stock for assets other than cash	Easy	5 min	Analytic	FN-Measurement		
Ex13-6	13-3	Selected stock transactions	Easy	15 min	Analytic	FN-Measurement		
Ex13-7	13-3	Issuing stock	Moderate	10 min	Analytic	FN-Measurement		
Ex13-8	13-3	Issuing stock	Easy	10 min	Analytic	FN-Measurement		
Ex13-9	13-4	Entries for cash dividends	Easy	10 min	Analytic	FN-Measurement		
Ex13-10	13-4	Entries for stock dividends	Moderate	15 min	Analytic	FN-Measurement		
Ex13-11	13-5	Treasury stock transactions	Moderate	15 min	Analytic	FN-Measurement		
Ex13-12	13-5, 13-6	Treasury stock transactions	Moderate	15 min	Analytic	FN-Measurement		
Ex13-13	13-5, 13-6	Treasury stock transactions	Moderate	15 min	Analytic	FN-Measurement		
Ex13-14	13-6	Reporting paid-in-capital	Easy	10 min	Analytic	FN-Measurement		
Ex13-15	13-6	Stockholders' equity section of balance sheet	Easy	10 min	Analytic	FN-Measurement		
Ex13-16	13-6	Stockholders' equity section of balance sheet	Easy	10 min	Analytic	FN-Measurement		
Ex13-18	13-6	Retained earnings statement	Easy	10 min	Analytic	FN-Measurement		
Ex13-17	13-6	Stockholders' equity section of balance sheet	Moderate	15 min	Analytic	FN-Measurement		
Ex13-19	13-6	Statement of stockholders' equity	Moderate	15 min	Analytic	FN-Measurement	Exl	
Ex13-20	13-7	Effect of stock split	Easy	5 min	Analytic	FN-Measurement		
Ex13-21	13-7	Effect of cash dividend and stock split	Easy	5 min	Analytic	FN-Measurement		
Ex13-22	13-7	Selected dividend transactions, stock split	Moderate	15 min	Analytic	FN-Measurement		
Ex13-23	FAI	Dividend yield	Easy	5 min	Analytic	FN-Measurement		
Ex13-24	FAI	Dividend yield	Easy	10 min	Analytic	FN-Measurement		
Ex13-25	FAI	Dividend yield	Moderate	10 min	Analytic	FN-Measurement		
Pr13-1A	13-3	Dividends on preferred and common stock	Moderate	1 hr	Analytic	FN-Measurement	Exl	
Pr13-2A	13-3	Stock transactions for corporate expansion	Moderate	45 min	Analytic	FN-Measurement		KA
Pr13-3A	13-3, 13-4, 13-5	Selected stock transactions	Moderate	1 hr	Analytic	FN-Measurement		KA
Pr13-4A	13-3, 13-4, 13-5, 13-6	Entries for selected corporate transactions	Difficult	1 hr	Analytic	FN-Measurement	Exl	KA
Pr13-5A	13-3, 13-4, 13-5, 13-7	Entries for selected corporate transactions	Moderate	1 hr	Analytic	FN-Measurement	Exl	KA
Pr13-1B	13-3	Dividends on preferred and common stock	Moderate	1 hr	Analytic	FN-Measurement	Exl	

Number	Objective	Description	Difficulty	Time	AACSB	AICPA	SS	GL
Pr13-2B	13-3	Stock transactions for corporate expansion	Moderate	45 min	Analytic	FN-Measurement		KA
Pr13-3B	13-3, 13-4, 13-5	Selected stock transactions	Moderate	1 hr	Analytic	FN-Measurement		KA
Pr13-4B	13-3, 13-4, 13-5, 13-6	Entries for selected corporate transactions	Difficult	1 hr	Analytic	FN-Measurement	Exl	KA
Pr13-5B	13-3, 13-4, 13-5, 13-7	Entries for selected corporate transactions	Moderate	1 hr	Analytic	FN-Measurement	Exl	KA
SA13-1	13-1	Board of directors' actions	Easy	10 min	Ethics	BB-Industry		
SA13-2	13-3	Ethics and professional conduct in business	Easy	10 min	Ethics	BB-Industry		
SA13-3	13-3	Issuing stock	Moderate	20 min	Analytic	FN-Measurement		
SA13-4	13-4	Dividends	Moderate	20 min	Analytic	FN-Measurement		
SA13-5	13-1	Profiling a corporation	Moderate	30 min	Analytic	BB-Industry		
SA13-6	13-1	Interpret stock exchange listing			Analytic	BB-Industry		

1. Each stockholder's liability for corporation debts is limited to the amount invested in the corporation. A corporation is responsible for its own obligations, and therefore, its creditors may not look beyond the assets of the corporation for satisfaction of their claims.

2. The large investments needed by large businesses are usually obtainable only through the pooling of the resources of many people. The corporation also has the advantages over proprietorships and partnerships of transferable shares of ownership, and thus the continuity of existence, and limited liability of its owners (stockholders).

3. No. Common stock with a higher par is not necessarily a better investment than common stock with a lower par because par is an amount assigned to the shares.

4. The broker is not correct. Corporations are not legally liable to pay dividends until the dividends are declared. If the company that issued the preferred stock has operating losses, it could omit dividends, first, on its common stock and, later, on its preferred stock.

5. Factors influencing the market price of a corporation's stock include the following:
   a. Financial condition, earnings record, and dividend record of the corporation.
   b. Its potential earning power.
   c. General business and economic conditions and prospects.

6. No. Premium on stock is additional paid-in capital.

7. a. Sufficient retained earnings, sufficient cash, and formal action by the board of directors.
   b. February 6, declaration date; March 9, record date; and April 5, payment date.

8. The company may not have had enough cash on hand to pay a dividend on the common stock, or resources may be needed for plant expansion, replacement of facilities, payment of liabilities, etc.

9. a. No change.
   b. Total equity is the same.

10. a. Current liability
    b. Stockholders' equity

11. a. Unissued stock has never been issued, but treasury stock has been issued as fully paid and has subsequently been reacquired.
    b. As a deduction from the total of other stockholders' equity accounts.

12. a. It has no effect on revenue or expense.
    b. It reduces stockholders' equity by $120,000.

13. a. It has no effect on revenue.
    b. It increases stockholders' equity by $158,000.

14. The primary advantage of the combined income and retained earnings statement is that it emphasizes net income as the connecting link between the income statement and the retained earnings portion of stockholders' equity.

15. The three classifications of restrictions on retained earnings are legal, contractual, and discretionary. Appropriations are normally reported in the notes to the financial statements.

16. Such prior period adjustments should be reported as an adjustment to the beginning balance of retained earnings.

17. The statement of stockholders' equity is normally prepared when there are significant changes in stock and other paid-in capital accounts.

18. The primary purpose of a stock split is to bring about a reduction in the market price per share and thus to encourage more investors to buy the company's shares.

PRACTICE EXERCISES

PE 13–1A

	Year 1	Year 2	Year 3
Amount distributed	$40,000	$10,000	$120,000
Preferred dividend (10,000 shares)	15,000	10,000	15,000
Common dividend (25,000 shares)	$25,000	$ 0	$105,000
Dividends per share:			
Preferred stock	$1.50	$1.00	$1.50
Common stock	$1.00	None	$4.20

PE 13–1B

	Year 1	Year 2	Year 3
Amount distributed	$20,000	$ 4,000	$40,000
Preferred dividend (5,000 shares)	7,500	4,000	7,500
Common dividend (10,000 shares)	$12,500	$ 0	$32,500
Dividends per share:			
Preferred stock	$1.50	$0.80	$1.50
Common stock	$1.25	None	$3.25

PE 13–2A

Aug. 3	Cash	5,760,000	
	Common Stock		4,500,000
	Paid-In Capital in Excess of Stated Value....		1,260,000
	(45,000 shares × $128).		
Sept. 22	Cash	150,000	
	Preferred Stock		150,000
	(2,000 shares × $75).		
Nov. 4	Cash	240,000	
	Preferred Stock		225,000
	Paid-In Capital in Excess of Par		15,000
	(3,000 shares × $80).		

PE 13–2B

July	6	Cash	960,000	
		Common Stock..		960,000
		(800,000 shares × $1.20).		
Aug.	30	Cash	500,000	
		Preferred Stock		500,000
		(10,000 shares × $50).		
Oct.	14	Cash	405,000	
		Preferred Stock		375,000
		Paid-In Capital in Excess of Par		30,000
		(7,500 shares × $54).		

PE 13–3A

July	16	Cash Dividends	48,000	
		Cash Dividends Payable.........................		48,000
Aug.	15	No entry required.		
Sept.	30	Cash Dividends Payable	48,000	
		Cash		48,000

PE 13–3B

Oct.	1	Cash Dividends	90,000	
		Cash Dividends Payable.........................		90,000
Nov.	1	No entry required.		
Dec.	24	Cash Dividends Payable	90,000	
		Cash		90,000

PE 13–4A

Feb.	13	Stock Dividends (300,000 × 3% × $63)...............	567,000	
		Stock Dividends Distributable (9,000 × $40)		360,000
		Paid-In Capital in Excess of Par—		
		Common Stock ($567,000 − $360,000)		207,000
Mar.	14	No entry required.		
Apr.	30	Stock Dividends Distributable...........................	360,000	
		Common Stock...		360,000

PE 13–4B

May 10 Stock Dividends (250,000 × 2% × $60)............... 300,000
        Stock Dividends Distributable (5,000 × $50)   250,000
        Paid-In Capital in Excess of Par—
        Common Stock ($300,000 – $250,000)   50,000

June 9 No entry required.

Aug. 1 Stock Dividends Distributable............................ 250,000
        Common Stock..   250,000

PE 13–5A

Jan. 24 Treasury Stock (6,000 × $18)............................. 108,000
        Cash   108,000

Mar. 15 Cash (4,500 × $21)... 94,500
        Treasury Stock (4,500 × $18).........................   81,000
        Paid-In Capital from Sale of
        Treasury Stock [4,500 × ($21 – $18)]   13,500

June 2 Cash (1,500 × $17)... 25,500
        Paid-In Capital from Sale of
        Treasury Stock [1,500 × ($18 – $17)]................... 1,500
        Treasury Stock (1,500 × $18).........................   27,000

PE 13–5B

Oct. 2 Treasury Stock (12,000 × $6)............................. 72,000
        Cash   72,000

Nov. 15 Cash (8,400 × $9)... 75,600
        Treasury Stock (8,400 × $6).........................   50,400
        Paid-In Capital from Sale of
        Treasury Stock [8,400 × ($9 – $6)]   25,200

Dec. 22 Cash (3,600 × $5)... 18,000
        Paid-In Capital from Sale of
        Treasury Stock [3,600 × ($6 – $5)]..................... 3,600
        Treasury Stock (3,600 × $6).........................   21,600

PE 13–6A

Stockholders' Equity

Paid-in capital:		
Common stock, $80 par (30,000 shares authorized, 25,000 shares issued).................	$ 2,000,000	
Excess of issue price over par............................	315,000	$ 2,315,000
From sale of treasury stock.................................		33,000
Total paid-in capital		$ 2,348,000
Retained earnings...		1,112,000
Total..		$ 3,460,000
Deduct treasury stock (2,000 shares at cost)..........		180,000
Total stockholders' equity		$ 3,280,000

PE 13–6B

Stockholders' Equity

Paid-in capital:		
Common stock, $75 par (50,000 shares authorized, 45,000 shares issued).................	$ 3,375,000	
Excess of issue price over par............................	485,000	$ 3,860,000
From sale of treasury stock.................................		18,000
Total paid-in capital		$ 3,878,000
Retained earnings...		1,452,000
Total..		$ 5,330,000
Deduct treasury stock (5,000 shares at cost)..........		420,000
Total stockholders' equity		$ 4,910,000

PE 13–7A

DYNAMIC LEADERS INC.
Retained Earnings Statement
For the Year Ended July 31, 2008

Retained earnings, August 1, 2007		$ 988,500
Net income	$325,000	
Less dividends declared	125,000	
Increase in retained earnings		200,000
Retained earnings, July 31, 2008..............................		$ 1,188,500

PE 13–7B

MAXIMA RETRACTORS INC.
Retained Earnings Statement
For the Year Ended October 31, 2008

Retained earnings, November 1, 2007		$ 2,906,000
Net income	$553,000	
Less dividends declared	300,000	
Increase in retained earnings		253,000
Retained earnings, October 31, 2008		$ 3,159,000

EXERCISES

Ex. 13–1

	1st Year	2nd Year	3rd Year	4th Year
a. Total dividend distributed	$ 40,000	$ 98,000	$ 120,000	$ 195,000
b. Preferred dividend	$ 40,000	$ 50,000	$ 50,000	$ 50,000
Preferred shares outstanding	/ 50,000	/ 50,000	/ 50,000	/ 50,000
Preferred dividend per share	$ 0.80	$ 1.00	$ 1.00	$ 1.00
Dividend for common shares (a. – b.)	$ —	$ 48,000	$ 70,000	$ 145,000
Common shares outstanding	—	/ 100,000	/ 100,000	/ 100,000
Common dividend per share	—	$ 0.48	$ 0.70	$ 1.45

Ex. 13–2

	1st Year	2nd Year	3rd Year	4th Year
a. Total dividend distributed	$ 6,000	$ 26,000	$ 4,000	$ 60,000
b. Preferred dividend	$ 6,000	$ 10,000	$ 4,000	$ 10,000
Preferred shares outstanding	/ 40,000	/ 40,000	/ 40,000	/ 40,000
Preferred dividend per share	$ 0.15	$ 0.25	$ 0.10	$ 0.25
Dividend for common shares (a. – b.)	$ —	$ 16,000	$ —	$ 50,000
Common shares outstanding	—	/ 50,000	—	/ 50,000
Common dividend per share	—	$ 0.32	—	$ 1.00

Ex. 13–3

a. Feb.   4 Cash.. 1,920,000

                Common Stock....................................   600,000

                Paid-In Capital in Excess of Par—

                Common Stock....................................   1,320,000

    Mar. 31 Cash.. 1,620,000

                Preferred Stock..................................   1,350,000

                Paid-In Capital in Excess of Par—

                Preferred Stock..................................   270,000

b. $3,540,000 ($1,920,000 + $1,620,000)

Ex. 13–4

a. July   17 Cash.. 5,400,000

                Common Stock....................................   750,000

                Paid-In Capital in Excess of

                Stated Value.....................................   4,650,000

    Sept. 20 Cash.. 800,000

                Preferred Stock..................................   500,000

                Paid-In Capital in Excess of Par—

                Preferred Stock..................................   300,000

b. $6,200,000 ($5,400,000 + $800,000)

Ex. 13–5

Nov. 10 Land.. 480,000

            Common Stock....................................   120,000

            Paid-In Capital in Excess of Par....................   360,000

Ex. 13–6

a. Cash 240,000

    Common Stock   240,000

b. Organizational Expenses 6,000

    Common Stock   6,000

    Cash 216,000

    Common Stock   216,000

c. Land 75,000

   Building... 240,000

    Interest Payable*...   2,200

    Mortgage Note Payable   200,000

    Common Stock   112,800

*An acceptable alternative would be to credit Interest Expense.

Ex. 13–7

Buildings 80,000

Land 100,000

   Preferred Stock...   160,000

   Paid-In Capital in Excess of Par—Preferred Stock   20,000

Cash... 450,000

   Common Stock   400,000

   Paid-In Capital in Excess of Par—Common Stock.......   50,000

Ex. 13–8

Feb.	19	Cash..	1,500,000	
		Common Stock		1,500,000
	27	Organizational Expenses	7,500	
		Common Stock		7,500
Mar.	13	Land..	80,000	
		Buildings	350,000	
		Equipment	45,000	
		Common Stock		450,000
		Paid-In Capital in Excess of Par—		
		Common Stock		25,000
May	6	Cash..	230,000	
		Preferred Stock....................................		200,000
		Paid-In Capital in Excess of Par—		
		Preferred Stock....................................		30,000

Ex. 13–9

July	2	Cash Dividends...	275,000	
		Cash Dividends Payable		275,000
Aug.	1	No entry required.		
Sept.	1	Cash Dividends Payable	275,000	
		Cash		275,000

Ex. 13–10

a. (1) Stock Dividends 720,000*

        Stock Dividends Distributable   600,000

        Paid-In Capital in Excess of Par—

        Common Stock   120,000

        *[($30,000,000/$100) × $120] × 2%

    (2) Stock Dividends Distributable 600,000

        Common Stock   600,000

b. (1) $34,500,000 ($30,000,000 + $4,500,000)

    (2) $50,600,000

    (3) $85,100,000 ($34,500,000 + $50,600,000)

c. (1) $35,220,000 ($34,500,000 + $720,000)

    (2) $49,880,000 ($50,600,000 − $720,000)

    (3) $85,100,000 ($35,220,000 + $49,880,000)

Ex. 13–11

a. May   2 Treasury Stock 216,000

             Cash   216,000

    Aug. 14 Cash 190,000

             Treasury Stock   180,000

             Paid-In Capital from Sale of

             Treasury Stock   10,000

    Nov.   7 Cash 35,000

             Paid-In Capital from Sale of

             Treasury Stock 1,000

             Treasury Stock   36,000

b. $9,000 credit

c. Mountain Springs may have purchased the stock to support the market price of the stock, to provide shares for resale to employees, or for reissuance to employees as a bonus according to stock purchase agreements.

Ex. 13–12

a. Sept.	9	Treasury Stock...	1,068,000	
		Cash		1,068,000
Oct.	31	Cash...	966,000	
		Treasury Stock		934,500
		Paid-In Capital from Sale of Treasury Stock		31,500
Dec.	4	Cash...	85,500	
		Treasury Stock		80,100
		Paid-In Capital from Sale of Treasury Stock		5,400

b. $36,900 ($31,500 + $5,400) credit

c. $53,400 (600 × $89) debit

d. The balance in the treasury stock account is reported as a deduction from the total of the paid-in capital and retained earnings.

Ex. 13–13

a. June	12	Treasury Stock...	720,000	
		Cash		720,000
Aug.	10	Cash...	450,000	
		Treasury Stock		432,000
		Paid-In Capital from Sale of Treasury Stock		18,000
Dec.	20	Cash...	282,000	
		Paid-In Capital from Sale of Treasury Stock..	6,000	
		Treasury Stock		288,000

b. $12,000 credit

c. Stockholders' Equity section

d. Tacoma Inc. may have purchased the stock to support the market price of the stock, to provide shares for resale to employees, or for reissuance to employees as a bonus according to stock purchase agreements.

Ex. 13–14

Stockholders' Equity

Paid-in capital:
Preferred 3% stock, $100 par
(50,000 shares authorized,
15,000 shares issued)................ $1,500,000
Excess of issue price over par....... 180,000 $1,680,000
Common stock, no par, $10 stated
value (500,000 shares author-
ized, 67,500 shares issued)....... $ 675,000
Excess of issue price over par....... 125,000 800,000
From sale of treasury stock............ 14,500
Total paid-in capital $2,494,500

Ex. 13–15

Stockholders' Equity

Paid-in capital:
Common stock, $50 par
(25,000 shares authorized,
18,000 shares issued)................ $900,000
Excess of issue price over par....... 110,000 $1,010,000
From sale of treasury stock............ 42,000
Total paid-in capital $1,052,000
Retained earnings................................. 3,178,000
Total... $4,230,000
Deduct treasury stock
(3,500 shares at cost)..................... 210,000
Total stockholders' equity $4,020,000

Ex. 13–16

<u>**Stockholders' Equity**</u>

Paid-in capital:

Preferred 3% stock, $75 par (20,000 shares authorized, 12,500 shares issued)	$937,500		
Excess of issue price over par	25,000	$ 962,500	
Common stock, $5 par (400,000 shares authorized 175,000 shares issued)	$875,000		
Excess of issue price over par	700,000	1,575,000	
From sale of treasury stock		16,000	
Total paid-in capital		$ 2,553,500	
Retained earnings		2,338,000	
Total		$ 4,891,500	
Deduct treasury common stock (22,000 shares at cost)		165,000	
Total stockholders' equity			$ 4,726,500

Ex. 13–17

STILLWATER CORPORATION
Retained Earnings Statement
For the Year Ended August 31, 2008

Retained earnings, September 1, 2007		$ 1,752,000
Net income	$378,000	
Less dividends declared	180,000	
Increase in retained earnings		198,000
Retained earnings, August 31, 2008		$ 1,950,000

Ex. 13–18

1. Retained earnings is not part of paid-in capital.

2. The cost of treasury stock should be *deducted* from the *total* stockholders' equity.

3. Dividends payable should be included as part of current liabilities and not as part of stockholders' equity.

4. Common stock should be included as part of paid-in capital.

5. The amount of shares of common stock issued of 60,000 times the par value per share of $50 should be extended as $3,000,000, not $3,900,000. The difference, $900,000, probably represents paid-in capital in excess of par.

6. Organizing costs should be expensed when incurred and not included as a part of stockholders' equity.

One possible corrected Stockholders' Equity section of the balance sheet is as follows:

Stockholders' Equity

Paid-in capital:			
Preferred 1% stock, $75 par			
(8,000 shares authorized and issued)	$ 600,000		
Excess of issue price over par	56,000	$ 656,000	
Common stock, $50 par (100,000 shares authorized,			
60,000 shares issued)	$ 3,000,000		
Excess of issue price over par	900,000	3,900,000	
Total paid-in capital		$ 4,556,000	
Retained earnings		1,203,000*	
		$ 5,759,000	
Deduct treasury stock (4,000 shares at cost)		320,000	
Total stockholders' equity		$ 5,439,000	

* $1,278,000 – $75,000. Since the organizing costs should have been expensed, the retained earnings should be $75,000 less.

Ex. 13–19

FAMILY GREETING CARDS INC.
Statement of Stockholders' Equity
For the Year Ended December 31, 2008

	Common Stock $3 Par	Paid-In Capital in Excess of Par	Treasury Stock	Retained Earnings	Total
Balance, Jan. 1, 2008	$600,000	$350,000	—	$2,108,000	$3,058,000
Issued 50,000 shares of common stock	150,000	100,000			250,000
Purchased 6,000 shares as treasury stock............................			$(24,000)		(24,000)
Net income......................				325,000	325,000
Dividends				(80,000)	(80,000)
Balance, Dec. 31, 2008 ...	$750,000	$450,000	$(24,000)	$2,353,000	$3,529,000

Ex. 13–20

a. 150,000 shares (50,000 × 3)

b. $60 per share ($180/3)

Ex. 13–21

	Assets	Liabilities	Stockholders' Equity
(1) Declaring a cash dividend	0	+	–
(2) Paying the cash dividend declared in (1)	–	–	0
(3) Authorizing and issuing stock certificates in a stock split	0	0	0
(4) Declaring a stock dividend	0	0	0
(5) Issuing stock certificates for the stock dividend declared in (4)	0	0	0

Ex. 13–22

Mar. 5 No entry required. The stockholders ledger would be revised to record the increased number of shares held by each stockholder.

May 15 Cash Dividends..	126,000*	
Cash Dividends Payable...............................		126,000

*[(15,000 shares × $2) + (800,000 shares × $0.12)] = $30,000 + $96,000 = $126,000

July 14 Cash Dividends Payable	126,000	
Cash		126,000

Nov. 15 Cash Dividends..	142,000*	
Cash Dividends Payable...............................		142,000

*[(15,000 shares × $2) + (800,000 shares × $0.14)] = $30,000 + $112,000 = $142,000

15 Stock Dividends...	240,000**	
Stock Dividends Distributable........................		200,000
Paid-In Capital in Excess of Par—Common Stock..		40,000

**(800,000 shares × 1% × $30) = $240,000

Dec. 15 Cash Dividends Payable	142,000	
Cash		142,000

15 Stock Dividends Distributable.............................	200,000	
Common Stock..		200,000

Ex. 13–23

$$\text{Dividend Yield} = \frac{\text{Cash Dividend per Share of Common Stock}}{\text{Market Price per Share of Common Stock}}$$

Dividend Yield: $\dfrac{\$1.95}{\$49.69} = 3.9\%$

Ex. 13–24

a. 2005: Dividend Yield = $0.91/$35.05 = 2.60%

   2004: Dividend Yield = $0.82/$36.50 = 2.25%

b. Dividends per share increased from $0.82 in 2004 to $0.91 in 2005. In addition, the dividend yield increased from 2.25% in 2004 to 2.60% in 2005. The increase in the dividend yield is a result of the $0.09 increase in dividends per share as well as the slight decrease in the closing stock price of $1.45 per share ($36.50 – $35.05). This is consistent with the following excerpt from the Investor Communications section of GE's Web site:

   GE has rewarded its shareowners with 30 consecutive years of dividend growth. GE's dividend yield is about 3.6% currently. We are committed to dividend growth in line with earnings growth.

Ex. 13–25

The investor would receive a return on the investment through share price appreciation as internally generated funds are used to fund growth and earnings opportunities. Thus, investors in eBay would likely approve of this policy, because the company is able to earn superior returns with internally generated earnings beyond what investors could likely earn on their own by investing dividend distributions.

PROBLEMS

Prob. 13–1A

1.

Year	Total Dividends	Preferred Dividends		Common Dividends	
		Total	Per Share	Total	Per Share
2003......................	$ 21,000	$21,000	$ 2.10	$ 0	$ 0
2004......................	50,000	30,000	3.00	20,000	0.20
2005......................	15,000	15,000	1.50	0	0
2006......................	80,000	30,000	3.00	50,000	0.50
2007......................	90,000	30,000	3.00	60,000	0.60
2008......................	140,000	30,000	3.00	110,000	1.10
			$15.60		$2.40

2. Average annual dividend for preferred: $2.60 per share ($15.60/6)

   Average annual dividend for common: $0.40 per share ($2.40/6)

3. a. 3.25% ($2.60/$80)

   b. 4.0% ($0.40/$10)

Prob. 13–2A

June	6	Building	1,200,000	
		Land	300,000	
		Common Stock		1,350,000
		Paid-In Capital in Excess of Par—		
		Common Stock		150,000
	14	Cash	540,000	
		Preferred Stock		375,000
		Paid-In Capital in Excess of Par—		
		Preferred Stock		165,000
	30	Cash	500,000	
		Mortgage Note Payable		500,000

Prob. 13–3A

a. Cash (12,000 × $62) 744,000

    Common Stock (12,000 × $40) 480,000

    Paid-In Capital in Excess of Par—Common

    Stock (12,000 × $22) 264,000

b. Cash (5,000 × $124) 620,000

    Preferred Stock (5,000 × $100) 500,000

    Paid-In Capital in Excess of Par—Preferred

    Stock (5,000 × $24) 120,000

c. Treasury Stock 580,000

    Cash 580,000

        ($580,000/10,000 shares) = $58 per share.

d. Cash 457,500

    Treasury Stock (7,500 × $58) 435,000

    Paid-In Capital from Sale of Treasury Stock 22,500

e. Cash 82,500

  Paid-In Capital from Sale of Treasury Stock 4,500

    Treasury Stock (1,500 × $58) 87,000

f. Cash Dividends 86,500

    Cash Dividends Payable 86,500

        (23,000 × $2) + [(70,000 + 12,000 – 10,000

        + 7,500 + 1,500) × $0.50].

g. Cash Dividends Payable 86,500

    Cash 86,500

Prob. 13–4A

1. and 2.

Common Stock

			Jan.	1	Bal.	3,800,000
			Mar.	3		200,000
			Aug.	15		120,000
			Dec.	31	Bal.	4,120,000

Paid-In Capital in Excess of Stated Value

			Jan.	1	Bal.	760,000
			Mar.	3		260,000
			July	1		240,000
			Dec.	31	Bal.	1,260,000

Retained Earnings

Dec.	31		460,500	Jan.	1	Bal.	4,390,000
				Dec.	31		639,500
				Dec.	31	Bal.	4,569,000

Treasury Stock

Jan.	1	Bal.	500,000	May	21		500,000
Sept.	30		230,000				
Dec.	31	Bal.	230,000				

Paid-In Capital from Sale of Treasury Stock

			May	21		150,000

Stock Dividends Distributable

Aug.	15		120,000	July	1		120,000

Stock Dividends

July	1		360,000	Dec.	31		360,000

Cash Dividends

Dec.	27		100,500	Dec.	31		100,500

Prob. 13–4A Continued

2.

Jan.	10	Cash Dividends Payable	71,000*	
		Cash		71,000
		*[(380,000 – 25,000) × $0.20]		
Mar.	3	Cash...	460,000	
		Common Stock (20,000 × $10)........................		200,000
		Paid-In Capital in Excess of Stated Value		260,000
May	21	Cash...	650,000	
		Treasury Stock (25,000 × $20)		500,000
		Paid-In Capital from Sale of Treasury Stock.		150,000
July	1	Stock Dividends...	360,000*	
		Stock Dividends Distributable (12,000 × $10)		120,000
		Paid-In Capital in Excess of Stated Value		240,000
		*(380,000 + 20,000) × 3% × $30		
Aug.	15	Stock Dividends Distributable............................	120,000	
		Common Stock		120,000
Sept.	30	Treasury Stock..	230,000	
		Cash		230,000
Dec.	27	Cash Dividends..	100,500*	
		Cash Dividends Payable		100,500
		*(380,000 + 20,000 + 12,000 – 10,000) × $0.25		
	31	Income Summary..	639,500	
		Retained Earnings..		639,500
	31	Retained Earnings	460,500	
		Stock Dividends		360,000
		Cash Dividends		100,500

Prob. 13–4A   Concluded

3.

EUREKA ENTERPRISES INC.
Retained Earnings Statement
For the Year Ended December 31, 2008

Retained earnings (January 1, 2008)..............................		$4,390,000
Net income	$ 639,500	
Less: Cash dividends	(100,500)	
Stock dividends	(360,000)	
Increase in retained earnings		179,000
Retained earnings (December 31, 2008).........................		$4,569,000

4.

Stockholders' Equity

Paid-in capital:		
Common stock, $10 stated value (500,000 shares		
authorized, 412,000 shares issued)..........................	$ 4,120,000	
Excess of issue price over stated value......................	1,260,000	
From sale of treasury stock...	150,000	
Total paid-in capital		$ 5,530,000
Retained earnings..		4,569,000
Total		$10,099,000
Deduct treasury stock (10,000 shares at cost)...................		230,000
Total stockholders' equity		$ 9,869,000

Prob. 13–5A

Jan. 3 No entry required. The stockholders ledger would be revised to record the increased number of shares held by each stockholder.

Feb. 20	Treasury Stock (50,000 × $32)	1,600,000	
	Cash		1,600,000
May 1	Cash Dividends...	73,000*	
	Cash Dividends Payable		73,000

*(30,000 × $0.80) + [(400,000 – 50,000) × $0.14]

June 1	Cash Dividends Payable	73,000	
	Cash		73,000
Aug. 5	Cash (42,000 × $39)	1,638,000	
	Treasury Stock (42,000 × $32)		1,344,000
	Paid-In Capital from Sale of Treasury Stock (42,000 × $7)		294,000
Nov. 15	Cash Dividends...	82,800*	
	Cash Dividends Payable		82,800

*(30,000 × $0.80) + [(400,000 – 8,000) × $0.15]

15	Stock Dividends (7,840 × $40)	313,600**	
	Stock Dividends Distributable (7,840 × $25)		196,000
	Paid-In Capital in Excess of Par—Common Stock (7,840 × $15)		117,600

**(400,000 – 8,000) × 2% × $40

Dec. 31	Cash Dividends Payable	82,800	
	Cash		82,800
31	Stock Dividends Distributable............................	196,000	
	Common Stock		196,000

Prob. 13–1B

1.

Year	Total Dividends	Preferred Dividends		Common Dividends	
		Total	Per Share	Total	Per Share
2003......................	$ 60,000	$20,000	$0.50	$40,000	$0.80
2004......................	8,000	8,000	0.20	0	0
2005......................	30,000	20,000	0.50	10,000	0.20
2006......................	40,000	20,000	0.50	20,000	0.40
2007......................	80,000	20,000	0.50	60,000	1.20
2008......................	115,000	20,000	0.50	95,000	1.90
			$2.70		$4.50

2. Average annual dividend for preferred: $0.45 per share ($2.70/6)
   Average annual dividend for common: $0.75 per share ($4.50/6)

3. a. 1.8% ($0.45/$25)

   b. 4.0% ($0.75/$18.75)

Prob. 13–2B

Jan.	6	Cash...	900,000	
		Mortgage Note Payable..................................		900,000
	15	Cash...	950,000	
		Preferred Stock...		800,000
		Paid-In Capital in Excess of Par—		
		Preferred Stock...		150,000
	31	Building	1,675,000	
		Land	250,000	
		Common Stock...		1,600,000
		Paid-In Capital in Excess of Par—		
		Common Stock...		325,000

Prob. 13–3B

a. Treasury Stock 650,000
     Cash 650,000
       ($650,000/25,000 shares) = $26 per share.

b. Cash 576,000
     Treasury Stock (18,000 × $26) 468,000
     Paid-In Capital from Sale of Treasury Stock 108,000

c. Cash (10,000 × $80) 800,000
     Preferred Stock (10,000 × $50) 500,000
     Paid-In Capital in Excess of Par—Preferred
     Stock (10,000 × $30) 300,000

d. Cash (40,000 × $30) 1,200,000
     Common Stock (40,000 × $15) 600,000
     Paid-In Capital in Excess of Par—Common
     Stock 600,000

e. Cash 150,000
    Paid-In Capital from Sale of Treasury Stock 6,000
     Treasury Stock (6,000 × $26) 156,000

f. Cash Dividends 123,900
     Cash Dividends Payable 123,900
       (60,000 X $1) + [(600,000 – 25,000 + 18,000
       + 40,000 + 6,000) × $0.10]

g. Cash Dividends Payable 123,900
     Cash 123,900

Prob. 13–4B

1. and 2.

Common Stock

			Jan.	1	Bal.	3,000,000
			Apr.	3		800,000
			Aug.	30		76,000
			Dec.	31	Bal.	3,876,000

Paid-In Capital in Excess of Stated Value

			Jan.	1	Bal.	600,000
			Apr.	3		800,000
			July	30		95,000
			Dec.	31	Bal.	1,495,000

Retained Earnings

Dec. 31		215,700	Jan.	1	Bal.	6,175,000
			Dec.	31		350,000
			Dec.	31	Bal.	6,309,300

Treasury Stock

Jan.	1	Bal.	280,000	Feb.	19		280,000
Nov.	7		600,000				
Dec.	31	Bal.	600,000				

Paid-In Capital from Sale of Treasury Stock

		Feb.	19	80,000

Stock Dividends Distributable

Aug.	30	76,000	July	30	76,000

Stock Dividends

July	30	171,000	Dec.	31	171,000

Cash Dividends

Dec.	30	44,700	Dec.	31	44,700

2.

Jan. 12	Cash Dividends Payable	35,000*	
	Cash		35,000
	*[(150,000 – 10,000) × $0.25]		
Feb. 19	Cash...	360,000	
	Treasury Stock		280,000
	Paid-In Capital from Sale of Treasury Stock.		80,000
Apr. 3	Cash...	1,600,000	
	Common Stock (40,000 × $20).......................		800,000
	Paid-In Capital in Excess of Stated Value.....		800,000
July 30	Stock Dividends...	171,000*	
	Stock Dividends Distributable (3,800 × $20)		76,000
	Paid-In Capital in Excess of Stated Value.....		95,000
	*(150,000 + 40,000) × 2% × $45		
Aug. 30	Stock Dividends Distributable............................	76,000	
	Common Stock		76,000
Nov. 7	Treasury Stock...	600,000	
	Cash		600,000
	($600,000/15,000 shares) = $40 per share.		
Dec. 30	Cash Dividends...	44,700*	
	Cash Dividends Payable		44,700
	*(150,000 + 40,000 + 3,800 – 15,000) × $0.25		
31	Income Summary..	350,000	
	Retained Earnings...		350,000
31	Retained Earnings	215,700	
	Stock Dividends		171,000
	Cash Dividends		44,700

3.

GPS ENTERPRISES INC.
Retained Earnings Statement
For the Year Ended December 31, 2008

Retained earnings (beginning of period).......................		$6,175,000
Net income	$350,000	
Less: Cash dividends..	(44,700)	
Stock dividends..	(171,000)	
Increase in retained earnings		134,300
Retained earnings (end of period)................................		$6,309,300

4.

Stockholders' Equity

Paid-in capital:		
Common stock, $20 stated value (250,000 shares		
authorized, 193,800 shares issued)....................	$ 3,876,000	
Excess of issue price over stated value	1,495,000	
From sale of treasury stock..................................	80,000	
Total paid-in capital		$ 5,451,000
Retained earnings..		6,309,300
Total...		$11,760,300
Deduct treasury stock (15,000 shares at cost).............		600,000
Total stockholders' equity		$11,160,300

Prob. 13–5B

Jan. 10 No entry required. The stockholders ledger would be revised to record the increased number of shares held by each stockholder.

Mar.	**1**	Cash Dividends..	185,000*	
		Cash Dividends Payable...............................		185,000

*(125,000 × $1) + (500,000 × $0.12)

Apr.	**30**	Cash Dividends Payable	185,000	
		Cash		185,000
July	**9**	Treasury Stock (40,000 × $16)	640,000	
		Cash		640,000
Aug.	**29**	Cash (30,000 × $21)	630,000	
		Treasury Stock (30,000 × $16).......................		480,000
		Paid-In Capital from Sale of Treasury		
		Stock (30,000 × $5)..		150,000
Sept.	**1**	Cash Dividends..	169,100*	
		Cash Dividends Payable...............................		169,100

*(125,000 × $1) + [(500,000 – 10,000) × $0.09]

	1	Stock Dividends (4,900 × $22)	107,800**	
		Stock Dividends Distributable (4,900 × $5) ...		24,500
		Paid-In Capital in Excess of Par—Common		
		Stock (4,900 × $17)..		83,300

**(500,000 – 10,000) × 1% × $22

Oct.	**31**	Cash Dividends Payable	169,100	
		Cash		169,100
	31	Stock Dividends Distributable............................	24,500	
		Common Stock...		24,500

SPECIAL ACTIVITIES

SA 13–1

At the time of this decision, the WorldCom board had come under intense scrutiny. This was the largest loan by a company to its CEO in history. The SEC began an investigation into this loan, and Bernie Ebbers was eventually terminated as the CEO, with this loan being cited as part of the reason. The board indicated that the decision to lend Ebbers this money was to keep him from selling his stock and depressing the share price. Thus, it claimed that it was actually helping shareholders by keeping these shares from being sold. However, this argument wasn't well received, given that the share price dropped from around $15 per share at the time of the loan to about $2.50 per share when Ebbers was terminated. In addition, critics were scornful of the low "sweetheart" interest rate given to Ebbers for this loan. In addition, many critics viewed the loan as risky, given that it was not supported by any personal assets. WorldCom has since entered bankruptcy proceedings, with the Ebbers loan still uncollected as of this writing.

Some press comments:

1. *When he borrowed money personally, he used his WorldCom stock as collateral. As these loans came due, he was unwilling to sell at "depressed prices" of $10 to $15 (it's now around $2.50). So WorldCom lent him the money to consolidate his loans, to the tune of $366 million. How a board of directors, representing you and me at the table, allowed this to happen is beyond comprehension. They should resign with Bernie. (Source: Andy Kessler, "Bernie Bites the Dust," The Wall Street Journal, May 1, 2002, p. A18.)*

2. *It was astonishing to read the other day that the board of directors of the United States' second-largest telecommunications company claims to have had its shareholders' interests in mind when it agreed to grant more than $430 million in low-interest loans to the company's CEO, mainly to meet margin calls on his stock.*

   Yet that's the level to which fiduciary responsibility seems to have sunk on the board of Clinton, Mississippi-based WorldCom, the deeply troubled telecom giant, as it sought to bail Bernard Ebbers out of the folly of speculating in shares of WorldCom itself. Sadly, WorldCom is hardly alone.

   "The very essence of why Mr. Ebbers was granted a loan was to protect shareholder value," said a WorldCom spokesman in mid-March, just as the U.S. Securities & Exchange Commission was unfurling a probe of the loan and 23 other matters related to WorldCom's finances.

SA 13–1   Concluded

Yes, folks, you read that right. On March 14, 2002, a spokesman for a publicly traded, $20 billion company actually stood up and declared that of all the uses to which the company could have put almost half-a-billion dollars, the best one by far—at least from the point of view of the shareholders—was to spend it on some sort of stock-parking scheme in order to keep the CEO out of bankruptcy court. (Source: Christopher Byron, "Bernie's Bad Idea," *Red Herring*, April 16, 2002.)

Note to Instructors: Bernie Ebbers is currently serving a 25-year prison sentence for conspiracy, securities fraud, and making false statements to securities regulators.

SA 13–2

Gigi and Ron are behaving in a professional manner as long as full and complete information is provided to potential investors in accordance with federal regulations for the sale of securities to the public. If such information is provided, the marketplace will determine the fair value of the company's stock.

SA 13–3

1. This case involves a transaction in which a security has been issued that has characteristics of both stock and debt. The primary argument for classifying the issuance of the common stock as debt is that the investors have a legal right to an amount equal to the purchase price (face value) of the security. This is similar to a note payable or a bond payable. In addition, the $100 payment could be argued to be equivalent to an interest payment, whose payment has been deferred until a later date.

    Arguments against classifying the security as debt include the fact that the investors will not receive fixed "annual" interest payments. In fact, if Las Animas Inc. does not generate any net sales, the investors do not have a right to receive any payments. One could argue that the payments of 2% of net sales are, in substance, a method of redeeming the stock. As indicated in the case, the stockholders must surrender their stock for $100 after the $5 million payment has been made. Overall, the arguments would seem to favor classifying the security as common stock.

SA 13–3 Concluded

2. In practice, the $5 million stock issuance would probably be classified as common stock. However, full disclosure should be made of the 2% of net sales and $100 payment obligations in the notes to the financial statements. In addition, as Las Animas Inc. generates net sales, a current liability should be recorded for the payment to stockholders. Such payments would be classified as dividend payments rather than as interest payments. Debra Allen should also investigate whether such payments might violate any loan agreements with the banks. Banks often restrict dividend payments in loan agreements. If such an agreement has been violated, Las Animas Inc. should notify the bank immediately and request a waiver of the violation.

SA 13–4

a. 500 shares × ($1.00/14) = $125

b. $1.00/34.51 = 2.9%

c. $34.51 + $0.19 = $34.70 (May 10, 2006, close price)
    -$0.19/$34.70 = .55% decrease

d. 500 shares × $34.51 = $17,255 plus brokerage commission

    The $17,255 paid for 500 shares of GE common stock goes to the seller of the common stock (another shareholder). The brokerage commission goes to the broker who facilitated the trade.

    Note to Instructors: You may wish to leave the answer as given, or go into greater detail about the NYSE specialist system. Namely, the specialist both buys and sells the GE common stock and acts as an intermediary between individual buyers and sellers. The specialist makes money on the bid/ask price spreads between buyers and sellers. The specialist creates an orderly market by matching supply and demand.

SA 13–5

1. Before a cash dividend is declared, there must be sufficient retained earnings and cash. On December 31, 2008, the retained earnings balance of $1,199,200 is available for use in declaring a dividend. This balance is sufficient for the payment of the normal quarterly cash dividend of $0.40 per share, which would amount to $16,000 ($0.40 × 40,000).

    Sentinel Inc.'s cash balance at December 31, 2008, is $64,000, of which $40,000 is committed as the compensating balance under the loan agreement. This leaves only $24,000 to pay the dividend of $16,000 and to finance normal operations in the future. Unless the cash balance can be expected to increase significantly in early 2009, it is questionable whether sufficient cash will be available to pay a cash dividend and to provide for future cash needs.

    Other factors that should be considered include the company's working capital (current assets – current liabilities) position and the loan provision pertaining to the current ratio, resources needed for plant expansion or replacement of facilities, future business prospects of the company, and forecasts for the industry and the economy in general. The working capital is $807,200 ($1,007,200 – $200,000) on December 31, 2008. The current ratio is therefore 5:1 ($1,007,200/$200,000) on December 31, 2008. However, after deducting the $600,000 committed to store modernization and product-line expansion, the ratio drops to 2:1 ($407,200/$200,000). If the cash dividend were declared and paid and the other current assets and current liabilities remain unchanged, the current ratio would drop to 1.956:1 ($391,200/$200,000), and this would violate the loan agreement. Further, working capital commitments for 2009 and any additional funds that might be required, such as funds for the replacement of fixed assets, would suggest that the declaration of a cash dividend for the fourth quarter of 2008 might not be wise.

2. Given the cash and working capital position of Sentinel Inc. on December 31, 2008, a stock dividend might be an appropriate alternative to a cash dividend.

    a. From the point of view of a stockholder, the declaration of a stock dividend would continue the dividend declaration trend of Sentinel Inc. In addition, although the amount of the stockholders' equity and proportional interest in the corporation would remain unchanged, the stockholders might benefit from an increase in the fair market value of their total holdings of Sentinel Inc. stock after distribution of the dividend.

    b. From the point of view of the board of directors, a stock dividend would continue the dividend trend, while the cash and working capital position of the company would not be jeopardized. Many corporations use stock dividends as a way to "plow back" retained earnings for use in acquiring new facilities or for expanding their operations. Sentinel Inc. has sufficient unissued common stock to declare a stock dividend without changing the amount authorized.

SA 13–6

Note to Instructors: The purpose of this activity is to familiarize students with sources of information about corporations and how that information is useful in evaluating the corporation's activities.

CHAPTER 14
INCOME TAXES, UNUSUAL INCOME ITEMS, AND INVESTMENTS IN STOCKS

QUESTION INFORMATION

Number	Objective	Description	Difficulty	Time	AACSB	AICPA	SS	GL
Q14-1	14-1		Easy	5 min	Analytic	FN-Measurement		
Q14-2	14-2		Easy	5 min	Analytic	FN-Measurement		
Q14-3	14-2		Easy	5 min	Analytic	FN-Measurement		
Q14-4	14-2		Easy	5 min	Analytic	FN-Measurement		
Q14-5	14-2		Easy	5 min	Analytic	FN-Measurement		
Q14-6	14-2		Easy	5 min	Analytic	FN-Measurement		
Q14-7	14-2		Easy	5 min	Analytic	FN-Measurement		
Q14-8	14-3		Easy	5 min	Analytic	FN-Measurement		
Q14-9	14-4		easy	5 min	Analytic	FN-Measurement		
Q14-10	14-5		Easy	5 min	Analytic	FN-Measurement		
Q14-11	14-5		Easy	5 min	Analytic	FN-Measurement		
Q14-12	14-5		Easy	5 min	Analytic	FN-Measurement		
Q14-13	14-5		Easy	5 min	Analytic	FN-Measurement		
Q14-14	14-5		Easy	5 min	Analytic	FN-Measurement		
Q14-15	14-5		Easy	5 min	Analytic	FN-Measurement		
Q14-16	14-5		Easy	5 min	Analytic	FN-Measurement		
PE14-1A	14-1	Deferred tax entries	Easy	5 min	Analytic	FN-Measurement		
PE14-1B	14-1	Deferred tax entries	Easy	5 min	Analytic	FN-Measurement		
PE14-2A	14-2	Journalize fixed asset impairment and re-structuring charge	Easy	5 min	Analytic	FN-Measurement		
PE14-2B	14-2	Journalize fixed asset impairment and re-structuring charge	Easy	5 min	Analytic	FN-Measurement		
PE14-3A	14-3	Calculate earnings per share	Easy	5 min	Analytic	FN-Measurement		
PE14-3B	14-3	Calculate earnings per share	Easy	5 min	Analytic	FN-Measurement		
PE14-4A	14-4	Comprehensive in-come	Easy	5 min	Analytic	FN-Measurement		
PE14-4B	14-4	Comprehensive in-come	Easy	5 min	Analytic	FN-Measurement		
PE14-5A	14-5	Temporary invest-ments	Easy	5 min	Analytic	FN-Measurement		
PE14-5B	14-5	Temporary invest-ments	Easy	5 min	Analytic	FN-Measurement		
PE14-6A	14-5	Equity method	Easy	5 min	Analytic	FN-Measurement		
PE14-6B	14-5	Equity method	Easy	5 min	Analytic	FN-Measurement		
Ex14-1	14-1	Income tax entries	Easy	15 min	Analytic	FN-Measurement		
Ex14-2	14-1	Deferred income taxes	Easy	10 min	Analytic	FN-Measurement		
Ex14-3	14-1	Deferred income taxes	Easy	10 min	Analytic	FN-Measurement		
Ex14-4	14-2	Fixed asset impair-ment	Easy	15 min	Analytic	FN-Measurement		
Ex14-5	14-2	Fixed asset impair-ment	Easy	10 min	Analytic	FN-Measurement		
Ex14-6	14-2	Restructuring charge	Easy	15 min	Analytic	FN-Measurement		

Number	Objective	Description	Difficulty	Time	AACSB	AICPA	SS	GL
Ex14-7	14-2	Restructuring charge	Moderate	20 min	Analytic	FN-Measurement		
Ex14-8	14-2	Restructuring charges and asset impairment	Easy	15 min	Analytic	FN-Measurement		
Ex14-9	14-2	Extraordinary item	Easy	5 min	Analytic	FN-Measurement		
Ex14-10	14-2	Extraordinary item	Easy	5 min	Analytic	FN-Measurement		
Ex14-11	14-2	Extraordinary items	Easy	5 min	Analytic	FN-Measurement		
Ex14-12	14-2	Identifying extraordinary items	Easy	10 min	Analytic	FN-Measurement		
Ex14-13	14-2, 14-3	Income statement	Easy	15 min	Analytic	FN-Measurement	Exl	
Ex14-14	14-2, 14-3	Income statement	Moderate	20 min	Analytic	FN-Measurement		
Ex14-15	14-3	Earnings per share with preferred stock	Easy	5 min	Analytic	FN-Measurement		
Ex14-16	14-4	Comprehensive income	Easy	10 min	Analytic	FN-Measurement		
Ex14-17	14-4, 14-5	Comprehensive income and temporary investments	Moderate	15 min	Analytic	FN-Measurement		
Ex14-18	14-4, 14-5	Comprehensive income and temporary investments	Moderate	20 min	Analytic	FN-Measurement		
Ex14-19	14-4, 14-5	Temporary investments and other comprehensive income	Moderate	15 min	Analytic	FN-Measurement		
Ex14-20	14-5	Temporary investments in marketable securities	Easy	10 min	Analytic	FN-Measurement		
Ex14-21	14-4, 14-5	Financial statement reporting of temporary investments	Moderate	20 min	Analytic	FN-Measurement	Exl	
Ex14-22	14-5	Entries for investment in stock, receipt of dividends, and sale of shares	Easy	10 min	Analytic	FN-Measurement		
Ex14-23	14-5	Entries for using equity method for stock investment	Easy	10 min	Analytic	FN-Measurement		
Ex14-24	14-5	Equity method for stock investment	Easy	5 min	Analytic	FN-Measurement		
Ex14-25	FAI	Price-earnings ratio	Easy	5 min	Analytic	FN-Measurement		
Ex14-26	FAI	Price-earnings ratio calculations	Moderate	10 min	Analytic	FN-Measurement		
Pr14-1A	14-1	Income tax allocation	Moderate	45 min	Analytic	FN-Measurement		
Pr14-2A	14-2, 14-3, 14-4	Income tax; income statement	Moderate	1 hr	Analytic	FN-Measurement	Exl	
Pr14-3A	14-1, 14-2, 14-3, 14-4, 14-5	Income statement; retained earnings statement; balance sheet	Difficult	1 1/2 hr	Analytic	FN-Measurement	Exl	
Pr14-4A	14-5	Entries for investments in stock	Moderate	45 min	Analytic	FN-Measurement		KA
Pr14-1B	14-1	Income tax allocation	Moderate	45 min	Analytic	FN-Measurement		
Pr14-2B	14-2, 14-3, 14-4	Income tax; income statement	Moderate	1 hr	Analytic	FN-Measurement	Exl	
Pr14-3B	14-1, 14-2, 14-3, 14-4, 14-5	Income statement; retained earnings statement; balance sheet	Difficult	1 1/2 hr	Analytic	FN-Measurement	Exl	
Pr14-4B	14-5	Entries for investments in stock	Moderate	45 min	Analytic	FN-Measurement		KA

Number	Objective	Description	Difficulty	Time	AACSB	AICPA	SS	GL
SA14-1	14-5	Equity method disclosure	Easy	5 min	Analytic	FN-Measurement		
SA14-2	14-2	Special charges analysis	Moderate	20 min	Analytic	FN-Measurement		
SA14-3	14-4	Comprehensive income	Easy	10 min	Analytic	FN-Measurement		
SA14-4	14-2	Ethics and professional behavior	Easy	5 min	Ethics	BB-Industry		
SA14-5	14-2	Reporting extraordinary item	Easy	5 min	Analytic	FN-Measurement		
SA14-6	14-2	Extraordinary items and discontinued operations	Moderate	45 min	Analytic	FN-Measurement		

EYE OPENERS

1. a. Current liability
   b. Long-term liability or deferred credit (following the Long-Term Liabilities section)

2. This is an example of a fixed asset impairment. Thus, a loss of $100 million should be disclosed on the income statement as a separate line item above the income from continuing operations, and the plant and equipment should be written down to their appraised value ($20 million).

3. The severance costs are a current period expense associated with downsizing operations. Thus, a restructuring charge should be recognized on the income statement (above income from continuing operations) and any liability recognized. As payments are made to employees, the liability is decreased.

4. Extraordinary items:
   Gain on condemnation of land, net of applicable income tax of $48,000 ....$72,000

5. The urban renewal agency's acquisition of the property may be viewed as a form of expropriation under paragraph 23 of *Accounting Principles Board Opinion No. 30*, "Reporting the Results of Operations—Reporting the Effects of Disposal of a Segment of a Business, and Extraordinary, Unusual and Infrequently Occurring Events and Transactions." Paragraph 23 says a gain or loss from sale or abandonment of property, plant, or equipment used in the business should be included as an extraordinary item if it is the direct result of an expropriation. Accordingly, the gain should be reported as an extraordinary item in the income statement.

6. The loss from discontinued operations of $2.3 billion should be identified on the income statement as discontinued operations and should follow the presentation of the results of continuing operations (sales less the customary costs and expenses). The data on discontinued operations (identity of the segment, date of disposal, etc.) should be disclosed in a note.

7. A change from one acceptable accounting method to another acceptable accounting method is treated as a retroactive restatement of prior period financial statements, as if the new accounting principle had been used at inception.

8. a. Yes, the $0.40-per-share gain should be reported as an extraordinary item.
   b. Operations appear to have declined. The earnings per share for the current year that is comparable to the preceding year's earnings per share of $1.10 is $0.98 ($1.38 – $0.40).

9. a. Examples of other comprehensive income items include foreign currency items, pension liability adjustments, and unrealized gains and losses on certain investments in debt and equity securities.
   b. No. Other comprehensive income does not affect the determination of net income or retained earnings.

10. A business may purchase stocks as a means of earning a return (income) on excess cash that it does not need for its normal operations. In other cases, a business may purchase the stock of another company as a means of developing or maintaining business relationships with the other company. A business may also purchase common stock as a means of gaining control of another company's operations.

11. On the balance sheet, temporary investments in marketable securities are reported at their fair market values, net of any applicable income taxes related to any unrealized gains or losses.

12. Unrealized gains or losses (net of applicable taxes) should be reported as either an addition to or deduction from net income in arriving at comprehensive income.

13. a. The equity method
    b. Investments

14. Investment in Gestalt Corporation

15. Investment in
    Affiliates 2,400,000
       Income of
          Affiliates 2,400,000

16. The financial statements of the parent and subsidiary are consolidated, or combined, into a single unified disclosure.

770

PRACTICE EXERCISES

PE 14–1A

Income Tax Expense	189,000	
Income Tax Payable		168,000
Deferred Income Tax Payable		21,000

Income tax expense based on $540,000 reported income at 35%...	$189,000
Income tax payable based on $480,000 taxable income at 35%......	168,000
Income tax deferred to future years..	$ 21,000

PE 14–1B

Income Tax Expense	36,000	
Income Tax Payable		30,400
Deferred Income Tax Payable		5,600

Income tax expense based on $90,000 reported income at 40%.....	$36,000
Income tax payable based on $76,000 taxable income at 40%........	30,400
Income tax deferred to future years..	$ 5,600

PE 14–2A

Dec. 15	Loss on Fixed Asset Impairment	46,000	
	Equipment		46,000
	Restructuring Charge	60,000*	
	Employee Termination Obligation................		60,000
	*15 employees × 4,000		

PE 14–2B

Dec. 23	Loss on Fixed Asset Impairment	320,000	
	Land		320,000
	Restructuring Charge	405,000*	
	Employee Termination Obligation................		405,000
	*45 employees × 9,000		

PE 14–3A

Earnings per share: $\dfrac{\$2{,}430{,}000 \ - \ \$270{,}000 \ ^*}{240{,}000} = \$9.00$ per share

*30,000 shares × $100 par value × 9% = $270,000

PE 14–3B

Earnings per share: $\dfrac{\$350{,}000 \ - \ \$35{,}000 \ ^*}{420{,}000} = \$0.75$ per share

*5,000 shares × $100 par value × 7% = $35,000

PE 14–4A

a. $117,400 = $104,000 + $13,400
b. $669,000 = $565,000 + $104,000
c. $84,400 = $71,000 + $13,400

PE 14–4B

a. $979,500 = $856,000 + $123,500
b. $4,316,000 = $3,460,000 + $856,000
c. $747,500 = $624,000 + $123,500

PE 14–5A

a.	Initial cost		$123,000
	Unrealized gain ($137,000 – $123,000)	$14,000	
	Less: Tax on unrealized gain ($14,000 × 40%)	5,600	
	Unrealized gain, net of tax		8,400
	Reported amount of marketable securities		$131,400
b.	Net income		$151,000
	Unrealized gain ($137,000 – $123,000)	$14,000	
	Less: Tax on unrealized gain ($14,000 × 40%)	5,600	
	Other comprehensive income, net of tax		8,400
	Comprehensive income		$159,400

PE 14–5B

a.	Initial cost		$56,000
	Unrealized loss ($56,000 – $49,700)	$6,300	
	Less: Tax benefit on unrealized loss ($6,300 × 35%)	2,205	
	Unrealized loss, net of tax		4,095
	Reported amount of marketable securities		$51,905
b.	Net income		$97,500
	Unrealized loss ($56,000 – $49,700)	$6,300	
	Less: Tax benefit on unrealized loss ($6,300 × 35%)	2,205	
	Other comprehensive loss, net of tax		4,095
	Comprehensive income		$93,405

PE 14–6A

Gilliam share of Forrester reported net income (35% × $675,000)	$236,250
Less Gilliam share of the Forrester dividend (35% × $155,000)	54,250
Increase in the investment in Forrester Company stock	$182,000

PE 14–6B

Miranda share of Orson reported net loss (25% × $300,000)	$ 75,000
Miranda share of the Orson dividend (25% × $40,000)	10,000
Decrease in the investment in Orson Company stock	$ 85,000

EXERCISES

Ex. 14–1

Apr.	15	Income Tax Expense...	90,000	
		Cash		90,000
June	15	Income Tax Expense...	90,000	
		Cash		90,000
Sept.	15	Income Tax Expense...	90,000	
		Cash		90,000
Dec.	31	Income Tax Expense...	110,000*	
		Income Tax Payable..		50,000**
		Deferred Income Tax Payable		60,000

*[($950,000 × 40%) − (3 × $90,000)] = $110,000
**[($800,000 × 40%) − (3 × $90,000)] = $50,000

Jan.	15	Income Tax Payable	50,000	
		Cash		50,000

Ex. 14–2

2007

Dec.	31	Income Tax Expense...	1,208,000	
		Deferred Income Tax Payable		168,000*
		Income Tax Payable..		1,040,000**

*$420,000 × 40% = $168,000
**$2,600,000 × 40% = $1,040,000

2008

Dec.	31	Income Tax Expense...	1,032,000	
		Deferred Income Tax Payable	168,000	
		Income Tax Payable..		1,200,000*

*$3,000,000 × 40% = $1,200,000

Ex. 14–3

2007

Dec.	31	Income Tax Expense	91,000*	
		Deferred Income Tax Asset	31,500	
		Income Tax Payable		122,500**

*$260,000 × 35% = $91,000
**$350,000 × 35% = $122,500

2008

Dec.	31	Income Tax Expense	141,750*	
		Deferred Income Tax Asset		31,500
		Income Tax Payable		110,250

*$405,000 × 35%

Ex. 14–4

a.

Depreciation expense per year: $\dfrac{\$90,000,000 - \$10,000,000}{10 \text{ years}} = \$8,000,000$ per year

December 31, 2008, net book value (carrying value) prior to impairment adjustment:

Fiber optic network cost	$90,000,000
Less accumulated depreciation	16,000,000
Fiber optic net book value	$74,000,000

b.

2008

Dec.	31	Loss from Fixed Asset Impairment	24,000,000*	
		Fixed Assets—Fiber Optic Network		24,000,000

*$74,000,000 – $50,000,000

c.

Balance sheet:

Fixed assets—Fiber optic network	$66,000,000*
Less accumulated depreciation	16,000,000
Fixed assets—Fiber optic network net book value.	$50,000,000

*$90,000,000 – $24,000,000

Ex. 14–5

a.

2008

Dec. 31 Loss from Fixed Asset Impairment...................... 152,000,000
        Fixed Assets—Buildings and Improvements   120,000,000
        Fixed Assets—Land.......................................   13,000,000
        Fixed Assets—Equipment.............................   19,000,000

b. On December 31, 2008, management determined that one of the resort properties was permanently impaired due to the discovery of an adjacent toxic chemical waste site. Bookings to this property have dropped significantly, and it was determined that the property had to be abandoned. As a result, a $152 million asset impairment loss was recognized in 2008, reflecting the fair value of assets associated with this site, as detailed in the following table:

	Original Cost	Impairment Loss	Fair Value
Land	$ 30,000,000	$ 13,000,000	$17,000,000
Buildings and improvements.....	120,000,000	120,000,000	0
Equipment	25,000,000	19,000,000	6,000,000
Total	$ 175,000,000	$ 152,000,000	$23,000,000

Ex. 14–6

a.

2008

Nov.	1	Restructuring Charge	4,680,000	
		Employee Termination Obligation		4,680,000

Average salary	$	65,000
Planned number of positions to be eliminated	×	180
Total annual salary eliminated		$11,700,000
Average tenure..	×	8 yrs.
Severance rate	×	5%
Total severance		$ 4,680,000

b.

2008

Dec.	21	Employee Termination Obligation	1,300,000	
		Cash		1,300,000

Average salary	$	65,000
Number of positions eliminated	×	50
Average tenure..	×	8 yrs.
Severance rate	×	5%
Total severance paid..		$1,300,000

c.

Balance sheet disclosure:

Current liabilities:

Employee termination obligation	$3,380,000

Note disclosure:

On November 1, 2008, the board of directors approved a plan to eliminate 180 headquarter positions due to a decline in demand for the company's products. A severance plan was approved and communicated to employees providing termination benefits to employees terminated between December 1, 2008, and April 1, 2009. Accordingly, a restructuring charge of $4,680,000 was recognized in 2008 for the accrued termination benefits. Of this amount, $1,300,000 was distributed to terminated employees in 2008. The remaining $3,380,000 was recognized as a current liability and will be paid to employees terminated during the first three months of 2009.

Ex. 14–7

a.

Closing and relocation costs	$ 600,000
Employee severance costs	3,024,000*
Contract termination costs	150,000
Total restructuring charge	$ 3,774,000

*Employee severance costs:

Number of hours per month	180 hrs.
Labor rate per hour	× $14.00
Monthly wage per employee	$ 2,520
Number of employees	× 300
Total monthly wages	$ 756,000
Severance rate	× 400%
Total termination benefit	$ 3,024,000

b.

2008
July	1	Restructuring Charge	3,774,000	
		Restructuring Obligation...............................		3,774,000

Note: The obligation is not "employee termination obligation" because there are several types of restructuring charges included in the total. Thus, the account Restructuring Obligation is used to represent the total obligation.

c.

2008
Oct.	15	Restructuring Obligation	756,000	
		Cash		756,000

$756,000 = $3,024,000/4

d. Balance sheet disclosure:

Current liability:

Restructuring obligation	$2,268,000

$2,268,000 = $756,000 × 3 remaining installments

Note: All other estimated restructuring payments were made in 2008.

Ex. 14–7　　　　**Concluded**

e. Note disclosure:

On July 1, 2008, the board of directors of the company approved and announced a restructuring plan that resulted in a $3,774,000 charge in 2008 consisting of the following items:

Closing and relocation costs	$ 600,000
Employee severance costs	3,024,000
Contract termination costs	150,000
Total restructuring charge	$ 3,774,000

The restructuring was caused by unfavorable publicity regarding the caffeine content of our juice products. The adverse publicity reduced the demand for our products, requiring us to consolidate operations by closing one of our juice plants and eliminating 300 direct labor positions. On December 31, 2008, there remains a current restructuring obligation of $2,268,000, primarily related to employee severance agreements.

Note: While no information was provided in the exercise, it is likely that the factory building is also impaired requiring a write-down and appropriate disclosures.

Ex. 14–8

a.

2008
Dec. 31 Loss from Fixed Asset Impairment.................... 13,600,000*
          Fixed Assets—Tractor-Trailers....................   13,600,000

     *($48,000,000 – $14,000,000) × (1 – 60%)

Note: The planned sale of 50 trucks is a future event. The asset impairment impacts all trucks, and thus should be recognized currently.

Dec. 31 Restructuring Charge 780,000*
          Employee Termination Obligation................   780,000

     *65 employees × $12,000

b. December 31, 2008, balance sheet disclosures:

Fixed assets:
Tractor-trailers	$34,400,000
Less accumulated depreciation...	(14,000,000)
Tractor-trailer net book value	$20,400,000

Current liabilities:
Employee termination obligation...	$780,000

Note disclosure:

On December 31, 2008, the board of directors approved and communicated a restructuring plan in response to low-cost competition in the company's service market. The plan calls for the sale of 50 tractor-trailers and elimination of 50 drivers and 15 staff personnel. Due to the general overcapacity in the transportation market, tractor-trailer market values are estimated to be 60% of the existing book value, causing us to recognize an unrecoverable loss on fixed asset impairment of $13,600,000 in 2008 for the entire fleet. In addition, a severance plan was approved for the eliminated positions. The charge for employee severance was $780,000 for 2008, all of which is currently payable at the end of the fiscal year. It is estimated that all severance obligations will be satisfied by the end of the first quarter in 2009.

c.

2009
Mar. 14 Employee Termination Obligation 780,000
          Cash   780,000

Ex. 14–9

No. Extraordinary items are events and transactions that are unusual and occur infrequently. It is not unusual for a company to insure the life of its president or to receive the proceeds of the policy upon his or her death. Since it does not meet both criteria, this gain is not an extraordinary item.

Ex. 14–10

To be classified as an extraordinary item for income statement reporting purposes, the item (event) must be (1) unusual from the typical operating activities of the business and (2) occurring infrequently. Although it would seem that the income from the Stabilization Act would meet these criteria, the airline industry (including Delta) did not report the income as an extraordinary item. Indeed, the complete costs and income from the September 11, 2001, terrorist incident were not accounted for as extraordinary items as explained below.

The text from the Emerging Issues Task Force, "Accounting for the Impact of the Terrorist Attacks of September 11, 2001," explains the reason for the decision:

The EITF reached a consensus that losses or costs resulting from the September 11 events should be included in the determination of income from continuing operations; thus, they should not be classified as extraordinary items. In the opinion of the Task Force, it would not be possible to isolate the effects of the September 11 events in a single line item, because of the difficulty in distinguishing losses that are directly attributable to such events from those that are not. Losses or costs associated with the events of September 11 may, however, be reported as a separate component of income from continuing operations if they are deemed to be either unusual or infrequently occurring in nature.

In the final analysis, the Task Force reached the foregoing decision based on its conclusion that users of financial statements would not be well served by separate reporting as an extraordinary item of only a portion of the impact of the September 11 events that strictly qualify for extraordinary classification under APB No. 30, Reporting the Results of Operations. Pursuant to Opinion 30, only losses or costs that can be clearly measured and irrefutably attributed to a specific event may be shown as an extraordinary item.

The Task Force acknowledges that, while the September 11 events no doubt contributed to the pace and severity of the economic slowdown, identifying the impact of those events would be subjective and difficult—if at all possible. Moreover, the Task Force points out that the most significant financial statement impact for many affected companies might be lost or reduced revenues; in accordance with Opinion 30, the measurement of an extraordinary item does not reflect an estimate of forgone sales or income.

Ex. 14–11

a. The Weyerhaeuser loss was reported as extraordinary. The Mount St. Helen's eruption was deemed extraordinary because the losses from its impact were specific and isolated. In addition, Mount St. Helens had not erupted for over 130 years, making it infrequent.

b. All losses associated with the 9/11 incident were not reported as extraordinary. See the extensive EITF (Emerging Issues Task Force) quote in Exercise 14–10, which in summary states that while the incident was unusual and infrequent, it would not be possible to limit the scope of possible losses associated with this event. The concern was that companies would identify as "extraordinary" indirect business losses as a result of the general decline in the economy as a result of this event. In the words of the EIFT, "it would not be possible to isolate the effects of the September 11 events in a single line item, because of the difficulty in distinguishing losses that are directly attributable to such events from those that are not."

c. Hurricane Katrina losses are not reported as extraordinary, mostly because hurricanes are not unusual or infrequent events on the Gulf Coast. The following is an excerpt that captures the basic essence of the argument.

Katrina Was Not "Extraordinary"

However, from a financial reporting standpoint, Hurricane Katrina was not an "extraordinary" event, according to at least two of the most prominent accounting bodies.

The American Institute of Certified Public Accountants (AICPA) advised its members that because a hurricane is a natural disaster "that is reasonably expected to reoccur," the losses it causes should not be considered extraordinary from a bookkeeping perspective, said a Bloomberg report. This is significant, because extraordinary events are separated from the usual run-of-business expenses in financial reports, and are typically ignored or downplayed by investors when they judge the financial performance of a company.

"There are people who say it's the magnitude of what Hurricane Katrina did that was extraordinary," AICPA director of accounting standards Daniel Noll told the wire service. "You can find accountants on the same block who will disagree on this guidance."

So, what does it take for a natural disaster to be deemed extraordinary? An earthquake that strikes an area with no known fault line or documented history of quake activity, Noll told Bloomberg.

Ex. 14–11   Concluded

The Financial Accounting Standards Board (FASB) also considers Katrina "ordinary" for accounting purposes. Larry Smith, the chairman of FASB's Emerging Issues Task Force, said on Wednesday that there were no plans to have the task force consider whether to label Katrina an extraordinary event, reported Bloomberg, citing board spokesman Gerard Carney.

Source: Stephen Taub, "Experts Advise Accountants Not to Classify Katrina-Related Expenses as Extraordinary," *CFO.com*, September 19, 2005.

Ex. 14–12

a. NR   e. NR
b. NR   f. E
c. NR   g. NR
d. NR   h. E

Ex. 14–13

WIND SURFER INC.
Income Statement
For the Year Ended June 30, 2008

Sales		$ 1,100,000
Cost of merchandise sold		467,500
Gross profit		$ 632,500
Operating expenses:		
Selling expenses	$125,500	
Administrative expenses	104,000	229,500
Special charges:		
Loss from fixed asset impairment		120,000
Restructuring charge		50,000
Income from continuing operations before income tax		$ 233,000
Income tax expense		93,200
Income from continuing operations		$ 139,800
Loss on discontinued operations, net of applicable		
income tax of $32,000		48,000
Income before extraordinary items		$ 91,800
Extraordinary item:		
Gain on condemnation of land, net of applicable		
income tax of $23,200		34,800
Net income		$ 126,600
Earnings per common share:		
Income from continuing operations		$ 6.99
Loss on discontinued operations		2.40
Income before extraordinary item		$ 4.59
Extraordinary item		1.74
Net income		$ 6.33

Ex. 14–14

1. The order of presentation of the unusual items is incorrect. The order should be as follows:

    Income from continuing operations

    Loss on discontinued operations

    Income before extraordinary items

    Extraordinary items

    Net income

2. The restructuring charge is not an extraordinary item but should be disclosed above income from continuing operations. The associated tax benefit should not be net against this amount but should be part of the tax on continuing operations.

3. The fixed asset impairment should be disclosed above income from continuing operations.

4. The earnings per share data are presented in the incorrect order—see (1) above.

5. The earnings per share computations are incorrect. The amount of preferred stock dividends ($20,000) should be subtracted from "income from continuing operations," "income before extraordinary item," and "net income" in computing the earnings per share of common stock.

6. A corrected presentation appears on the next page.

Ex. 14–14   Concluded

AUDIO AFFECTION INC.
Income Statement
For the Year Ended December 31, 2008

Net sales...		$967,000
Cost of merchandise sold..		578,000
Gross profit		$389,000
Operating expenses:		
Selling expenses	$127,000	
Administrative expenses...	142,000	269,000
Special charges:		
Restructuring charge	$ 20,000	
Fixed asset impairment..	24,000	44,000
Income from continuing operations before income tax		$ 76,000
Income tax expense...		40,000*
Income from continuing operations................................		$ 36,000
Loss on discontinued operations (net of applicable		
income tax of $15,000)		(22,500)
Income before extraordinary items		$ 13,500
Extraordinary item:		
Gain on condemnation of land, net of applicable		
income tax of $20,000		30,000
Net income		$ 43,500
Earnings per common share:		
Income from continuing operations		
[($36,000 – $20,000)/50,000 shares]......................		$ 0.32
Loss on discontinued operations		(0.45)
Income before extraordinary item		$ (0.13)
Extraordinary item		0.60
Net income		$ 0.47

*$48,000 – $8,000 tax benefit from restructuring charge

Ex. 14–15

Basic earnings per share when there is preferred stock is determined as follows:

$$\text{Earnings per Common Share} = \frac{\text{Net Income} - \text{Preferred Stock Dividends}}{\text{Number of Common Shares Outstanding}}$$

$$\text{Earnings per Common Share} = \frac{\$150,600 - (2,000 \text{ pref. shares} \times \$6 \text{ per share})}{90,000 \text{ common shares}}$$

Earnings per Common Share = $1.54 per share

Ex. 14–16

a.

Retained earnings, December 31, 2007	$ 1,483,000
Plus net income...	460,000
	$ 1,943,000
Less dividends	250,000
Retained earnings, December 31, 2008	$ 1,693,000

b.

Accumulated other comprehensive income, December 31, 2007	$171,000
Less unrealized loss from temporary investments	45,000
Accumulated other comprehensive income, December 31, 2008	$126,000

Ex. 14–17

a. $75,000	$250,000 – $175,000
b. $9,000	$1,000 – ($8,000)
c. $84,000	$75,000 + $9,000
d. $41,000	$32,000 + $9,000
e. $104,000	$100,000 + $4,000
f. $45,000	$41,000 + $4,000
g. $350,000	$250,000 + $100,000
h. $5,000	$1,000 + $4,000

Ex. 14–18

a.

MANGO CORPORATION
Statement of Comprehensive Income
For the Year Ended December 31, 2008

Net income	$150,000
Other comprehensive income:	
Unrealized gain on investment portfolio, net of tax	55,000
Total comprehensive income	$205,000

b.

MANGO CORPORATION
Stockholders' Equity
December 31, 2008

Common stock...	$ 35,000
Paid-in capital in excess of par value	350,000
Retained earnings..	585,000*
Accumulated other comprehensive income...............................	10,000**
Total	$980,000

*$435,000 + $150,000
**($45,000) + $55,000

Ex. 14–19

a. 2008

Unrealized loss [10,000 shares × ($20 – $16)]..........	$40,000
Less tax benefit on unrealized loss (40% rate)	16,000
Unrealized loss, net of income tax benefit	$24,000

2009

Unrealized gain [10,000 shares × ($25 – $16)]..........	$90,000
Less taxes on unrealized gain (40% rate).................	36,000
Unrealized gain, net of income tax...........................	$54,000

Note: The tax benefit and expense give rise to temporary differences, since gains and losses are only included for tax purposes at the time of sale.

b.

Dec. 31, 2008

Accumulated Other Comprehensive Loss	$24,000

Dec. 31, 2009

Accumulated Other Comprehensive Income	$30,000*

*($24,000) + $54,000 = $30,000

c. The Accumulated Other Comprehensive Income or Deficit is disclosed in the Stockholders' Equity section of the balance sheet, separately from the retained earnings or paid-in capital accounts.

Ex. 14–20

a.	Marketable Securities	57,000	
	Cash...		57,000
b.	Cash	2,150	
	Dividend Revenue..		2,150

Ex. 14–21

a.

GEO-METRICS CORPORATION
Balance Sheet
December 31, 2008

Assets

Current assets:
    Temporary investments in marketable securities,
      at cost $57,000
    Plus unrealized gain (net of applicable income
      tax benefit of $1,200)... 1,800* $58,800

*Computation:
    Market:
      M-Labs Inc.: 1,000 shares × $25 .... $ 25,000
      Spectrum Corp.: 2,500 shares × $14   35,000
                                                     $ 60,000
      Cost ($19,000 + $38,000)   57,000
      Unrealized gain .... $ 3,000
      Taxes on unrealized gain ($3,000 × 40%)   1,200
      Unrealized gain, net of applicable tax benefit .... $ 1,800

b.

GEO-METRICS CORPORATION
Statement of Comprehensive Income
For the Year Ended December 31, 2008

Net income $100,000
Other comprehensive income:
    Unrealized gain on temporary investments in marketable
    securities (net of applicable income tax of $1,200)..................... 1,800
Comprehensive income $101,800

Ex. 14–22

a. Investment in Bat Co. Stock.. 163,200*
    Cash.. 163,200
    *(4,000 shares × $40.75) + $200

b. Cash 7,000
    Dividend Revenue.. 7,000
        (No entry for stock dividends; carrying
        amount per share of stock is now
        $163,200/4,080, or $40.)

c. Cash 52,935*
    Investment in Bat Co. Stock 40,000
    Gain on Sale of Investments.................................... 12,935
    *(1,000 shares × $53) − $65

Ex. 14–23

a. Investment in May Corp. Stock 750,000
    Income of May Corp.. 750,000
        ($3,000,000 × 70,000/280,000)

b. Cash 266,000
    Investment in May Corp. Stock................................. 266,000
        (70,000 shares × $3.80)

Ex. 14–24

	(in millions)
Investment in Sour Company stock, December 31, 2007..................	$135
Plus equity earnings in Sour Company	15
Less dividends received	4*
Investment in Sour Company stock, December 31, 2008..................	$146

*The Sour Company investment is accounted for under the equity method, since there are equity earnings from this investment. Since there were no purchases or sales of Sour Company stock, there must have been a dividend received. This would explain how the ending balance of the investment account went from $150 to $146. Since the investment is accounted for under the equity method, the market value is not used for valuation purposes.

Ex. 14–25

$$\text{Earnings per Share} = \frac{\text{Net Income} - \text{Preferred Dividends}}{\text{Common Shares Outstanding}}$$

Earnings per share: $\dfrac{\$672{,}000 - (\$800{,}000 \times 6\%)}{120{,}000} = \$5.20$ per common share

$$\text{Price-Earnings Ratio} = \frac{\text{Price per Share}}{\text{Earnings per Share}}$$

Price-earnings ratio: $\dfrac{\$72.80}{\$5.20} = 14$

Ex. 14–26

a.

$$\text{Price-Earnings Ratio} = \frac{\text{Market Price per Share of Common Stock}}{\text{Earnings per Share of Common Stock (basic)}}$$

Price-earnings ratio, 2005: $\dfrac{\$56}{\$5.76}$, 9.7

Price-earnings ratio, 2004: $\dfrac{\$51}{\$3.91}$, 13.0

Price-earnings ratio, 2003: $\dfrac{\$41}{\$3.24}$, 12.7

b. The price-earnings ratio decreased from 12.7 to 9.7, or 24% [(12.7 − 9.7)/12.7]. During this time frame, the U.S. economy was expanding and the demand for oil was increasing. In addition, the price of oil was increasing. As a result, ExxonMobil had some of the strongest net income in its history during 2005. The price-earnings ratio grew to reflect this favorable increase in net income. It is interesting, however, that the price-earnings ratio declined over these last three years. Since ExxonMobil is experiencing record net income, investors are taking a more cautious tone. That is, they are not assuming this strong net income will necessarily continue into the future. As a result, the price-earnings ratio is actually below the general market price-earnings ratio, which during this time was around 17.

PROBLEMS

Prob. 14–1A

1. and 2.

Year	Income Tax Deducted on Income Statement	Income Tax Payments for the Year	Deferred Income Tax Payable	
			Year's Addition (Deduction)	Year-End Balance
First	$100,000	$ 80,000	$20,000	$20,000
Second	120,000	112,000	8,000	28,000
Third	200,000	216,000	(16,000)	12,000
Fourth	160,000	172,000	(12,000)	0
Total	$580,000	$580,000	$ 0	

Prob. 14–2A

XTREME WORLD INC.
Income Statement
For the Year Ended June 30, 2008

Sales			$ 865,000
Cost of merchandise sold			345,000
Gross profit			$ 520,000
Operating expenses:			
Selling expenses:			
Sales commissions expense	$130,000		
Advertising expense	57,000		
Depreciation expense—store equipment	45,000		
Miscellaneous selling expense	14,000		
Total selling expenses		$246,000	
Administrative expenses:			
Office salaries expense...........................	$ 70,000		
Rent expense	25,000		
Depreciation expense—office equipment	16,000		
Insurance expense	9,000		
Miscellaneous administrative expense....	11,000		
Total administrative expenses		131,000	
Special charges:			
Loss from fixed asset impairment...............	$ 40,000		
Restructuring charge	50,000		
Total special charges		90,000	
Total expenses....................................			467,000
Income from continuing operations before			
other income and expenses			$ 53,000
Other income and expenses:			
Interest expense			18,000
Income from continuing operations before			
income tax..			$ 35,000
Income tax expense..................................			10,500
Income from continuing operations................			$ 24,500
Gain on discontinued operations....................	$ 38,000		
Less applicable income tax	11,400		26,600
Income before extraordinary item			$ 51,100
Extraordinary item:			
Loss from condemnation of land	$ 24,000		
Less applicable income tax	7,200		(16,800)
Net income			$ 34,300

Prob. 14–2A   Concluded

Earnings per share:

Income from continuing operations.............	$	4.90
Gain on discontinued operations.................		5.32
Income before extraordinary item	$	10.22
Extraordinary item		(3.36)
Net income	$	6.86

Note: Unrealized gain on temporary investments would be an other comprehensive income item, not included on the income statement in determining net income.

Prob. 14–3A

1.

AMANA BREAD CORPORATION
Income Statement
For the Year Ended October 31, 2008

Sales		$955,000
Cost of merchandise sold...............................		458,000
Gross profit		$497,000
Operating expenses:		
Selling expenses	$224,000	
Administrative expenses............................	80,000	
Loss from fixed asset impairment	35,000	
Restructuring charge	65,000	
Total expenses		404,000
Income from operations..................................		$ 93,000
Other expenses:		
Interest expense	$ (5,000)	
Interest revenue	4,000	(1,000)
Income from continuing operations before income tax.		$ 92,000
Income tax expense...		36,800
Income from continuing operations...............		$ 55,200
Loss from discontinued operations................	$ 60,000	
Less applicable income tax	24,000	36,000
Income before extraordinary item		$ 19,200
Extraordinary item:		
Gain on condemnation of land	$ 80,000	
Less applicable income tax	32,000	48,000
Net income		$ 67,200
Earnings per common share:		
Income from continuing operations..........		$ 0.49*
Loss on discontinued operations		0.45
Income before extraordinary item		$ 0.04
Extraordinary item		0.60
Net income......................................		$ 0.64

*($55,200 – $16,000)/80,000 common shares

Prob. 14–3A   Continued

2.

AMANA BREAD CORPORATION
Retained Earnings Statement
For the Year Ended October 31, 2008

Retained earnings, November 1, 2007			$1,277,250
Net income		$67,200	
Less dividends declared:			
Cash dividends	$51,000		
Stock dividends	12,000	63,000	
Increase in retained earnings			4,200
Retained earnings, October 31, 2008			$1,281,450

3.

AMANA BREAD CORPORATION
Balance Sheet
October 31, 2008

Assets

Current assets:			
Cash...		$ 165,300	
Temporary investments in marketable			
securities (at cost)	$122,000		
Less unrealized loss in temporary			
investments	28,000	94,000	
Accounts receivable.............................	$185,000		
Less allowance for doubtful accounts	5,400	179,600	
Notes receivable		42,500	
Merchandise inventory, at lower of cost			
(FIFO) or market		122,000	
Interest receivable		2,500	
Prepaid expenses		2,600	
Total current assets..........................			$ 608,500
Property, plant, and equipment:			
Equipment...	$1,958,000		
Less accumulated depreciation	465,000		
Total property, plant, and equipment			1,493,000
Intangible assets:			
Patents..			14,000
Total assets			$ 2,115,500

Liabilities

Current liabilities:

Accounts payable	$ 47,800	
Employee termination obligation	45,000	
Income tax payable	11,200	
Dividends payable	12,750	
Deferred income taxes payable	5,400	
Total current liabilities		$ 122,150
Deferred credits:		
Deferred income taxes payable		22,900
Total liabilities		$ 145,050

Stockholders' Equity

Paid-In capital:

Preferred 8% stock, $100 par (10,000 shares authorized; 2,000 shares issued)	$200,000		
Excess of issue price over par	8,000	$ 208,000	
Common stock, $1 par (100,000 shares authorized; 82,000 shares issued)	$ 82,000		
Excess of issue price over par	451,000	533,000	
From sale of treasury stock		16,000	
Total paid-in capital		$ 757,000	
Retained earnings		1,281,450	
		$2,038,450	
Deduct treasury common stock (2,000 shares at cost)		40,000	
Less accumulated other comprehensive loss		28,000	
Total stockholders' equity			1,970,450
Total liabilities and stockholders' equity			$ 2,115,500

Prob. 14–4A

2006

Jan.	3	Investment in Nichols Corporation Stock	220,480	
		Cash		220,480
July	2	Cash	5,000	
		Dividend Revenue		5,000
Dec.	5	Cash	5,400	
		Dividend Revenue		5,400

2009

Jan.	2	Investment in Telico Inc. Stock	540,000	
		Cash		540,000
July	6	Cash	5,000	
		Dividend Revenue		5,000

Memo—Received a dividend of 160 shares of
Nichols Corporation stock. Number of shares
held, 4,160. Cost basis per share,
$220,480/4,160 shares = $53.00.

Oct.	23	Cash	54,260	
		Investment in Nichols Corporation Stock		42,400*
		Gain on Sale of Investments		11,860

*800 shares × $53 per share

Dec.	10	Cash	5,040	
		Dividend Revenue		5,040

(4,160 – 800 = 3,360 shares;
3,360 × $1.50 = $5,040).

	31	Cash	38,000	
		Investment in Telico Inc. Stock		38,000
	31	Investment in Telico Inc. Stock	65,000	
		Income of Telico Inc.		65,000

($260,000 × 25% = $65,000).

[*Note:* 25% = 32,000 shares/128,000 shares from January 2, 2009.]

Prob. 14–1B

1. and 2.

Year	Income Tax Deducted on Income Statement	Income Tax Payments for the Year	Deferred Income Tax Payable	
			Year's Addition (Deduction)	Year-End Balance
First	$ 17,500	$ 12,250	$ 5,250	$5,250
Second	22,750	21,000	1,750	7,000
Third	31,500	34,300	(2,800)	4,200
Fourth	35,000	39,200	(4,200)	0
Total	$106,750	$106,750	$ 0	

Prob. 14–2B

ATV INC.
Income Statement
For the Year Ended March 31, 2008

Sales			$2,800,000
Cost of merchandise sold			1,640,000
Gross profit			$1,160,000
Operating expenses:			
Selling expenses:			
Sales salaries expense	$160,000		
Advertising expense	36,000		
Depreciation expense—store equipment	145,000		
Miscellaneous selling expense	25,000		
Total selling expenses		$366,000	
Administrative expenses:			
Office salaries expense	$230,000		
Rent expense	100,000		
Depreciation expense—office equipment	32,000		
Miscellaneous administrative expense....	41,000		
Total administrative expenses		403,000	
Special charges:			
Loss from fixed asset impairment	$ 32,000		
Restructuring charge	70,000		
Total special charges		102,000	
Total expenses			871,000
Income from continuing operations before			
other income and expenses			$ 289,000
Other income and expenses:			
Interest revenue			25,000
Income from continuing operations before			
income tax			$ 314,000
Income tax expense			94,200
Income from continuing operations			$ 219,800
Loss from discontinued operations	$ 78,000		
Less applicable income tax	23,400		54,600
Income before extraordinary item			$ 165,200
Extraordinary item:			
Gain on condemnation of land	$ 54,000		
Less applicable income tax	16,200		37,800
Net income			$ 203,000
Earnings per share:			
Income from continuing operations			$ 10.99
Loss from discontinued operations			(2.73)
Income before extraordinary item			$ 8.26
Extraordinary item			1.89
Net income			$ 10.15

Note: Unrealized loss on temporary investments would be an other comprehensive income item, not included on the income statement in determining net income.

Prob. 14–3B

1.

DISK N' DAT CORPORATION
Income Statement
For the Year Ended August 31, 2008

Sales		$550,000
Cost of merchandise sold		232,000
Gross profit		$318,000
Expenses:		
Selling expenses	$60,000	
Administrative expenses	23,000	
Loss from fixed asset impairment	14,000	
Restructuring charge	45,000	
Total expenses		142,000
Income from operations		$176,000
Other expenses:		
Interest expense	$ (3,000)	
Interest revenue	2,500	(500)
Income from continuing operations before income tax		$175,500
Income tax expense		70,200
Income from continuing operations		$105,300
Loss from discontinued operations	$36,000	
Less applicable income tax	14,400	21,600
Income before extraordinary item		$ 83,700
Extraordinary item:		
Gain on condemnation of land	$75,000	
Less applicable income tax	30,000	45,000
Net income		$128,700
Earnings per common share:		
Income from continuing operations		$ 2.14*
Loss on discontinued operations		0.48
Income before extraordinary item		$ 1.66
Extraordinary item		1.00
Net income		$ 2.66

*($105,300 – $9,000)/45,000 shares

Prob. 14–3B   Continued

2.

DISK N' DAT CORPORATION
Retained Earnings Statement
For the Year Ended August 31, 2008

Retained earnings, September 1, 2007		$397,950
Net income	$128,700	
Less dividends declared:		
Cash dividends	$30,000	
Stock dividends	5,000	35,000
Increase in retained earnings		93,700
Retained earnings, August 31, 2008		$491,650

3.

DISK N' DAT CORPORATION
Balance Sheet
August 31, 2008

Assets

Current assets:			
Cash..		$ 87,500	
Temporary investments in marketable			
equity securities (at cost)..................	$125,000		
Plus unrealized gain................................	9,000	134,000	
Accounts receivable..............................	$ 28,000		
Less allowance for doubtful accounts	2,500	25,500	
Merchandise inventory, at lower of			
cost (FIFO) or market.........................		87,000	
Interest receivable		500	
Prepaid expenses		15,900	
Total current assets...........................			$ 350,400
Property, plant, and equipment:			
Equipment..		$1,350,000	
Less accumulated depreciation		145,000	
Total property, plant, and equipment			1,205,000
Intangible assets:			
Patents..			40,000
Total assets			$1,595,400

Liabilities

Current liabilities:

Accounts payable	$ 12,000	
Employee termination obligation	30,000	
Income tax payable................................	21,450	
Dividends payable	7,500	
Deferred income taxes payable............	4,700	
Total current liabilities........................		$ 75,650

Deferred credits:

Deferred income taxes payable............		8,100
Total liabilities...		$ 83,750

Stockholders' Equity

Paid-in capital:

Preferred 6% stock, $100 par (30,000 shares authorized; 1,500 shares issued)..........................	$150,000		
Excess of issue price over par.............	20,000	$ 170,000	
Common stock, $1 par (100,000 shares authorized; 46,000 shares issued)	$ 46,000		
Excess of issue price over par.............	820,000	866,000	
From sale of treasury stock..................		5,000	
Total paid-in capital		$1,041,000	
Retained earnings...		491,650	
		$1,532,650	
Deduct treasury common stock (1,000 shares at cost)		30,000	
Plus accumulated other comprehensive income		9,000	
Total stockholders' equity			1,511,650
Total liabilities and stockholders' equity			$1,595,400

Prob. 14-4B

2006

Feb.	10	Investment in Mode Corporation Stock.............	288,864	
		Cash		288,864
July	15	Cash	8,800	
		Dividend Revenue		8,800
Dec.	15	Cash	9,200	
		Dividend Revenue		9,200

2009

Jan.	3	Investment in Applause Inc. Stock	675,000	
		Cash		675,000
Apr.	14	Cash	8,800	
		Dividend Revenue		8,800

> Memo—Received a dividend of 160 shares of Mode Corporation stock. Number of shares held, 8,160. Cost basis per share, $288,864/8,160 shares = $35.40.

July	26	Cash	31,875	
		Loss on Sales of Investments	3,525	
		Investment in Mode Corporation Stock.........		35,400
Dec.	15	Cash	8,592	
		Dividend Revenue		8,592
		(8,160 − 1,000 = 7,160 shares; 7,160 × $1.20 = $8,592).		
	31	Cash	12,500	
		Investment in Applause Inc. Stock		12,500
	31	Investment in Applause Inc. Stock	97,500	
		Income of Applause Inc.		97,500
		($325,000 × 30% = $97,500).		

[*Note:* 30% = 30,000 shares/100,000 shares from January 3, 2009.]

SPECIAL ACTIVITIES

SA 14-1

Yes. In this case, the equity method is required because Goodyear owns enough of the voting stock of the investee to have a significant influence over its operating and financing policies.

SA 14-2

1.

MERCURY SHOES INC.
Vertical Analysis of Income Statement
For the Years Ended December 31, 2008 and 2007

	2008		2007	
Sales	$510,000	100.0%	$430,000	100.0%
Cost of merchandise sold	224,400	44.0	193,500	45.0
Gross profit	$285,600	56.0	$236,500	55.0
Selling and administrative expenses	122,400	24.0	107,500	25.0
Loss on fixed asset impairment	127,500	25.0		0.0
Income from operations	$ 35,700	7.0	$129,000	30.0
Income tax expense	14,280	2.8	51,600	12.0
Net income	$ 21,420	4.2%	$ 77,400	18.0%

2. The operating income is 30% of sales in 2007 but only 7% of sales in 2008. Net income dropped from $77,400 to $21,420. This would seem to indicate a large reduction in performance in 2008. However, the loss on the fixed asset impairment, which is unusual, is 25% of sales. Without this loss, the income from operations would have been 32% of sales, or 2 points better than 2007. Combining this with growing sales from $430,000 to $510,000 would indicate that the company is doing well on a recurring basis.

There is some concern that management was unable to successfully complete the software project. Order management is an important capability for a retailer, so this event should not be completely ignored. The loss clearly indicates a failed effort at meeting an important operational objective. This need is still outstanding, will require future effort, and may limit future growth. However, the financial numbers would seem to indicate that the recurring, or core, earnings and growth are on track.

SA 14–3

a. The "other" comprehensive income or loss for the period is the difference in the accumulated other comprehensive income (loss) shown on the balance sheet [($170) – ($131)] between the two comparative periods, or a $39 other comprehensive loss.

b. The other comprehensive loss items are adjustments to stockholders' equity that do not flow through the income statement. The FASB created this category of disclosure to recognize economic events that impact stockholders' equity but are considered too controversial to be included in earnings. In a sense, this is a "middle ground" solution where the items are not ignored, nor are they considered part of net income.

Note to Instructors: The common stock balance of $0 for December 31, 2005, is the result of common stock repurchase and retirement. This does not mean that there are no shares outstanding. Rather, the company has been able to essentially eliminate the book value of the original equity investment through share repurchases. This is highly unusual and an interesting item to point out in discussing this activity.

SA 14–4

No. Although Dillon will not be lying about the amount of total earnings per share of $1.05, it would be clearly misleading not to identify the impact of the extraordinary gain of $0.20 related to the selling of the land. In addition to being unethical and unprofessional, Dillon may violate federal securities laws if he sells his stock after the announcement. In this case, it might be alleged that Dillon traded on "insider" information for his own profit.

SA 14–5

To be classified as an extraordinary item, an event must meet both of the following requirements:

a. Unusual nature—The event should be significantly different from the typical or the normal operating activities of the entity.

b. Infrequent occurrence—The event should not be expected to recur often.

Events that meet both of the preceding requirements are uncommon. Usually, extraordinary items result from natural disasters, such as floods, earthquakes, and fires. Thus, your first impression might be that the frost damage for Sunshine Fruit would qualify as an extraordinary item. However, this is not the case. In an accounting interpretation of a similar case, it was ruled that frost damage experienced by a Florida citrus grower did not meet the criterion of "infrequent" in occurrence. Frost damage is normally experienced in Florida every three to four years. Thus, the history of past losses would suggest that such damage can be expected to occur again in the foreseeable future. The fact that Sunshine Fruit had not had frost damage in the previous five years is not sufficient to meet the infrequency of occurrence criterion. It would, however, be acceptable to identify the losses from frost damage as a separate line item above the income from continuing operations.

SA 14–6

Note to Instructors: The purpose of this activity is to familiarize students with extraordinary items and discontinued operations reported by real companies and to determine the impact of these items on earnings per share.

The following is an example from Reynolds American Inc.'s comparative income statements, beginning with income for continuing operations before taxes:

Reynolds American Inc.
CONSOLIDATED STATEMENTS OF INCOME (LOSS)
(Dollars in Millions, Except Per Share Amounts)

	For the Years Ended December 31,		
	2005	2004	2003
Income (loss) from continuing operations before income taxes..	$ 1,416	$ 829	$(3,918)
Provision for (benefit from) income taxes	431	202	(229)
Income (loss) from continuing operations	985	627	(3,689)
Discontinued operations:			
Gain on sale of discontinued businesses, net of income taxes (2005—$1; 2004—$6; 2003—$97).....	2	12	122
Income (loss) before extraordinary item	987	639	(3,567)
Extraordinary item—gain on acquisition	55	49	121
Net income (loss)	$ 1,042	$ 688	$(3,446)
Basic income (loss) per share:			
Income (loss) from continuing operations	$ 6.68	$ 5.66	$(44.08)
Gain on sale of discontinued businesses	0.01	0.111.46	
Extraordinary item...	0.38	0.44	1.45
Net income (loss)	$ 7.07	$ 6.21	$(41.17)

CHAPTER 15
BONDS PAYABLE AND
INVESTMENTS IN BONDS

QUESTION INFORMATION

Number	Objective	Description	Difficulty	Time	AACSB	AICPA	SS	GL
Q15-1	15-2		Easy	5 min	Analytic	FN-Measurement		
Q15-2	15-2		Easy	5 min	Analytic	FN-Measurement		
Q15-3	15-2		Easy	5 min	Analytic	FN-Measurement		
Q15-4	15-2		Easy	5 min	Analytic	FN-Measurement		
Q15-5	15-2		Easy	5 min	Analytic	FN-Measurement		
Q15-6	15-2		Easy	5 min	Analytic	FN-Measurement		
Q15-7	15-2		Easy	5 min	Analytic	FN-Measurement		
Q15-8	15-2		Easy	5 min	Analytic	FN-Measurement		
Q15-9	15-3		Easy	5 min	Analytic	FN-Measurement		
Q15-10	15-3		Easy	5 min	Analytic	FN-Measurement		
Q15-11	15-3		Easy	5 min	Analytic	FN-Measurement		
Q15-12	15-3		Easy	5 min	Analytic	FN-Measurement		
Q15-13	15-4		Easy	5 min	Analytic	FN-Measurement		
Q15-14	15-5		Easy	5 min	Analytic	FN-Measurement		
Q15-15	15-6		Easy	5 min	Analytic	FN-Measurement		
PE15-1A	15-1	Determining the effect of alternative financing plans on earnings per share	Easy	5 min	Analytic	FN-Measurement		
PE15-1B	15-1	Determining the effect of alternative financing plans on earnings per share	Easy	5 min	Analytic	FN-Measurement		
PE15-2A	15-2	Determine the present value of a future amount	Easy	5 min	Analytic	FN-Measurement		
PE15-2B	15-2	Determine the present value of a future amount	Easy	5 min	Analytic	FN-Measurement		
PE15-3A	15-2	Determine the present value of a bond	Easy	5 min	Analytic	FN-Measurement		
PE15-3B	15-2	Determine the present value of a bond	Easy	5 min	Analytic	FN-Measurement		
PE15-4A	15-3	Record the issuance of bonds payable	Easy	5 min	Analytic	FN-Measurement		
PE15-4B	15-3	Record the issuance of bonds payable	Easy	5 min	Analytic	FN-Measurement		
PE15-5A	15-3	Record the interest for bonds payable	Easy	5 min	Analytic	FN-Measurement		
PE15-5B	15-3	Record the interest for bonds payable	Easy	5 min	Analytic	FN-Measurement		
PE15-6A	15-3	Record the issuance of bonds payable	Easy	5 min	Analytic	FN-Measurement		
PE15-6B	15-3	Record the issuance of bonds payable	Easy	5 min	Analytic	FN-Measurement		
PE15-7A	15-3	Record the interest for bonds payable	Easy	5 min	Analytic	FN-Measurement		
PE15-7B	15-3	Record the interest for bonds payable	Easy	5 min	Analytic	FN-Measurement		

Number	Objective	Description	Difficulty	Time	AACSB	AICPA	SS	GL
PE15-8A	15-4	Record the redemption of bonds payable	Easy	5 min	Analytic	FN-Measurement		
PE15-8B	15-4	Record the redemption of bonds payable	Easy	5 min	Analytic	FN-Measurement		
PE15-9A	15-5	Record the purchase of a bond investment	Easy	5 min	Analytic	FN-Measurement		
PE15-9B	15-5	Record the purchase of a bond investment	Easy	5 min	Analytic	FN-Measurement		
Ex15-1	15-1	Effect of financing on earnings per share	Easy	10 min	Analytic	FN-Measurement		
Ex15-2	15-1	Evaluating alternative financing plans	Easy	5 min	Analytic	FN-Measurement		
Ex15-3	15-1	Corporate financing	Easy	5 min	Analytic	FN-Measurement		
Ex15-4	15-2	Present value of amounts due	Easy	10 min	Analytic	FN-Measurement		
Ex15-5	15-2	Present value of an annuity	Easy	10 min	Analytic	FN-Measurement		
Ex15-6	15-2	Present value of an annuity	Easy	5 min	Analytic	FN-Measurement		
Ex15-7	15-2	Present value of an annuity	Easy	5 min	Analytic	FN-Measurement		
Ex15-8	15-2, 15-3	Present value of bonds payable, discount	Easy	5 min	Analytic	FN-Measurement		
Ex15-9	15-2, 15-3	Present value of bonds payable, premium	Easy	5 min	Analytic	FN-Measurement		
Ex15-10	15-2, 15-3	Bond price	Easy	5 min	Analytic	FN-Measurement		
Ex15-11	15-3	Entries for issuing bonds	Easy	10 min	Analytic	FN-Measurement		
Ex15-12	15-3	Entries for issuing bonds and amortizing discount by straight-line method	Easy	15 min	Analytic	FN-Measurement		
Ex15-13	15-2, 15-3	Computing bond proceeds, entries for bond issuing, and amortizing premium by straight-line method	Easy	10 min	Analytic	FN-Measurement		
Ex15-14	15-3, 15-4	Entries for issuing and calling bonds, loss	Easy	10 min	Analytic	FN-Measurement		
Ex15-15	15-3, 15-4	Entries for issuing and calling bonds, gain	Easy	10 min	Analytic	FN-Measurement		
Ex15-16	15-4, 15-6	Reporting bonds	Easy	5 min	Analytic	FN-Measurement		
Ex15-17	15-5	Amortizing discount on bond investment	Easy	5 min	Analytic	FN-Measurement		
Ex15-18	15-5	Entries to purchase and sale of investments in bonds, loss	Easy	10 min	Analytic	FN-Measurement		
Ex15-19	15-5	Entries to purchase and sale of investments in bonds, gain	Easy	10 min	Analytic	FN-Measurement		
Ex15-20	FAI	Number of times interest charges earned	Easy	10 min	Analytic	FN-Measurement		
Ex15-21	Appendix	Amortize discount by interest method	Easy	15 min	Analytic	FN-Measurement		

Number	Objective	Description	Difficulty	Time	AACSB	AICPA	SS	GL
Ex15-22	Appendix	Amortize premium by interest method	Moderate	15 min	Analytic	FN-Measurement		
Ex15-23	Appendix	Computing bond proceeds, amortizing premium by interest method, and interest expense	Moderate	15 min	Analytic	FN-Measurement		
Ex15-24	Appendix	Compute bond proceeds, amortizing discount by interest method, and interest expense	Moderate	15 min	Analytic	FN-Measurement		
Pr15-1A	15-1	Effects of financing on earnings per share	Moderate	1 1/2 hr	Analytic	FN-Measurement	Exl	
Pr15-2A	15-2, 15-3	Present value, bond premium, entries for bonds payable transactions	Moderate	1 hr	Analytic	FN-Measurement		KA
Pr15-3A	15-2, 15-3	Present value, bond discount, entries for bonds payable transactions	Moderate	1 hr	Analytic	FN-Measurement		KA
Pr15-4A	15-3, 15-4	Entries for bonds payable transactions	Moderate	1 hr	Analytic	FN-Measurement	Exl	KA
Pr15-5A	15-5	Entries for bond investments	Moderate	1 1/4 hr	Analytic	FN-Measurement	Exl	KA
Pr15-6A	Appendix	Entries for bonds payable transactions, interest method of amortizing bond premium	Moderate	45 min	Analytic	FN-Measurement		
Pr15-7A	Appendix	Entries for bonds payable transactions, interest method of amortizing bond discount	Moderate	45 min	Analytic	FN-Measurement		
Pr15-1B	15-1	Effects of financing on earnings per share	Moderate	1 1/2 hr	Analytic	FN-Measurement	Exl	
Pr15-2B	15-2, 15-3	Present value, bond premium, entries for bonds payable transactions	Moderate	1 hr	Analytic	FN-Measurement		KA
Pr15-3B	15-2, 15-3	Present value, bond discount, entries for bonds payable transactions	Moderate	1 hr	Analytic	FN-Measurement		KA
Pr15-4B	15-3, 15-4	Entries for bonds payable transactions	Moderate	1 hr	Analytic	FN-Measurement	Exl	KA
Pr15-5B	15-5	Entries for bond investments	Moderate	1 1/4 hr	Analytic	FN-Measurement	Exl	KA
Pr15-6B	Appendix	Entries for bonds payable transactions, interest method of amortizing bond premium	Moderate	45 min	Analytic	FN-Measurement		
Pr15-7B	Appendix	Entries for bonds payable transactions, interest method of amortizing bond discount	Moderate	45 min	Analytic	FN-Measurement		

Number	Objective	Description	Difficulty	Time	AACSB	AICPA	SS	GL
Comp Problem 4	15-1, 15-2, 15-2, 15-4, 15-5, 15-6	Journalize transactions, prepare financial statements	Difficult	3 hr	Analytic	FN-Measurement		
SA15-1	15-2	General Electric bond issuance	Easy	5 min	Ethics	BB-Industry		
SA15-2	15-2	Ethics and professional conduct in business	Easy	5 min	Ethics	BB-Industry		
SA15-3	15-2	Present values	Easy	10 min	Analytic	FN-Measurement		
SA15-4	15-1	Preferred stock vs. bonds	Easy	5 min	Analytic	FN-Measurement		
SA15-5	15-2, 15-3	Investing in bonds	Moderate	15 min	Analytic	FN-Measurement		
SA15-6	15-1	Investing in bonds	Easy	20 min	Analytic	FN-Measurement		
SA15-7	15-2	Financing business expansion	Moderate	30 min	Analytic	FN-Measurement		

EYE OPENERS

1. (1) To pay the face (maturity) amount of the bonds at a specified date. (2) To pay periodic interest at a specified percentage of the face amount.

2. a. Bonds that may be exchanged for other securities under specified conditions.

   b. The issuing corporation reserves the right to redeem the bonds before the maturity date.

   c. Bonds issued on the basis of the general credit of the corporation.

3. The phrase "time value of money" means that an amount of cash to be received today is worth more than the same amount of cash to be received in the future. This is because cash on hand today can be invested to earn income.

4. (b) $9,000 to be received at the end of each of the next two years has the higher present value because cash that is received earlier can be invested to earn income.

5. Less than face amount. Because comparable investments in bonds provide a market interest rate (10%) that is greater than the rate on the bond being purchased (9%), the bond will sell at a discount as the market's means of equalizing the two interest rates.

6. a. Greater than $5,000,000

   b. 1. $5,000,000
      2. 5%
      3. 7%
      4. $5,000,000

7. Less than the contract rate

8. a. Premium
   b. $125,000
   c. Premium on Bonds Payable

9. a. Debit Interest Expense
      Credit Discount on Bonds Payable
   b. Debit Premium on Bonds Payable
      Credit Interest Expense

10. No. Because zero-coupon bonds do not provide for interest payments, they will sell at a discount.

11. The purpose of a bond sinking fund is to accumulate over the life of a bond issue enough funds to pay the indebtedness at the maturity date.

12. The bond issue that is callable is more risky for investors, because the company may redeem (call) the bond issue if interest rates fall. In addition, since the bonds may be called at their face amount, they will sell for a lower value than the noncallable bond issue.

13. A loss of $7,000 [($500,000 × 0.97) − ($500,000 − $22,000)]

14. Under the caption "Investments"

15. At their cost less any amortized premium or plus any amortized discount

PRACTICE EXERCISES

PE 15–1A

	Plan 1	Plan 2
Earnings before bond interest and income tax...............	$400,000	$400,000
Bond interest..	120,000[1]	60,000[3]
Balance..	$280,000	$340,000
Income tax..	112,000[2]	136,000[4]
Net income	$168,000	$204,000
Dividends on preferred stock	0	140,000
Earnings available for common stock	$168,000	$ 64,000
Number of common shares	/100,000	/ 80,000
Earnings per share on common stock...........................	$ 1.68	$ 0.80

[1]$1,000,000 × 12%
[2]$280,000 × 40%
[3]$500,000 × 12%
[4]$340,000 × 40%

PE 15–1B

	Plan 1	Plan 2
Earnings before bond interest and income tax...............	$ 500,000	$ 500,000
Bond interest..	270,000[1]	216,000[3]
Balance	$ 230,000	$ 284,000
Income tax..	92,000[2]	113,600[4]
Net income	$ 138,000	$ 170,400
Dividends on preferred stock	0	120,000
Earnings available for common stock	$ 138,000	$ 50,400
Number of common shares	/ 150,000	/ 120,000
Earnings per share on common stock...........................	$ 0.92	$ 0.42

[1]$3,000,000 × 9%
[2]$230,000 × 40%
[3]$2,400,000 × 9%
[4]$284,000 × 40%

PE 15–2A

$3,558.45. [$7,000 × 0.50835 (Present value of $1 for 10 periods at 7%)]

PE 15–2B

$1,357.05. [$3,000 × 0.45235 (Present value of $1 for 7 periods at 12%)]

PE 15–3A

Present value of face amount of $150,000 due in 10 years, at 7% compounded annually: $150,000 × 0.50835 (present value factor of $1 for 10 periods at 7%).....................	$ 76,252*
Present value of 10 annual interest payments of $10,500, at 7% interest compounded annually: $10,500 × 7.02358 (present value of annuity of $1 for 10 periods at 7%)	73,748
Total present value of bonds	$150,000

*Rounded to the nearest dollar.

PE 15–3B

Present value of face value of $80,000 due in 5 years, at 10% compounded annually: $80,000 × 0.62092 (present value factor of $1 for 5 periods at 10%).....................	$49,674*
Present value of 5 annual interest payments of $8,000, at 10% interest compounded annually: $8,000 × 3.79079 (present value of annuity of $1 for 5 periods at 10%)..............	30,326*
Total present value of bonds	$80,000

*Rounded to the nearest dollar.

PE 15–4A

Cash...	463,202	
Discount on Bonds Payable	36,798	
Bonds Payable...		500,000

PE 15–4B

Cash...	1,330,403	
Discount on Bonds Payable	169,597	
Bonds Payable...		1,500,000

PE 15–5A

Interest Expense..	26,840	
Discount on Bonds Payable...		1,840
Cash		25,000

      Paid interest and amortized the bond discount ($36,798/20).

PE 15–5B

Interest Expense..	76,960	
Discount on Bonds Payable...		16,960
Cash		60,000

      Paid interest and amortized the bond discount ($169,597/10).

PE 15–6A

Cash	2,154,429	
Premium on Bonds Payable...		154,429
Bonds Payable		2,000,000

PE 15–6B

Cash	1,065,040	
Premium on Bonds Payable...		65,040
Bonds Payable		1,000,000

PE 15–7A

Interest Expense..	104,557	
Premium on Bonds Payable	15,443	
Cash		120,000

      Paid interest and amortized the bond premium ($154,429/10).

PE 15–7B

Interest Expense	46,748	
Premium on Bonds Payable	3,252	
Cash..		50,000

     Paid interest and amortized the bond premium
     ($65,040/20).

PE 15–8A

Bonds Payable	700,000	
Loss on Redemption of Bonds...	45,000	
Discount on Bonds Payable		60,000
Cash..		685,000

PE 15–8B

Bonds Payable	250,000	
Premium on Bonds Payable	20,000	
Gain on Redemption of Bonds..		25,000
Cash..		245,000

PE 15–9A

a. 2008

Sept. 1	Investment in Maxtech Corporation Bonds ...	56,000	
	Interest Revenue	1,400	
	Cash..		57,400

b. 2008

Dec. 31	Investment in Maxtech Corporation Bonds ...	505*	
	Interest Revenue.......................................		505

     *[($70,000 – $56,000)/111 months] × 4 months.

PE 15–9B

a. 2008
    Mar. 1 Investment in PUA-Tech Corporation Bonds ...   40,000
             Interest Revenue   1,250
                 Cash...   41,250

b. 2008
    Dec. 31 Investment in PUA-Tech Corporation Bonds ...   901*
                 Interest Revenue..   901

            *[($50,000 – $40,000)/111 months] × 10 months.

EXERCISES

Ex. 15–1

		Bliss Co.
a.	Earnings before bond interest and income tax............	$ 1,000,000
	Bond interest..	240,000
	Balance	$ 760,000
	Income tax	304,000
	Net income..	$ 456,000
	Dividends on preferred stock......................................	320,000
	Earnings available for common stock.........................	$ 136,000
	Earnings per share on common stock.........................	$ 0.68
b.	Earnings before bond interest and income tax............	$ 1,800,000
	Bond interest..	240,000
	Balance	$ 1,560,000
	Income tax	624,000
	Net income..	$ 936,000
	Dividends on preferred stock......................................	320,000
	Earnings available for common stock.........................	$ 616,000
	Earnings per share on common stock.........................	$ 3.08
c.	Earnings before bond interest and income tax............	$ 3,200,000
	Bond interest..	240,000
	Balance	$ 2,960,000
	Income tax	1,184,000
	Net income..	$ 1,776,000
	Dividends on preferred stock......................................	320,000
	Earnings available for common stock.........................	$ 1,456,000
	Earnings per share on common stock.........................	$ 7.28

Ex. 15–2

Factors other than earnings per share that should be considered in evaluating financing plans include: bonds represent a fixed annual interest requirement, while dividends on stock do not; bonds require the repayment of principal, while stock does not; and common stock represents a voting interest in the ownership of the corporation, while bonds do not.

Ex. 15–3

Williams-Sonoma's major source of financing is common stock. It has long-term debt, excluding current installments, of $14,490,000, compared to stockholders' equity of $1,125,318,000.

Ex. 15–4

a. $200,000/1.07 = $186,916
   $186,916/1.07 = $174,688
   $174,688/1.07 = $163,260

b. $200,000 × 0.81630 = $163,260

Ex. 15–5

a. First Year: $75,000 × 0.95238 = $ 71,428.50
   Second Year: $75,000 × 0.90703 =   68,027.25
   Third Year: $75,000 × 0.86384 =   64,788.00
   Fourth Year: $75,000 × 0.82270 =   61,702.50
   Total present value $265,946.25

b. $75,000 × 3.54595 = $265,946.25

Ex. 15–6

$2,000,000 × 12.46221 = $24,924,420

Ex. 15–7

No. The present value of your winnings using an interest rate of 10% is $17,027,120 ($2,000,000 × 8.51356), which is more than one-half of the present value of your winnings using an interest rate of 5% ($24,924,420; see Ex. 15–6). This is because of the effect of compounding the interest. That is, compound interest functions are not linear functions, but use exponents.

Ex. 15–8

Present value of $1 for 10 (semiannual) periods at 5% (semiannual rate)	0.61391	
Face amount of bonds..	× $20,000,000	$12,278,200
Present value of an annuity of $1 for 10 periods at 5%	7.72174	
Semiannual interest payment...................................	× $900,000	6,949,566
Total present value (proceeds)..............................		$19,227,766

Ex. 15–9

Present value of $1 for 10 (semiannual) periods at 5.5% (semiannual rate)	0.58543	
Face amount of bonds..	× $15,000,000	$ 8,781,450
Present value of an annuity of $1 for 10 periods at 5.5%	7.53763	
Semiannual interest payment...................................	× $900,000	6,783,867
Total present value (proceeds)..............................		$15,565,317

Ex. 15–10

The bonds were selling at a premium. This is indicated by the selling price of 108.89, which is stated as a percentage of face amount and is more than par (100%). The market rate of interest for similar quality bonds was lower than 6.375%, and this is why the bonds were selling at a premium.

Ex. 15–11

May 1	Cash...	12,000,000	
	Bonds Payable...		12,000,000
Nov. 1	Interest Expense..	480,000	
	Cash		480,000
Dec. 31	Interest Expense..	160,000*	
	Interest Payable..		160,000

*12,000,000 × 8% × 2/12.

Ex. 15–12

a. 1. Cash.. 11,116,854
      Discount on Bonds Payable 883,146
          Bonds Payable..   12,000,000

   2. Interest Expense... 600,000
         Cash   600,000

   3. Interest Expense... 600,000
         Cash   600,000

   4. Interest Expense... 176,629
         Discount on Bonds Payable   176,629
         $883,146/5 years = $176,629.

b. Annual interest paid... $1,200,000
  Plus discount amortized..   176,629
  Interest expense for first year $1,376,629

Note: The following data in support of the proceeds of the bond issue stated in the exercise are presented for the instructor's information. Students are not required to make the computations.

Present value of $1 for 10 (semiannual)
periods at 6% (semiannual rate) 0.55840
Face amount.. × $12,000,000 $ 6,700,800

Present value of annuity of $1 for 10
periods at 6%...   7.36009
Semiannual interest payment .... × $600,000   4,416,054

Total present value of bonds payable $11,116,854

Ex. 15–13

a.

Cash	4,301,504	
Premium on Bonds Payable		301,504
Bonds Payable		4,000,000

Note: The following data are in support of the determination of the proceeds of the bond issue stated in the exercise:

Present value of $1 for 10 (semiannual) periods at 5.5% (semiannual rate)	0.58543	
Face amount	× $4,000,000	$ 2,341,720
Present value of an annuity of $1 for 10 periods at 5.5%	7.53763	
Semiannual interest payment	× $260,000	1,959,784
Proceeds		$ 4,301,504

b.

Interest Expense	229,850	
Premium on Bonds Payable	30,150*	
Cash		260,000**

  *$301,504/10 semiannual payments.
  **$4,000,000 × 13% × 6/12.

Ex. 15–14

2008

Apr.	1	Cash	7,000,000	
		Bonds Payable		7,000,000
Oct.	1	Interest Expense	315,000	
		Cash		315,000

2012

Oct.	1	Bonds Payable	7,000,000	
		Loss on Redemption of Bonds	210,000	
		Cash		7,210,000

Ex. 15–15

2008					
Jan.	1	Cash..	4,000,000	
		Bonds Payable...		4,000,000
July	1	Interest Expense...	140,000	
		Cash		140,000
2014					
July	1	Bonds Payable..	4,000,000	
		Gain on Redemption of Bonds.......................		160,000
		Cash		3,840,000

Ex. 15–16

1. The significant loss on redemption of the series X bonds should be reported in the Other Income and Expense section of the income statement, rather than as an extraordinary loss.

2. The series Y bonds outstanding at the end of the current year should be reported as a noncurrent liability on the balance sheet because they are to be paid from funds set aside in a sinking fund.

Ex. 15–17

The discount of $4,180 ($5,000 – $820) is amortized as interest revenue over the life of the bonds, using the straight-line method (illustrated in this chapter) or the interest method (illustrated in the appendix to this chapter).

Ex. 15–18

a. Investment in Sanhueza Co. Bonds 612,000
Interest Revenue 10,500
   Cash   622,500

b. Cash 21,000
   Interest Revenue   21,000

c. Interest Revenue 960
   Investment in Sanhueza Co. Bonds   960

d. Cash 591,500
Loss on Sale of Investments 18,720
   Investment in Sanhueza Co. Bonds   606,720
   Interest Revenue   3,500

Ex. 15–19

a. Investment in Blaga Co. Bonds 436,500
Interest Revenue 9,000
   Cash   445,500

b. Cash 18,000
   Interest Revenue   18,000

c. Investment in Blaga Co. Bonds 1,080
   Interest Revenue   1,080

d. Cash 457,500
   Investment in Blaga Co. Bonds   442,440
   Gain on Sale of Investments   12,060
   Interest Revenue   3,000

Ex. 15–20

a. Current year:

Number of times interest charges earned: $6.6 = \dfrac{\$489{,}000{,}000 + \$88{,}000{,}000}{\$88{,}000{,}000}$

Preceding year:

Number of times interest charges earned: $8.8 = \dfrac{\$708{,}000{,}000 + \$91{,}000{,}000}{\$91{,}000{,}000}$

b. The number of times interest charges earned has declined from 8.8 to 6.6 in the current year. Although Southwest Airlines has adequate earnings to pay interest, the decline in this ratio may cause concern among debtholders.

Appendix Ex. 15–21

a.
1. Cash... 9,785,645
   Discount on Bonds Payable 1,214,355
      Bonds Payable..   11,000,000

2. Interest Expense...................................... 495,000
      Cash   495,000

3. Interest Expense...................................... 495,000
      Cash   495,000

4. Interest Expense...................................... 189,806
      Discount on Bonds Payable   189,806

Computations:
$9,785,645 × 6% = $587,139
$587,139 – $495,000 = $92,139 first semiannual amortization
$9,785,645 + $92,139 = $9,877,784
$9,877,784 × 6% = $592,667
$592,667 – $495,000 = $97,667 second semiannual amortization
$92,139 + $97,667 = $189,806 amortization for first year

Note: The following data in support of the proceeds of the bond issue stated in the exercise are presented for the instructor's information. Students are not required to make the computations.

Present value of $1 for 10 (semiannual)
   periods at 6% (semiannual rate)........................   0.55840
Face amount... × $11,000,000 $ 6,142,400

Present value of annuity of $1 for
   10 periods at 6% 7.36009
Semiannual interest payment .... × $495,000   3,643,245
Total present value of bonds payable .... $ 9,785,645

b. Annual interest paid... $ 990,000
    Plus discount amortized...   189,806
    Interest expense for first year .... $ 1,179,806

Appendix Ex. 15–22

a. 1. Cash 2,688,440

    Premium on Bonds Payable 188,440

    Bonds Payable 2,500,000

2. Interest Expense 162,500

    Cash 162,500

3. Interest Expense 162,500

    Cash 162,500

4. Premium on Bonds Payable 30,077

    Interest Expense 30,077

Computations:

$2,688,440 × 5.5% = $147,864

$162,500 – $147,864 = $14,636 first semiannual amortization

$2,688,440 – $14,636 = $2,673,804

$2,673,804 × 5.5% = $147,059

$162,500 – $147,059 = $15,441 second semiannual amortization

$14,636 + $15,441 = $30,077 first year amortization

b. Annual interest paid $325,000

Less premium amortized 30,077

Interest expense for first year $294,923

Appendix Ex. 15–23

a. Present value of $1 for 10 (semiannual)
   periods at 5.5% (semiannual rate)...................... 0.58543
   Face amount.. × $22,000,000 $12,879,460

   Present value of annuity of $1 for 10
   periods at 5.5% 7.53763
   Semiannual interest payment .... × $1,540,000   11,607,950
   Proceeds of bond sale.. $24,487,410

b. First semiannual interest payment.......................... $ 1,540,000
   5.5% of carrying amount of $24,487,410   1,346,808
   Premium amortized... $ 193,192

c. Second semiannual interest payment................... $ 1,540,000
   5.5% of carrying amount of $24,294,218*   1,336,182
   Premium amortized... $ 203,818

   *$24,487,410 – $193,192 = $24,294,218

d. Annual interest paid... $ 3,080,000
   Less premium amortized...   397,010*
   Interest expense for first year............................... $ 2,682,990

   *$193,192 + $203,818 = $397,010.

Appendix Ex. 15–24

a. Present value of $1 for 10 (semiannual)
periods at 5% (semiannual rate)........................ 0.61391
Face amount... × $27,500,000 $16,882,525

Present value of annuity of $1 for 10 periods at 5%... 7.72174
Semiannual interest payment .... × $1,100,000   8,493,914
Proceeds of bond sale... $25,376,439

b. 5% of carrying amount of $25,376,439 .... $ 1,268,822
First semiannual interest payment........................   1,100,000
Discount amortized.. $ 168,822

c. 5% of carrying amount of $25,545,261*................. $ 1,277,263
Second semiannual interest payment....................   1,100,000
Discount amortized.. $ 177,263

*$25,376,439 + $168,822 = $25,545,261.

d. Annual interest paid... $ 2,200,000
Plus discount amortized...   346,085*
Interest expense first year...................................... $ 2,546,085

*$168,822 + $177,263 = $346,085.

PROBLEMS

Prob. 15–1A

1.

	Plan 1	Plan 2	Plan 3
Earnings before interest and income tax	$20,000,000	$20,000,000	$20,000,000
Deduct interest on bonds.............................	—	—	1,600,000
Income before income tax	$20,000,000	$20,000,000	$18,400,000
Deduct income tax......................................	8,000,000	8,000,000	7,360,000
Net income	$12,000,000	$12,000,000	$11,040,000
Dividends on preferred stock	—	800,000	400,000
Available for dividends on common stock ...	$12,000,000	$11,200,000	$10,640,000
Shares of common stock outstanding..........	/ 4,000,000	/ 2,000,000	/ 1,000,000
Earnings per share on common stock..........	$ 3.00	$ 5.60	$ 10.64

2.

	Plan 1	Plan 2	Plan 3
Earnings before interest and income tax	$ 2,600,000	$ 2,600,000	$ 2,600,000
Deduct interest on bonds.............................	—	—	1,600,000
Income before income tax	$ 2,600,000	$ 2,600,000	$ 1,000,000
Deduct income tax......................................	1,040,000	1,040,000	400,000
Net income	$ 1,560,000	$ 1,560,000	$ 600,000
Dividends on preferred stock	—	800,000	400,000
Available for dividends on common stock ...	$ 1,560,000	$ 760,000	$ 200,000
Shares of common stock outstanding..........	/ 4,000,000	/ 2,000,000	/ 1,000,000
Earnings per share on common stock..........	$ 0.39	$ 0.38	$ 0.20

Prob. 15–1A   Concluded

3. The principal advantage of Plan 1 is that it involves only the issuance of common stock, which does not require a periodic interest payment or return of principal, and a payment of preferred dividends is not required. It is also more attractive to common shareholders than is Plan 2 or 3 if earnings before interest and income tax is $2,600,000. In this case, it has the largest EPS ($0.39). The principal disadvantage of Plan 1 is that it requires an additional investment by present common shareholders to retain their current interest in the company. Also, if earnings before interest and income tax is $20,000,000, this plan offers the lowest EPS ($3.00) on common stock.

The principal advantage of Plan 3 is that little additional investment would need to be made by common shareholders for them to retain their current interest in the company. Also, it offers the largest EPS ($10.64) if earnings before interest and income tax is $20,000,000. Its principal disadvantage is that the bonds carry a fixed annual interest charge and require the payment of principal. It also requires a dividend payment to preferred stockholders before a common dividend can be paid. Finally, Plan 3 provides the lowest EPS ($0.20) if earnings before interest and income tax is $2,600,000.

Plan 2 provides a middle ground in terms of the advantages and disadvantages described in the preceding paragraphs for Plans 1 and 3.

Prob. 15–2A

1.

Cash	844,077*		
Premium on Bonds Payable		44,077	
Bonds Payable		800,000	

*Present value of $1 for 20 (semiannual)		
periods at 6.5% (semiannual rate)...................	0.28380	
Face amount...	× $800,000	$227,040
Present value of an annuity of $1 for 20		
periods at 6.5%	11.01851	
Semiannual interest payment	× $56,000	617,037
Proceeds of bond issue.......................................		$844,077

2.

a.	Interest Expense...	53,796	
	Premium on Bonds Payable ($44,077/20)	2,204	
	Cash		56,000
b.	Interest Expense...	53,796	
	Premium on Bonds Payable	2,204	
	Cash		56,000

3. $53,796

4. Yes. Investors will be willing to pay more than the face amount of the bonds when the interest payments they will receive from the bonds exceed the amount of interest that they could receive from investing in other bonds.

Prob. 15–3A

1.
Cash	11,783,070*	
Discount on Bonds Payable	716,930	
Bonds Payable		12,500,000

*Present value of $1 for 20 (semiannual) periods at 6% (semiannual rate)	0.31180	
Face amount	× $12,500,000	$ 3,897,500
Present value of an annuity of $1 for 20 periods at 6%	11.46992	
Semiannual interest payment	× $687,500	7,885,570
Proceeds of bond issue		$11,783,070

2.
a.	Interest Expense	723,347	
	Discount on Bonds Payable ($716,930/20)		35,847
	Cash		687,500
b.	Interest Expense	723,347	
	Discount on Bonds Payable		35,847
	Cash		687,500

3. $723,347

4. Yes. Investors will not be willing to pay the face amount of the bonds when the interest payments they will receive from the bonds are less than the amount of interest that they could receive from investing in other bonds.

Prob. 15–4A

1.

2007

July	1	Cash..		20,880,780	
		Premium on Bonds Payable..................			1,880,780
		Bonds Payable.......................................			19,000,000
Dec.	31	Interest Expense...................................		1,140,000	
		Cash			1,140,000
	31	Premium on Bonds Payable		134,341	
		Interest Expense.....................................			134,341
	31	Income Summary.....................................		1,005,659	
		Interest Expense.....................................			1,005,659

2008

June	30	Interest Expense..		1,140,000	
		Cash			1,140,000
Dec.	31	Interest Expense..		1,140,000	
		Cash			1,140,000
	31	Premium on Bonds Payable		268,682	
		Interest Expense.....................................			268,682
	31	Income Summary.....................................		2,011,318	
		Interest Expense.....................................			2,011,318

2009

July	1	Bonds Payable		19,000,000	
		Premium on Bonds Payable		1,343,416	
		Gain on Redemption on Bonds..............			1,058,416
		Cash ($19,000,000 × 101.5%)..................			19,285,000

2. a. 2007: $1,005,659

   b. 2008: $2,011,318

3.

Initial carrying amount of bonds....................................	$20,880,780
Premium amortized on December 31, 2007	(134,341)
Premium amortized on December 31, 2008	(268,682)
Carrying amount of bonds, December 31, 2008	$20,477,757

Prob. 15–5A

2007

Date	Account	Debit	Credit
Sept. 1	Investment in Wilson Company Bonds	578,580	
	Interest Revenue ($600,000 × 10% × 2/12).........	10,000	
	Cash		588,580
Dec. 31	Cash..	30,000	
	Interest Revenue		30,000
31	Investment in Wilson Company Bonds	360*	
	Interest Revenue		360

*[($600,000 − $578,580)/238 months]x4.

2012

Date	Account	Debit	Credit
June 30	Cash..	30,000	
	Interest Revenue		30,000
Oct. 31	Investment in Wilson Company Bonds	450	
	Interest Revenue		450
31	Cash..	300,600*	
	Loss on Sale of Investments	1,480	
	Investment in Wilson Company Bonds		292,080
	Interest Revenue		10,000

*($300,000 × 0.97) + ($300,000 × 10% × 4/12) − $400

Date	Account	Debit	Credit
Dec. 31	Cash..	15,000	
	Interest Revenue		15,000
31	Investment in Wilson Company Bonds	540	
	Interest Revenue		540

Appendix Prob. 15–6A

1. a. Interest Expense.. 54,865
        Premium on Bonds Payable
        [$56,000 – (6.5% × $844,077)].................................. 1,135
            Cash 56,000

    b. Interest Expense.. 54,791
        Premium on Bonds Payable
        [$56,000 – (6.5% × $842,942)].................................. 1,209
            Cash 56,000

2. $54,865

Appendix Prob. 15–7A

1. a. Interest Expense.. 706,984
        Discount on Bonds Payable
        [($687,500 – (6% × $11,783,070)] 19,484
            Cash 687,500

    b. Interest Expense.. 708,153
        Discount on Bonds Payable
        [$687,500 – (6% × $11,802,554)] 20,653
            Cash 687,500

2. $706,984

Prob. 15–1B

1.

	Plan 1	Plan 2	Plan 3
Earnings before interest and income tax	$30,000,000	$30,000,000	$30,000,000
Deduct interest on bonds.............................	—	—	1,200,000
Income before income tax	$30,000,000	$30,000,000	$28,800,000
Deduct income tax...	12,000,000	12,000,000	11,520,000
Net income	$18,000,000	$18,000,000	$17,280,000
Dividends on preferred stock	—	600,000	300,000
Available for dividends on common stock ...	$18,000,000	$17,400,000	$16,980,000
Shares of common stock outstanding..........	/ 7,500,000	/ 3,750,000	/ 1,875,000
Earnings per share on common stock..........	$ 2.40	$ 4.64	$ 9.06

2.

	Plan 1	Plan 2	Plan 3
Earnings before interest and income tax	$ 1,800,000	$ 1,800,000	$ 1,800,000
Deduct interest on bonds.............................	—	—	1,200,000
Income before income tax	$ 1,800,000	$ 1,800,000	$ 600,000
Deduct income tax...	720,000	720,000	240,000
Net income	$ 1,080,000	$ 1,080,000	$ 360,000
Dividends on preferred stock	—	600,000	300,000
Available for dividends on common stock ...	$ 1,080,000	$ 480,000	$ 60,000
Shares of common stock outstanding..........	/ 7,500,000	/ 3,750,000	/ 1,875,000
Earnings per share on common stock..........	$ 0.14	$ 0.13	$ 0.03

Prob. 15–1B   Concluded

3. The principal advantage of Plan 1 is that it involves only the issuance of common stock, which does not require a periodic interest payment or return of principal, and a payment of preferred dividends is not required. It is also more attractive to common shareholders than is Plan 2 or 3 if earnings before interest and income tax is $1,800,000. In this case, it has the largest EPS ($0.14). The principal disadvantage of Plan 1 is that it requires an additional investment by present common shareholders to retain their current interest in the company. Also, if earnings before interest and income tax is $30,000,000, this plan offers the lowest EPS ($2.40) on common stock.

The principal advantage of Plan 3 is that little additional investment would need to be made by common shareholders for them to retain their current interest in the company. Also, it offers the largest EPS ($9.06) if earnings before interest and income tax is $30,000,000. Its principal disadvantage is that the bonds carry a fixed annual interest charge and require the payment of principal. It also requires a dividend payment to preferred stockholders before a common dividend can be paid. Finally, Plan 3 provides the lowest EPS ($0.03) if earnings before interest and income tax is $1,800,000.

Plan 2 provides a middle ground in terms of the advantages and disadvantages described in the preceding paragraphs for Plans 1 and 3.

Prob. 15–2B

1. Cash 18,375,706*

    Premium on Bonds Payable 2,375,706

    Bonds Payable 16,000,000

*Present value of $1 for 14 (semiannual)

    periods at 5% (semiannual rate)....................... 0.50507

Face amount... × $16,000,000 $ 8,081,120

Present value of an annuity of $1 for 14

    periods at 5% 9.89864

Semiannual interest payment .... × $1,040,000   10,294,586

Proceeds of bond issue... $18,375,706

2. a. Interest Expense.. 870,307

    Premium on Bonds Payable ($2,375,706/14).... 169,693

       Cash 1,040,000

  b. Interest Expense.. 870,307

    Premium on Bonds Payable 169,693

       Cash 1,040,000

3. $870,307

4. Yes. Investors will be willing to pay more than the face amount of the bonds when the interest payments they will receive from the bonds exceed the amount of interest that they could receive from investing in other bonds.

Prob. 15–3B

1. Cash 20,344,863*
   Discount on Bonds Payable.................................... 1,655,137
      Bonds Payable   22,000,000

   *Present value of $1 for 40 (semiannual)
      periods at 6% (semiannual rate)......................... 0.09722
   Face amount... × $22,000,000 $ 2,138,840
   Present value of an annuity of $1 for 40
      periods at 6% 15.04630
   Semiannual interest payment .... × $1,210,000   18,206,023
                                                 $20,344,863

2. a. Interest Expense... 1,251,378
       Discount on Bonds Payable
       ($1,655,137/40)...   41,378
       Cash   1,210,000

   b. Interest Expense... 1,251,378
       Discount on Bonds Payable   41,378
       Cash   1,210,000

3. $1,251,378

4. Yes. Investors will not be willing to pay the face amount of the bonds when
   the interest payments they will receive from the bonds are less than the
   amount of interest that they could receive from investing in other bonds.

Prob. 15–4B

1.

2007

July	1	Cash...	11,252,273	
		Discount on Bonds Payable	747,727	
		Bonds Payable..		12,000,000
Dec.	31	Interest Expense...	540,000	
		Cash		540,000
	31	Interest Expense...	37,386	
		Discount on Bonds Payable		37,386
	31	Income Summary..	577,386	
		Interest Expense..		577,386

2008

June	30	Interest Expense...	540,000	
		Cash		540,000
Dec.	31	Interest Expense...	540,000	
		Cash		540,000
	31	Interest Expense...	74,772	
		Discount on Bonds Payable		74,772
	31	Income Summary..	1,154,772	
		Interest Expense..		1,154,772

2009

June	30	Bonds Payable..	12,000,000	
		Loss on Redemption of Bonds...................	358,183	
		Discount on Bonds Payable		598,183
		Cash		11,760,000

2. **a.** 2007: $577,386

    b. 2008: $1,154,772

3.

Initial carrying amount of bonds...................................	$11,252,273
Discount amortized on December 31, 2007	37,386
Discount amortized on December 31, 2008	74,772
Carrying amount of bonds, December 31, 2008	$11,364,431

Prob. 15–5B

2007

Sept. 1	Investment in Ivan Company Bonds...................	853,100	
	Interest Revenue ($800,000 × 9% × 2/12)...........	12,000	
	Cash		865,100
Dec. 31	Cash ($800,000 × 9% × 6/12)...............................	36,000	
	Interest Revenue		36,000
31	Interest Revenue..	1,800	
	Investment in Ivan Company Bonds..............		1,800

2013

June 30	Cash...	36,000	
	Interest Revenue		36,000
Aug. 31	Interest Revenue..	1,800	
	Investment in Ivan Company Bonds..............		1,800
31	Cash...	413,500*	
	Gain on Sale of Investments		1,900
	Investment in Ivan Company Bonds..............		405,600
	Interest Revenue		6,000

*($400,000 × 1.02) + ($400,000 × 9% × 2/12) − $500.

Dec. 31	Cash...	18,000	
	Interest Revenue		18,000
31	Interest Revenue..	2,700	
	Investment in Ivan Company Bonds..............		2,700

Appendix Prob. 15–6B

1. a. Interest Expense 918,785
      Premium on Bonds Payable
      [$1,040,000 – (5% × $18,375,706)] 121,215
         Cash   1,040,000

   b. Interest Expense 912,725
      Premium on Bonds Payable
      [$1,040,000 – (5% × $18,254,491)] 127,275
         Cash   1,040,000

2. $918,785

Appendix Prob. 15–7B

1. a. Interest Expense 1,220,692
      Discount on Bonds Payable
      [($20,344,863 × 6%) – $1,210,000]   10,692
         Cash   1,210,000

   b. Interest Expense 1,221,333
      Discount on Bonds Payable
      [($20,355,555 × 6%) – $1,210,000]   11,333
         Cash   1,210,000

2. $1,220,692

COMPREHENSIVE PROBLEM 4

1. a. Cash... 812,500
     Common Stock...   375,000
     Paid-In Capital in Excess of Par—
     Common Stock...   437,500

  b. Cash... 1,600,000
     Preferred Stock...   1,250,000
     Paid-In Capital in Excess of Par—
     Preferred Stock...   350,000

  c. Cash... 16,869,339
     Bonds Payable...   15,000,000
     Premium on Bonds Payable........................   1,869,339

    Computations:
    Present value of face amount of $15,000,000 com-
    pounded semiannually × 0.37689 [present value of
    $1 for 20 (semiannual) periods at 5%
    (semiannual rate)]... $ 5,653,350
    Present value of semiannual interest payments of
      $900,000 at 5% compounded semiannually:
      $900,000 × 12.46221 (present value of annuity
      of $1 for 20 periods at 5%)................................   11,215,989
    Total present value of bonds.................................. $16,869,339

  d. Cash Dividends ($0.25 × 125,000) + (2.5 × 18,750). 78,125
     Cash Dividends Payable.............................   78,125

  e. Cash Dividends Payable................................. 78,125
     Cash..   78,125

  f. Bonds Payable... 500,000
    Premium on Bonds Payable........................... 6,150
     Cash..   505,000
     Gain on Redemption of Bonds....................   1,150

  g. Treasury Stock.. 390,625
     Cash..   390,625

h. Stock Dividends.. 151,406*
   Cash Dividends... 46,875
      Stock Dividends Distributable........................... 71,250
      Paid-In Capital in Excess of Par—
      Common Stock... 80,156
      Cash Dividends Payable.................................. 46,875

   *125,000 – 6,250 = 118,750
    118,750 × 2% = 2,375
    2,375 × $63.75 = $151,406

i. Stock Dividends Distributable............................. 71,250
   Cash Dividends Payable 46,875
      Common Stock... 71,250
      Cash 46,875

j. Investment in Lewis Sports Inc. Bonds................. 145,500
   Interest Revenue.. 5,625
      Cash 151,125

k. Cash... 271,875
      Treasury Stock 234,375
      Paid-In Capital from Sale of Treasury Stock..... 37,500

l. Interest Expense.. 806,533
   Premium on Bonds Payable 93,467
      Cash 900,000

   Computations:
   Semiannual interest payment................................ $900,000
   Amortization premium [($1,869,339/120 months)
      × 6 months, rounded] 93,467
   Interest expense $806,533

m. Interest Receivable.. 7,500
      Interest Revenue 7,500
         Interest accrued for four months.

   Computation: $150,000 × 15% × 4/12 = $7,500

   Investment in Lewis Sports Inc. Bonds................. 120
      Interest Revenue 120
         Amortization of discounts for four months.

2. a.

DELHOME PRODUCTS INC.
Income Statement
For the Year Ended July 31, 2008

Sales			$ 6,300,000
Cost of merchandise sold..............................			3,498,750
Gross profit			$ 2,801,250
Operating expenses:			
Selling expenses:			
Sales salaries expense.........................	$360,000		
Sales commissions.............................	195,000		
Advertising expense	150,000		
Depreciation expense—store buildings			
and equipment	90,000		
Delivery expense.................................	27,000		
Store supplies expense	20,000		
Miscellaneous selling expense...........	13,750	$855,750	
Administrative expenses:			
Office salaries expense	$170,000		
Office rent expense.............................	50,000		
Depreciation expense—office buildings			
and equipment	25,000		
Office supplies expense......................	10,000		
Miscellaneous administrative expense	7,500	262,500	
Special charges:			
Restructuring charges..........................	$ 93,750		
Fixed asset impairment	187,500	281,250	
Total expenses			1,399,500
Income from operations................................			$ 1,401,750
Other expenses and income:			
Interest revenue..		$ 2,025	
Gain on redemption of bonds (net of			
applicable income tax of $150)		1,000	
Interest expense		(778,266)	(775,241)
Income from continuing operations before			
income tax...			$ 626,509
Income tax..			247,509
Income from continuing operations.............			$ 379,000
Loss from disposal of a discontinued			
operations		$250,000	
Less applicable income tax		100,000	150,000
Net income			$ 229,000

Comp. Prob. 4   Continued

Earnings per common share:
Income from continuing operations.....................................	$1.53*
Loss on discontinued operations	1.20
Net income	$0.33

*($379,000 – $187,500 preferred dividends)/125,000 common shares.

b.

DELHOME PRODUCTS INC.
Retained Earnings Statement
For the Year Ended July 31, 2008

Retained earnings, August 1, 2007		$2,302,970
Net income for year	$229,000	
Less dividends:		
Cash dividends...	$310,315	
Stock dividends..	151,406	461,721
Decrease in retained earnings.......................		232,721
Retained earnings, July 31, 2008...................		$2,070,249

c.

DELHOME PRODUCTS INC.
Balance Sheet
July 31, 2008

Assets

Current assets:

Cash..		$ 250,000	
Accounts receivable..............................	$ 562,500		
Less allowance for doubtful accounts ..	43,750	518,750	
Notes receivable......................................		156,250	
Merchandise inventory, at lower of cost (fifo) or market		850,000	
Interest receivable...................................		7,500	
Prepaid expenses.....................................		31,250	
Total current assets..............................			$ 1,813,750

Investments:

Investment in Lewis Sports Inc. bonds			145,620

Property, plant, and equipment:

Store buildings and equipment..............	$21,920,876		
Less accumulated depreciation.............	4,428,750	$17,492,126	
Office buildings and equipment..............	$ 7,412,500		
Less accumulated depreciation.............	1,670,650	5,741,850	
Total property, plant, and equipment..			23,233,976

Intangible assets:

Goodwill			540,000
Total assets			$25,733,346

Comp. Prob. 4   Concluded

Liabilities

Current liabilities:

Accounts payable	$ 212,000	
Employee termination obligation	81,250	
Income tax payable	40,000	
Dividends payable	37,500	
Deferred income tax payable	17,500	
Total current liabilities		$ 388,250
Long-term liabilities:		
Bonds payable, 11%, due 2018	$14,500,000	
Add premium on bonds payable	1,769,722	16,269,722
Deferred credits:		
Deferred income tax payable		33,875
Total liabilities		$16,691,847

Stockholders' Equity

Paid-in capital:

Preferred 8% stock, $125 par (30,000 shares authorized; 18,750 shares issued)	$ 2,343,750	
Excess of issue price over par	300,000	$ 2,643,750
Common stock, $30 par (400,000 shares authorized; 124,875 shares issued)	$ 3,746,250	
Excess of issue price over par	700,000	4,446,250
From sale of treasury stock		37,500
Total paid-in capital		$ 7,127,500
Retained earnings		2,070,249
Total		$ 9,197,749
Deduct treasury common stock (2,500 shares at cost)		156,250
Total stockholders' equity		9,041,499
Total liabilities and stockholders' equity		$25,733,346

SPECIAL ACTIVITIES

SA 15–1

GE Capital's action was legal, but caused a great public relations stir at the time. Some quotes:

"A lot of people feel like they have been sorely used," said one bond fund manager. "There was nothing illegal about it, but it was nasty."

The fund manager said that GE Capital's decision to upsize its bond issue to $11 billion from $6 billion midway through the offering ordinarily wouldn't have upset bondholders.

"But then to find out two days later that they had filed a $50 billion shelf?" he said. "People buy GE because it's like buying Treasurys, not because they want to get jerked around."

GE Capital's action was probably ethical, even though it caused some stir. In its own defense, it stated:

In a statement released late Thursday, GE Capital said "with the $11 billion bond issuance of March 13, GE Capital exhausted its existing debt shelf registration; consequently, on March 20, GE Capital filed a $50 billion shelf registration."

The release said the shelf filing was not an offering and that it would be used in part to roll over $31 billion in maturing long-term debt.

In retrospect, GE Capital could have been a little more forthcoming about its financing plans prior to selling the $11 billion on bonds, but there was nothing unethical or illegal about its disclosures.

> Source: "GE Capital Timing on $50B Shelf Filing Added To Backlash," *Dow Jones Capital Markets Report*, March 22, 2002, Copyright (c) 2002, Dow Jones & Company, Inc.

SA 15–2

Without the consent of the bondholders, Bob's use of the sinking fund cash to temporarily alleviate the shortage of funds would violate the bond indenture contract and the trust of the bondholders. It would therefore be unprofessional. In addition, the use of Bob's brother-in-law as trustee of the sinking fund is a potential conflict of interest that could be considered unprofessional.

SA 15–3

Receive $5,000,000 today:

Present value of $5,000,000 today = $5,000,000

Receive $2,000,000 today, plus $600,000 per year for 10 years:

Present value of $2,000,000 today = $2,000,000

Present value of annual payments = $600,000 × 6.41766 (Present value of an annuity of $1 for 10 periods at 9%) = $3,850,596

Total value = Present value of $2,000,000 + Present value of annual payments

Total value = $2,000,000 + $3,850,596 = $5,850,596

Receive $1,000,000 per year for 10 years:

Present value of annual payments = $1,000,000 × 6.41766 (Present value of an annuity of $1 for 10 periods at 9%) = $6,417,660

The option that has the highest value in terms of present value is to receive $1,000,000 per year for 10 years.

SA 15–4

The primary advantage of issuing preferred stock rather than bonds is that the preferred stock does not obligate Beacon to pay dividends, while interest on bonds must be paid. That is, the issuance of bonds will require annual interest payments, thus necessitating a periodic (probably semiannual) cash outflow. Given St. Seniors volatility of operating cash flows, the required interest payments might strain Beacon's liquidity. In the extreme, this could even lead to a bankruptcy of Beacon.

The issuance of bonds has the advantage of providing a tax deduction for interest expense. This would tend to reduce the net (after-tax) cost of the bonds. Probably the safest alternative is for Beacon to issue preferred stock. Of course, another alternative might be to issue a combination of preferred stock and bonds.

SA 15–5

1. The following table lists the face value, coupon rate, and maturity of each bond issue.

Face Value	Coupon Rate	Maturity Date
$243 million	9.875%	November 1, 2021
$250 million	9.625%	March 15, 2022
$250 million	9.500%	May 15, 2022
$240 million	9.125%	July 1, 2022
$250 million	8.250%	March 1, 2023
$250 million	8.125%	June 15, 2023

2. Georgia-Pacific may have called these bond issues early for a number of reasons. These reasons might include refinancing at lower interest rates, using cash flows from operations to reduce leverage, refinancing debt with equity through an initial public offering (IPO) or a secondary offering, using the funds from the sale of a subsidiary to reduce leverage (as was the case with Georgia-Pacific in this example), or refinancing fixed rate debt with variable rate debt in anticipation of falling interest rates.

SA 15–6

Note to Instructors: The purpose of this activity is to familiarize students with bonds as an investment and the sources of information about bonds.

SA 15–7

1.

	Plan 1	Plan 2
Shares of common stock	160,000	247,500
Earnings before bond interest and income tax	$700,000	$700,000
Deduct interest on bonds	350,000	227,500
Income before income tax	$350,000	$472,500
Deduct income tax	140,000	189,000
Net income	$210,000	$283,500
Earnings per share on common stock	$ 1.31*	$ 1.15**

*210,000/160,000
**283,500/(160,000 + 87,500)

2. a. Factors to be considered in addition to earnings per share:
   1. There is a definite legal obligation to pay interest on bonds, but there is no definite commitment to pay dividends on common stock. Therefore, if net income should drop substantially, bonds would be less desirable than common stock.
   2. If the bonds are issued, there is a definite commitment to repay the principal in 20 years. In case of liquidation, the claims of the bondholders would rank ahead of the claims of the common stockholders.
   3. Present stockholders must purchase the new stock if they are to retain their proportionate control and financial interest in the corporation.

   b. Since the net income has been relatively stable in the past and anticipated earnings under Plan 1 offer earnings per share of $1.31 for the common stockholder, Plan 1 appears to be somewhat more advantageous for present stockholders.

SA 15–8

Note to Instructors: The purpose of this activity is to familiarize students with bond ratings and the importance of bond ratings to the issuer as well as to the investor.

SA 15–9

1. 2003: $22
    2004: $1,703
    2005: $1,975

2. 2003: 11,620.9 = ($255,638 + $22)/$22
    2004: 183.2 = ($310,205 + $1,703)/$1,703
    2005: 177.6 = ($348,798 + $1,975)/$1,975

    While the company's ratio decreased significantly between 2003 and 2004, this was due to the fact that the company had virtually no interest expense before 2004. The company's current ratio of 177.6 times is still extremely
    favorable.

CHAPTER 16
STATEMENT OF CASH FLOWS

QUESTION INFORMATION

Number	Objective	Description	Difficulty	Time	AACSB	AICPA	SS	GL
Q16-1	16-3		Easy	5 min	Analytic	FN-Measurement		
Q16-2	16-2		Easy	5 min	Analytic	FN-Measurement		
Q16-3	16-1		Easy	5 min	Analytic	FN-Measurement		
Q16-4	16-1		Easy	5 min	Analytic	FN-Measurement		
Q16-5	16-2		Easy	5 min	Analytic	FN-Measurement		
Q16-6	16-2		Easy	5 min	Analytic	FN-Measurement		
Q16-7	16-2		Easy	5 min	Analytic	FN-Measurement		
Q16-8	16-1		Easy	5 min	Analytic	FN-Measurement		
Q16-9	16-1		Easy	5 min	Analytic	FN-Measurement		
Q16-10	16-2, 16-3		Easy	5 min	Analytic	FN-Measurement		
Q16-11	16-1, 16-3		Easy	5 min	Analytic	FN-Measurement		
Q16-12	16-1		Easy	5 min	Analytic	FN-Measurement		
PE16-1A	16-1	Classifying cash flows	Easy	5 min	Analytic	FN-Measurement		
PE16-1B	16-1	Classifying cash flows	Easy	5 min	Analytic	FN-Measurement		
PE16-2A	16-2	Adjustments to net income—indirect method	Easy	5 min	Analytic	FN-Measurement		
PE16-2B	16-2	Adjustments to net income—indirect method	Easy	5 min	Analytic	FN-Measurement		
PE16-3A	16-2	Changes in current operating assets and liabilities—indirect method	Easy	5 min	Analytic	FN-Measurement		
PE16-3B	16-2	Changes in current operating assets and liabilities—indirect method	Easy	5 min	Analytic	FN-Measurement		
PE16-4A	16-2	Reporting cash flows from operating activities—indirect method	Easy	10 min	Analytic	FN-Measurement		
PE16-4B	16-2	Reporting cash flows from operating activities—indirect method	Easy	10 min	Analytic	FN-Measurement		
PE16-5A	16-2	Reporting land transactions on the statement of cash flows	Easy	5 min	Analytic	FN-Measurement		
PE16-5B	16-2	Reporting land transactions on the statement of cash flows	Easy	5 min	Analytic	FN-Measurement		
PE16-6A	16-3	Cash received from customers—direct method	Easy	5 min	Analytic	FN-Measurement		
PE16-6B	16-3	Cash received from customers—direct method	Easy	5 min	Analytic	FN-Measurement		
PE16-7A	16-3	Cash payments for merchandise—direct method	Easy	5 min	Analytic	FN-Measurement		

Number	Objective	Description	Difficulty	Time	AACSB	AICPA	SS	GL
PE16-7B	16-3	Cash payments for merchandise—direct method	Easy	5 min	Analytic	FN-Measurement		
Ex16-1	16-1	Cash flows for operating activities-net loss	Easy	5 min	Analytic	FN-Measurement		
Ex16-2	16-1	Effects of transactions on cash flows	Easy	10 min	Analytic	FN-Measurement		
Ex16-3	16-1	Classifying cash flows	Easy	10 min	Analytic	FN-Measurement		
Ex16-4	16-2	Cash flows from operating activities-indirect method	Easy	10 min	Analytic	FN-Measurement		
Ex16-5	16-2	Cash flows from operating activities-indirect method	Easy	10 min	Analytic	FN-Measurement		
Ex16-6	16-1, 16-2	Cash flows from operating activities-indirect method	Easy	10 min	Analytic	FN-Measurement		
Ex16-7	16-1, 16-2	Cash flows from operating activities-indirect method	Easy	10 min	Analytic	FN-Measurement		
Ex16-8	16-2	Determining cash payments to stockholders	Easy	5 min	Analytic	FN-Measurement		
Ex16-9	16-2	Reporting changes in equipment on statement of cash flows	Easy	5 min	Analytic	FN-Measurement		
Ex16-10	16-2	Reporting changes in equipment on statement of cash flows	Easy	5 min	Analytic	FN-Measurement		
Ex16-11	16-2	Reporting land transactions on statement of cash flows	Easy	5 min	Analytic	FN-Measurement		
Ex16-12	16-2	Reporting stockholders' equity items on statement of cash flows	Moderate	10 min	Analytic	FN-Measurement		
Ex16-13	16-2	Reporting land acquisition for cash and mortgage note on statement of cash flows	Easy	5 min	Analytic	FN-Measurement		
Ex16-14	16-2	Reporting issuance and retirement of long-term debt	Moderate	10 min	Analytic	FN-Measurement		
Ex16-15	16-2	Determining net income from cash flow from operating activities	Moderate	10 min	Analytic	FN-Measurement		
Ex16-16	16-2	Cash flows from operating activities-indirect method	Moderate	15 min	Analytic	FN-Measurement	Exl	
Ex16-17	16-2	Statement of cash flows	Moderate	20 min	Analytic	FN-Measurement	Exl	
Ex16-18	16-2	Statement of cash flows-indirect method	Moderate	15 min	Analytic	FN-Measurement		
Ex16-19	16-3	Cash flows from operating activities-direct method	Easy	5 min	Analytic	FN-Measurement		
Ex16-20	16-3	Cash paid for merchandise purchases	Easy	5 min	Analytic	FN-Measurement		

Number	Objective	Description	Difficulty	Time	AACSB	AICPA	SS	GL
Ex16-21	16-3	Determining selected amounts for cash flows from operating activities-direct method	Easy	10 min	Analytic	FN-Measurement		
Ex16-22	16-3	Cash flows from operating activities-direct method	Moderate	15 min	Analytic	FN-Measurement		
Ex16-23	16-3	Cash flows from operating activities-direct method	Moderate	15 min	Analytic	FN-Measurement		
Ex16-24	FAI	Free cash flow	Easy	5 min	Analytic	FN-Measurement		
Ex16-25	FAI	Free cash flow	Easy	5 min	Analytic	FN-Measurement		
Pr16-1A	16-2	Statement of cash flows-indirect method	Moderate	1 1/4 hr	Analytic	FN-Measurement	Exl	
Pr16-2A	16-2	Statement of cash flows-indirect method	Moderate	1 1/2 hr	Analytic	FN-Measurement	Exl	
Pr16-3A	16-2	Statement of cash flows-indirect method	Moderate	1 1/2 hr	Analytic	FN-Measurement	Exl	
Pr16-4A	16-3	Statement of cash flows-direct method	Moderate	1 1/4 hr	Analytic	FN-Measurement	Exl	KA
Pr16-5A	16-3	Statement of cash flows-direct method applied to PR 16-1A	Moderate	1 1/4 hr	Analytic	FN-Measurement	Exl	
Pr16-1B	16-2	Statement of cash flows-indirect method	Moderate	1 1/4 hr	Analytic	FN-Measurement	Exl	
Pr16-2B	16-2	Statement of cash flows-indirect method	Moderate	1 1/2 hr	Analytic	FN-Measurement	Exl	
Pr16-3B	16-2	Statement of cash flows-indirect method	Moderate	1 1/2 hr	Analytic	FN-Measurement	Exl	
Pr16-4B	16-3	Statement of cash flows-direct method	Moderate	1 1/4 hr	Analytic	FN-Measurement	Exl	KA
Pr16-5B	16-3	Statement of cash flows-direct method applied to PR 16-1A	Moderate	1 1/4 hr	Analytic	FN-Measurement	Exl	
SA16-1	16-1	Ethics and professional conduct in business	Easy	5 min	Ethics	BB-Industry		
SA16-2	16-1	Using the statement of cash flows	Easy	5 min	Analytic	FN-Measurement		
SA16-3	16-2	Analysis of cash flow from operations	Easy	5 min	Analytic	FN-Measurement		
SA16-4	16-2	Analysis of cash flow from operations	Moderate	20 min	Analytic	FN-Measurement		
SA16-5	16-2, 16-3	Statement of cash flows	Moderate	45 min	Analytic	FN-Measurement		

EYE OPENERS

1. It is costly to accumulate the data needed.

2. It focuses on the differences between net income and cash flows from operating activities, and the data needed are generally more readily available and less costly to obtain than is the case for the direct method.

3. In a separate schedule of noncash investing and financing activities accompanying the statement of cash flows.

4. **a.** No effect
   b. No

5. The $25,000 increase must be added to income from operations because the amount of cash paid to merchandise creditors was $25,000 less than the amount of purchases included in the cost of goods sold.

6. The $15,000 decrease in salaries payable should be deducted from income to determine the amount of cash flows from operating activities. The effect of the decrease in the amount of salaries owed was to pay $15,000 more cash during the year than had been recorded as an expense.

7. **a.** $9,000 gain
   b. Cash inflow of $84,000

   c. The gain of $9,000 would be deducted from net income in determining net cash flow from operating activities; $84,000 would be reported as cash flow from investing activities.

8. Cash flow from financing activities—issuance of bonds, $4,200,000

9. **a.** Cash flow from investing activities—disposal of fixed assets, $12,000
   The $12,000 gain on asset disposal should be deducted from net income in determining cash flow from operating activities under the indirect method.

   b. No effect

10. The same. The amount reported as the net cash flow from operating activities is not affected by the use of the direct or indirect method.

11. Cash received from customers, cash payments for merchandise, cash payments for operating expenses, cash payments for interest, cash payments for income taxes.

12. Reported in a separate schedule, as follows:
    Schedule of noncash financing activities:
    Issuance of stock for
     acquisitions.................... $128 million

PRACTICE EXERCISE

PE 16–1A

a. Financing
b. Operating
c. Investing

d. Investing
e. Operating
f. Operating

PE 16–1B

a. Operating
b. Financing
c. Investing

d. Financing
e. Operating
f. Operating

PE 16–2A

Net income	$ 90,000
Adjustments to reconcile net income to net cash flow from operating activities:	
Depreciation	8,000
Amortization	5,200
Loss from sale of investments	6,000
Net cash flows from operating activities	$109,200

PE 16–2B

Net income	$125,000
Adjustments to reconcile net income to net cash flow from operating activities:	
Depreciation	3,500
Amortization	1,800
Gain from sale of land	(12,500)
Net cash flows from operating activities	$117,800

PE 16–3A

Net income	$110,000
Adjustments to reconcile net income to net cash flow from operating activities:	
Changes in current operating assets and liabilities:	
Decrease in accounts receivable......................................	2,000
Increase in inventory..	(2,500)
Increase in accounts payable..	1,300
Net cash flow from operating activities	$110,800

PE 16–3B

Net income	$290,000
Adjustments to reconcile net income to net cash flow from operating activities:	
Changes in current operating assets and liabilities:	
Increase in accounts receivable	(7,500)
Increase in inventory..	(21,000)
Increase in accounts payable..	19,500
Net cash flow from operating activities	$281,000

PE 16–4A

Cash flows from operating activities:		
Net income	$ 85,000	
Adjustments to reconcile net income to net cash flow from operating activities:		
Depreciation...	14,000	
Gain from disposal of equipment	(10,500)	
Changes in current operating assets and liabilities:		
Decrease in accounts receivable........................	6,000	
Decrease in accounts payable	(1,800)	
Net cash flow from operating activities..................		$92,700

PE 16–4B

Cash flows from operating activities:
Net income $150,000
Adjustments to reconcile net income to net cash
  flow from operating activities:
    Depreciation.. 25,000
    Loss from disposal of equipment......................... 14,300
Changes in current operating assets and liabilities:
    Increase in accounts receivable .... (9,400)
    Increase in accounts payable................................ 4,300
Net cash flow from operating activities................... $184,200

PE 16–5A

The loss on sale of land is deducted from net income as shown below:
  Loss on sale of land... $ 15,000

The purchase and sale of land is reported as part of cash flows from investing activities as shown below:
    Cash received for sale of land.. 90,000
    Cash paid for purchase of land.. (200,000)

PE 16–5B

The gain on sale of land is deducted from net income as shown below:
  Gain on sale of land .... $ (55,000)

The purchase and sale of land is reported as part of cash flows from investing activities as shown below:
    Cash received for sale of land.. 375,000
    Cash paid for purchase of land.. (500,000)

PE 16–6A

Sales $623,000
Deduct increase in accounts receivable... 48,000
Cash received from customers $575,000

PE 16–6B

Sales	$58,400
Add decrease in accounts receivable	2,100
Cash received from customers	$60,500

PE 16–7A

Cost of merchandise sold	$568,000
Deduct decrease in inventories	(39,000)
Add decrease in accounts payable	28,000
Cash paid for merchandise	$557,000

PE 16–7B

Cost of merchandise sold	$111,000
Add increase in inventories	8,400
Deduct increase in accounts payable	(5,700)
Cash paid for merchandise	$113,700

EXERCISES

Ex. 16–1

There were net additions, such as depreciation and amortization of intangible assets of $1.133 billion, to the net loss reported on the income statement to convert the net loss from the accrual basis to the cash basis. For example, depreciation is an expense in determining net income, but it does not result in a cash outflow. Thus, depreciation is added back to the net loss in order to determine cash flow from operations.

The cash from operating activities detail is provided as follows for class discussion:

Northwest Airlines Corporation
Cash Flows from Operating Activities
(selected from Statement of Cash Flows)
(in millions)

CASH FLOWS FROM OPERATING ACTIVITIES	
Net income (loss)	$(862)
Adjustments to reconcile net income (loss) to net cash flow provided by operating activities:	
Depreciation and amortization	731
Income tax expense (benefit)	1
Net receipts (payments) of income taxes	(3)
Pension and other postretirement benefit contributions less than expense	190
Net loss (earnings) of affiliates	(8)
Net loss (gain) on disposition of property, equipment and other	(95)
Other, net	77
Changes in certain assets and liabilities:	
Decrease (increase) in accounts receivable	46
Decrease (increase) in flight equipment spare parts	7
Decrease (increase) in supplies, prepaid expenses and other	(60)
Increase (decrease) in air traffic liability	191
Increase (decrease) in accounts payable....................................	27
Increase (decrease) in other liabilities	19
Increase (decrease) in accrued liabilities	10
Net cash provided by (used in) operating activities	$ 271

Ex. 16–2

a.	Cash receipt, $450,000	e.	Cash receipt, $98,000
b.	Cash receipt, $36,000	f.	Cash payment, $52,500
c.	Cash payment, $250,000	g.	Cash payment, $500,500
d.	Cash payment, $300,000	h.	Cash payment, $40,000

Ex. 16–3

a.	financing	g.	financing
b.	operating	h.	financing
c.	investing	i.	investing
d.	financing	j.	financing
e.	investing	k.	financing
f.	investing		

Ex. 16–4

a.	deducted	g.	deducted
b.	deducted	h.	deducted
c.	added	i.	deducted
d.	added	j.	added
e.	added	k.	added
f.	added		

Ex. 16–5

Net income	$92,000	
Adjustments to reconcile net income to net cash flow from operating activities:		
Depreciation	18,600	
Changes in current operating assets and liabilities:		
Increase in accounts receivable...............................	(1,200)	
Decrease in inventories	1,900	
Increase in prepaid expenses...................................	(500)	
Increase in accounts payable...................................	3,100	
Decrease in wages payable	(2,200)	
Net cash flow from operating activities		$111,700

Ex. 16–6

a. Cash flows from operating activities:

Net income...	$165,300	
Adjustments to reconcile net income to net cash flow from operating activities:		
Depreciation	46,700	
Changes in current operating assets and liabilities:		
Decrease in accounts receivable..............................	3,800	
Increase in inventories	(10,800)	
Decrease in prepaid expenses..................................	600	
Decrease in accounts payable..................................	(2,800)	
Increase in salaries payable.......................................	300	
Net cash flow from operating activities		$203,100

b. Yes. The amount of cash flows from operating activities reported on the statement of cash flows is not affected by the method of reporting such flows.

Ex. 16–7

Cash flows from operating activities:

Net income	$186,000	
Adjustments to reconcile net income to net cash flow from operating activities:		
Depreciation..	24,500	
Gain on disposal of equipment..............................	(10,200)	
Changes in current operating assets and liabilities:		
Increase in accounts receivable	(4,400)	
Decrease in inventories	2,000	
Decrease in prepaid insurance	800	
Decrease in accounts payable	(2,700)	
Increase in taxes payable	900	
Net cash flow from operating activities...................		$196,900

Note: The change in dividends payable would be used to adjust the dividends declared in obtaining the cash paid for dividends in the financing activities section of the statement of cash flows.

Ex. 16–8

Dividends declared	$120,000
Add decrease in dividends payable	5,000
Dividends paid to stockholders during the year	$125,000

The company probably had four quarterly payments—the first one being $35,000 declared in the preceding year and three payments of $30,000 each—of dividends declared and paid during the current year. Thus, $125,000 [$35,000 + (3 × $30,000)] is the amount of cash payments to stockholders. The $30,000 of dividends payable at the end of the year will be paid in the next year.

Ex. 16–9

Cash flows from investing activities:
    Cash received from sale of equipment $41,000

[The loss on the sale, $4,000 ($41,000 proceeds from sale less $45,000 book value), would be added to net income in determining the cash flows from operating activities if the indirect method of reporting cash flows from operations is used.]

Ex. 16–10

Cash flows from investing activities:
    Cash received from sale of equipment $15,000

[The gain on the sale, $2,000 ($15,000 proceeds from sale less $13,000 book value), would be deducted from net income in determining the cash flows from operating activities if the indirect method of reporting cash flows from operations is used.]

Ex. 16–11

Cash flows from investing activities:

Cash received from sale of land	$365,000
Less: Cash paid for purchase of land	400,000

(The gain on the sale of land, $115,000, would be deducted from net income in determining the cash flows from operating activities if the indirect method of reporting cash flows from operations is used.)

Ex. 16–12

Cash flows from financing activities:

Cash received from sale of common stock................ $496,000

Less: Cash paid for dividends..................................... 124,000

Note: The stock dividend is not disclosed on the statement of cash flows.

Ex. 16–13

Cash flows from investing activities:

Cash paid for purchase of land $326,000

A separate schedule of noncash investing and financing activities would report the purchase of $400,000 land with a long-term mortgage note, as follows:

Purchase of land by issuing long-term mortgage note $400,000

Ex. 16–14

Cash flows from financing activities:

Cash received from issuing bonds payable............... $330,000

Less: Cash paid to redeem bonds payable................ 70,000

Note: The discount amortization of $1,600 would be shown as an adjusting item (increase) in the cash flows from operating activities section under the indirect method.

Ex. 16–15

Net cash flow from operating activities		$86,700
Add: Increase in accounts receivable	$4,300	
Increase in prepaid expenses	700	
Decrease in income taxes payable	2,000	
Gain on sale of investments	3,400	10,400
		$97,100
Deduct: Depreciation	$8,500	
Decrease in inventories	5,600	
Increase in accounts payable	1,200	15,300
Net income, per income statement		$81,800

Note to Instructors: The net income must be determined by working backward through the cash flows from operating activities section of the statement of cash flows. Hence, those items which were added (deducted) to determine net cash flow from operating activities must be deducted (added) to determine net income.

Ex. 16–16

a.

JONES SODA CO.
Cash Flows from Operating Activities
(in thousands)

Cash flows from operating activities:		
Net income	$1,330	
Adjustments to reconcile net income to net cash flow from operating activities:		
Depreciation	193	
Stock-based compensation expense (noncash) ..	20	
Changes in current operating assets and liabilities:		
Increase in accounts receivable	(1,328)	
Increase in inventories	(1,550)	
Increase in prepaid expenses	(124)	
Increase in accounts payable................................	686	
Net cash flow used in operating activities		$(773)

b. Jones Soda is a very profitable company, but is using cash in operating activities (a negative cash flow). The reason is the large increases in accounts receivable and inventory. The current assets and liabilities are all increasing because Jones Soda is expanding rapidly. Thus, the negative cash flows from operating activities should not be too much of a concern to management.

Ex. 16–17

ALLIANCE STRUCTURES INC.
Statement of Cash Flows
For the Year Ended December 31, 2008

Cash flows from operating activities:		
Net income	$ 40	
Adjustments to reconcile net income to net cash		
flow from operating activities:		
Depreciation...	4	
Loss on sale of land....................................	5	
Changes in current operating assets and liabilities:		
Increase in accounts receivable	(3)	
Increase in inventories	(3)	
Increase in accounts payable............................	7	
Net cash flow from operating activities...................		$ 50
Cash flows from investing activities:		
Cash received from sale of land	$ 15	
Less cash paid for purchase of equipment	10	
Net cash flow provided by investing activities		5
Cash flows from financing activities:		
Cash received from sale of common stock..............	$ 23	
Less cash paid for dividends	11*	
Net cash flow provided by financing activities		12
Increase in cash..		$ 67
Cash at the beginning of the year		23
Cash at the end of the year		$ 90

*$12 – $1 = $11

Ex. 16–18

1. The increase in accounts receivable should be deducted from net income in the cash flows from operating activities section.

2. The gain from sale of investments should be deducted from net income in the cash flows from operating activities section.

3. The increase in accounts payable should be added to net income in the cash flows from operating activities section.

4. Cash paid for dividends should be deducted from cash received from the sale of common stock in the cash flows from financing activities section.

Ex. 16–18   Concluded

5. The correct amount of cash at the beginning of the year, $83,600, should be added to the increase in cash.

6. The final amount should be the amount of cash at the end of the year, $123,900.

A correct statement of cash flows would be as follows:

WHOLE LIFE NUTRITION PRODUCTS INC.
Statement of Cash Flows
For the Year Ended December 31, 2008

Cash flows from operating activities:		
Net income		$123,400
Adjustments to reconcile net income to net cash flow from operating activities:		
Depreciation		35,000
Gain on sale of investments		(6,000)
Changes in current operating assets and liabilities:		
Increase in accounts receivable		(9,500)
Increase in inventories		(12,300)
Increase in accounts payable		3,700
Decrease in accrued expenses		(900)
Net cash flow from operating activities		$133,400
Cash flows from investing activities:		
Cash received from sale of investments		$ 85,000
Less: Cash paid for purchase of land	$ 90,000	
Cash paid for purchase of equipment	150,100	240,100
Net cash flow used for investing activities		(155,100)
Cash flows from financing activities:		
Cash received from sale of common stock		$107,000
Less: Cash paid for dividends		45,000
Net cash flow provided by financing activities		62,000
Increase in cash		$ 40,300
Cash at the beginning of the year		83,600
Cash at the end of the year		$123,900

Ex. 16–19

a. Sales $450,000
   Plus decrease in accounts receivable balance........ 21,000
   Cash received from customers $471,000

b. Income tax expense.. $ 35,000
   Plus decrease in income tax payable 3,100
   Cash payments for income tax................................ $ 38,100

Ex. 16–20

Cost of merchandise sold.. $8,639*
Add increase in merchandise inventories...................... 291
Deduct increase in accounts payable............................ (125)
Cash paid for merchandise... $8,805

*In millions

Ex. 16–21

a. Cost of merchandise sold... $345,000
   Add decrease in accounts payable 3,300
                                                                               $348,300
   Deduct decrease in inventories............................... 5,200
   Cash payments for merchandise $343,100

b. Operating expenses other than depreciation........... $ 60,000
   Add decrease in accrued expenses.......................... 400
                                                                               $ 60,400
   Deduct decrease in prepaid expenses 500
   Cash payments for operating expenses................... $ 59,900

Ex. 16–22

Cash flows from operating activities:			
Cash received from customers		$466,500[1]	
Deduct: Cash payments for merchandise ...	$269,700[2]		
Cash payments for operating expenses.....................................	87,900[3]		
Cash payments for income tax	21,700[4]	379,300	
Net cash flow from operating activities.........			$ 87,200

Computations:

1. Sales..		$456,000
Add decrease in accounts receivable.............................		10,500
Cash received from customers		$466,500

2. Cost of merchandise sold...		$259,000
Add: Increase in inventories..	$ 3,500	
Decrease in accounts payable	7,200	10,700
Cash payments for merchandise		$269,700

3. Operating expenses other than depreciation		$ 92,400
Deduct: Decrease in prepaid expenses.........................	$ 3,400	
Increase in accrued expenses	1,100	4,500
Cash payments for operating expenses.........................		$ 87,900

4. Income tax expense		$ 19,300
Add decrease in income tax payable.............................		2,400
Cash payments for income tax		$ 21,700

Ex. 16–23

Cash flows from operating activities:

Cash received from customers			$182,100[1]
Deduct: Cash payments for merchandise ...	$ 70,000[2]		
Cash payments for operating expenses......................................	49,100[3]		
Cash payments for income tax	15,400	134,500	
Net cash flow from operating activities.........			$ 47,600

Computations:

1. Sales...	$184,000
Deduct increase in accounts receivable	1,900
Cash received from customers	$182,100
2. Cost of merchandise sold...	$ 67,000
Add increase in inventories..	5,000
	$ 72,000
Deduct increase in accounts payable	2,000
Cash payments for merchandise	$ 70,000
3. Operating expenses other than depreciation	$ 49,000
Add decrease in accrued expenses..	700
	$ 49,700
Deduct decrease in prepaid expenses	600
Cash payments for operating expenses...	$ 49,100

Ex. 16–24

Cash flows from operating activities	$120,000
Less cash paid for maintaining property, plant, and equipment	27,000*
Free cash flow	$ 93,000

*Property, plant, and equipment to maintain productive capacity: $45,000 × 60% = $27,000

Ex. 16–25

		Fiscal year ended January 29, 2006 <u>(all numbers in thousands)</u>
Cash flows from operating activities		$ 348,373
Less: Capital expenditure to maintain existing		
capacity:		
Purchases of property and equipment.........	$151,788	
Percent to maintain productive capacity	<u>× 70%</u>	<u>(106,252)</u>
Free cash flow...		<u>$ 241,121</u>

Prob. 16–1A

OAK AND TILE FLOORING CO.
Statement of Cash Flows
For the Year Ended June 30, 2008

Cash flows from operating activities:		
Net income	$ 65,900	
Adjustments to reconcile net income to net cash flow from operating activities:		
Depreciation	7,300	
Loss on sale of investments	5,000	
Changes in current operating assets and liabilities:		
Increase in accounts receivable	(9,300)	
Increase in inventories	(4,200)	
Increase in accounts payable	5,700	
Increase in accrued expenses	1,800	
Net cash flow from operating activities.........		$ 72,200
Cash flows from investing activities:		
Cash received from sale of investments	$ 45,000	
Less: Cash paid for purchase of land $145,000		
Cash paid for purchase of equipment 39,500	184,500	
Net cash flow used for investing activities		(139,500)
Cash flows from financing activities:		
Cash received from sale of common stock...	$126,000	
Less cash paid for dividends	47,500*	
Net cash flow provided by financing activities		78,500
Increase in cash...		$ 11,200
Cash at the beginning of the year		23,500
Cash at the end of the year		$ 34,700

*$50,000 + $10,000 − $12,500 = $47,500

Prob. 16–1A   Concluded

	A	B	C		D		E	
		OAK AND TILE FLOORING CO.						
		Spreadsheet (Work Sheet) For Statement of Cash Flows						
		For the Year Ended June 30, 2008						
		Balance	**Transactions**				**Balance**	
		June 30, 2007	**Debit**		**Credit**		June 30, 2008	
1	Cash	23,500	(m)	11,200			34,700	1
2	Accounts receivable	92,300	(l)	9,300			101,600	2
3	Inventories	142,100	(k)	4,200			146,300	3
4	Investments	50,000			(j)	50,000	0	4
5	Land	0	(i)	145,000			145,000	5
6	Equipment	175,500	(h)	39,500			215,000	6
7	Accum. dep.—equipment	(41,300)			(g)	7,300	(48,600)	7
8	Accounts payable	(95,200)			(f)	5,700	(100,900)	8
9	Accrued expenses	(13,200)			(e)	1,800	(15,000)	9
10	Dividends payable	(10,000)			(d)	2,500	(12,500)	10
11	Common stock	(50,000)			(c)	6,000	(56,000)	11
12	Paid-in capital in excess of par—common stock	(100,000)			(c)	120,000	(220,000)	12
13	Retained earnings	(173,700)	(b)	50,000	(a)	65,900	(189,600)	13
14	Totals	0		259,200		259,200	0	14
15	Operating activities:							15
16	Net income		(a)	65,900				16
17	Depreciation		(g)	7,300				17
18	Loss on sale of investments		(j)	5,000				18
19	Increase in accounts receivable				(l)	9,300		19
20	Increase in inventories				(k)	4,200		20
21	Increase in accounts payable		(f)	5,700				21
22	Increase in accrued expenses		(e)	1,800				22
23	Investing activities:							23
24	Purchase of equipment				(h)	39,500		24
25	Purchase of land				(i)	145,000		25
26	Sale of investments		(j)	45,000				26
27	Financing activities:							27
28	Declaration of cash dividends				(b)	50,000		28
29	Sale of common stock		(c)	126,000				29
30	Increase in dividends payable		(d)	2,500				30
31	Net increase in cash				(m)	11,200		31
32	Totals			259,200		259,200		32

Prob. 16–2A

PORTABLE LUGGAGE COMPANY
Statement of Cash Flows
For the Year Ended December 31, 2008

Cash flows from operating activities:		
Net income	$204,800	
Adjustments to reconcile net income to net cash flow from operating activities:		
Depreciation..	29,500	
Patent amortization	5,500	
Changes in current operating assets and liabilities:		
Increase in accounts receivable	(29,100)	
Decrease in inventories	53,500	
Increase in prepaid expenses	(2,500)	
Decrease in accounts payable	(35,600)	
Decrease in salaries payable	(4,400)	
Net cash flow from operating activities........................		$ 221,700
Cash flows from investing activities:		
Cash paid for construction of building..........................	$230,000	
Net cash flow used for investing activities		(230,000)
Cash flows from financing activities:		
Cash received from issuance of mortgage note...........	$ 90,000	
Less: Cash paid for dividends	49,000*	
Net cash flow provided by financing activities.............		41,000
Increase in cash...		$ 32,700
Cash at the beginning of the year		143,200
Cash at the end of the year..		$ 175,900
Schedule of Noncash Financing and Investing Activities:		
Issuance of common stock to retire bonds		$ 154,000

*$52,000 + $10,000 − $13,000 = $49,000

	A	B	C		D		E	
			Transactions					
		Balance					Balance	
		Dec. 31, 2007	Debit		Credit		Dec. 31, 2008	
	PORTABLE LUGGACE COMPANY							
	Spreadsheet (Work Sheet) For Statement of Cash Flows							
	For the Year Ended December 31, 2008							
1	Cash	143,200	(p)	32,700			175,900	1
2	Accounts receivable (net)	235,000	(o)	29,100			264,100	2
3	Inventories	405,800			(n)	53,500	352,300	3
4	Prepaid expenses	10,000	(m)	2,500			12,500	4
5	Land	120,000					120,000	5
6	Buildings	450,000	(l)	230,000			680,000	6
7	Accum. dep.—buildings	(164,500)			(k)	20,500	(185,000)	7
8	Machinery and equipment	310,000					310,900	8
9	Accum. dep.—machinery and equipment	(76,000)			(j)	9,000	(85,000)	9
10	Patents	48,000			(i)	5,500	42,500	10
11	Accounts payable	(367,900)	(h)	35,600			(332,300)	11
12	Dividends payable	(10,000)			(g)	3,000	(13,000)	12
13	Salaries payable	(34,600)	(f)	4,400			(30,200)	13
14	Mortgage note payable	0			(e)	90,000	(90,000)	14
15	Bonds payable	(154,000)	(d)	154,000			0	15
16	Common stock	(20,000)			(c)	4,000	(24,000)	16
17	Paid-in capital in excess of par—common stock	(50,000)			(c)	150,000	(200,000)	17
18	Retained earnings	(845,000)	(b)	52,000	(a)	204,800	(997,800)	18
19	Totals	0		540,300		540,300	0	19

	Balance, Dec. 31, 2007	Transactions		Balance, Dec. 31, 2008
		Debit	Credit	
Operating activities:				
Net income		(a) 204,800		
Depreciation—buildings		(k) 20,500		
Depreciation—machinery and equipment		(j) 9,000		
Amortization of patents		(i) 5,500		
Increase in accounts receivable			(o) 29,100	
Decrease in inventories		(n) 53,500		
Increase in prepaid expenses			(m) 2,500	
Decrease in accounts payable			(h) 35,600	
Decrease in salaries payable ..			(f) 4,400	
Investing activities:				
Construction of building			(l) 230,000	
Financing activities:				
Declaration of cash dividends			(b) 52,000	
Issuance of mortgage note payable...............................		(e) 90,000		
Increase in dividends payable		(g) 3,000		
Schedule of noncash investing and financing activities:				
Issuance of common stock to retire bonds		(c) 154,000	(d) 154,000	
Net increase in cash			(p) 32,700	
Totals...		540,300	540,300	

Prob. 16–3A

RESTON SUPPLY CO.
Statement of Cash Flows
For the Year Ended December 31, 2008

Cash flows from operating activities:			
Net income		$ 28,600	
Adjustments to reconcile net income to net cash flow from operating activities:			
Depreciation		10,400	
Gain on sale of land		(9,000)	
Changes in current operating assets and liabilities:			
Increase in accounts receivable		(14,300)	
Increase in inventories		(8,000)	
Decrease in prepaid expenses		1,200	
Decrease in accounts payable		(5,600)	
Increase in income tax payable		800	
Net cash flow from operating activities			$ 4,100
Cash flows from investing activities:			
Cash received from land sold		$ 69,000	
Less: Cash paid for acquisition of building	$150,000		
Cash paid for purchase of equipment	29,800	179,800	
Net cash flow used for investing activities			(110,800)
Cash flows from financing activities:			
Cash received from issuance of bonds payable	$ 50,000		
Cash received from issuance of common stock	63,000	$113,000	
Less cash paid for dividends		12,000	
Net cash flow provided by financing activities			101,000
Decrease in cash			$ (5,700)
Cash at the beginning of the year			51,200
Cash at the end of the year			$ 45,500

Prob. 16–3A   Concluded

	A	B	C		D		E	
		RESTON SUPPLY CO.						
		Spreadsheet (Work Sheet) For Statement of Cash Flows						
		For the Year Ended December 31, 2008						
		Balance	**Transactions**				**Balance**	
		Dec. 30, 2007	**Debit**		**Credit**		**Dec. 30, 2008**	
1	Cash	51,200			(p)	5,700	45,500	1
2	Accounts receivable	92,400	(i)	14,300			106,700	2
3	Inventories	131,200	(h)	8,000			139,200	3
4	Prepaid expenses	4,000			(g)	1,200	2,800	4
5	Land	210,000			(m)	60,000	150,000	5
6	Buildings	150,000	(l)	150,000			300,000	6
7	Accum. dep.—buildings	(55,500)			(f)	4,700	(60,200)	7
8	Equipment	80,300			(k)	10,000	100,100	8
9	Accum. dep.—equipment	(24,500)	(k)	10,000	(e)	5,700	(20,200)	9
10	Accounts payable	(95,600)	(d)	5,600			(90,000)	10
11	Income tax payable	(3,200)			(c)	800	(4,000)	11
12	Bonds payable	0			(n)	50,000	(50,000)	12
13	Common stock	(30,000)			(o)	3,000	(33,000)	13
14	Paid-in capital in excess of par—common stock	(120,000)			(o)	60,000	(180,000)	14
15	Retained earnings	(390,000)	(b)	12,000	(a)	28,600	(406,900)	15
16	Totals	0		229,700		229,700	0	16
17	Operating activities:							17
18	Net income		(a)	28,600				18
19	Depreciation—equipment		(e)	5,700				19
20	Depreciation—buildings		(f)	4,700				20
21	Gain on sale of land				(m)	9,000		21
22	Increase in accounts receivable				(i)	14,300		22
23	Increase in inventories				(h)	8,000		23
24	Decrease in prepaid expenses		(g)	1,200				24
25	Decrease in accounts payable				(d)	5,600		25
26	Increase in income tax payable		(c)	800				26
27	Investing activities:							27
28	Purchase of equipment				(j)	29,800		28
29	Acquisition of building				(l)	150,000		29
30	Sale of land		(m)	69,000				30
31	Financing activities:							31
32	Payment of cash dividends				(b)	12,000		32
33	Issuance of bonds payable		(n)	50,000				33
34	Issuance of common stock		(o)	63,000				34
35	Net decrease in cash		(p)	5,700				35
36	Totals			228,700		228,700		36

Prob. 16–4A

GREEN EARTH LAWN AND GARDEN INC.
Statement of Cash Flows
For the Year Ended December 31, 2009

Cash flows from operating activities:			
Cash received from customers		$923,700[1]	
Deduct: Cash payments for			
merchandise	$472,200[2]		
Cash payments for operating			
expenses	281,300[3]		
Cash payments for income tax.....	62,300	815,800	
Net cash flow from operating activities......			$ 107,900
Cash flows from investing activities:			
Cash received from sale of investments		$122,000	
Less: Cash paid for land	$200,000		
Cash paid for equipment...................	50,000	250,000	
Net cash flow used for investing			
activities			(128,000)
Cash flows from financing activities:			
Cash received from sale of			
common stock		$102,000	
Less cash paid for dividends		86,300*	
Net cash flow used for			
financing activities			15,700
Decrease in cash			$ (4,400)
Cash at the beginning of the year			142,300
Cash at the end of the year..............................			$ 137,900

Schedule Reconciling Net Income with Cash Flows from Operating Activities:

Net income	$ 117,900
Adjustments to reconcile net income to net cash flow from	
operating activities:	
Depreciation expense	23,600
Gain on sale of investments..	(32,000)
Changes in current operating assets and liabilities:	
Increase in accounts receivable	(16,300)
Increase in inventories	(6,400)
Increase in accounts payable...	23,500
Decrease in accrued expense	(2,400)
Net cash flow from operating activities....................................	$ 107,900

*Dividends paid: $88,300 + $19,000 − $21,000 = $86,300

Prob. 16–4A   Concluded

Computations:

1. Sales $940,000
   Deduct increase in accounts receivable 16,300
   Cash received from customers $923,700

2. Cost of merchandise sold... $489,300
   Add increase in inventories... 6,400
   $495,700
   Deduct increase in accounts payable 23,500
   Cash payments for merchandise $472,200

3. Operating expenses other than depreciation $278,900
   Add decrease in accrued expenses.............................. 2,400
   Cash payments for operating expenses....................... $281,300

Prob. 16–5A

OAK AND TILE FLOORING CO.
Statement of Cash Flows
For the Year Ended June 30, 2008

Cash flows from operating activities:			
Cash received from customers		$ 954,100[1]	
Deduct: Cash payments for merchandise	$660,600[2]		
Cash payments for operating			
expenses	193,200[3]		
Cash payments for income tax.....	28,100	881,900	
Net cash flow from operating activities......			$ 72,200
Cash flows from investing activities:			
Cash received from sale of investments		$ 45,000	
Less: Cash paid for purchase of land	$145,000		
Cash paid for purchase of			
equipment	39,500	184,500	
Net cash flow used for investing			
activities			(139,500)
Cash flows from financing activities:			
Cash received from sale of common			
stock		$ 126,000	
Less cash paid for dividends		47,500*	
Net cash flow provided by financing			
activities			78,500
Increase in cash..			$ 11,200
Cash at the beginning of the year			23,500
Cash at the end of the year..............................			$ 34,700

Schedule Reconciling Net Income with Cash Flows from Operating Activities:	
Net income	$ 65,900
Adjustments to reconcile net income to net cash flow	
from operating activities:	
Depreciation expense...	7,300
Loss on sale of investments	5,000
Changes in current operating assets and liabilities:	
Increase in accounts receivable	(9,300)
Increase in inventories	(4,200)
Increase in accounts payable	5,700
Increase in accrued expenses	1,800
Net cash flow from operating activities.........................	$ 72,200

*Dividends paid: $50,000 + $10,000 − $12,500 = $47,500

Prob. 16–5A   Concluded

Computations:

1. Sales $963,400
   Deduct increase in accounts receivable 9,300
   Cash received from customers $954,100

2. Cost of merchandise sold.. $662,100
   Add increase in inventories... 4,200
                                                                                           $666,300
   Deduct increase in accounts payable 5,700
   Cash payments for merchandise $660,600

3. Operating expenses other than depreciation $195,000
   Deduct increase in accrued expenses 1,800
   Cash payments for operating expenses....................... $193,200

Prob. 16–1B

GOLD MEDAL SPORTING GOODS INC.
Statement of Cash Flows
For the Year Ended December 31, 2008

Cash flows from operating activities:			
Net income		$ 94,400	
Adjustments to reconcile net income to net cash flow from operating activities:			
Depreciation		11,500	
Gain on sale of investments		(25,000)	
Changes in current operating assets and liabilities:			
Increase in accounts receivable		(11,800)	
Increase in inventories		(15,400)	
Increase in accounts payable		14,700	
Decrease in accrued expenses		(6,500)	
Net cash flow from operating activities			$ 61,900
Cash flows from investing activities:			
Cash received from sale of investments		$175,000	
Less: Cash paid for purchase of land	$205,000		
Cash paid for purchase of equipment	95,000	300,000	
Net cash flow used for investing activities			(125,000)
Cash flows from financing activities:			
Cash received from sale of common stock		$145,000	
Less cash paid for dividends		57,000*	
Net cash flow provided by financing activities			88,000
Increase in cash			$ 24,900
Cash at the beginning of the year			366,200
Cash at the end of the year			$ 391,100

*$60,000 + $12,000 − $15,000 = $57,000

GOLD MEDAL SPORTING GOODS, INC.
Spreadsheet (Work Sheet) for Statement of Cash Flows
For the Year Ended December 31, 2008

	Balance, Dec. 31, 2007	Transactions Debit		Transactions Credit		Balance, Dec. 31, 2008
Cash...	366,200	(m)	24,900			391,100
Accounts receivable	130,600	(l)	11,800			142,400
Inventories	385,700	(k)	15,400			401,100
Investments....................................	150,000			(j)	150,000	0
Land...	0	(i)	205,000			205,000
Equipment......................................	345,700	(h)	95,000			440,700
Accumulated depreciation—						
equipment..................................	(92,500)			(g)	11,500	(104,000)
Accounts payable	(253,100)			(f)	14,700	(267,800)
Accrued expenses	(32,900)	(e)	6,500			(26,400)
Dividends payable	(12,000)			(d)	3,000	(15,000)
Common stock................................	(60,000)			(c)	20,000	(80,000)
Paid-in capital in excess of par—						
common stock	(175,000)			(c)	125,000	(300,000)
Retained earnings..........................	(752,700)	(b)	60,000	(a)	94,400	(787,100)
Totals...	0		418,600		418,600	0
Operating activities:						
Net income		(a)	94,400			
Depreciation		(g)	11,500			
Gain on sale of investments ...				(j)	25,000	
Increase in accounts						
receivable				(l)	11,800	
Increase in inventories				(k)	15,400	
Increase in accounts payable		(f)	14,700			
Decrease in accrued expenses				(e)	6,500	
Investing activities:						
Purchase of equipment				(h)	95,000	
Purchase of land......................				(i)	205,000	
Sale of investments		(j)	175,000			
Financing activities:						
Declaration of cash dividends				(b)	60,000	
Sale of common stock.............		(c)	145,000			
Increase in dividends payable		(d)	3,000			
Net increase in cash				(m)	24,900	
Totals...			443,600		443,600	

Prob. 16–2B

AIR GLIDE ATHLETIC APPAREL CO.
Statement of Cash Flows
For the Year Ended December 31, 2008

Cash flows from operating activities:			
Net income		$ 81,300	
Adjustments to reconcile net income to net cash flow from operating activities:			
Depreciation		26,100	
Changes in current operating assets and liabilities:			
Decrease in accounts receivable		5,400	
Increase in merchandise inventory		(7,000)	
Increase in prepaid expenses		(1,200)	
Increase in accounts payable		3,900	
Net cash flow from operating activities			$ 108,500
Cash flows from investing activities:			
Cash paid for equipment		$ 50,900	
Net cash flow used for investing activities			(50,900)
Cash flows from financing activities:			
Cash received from sale of common stock		$ 85,000	
Less: Cash paid for dividends	$ 48,000		
Cash paid to retire mortgage note payable	105,000	153,000	
Net cash flow used in financing activities			(68,000)
Decrease in cash			$ (10,400)
Cash at the beginning of the year			56,200
Cash at the end of the year			$ 45,800

Prob. 16–2B   Concluded

AIR GLIDE ATHLETIC APPAREL CO.
Spreadsheet (Work Sheet) for Statement of Cash Flows
For the Year Ended December 31, 2008

	Balance, Dec. 31, 2007	Transactions		Balance, Dec. 31, 2008
		Debit	Credit	
Cash...	56,200		(l) 10,400	45,800
Accounts receivable	75,600		(k) 5,400	70,200
Merchandise inventory..................	93,500	(j) 7,000		100,500
Prepaid expenses	3,000	(i) 1,200		4,200
Equipment......................................	167,800	(h) 50,900	(g) 14,000	204,700
Accumulated depreciation—				
equipment....................................	(41,300)	(g) 14,000	(f) 26,100	(53,400)
Accounts payable	(74,300)		(e) 3,900	(78,200)
Mortgage note payable..................	(105,000)	(d) 105,000		0
Common stock...............................	(10,000)		(c) 5,000	(15,000)
Paid-in capital in excess of par—				
common stock	(100,000)		(c) 80,000	(180,000)
Retained earnings..........................	(65,500)	(b) 48,000	(a) 81,300	(98,800)
Totals...	0	226,100	226,100	0
Operating activities:				
Net income		(a) 81,300		
Depreciation		(f) 26,100		
Decrease in accounts receivables.........................		(k) 5,400		
Increase in merchandise inventory............................			(j) 7,000	
Increase in prepaid expenses			(i) 1,200	
Increase in accounts payable		(e) 3,900		
Investing activities:				
Purchase of equipment			(h) 50,900	
Financing activities:				
Payment of cash dividends			(b) 48,000	
Sale of common stock.............		(c) 85,000		
Payment of mortgage note payable...............................			(d) 105,000	
Net decrease in cash		(l) 10,400		
Totals...		212,100	212,100	

Prob. 16–3B

RISE N' SHINE JUICE CO.
Statement of Cash Flows
For the Year Ended December 31, 2008

Cash flows from operating activities:			
Net loss		$ (11,700)	
Adjustments to reconcile net income to net cash flow from operating activities:			
Depreciation		23,800	
Loss on sale of land...............................		6,000	
Changes in current operating assets and liabilities:			
Increase in accounts receivable		(28,600)	
Increase in inventories		(45,100)	
Decrease in prepaid expenses...............		2,500	
Decrease in accounts payable...............		(15,300)	
Net cash flow from operating activities......			$ (68,400)
Cash flows from investing activities:			
Cash received from land sold		$ 64,000	
Less: Cash paid for acquisition of building...................................	$240,000		
Cash paid for purchase of equipment................................	44,600	284,600	
Net cash flow used for investing activities			(220,600)
Cash flows from financing activities:			
Cash received from issuance of bonds payable...	$115,000		
Cash received from issuance of common stock	168,000	$ 283,000	
Less cash paid for dividends		14,000	
Net cash flow provided by financing activities			269,000
Decrease in cash			$ (20,000)
Cash at the beginning of the year			412,300
Cash at the end of the year.............................			$ 392,300

RISE N' SHINE JUICE CO.
Spreadsheet (Work Sheet) for Statement of Cash Flows
For the Year Ended December 31, 2008

	Balance, Dec. 31, 2007	Transactions Debit		Transactions Credit		Balance, Dec. 31, 2008
Cash	412,300			(o)	20,000	392,300
Accounts receivable	325,600	(g)	28,600			354,200
Inventories	497,000	(h)	45,100			542,100
Prepaid expenses	15,000			(f)	2,500	12,500
Land	205,000			(l)	70,000	135,000
Buildings	385,000	(k)	240,000			625,000
Accumulated depreciation— buildings	(163,400)			(e)	11,200	(174,600)
Equipment	194,300	(i)	44,600	(j)	20,000	218,900
Accumulated depreciation— equipment	(67,800)	(j)	20,000	(d)	12,600	(60,400)
Accounts payable	(409,500)	(c)	15,300			(394,200)
Bonds payable	0			(m)	115,000	(115,000)
Common stock	(50,000)			(n)	8,000	(58,000)
Paid-in capital in excess of par— common stock	(240,000)			(n)	160,000	(400,000)
Retained earnings	(1,103,500)	(a)	11,700			(1,077,800)
		(b)	14,000			
Totals	0		419,300		419,300	0
Operating activities:						
Net loss				(a)	11,700	
Depreciation—equipment		(d)	12,600			
Depreciation—buildings		(e)	11,200			
Loss on sale of land		(l)	6,000			
Increase in accounts receivable				(g)	28,600	
Increase in inventories				(h)	45,100	
Decrease in prepaid expenses		(f)	2,500			
Decrease in accounts payable				(c)	15,300	
Investing activities:						
Purchase of equipment				(i)	44,600	
Acquisition of building				(k)	240,000	
Sale of land		(l)	64,000			
Financing activities:						
Payment of cash dividends				(b)	14,000	
Issuance of bonds payable		(m)	115,000			
Issuance of common stock		(n)	168,000			
Net decrease in cash		(o)	20,000			
Totals			399,300		399,300	

Prob. 16–4B

HOME AND HEARTH INC.
Statement of Cash Flows
For the Year Ended December 31, 2009

Cash flows from operating activities:			
Cash received from customers		$3,733,600[1]	
Deduct: Cash payments for merchandise..........................	$1,535,600[2]		
Cash payments for operating expenses...............................	1,941,400[3]		
Cash payments for income tax ...	63,000	3,540,000	
Net cash flow from operating activities......			$ 193,600
Cash flows from investing activities:			
Cash received from sale of investments....		$ 110,000	
Less: Cash paid for purchase of land........	$ 325,000		
Cash paid for purchase of equipment	125,000	450,000	
Net cash flow used for investing activities			(340,000)
Cash flows from financing activities:			
Cash received from sale of common stock		$ 144,000	
Less cash paid for dividends		20,100*	
Net cash flow provided by financing activities..			123,900
Decrease in cash			$ (22,500)
Cash at the beginning of the year			424,600
Cash at the end of the year..............................			$ 402,100

Reconciliation of Net Income with Cash Flows from Operating Activities:	
Net income	$ 146,000
Adjustments to reconcile net income to net cash flow from operating activities:	
Depreciation	27,400
Loss on sale of investments	40,000
Changes in current operating assets and liabilities:	
Increase in accounts receivable	(12,100)
Increase in inventories	(17,700)
Increase in accounts payable	14,600
Decrease in accrued expenses...	(4,600)
Net cash flow from operating activities.........................	$ 193,600

*Dividends paid: $21,600 + $4,000 – $5,500 = $20,100

Prob. 16–4B   Concluded

Computations:

1. Sales $3,745,700
   Deduct increase in accounts receivable 12,100
   Cash received from customers $3,733,600

2. Cost of merchandise sold... $1,532,500
   Add increase in inventories.. 17,700
                                                                                        $1,550,200
   Deduct increase in accounts payable 14,600
   Cash payments for merchandise $1,535,600

3. Operating expenses other than depreciation $1,936,800
   Add decrease in accrued expenses.............................. 4,600
   Cash payments for operating expenses....................... $1,941,400

Prob. 16–5B

GOLD MEDAL SPORTING GOODS INC.
Statement of Cash Flows
For the Year Ended December 31, 2008

Cash flows from operating activities:

Cash received from customers		$1,620,700[1]	
Deduct: Cash payments for merchandise	$909,000[2]		
Cash payments for operating expenses.....................................	615,500[3]		
Cash payments for income tax........	34,300	1,558,800	
Net cash flow from operating activities.........			$ 61,900

Cash flows from investing activities:

Cash received from sale of investments		$ 175,000	
Less: Cash paid for land	$205,000		
Cash paid for equipment.....................	95,000	300,000	
Net cash flow used for investing activities ...			(125,000)

Cash flows from financing activities:

Cash received from sale of common stock...		$ 145,000	
Less cash paid for dividends		57,000[4]	
Net cash flow provided by financing activities			88,000
Increase in cash...			$ 24,900
Cash at the beginning of the year			366,200
Cash at the end of the year.................................			$ 391,100

Reconciliation of Net Income with Cash Flows from Operating Activities:

Net income	$ 94,400
Adjustments to reconcile net income to net cash flow from operating activities:	
Depreciation	11,500
Gain on sale of investments	(25,000)
Changes in current operating assets and liabilities:	
Increase in accounts receivable	(11,800)
Increase in inventories	(15,400)
Increase in accounts payable	14,700
Decrease in accrued expenses...................................	(6,500)
Net cash flow from operating activities...........................	$ 61,900

Prob. 16–5B   Concluded

Computations:

1. Sales .... $ 1,632,500
   Deduct increase in accounts receivable 11,800
   Cash received from customers .... $ 1,620,700

2. Cost of merchandise sold .... $ 908,300
   Add increase in inventories 15,400
                                                                $ 923,700
   Deduct increase in accounts payable 14,700
   Cash payments for merchandise .... $ 909,000

3. Operating expenses other than
        depreciation .... $ 609,000
   Add decrease in accrued expenses 6,500
   Cash payments for operating expenses .... $ 615,500

4. Cash dividends declared .... $ 60,000
   Deduct increase in dividends payable 3,000
   Cash paid for dividends .... $ 57,000

SPECIAL ACTIVITIES

SA 16–1

Although this situation might seem harmless at first, it is, in fact, a violation of generally accepted accounting principles. The operating cash flow per share figure should not be shown on the face of the income statement. The income statement is constructed under accrual accounting concepts, while operating cash flow "undoes" the accounting accruals. Thus, unlike Linda's assertion that this information would be useful, more likely the information could be confusing to users. Some users might not be able to distinguish between earnings and operating cash flow per share—or how to interpret the difference. By agreeing with Linda, Ben has breached his professional ethics because the disclosure would violate generally accepted accounting principles. On a more subtle note, Linda is being somewhat disingenuous. Apparently, Linda is not pleased with this year's operating performance and would like to cover the earnings "bad news" with some cash flow "good news" disclosures. An interesting question is: Would Linda be as interested in the dual per share disclosures in the opposite scenario—with earnings per share improving and cash flow per share deteriorating? Probably not.

SA 16–2

Start-up companies are unique in that they frequently will have negative retained earnings and operating cash flows. The negative retained earnings are often due to losses from high start-up expenses. The negative operating cash flows are typical because growth requires cash. Growth must be financed with cash before the cash returns. For example, a company must expend cash to make the service in Period 1 before selling it and receiving cash in Period 2. The start-up company constantly faces spending cash today for the next period's growth. For Aspen Technologies Inc., the money spent on salaries to develop the business is a cash outflow that must occur before the service provides revenues. In addition, the company must use cash to market its service to potential customers. In this situation, the only way the company stays in business is from the capital provided by the owners. This owner-supplied capital is the lifeblood of a start-up company. Banks will not likely lend money on this type of venture (except with assets as security). Aspen Technologies Inc. could be a good investment. It all depends on whether the new service has promise. The financial figures will not reveal this easily. Only actual sales will reveal if the service is a hit. Until this time the company is at risk. If the service is not popular, the company will have no cash to fall back on—it will likely go bankrupt. If, however, the service is successful, then Aspen Technologies Inc. should become self-sustaining and provide a good return for the shareholders.

SA 16–3

The senior vice president is very focused on profitability but has been bleeding cash. The increase in accounts receivable and inventory is striking. Apparently, the new credit card campaign has found many new customers, since the accounts receivable is growing. Unfortunately, it appears as though the new campaign has done a poor job of screening creditworthiness in these new customers. In other words, there are many new credit card purchasers—unfortunately, they do not appear to be paying off their balances. The new merchandise purchases appear to be backfiring. The company has received some "good deals," except that they are only "good deals" if it can resell the merchandise. If the merchandise has no customer appeal, then that would explain the inventory increase. In other words, the division is purchasing merchandise that sits on the shelf, regardless of pricing. The reduction in payables is the result of the division becoming overdue on payments. The memo reports that most of the past due payables have been paid. This situation is critical in the retailing business. A retailer cannot afford a poor payment history, or it will be denied future merchandise shipments. This is a signal of severe cash problems. Overall, the picture is of a retailer having severe operating cash flow difficulties.

Note to Instructors: This scenario is essentially similar to Kmart's path to eventual bankruptcy. It reported earnings, while having significant negative cash flows from operations due to expanding credit too liberally (increases in accounts receivable) and purchasing too much unsaleable inventory (increases in inventory). Eventually, Kmart's inventory write-down resulted in significant losses about the time it entered bankruptcy.

SA 16–4

a. 1. Normal practice for determining the amount of cash flows from operating activities during the year is to begin with the reported net income. This net income must ordinarily be adjusted upward and/or downward to determine the amount of cash flows. Although many operating expenses decrease cash, depreciation does not do so. The amount of net income understates the amount of cash flows provided by operations to the extent that depreciation expense is deducted from revenue. Accordingly, the depreciation expense for the year must be added back to the reported net income in arriving at cash flows from operating activities.

   2. Generally accepted accounting principles require that significant transactions affecting future cash flows should be reported in a separate schedule to the statement, even though they do not affect cash. Accordingly, even though the issuance of the common stock for land does not affect cash, the transaction affects future cash flows and must be reported.

   3. The $50,000 cash received from the sale of the investments is reported in the cash flows from investing activities section. Since the sale included a gain of $8,000, to avoid double reporting of this amount, the gain is deducted from net income to remove it from the determination of cash flows from operating activities.

   4. The balance sheets for the last two years will indicate the increase in cash but will not indicate the firm's activities in meeting its financial obligations, paying dividends, and maintaining and expanding operating capacity. Such information, as provided by the statement of cash flows, assists creditors in assessing the firm's solvency and profitability—two very important factors bearing on the evaluation of a potential loan.

b. The statement of cash flows indicates a strong liquidity position for Cabinet Craft Inc. The increase in cash of $97,800 for the past year is more than adequate to cover the $50,000 of new building and store equipment costs that will not be provided by the loan. Thus, the statement of cash flows most likely will enhance the company's chances of receiving a loan. However, other information, such as a projection of future earnings, a description of collateral pledged to support the loan, and an independent credit report, would normally be considered before a final loan decision is made.

SA 16–5

a. and b.

Recent statements of cash flows for Johnson & Johnson and AMR Corp. (American Airlines) are shown on the following pages. The actual analysis may be different due to updated information. However, this answer shows the structure for a possible response.

<u>Johnson & Johnson</u>

Johnson & Johnson (J&J) is a powerful generator of cash flows from operating activities, with over $11 billion in cash flows. This is enough to support over $2 billion in new investment, with the remainder available for dividends and repurchases of common stock. Overall, the statement of cash flows indicates very favorable cash flows for J&J. J&J's free cash flow is approximately $9.3 billion for the year ($11.9 – $2.6).

JOHNSON & JOHNSON
Consolidated Statements of Cash Flows
1-Jan-06

In Millions For Period Ended Jan 1, 2006	<u>01/01/06</u>
CASH FLOWS FROM OPERATING ACTIVITIES:	
Net earnings	$10,411
Adjustments to reconcile net earnings to cash flows:	
Depreciation and amortization of property and intangibles	2,093
Purchased in-process research and development	362
Deferred tax provision	(46)
Accounts receivable allowances	(31)
Changes in assets and liabilities, net of effects from acquisitions:	
Increase in accounts receivable	(568)
(Increase)/decrease in inventories	(396)
(Decrease)/increase in accounts payable and accrued liabilities	(911)
(Decrease)/(increase) in other current and non-current assets	620
Increase in other current and non-current liabilities	343
NET CASH FLOWS FROM OPERATING ACTIVITIES	$11,877
CASH FLOWS FROM INVESTING ACTIVITIES:	
Additions to property, plant and equipment	(2,632)
Proceeds from the disposal of assets	154
Acquisitions, net of cash acquired (Note 17)	(987)
Purchases of investments	(5,660)
Sales of investments	9,187
Other (primarily intangibles)	(341)
NET CASH USED BY INVESTING ACTIVITIES	$ (279)

SA 16–5   Continued

In Millions For Period Ended Jan 1, 2006	01/01/06
CASH FLOWS FROM FINANCING ACTIVITIES	
Dividends to shareholders	$ (3,793)
Repurchase of common stock	(1,717)
Proceeds from short-term debt	1,215
Retirement of short-term debt	(732)
Proceeds from long-term debt	6
Retirement of long-term debt	(196)
Proceeds from the exercise of stock options	696
NET CASH USED BY FINANCING ACTIVITIES	$ (4,521)
Effect of exchange rate changes on cash and cash equivalents	(225)
Increase in cash and cash equivalents	$ 6,852
Cash and cash equivalents, beginning of year (Note 1)	9,203
CASH AND CASH EQUIVALENTS, END OF YEAR (NOTE 1)	16,055
SUPPLEMENTAL SCHEDULE OF NONCASH INVESTING AND FINANCING ACTIVITIES	
Treasury stock issued for employee compensation and stock option plans, net of cash proceeds	818
Conversion of debt	369

AMR Corp.

AMR is weaker than J&J. AMR had cash flows from operating activities of over $1 billion. In addition, AMR had net negative cash flows from investing activities of approximately $1.5 billion. As a result, AMR needed sources of cash from financing activities. The net sources of cash from financing activities was $533 million. AMR generates sufficient cash from operations to maintain the necessary investment in its fixed assets. Free cash flow is approximately $343 million ($1,024 – $681). However, AMR does not generate cash at nearly the same amount as Johnson & Johnson.

SA 16–5   **Continued**

AMR CORP.
Consolidated Statements of Cash Flows
31-Dec-05

In Millions For Period Ended Dec 31, 2005	12/31/05
Cash Flow from Operating Activities:	
Net loss	$ (861)
Adjustments to reconcile net loss to net cash provided (used) by operating activities:	
Depreciation...	1,033
Amortization..	131
Provisions for asset impairments and restructuring charges	134
Redemption payments under operating leases for special facility revenue bonds...	(104)
Change in assets and liabilities:	
Decrease (increase) in receivables.................................	(156)
Decrease (increase) in inventories	(59)
Increase (decrease) in accounts payable and accrued liabilities	250
Increase (decrease) in air traffic liability	432
Increase (decrease) in other liabilities and deferred credits........	197
Other, net	27
Net cash (used) provided by operating activities	$ 1,024
Cash Flow from Investing Activities:	
Capital expenditures, including purchase deposits on flight equipment..	(681)
Net increase in short-term investments	(867)
Net decrease (increase) in restricted cash and short-term investments..	(32)
Proceeds from sale of equipment and property and other investments..	40
Other..	1
Net cash used for investing activities..	$(1,539)

SA 16–5 Concluded

In Millions For Period Ended Dec 31, 2005	12/31/05
Cash Flow from Financing Activities:	
Payments on long-term debt and capital lease obligations	$(1,131)
Proceeds from:	
Issuance of long-term debt and special facility bond transactions	1,252
Issuance of common stock, net of issuance costs	223
Securitization transactions	133
Exercise of stock options	56
Net cash provided by financing activities	$ 533
Net increase in cash	18
Cash at beginning of year	120
Cash at end of year	138
Activities Not Affecting Cash	
Funding of construction and debt service reserve accounts	284
Capital lease obligations incurred	13

CHAPTER 17
FINANCIAL STATEMENT ANALYSIS

QUESTION INFORMATION

Number	Objective	Description	Difficulty	Time	AACSB	AICPA	SS	GL
Q17-1	17-1		Easy	5 min	Analytic	FN-Measurement		
Q17-2	17-1		Easy	5 min	Analytic	FN-Measurement		
Q17-3	17-1		Easy	5 min	Analytic	FN-Measurement		
Q17-4	17-1		Easy	5 min	Analytic	FN-Measurement		
Q17-5	17-2		Easy	5 min	Analytic	FN-Measurement		
Q17-6	17-2		Easy	5 min	Analytic	FN-Measurement		
Q17-7	17-2		Easy	5 min	Analytic	FN-Measurement		
Q17-8	17-2		Easy	5 min	Analytic	FN-Measurement		
Q17-9	17-2		Easy	5 min	Analytic	FN-Measurement		
Q17-10	17-2		Easy	5 min	Analytic	FN-Measurement		
Q17-11	17-3		Easy	5 min	Analytic	FN-Measurement		
Q17-12	17-3		Easy	5 min	Analytic	FN-Measurement		
Q17-13	17-3		Easy	5 min	Analytic	FN-Measurement		
Q17-14	17-3		Easy	5 min	Analytic	FN-Measurement		
Q17-15	17-3		Easy	5 min	Analytic	FN-Measurement		
Q17-16	17-3		Easy	5 min	Analytic	FN-Measurement		
PE17-1A	17-1	Horizontal analysis	Easy	5 min	Analytic	FN-Measurement		
PE17-1B	17-1	Horizontal analysis	Easy	5 min	Analytic	FN-Measurement		
PE17-2A	17-1	Common-size financial statements	Easy	5 min	Analytic	FN-Measurement		
PE17-2B	17-1	Common-size financial statements	Easy	5 min	Analytic	FN-Measurement		
PE17-3A	17-1	Current position analysis	Easy	5 min	Analytic	FN-Measurement		
PE17-3B	17-1	Current position analysis	Easy	5 min	Analytic	FN-Measurement		
PE17-4A	17-1	Accounts receivable analysis	Easy	5 min	Analytic	FN-Measurement		
PE17-4B	17-1	Accounts receivable analysis	Easy	5 min	Analytic	FN-Measurement		
PE17-5A	17-2	Inventory analysis	Easy	5 min	Analytic	FN-Measurement		
PE17-5B	17-2	Inventory analysis	Easy	5 min	Analytic	FN-Measurement		
PE17-6A	17-2	Ratio of fixed assets to long-term liabilities and ratio of liabilities to stockholders' equity	Easy	5 min	Analytic	FN-Measurement		
PE17-6B	17-2	Ratio of fixed assets to long-term liabilities and ratio of liabilities to stockholders' equity	Easy	5 min	Analytic	FN-Measurement		
PE17-7A	17-2	Times interest charges are earned	Easy	5 min	Analytic	FN-Measurement		
PE17-7B	17-2	Times interest charges are earned	Easy	5 min	Analytic	FN-Measurement		
PE17-8A	17-2	Ratio of net sales to total assets	Easy	5 min	Analytic	FN-Measurement		
PE17-8B	17-3	Ratio of net sales to total assets	Easy	5 min	Analytic	FN-Measurement		
PE17-9A	17-3	Rate earned on total assets	Easy	5 min	Analytic	FN-Measurement		

Number	Objective	Description	Difficulty	Time	AACSB	AICPA	SS	GL
PE17-9B	17-3	Rate earned on total assets	Easy	5 min	Analytic	FN-Measurement		
PE17-10A	17-3	Rate earned on stockholders' equity and rate earned on common stockhold- ers' equity	Easy	5 min	Analytic	FN-Measurement		
PE17-10B	17-3	Rate earned on stockholders' equity and rate earned on common stockhold- ers' equity	Easy	5 min	Analytic	FN-Measurement		
PE17-11A	17-3	Earnings per share on common stock	Easy	5 min	Analytic	FN-Measurement		
PE17-11B	17-3	Earnings per share on common stock	Easy	5 min	Analytic	FN-Measurement		
PE17-12A	17-3	Price-earnings ratio	Easy	5 min	Analytic	FN-Measurement		
PE17-12B	17-3	Price-earnings ratio	Easy	5 min	Analytic	FN-Measurement		
Ex17-1	17-1	Vertical analysis of income statement	Easy	15 min	Analytic	FN-Measurement	Exl	
Ex17-2	17-1	Vertical analysis of income statement	Easy	15 min	Analytic	FN-Measurement	Exl	
Ex17-3	17-1	Common-size income statement	Easy	15 min	Analytic	FN-Measurement	Exl	
Ex17-4	17-1	Vertical analysis of balance sheet	Easy	20 min	Analytic	FN-Measurement	Exl	
Ex17-5	17-1	Horizontal analysis of the income statement	Easy	20 min	Analytic	FN-Measurement	Exl	
Ex17-6	17-2	Current position analysis	Easy	10 min	Analytic	FN-Measurement		
Ex17-7	17-2	Current position analysis	Easy	10 min	Analytic	FN-Measurement		
Ex17-8	17-2	Current position analysis	Moderate	15 min	Analytic	FN-Measurement		
Ex17-9	17-2	Accounts receivable analysis	Easy	10 min	Analytic	FN-Measurement		
Ex17-10	17-2	Accounts receivable analysis	Easy	10 min	Analytic	FN-Measurement		
Ex17-11	17-2	Inventory analysis	Easy	10 min	Analytic	FN-Measurement		
Ex17-12	17-2	Inventory analysis	Easy	10 min	Analytic	FN-Measurement		
Ex17-13	17-2	Ratio of liabilities to stockholders' equity and number of times interest charges earned	Easy	10 min	Analytic	FN-Measurement		
Ex17-14	17-2	Ratio of liabilities to stockholders' equity and number of times interest charges earned	Easy	15 min	Analytic	FN-Measurement		
Ex17-15	17-2	Ratio of liabilities to stockholders' equity and fixed assets to long-term liabilities	Easy	10 min	Analytic	FN-Measurement		
Ex17-16	17-2	Ratio of liabilities to stockholders' equity and fixed assets to long-term liabilities	Easy	10 min	Analytic	FN-Measurement		
Ex17-17	17-3	Profitability ratios	Easy	10 min	Analytic	FN-Measurement		
Ex17-18	17-3	Profitability ratios	Easy	15 min	Analytic	FN-Measurement		

Number	Objective	Description	Difficulty	Time	AACSB	AICPA	SS	GL
Ex17-19	17-3	Six measures of solvency of profitability	Moderate	20 min	Analytic	FN-Measurement		
Ex17-20	17-3	Six measures of solvency of profitability	Moderate	20 min	Analytic	FN-Measurement		
Ex17-21	17-3	Earnings per share, price-earnings ratio, dividend yield	Easy	15 min	Analytic	FN-Measurement		
Ex17-22	17-3	Earnings per share	Easy	10 min	Analytic	FN-Measurement		
Ex17-23	17-3	Price-earnings ratio; dividend yield	Easy	10 min	Analytic	FN-Measurement		
Pr17-1A	17-1	Horizontal analysis for income statement	Moderate	1 hr	Analytic	FN-Measurement	Exl	KA
Pr17-2A	17-1	Vertical analysis for income statement	Moderate	1 hr	Analytic	FN-Measurement	Exl	KA
Pr17-3A	17-2	Effects of transactions on current position analysis	Moderate	1 hr	Analytic	FN-Measurement	Exl	
Pr17-4A	17-2,17-3	Nineteen measures of solvency and profitability	Moderate	2 hr	Analytic	FN-Measurement	Exl	
Pr17-5A	17-2,17-3	Solvency and profitability trend analysis	Moderate	1 1/2 hr	Analytic	FN-Measurement		
Pr17-1B	17-1	Horizontal analysis for income statement	Moderate	1 hr	Analytic	FN-Measurement	Exl	KA
Pr17-2B	17-1	Vertical analysis for income statement	Moderate	1 hr	Analytic	FN-Measurement	Exl	KA
Pr17-3B	17-2	Effects of transactions on current position analysis	Moderate	1 hr	Analytic	FN-Measurement	Exl	
Pr17-4B	17-2, 17-3	Nineteen measures of solvency and profitability	Moderate	2 hr	Analytic	FN-Measurement	Exl	
Pr17-5B	17-2, 17-3	Solvency and profitability trend analysis	Moderate	1 1/2 hr	Analytic	FN-Measurement		
W-S FSA	17-1, 17-2, 17-3	Financial statement analysis	Moderate	1 1/2 hr	Analytic	FN-Measurement		
SA17-1	17-2	Analysis of financial corporate growth	Easy	5 min	Analytic	FN-Measurement		
SA17-2	17-2	receivables and inventory turnover	Moderate	10 min	Analytic	FN-Measurement		
SA17-3	17-1	Vertical analysis	Easy	15 min	Analytic	FN-Measurement		
SA17-4	17-3	Profitability and stockholders' equity	Moderate	20 min	Analytic	FN-Measurement		
SA17-5	17-2, 17-3	Projecting financial statements	Moderate	30 min	Analytic	FN-Measurement		
SA17-6	17-2, 17-3	Comprehensive profitability and solvency analysis	Easy	15 min	Analytic	FN-Measurement		

1. Horizontal analysis is the percentage analysis of increases and decreases in corresponding statements. The percent change in the cash balances at the end of the preceding year from the end of the current year is an example. Vertical analysis is the percentage analysis showing the relationship of the component parts to the total in a single statement. The percent of cash as a portion of total assets at the end of the current year is an example.

2. Comparative statements provide information as to changes between dates or periods. Trends indicated by comparisons may be far more significant than the data for a single date or period.

3. Before this question can be answered, the increase in net income should be compared with changes in sales, expenses, and assets devoted to the business for the current year. The return on assets for both periods should also be compared. If these comparisons indicate favorable trends, the operating performance has improved; if not, the apparent favorable increase in net income may be offset by unfavorable trends in other areas.

4. You should first determine if the expense amount in the base year (denominator) is significant. An 80% or more increase of a very small expense item may be of little concern. However, if the expense amount in the base year is significant, then over an 80% increase may require further investigation.

5. Generally, the two ratios would be very close, because most service businesses sell services and hold very little inventory.

6. The amount of working capital and the change in working capital are just two indicators of the strength of the current position. A comparison of the current ratio and the quick ratio, along with the amount of working capital, gives a better analysis of the current position. Such a comparison shows:

	Current Year	Preceding Year
Working capital	$40,000	$48,000
Current ratio	1.8	2.6
Quick ratio	0.7	1.2

It is apparent that, although working capital has decreased, the current ratio has fallen from 2.6 to 1.8, and the quick ratio has fallen from 1.2 to 0.7.

7. The bulk of Wal-Mart sales are to final customers that pay with credit cards or cash. In either case, there is no accounts receivable. Procter & Gamble, in contrast, sells almost exclusively to other businesses, such as Wal-Mart. Such sales are "on account," and thus, create accounts receivable that must be collected. A recent financial statement showed Wal-Mart's accounts receivable turning 109 times, while Procter & Gamble's turned only 13 times.

8. No, an accounts receivable turnover of 5 with sales on a n/45 basis is not satisfactory. It indicates that accounts receivable are collected, on the average, in one-fifth of a year, or approximately 73 days from the date of sale. Assuming that some customers pay within the 45-day term, it indicates that other accounts are running beyond 73 days. It is also possible that there is a substantial amount of past-due accounts of doubtful collectibility on the books.

9. a. A high inventory turnover minimizes the amount invested in inventories, thus freeing funds for more advantageous use. Storage costs, administrative expenses, and losses caused by obsolescence and adverse changes in prices are also kept to a minimum.

   b. Yes. The inventory turnover could be high because the quantity of inventory on hand is very low. This condition might result in the lack of sufficient goods on hand to meet sales orders.

c. Yes. The inventory turnover relates to the "turnover" of inventory during the year, while the number of days' sales in inventory relates to the amount of inventory on hand at the end of the year. Therefore, a business could have a high inventory turnover *for the year*, yet have a high number of days' sales in inventory at the *end of the year.*

10. The ratio of fixed assets to long-term liabilities increased from 2.5 for the preceding year to 3.0 for the current year, indicating that the company is in a stronger position now than in the preceding year to borrow additional funds on a long-term basis.

11. a. The rate earned on total assets adds interest expense to the net income, which is divided by average total assets. It measures the profitability of total assets, without regard for how the assets are financed. The rate earned on stockholders' equity divides net income by average total stockholders' equity. It measures the profitability of the stockholders' investment.

   b. The rate earned on stockholders' equity is normally higher than the rate earned on total assets. This is because of leverage, which compensates stockholders for the higher risk of their investments.

12. a. Due to leverage, the rate on stockholders' equity will often be greater than the rate on total assets. This occurs because the amount earned on assets acquired through the use of funds provided by creditors exceeds the interest charges paid to creditors.

   b. Higher. The concept of leverage applies to preferred stock as well as debt. The rate earned on common stockholders' equity ordinarily exceeds the rate earned on total stockholders' equity because the amount earned on assets acquired through the use of funds provided by preferred stockholders normally exceeds the dividends paid to preferred stockholders.

13. The earnings per share in the preceding year were $30 per share ($60/2), adjusted for the stock split in the latest year.

14. A share of common stock is currently selling at 10 times current annual earnings.

15. The dividend yield on common stock is a measure of the rate of return to common stockholders in terms of cash dividend distributions. Companies in growth industries typically reinvest a significant portion of the amount earned in common stockholders' equity to expand operations rather than to return earnings to stockholders in the form of cash dividends.

16. During periods when sales are increasing, it is likely that a company will increase its inventories and expand its plant. Such situations frequently result in an increase in current liabilities out of proportion to the increase in current assets and thus lower the current ratio.

PRACTICE EXERCISE

PE 17–1A

Marketable securities	$13,200 increase ($68,200 – $55,000), or 24%
Inventory	$1,300 decrease ($63,700 – $65,000), or –2%

PE 17–1B

Accounts payable	$21,600 increase ($141,600 – $120,000), or 18%
Long-term debt	$25,000 increase ($150,000 – $125,000), or 20%

PE 17–2A

	Amount	Percentage	
Sales	$400,000	100%	($400,000/$400,000)
Cost of goods sold	340,000	85	($340,000/$400,000)
Gross profit	$ 60,000	15%	($60,000/$400,000)

PE 17–2B

	Amount	Percentage	
Sales	$250,000	100%	($250,000/$250,000)
Gross profit	100,000	40	($100,000/$250,000)
Net income	50,000	20	($50,000/$250,000)

PE 17–3A

a. Current Ratio = Current Assets/Current Liabilities
    Current Ratio = ($125,000 + $40,000 + $30,000 + $120,000)/$150,000
    Current Ratio = 2.1

b. Quick Ratio = Quick Assets/Current Liabilities
    Quick Ratio = ($125,000 + $40,000 + $30,000)/$150,000
    Quick Ratio = 1.3

PE 17–3B

a. Current Ratio = Current Assets/Current Liabilities

   Current Ratio = ($275,000 + $200,000 + $625,000 + $300,000)/$800,000

   Current Ratio = 1.8

b. Quick Ratio = Quick Assets/Current Liabilities

   Quick Ratio = ($275,000 + $200,000 + $625,000)/$800,000

   Quick Ratio = 1.4

PE 17–4A

a. Accounts Receivable Turnover = Net Sales/Average Accounts Receivable

   Accounts Receivable Turnover = $450,000/$37,500

   Accounts Receivable Turnover = 12.0

b. Number of Days' Sales in Receivables = Average Accounts Receivable/
   Average Daily Sales

   Number of Days' Sales in Receivables = $37,500/($450,000/365)
                                        = $37,500/$1,233

   Number of Days' Sales in Receivables = 30.4 days

PE 17–4B

a. Accounts Receivable Turnover = Net Sales/Average Accounts Receivable

   Accounts Receivable Turnover = $225,000/$25,000

   Accounts Receivable Turnover = 9.0

b. Number of Days' Sales in Receivables = Average Accounts Receivable/
   Average Daily Sales

   Number of Days' Sales in Receivables = $25,000/($225,000/365) = $25,000/$616

   Number of Days' Sales in Receivables = 40.6 days

PE 17–5A

a. Inventory Turnover = Cost of Goods Sold/Average Inventory
Inventory Turnover = $465,000/$71,500
Inventory Turnover = 6.5

b. Number of Days' Sales in Inventory = Average Inventory/Average Daily Cost
of Goods Sold
Number of Days' Sales in Inventory = $71,500/($465,000/365) = $71,500/$1,274
Number of Days' Sales in Inventory = 56.1 days

PE 17–5B

a. Inventory Turnover = Cost of Goods Sold/Average Inventory
Inventory Turnover = $330,000/$55,000
Inventory Turnover = 6.0

b. Number of Days' Sales in Inventory = Average Inventory/Average Daily Cost
of Goods Sold
Number of Days' Sales in Inventory = $55,000/($330,000/365) = $55,000/$904
Number of Days' Sales in Inventory = 60.8 days

PE 17–6A

a. Fixed Asset Turnover Ratio = Fixed Assets/Long-Term Liabilities
Fixed Asset Turnover Ratio = $700,000/$218,750
Fixed Asset Turnover Ratio = 3.2

b. Ratio of Liabilities to Total Stockholders' Equity = Total Liabilities/Total
Stockholders' Equity
Ratio of Liabilities to Total Stockholders' Equity = $235,000/$940,000
Ratio of Liabilities to Total Stockholders' Equity = 0.3

PE 17–6B

a. Fixed Asset Turnover Ratio = Fixed Assets/Long-Term Liabilities
    Fixed Asset Turnover Ratio = $900,000/$625,000
    Fixed Asset Turnover Ratio = 1.4

b. Ratio of Liabilities to Total Stockholders' Equity = Total Liabilities/Total Stockholders' Equity
    Ratio of Liabilities to Total Stockholders' Equity = $850,000/$500,000
    Ratio of Liabilities to Total Stockholders' Equity = 1.7

PE 17–7A

Number of Times Interest Charges Are Earned = (Income Before Income Tax + Interest Expense)/Interest Expense
Number of Times Interest Charges Are Earned = ($375,000 + $120,000)/$120,000
Number of Times Interest Charges Are Earned = 4.1

PE 17–7B

Number of Times Interest Charges Are Earned = (Income Before Income Tax + Interest Expense)/Interest Expense
Number of Times Interest Charges Are Earned = ($625,000 + $160,000)/$160,000
Number of Times Interest Charges Are Earned = 4.9

PE 17–8A

Ratio of Net Sales to Assets = Net Sales/Average Total Assets
Ratio of Net Sales to Assets = $1,170,000/$650,000
Ratio of Net Sales to Assets = 1.8

PE 17–8B

Ratio of Net Sales to Assets = Net Sales/Average Total Assets
Ratio of Net Sales to Assets = $1,520,000/$950,000
Ratio of Net Sales to Assets = 1.6

PE 17–9A

Rate Earned on Total Assets = (Net Income + Interest Expense)/
Average Total Assets

Rate Earned on Total Assets = ($225,000 + $20,000)/$3,250,000

Rate Earned on Total Assets = $245,000/$3,250,000

Rate Earned on Total Assets = 7.5%

PE 17–9B

Rate Earned on Total Assets = (Net Income + Interest Expense)/
Average Total Assets

Rate Earned on Total Assets = ($115,000 + $10,000)/$1,250,000

Rate Earned on Total Assets = $125,000/$1,250,000

Rate Earned on Total Assets = 10.0%

PE 17–10A

a. Rate Earned on Stockholders' Equity = Net Income/Average Stockholders'
Equity

Rate Earned on Stockholders' Equity = $225,000/$1,750,000

Rate Earned on Stockholders' Equity = 12.9%

b. Rate Earned on Common Stockholders' Equity = (Net Income – Preferred Dividends)/Average Common
Stockholders' Equity

Rate Earned on Common Stockholders' Equity = ($225,000 – $20,000)/
$1,000,000

Rate Earned on Common Stockholders' Equity = 20.5%

PE 17–10B

a. Rate Earned on Stockholders' Equity = Net Income/Average Stockholders' Equity

   Rate Earned on Stockholders' Equity = $115,000/$850,000

   Rate Earned on Stockholders' Equity = 13.5%

b. Rate Earned on Common Stockholders' Equity = (Net Income – Preferred Dividends)/Average Common Stockholders' Equity

   Rate Earned on Common Stockholders' Equity = ($115,000 – $10,000)/$750,000

   Rate Earned on Common Stockholders' Equity = 14%

PE 17–11A

a. Earnings per Share on Common Stock = (Net Income – Preferred Dividends)/Shares of Common Stock Outstanding

   Earnings per Share = ($115,000 – 15,000)/20,000

   Earnings per Share = $5.00

b. Price-Earnings Ratio = Market Price per Share of Common Stock/Earnings per Share on Common Stock

   Price-Earnings Ratio = $65.00/$5.00

   Price-Earnings Ratio = 13.0

PE 17–11B

a. Earnings per Share on Common Stock = (Net Income – Preferred Dividends)/Shares of Common Stock Outstanding

   Earnings per Share = ($525,000 – 25,000)/50,000

   Earnings per Share = $10.00

b. Price-Earnings Ratio = Market Price per Share of Common Stock/Earnings per Share on Common Stock

   Price-Earnings Ratio = $75.00/$10.00

   Price-Earnings Ratio = 7.5

Ex. 17–1

a.

JAZZ-TECH COMMUNICATIONS CO.
Comparative Income Statement
For the Years Ended December 31, 2008 and 2007

	2008		2007	
	Amount	Percent	Amount	Percent
Sales	$750,000	100.0%	$600,000	100.0%
Cost of goods sold	450,000	60.0	312,000	52.0
Gross profit	$300,000	40.0%	$288,000	48.0%
Selling expenses.........................	$120,000	16.0%	$126,000	21.0%
Administrative operating				
expenses	105,000	14.0	84,000	14.0
Total expenses............................	$225,000	30.0%	$210,000	35.0%
Income from operations	$ 75,000	10.0%	$ 78,000	13.0%
Income tax expense...................	37,500	5.0	30,000	5.0
Net income	$ 37,500	5.0%	$ 48,000	8.0%

b. The vertical analysis indicates that the cost of goods sold as a percent of sales increased by 8 percentage points (60% – 52%) between 2007 and 2008. However, the selling expenses improved by 5 percentage points. Thus, the net income as a percent of sales dropped by 3 percentage points.

Ex. 17–2

a.

Speedway Motorsports, Inc.
Comparative Income Statement (in thousands of dollars)
For the Years Ended December 31, 2004 and 2003

	2004		2003	
Revenues:				
Admissions	$156,718	35.1%	$150,253	37.1%
Event-related revenue	137,074	30.7	127,055	31.4
NASCAR broadcasting revenue	110,016	24.6	90,682	22.4
Other operating revenue.................	42,711	9.6	36,539	9.0
Total revenue.............................	$446,519	100.0%	$404,529	100.0%*
Expenses and other:				
Direct expense of events	$ 81,432	18.2%	$ 77,962	19.3%
NASCAR purse and sanction fees .	78,473	17.6	69,691	17.2
Other direct expenses.....................	102,053	22.9	101,408	25.1
General and administrative	65,152	14.6	58,698	14.5
Total expenses and other..........	$327,110	73.3%	$307,759	76.1%
Income from continuing operations....	$119,409	26.7%	$ 96,770	23.9%

*Rounded to the nearest tenth of a percent.

b. While overall revenue increased some between the two years, the overall mix of revenue sources did change somewhat. The NASCAR broadcasting revenue increased as a percent of total revenue by two percentage points, while the percent of admissions revenue to total revenue decreased by two percentage points as well. The expenses as a percent of total revenue shifted the most between the direct event expenses and other direct expenses. That is, the direct event expenses as a percent of total revenue declined one percentage point, while the other direct expenses as a percent of total revenue decreased by over two percentage points. Overall, the income from continuing operations increased a solid 2.8 percentage points of total revenue between the two years, which is a favorable trend. As a further note, the income from continuing operations as a percent of sales exceeds 25% in the most recent year, which is excellent. Apparently, owning and operating motor speedways is a business that produces high operating profit margins.

Note to Instructors: The high operating margin is probably necessary to compensate for the extensive investment in speedway assets.

Ex. 17–3

a.

JARIBO COMMUNICATIONS COMPANY
Common-Size Income Statement
For the Year Ended December 31, 20—

	Jaribo Communications Company		Communications Industry Average
	Amount	Percent	
Sales	$ 1,265,000	101.2%	101.0%
Sales returns and allowances	15,000	1.2	1.0
Net sales...	$ 1,250,000	100.0%	100.0%
Cost of goods sold	450,000	36.0	41.0
Gross profit	$ 800,000	64.0%	59.0%
Selling expenses.......................................	$ 525,000	42.0%	38.0%
Administrative expenses..............................	143,750	11.5	10.5
Total operating expenses	$ 668,750	53.5%	48.5%
Operating income	$ 131,250	10.5%	10.5%
Other income..	22,500	1.8	1.2
	$ 153,750	12.3%	11.7%
Other expense...	18,750	1.5	1.7
Income before income tax	$ 135,000	10.8%	10.0%
Income tax expense....................................	50,000	4.0	4.0
Net income	$ 85,000	6.8%	6.0%

b. The cost of goods sold is 5 percentage points lower than the industry average, but the selling expenses and administrative expenses are four percentage points and 1 percentage point higher than the industry average. The combined impact is for net income as a percent of sales to be 0.8 percentage point better than the industry average. Apparently, the company is managing the cost of manufacturing product better than the industry but has slightly higher selling and administrative expenses relative to the industry. The cause of the higher selling and administrative expenses as a percent of sales, relative to the industry, can be investigated further.

Ex. 17–4

DOVER HOT TUB COMPANY
Comparative Balance Sheet
December 31, 2008 and 2007

	2008		2007	
	Amount	Percent	Amount	Percent
Current assets............................	$ 768,000	64.0%	$ 250,000	25.0%
Property, plant, and equipment.	336,000	28.0	650,000	65.0
Intangible assets.........................	96,000	8.0	100,000	10.0
Total assets.................................	$1,200,000	100.0%	$1,000,000	100.0%
Current liabilities	$ 270,000	22.5%	$ 175,000	17.5%
Long-term liabilities...................	300,000	25.0	255,000	25.5
Common stock............................	60,000	5.0	70,000	7.0
Retained earnings.......................	570,000	47.5	500,000	50.0
Total liabilities and stockholders' equity..............	$1,200,000	100.0%	$1,000,000	100.0%

Ex. 17–5

a.

WEB-PICS COMPANY
Comparative Income Statement
For the Years Ended December 31, 2008 and 2007

	2008	2007	Increase (Decrease)	
	Amount	Amount	Amount	Percent
Sales	$117,000	$150,000	$(33,000)	– 22.0%
Cost of goods sold	56,000	70,000	(14,000)	– 20.0%
Gross profit	$ 61,000	$ 80,000	$(19,000)	– 23.8%
Selling expenses..........................	$ 36,000	$ 37,500	$ (1,500)	– 4.0%
Administrative expenses...........	12,500	10,000	2,500	25.0%
Total operating expenses	$ 48,500	$ 47,500	$ 1,000	2.1%
Income before income tax	$ 12,500	$ 32,500	$(20,000)	– 61.5%
Income tax expense....................	2,000	10,000	(8,000)	– 80.0%
Net income	$ 10,500	$ 22,500	$(12,000)	– 53.3%

b. The net income for Web-Pics Company decreased by approximately 53.3% from 2007 to 2008. This decrease was the combined result of a decrease in sales of 22% and higher expenses. The cost of goods sold decreased at a slower rate than the decrease in sales, thus causing gross profit to decrease more than the decrease in sales. In addition, administrative expenses increased significantly between 2007 and 2008.

Ex. 17–6

a. (1) Working Capital = Current Assets – Current Liabilities

   2008: $1,265,000 = $1,840,000 – $575,000

   2007: $1,044,000 = $1,624,000 – $580,000

   (2) Current Ratio = $\dfrac{\text{Current Assets}}{\text{Current Liabilities}}$

   2008: $\dfrac{\$1,840,000}{\$575,000} = 3.2$ 2007: $\dfrac{\$1,624,000}{\$580,000} = 2.8$

   (3) Quick Ratio = $\dfrac{\text{Quick Assets}}{\text{Current Liabilities}}$

   2008: $\dfrac{\$1,035,000}{\$575,000} = 1.8$ 2007: $\dfrac{\$986,000}{\$580,000} = 1.7$

b. The liquidity of Outdoor Suppliers has improved from the preceding year to the current year. The working capital, current ratio, and quick ratio have all increased. Most of these changes are the result of a decrease in current liabilities, specifically accounts (notes) payable, combined with an increase in the current assets.

Ex. 17–7

a. (1) Current Ratio = $\dfrac{\text{Current Assets}}{\text{Current Liabilities}}$

   Dec. 31, 2005: $\dfrac{\$10,454}{\$9,406} = 1.1$ Dec. 25, 2004: $\dfrac{\$8,639}{\$7,152} = 1.2$

   (2) Quick Ratio = $\dfrac{\text{Quick Assets}}{\text{Current Liabilities}}$

   Dec. 31, 2005: $\dfrac{\$8,143}{\$9,406} = 0.9$ Dec. 25, 2004: $\dfrac{\$6,444}{\$7,152} = 0.9$

b. The liquidity of PepsiCo has decreased some over this time period. Both the current and quick ratios have decreased. The current ratio decreased from 1.2 to 1.1, and the quick ratio remained constant at 0.9. However, these trends are slight. PepsiCo is a strong company with ample resources for meeting short-term obligations.

Ex. 17–8

a. The working capital, current ratio, and quick ratio are calculated incorrectly. The working capital and current ratio incorrectly include intangible assets and property, plant, and equipment as a part of current assets. Both are noncurrent. The quick ratio has both an incorrect numerator (quick assets) and denominator. The numerator of the quick ratio incorrectly includes intangible assets, which are noncurrent. The denominator is also incorrect, as it does not include accrued liabilities. The denominator of the quick ratio should be total current liabilities.

The correct calculations are as follows:

Working Capital = Current Assets – Current Liabilities
$480,500 – $400,000 = $80,500

$$\text{Current Ratio} = \frac{\text{Current Assets}}{\text{Current Liabilities}}$$

$$\frac{\$480,500}{\$400,000} = 1.2$$

$$\text{Quick Ratio} = \frac{\text{Quick Assets}}{\text{Current Liabilities}}$$

$$\frac{\$190,000 + \$95,000 + \$171,000}{\$400,000} = 1.1$$

b. Unfortunately, the working capital, current ratio, and quick ratio are all below the minimum threshold required by the bond indenture. This may require the company to renegotiate the bond contract, including a possible unfavorable change in the interest rate.

Ex. 17–9

a. (1) Accounts Receivable Turnover = $\dfrac{\text{Net Sales on Account}}{\text{Average Monthly Accounts Receivable}}$

2008: $\dfrac{\$540,000}{\$78,261} = 6.9$ 2007: $\dfrac{\$500,000}{\$80,645} = 6.2$

(2) Number of Days' Sales in Receivables = $\dfrac{\text{Average Accounts Receivable}}{\text{Average Daily Sales on Account}}$

2008: $\dfrac{\$80,476^1}{\$1,479^2} = 54.4$ days

2007: $\dfrac{\$83,562^3}{\$1,370^4} = 61.0$ days

[1] $\$80,476 = (\$75,452 + \$85,500)/2$

[2] $\$1,479 = \$540,000/365$ days

[3] $\$83,562 = (\$85,500 + \$81,624)/2$

[4] $\$1,370 = \$500,000/365$ days

b. The collection of accounts receivable has improved. This can be seen in both the increase in accounts receivable turnover and the reduction in the collection period. The credit terms require payment in 60 days. In 2007, the collection period exceeded these terms. However, the company apparently became more aggressive in collecting accounts receivable or more restrictive in granting credit to customers. Thus, in 2008, the collection period is within the credit terms of the company.

Ex. 17–10

a. (1) Accounts Receivable Turnover = $\dfrac{\text{Net Sales on Account}}{\text{Average Accounts Receivable}}$

May: $\dfrac{\$14,441}{(\$2,294 + \$1,788)/2} = 7.1$

Federated: $\dfrac{\$15,630}{(\$3,418 + \$3,213)/2} = 4.7$

(2) Number of Days' Sales in Receivables = $\dfrac{\text{Accounts Receivable}}{\text{Average Daily Sales on Account}}$

May: $\dfrac{(\$2,294 + \$1,788)/2}{\$39.6^1} = 51.5 \text{ days}$

Federated: $\dfrac{(\$3,418 + \$3,213)/2}{\$42.8^2} = 77.5 \text{ days}$

[1]$39.6 = $14,441/365 days
[2]$42.8 = $15,630/365 days

b. May's accounts receivable turnover is much higher than Federated's (7.1 for May vs. 4.7 for Federated). The number of days' sales in receivables is lower for May than for Federated (51.5 days for May vs. 77.5 days for Federated). These differences indicate that May is able to turn over its receivables more quickly than Federated. As a result, it takes May less time to collect its receivables.

Ex. 17–11

a. (1) $\text{Inventory Turnover} = \dfrac{\text{Cost of Goods Sold}}{\text{Average Inventory}}$

Current Year: $\dfrac{\$492,000}{(\$67,200 + \$64,000)/2} = 7.5$

Preceding Year: $\dfrac{\$528,200}{(\$44,000 + \$67,200)/2} = 9.5$

(2) $\text{Number of Days' Sales in Inventory} = \dfrac{\text{Average Inventory}}{\text{Average Daily Cost of Goods Sold}}$

Current Year: $\dfrac{(\$64,000 + \$67,200)/2}{\$1,348^{1}} = 48.7 \text{ days}$

Preceding Year: $\dfrac{(\$67,200 + \$44,000)/2}{\$1,447^{2}} = 38.4 \text{ days}$

[1]$\$1,348 = \$492,000/365 \text{ days}$

[2]$\$1,447 = \$528,200/365 \text{ days}$

b. The inventory position of the business has deteriorated. The inventory turnover has decreased, while the number of days' sales in inventory has increased. The sales volume has declined faster than the inventory has declined, thus resulting in the deteriorating inventory position.

Ex. 17–12

a. (1) Inventory Turnover = $\dfrac{\text{Cost of Goods Sold}}{\text{Average Inventory}}$

Dell: $\dfrac{\$45,620}{(\$459 + \$576)/2} = 88.2$

HP: $\dfrac{\$66,440}{(\$7,071 + \$6,877)/2} = 9.5$

(2) Number of Days' Sales in Inventory = $\dfrac{\text{Average Inventory}}{\text{Average Daily Cost of Goods Sold}}$

Dell: $\dfrac{(\$459 + \$576)/2}{\$125^1} = 4.1$ days

HP: $\dfrac{(\$7,071 + \$6,877)/2}{\$182^2} = 38.3$ days

[1] $\$125 = \$45,620/365$ days

[2] $\$182 = \$66,440/365$ days

b. Dell has a much higher inventory turnover ratio than does HP (88.2 vs. 9.5 for HP). Likewise, Dell has a much smaller number of days' sales in inventory (4.1 days vs. 38.3 days for HP). These significant differences are a result of Dell's make-to-order strategy. Dell has successfully developed a manufacturing process that is able to fill a customer order quickly. As a result, Dell does not need to prebuild computers to inventory. HP, in contrast, prebuilds computers, printers, and other equipment to be sold by retail stores and other retail channels. In this industry, there is great obsolescence risk in holding computers in inventory. New technology can make an inventory of computers difficult to sell; therefore, inventory is costly and risky. Dell's operating strategy is considered revolutionary and is now being adopted by many both in and out of the computer industry. Indeed, at the time of this writing, HP and Gateway, Inc., are changing their practices to mirror those of Dell. Apple Computer, Inc., also employs similar manufacturing techniques, and thus enjoys excellent inventory efficiency.

Ex. 17–13

a. Ratio of Liabilities to Stockholders' Equity $= \dfrac{\text{Total Liabilities}}{\text{Total Stockholders' Equity}}$

Dec. 31, 2008: $\dfrac{\$2,160,000}{\$4,364,800} = 0.5$ Dec. 31, 2007: $\dfrac{\$2,464,000}{\$3,520,000} = 0.7$

b. Number of Times Bond Interest Charges Are Earned $= \dfrac{\text{Income Before Tax + Interest Expense}}{\text{Interest Expense}}$

Dec. 31, 2008: $\dfrac{\$844,800 + \$192,000\,^{*}}{\$192,000} = 5.4$

Dec. 31, 2007: $\dfrac{\$537,600 + \$224,000\,^{**}}{\$224,000} = 3.4$

*($1,600,000 + $320,000) × 10% = $192,000
**($1,920,000 + $320,000) × 10% = $224,000

c. Both the ratio of liabilities to stockholders' equity and the number of times bond interest charges were earned have improved significantly from 2007 to 2008. These results are the combined result of a larger income before taxes and lower serial bonds payable in the year 2008 compared to 2007.

Ex. 17–14

a. Ratio of Liabilities to Stockholders' Equity = $\dfrac{\text{Total Liabilities}}{\text{Total Stockholders' Equity}}$

Hasbro: $\dfrac{\$1{,}600{,}936{,}000}{\$1{,}639{,}724{,}000} = 1.0$

Mattel, Inc.: $\dfrac{\$2{,}370{,}680{,}000}{\$2{,}385{,}812{,}000} = 1.0$

b.

Number of Times Interest Charges Are Earned $= \dfrac{\text{Interest Before Tax} + \text{Interest Expense}}{\text{Interest Expense}}$

Hasbro: $\dfrac{\$293{,}012{,}000 + \$31{,}698{,}000}{\$31{,}698{,}000} = 10.2$

Mattel, Inc.: $\dfrac{\$730{,}817{,}000 + \$77{,}764{,}000}{\$77{,}764{,}000} = 10.4$

c. Both companies carry a moderate proportion of debt to the stockholders' equity, at nearly 1.0 times stockholders' equity. The companies' debt as a percent of stockholders' equity is very similar. Both companies also have very strong interest coverage, earning in excess of 10 times interest charges. Together, these ratios indicate that both companies provide creditors with a margin of safety, and that earnings appear more than enough to make interest payments.

Ex. 17–15

a. Ratio of Liabilities to Stockholders' Equity = $\dfrac{\text{Total Liabilities}}{\text{Total Stockholders' Equity}}$

H.J. Heinz: $\dfrac{\$2,587,068 + \$4,121,984 + \$1,266,093}{\$2,602,573} = 3.1$

Hershey: $\dfrac{\$1,518,223 + \$942,755 + \$813,182}{\$1,021,076} = 3.2$

b. Ratio of Fixed Assets to Long-Term Liabilities = $\dfrac{\text{Fixed Assets (net)}}{\text{Long-Term Liabilities}}$

H.J. Heinz: $\dfrac{\$2,163,938}{\$4,121,984} = 0.5$

Hershey: $\dfrac{\$1,659,138}{\$942,755} = 1.8$

c. H.J. Heinz uses more debt than does Hershey. While the total liabilities to stockholders' equity ratio is similar for both companies (3.1 vs. 3.2), the ratio of fixed assets is very different. H.J. Heinz has a much lower ratio of fixed assets to long-term liabilities than Hershey. This ratio divides the property, plant, and equipment (net) by the long-term debt. The denominator should not include the other long-term liabilities such as pensions and deferred tax credits because these items are not related to financing fixed assets. The ratio for H.J. Heinz is aggressive with only 50% of fixed assets covering the long-term debt. That is, the creditors of H.J. Heinz have 50 cents of property, plant, and equipment covering every dollar of long-term debt. The same ratio for Hershey shows fixed assets covering 1.8 times the long-term debt. That is, Hershey's creditors have $1.80 of property, plant, and equipment covering every dollar of long-term debt. This would suggest that Hershey has stronger creditor protection and borrowing capacity than does H.J. Heinz.

Ex. 17–16

a. Ratio of Net Sales to Total Assets: $\dfrac{\text{Net Sales}}{\text{Total Assets}}$

YRC Worldwide: $\dfrac{\$6,767,485}{\$3,545,199} = 1.9$

Union Pacific: $\dfrac{\$12,215,000}{\$34,041,500} = 0.4$

C.H. Robinson Worldwide, Inc.: $\dfrac{\$4,341,538}{\$994,423} = 4.4$

b. The ratio of net sales to assets measures the number of sales dollars earned for each dollar of assets. The greater the number of sales dollars earned for every dollar of assets, the more efficient a firm is in using assets. Thus, the ratio is a measure of the efficiency in using assets. The three companies are different in their efficiency in using assets, because they are different in the nature of their operations. Union Pacific earns only 40 cents for every dollar of assets. This is because Union Pacific is very asset intensive. That is, Union Pacific must invest in locomotives, railcars, terminals, tracks, right-of-way, and information systems in order to earn revenues. These investments are significant. YRC Worldwide is able to earn $1.90 for every dollar of assets, and thus, is able to earn more revenue for every dollar of assets than the railroad. This is because the motor carrier invests in trucks, trailers, and terminals, which require less investment per dollar of revenue than does the railroad. Moreover, the motor carrier does not invest in the highway system, because the government owns the highway system. Thus, the motor carrier has no investment in the transportation network itself unlike the railroad. C.H. Robinson Worldwide, Inc., the transportation arranger, hires transportation services from motor carriers and railroads, but does not own these assets itself. The transportation arranger has assets in accounts receivable and information systems but does not require transportation assets; thus, it is able to earn the highest revenue per dollar of assets.

Ex. 17–16   Concluded

Note to Instructors: Students may wonder how asset-intensive companies overcome their asset efficiency disadvantages to competitors with better asset efficiencies, as in the case between railroads and motor carriers. Asset efficiency is part of the financial equation; the other part is the profit margin made on each dollar of sales. Thus, companies with high asset efficiency often operate on thinner margins than do companies with lower asset efficiency. For example, the motor carrier must pay highway taxes, which lowers its operating margins when compared to railroads that own their right-of-way, and thus do not have the tax expense of the highway. While not required in this exercise, the railroad has the highest profit margins, the motor carrier is in the middle, while the transportation arranger operates on very thin margins.

Ex. 17–17

a. $\text{Rate Earned on Total Assets} = \dfrac{\text{Net Income} + \text{Interest Expense}}{\text{Average Total Assets}}$

2008: $\dfrac{\$112,500 + \$15,000}{\$1,100,000^*} = 11.6\%$ 2007: $\dfrac{\$135,000 + \$15,000}{\$960,000^{**}} = 15.6\%$

*($1,160,000 + $1,040,000)/2   **($1,040,000 + $880,000)/2

$\text{Rate Earned on Stockholders' Equity} = \dfrac{\text{Net Income}}{\text{Average Stockholders' Equity}}$

2008: $\dfrac{\$112,500}{\$897,050^*} = 12.5\%$ 2007: $\dfrac{\$135,000}{\$786,100^{**}} = 17.2\%$

*($946,900 + $847,200)/2   **($847,200 + $725,000)/2

$\text{Rate Earned on Common Stockholders' Equity} = \dfrac{\text{Net Income} - \text{Preferred Dividends}}{\text{Average Common Stockholders' Equity}}$

2008: $\dfrac{\$112,500 - \$12,800}{\$737,050^*} = 13.5\%$ 2007: $\dfrac{\$135,000 - \$12,800}{\$626,100^{**}} = 19.5\%$

*($786,900 + $687,200)/2   **($687,200 + $565,000)/2

b.   The profitability ratios indicate that Berry's profitability has deteriorated. Most of this change is from net income falling from $135,000 in 2007 to $112,500 in 2008. The cost of debt is 10%. Since the rate of return on assets exceeds this amount in either year, there is positive leverage from use of debt. However, this leverage is greater in 2007 because the rate of return on assets exceeds the cost of debt by a greater amount in 2007.

Ex. 17–18

a. Rate Earned on Total Assets = $\dfrac{\text{Net Income} + \text{Interest Expense}}{\text{Average Total Assets}}$

Fiscal Year 2005: $\dfrac{\$81,872 + \$2,083}{(\$1,492,906 + \$1,327,338)/2} = 6.0\%$

Fiscal Year 2004: $\dfrac{\$63,276 + \$3,641}{(\$1,327,338 + \$1,256,397)/2} = 5.2\%$

b. Rate Earned on Stockholders' Equity = $\dfrac{\text{Net Income}}{\text{Average Total Stockholders' Equity}}$

Fiscal Year 2004: $\dfrac{\$81,872}{(\$1,034,482 + \$962,744)/2} = 8.2\%$

Fiscal Year 2004: $\dfrac{\$63,276}{(\$926,744 + \$818,856)/2} = 7.2\%$

c. Both the rate earned on total assets and the rate earned on stockholders' equity have increased over the two-year period. The rate earned on total assets increased from 5.2% to 6.0%, and the rate earned on stockholders' equity increased from 7.2% to 8.2%. The rate earned on stockholders' equity exceeds the rate earned on total assets due to the positive use of leverage.

d. During fiscal 2005, Ann Taylor's results were weak compared to the industry average. The rate earned on total assets for Ann Taylor was less than the industry average (6.0% vs. 8.2%). The rate earned on stockholders' equity was less than the industry average (8.2% vs. 16.7%). These relationships suggest that Ann Taylor has less leverage than the industry, on average.

Ex. 17–19

a. Ratio of Fixed Assets to Long-Term Liabilities $= \dfrac{\text{Fixed Assets}}{\text{Long-Term Liabilities}}$

$\dfrac{\$1,200,000}{\$825,000} = 1.5$

b. Ratio of Liabilities to Stockholders' Equity $= \dfrac{\text{Total Liabilities}}{\text{Total Stockholders' Equity}}$

$\dfrac{\$885,000}{\$1,785,900} = 0.5$

c. Ratio of Net Sales to Assets $= \dfrac{\text{Net Sales}}{\text{Average Total Assets (excluding investments)}}$

$\dfrac{\$3,600,000}{\$2,357,950^*} = 1.5$

*[($2,525,000 + $2,670,900)/2] – $240,000. The end-of-period total assets are equal to the sum of total liabilities ($885,000) and stockholders' equity ($1,785,900).

d. Rate Earned on Total Assets $= \dfrac{\text{Net Income} + \text{Interest Expense}}{\text{Average Total Assets}}$

$\dfrac{\$216,000 + \$66,000}{\$2,597,950^*} = 10.9\%$

*($2,525,000 + $2,670,900)/2

e. Rate Earned on Stockholders' Equity $= \dfrac{\text{Net Income}}{\text{Average Stockholders' Equity}}$

$\dfrac{\$216,000}{\$1,717,950^*} = 12.6\%$

*[($250,000 + $800,000 + $600,000) + $1,785,900]/2

f. Rate Earned on Common Stockholders' Equity $= \dfrac{\text{Net Income} - \text{Preferred Dividends}}{\text{Average Common Stockholders' Equity}}$

$\dfrac{\$216,000 - \$22,500}{\$1,467,950^*} = 13.2\%$

* [($800,000 + $735,900) + ($800,000 + $600,000)]/2

Ex. 17–20

a. $\dfrac{\text{Number of Times Bond}}{\text{Interest Charges Are Earned}} = \dfrac{\text{Income Before Tax} + \text{Interest Expense}}{\text{Interest Expense}}$

$\dfrac{\$625,000 + \$225,000}{\$225,000} = 3.8 \text{ times}$

b. $\text{Number of Times Preferred Dividends Are Earned} = \dfrac{\text{Net Income}}{\text{Preferred Dividends}}$

$\dfrac{\$450,000}{\$62,500} = 7.2 \text{ times}$

c. $\text{Earnings per Share on Common Stock} = \dfrac{\text{Net Income} - \text{Preferred Dividends}}{\text{Common Shares Outstanding}}$

$\dfrac{\$450,000 - \$62,500}{250,000 \text{ shares}} = \$1.55$

d. $\text{Price-Earnings Ratio} = \dfrac{\text{Market Price per Share}}{\text{Earnings per Share}}$

$\dfrac{\$25}{\$1.55} = 16.1$

e. $\text{Dividends per Share of Common Stock} = \dfrac{\text{Common Dividends}}{\text{Common Shares Outstanding}}$

$\dfrac{\$125,000}{250,000 \text{ shares}} = \$0.50$

f. $\text{Dividend Yield} = \dfrac{\text{Common Dividend per Share}}{\text{Share Price}}$

$\dfrac{\$0.50}{\$25.00} = 2.0\%$

Ex. 17–21

a. Earnings per Share $= \dfrac{\text{Net Income} - \text{Preferred Dividends}}{\text{Common Shares Outstanding}}$

$\dfrac{\$450,000 - \$45,000}{300,000 \text{ shares}} = \$1.35$

b. Price-Earnings Ratio $= \dfrac{\text{Market Price per Share}}{\text{Earnings per Share}}$

$\dfrac{\$20.00}{\$1.35} = 14.8$

c. Dividends per Share $= \dfrac{\text{Common Dividends}}{\text{Common Shares Outstanding}}$

$\dfrac{\$75,000}{300,000 \text{ shares}} = \$0.25$

d. Dividend Yield $= \dfrac{\text{Common Dividend per Share}}{\text{Share Price}}$

$\dfrac{\$0.25}{\$20.00} = 1.3\%$

Ex. 17–22

a. Earnings per share on income before extraordinary items:

Net income..	$1,250,000
Less gain on condemnation...	(360,000)
Plus loss from flood damage	235,000
Income before extraordinary items	$1,125,000

Earnings Before Extraordinary Items per Share on Common Stock =

$\dfrac{\text{Income Before Extraordinary Items} - \text{Preferred Dividends}}{\text{Common Shares Outstanding}}$

$\dfrac{\$1,125,000 - \$500,000}{250,000 \text{ shares}} = \$2.50 \text{ per share}$

b. Earnings per Share on Common Stock $= \dfrac{\text{Net Income} - \text{Preferred Dividends}}{\text{Common Shares Outstanding}}$

$\dfrac{\$1,250,000 - \$500,000}{250,000 \text{ shares}} = \$3.00 \text{ per share}$

Ex. 17–23

a. $\text{Price-Earnings Ratio} = \dfrac{\text{Market Price per Share}}{\text{Earnings per Share}}$

Bank of America: $\dfrac{\$44.47}{\$4.15} = 10.7$

eBay: $\dfrac{\$41.60}{\$0.78} = 53.3$

Coca-Cola: $\dfrac{\$41.19}{\$2.04} = 20.2$

$\text{Dividend Yield} = \dfrac{\text{Dividend per Share}}{\text{Market Price per Share}}$

Bank of America: $\dfrac{\$2.00}{\$44.47} = 4.5\%$

eBay: $\dfrac{\$0.00}{\$41.60} = 0\%$

Coca-Cola: $\dfrac{\$1.12}{\$41.19} = 2.7\%$

b. Bank of America has the largest dividend yield, but the smallest price-earnings ratio. Stock market participants value Bank of America common stock on the basis of its dividend. The dividend is an attractive yield at this date. Because of this attractive yield, stock market participants do not expect the share price to grow significantly, hence the low price-earnings valuation. This is a typical pattern for companies that pay high dividends. eBay shows the opposite extreme. eBay pays no dividend, and thus has no dividend yield. However, eBay has the largest price-earnings ratio of the three companies. Stock market participants are expecting a return on their investment from appreciation in the stock price. Some would say that the stock is priced very aggressively at 53.3 times earnings. Coca-Cola is priced in between the other two companies. Coca-Cola has a moderate dividend producing a yield of 2.7%. The price-earnings ratio is near 20, which is close to the market average at this writing. Thus, Coca-Cola is expected to produce shareholder returns through a combination of some share price appreciation and a small dividend.

PROBLEMS

Prob. 17–1A

1.

DOANE INC.
Comparative Income Statement
For the Years Ended December 31, 2008 and 2007

	2008	2007	Increase (Decrease) Amount	Percent
Sales	$91,500	$73,200	$18,300	25.0%
Sales returns and allowances	1,440	1,200	240	20.0%
Net sales..........................	$90,060	$72,000	$18,060	25.1%
Cost of goods sold	50,400	42,000	8,400	20.0%
Gross profit	$39,660	$30,000	$ 9,660	32.2%
Selling expenses...................	$16,560	$14,400	$ 2,160	15.0%
Administrative expenses............	10,800	9,600	1,200	12.5%
Total operating expenses	$27,360	$24,000	$ 3,360	14.0%
Income from operations.............	$12,300	$ 6,000	$ 6,300	105.0%
Other income........................	600	600	0	0.0%
Income before income tax	$12,900	$ 6,600	$ 6,300	95.5%
Income tax expense.................	2,880	1,440	1,440	100.0%
Net income	$10,020	$ 5,160	$ 4,860	94.2%

2. The profitability has significantly improved. Net sales have increased by 25.1% over the 2007 base year. In addition, however, cost of goods sold, selling expenses, and administrative expenses grew at a slower rate. Increasing sales combined with costs that increase at a slower rate results in strong earnings growth. In this case, net income grew 94.2% over the base year.

Prob. 17–2A

1.

DUSAN WATER SUPPLIES INC.
Comparative Income Statement
For the Years Ended December 31, 2008 and 2007

	2008 Amount	2008 Percent	2007 Amount	2007 Percent
Sales	$ 255,000	102.0%	$ 214,000	101.9%
Sales returns and allowances	5,000	2.0	4,000	1.9
Net sales..	$ 250,000	100.0%	$ 210,000	100.0%
Cost of goods sold	142,500	57.0	121,800	58.0
Gross profit	$ 107,500	43.0%	$ 88,200	42.0%
Selling expenses..................................	$ 100,000	40.0%	$ 50,400	24.0%
Administrative expenses.....................	20,000	8.0	16,800	8.0
Total operating expenses	$ 120,000	48.0%	$ 67,200	32.0%
Income from operations......................	$ (12,500)	(5.0)%	$ 21,000	10.0%
Other income...	6,250	2.5	4,200	2.0
Income before income tax	$ (6,250)	(2.5)%	$ 25,200	12.0%
Income tax expense (benefit).............	(2,500)	1.0	8,400	4.0
Net income (loss).................................	$ (3,750)	(1.5)%	$ 16,800	8.0%

2. The net income as a percent of sales has declined. All the costs and expenses, other than selling expenses, have maintained their approximate cost as a percent of sales relationship between 2007 and 2008. Selling expenses as a percent of sales, however, have grown from 24.0% to 40.0% of sales. Apparently, the new advertising campaign has not been successful. The increased expense has not produced sufficient sales to maintain relative profitability. Thus, selling expenses as a percent of sales have increased.

Prob. 17–3A

1. a. Working Capital = Current Assets – Current Liabilities

   $953,000 – $429,500 = $523,500

   b. Current Ratio = $\dfrac{\text{Current Assets}}{\text{Current Liabilities}}$

   $\dfrac{\$953,000}{\$429,500} = 2.2$

   c. Quick Ratio = $\dfrac{\text{Quick Assets}}{\text{Current Liabilities}}$

   $\dfrac{\$195,000 + \$92,500 + \$293,000}{\$429,500} = 1.4$

2.

| | | | | Supporting Calculations | | |
Transaction	Working Capital	Current Ratio	Quick Ratio	Current Assets	Quick Assets	Current Liabilities
a.	$523,500	2.2	1.4	$ 953,000	$580,500	$429,500
b.	523,500	2.5	1.4	869,000	496,500	345,500
c.	523,500	2.1	1.2	1,008,000	580,500	484,500
d.	523,500	2.3	1.4	920,500	548,000	397,000
e.	485,500	2.0	1.2	953,000	580,500	467,500
f.	523,500	2.2	1.4	953,000	580,500	429,500
g.	708,500	2.6	1.8	1,138,000	765,500	429,500
h.	523,500	2.2	1.4	953,000	580,500	429,500
i.	698,500	2.6	1.8	1,128,000	755,500	429,500
j.	523,500	2.2	1.3	953,000	565,500	429,500

Prob. 17–4A

1. **Working capital:** $1,231,500 − $342,000 = $889,500

Ratio	Numerator	Denominator	Calculated Value
2. Current ratio	$1,231,500	$342,000	3.6
3. Quick ratio	$779,000	$342,000	2.3
4. Accounts receivable turnover	$3,360,000	($260,000 + $196,500)/2	14.7
5. Number of days' sales in receivables	($260,000 + $196,500)/2	($3,360,000/365)	24.8
6. Inventory turnover.........	$1,500,000	($425,000 + $332,500)/2	4.0
7. Number of days' sales in inventory....................	($425,000 + $332,500)/2	($1,500,000/365)	92.2
8. Ratio of fixed assets to long-term liabilities	$2,575,000	$1,100,000	2.3
9. Ratio of liabilities to stockholders' equity	$1,442,000	$2,684,000	0.5
10. Number of times interest charges earned..............	$598,000 + $98,000	$98,000	7.1
11. Number of times preferred dividends earned	$430,000	$12,500	34.4
12. Ratio of net sales to assets............................	$3,360,000	($3,806,500 + $2,841,500)/2	1.0
13. Rate earned on total assets............................	$430,000 + $98,000	($4,126,000 + $3,091,500)/2	14.6%
14. Rate earned on stock-holders' equity...............	$430,000	($2,684,000 + $2,306,500)/2	17.2%
15. Rate earned on common stock-holders' equity...............	($430,000 − $12,500)	($2,184,000 + $1,806,500)/2	20.9%
16. Earnings per share on common stock	($430,000 − $12,500)	40,000	$10.44
17. Price-earnings ratio	$55.00	$10.44	5.3
18. Dividends per share of common stock	$40,000	40,000	$1.00
19. Dividend yield................	$1.00	$55.00	1.8%

Prob. 17–5A

1. a.

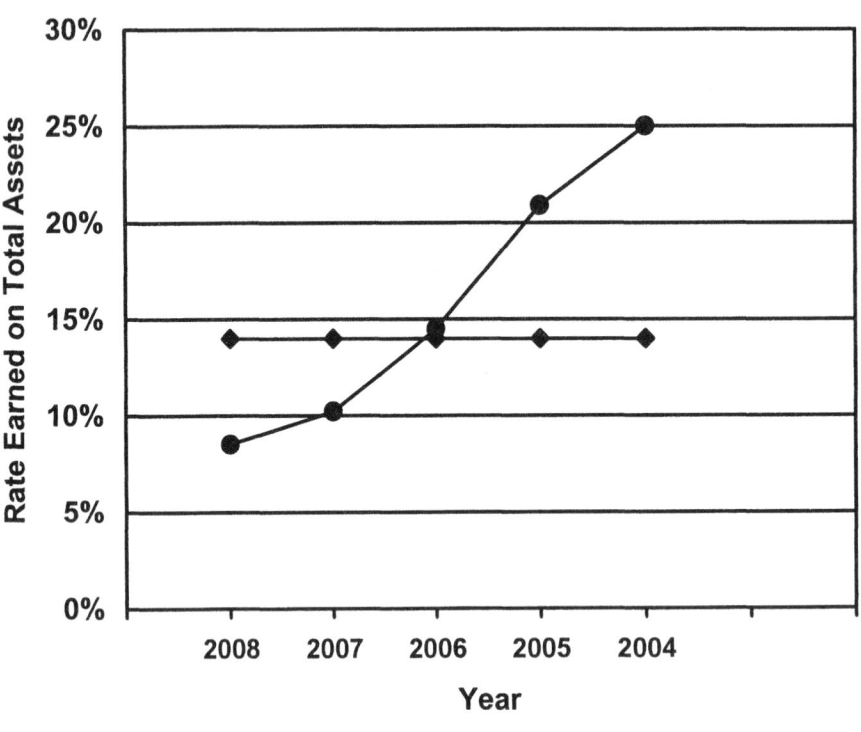

——◆—— Industry rate earned on total assets
——●—— Shore's rate earned on total assets

$$\text{Rate Earned on Total Assets} = \frac{\text{Net Income} + \text{Interest Expense}}{\text{Average Total Assets}}$$

2008: $\dfrac{\$184{,}800}{\$2{,}170{,}000} = 8.5\%$ 　　　　 2005: $\dfrac{\$322{,}000}{\$1{,}540{,}000} = 20.9\%$

2007: $\dfrac{\$203{,}000}{\$1{,}995{,}000} = 10.2\%$ 　　　　 2004: $\dfrac{\$315{,}000}{\$1{,}260{,}000} = 25.0\%$

2006: $\dfrac{\$259{,}000}{\$1{,}785{,}000} = 14.5\%$

Prob. 17–5A   Continued

1. b.

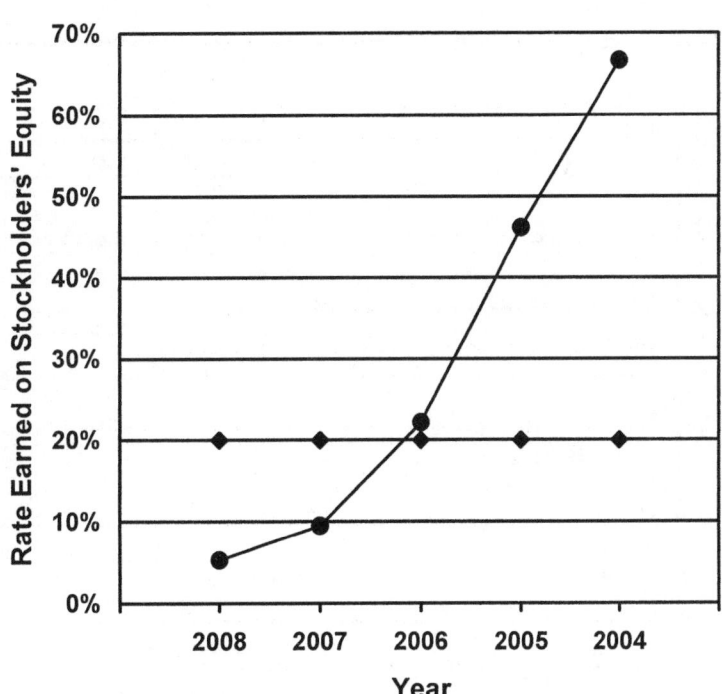

———◆——— Industry rate earned on stockholders' equity
———●——— Shore's rate earned on stockholders' equity

$$\text{Rate Earned on Stockholders' Equity} = \frac{\text{Net Income}}{\text{Average Total Stockholders' Equity}}$$

2008: $\dfrac{\$42,000}{\$791,000} = 5.3\%$ 2005: $\dfrac{\$210,000}{\$455,000} = 46.2\%$

2007: $\dfrac{\$70,000}{\$735,000} = 9.5\%$ 2004: $\dfrac{\$210,000}{\$315,000} = 66.7\%$

2006: $\dfrac{\$140,000}{\$630,000} = 22.2\%$

1. c.

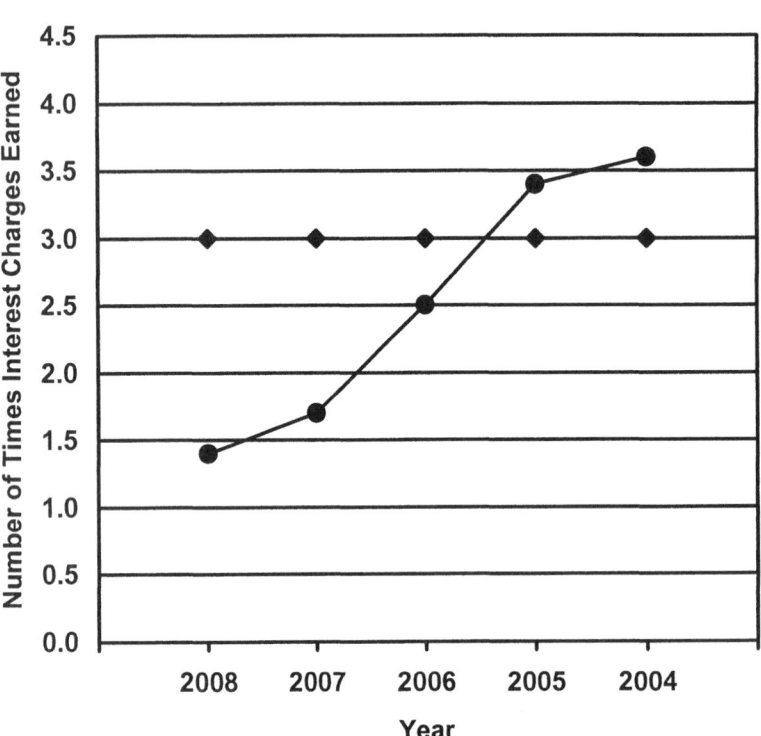

—◆—Industry number of times interest charges earned
—●—Shore's number of times interest charges earned

$$\begin{array}{c}\text{Number of Times} \\ \text{Interest Charges} \\ \text{Earned}\end{array} = \frac{\text{Net Income} + \text{Income Tax Expense} + \text{Interest Expense}}{\text{Interest Expense}}$$

2008: $\dfrac{\$197{,}400}{\$142{,}800} = 1.4$ 2005: $\dfrac{\$385{,}000}{\$112{,}000} = 3.4$

2007: $\dfrac{\$224{,}000}{\$133{,}000} = 1.7$ 2004: $\dfrac{\$378{,}000}{\$105{,}000} = 3.6$

2006: $\dfrac{\$301{,}000}{\$119{,}000} = 2.5$

Prob. 17–5A   Continued

1. d.

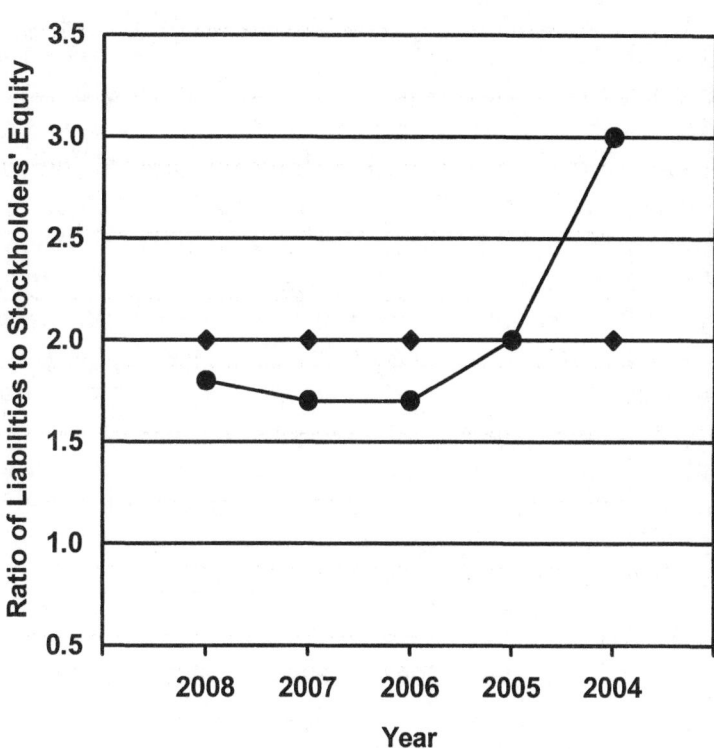

—◆— Industry ratio of liabilities to stockholders' equity

—●— Shore's ratio of liabilities to stockholders' equity

$$\text{Ratio of Liabilities to Stockholders' Equity} = \frac{\text{Total Liabilities}}{\text{Total Stockholders' Equity}}$$

2008: $\dfrac{\$1,428,000}{\$812,000} = 1.8$ 2005: $\dfrac{\$1,120,000}{\$560,000} = 2.0$

2007: $\dfrac{\$1,330,000}{\$770,000} = 1.7$ 2004: $\dfrac{\$1,050,000}{\$350,000} = 3.0$

2006: $\dfrac{\$1,190,000}{\$700,000} = 1.7$

Note: Total liabilities are determined by subtracting stockholders' equity (ending balance) from the total assets (ending balance).

2. Both the rate earned on total assets and the rate earned on stockholders' equity have been moving in a negative direction in the last five years. Both measures have moved below the industry average over the last two years. The cause of this decline is driven by a rapid decline in earnings. The use of debt can be seen from the ratio of liabilities to stockholders' equity. The ratio has declined over the time period and has declined below the industry average. Thus, the level of debt relative to the stockholders' equity has gradually improved over the five years. Unfortunately, the earnings have declined at a faster rate, causing the rate earned on stockholders' equity to decline. The rate earned on total assets ran below the interest cost on debt in 2007 and 2008, causing the rate earned on stockholders' equity to drop below the rate earned on total assets. This is an example of negative leverage. The number of times interest charges were earned has been falling below the industry average for several years. This is the result of low profitability combined with high interest costs (10%). The number of times interest is earned has fallen to a dangerously low level in 2008. The low profitability and time interest charges are earned in 2008, as well as the five-year trend, should be a major concern to the company's management, stockholders, and creditors.

Prob. 17–1B

1.

PHOENIX TECHNOLOGY COMPANY
Comparative Income Statement
For the Years Ended December 31, 2008 and 2007

	2008	2007	Increase (Decrease) Amount	Percent
Sales	$385,000	$343,200	$ 41,800	12.2%
Sales returns and allowances	4,800	3,200	1,600	50.0%
Net sales...	$380,200	$340,000	$ 40,200	11.8%
Cost of goods sold	180,000	144,000	36,000	25.0%
Gross profit	$200,200	$196,000	$ 4,200	2.1%
Selling expenses............................	$ 87,400	$ 76,000	$ 11,400	15.0%
Administrative expenses..............	30,000	24,000	6,000	25.0%
Total operating expenses	$117,400	$100,000	$ 17,400	17.4%
Income from operations................	$ 82,800	$ 96,000	$ (13,200)	(13.8)%
Other income..................................	1,600	1,600	0	0.0%
Income before income tax	$ 84,400	$ 97,600	$ (13,200)	(13.5)%
Income tax expense.......................	36,800	32,000	4,800	15.0%
Net income	$ 47,600	$ 65,600	$ (18,000)	(27.4)%

2. Net income has declined from 2007 to 2008. Net sales have increased by 11.8%; however, cost of goods sold has increased by 25.0%, causing the gross profit to grow at a rate less than sales relative to the base year. In addition, total operating expenses have increased at a faster rate than sales (17.4% increase vs. 11.8% net sales increase). Increases in costs and expenses that are higher than the increase in sales have caused the net income to decline by 27.4%.

Prob. 17–2B

1.

ACEDIA TECHNOLOGY COMPANY
Comparative Income Statement
For the Years Ended December 31, 2008 and 2007

	2008		2007	
	Amount	Percent	Amount	Percent
Sales	$ 755,000	100.7%	$ 676,000	100.9%
Sales returns and allowances ..	5,000	0.7	6,000	0.9
Net sales	$ 750,000	100.0%	$ 670,000	100.0%
Cost of goods sold	292,500	39.0	274,700	41.0
Gross profit	$ 457,500	61.0%	$ 395,300	59.0%
Selling expenses.........................	$ 172,500	23.0%	$ 160,800	24.0%
Administrative expenses...........	82,500	11.0	80,400	12.0
Total operating expenses	$ 255,000	34.0%	$ 241,200	36.0%
Income from operations.............	$ 202,500	27.0%	$ 154,100	23.0%
Other income.............................	7,500	1.0	6,700	1.0
Income before income tax	$ 210,000	28.0%	$ 160,800	24.0%
Income tax expense...................	60,000	8.0	53,600	8.0
Net income	$ 150,000	20.0%	$ 107,200	16.0%

2. The vertical analysis indicates that the costs (cost of goods sold, selling expenses, and administrative expenses) as a percent of sales improved from 2007 to 2008. As a result, net income as a percent of sales increased from 16.0% to 20.0%. The sales promotion campaign appears successful. The selling expenses as a percent of sales declined, suggesting that the increased cost was more than made up by increased sales.

Prob. 17–3B

1. a. **Working Capital = Current Assets – Current Liabilities**

$$\$2,008,000 - \$944,000 = \$1,064,000$$

b. **Current Ratio** = $\dfrac{\text{Current Assets}}{\text{Current Liabilities}}$

$$\dfrac{\$2,008,000}{\$944,000} = 2.1$$

c. **Quick Ratio** = $\dfrac{\text{Quick Assets}}{\text{Current Liabilities}}$

$$\dfrac{\$384,000 + \$176,000 + \$608,000}{\$944,000} = 1.2$$

2.

				Supporting Calculations		
Transaction	Working Capital	Current Ratio	Quick Ratio	Current Assets	Quick Assets	Current Liabilities
a.	$1,064,000	2.1	1.2	$2,008,000	$1,168,000	$ 944,000
b.	1,064,000	2.2	1.3	1,918,000	1,078,000	854,000
c.	1,064,000	2.0	1.1	2,128,000	1,168,000	1,064,000
d.	1,064,000	2.2	1.3	1,943,000	1,103,000	879,000
e.	1,031,500	2.1	1.2	2,008,000	1,168,000	976,500
f.	1,064,000	2.1	1.2	2,008,000	1,168,000	944,000
g.	1,224,000	2.3	1.4	2,168,000	1,328,000	944,000
h.	1,064,000	2.1	1.2	2,008,000	1,168,000	944,000
i.	1,489,000	2.6	1.7	2,433,000	1,593,000	944,000
j.	1,064,000	2.1	1.2	2,008,000	1,152,000	944,000

Prob. 17–4B

1. Working Capital: $754,500 – $225,000 = $529,500

	Ratio	Numerator	Denominator	Calculated Value
2.	Current ratio	$754,500	$225,000	3.4
3.	Quick ratio	$660,000	$225,000	2.9
4.	Accounts receivable turnover	$1,050,000	($160,000 + $132,000)/2	7.2
5.	Number of days' sales in receivables	($160,000 + $132,000)/2	($1,050,000/365)	50.8
6.	Inventory turnover.........	$300,000	($67,500 + $41,500)/2	5.5
7.	Number of days' sales in inventory..........	($67,500 + $41,500)2	($300,000/365)	66.3
8.	Ratio of fixed assets to long-term liabilities	$950,000	$740,000	1.3
9.	Ratio of liabilities to stockholders' equity	$965,000	$1,049,500	0.9
10.	Number of times interest charges earned	$352,250 + $64,000	$64,000	6.5
11.	Number of times preferred dividends earned	$321,500	$10,000	32.2
12.	Ratio of net sales to assets...........................	$1,050,000	($1,704,500 + $1,105,000)/2	0.7
13.	Rate earned on total assets...........................	$321,500 + $64,000	($2,014,500 + $1,265,000)/2	23.5%
14.	Rate earned on stockholders' equity...............	$321,500	($1,049,500 + $565,000)/2	39.8%
15.	Rate earned on common stockholders' equity...............	($321,500 – $10,000)	($849,500 + $465,000)/2	47.4%
16.	Earnings per share on common stock	($321,500 – $10,000)	28,000	$11.13
17.	Price-earnings ratio	$15.00	$11.13	1.3
18.	Dividends per share of common stock	$7,000	28,000	$0.25
19.	Dividend yield................	$0.25	$15.00	1.7%

Prob. 17–5B

1. a.

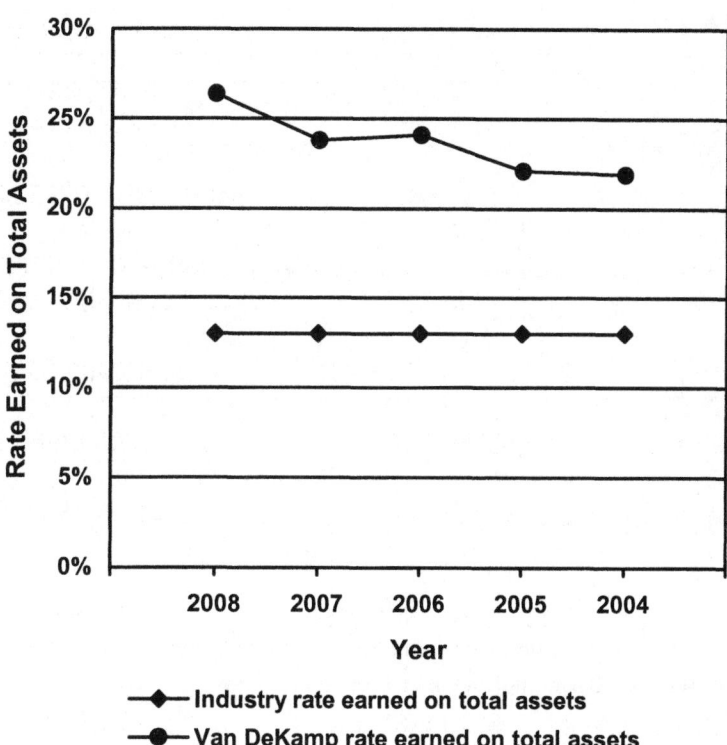

$$\text{Rate Earned on Total Assets} = \frac{\text{Net Income } + \text{ Interest Expense}}{\text{Average Total Assets}}$$

2008: $\dfrac{\$2,086,800}{\$7,917,500} = 26.4\%$ 2005: $\dfrac{\$762,000}{\$3,450,000} = 22.1\%$

2007: $\dfrac{\$1,434,000}{\$6,025,000} = 23.8\%$ 2004: $\dfrac{\$585,000}{\$2,700,000} = 21.7\%$

2006: $\dfrac{\$1,102,500}{\$4,575,000} = 24.1\%$

1. b.

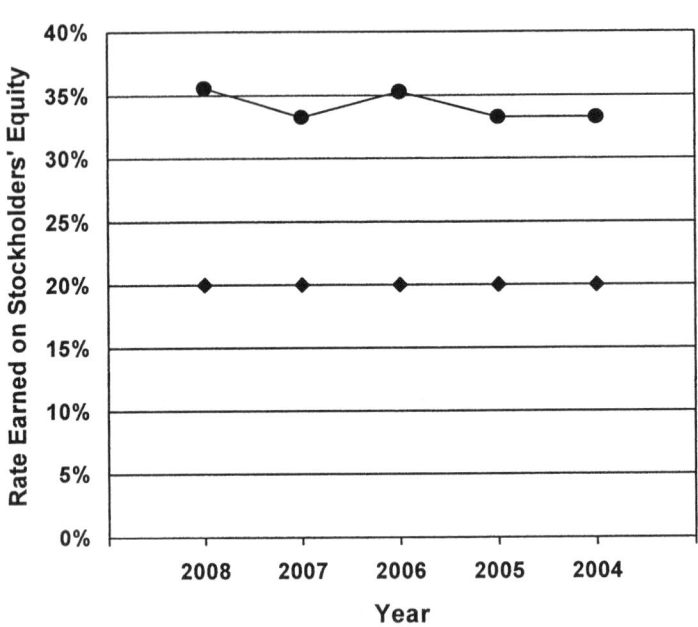

—◆—Industry rate earned on stockholders' equity
—●—Van DeKamp rate earned on stockholders' equity

$$\text{Rate Earned on Stockholders' Equity} = \frac{\text{Net Income}}{\text{Average Total Stockholders' Equity}}$$

2008: $\dfrac{\$1,815,000}{\$5,107,500} = 35.5\%$ 2005: $\dfrac{\$600,000}{\$1,800,000} = 33.3\%$

2007: $\dfrac{\$1,200,000}{\$3,600,000} = 33.3\%$ 2004: $\dfrac{\$450,000}{\$1,350,000} = 33.3\%$

2006: $\dfrac{\$900,000}{\$2,550,000} = 35.3\%$

Prob. 17–5B   Continued

1. c.

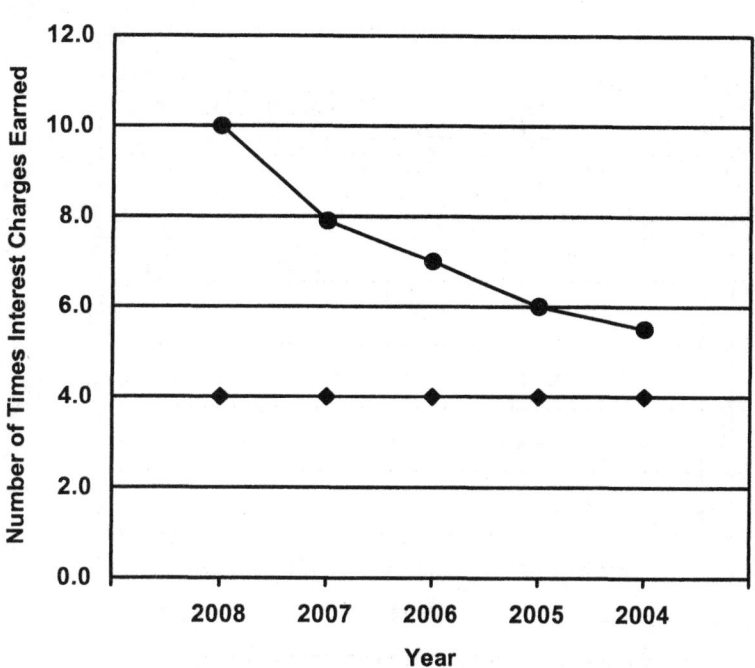

─◆─ Industry number of times interest charges earned
─●─ Van DeKamp number of times interest charges earned

$$\begin{matrix} \text{Number of Times} \\ \text{Interest Charges} \\ \text{Earned} \end{matrix} = \frac{\text{Net Income} + \text{Income Tax Expense} + \text{Interest Expense}}{\text{Interest Expense}}$$

2008: $\dfrac{\$2,722,050}{\$271,800} = 10.0$ 2005: $\dfrac{\$972,000}{\$162,000} = 6.0$

2007: $\dfrac{\$1,854,000}{\$234,000} = 7.9$ 2004: $\dfrac{\$742,500}{\$135,000} = 5.5$

2006: $\dfrac{\$1,417,500}{\$202,500} = 7.0$

Prob. 17–5B   Continued

1.   d.

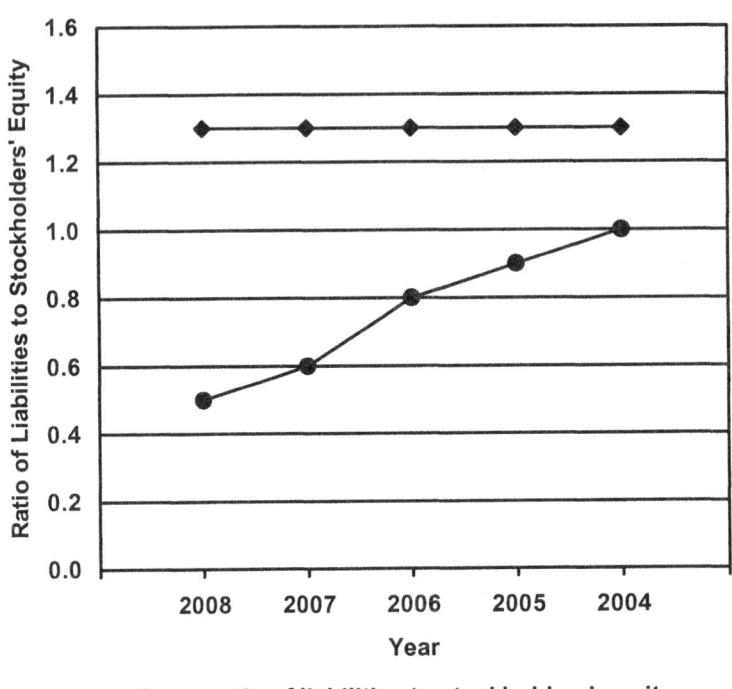

$$\text{Ratio of Liabilities to Stockholders' Equity} = \frac{\text{Total Liabilities}}{\text{Total Stockholders' Equity}}$$

2008: $\dfrac{\$3,020,000}{\$6,015,000} = 0.5$ 2005: $\dfrac{\$1,800,000}{\$2,100,000} = 0.9$

2007: $\dfrac{\$2,600,000}{\$4,200,000} = 0.6$ 2004: $\dfrac{\$1,500,000}{\$1,500,000} = 1.0$

2006: $\dfrac{\$2,250,000}{\$3,000,000} = 0.8$

Note: The total liabilities are the difference between the total assets and total stockholders' equity ending balances.

Prob. 17–5B   Concluded

2. Both the rate earned on total assets and rate earned on stockholders' equity are above the industry average for all five years. The rate earned on total assets is actually improving gradually. The rate earned on stockholders' equity exceeds the rate earned on total assets, providing evidence of the positive use of leverage. The company is clearly growing earnings as fast as the asset and equity base. In addition, the ratio of liabilities to stockholders' equity indicates that the proportion of debt to stockholders' equity has been declining over the period. The firm is adding to debt at a slower rate than the assets are growing from earnings. The number of times interest charges were earned ratio is improving during this time period. Again, the firm is increasing earnings faster than the increase in interest charges. Overall, these ratios indicate excellent financial performance coupled with appropriate use of debt (leverage).

WILLIAMS-SONOMA, INC., PROBLEM

1. a. Working capital (in thousands):

    2005: $492,772 ($1,083,164 – $590,392)
    2004: $351,608 ($873,765 – $522,157)

    b. Current ratio:

    2005: 1.8 ($1,083,164/$590,392)
    2004: 1.6 ($873,765/$552,157)

    c. Quick ratio:

    2005: 0.7 ($412,002/$590,392)
    2004: 0.5 ($281,730/$552,157)

    d. Accounts receivable turnover:

    2005: 75.7 {$3,538,947/[($51,020 + $42,520)/2]}
    2004: 84.7 {$3,136,931/[($42,520 + $31,573)/2]}

    e. Number of days' sales in receivables:

    2005: 4.8 [($51,020 + $42,520)/2]/($3,538,947/365)
    2004: 4.3 [($42,520 + $31,573)/2]/($3,136,931/365)

    f. Inventory turnover:

    2005: 4.3 {$2,103,465/[($520,292 + $452,421)/2]}
    2004: 4.4 {$1,865,786/[($452,421 + $404,100)/2]}

    g. Number of days' sales in inventory:

    2005: 84.4 {[($520,292 + $452,421)/2]/($2,103,465/365)}
    2004: 83.8 {[($452,421 + $404,100)/2]/($1,865,786/365)}

    h. Ratio of liabilities to stockholders' equity:

    2005: 0.8 ($856,302/$1,125,318)
    2004: 0.8 ($787,883/$957,662)

    i. Ratio of net sales to average total assets:

    2005: 1.9 {$3,538,947/[($1,981,620 + $1,745,545)/2]}
    2004: 2.0 {$3,136,931/[($1,745,545 + $1,470,735)/2]}

    j. Rate earned on average total assets:

    2005: 11.6% {($214,866 + $1,975)/[($1,981,620 + $1,745,545)/2]}
    2004: 12.0% {($191,234 + $1,703)/[($1,745,545 + $1,470,735)/2]}

    k. Rate earned on average common stockholders' equity:

    2005: 20.6% {$214,866/[($1,125,318 + $957,662)/2]}
    2004: 21.7% {$191,234/[($957,662 + $804,591)/2]}

Williams-Sonoma, Inc., Problem   Continued

   l. **Price-earnings ratio:**

       2005: 21.8 ($40.62/$1.86)
       2004: 20.9 ($34.53/$1.65)

  m. **Percentage relationship of net income to net sales:**

       2005: 6.1% ($214,866/$3,538,947)
       2004: 6.1% ($191,234/$3,136,931)

2. Before reaching definitive conclusions, each measure should be compared with past years, industry averages, and similar firms in the industry.

   a. The working capital increased significantly.

   b. and c. The current ratio and the quick ratio increased during 2005.

   d. and e. The accounts receivable turnover and number of days' sales in receivables indicate a slight decrease in the efficiency of collecting accounts receivable. The accounts receivable turnover decreased from 84.7 to 75.7. The number of days' sales in receivables increased from 4.3 to 4.8. Both measures indicate, however, that Williams-Sonoma has significant cash sales, since the turnover is so high and the average collection period is so short. If the credit sales were known, these ratios could be calculated with net credit sales on account in the numerator. The resulting calculations could be compared to Williams-Sonoma's credit policy.

   f. and g. The results of these two analyses showed a slight decrease in the inventory turnover and an increase in the number of days' sales in inventory. Both trends are small. Inventory management is critical to a retailer, so this ratio trend should be watched in the future.

   h. The margin of protection to the creditors remained constant. Overall, there is excellent protection to creditors.

   i. These analyses indicate a slight decrease in the effectiveness in the use of the assets to generate revenues.

   j. The rate earned on average total assets decreased slightly during 2005. Overall, rates earned on assets that exceed 10% are usually considered good performance.

   k. The rate earned on average common stockholders' equity in 2005 decreased slightly. This is also evidence of the positive use of leverage, since the rate earned on stockholders' equity exceeds the rate earned on assets. The rates earned on average common stockholders' equity shown for these two years would be considered excellent performance.

Williams-Sonoma, Inc., Problem   Concluded

l. The price-earnings ratio increased slightly from 2004 to 2005. This increase accompanied an overall increase in price-earnings ratios for the whole market during this time. In addition, market participants are revaluing Williams-Sonoma's growth prospects upward.

m. The percent of net income to net sales remained constant at 6.1%.

SPECIAL ACTIVITIES

SA 17–1

This position does not allow the shareholders to take advantage of leverage. As a result, the return on shareholders' equity cannot be improved by using debt. In contrast, a low or no debt load does provide the company great flexibility in the case of a national calamity. However, the "no debt" position only makes sense within the "national calamity" scenario. Within normal business operations, most companies can assume some debt without much loss of flexibility or control. Ice Mountain Brewery is competing against companies that will not be so inclined to avoid debt. As a result, they will likely be able to grow faster than Ice Mountain. The Ice Mountain management should consider the risk of not being able to keep up with the competition because of their conservative financing policies.

SA 17–2

Steve is concerned about the inventory and accounts receivable levels because he must determine their value. Inventory that cannot be sold (or sold at a large discount) or accounts receivable that cannot be collected must be written down to reflect their reduced value. Steve has conducted the ratio analysis and interviewed Tony to help make this determination. The inventory and accounts receivable levels have grown alarmingly. Tony's response to Steve is not reassuring. The inventory represents obsolete technology that is left over after the holiday season. The accounts receivable have apparently grown from loosening the credit standards. Steve may need to insist on write-downs of the inventory and accounts receivable balances to reflect their net realizable values. Tony is correct in pointing out that the current ratio has probably improved. Thus, although Tony calls this "good," it is only such if the current assets in the numerator are fairly valued. Under these circumstances, the current ratio is probably overstated because the inventory and accounts receivable balances are inflated relative to their net realizable values.

SA 17–3

DELL INC. AND APPLE COMPUTER, INC.
Common-Size Statements

	Dell Inc.	Apple Computer, Inc.
Sales (net)...	100.0%	100.0%
Cost of goods sold	82.2	71.0
Gross profit	17.8%	29.0%
Operating expenses:		
Selling, general, and administrative ...	9.2%	13.3%
Research and development.................	0.8	3.8
Total operating expenses	10.0%	17.2%*
Operating income	7.8%	11.8%

*Rounded to the nearest tenth of a percent.

The common-size analysis indicates that Dell and Apple are very different computer companies. Dell's income from operations is 7.8% of sales, while Apple's was 11.8% of sales. There is a 4 percentage point difference between the two companies. What explains this difference? The gross profit for Dell was 17.8% of sales, which is fairly narrow. Apple, in contrast, had a gross profit of 29.0% of sales, which is over 11 points better than Dell's. This suggests Apple is able to charge higher prices than Dell for its products (assuming that they are both equally efficient in making products). Apple's selling, general, and administrative expenses are at about 13.3% of sales, while Dell's is only 9.2% of sales. Dell designed the business for efficiency; thus, it operates on a low-cost structure. The selling, general, and administrative expenses do not include expensive advertising campaigns, complex sales channel administration, or complex product support activities. Apple, in contrast, has larger selling, general, and administrative costs as a percent of sales. It attempts to sell a unique machine to a unique audience. This requires significant SG&A effort. Another big difference between the two companies is in research and development. Dell's R&D is a narrow 0.8% of sales, while Apple's is 3.8% of sales. Essentially, Dell focuses its R&D effort on the final assembly of the computer. Dell relies on its suppliers to develop innovation in the components and operating system software (Microsoft). Apple, on the other hand, must constantly spend R&D on computers, peripherals, and its own operating system software. This is because Apple chooses not to follow the industry standards and thus must pave its own way on both hardware and software. This feature of Apple also contributes to its larger selling, general, and administrative costs as a percent of sales. The higher gross profit as a percentage of sales for Apple carries through to its income from operations, generating a significantly higher operating income as a percentage of sales compared to Dell.

SA 17–4

1. a. Rate Earned on Total Assets = $\dfrac{\text{Net Income} + \text{Interest Expense}}{\text{Average Total Assets}}$

2005: $\dfrac{\$2,024 + \$7,643}{\$287,669} = 3.4\%$

2004: $\dfrac{\$3,487 + \$7,071}{\$308,032} = 3.4\%$

2003: $\dfrac{(\$495) + \$7,643}{\$293,678} = 2.4\%$

   b. Rate Earned on Total Stockholders' Equity = $\dfrac{\text{Net Income}}{\text{Average Total Stockholders' Equity}}$

2005: $\dfrac{\$2,024}{\$14,501} = 14.0\%$

2004: $\dfrac{\$3,487}{\$13,848} = 25.2\%$

2003: $\dfrac{\$495}{\$8,532} = 5.8\%$

   c. Earnings per Share = $\dfrac{\text{Net Income} - \text{Preferred Dividends}}{\text{Common Shares Outstanding}}$

2005: $\dfrac{\$2,024}{\$1,846} = \$1.10$

2004: $\dfrac{\$3,487}{1,830} = \$1.91$

2003: $\dfrac{\$495}{1,832} = \$0.27$

SA 17–4 **Continued**

d. Dividend Yield = $\dfrac{\text{Dividend per Share of Common Stock}}{\text{Market Price per Share of Common Stock}}$

2005: $\dfrac{\$0.40}{\$11.22}$ = 3.6%

2004: $\dfrac{\$0.40}{\$14.98}$ = 2.7%

2003: $\dfrac{\$0.40}{\$11.95}$ = 3.3%

e. Price-Earnings Ratio = $\dfrac{\text{Market Price per Share of Common Stock}}{\text{Earnings per Share of Common Stock}}$

2005: $\dfrac{\$11.22}{\$1.10}$ = 10.2%

2004: $\dfrac{\$14.98}{\$1.91}$ = 7.8

2003: $\dfrac{\$11.95}{\$0.27}$ = 44.3

2. Ratio of Average Liabilities to Average Stockholders' Equity = Average Liabilities/ Average Stockholders' Equity

2005: $\dfrac{\$287,669 - \$14,501}{\$14,501}$ = 18.8

SA 17–4   Concluded

3. Ford's leverage is the result of its financing segment. The nature of financial institutions is to acquire debt money at a low interest rate and lend it out at a higher interest rate. This is inherently a low-risk business that allows financial institutions to acquire extensive debt resources with very little equity. Banks acquire deposits (debt) in this manner. Thus, financial institutions often have equity less than 10% of total assets. Ford's financing business skews the leverage ratio so that it does not appear like a normal manufacturer.

4. Ford's profitability, as measured by earnings per share, dramatically improved from 2003 levels as the recession from the early part of the decade receded. The rate earned on total assets improved moderately, while the rate earned on stockholders' equity improved significantly. The dividend yield did not change significantly during the period and remained near the 3% level. The price-earnings (P/E) ratio is interesting. In 2003, the earnings per share was slightly positive, but the stock price declined slightly, causing a P/E ratio of over 44, indicating the market's expectation for Ford's profitability to improve. In 2004, Ford had good earnings per share, but the stock price only increased moderately. Thus, the expected increase in earnings was realized, but the P/E dropped to near 8 and remained in that range in 2005. Apparently, stock market participants were not willing to pay a high price for future earnings because of the concern that Ford's profitability may be vulnerable to a future downturn. Shareholders know from history that Ford is a cyclical business. When the economy is going well, the market price will not bid up the stock price with the earnings, causing the P/E ratio to be depressed. In a sense, stockholders know it is only a matter of time before fortunes reverse. When the economy moves into recession, the stock price drops, but not as dramatically as the profitability. Thus, the P/E increases. Again, stockholders know it is only a matter of time before economic fortunes reverse back up.

SA 17–5

The following is an example of a solution. A student's actual solution will depend on the year of analysis.

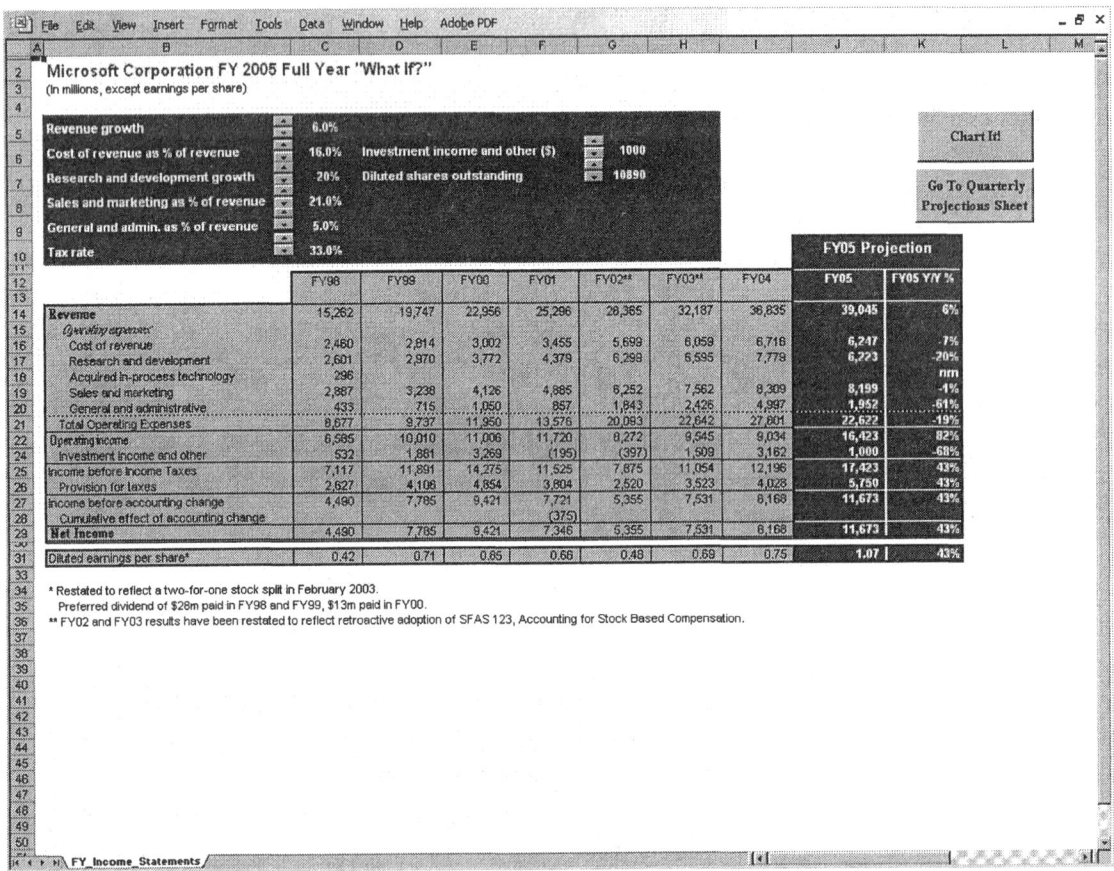

SA 17–6

1.

a. Rate Earned on Total Assets = $\dfrac{\text{Net Income} + \text{Interest Expense}}{\text{Average Total Assets}}$

Marriott: $\dfrac{\$596 + \$99}{\$8,423} = 8.3\%$

Hilton: $\dfrac{\$238 + \$274}{\$8,213} = 6.2\%$

b. Rate Earned on Total Stockholders' Equity = $\dfrac{\text{Net Income}}{\text{Average Total Stockholders' Equity}}$

Marriott: $\dfrac{\$596}{\$3,960} = 15.1\%$

Hilton: $\dfrac{\$238}{\$2,404} = 9.9\ \%$

c. Number of
Times Interest $= \dfrac{\text{Income Before Income Tax Expense} + \text{Interest Expense}}{\text{Interest Expense}}$
Charges Are Earned

Marriott: $\dfrac{\$696 + \$99}{\$99} = 8.0$

Hilton: $\dfrac{\$365 + \$274}{\$274} = 2.3$

d. Ratio of Liabilities to Stockholders' Equity = $\dfrac{\text{Total Liabilities}}{\text{Total Stockholders' Equity}}$

Marriott: $\dfrac{\$4,587}{\$4,081} = 1.1$

Hilton: $\dfrac{\$5,674}{\$2,568} = 2.2$

SA 17–6 **Concluded**

Summary Table:

	Marriott	Hilton
Rate earned on total assets	8.3%	6.2%
Rate earned on total stockholders' equity	15.1%	9.9%
Number of times interest charges are earned	8.0	2.3
Ratio of liabilities to stockholders' equity	1.1	2.2

2. Marriott has a higher rate earned on total assets (8.3% vs. 6.2%), and a higher rate on stockholders' equity (15.1% vs. 9.9%), compared to Hilton. Hilton's weaker performance relative to Marriott appears to be due to its inability to manage its debt. Hilton has much more leverage than Marriott. This is confirmed by the ratio of liabilities to stockholders' equity, which shows the relative debt held by Marriott is 1.1 times stockholders' equity, compared to 2.2 times for Hilton. The number of times interest charges are earned shows that Marriott covers its interest charges 8.0 times. The comparable number for Hilton is 2.3, which is marginally sufficient. Hilton's higher debt level is generating large interest expense, which is negatively affecting the rate earned on total assets and stockholders' equity. In summary, Hilton's high debt level is affecting the company's ability to earn returns for stockholders.

APPENDIX B
REVERSING ENTRIES

Ex. B–1

a. (1) Sales Salaries Expense 8,400

             Salaries Payable   8,400

                Accrued salaries ($2,800 × 3).

    (2) Accounts Receivable 7,975

             Fees Earned   7,975

                Accrued fees earned.

b. (1) Salaries Payable 8,400

             Sales Salaries Expense   8,400

                Reversing entry.

    (2) Fees Earned 7,975

             Accounts Receivable   7,975

                Reversing entry.

Ex. B–2

a. (1) Wages Expense 1,875

             Wages Payable   1,875

                Accrued wages ($9,375/5).

    (2) Accounts Receivable 6,100

              Fees Earned   6,100

                Accrued fees earned.

b. (1) Wages Payable 1,875

             Wages Expense   1,875

                Reversing entry.

    (2) Fees Earned 6,100

              Accounts Receivable   6,100

                Reversing entry.

Ex. B–3

a. (1) Payment (last payday in year)

(2) Adjusting (accrual of wages at end of year)

(3) Closing

(4) Reversing

(5) Payment (first payday in following year)

b. (1) Wages Expense.. 62,500
      Cash..   62,500

(2) Wages Expense.. 12,500
      Wages Payable..   12,500
        Accrued wages.

(3) Income Summary 1,760,300
      Wages Expense   1,760,300

(4) Wages Payable... 12,500
      Wages Expense   12,500
        Reversing entry.

(5) Wages Expense.. 60,000
      Cash..   60,000

Ex. B–4

a. (1) Payment (last payday in year)

(2) Adjusting (accrual of wages at end of year)

(3) Closing

(4) Reversing

(5) Payment (first payday in following year)

b.

(1) Salaries Expense	30,000	
Cash...		30,000
(2) Salaries Expense	10,000	
Salaries Payable		10,000
Accrued salaries.		
(3) Income Summary	1,510,000	
Salaries Expense		1,510,000
(4) Salaries Payable...	10,000	
Salaries Expense		10,000
Reversing entry.		
(5) Salaries Expense	30,000	
Cash...		30,000

APPENDIX C
END-OF-PERIOD SPREADSHEET (WORK SHEET) FOR A MERCHANDISING BUSINESS

Prob. C–1

1. [The solution to Part 1 can be found on the following pages.]

2.

STONES CO.
Income Statement
For the Year Ended December 31, 2008

Revenue from sales:			
Sales		$775,000	
Less: Sales returns and allowances	$11,900		
Sales discounts	7,100	19,000	
Net sales			$756,000
Cost of merchandise sold			463,200
Gross profit			$292,800
Expenses:			
Selling expenses:			
Sales salaries expense	$79,000		
Advertising expense	25,000		
Depreciation expense—store equipment	5,000		
Store supplies expense	3,150		
Miscellaneous selling expense	1,600		
Total selling expenses		$113,750	
Administrative expenses:			
Office salaries expense	$34,500		
Rent expense	16,000		
Insurance expense	3,700		
Depreciation expense—office equipment	2,800		
Office supplies expense	1,500		
Miscellaneous administrative expense	1,650		
Total administrative expenses		60,150	
Total expenses			173,900
Income from operations			$118,900
Other income and expense:			
Rent revenue		$ 600	
Interest expense		(11,600)	(11,000)
Net income			$107,900

Prob. C–1   Continued

1.

STONES CO.
End-of-Period Spreadsheet (Work Sheet)
For the Year Ended December 31, 2008

#	Account Title	Unadjusted Trial Balance Dr.	Unadjusted Trial Balance Cr.	Adjustments Dr.	Adjustments Cr.	Adjusted Trial Balance Dr.	Adjusted Trial Balance Cr.	Income Statement Dr.	Income Statement Cr.	Balance Sheet Dr.	Balance Sheet Cr.
1	Cash	9,000				9,000				9,000	
2	Accounts Receivable	72,500				72,500				72,500	
3	Merchandise Inventory	165,000			(a) 6,000	159,000				159,000	
4	Prepaid Insurance	9,700			(b) 3,700	6,000				6,000	
5	Store Supplies	4,200			(c) 3,100	1,100				1,100	
6	Office Supplies	2,100			(d) 1,500	600				600	
7	Store Equipment	160,000				160,000				160,000	
8	Acc. Depr.—Store Equip.		40,300		(e) 5,000		45,300				45,300
9	Office Equipment	70,000				70,000				70,000	
10	Acc. Depr.—Office Equip.		17,200		(f) 2,800		20,000				20,000
11	Accounts Payable		66,700				66,700				66,700
12	Salaries Payable				(g) 3,100		3,100				3,100
13	Unearned Rent		1,200	(h) 600			600				600
14	Note Payable (final payment due 2016)		125,000				125,000				125,000
15	Chang Yu, Capital		134,600				134,600				134,600
16	Chang Yu, Drawing	25,000				25,000				25,000	
17	Sales		775,000				775,000		775,000		
18	Sales Returns and Allow.	11,900				11,900		11,900			
19	Sales Discounts	7,100				7,100		7,100			
20	Cost of Merchandise Sold	457,200		(a) 6,000		463,200		463,200			
21	Sales Salaries Expense	76,400		(g) 2,600		79,000		79,000			
22	Advertising Expense	25,000				25,000		25,000			

#	Account	Trial Balance Dr	Trial Balance Cr	Adjustments Dr	Adjustments Cr	Adjusted Trial Balance Dr	Adjusted Trial Balance Cr	Income Statement Dr	Income Statement Cr	Balance Sheet Dr	Balance Sheet Cr
23	Depr. Exp.—Store Equip.			(e) 5,000		5,000		5,000			
24	Store Supplies Expense			(c) 3,150		3,150		3,150			
25	Misc. Selling Expense	1,600				1,600		1,600			
26	Office Salaries Expense	34,000		(g) 500		34,500		34,500			
27	Rent Expense	16,000				16,000		16,000			
28	Insurance Expense			(b) 3,700		3,700		3,700			
29	Depr. Exp.—Office Equip.			(f) 2,800		2,800		2,800			
30	Office Supplies Expense			(d) 1,500		1,500		1,500			
31	Misc. Admin. Expense	1,650				1,650		1,650			
32	Rent Revenue				(h) 600		600		600		
33	Interest Expense	11,600				11,600		11,600			
34		1,160,000	1,160,000	25,850	25,850	1,170,900	1,170,900	667,700	775,600	503,200	395,300
35	Net Income							107,900			107,900
36								775,600	775,600	503,200	503,200

3.

STONES CO.
Statement of Owner's Equity
For the Year Ended December 31, 2008

Chang Yu, capital, January 1, 2008......................................		$134,600
Net income for the year..	$107,900	
Less withdrawals..	25,000	
Increase in owner's equity...		82,900
Chang Yu, capital, December 31, 2008		$217,500

Prob. C–1   **Continued**

4.

STONES CO.
Balance Sheet
December 31, 2008

<u>Assets</u>

Current assets:

Cash..	$ 9,000	
Accounts receivable................................	72,500	
Merchandise inventory	159,000	
Prepaid insurance	6,000	
Store supplies..	1,100	
Office supplies...	600	
Total current assets		$248,200

Property, plant, and equipment:

Store equipment	$160,000		
Less accumulated depreciation............	45,300	$114,700	
Office equipment	$ 70,000		
Less accumulated depreciation............	20,000	50,000	
Total property, plant, and			
equipment			164,700
Total assets			$412,900

<u>Liabilities</u>

Current liabilities:

Accounts payable.....................................	$ 66,700	
Note payable (current portion)	25,000	
Salaries payable	3,100	
Unearned rent...	600	
Total current liabilities		$ 95,400

Long-term liabilities:

Note payable (final payment due 2016) ...		100,000
Total liabilities...		$195,400

<u>Owner's Equity</u>

Chang Yu, capital..		217,500
Total liabilities and owner's equity		$412,900

5.

Cost of Merchandise Sold...	6,000	
Merchandise Inventory		6,000
Insurance Expense..	3,700	
Prepaid Insurance		3,700
Store Supplies Expense...	3,150	
Store Supplies		3,150
Office Supplies Expense..	1,500	
Office Supplies		1,500
Depreciation Expense—Store Equipment..................	5,000	
Accum. Depreciation—Store Equipment..............		5,000
Depreciation Expense—Office Equipment.................	2,800	
Accum. Depreciation—Office Equipment.............		2,800
Sales Salaries Expense...	2,600	
Office Salaries Expense..	500	
Salaries Payable		3,100
Unearned Rent	600	
Rent Revenue		600

6.

Sales	775,000	
Rent Revenue	600	
Income Summary		775,600
Income Summary	667,700	
Sales Returns and Allowances		11,900
Sales Discounts		7,100
Cost of Merchandise Sold		463,200
Sales Salaries Expense		79,000
Advertising Expense		25,000
Depreciation Expense—Store Equipment		5,000
Store Supplies Expense		3,150
Miscellaneous Selling Expense		1,600
Office Salaries Expense		34,500
Rent Expense		16,000
Insurance Expense		3,700
Depreciation Expense—Office Equipment		2,800
Office Supplies Expense		1,500
Miscellaneous Administrative Expense		1,650
Interest Expense		11,600
Income Summary	107,900	
Change Yu, Capital		107,900
Change Yu, Capital	25,000	
Change Yu, Drawing		25,000

Prob. C-2

1.

LECLASSIC SPORTS CO.
End-of-Period Spreadsheet (Work Sheet)
For the Year Ended December 31, 2008

	Account Title	Unadjusted Trial Balance Dr.	Unadjusted Trial Balance Cr.	Adjustments Dr.	Adjustments Cr.	Adjusted Trial Balance Dr.	Adjusted Trial Balance Cr.	Income Statement Dr.	Income Statement Cr.	Balance Sheet Dr.	Balance Sheet Cr.
1	Cash	18,000				18,000				18,000	
2	Accounts Receivable	42,500				42,500				42,500	
3	Merchandise Inventory	215,000			(a) 5,000	210,000				210,000	
4	Prepaid Insurance	9,700			(b) 6,800	2,900				2,900	
5	Store Supplies	4,200			(c) 3,050	1,200				1,200	
6	Office Supplies	2,100			(d) 1,350	750				750	
7	Store Equipment	182,000				182,000				182,000	
8	Acc. Depr.—Store Equip.		40,300		(e) 7,500		47,800				47,800
9	Office Equipment	60,000				60,000				60,000	
10	Acc. Depr.—Office Equip.		17,200		(f) 3,800		21,000				21,000
11	Accounts Payable		56,700				56,700				56,700
12	Salaries Payable				(g) 4,100		4,100				4,100
13	Unearned Rent		1,200	(h) 800			400				400
14	Note Payable (final payment due 2013)		125,000				125,000				125,000
15	Tanya Brill, Capital		217,600				217,600				217,600
16	Tanya Brill, Drawing	5,000				5,000				5,000	
17	Sales		875,000				875,000		875,000		
18	Sales Returns and Allow.	13,900				13,900		13,900			
19	Sales Discounts	7,100				7,100		7,100			
20	Cost of Merchandise Sold	557,000		(a) 5,000		562,000		562,000			
21	Sales Salaries Expense	81,400		(g) 2,600		84,000		84,000			
22	Advertising Expense	45,000				45,000		45,000			

	Account	Trial Balance Dr	Trial Balance Cr	Adjustments Dr	Adjustments Cr	Adjusted Trial Balance Dr	Adjusted Trial Balance Cr	Income Statement Dr	Income Statement Cr	Balance Sheet Dr	Balance Sheet Cr	
23	Depr. Exp.—Store Equip.			(e) 7,500		7,500		7,500				23
24	Delivery Expense	6,000				6,000		6,000				24
25	Store Supplies Expense			(c) 3,050		3,050		3,050				25
26	Misc. Selling Expense	1,600				1,600		1,600				26
27	Office Salaries Expense	44,000		(g) 1,500		45,500		45,500				27
28	Rent Expense	25,200				25,200		25,200				28
29	Insurance Expense			(b) 6,800		6,800		6,800				29
30	Depr. Exp.—Office Equip.			(f) 3,800		3,800		3,800				30
31	Office Supplies Expense			(d) 1,350		1,350		1,350				31
32	Misc. Admin. Expense	1,650				1,650		1,650				32
33	Rent Revenue				(h) 800		800		800			33
34	Interest Expense	11,600				11,600		11,600				34
35		1,333,000	1,333,000	32,400	32,400	1,348,400	1,348,400	826,050	875,800	522,350	472,600	35
36	Net Income							49,750			49,750	35
36								875,800	875,800	522,350	522,350	

977

2.

LECLASSIC SPORTS CO.
Income Statement
For the Year Ended December 31, 2008

Revenue from sales:			
Sales		$875,000	
Less: Sales returns & allow.	$ 13,900		
Sales discounts	7,100	21,000	
Net sales			$ 854,000
Cost of merchandise sold			562,000
Gross profit			$ 292,000
Expenses:			
Selling expenses:			
Sales salaries expense	$ 84,000		
Advertising expense	45,000		
Depr. exp.—store equip.	7,500		
Delivery expense	6,000		
Store supplies expense	3,050		
Misc. selling expense	1,600		
Total selling expenses		$147,150	
Administrative expenses:			
Office salaries expense	$ 45,500		
Rent expense	25,200		
Insurance expense	6,800		
Depr. exp.—office equip.	3,800		
Office supplies expense	1,350		
Misc. administrative exp.	1,650		
Total admin. expenses		84,300	
Total expenses			231,450
Income from operations			$ 60,550
Other income and expense:			
Rent revenue		$ 800	
Interest expense		(11,600)	(10,800)
Net income			$ 49,750

Prob. C–2   Continued

3.

LECLASSIC SPORTS CO.
Statement of Owner's Equity
For the Year Ended December 31, 2008

Tanya Brill, capital, January 1, 2008		$217,600
Net income for the year	$49,750	
Less withdrawals	5,000	
Increase in owner's equity		44,750
Tanya Brill, capital, December 31, 2008		$262,350

4.

LECLASSIC SPORTS CO.
Balance Sheet
December 31, 2008

Assets

Current assets:

Cash..	$ 18,000	
Accounts receivable.................................	42,500	
Merchandise inventory	210,000	
Prepaid insurance	2,900	
Store supplies...	1,200	
Office supplies..	750	
Total current assets.............................		$275,350

Fixed assets:

Store equipment	$182,000		
Less accumulated depreciation..........	47,800	$134,200	
Office equipment	$ 60,000		
Less accumulated depreciation..........	21,000	39,000	
Total fixed assets............................			173,200
Total assets			$448,550

Liabilities

Current liabilities:

Accounts payable......................................	$ 56,700	
Note payable (current portion)	15,000	
Salaries payable	4,100	
Unearned rent	400	
Total current liabilities.........................		$ 76,200

Long-term liabilities:

Note payable (final payment, 2013)..........		110,000
Total liabilities..		$186,200

Owner's Equity

Tanya Brill, capital		262,350
Total liabilities and owner's equity		$448,550

5. Cost of Merchandise Sold.. 5,000

    Merchandise Inventory... 5,000

    Insurance Expense 6,800

    Prepaid Insurance.. 6,800

    Store Supplies Expense 3,050

    Store Supplies.. 3,050

    Office Supplies Expense 1,350

    Office Supplies... 1,350

    Depreciation Expense—Store Equipment 7,500

    Accumulated Depreciation—Store Equipment 7,500

    Depreciation Expense—Office Equipment 3,800

    Accumulated Depreciation—Office Equipment 3,800

    Sales Salaries Expense 2,600
    Office Salaries Expense 1,500

    Salaries Payable 4,100

    Unearned Rent.. 800

    Rent Revenue.. 800

6. Sales 875,000
   Rent Revenue 800
      Income Summary   875,800

   Income Summary 826,050
      Sales Returns and Allowances   13,900
      Sales Discounts   7,100
      Cost of Merchandise Sold   562,000
      Sales Salaries Expense   84,000
      Advertising Expense   45,000
      Depreciation Expense—Store Equipment   7,500
      Delivery Expense   6,000
      Store Supplies Expense   3,050
      Miscellaneous Selling Expense   1,600
      Office Salaries Expense   45,500
      Rent Expense   25,200
      Insurance Expense   6,800
      Depreciation Expense—Office Equipment   3,800
      Office Supplies Expense   1,350
      Miscellaneous Administrative Expense   1,650
      Interest Expense   11,600

   Income Summary 49,750
      Tanya Brill, Capital   49,750

   Tanya Brill, Capital 5,000
      Tanya Brill, Drawing   5,000